Matching Supply with Demand

An Introduction to Operations Management

Matching Supply with Demand

An Introduction to Operations Management

Fourth Edition

Gérard Cachon
The Wharton School, University of Pennsylvania

Christian Terwiesch
The Wharton School, University of Pennsylvania

McGraw Hill Education (India) Private Limited

MATCHING SUPPLY WITH DEMAND: AN INTRODUCTION TO OPERATIONS MANAGEMENT, FOURTH EDITION

McGraw Hill Education (India) Reprint 2023

Fourth reprint 2025

Reprinted in India by arrangement with McGraw Hill LLC, New York

Sales territories: India, Pakistan, Nepal, Bangladesh, Sri Lanka and Bhutan

Library of Congress Cataloging-in-Publication Data

Names: Cachon, Gérard, author. | Terwiesch, Christian, author.
Title: Matching supply with demand : an introduction to operations management / Gerard Cachon, The Wharton School, University of Pennsylvania, Christian Terwiesch, The Wharton School, University of Pennsylvania.
Description: Fourth edition. | New York, NY : McGraw-Hill Education, [2018] | Includes bibliographical references and index.
Identifiers: LCCN 2018026074| ISBN 9780078096655 (alk. paper) | ISBN 0078096650 (alk. paper)
Subjects: LCSH: Production management.
Classification: LCC TS155 .C13 2018 | DDC 658.5--dc23
LC record available at https://lccn.loc.gov/2018026074

ISBN-13: 978-93-5532-505-1
ISBN-10: 93-5532-505-3

04 05 06 07 08 RAJ 29 28 27 26 25

Published by McGraw Hill Education (India) Private Limited,
Anjana Complex, No:5/90A, Butt Road, St. Thomas Mount, Chennai – 600016, Tamil Nadu, India,

Printed and bound in India at Rajkamal Electric Press, Kundli-131028, Haryana

Cover Designer: Neeraj Dayal
Cover Image Source: Shutterstock

Visit us at: www.mheducation.co.in
Toll free in India: 1800 103 5875
Write to us at: support.india@mheducation.com
CIN: U80302TN2010PTC111532

To the teachers, colleagues, and professionals who shared with us their knowledge.

About the Authors

Gérard Cachon *The Wharton School, University of Pennsylvania*

Professor Cachon is the Fred R. Sullivan Professor of Operations, Information, and Decisions at The Wharton School of the University of Pennsylvania, where he teaches a variety of undergraduate, MBA, executive, and PhD courses in operations management. His research focuses on operations strategy, and in particular, on how operations are used to gain competitive advantage.

His administrative responsibilities have included Chair of the Operations, Information and Decisions Department, Vice Dean of Strategic Initiatives for the Wharton School, and President of the Manufacturing and Service Operations Society. He has been named an INFORMS Fellow and a Distinguished Fellow of the Manufacturing and Service Operations Society.

His articles have appeared in *Harvard Business Review, Management Science, Marketing Science, Manufacturing & Service Operations Management,* and *Operations Research.* He is the former editor-in-chief of *Manufacturing & Service Operations Management* and *Management Science.* He has consulted with a wide range of companies, including 4R Systems, Ahold, Americold, Campbell Soup, Gulfstream Aerospace, IBM, Medtronic, and O'Neill.

Before joining The Wharton School in July 2000, Professor Cachon was on the faculty at the Fuqua School of Business, Duke University. He received a PhD from The Wharton School in 1995.

He is an avid proponent of bicycle commuting (and other environmentally friendly modes of transportation). Along with his wife and four children he enjoys hiking, scuba diving, and photography.

Christian Terwiesch *The Wharton School, University of Pennsylvania*

Professor Terwiesch is the Andrew M. Heller Professor of Operations, Information, and Decisions at the Wharton School of the University of Pennsylvania. He is also a Senior Fellow of the Leonard Davis Institute for Health Economics, a Co-Director of the Mack Institute of Innovation Management, and holds a faculty appointment in Penn's Perelman School of Medicine. His research on operations management, research and development, and innovation management appears in many of the leading academic journals, including *Management Science, Operations Research, Marketing Science,* and *Organization Science.* He has received numerous teaching awards for his courses in Wharton's MBA and executive education programs.

Professor Terwiesch has researched with and consulted for various organizations, including a project on concurrent engineering for BMW, supply chain management for Intel and Medtronic, and product customization for Dell. Most of his current work relates to health care and innovation management. In the health care arena, some of Professor Terwiesch's recent projects include the analysis of capacity allocation for cardiac surgery procedures at the University of California–San Francisco and at Penn Medicine, the impact of emergency room crowding on hospital capacity and revenues (also at Penn Medicine), and the usage of intensive care beds in the Children's Hospital of Philadelphia. In the innovation area, recent projects include the management of the clinical development portfolio at Merck, the development of open innovation systems, and the design of patient-centered care processes in the Veterans Administration hospital system.

Professor Terwiesch's latest book, *Innovation Tournaments,* outlines a novel, process-based approach to innovation management. The book was featured by *BusinessWeek,* the *Financial Times,* and the *Sloan Management Review.*

Acknowledgements

We would like to acknowledge the many people who have helped us in so many different ways with this ongoing project.

We begin with the 2004 Wharton MBA class that weathered through our initial version of the text. It is not practical for us to name every student that shared comments with us, but we do wish to name the students who took the time to participate in our focus groups: Gregory Ames, Maria Herrada-Flores, Justin Knowles, Karissa Kruse, Sandeep Naik, Jeremy Stackowitz, Charlotte Walsh, and Thomas (TJ) Zerr. The 2005 MBA class enjoyed a much more polished manuscript, but nevertheless contributed numerous suggestions and identified remaining typos and errors (much to our chagrin). Since then, we have continued to receive feedback from our undergraduate, MBA, and executive MBA students at Wharton. In addition to Wharton students, we received helpful feedback from students at Texas A&M, the University of Toronto, and INSEAD.

Along with our students, we would like to thank our co-teachers in the core: Naren Agrawal, Krishnan Anand, Omar Besbes, Morris Cohen, Marshall Fisher, Richard Lai, Chris Lee, Pranab Majumder, Serguei Netessine, Kathy Pearson, Taylor Randall, Nicolas Reinecke, Daniel Snow, Stephan Spinler, Anita Tucker, Karl Ulrich, Senthil Veeraraghavan, and Yu-Sheng Zheng. In addition to useful pedagogical advice and quality testing, they shared many of their own practice problems and questions.

This book is not the first book in Operations Management, nor will it be the last. We hope we have incorporated the best practices of existing books while introducing our own innovations. The book by Anupindi et al. as well as the article by Harrison and Loch were very helpful to us, as they developed the process view of operations underlying Chapters 2 through 9. The book by Chase and Aquilano was especially useful for Chapter 7. We apply definitions and terminology from those sources whenever possible without sacrificing our guiding principles.

We also have received some indirect and direct assistance from faculty at other universities. Garrett van Ryzin's (Columbia) and Xavier de Groote's (INSEAD) inventory notes were influential in the writing of Chapters 2 and 16, and the revenue management note by Serguei Netessine (Wharton) and Rob Shumsky (Dartmouth) was the starting point for Chapter 18. The process analysis, queuing, and inventory notes and articles written by Martin Lariviere (Northwestern), Michael Harrison (Stanford), and Christoph Loch (INSEAD) were also influential in several of our chapters. Martin, being a particularly clever question designer, was kind enough to share many of his questions with us.

Matthew Drake (Duquesne University) provided us with invaluable feedback during his meticulous accuracy check of both the text and the solutions, and we thank him for his contribution.

Several brave souls actually read the entire manuscript and responded with detailed comments. These reviewers included Leslie M. Bobb (Bernard M. Baruch College), Sime Curkovic (Western Michigan University–Kalamazoo), Scott Dobos (Indiana University–Bloomington), Ricki Ann Kaplan (East Tennessee State University), and Kathy Stecke (University of Texas at Dallas).

Our Ph.D. student "volunteers," Karan Girotra, Diwas KC, Marcelo Olivares, and Fuqiang Zhang, as well as Ruchika Lal and Bernd Terwiesch, took on the tedious job of quality testing. Robert Batt, Santiago Gallino, Antonio Moreno, Greg Neubecker, Michael Van Pelt, and Bethany Schwartz helped to collect and analyze data and could frequently solve practice problems faster than we could. The text is much cleaner due to their efforts.

The many cases and practical examples that illustrate the core concepts of this book reflect our extensive collaboration with several companies, including the University of Pennsylvania Hospital System in the Philadelphia region, the Circored plant in Trinidad, the Xootr factory in New Hampshire, the An-ser call center in Wisconsin, the operations group at O'Neill in California, and the supply chain group at Medtronic in Minnesota. We have benefited from countless visits and meetings with their management teams. We thank the people of these organizations, whose role it is to match supply and demand in the "real world," for sharing their knowledge, listening to our ideas, and challenging our models. Special thanks go to Jeff Salomon and his team (Interventional Radiology), Karl Ulrich (Xootr), Allan Fromm (An-ser), Cherry Chu and John Pope (O'Neill), and Frederic Marie and John Grossman (Medtronic). Allan Fromm deserves extra credit, as he was not only willing to share with us his extensive knowledge of service operations that he gathered as a CEO of a call center company but also proofread the entire manuscript and tackled most of the practice problems. Special thanks also to the McKinsey operations practice, in particular Stephen Doig, John Drew, and Nicolas Reinecke, for sharing their practical experience on Lean Operations and the Toyota Production System.

We especially thank our friend, colleague, and cycling partner Karl Ulrich, who has been involved in various aspects of the book, starting from its initial idea to the last details of the design process, including the cover design.

Through each edition of this text we have been supported by a fantastic team at McGraw Hill: Chuck Synovec, Noelle Bathurst, Tobi Philips, Harper Christopher, and Fran Simon.

Finally, we thank our family members, some of whom were surely unwilling reviewers who nevertheless performed their family obligation with a cheerful smile.

Gérard Cachon

Christian Terwiesch

Preface

This book represents our view of the essential body of knowledge for an introductory operations management course. It has been successfully used with all types of students, from freshmen taking an introductory course in operations management, to MBAs, to executive MBAs, and even PhD students.

Our guiding principle in the development of *Matching Supply with Demand* has been "real operations, real solutions." "Real operations" means that most of the chapters in this book are written from the perspective of a specific company so that the material in this text will come to life by discussing it in a real-world context. Companies and products are simply easier to remember than numbers and equations. We have chosen a wide variety of companies, small and large, representing services, manufacturing, and retailing alike. While obviously not fully representative, we believe that—taken together—these cases provide a realistic picture of operations management problems today.

"Real solutions" means that we do not want equations and models to merely provide students with mathematical gymnastics for the sake of an intellectual exercise. We feel that professional training, even in a rigorous academic setting, requires tools and strategies that students can implement in practice. We achieve this by demonstrating how to apply our models from start to finish in a realistic operational setting. Furthermore, we openly address the implementation challenges of each model/strategy we discuss so that students know what to expect when the "rubber hits the pavement."

To fully deliver on "real operations, real solutions," we also must adhere to the principle of "real simple." Do not worry; "real simple" does not mean plenty of "blah-blah" without any analytical rigor. Quite the contrary. To us, "real simple" means hard analysis that is made easy to learn. This is crucial for an operations text. Our objective is to teach business leaders, not tacticians. Thus, we need students to be able to quickly develop a foundation of formal models so that they have the time to explore the big picture, that is, how operations can be transformed to provide an organization with sustainable competitive advantage and/or superior customer service. Students who get bogged down in details, equations, and analysis are not fully capturing the valuable insights they will need in their future career.

So how do we strive for "real simple"? First, we recognize that not every student comes to this material with an engineering/math background. As a result, we tried to use as little mathematical notation as possible, to provide many real-world examples, and to adhere to consistent terminology and phrasing. Second, we provide various levels of detail for each analysis. For example, every little step in an analysis is described in the text via an explicit example; then a summary of the process is provided in a "how to" exhibit, a brief listing of key notation and equations is provided at the end of each chapter, and, finally, solved practice problems are offered to reinforce learning. While we do humbly recognize, given the quantitative sophistication of this text, that "much simpler" might be more accurate than "real simple," we nevertheless hope that students will be pleasantly surprised to discover that their analytical capabilities are even stronger than they imagined.

The initial version of *Matching Supply with Demand* made its debut in portions of the operations management core course at Wharton in the 2002–2003 academic year. This edition incorporates the feedback we have received over the last 16 years from many students, executives, and colleagues, both at Wharton and abroad.

Gérard Cachon

Christian Terwiesch

Changes to This Edition

The fourth edition has benefited from the comments and suggestions from students, faculty, and practitioners from around the world.

The implemented changes can be divided into three categories: an update of data and case examples, the addition of two chapters related to content that was not previously covered in the book, and an overall streamlining of the exposition of the existing content.

The world has changed again between this and the previous edition. Ride sharing, apartment sharing, and electric vehicles were not yet a thing "back then." Consequently, we have updated data and examples to try to maintain the timeliness of the content.

We have added two new chapters to this book. The first new chapter is about forecasting, which is an absolutely essential input to all operations models. The growth of available data only makes forecasting more relevant. The second new chapter is on scheduling. We covered scheduling in early texts, but not to the extent the topic deserves given our continued emphasis on service operations. Now we provide a dedicated and more extensive coverage of scheduling.

We have made a number of small changes that make the material easier for students to absorb. For example, we have streamlined the exposition of labor utilization calculations and we have de-emphasized the use of the expected loss function in the newsvendor and order-up-to models. Instead of the loss function, we provide the "expected inventory function," which allows students to arrive at the necessary answer with fewer steps. Furthermore, we find that students are able to intuitively grasp what the inventory function does better than the loss function.

Resources for Instructors and Students

Instructor Resources

The Instructor's Edition within Connect is password-protected and a convenient place for instructors to access course supplements that include the complete solutions to all problems and cases, PowerPoint slides that include both lecture materials for nearly every chapter and nearly all the figures (including all the spreadsheets) in the book, and the Test Bank, which now includes filters for topic, learning objective, and level of difficulty for choosing questions and reporting on them, and is available in two ways:

- As Word files, with both question-only and answer files.
- In TestGen, a desktop test generator and editing application for instructors to provide printed tests that can incorporate both McGraw-Hill's and instructors' questions.

Student Resources

For the convenience of students, we are providing the website www.mheducation.co.in (see the inside back cover for more details) that will contain Case Materials and Excel files.

Brief Contents

Table of Contents

Chapter 1

Introduction

A central premise in economics is that prices adjust to match supply with demand: if there is excess demand, prices rise; if there is excess supply, prices fall. But while an economist may find comfort with this theory, managers in practice often do not. To them excess demand means lost revenue and excess supply means wasted resources. They fully understand that matching supply with demand is extremely difficult and requires more tools than just price adjustments.

Consider the following examples:

- In 2017, Tesla began shipping its very popular electric car, the Model 3. While they hoped to quickly achieve a production rate of 5,000 vehicles per week, they were far behind that goal. Meanwhile, well over 500,000 customers were waiting for their preordered car.
- In New York, taxi cab medallions, a regulatory requirement in most cities, once were traded for upwards of $1 million. With the emergence of new mobility services such as Uber and Lyft, these prices have plummeted. A reason for the success of these platforms is their flexibility to provide more driver capacity when and where needed.
- The city of Hamburg, Germany, completed the Elbphilharmonie, a world-class concert house with a spectacular design. Project management for this new musical venue was also spectacular, but for very different reasons. In 2005, the local government predicted construction costs to be 186 million euros and an opening of 2009. The final bill, however, was 789 million euros and it took until 2016 to complete the work.
- 30-year-old John Verrier entered an emergency department in the Bronx at 10 p.m. at night complaining about a rash. He was found dead over eight hours later, still stuck in the waiting room. Throughout the country, emergency room waiting times exceed two hours.
- GoPro launched a consumer drone, the Karma, with much fanfare. Unfortunately, only one month after launch, GoPro was forced to recall the drone because a dangerous malfunction could cause the drone to lose power and fall to the ground. GoPro was able to relaunch the Karma three months later, but missed the crucial holiday season due to the quality defect.

All of these cases have in common that they suffer from a mismatch between demand and supply, with respect either to their timing or to their quantities.

This book is about how firms can design their operations to better match supply with demand. Our motivation is simply stated: by better matching supply with demand, a firm gains a significant competitive advantage over its rivals. A firm can achieve this better match through the implementation of the rigorous models and the operational strategies we outline in this book.

To somewhat soften our challenge to economic theory, we do acknowledge it is possible to mitigate demand–supply mismatches by adjusting prices. For example, the effective market price for the Tesla Model 3 did rise, as became visible in the product's preowned price exceeding the list price. But, this price adjustment was not under Tesla's control, nor did Tesla collect the extra surplus from it. In other words, we view that price adjustment as a symptom of a problem, rather than evidence of a healthy system. Moreover, in many other cases, price adjustments are impossible. The time period between the initiation of demand and the fulfillment through supply is too short or there are too few buyers and sellers in the market. There simply is no market for emergency care in operating rooms or waiting times in call centers.

Why is matching supply with demand difficult? The short answer is that demand can vary, in either predictable or unpredictable ways, and supply is inflexible. On average, an organization might have the correct amount of resources (people, product, and/or equipment), but most organizations find themselves frequently in situations with resources in the wrong place, at the wrong time, and/or in the wrong quantity. Furthermore, shifting resources across locations or time is costly, hence the inflexibility in supply. For example, physicians are not willing to rush back and forth to the hospital as they are needed and retailers cannot afford to immediately move product from one location to another. While it is essentially impossible to always achieve a perfect match between supply and demand, successful firms continually strive for that goal.

Table 1.1 provides a sample of industries that we will discuss in this book and describes their challenge to match supply with demand. Take the airline industry (last column in Table 1.1.). Over the last two decades, most large airlines operating in the United States were able to increase their aircraft load factor (the percentage of seats on a plane that are utilized by a paying customer) from about 70–75 percent to over 80 percent. What might be annoying to us as consumers because of more congested boarding processes, a packed cabin, and an increased likelihood of being bumped on a flight, is critical to the financial success of the airlines. Transporting one more passenger on a flight increases the costs of operating the flight only by a very small number. Revenue, in contrast, grows significantly, and, given this combination, profits can double or triple by increasing the load factor by a few percentage points.

TABLE 1.1 Examples of Supply–Demand Mismatches

	Retailing	Iron Ore Plant	Emergency Room	Pacemakers	Air Travel
Supply	Consumer electronics	Iron ore	Medical service	Medical equipment	Seats on specific flight
Demand	Consumers buying a new video system	Steel mills	Urgent need for medical service	Heart surgeon requiring pacemaker at exact time and location	Travel for specific time and destination
Supply exceeds demand	High inventory costs; few inventory turns	Prices fall	Doctors, nurses, and infrastructure are underutilized	Pacemaker sits in inventory	Empty seat
Demand exceeds supply	Forgone profit opportunity; consumer dissatisfaction	Prices rise	Crowding and delays in the ER; potential diversion of ambulances	Forgone profit (typically not associated with medical risk)	Overbooking; customer has to take different flight (profit loss)
Actions to match supply and demand	Forecasting; quick response	If prices fall too low, production facility is shut down	Staffing to predicted demand; priorities	Distribution system holding pacemakers at various locations	Dynamic pricing; booking policies

(continued)

TABLE 1.1 Concluded

	Retailing	Iron Ore Plant	Emergency Room	Pacemakers	Air Travel
Managerial importance	Per-unit inventory costs for consumer electronics retailing all too often exceed net profits	Prices are so competitive that the primary emphasis is on reducing the cost of supply	Delays in treatment or transfer have been linked to death	Most products (valued $20k) spend 4–5 months waiting in a trunk of a salesperson before being used	About 30% of all seats fly empty; a 1–2% increase in seat utilization makes the difference between profits and losses
Reference	Chapter 2, The Process View of the Organization; Chapter 14, Betting on Uncertain Demand: The Newsvendor Model; Chapter 15, Assemble-to-Order, Make-to-Order, and Quick Response with Reactive Capacity	Chapter 3, Understanding the Supply Process: Evaluating Process Capacity; Chapter 4, Estimating and Reducing Labor Costs	Chapter 9, Variability and Its Impact on Process Performance: Waiting Time Problems; Chapter 10, The Impact of Variability on Process Performance: Throughput Losses	Chapter 16, Service Levels and Lead Times in Supply Chains: The Order-up-to Inventory Model	Chapter 18, Revenue Management with Capacity Controls

This illustrates a critical lesson: even a seemingly small improvement in operations can have a significant effect on a firm's profitability precisely because, for most firms, their profit (if they have a profit) is a relatively small percentage of their revenue. Hence, improving the match between supply and demand is a critically important responsibility for a firm's management.

The other examples in Table 1.1 are drawn from a wide range of settings: health care delivery and devices, retailing, and heavy industry. Each suffers significant consequences due to demand–supply mismatches, and each requires specialized tools to improve and manage its operations.

To conclude our introduction, we strongly believe that effective operations management is about effectively matching supply with demand. Organizations that take the design of their operations seriously and aggressively implement the tools of operations management will enjoy a significant performance advantage over their competitors. This lesson is especially relevant for senior management given the razor-thin profit margins firms must deal with in modern competitive industries.

1.1 Learning Objectives and Framework

In this book, we look at organizations as entities that must match the supply of what they produce with the demand for their product. In this process, we will introduce a number of quantitative models and qualitative strategies, which we collectively refer to as the "tools of operations management." By "quantitative model" we mean some mathematical procedure or equation that takes inputs (such as a demand forecast, a processing rate, etc.) and outputs a number that either instructs a manager on what to do (how much inventory to buy, how many nurses to have on call, etc.) or informs a manager about a relevant performance measure (e.g., the average time a customer waits for service, the average number of patients in the emergency room, etc.). By "qualitative strategy" we mean a guiding principle: for example, increase the flexibility of your production facilities, decrease the variety of products offered, serve customers in priority order, and so forth. The next section gives a brief description of the key models and strategies we cover. Our learning objective for this book, put as succinctly as we can, is to teach students how and when to implement the tools of operations management.

Just as the tools of operations management come in different forms, they can be applied in different ways:

1. Operations management tools can be applied to ensure that resources are used as efficiently as possible; that is, the most is achieved with what we have.
2. Operations management tools can be used to make desirable trade-offs between competing objectives.
3. Operations management tools can be used to redesign or restructure our operations so that we can improve performance along multiple dimensions simultaneously.

We view our diverse set of tools as complementary to each other. In other words, our focus is neither exclusively on the quantitative models nor exclusively on the qualitative strategies. Without analytical models, it is difficult to move beyond the "blah-blah" of strategies and without strategies, it is easy to get lost in the minutia of tactical models. Put another way, we have designed this book to provide a rigorous operations management education for a strategic, high-level manager or consultant.

We will apply operations tools to firms that produce services and goods in a variety of environments—from apparel to health care, from call centers to pacemakers, and from kick scooters to iron ore fines. We present many diverse settings precisely because there does not exist a "standard" operational environment. Hence, there does not exist a single tool that applies to all firms. By presenting a variety of tools and explaining their pros and cons, students will gain the capability to apply this knowledge no matter what operational setting they encounter.

Consider how operations tools can be applied to a call center. A common problem in this industry is to find an appropriate number of customer service representatives to answer incoming calls. The more representatives we hire, the less likely incoming calls will have to wait; thus, the higher will be the level of service we provide. However, labor is the single largest driver of costs in a call center, so, obviously, having more representatives on duty also will increase the costs we incur per call.

The first use of operations management tools is to ensure that resources are used as effectively as possible. Assume we engage in a benchmarking initiative with three other call centers and find that the performance of our competitors behaves according to Figure 1.1: Competitor A is providing faster response times but also has higher costs. Competitor B has longer response times but has lower costs. Surprisingly, we find that competitor C outperforms us on both cost and service level. How can this be?

It must be that there is something that competitor C does in the operation of the call center that is smarter than what we do. Or, in other words, there is something that we do in our operations that is inefficient or wasteful. In this setting, we need to use our tools to move the firm toward the frontier illustrated in Figure 1.1. The frontier is the line that includes all benchmarks to the lower left; that is, no firm is outside the current frontier. For example, a premium service might be an important element of our business strategy, so we may choose not to compromise on service. And we could have a target that at least 90 percent of the incoming calls will be served within 10 seconds or less. But given that target, we should use our quantitative tools to ensure that our labor costs are as low as possible, that is, that we are at least on the efficiency frontier.

The second use of operations management tools is to find the right balance between our competing objectives, high service and low cost. This is similar to what is shown in Figure 1.2. In such a situation, we need to quantify the costs of waiting as well as the costs of labor and then recommend the most profitable compromise between these two objectives.

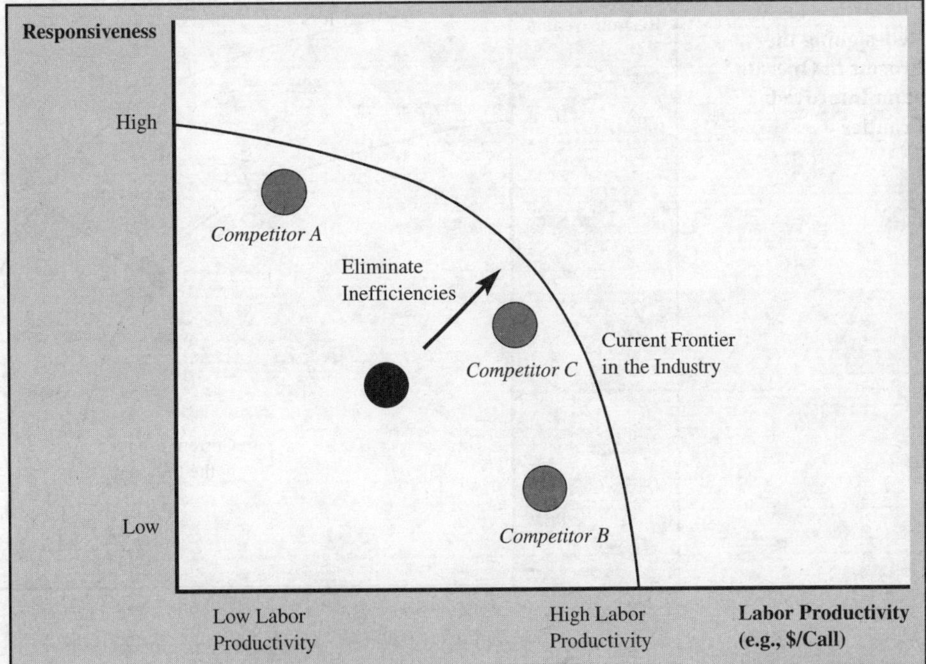

FIGURE 1.1 **Local Improvement of Operations by Eliminating Inefficiencies**

Moving to the frontier of efficiency and finding the right spot on the frontier are surely important. But outstanding companies do not stop there. The third use for our operations management tools is to fundamentally question the design of the current system itself. For example, a call center might consider merging with or acquiring another call center to gain scale economies. Alternatively, a call center might consider an investment in the development of a new technology leading to shorter call durations.

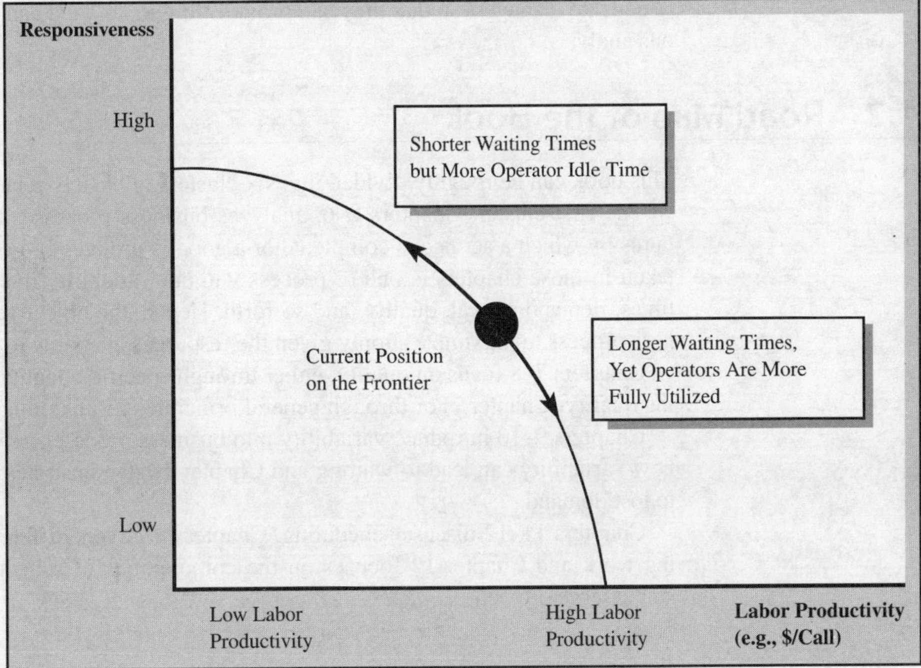

FIGURE 1.2 **Trade-Off between Labor Productivity and Responsiveness**

FIGURE 1.3 **Redesigning the Process to Operate at an Improved Frontier**

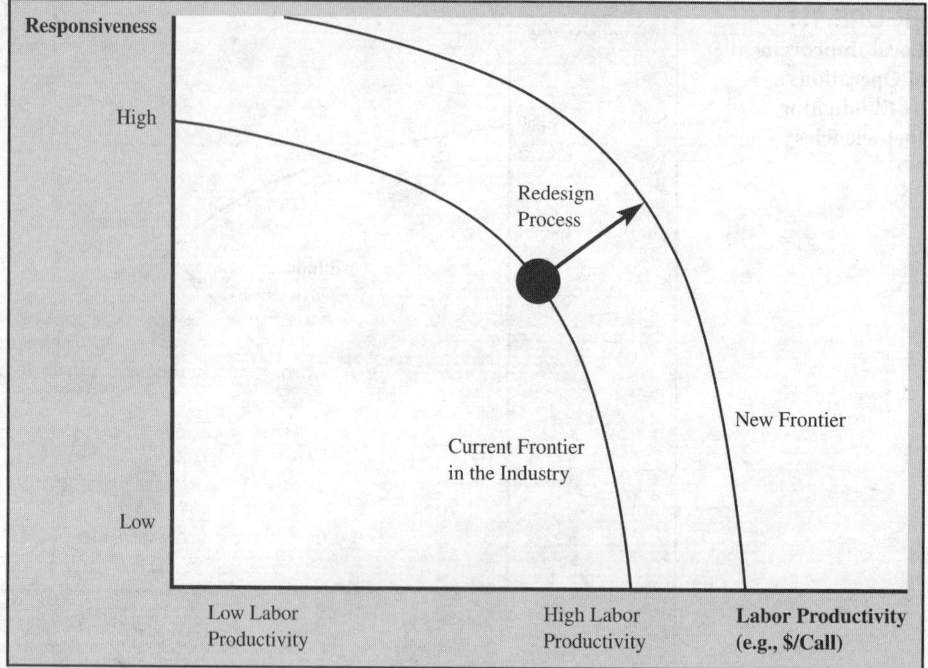

In such cases, a firm pushes the envelope, that is, moves the frontier of what previously was infeasible (see Figure 1.3). Hence, a firm is able to achieve faster responsiveness and higher labor productivity. But, unfortunately, there are few free lunches: while we have improved both customer service and labor productivity, pushing out the frontier generally requires some investments in time and effort. Hence, we need to use our tools to quantify the improvements we can achieve so that we can decide whether the effort is justifiable. It is easy to tell a firm that investing in technology can lead to shorter call durations, faster service, and higher labor productivity, but is that investment worthwhile? Our objective is to educate managers so that they can provide "big ideas" and can back them up with rigorous analysis.

1.2 Road Map of the Book

This book can be roughly divided into six clusters of closely related chapters.

The first cluster, Chapters 2–6, analyzes business processes (the methods and procedures by which a service is completed or a good is produced). For the most part, the view taken in those chapters is one of process without variability in service times, production times, demand arrival, quality, and so forth. Hence, the objective is to organize the business process to maximize supply given the resources available to the firm.

Chapters 7–8 focus on quality, either through specific quantitative methods for managing quality (Chapter 7) or through general principles for maximizing quality (Chapter 8).

Chapters 9–10 introduce variability into business process analysis. Chapter 9 discusses how variability can lead to waiting and Chapter 10 demonstrates how variability can lead to lost demand.

Chapters 11–12 discuss scheduling. Chapter 11 covers different methods for sequencing work and Chapter 12 focuses on the complexities of scheduling the activities for a single large project.

Chapters 13–16 discuss inventory control, information management, and process flexibility. Issues include demand forecasting, stocking quantities, performance measures, and response times.

Chapters 17–19 conclude the book with several strategic topics, including ways to mitigate risks, trying to influence demand through pricing, and coordinating the supply chain.

The following provides a more detailed summary of the contents of each chapter:

- Chapter 2 defines a process, introduces the basic process performance metrics, and provides a framework for characterizing processes (the product–process matrix). Little's Law is introduced, an essential formula for understanding business processes and the link between operations management and financial accounting.
- Chapter 3 introduces process analysis tools from the perspective of a manager (as opposed to an engineer): how to determine the capacity of a process and how to compute process utilization.
- Chapter 4 looks at assembly operations with a specific focus on labor costs, an extremely important performance metric. It frequently drives location decisions (consider the current debate related to offshoring) and has—especially in service operations—a major impact on the bottom line. We define measures such as labor content, labor utilization, and idle time. We also introduce the concept of line balancing.
- Chapter 5 studies production in the presence of setup times and setup costs (the EOQ model). A key issue is the impact of product variety on production performance.
- Chapter 6 connects the operational details of process analysis with key financial performance measures for a firm, such as return on invested capital. Through this chapter we discover how to make process improvement translate into enhanced financial performance for the organization.
- Chapter 7 details the tools of quality management, including statistical process control, six-sigma, and robust design.
- Chapter 8 describes how Toyota, via its world-famous collection of production strategies called the Toyota Production System, achieves high quality and low cost.
- Chapter 9 explores the consequences of variability on a process. As we will discuss in the context of a call center, variability can lead to long customer waiting times and thereby is a key enemy in all service organizations. We discuss how an organization should handle the trade-off between a desire for minimizing the investment into capacity (e.g., customer service representatives) while achieving a good service experience for the customer.
- Chapter 10 continues the discussion of variability and its impact on service quality. As we will discuss in the context of emergency medicine, variability frequently can lead to situations in which demand has to be turned away because of insufficient capacity. This has substantial implications, especially in the health care environment.
- Chapter 11 continues the theme of waiting times by discussing decisions related to sequencing (In which order should waiting units of demand be served?) and scheduling (Should we promise units of supply to our customers ahead of time?).
- Chapter 12 investigates project management, a process that is designed for a single, somewhat unique, project such as a ship, a new building, or a satellite.
- Chapter 13 introduces ways to plan for future demand based on forecasting techniques. While we cannot predict the future, we should try to learn as much as possible from demand realizations of the past.
- Chapter 14 focuses on the management of seasonal goods with only one supply opportunity. The newsvendor model allows a manager to strike the correct balance between too much supply and too little supply.

- Chapter 15 expands upon the setting of the previous chapter by allowing additional supply to occur in the middle of the selling season. This "reactive capacity" allows a firm to better respond to early season sales information.
- Chapter 16 continues the discussion of inventory management with the introduction of lead times. The order-up-to model is used to choose replenishment quantities that achieve target availability levels (such as an in-stock probability).
- Chapter 17 highlights numerous risk-pooling strategies to improve inventory management within the supply chain: for example, location pooling, product pooling, universal design, delayed differentiation (also known as postponement), and capacity pooling.
- Chapter 18 covers revenue management. In particular, the focus is on the use of booking limits and overbooking to better match demand to supply when supply is fixed.
- Chapter 19 identifies the bullwhip effect as a key issue in the effective operation of a supply chain and offers coordination strategies for firms to improve the performance of their supply chain.

Some of the chapters are designed to be "entry level" chapters, that is, chapters that can be read independently from the rest of the text. Other chapters are more advanced, so they at least require some working knowledge of the material in another chapter. Table 1.2 summarizes the contents of the chapters and indicates prerequisite chapters.

TABLE 1.2 Chapter Summaries and Prerequisites

Chapter	Managerial Issue	Key Qualitative Framework	Key Quantitative Tool	Prerequisite Chapters
2: The Process View of the Organization	Understanding business processes at a high level; process performance measures, inventory, flow time, and flow rate	Product–process matrix; focus on process flows	Little's Law Inventory turns and inventory costs	None
3: Understanding the Supply Process: Evaluating Process Capacity	Understanding the details of a process	Process flow diagram; finding and removing a bottleneck	Computing process capacity and utilization	Chapter 2
4: Estimating and Reducing Labor Costs	Labor costs	Line balancing; division of labor	Computing labor costs, labor utilization Minimizing idle time	Chapters 2, 3
5: Batching and Other Flow Interruptions: Setup Times and the Economic Order Quantity Model	Setup time and setup costs; managing product variety	Achieving a smooth process flow; deciding about setups and ordering frequency	EOQ model Determining batch sizes	Chapters 2, 3
6: The Link between Operations and Finance	Process improvement to enhance corporate performance	Return on Invested Capital (ROIC) tree	Computing ROIC	Chapters 2, 3
7: Quality and Statistical Process Control	Defining and improving quality	Statistical process control; six-sigma	Computing process capability; creating a control chart	None
8: Lean Operations and the Toyota Production System	Process improvement for competitive advantage	Lean operations; Toyota Production System	—	None

(continued)

TABLE 1.2 Concluded

Chapter	Managerial Issue	Key Qualitative Framework	Key Quantitative Tool	Prerequisite Chapters
9: Variability and Its Impact on Process Performance: Waiting Time Problems	Waiting times in service processes	Understanding congestion; pooling service capacity	Waiting time formula	None
10: The Impact of Variability on Process Performance: Throughput Losses	Lost demand in service processes	Role of service buffers; pooling	Erlang loss formula Probability of diverting demand	Chapter 9
11: Scheduling to Prioritize Demand	How to set priorities and how to reserve capacity	Priority rules and appointment systems	First-come-first-served; SPT rule	Chapter 9
12: Project Management	Time to project completion	Critical path	Critical path analysis	Chapters 2, 3
13: Forecasting	How to use past data about demand to predict future demand realizations	Time series–based forecasting	Exponential smoothing / demand patterns	None
14: Betting on Uncertain Demand: The Newsvendor Model	Choosing stocking levels for seasonal-style goods	Improving the forecasting process	Forecasting demand The newsvendor model for choosing stocking quantities and evaluating performance measures	None
15: Assemble-to-Order, Make-to-Order, and Quick Response with Reactive Capacity	How to use reactive capacity to reduce demand–supply mismatch costs	Value of better demand information; assemble-to-order and make-to-order strategies	Reactive capacity models	Chapter 14
16: Service Levels and Lead Times in Supply Chains: The Order-up-to Inventory Model	Inventory management with numerous replenishments	Impact of lead times on performance; how to choose an appropriate objective function	The order-up-to model for inventory management and performance-measure evaluation	Chapter 14 is highly recommended
17: Risk Pooling Strategies to Reduce and Hedge Uncertainty	How to better design the supply chain or a product or a service to better match supply with demand	Quantifying, reducing, avoiding, and hedging uncertainty	Newsvendor and order-up-to models	Chapters 14 and 16
18: Revenue Management with Capacity Controls	How to manage demand when supply is fixed	Reserving capacity for high-paying customers; accepting more reservations than available capacity	Booking limit/protection level model; overbooking model	Chapter 14
19: Supply Chain Coordination	How to manage demand variability and inventory across the supply chain	Bullwhip effect; supply chain contracts	Supply chain contract model	Chapter 14

Chapter 

The Process View of the Organization

Matching supply and demand would be easy if business processes would be instantaneous and could immediately create any amount of supply to meet demand. Understanding the questions of "Why are business processes not instantaneous?" and "What constrains processes from creating more supply?" is thereby at the heart of operations management. To answer these questions, we need to take a detailed look at how business processes actually work. In this chapter, we introduce some concepts fundamental to process analysis. The key idea of the chapter is that it is not sufficient for a firm to create great products and services; the firm also must design and improve its business processes that supply its products and services.

To get more familiar with the process view of a firm, we now take a detailed look behind the scenes of a particular operation, namely the Department of Interventional Radiology at Presbyterian Hospital in Philadelphia.

2.1 Presbyterian Hospital in Philadelphia

Interventional radiology is a subspecialty field of radiology that uses advanced imaging techniques such as real-time X-rays, ultrasound, computed tomography, and magnetic resonance imaging to perform minimally invasive procedures.

Over the past decades, interventional radiology procedures have begun to replace an increasing number of standard "open surgical procedures" for a number of reasons. Instead of being performed in an operating room, interventional radiology procedures are performed in an angiography suite (see Figure 2.1). Although highly specialized, these rooms are less expensive to operate than conventional operating rooms. Interventional procedures are often safer and have dramatically shorter recovery times compared to traditional surgery. Also, an interventional radiologist is often able to treat diseases such as advanced liver cancer that cannot be helped by standard surgery.

Although we may not have been in the interventional radiology unit, many, if not most, of us have been in a radiology department of a hospital at some point in our life. From the perspective of the patient, the following steps need to take place before the patient can go home or return to his or her hospital unit. In process analysis, we refer to these steps as *activities:*

- Registration of the patient.
- Initial consultation with a doctor; signature of the consent form.

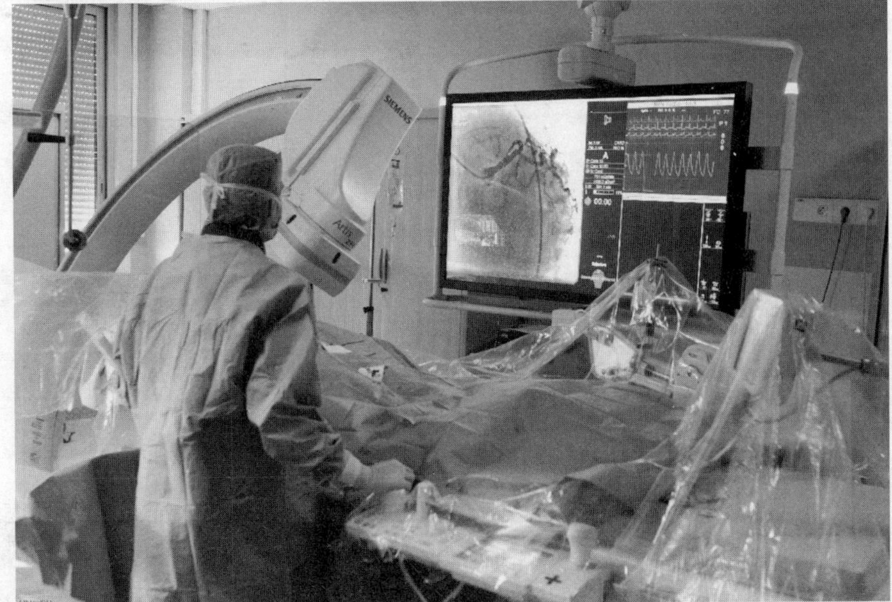

FIGURE 2.1
Example of a Procedure in an Interventional Radiology Unit

Source: Burger/Phanie/Alamy Stock Photo

- Preparation for the procedure.
- The actual procedure.
- Removal of all equipment.
- Recovery in an area outside the angiography suite.
- Consultation with the doctor.

Figure 2.2 includes a graphical representation of these steps, called a *Gantt diagram* (named after the 19th-century industrialist Henry Gantt). It provides several useful pieces of information.

First, the Gantt chart allows us to see the process steps and their durations, which are also called *activity times* or *processing times*. The duration simply corresponds to the length of the corresponding bars. Second, the Gantt diagram also illustrates the dependence between the various process activities. For example, the consultation with the doctor can only occur once the patient has arrived and been registered. In contrast, the preparation of the angiography suite can proceed in parallel to the initial consultation.

You might have come across Gantt charts in the context of project management. Unlike process analysis, project management is typically concerned with the completion of one single project. (See Chapter 12 for more details on project management.) The most well-known concept of project management is the *critical path*. The critical path is composed of all those activities that—if delayed—would lead to a delay in the overall completion time of the project, or—in this case—the time the patient has completed his or her stay in the radiology unit.

In addition to the eight steps described in the Gantt chart of Figure 2.2, most of us associate another activity with hospital care: waiting. Strictly speaking, waiting is not really an activity, as it does not add any value to the process. However, waiting is nevertheless relevant. It is annoying for the patient and can complicate matters for the hospital unit. For this reason, waiting times take an important role in operations management. Figure 2.3 shows the actual durations of the activities for a patient arriving at 12:30, as well as the time the patient needs to wait before being moved to the angiography suite.

FIGURE 2.2
Gantt Chart Summarizing the Activities for Interventional Radiology

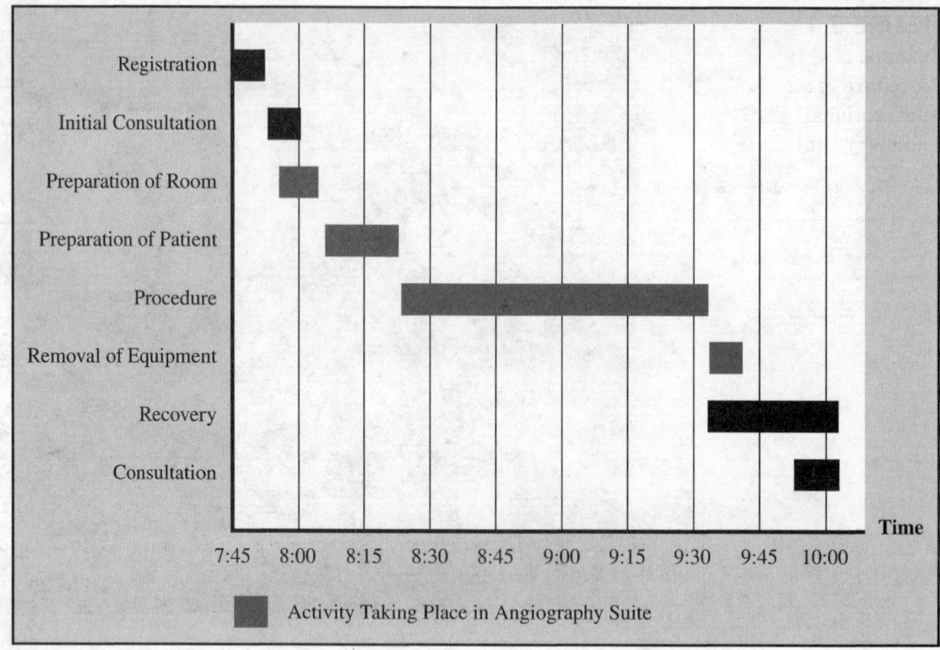

But why is there waiting time? Waiting is—to stay in the medical language for the moment—a symptom of supply–demand mismatch. If supply would be unlimited, our visit to the hospital would be reduced to the duration of the activities outlined in Figure 2.2 (the critical path). Imagine visiting a hospital in which all the nurses, technicians, doctors, and hospital administrators would just care for you!

FIGURE 2.3
Gantt Chart Summarizing the Activities for a Patient Arriving at 12:30

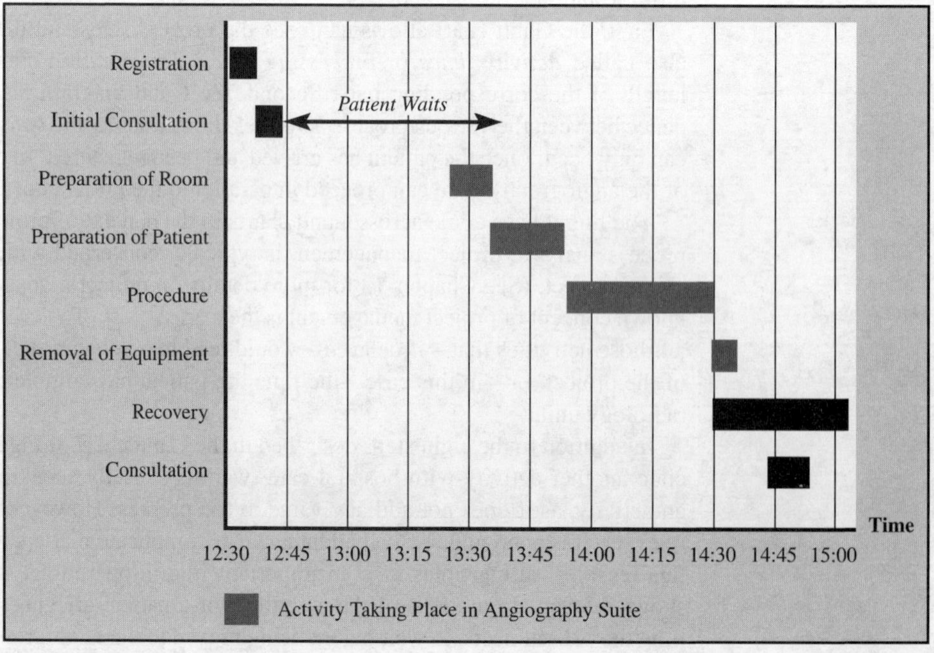

Given that few of us are in a position to receive the undivided attention of an entire hospital unit, it is important that we not only take the egocentric perspective of the patient, but look at the hospital operations more broadly. From the perspective of the hospital, there are many patients "flowing" through the process.

The people and the equipment necessary to support the interventional radiology process deal with many patients, not just one. We refer to these elements of the process as the *process resources*. Consider, for example, the perspective of the nurse and how she/he spends her/his time in the department of interventional radiology. Obviously, radiology from the viewpoint of the nurse is not an exceptional event, but a rather repetitive endeavor. Some of the nurse's work involves direct interaction with the patient; other work—while required for the patient—is invisible to the patient. This includes the preparation of the angiography suite and various aspects of medical record keeping.

Given this repetitive nature of work, the nurse as well as the doctors, technicians, and hospital administrators think of interventional radiology as a process, not a project. Over the course of the day, they see many patients come and go. Many hospitals, including Presbyterian Hospital in Philadelphia, have a "patient log" that summarizes at what times patients arrive at the unit. This patient log provides a picture of demand on the corresponding day. The patient log for December 2 is summarized by Table 2.1.

Many of these arrivals were probably scheduled some time in advance. Our analysis here focuses on what happens to the patient once he/she has arrived in the interventional radiology unit. A separate analysis could be performed, looking at the process starting with a request for diagnostics up to the arrival of the patient.

Given that the resources in the interventional radiology unit have to care for 11 patients on December 2, they basically need to complete the work according to 11 Gantt charts of the type outlined in Figure 2.2. This—in turn—can lead to waiting times. Waiting times arise when several patients are "competing" for the same limited resource, which is illustrated by the following two examples.

First, observe that the critical path for a typical patient takes about 2 hours. Note further that we want to care for 11 patients over a 10-hour workday. Consequently, we will have to take care of several patients at once. This would not be a problem if we had unlimited resources, nurses, doctors, space in the angiography suites, and so forth. However, given the resources that we have, if the Gantt charts of two patients are requesting the same resource simultaneously, waiting times result. For example, the second patient might require the initial consultation with the doctor at a time when the doctor is in the middle of the procedure for patient 1. Note also that patients 1, 4, 5, 6, 8, and 9 are assigned to the same room (the unit has a main room and a second room used for simpler cases), and thus they are also potentially competing for the same resource.

TABLE 2.1 Patient Log on December 2

Number	Patient Name	Arrival Time	Room Assignment
1		7:35	Main room
2		7:45	
3		8:10	
4		9:30	Main room
5		10:15	Main room
6		10:30	Main room
7		11:05	
8		12:35	Main room
9		14:30	Main room
10		14:35	
11		14:40	

FIGURE 2.4
Time Patient Spent in the Interventional Radiology Unit (for Patients Treated in Main Room Only), Including Room Preparation Time

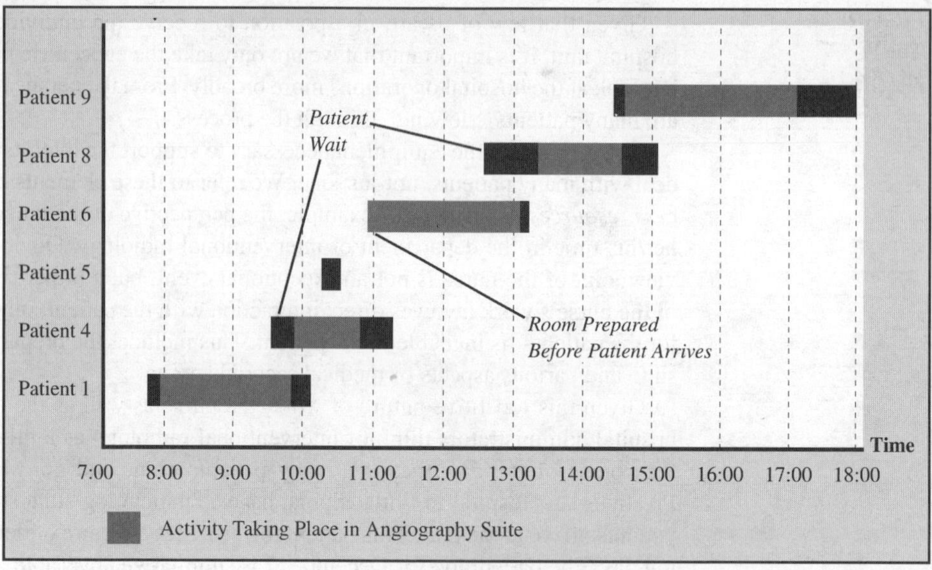

FIGURE 2.5
Usage of the Main Room

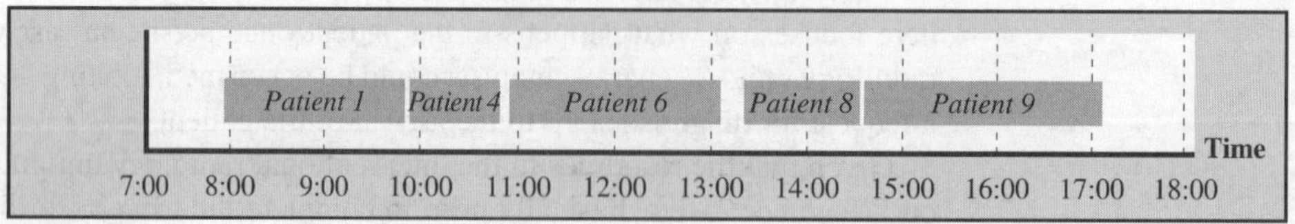

A second source of waiting time lies in the unpredictable nature of many of the activities. Some patients will take much longer in the actual procedure than others. For example, patient 1 spent 1:50 hours in the procedure, while patient 9 was in the procedure for 2:30 hours (see Figure 2.4). As an extreme case, consider patient 5, who refused to sign the consent form and left the process after only 15 minutes.

Such uncertainty is undesirable for resources, as it leaves them "flooded" with work at some moments in the day and "starved" for work at other moments. Figure 2.5 summarizes at what moments in time the angiography suite was used on December 2.

By now, we have established two views to the interventional radiology:

- The view of the patient for whom the idealized stay is summarized by Figure 2.2. Mismatches between supply and demand from the patient's perspective mean having a unit of demand (i.e., the patient) wait for a unit of supply (a resource).
- The view of the resources (summarized by Figure 2.5), which experience demand–supply mismatches when they are sometimes "flooded" with work, followed by periods of no work.

As these two perspectives are ultimately two sides of the same coin, we are interested in bringing these two views together. This is the fundamental idea of process analysis.

2.2 Three Measures of Process Performance

At the most aggregate level, a process can be thought of as a "black box" that uses *resources* (labor and capital) to transform *inputs* (undiagnosed patients, raw materials, unserved customers) into *outputs* (diagnosed patients, finished goods, served customers). This is shown

FIGURE 2.6
The Process View of an Organization

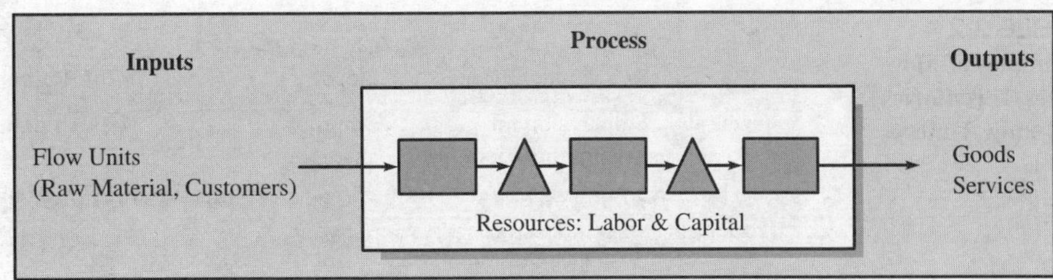

in Figure 2.6. Chapter 3 explains the details of constructing figures like Figure 2.6, which are called *process flow diagrams*. When analyzing the processes that lead to the supply of goods and services, we first define our unit of analysis.

In the case of the interventional radiology unit, we choose patients as our *flow unit*. Choosing the flow unit is typically determined by the type of product or service the supply process is dealing with; for example, vehicles in an auto plant, travelers for an airline, or gallons of beer in a brewery.

As suggested by the term, flow units flow through the process, starting as input and later leaving the process as output. With the appropriate flow unit defined, we next can evaluate a process based on three fundamental process performance measures:

- The number of flow units contained within the process is called the *inventory* (in a production setting, it is referred to as *work-in-process, WIP*). Given that our focus is not only on production processes, inventory could take the form of the number of insurance claims or the number of tax returns at the IRS. There are various reasons why we find inventory in processes, which we discuss in greater detail below. While many of us might initially feel uncomfortable with the wording, the inventory in the case of the interventional radiology unit is a group of patients.
- The time it takes a flow unit to get through the process is called the *flow time*. The flow time takes into account that the item (flow unit) may have to wait to be processed because there are other flow units (inventory) in the process potentially competing for the same resources. Flow time is an especially important performance metric in service environments or in other business situations that are sensitive to delays, such as make-to-order production, where the production of the process only begins upon the arrival of the customer order. In a radiology unit, flow time is something that patients are likely to care about: it measures the time from their arrival at the interventional radiology unit to the time patients can go home or return to their hospital unit.
- Finally, the rate at which the process is delivering output (measured in [flow units/unit of time], e.g., units per day) is called the *flow rate* or the *throughput rate*. The maximum rate with which the process can generate supply is called the *capacity* of the process. For December 2, the throughput of the interventional radiology unit was 11 patients per day.

Table 2.2 provides several examples of processes and their corresponding flow rates, inventory levels, and flow times.

You might be somewhat irritated that we have moved away from the idea of supply and demand mismatch for a moment. Moreover, we have not talked about profits so far. However, note that increasing the maximum flow rate (capacity) avoids situations where we have insufficient supply to match demand. From a profit perspective, a higher flow rate translates directly into more revenues (you can produce a unit faster and thus can produce more units), assuming your process is currently *capacity-constrained*, that is, there is sufficient demand that you could sell any additional output you make.

TABLE 2.2
Examples of Flow Rates, Inventories, and Flow Times

	U.S. Immigration	Champagne Industry	MBA Program	Large PC Manufacturer
Flow unit	Application for immigration benefit	Bottle of champagne	MBA student	Computer
Flow rate/ throughput	Approved or rejected visa cases: 6.3 million per year	260 million bottles per year	600 students per year	5,000 units per day
Flow time	Average processing time: 7.6 months	Average time in cellar: 3.46 years	2 years	10 days
Inventory	Pending cases: 4.0 million cases	900 million bottles	1,200 students	50,000 computers

Shorter flow times reduce the time delay between the occurrence of demand and its fulfillment in the form of supply. Shorter flow times therefore also typically help to reduce demand–supply mismatches. In many industries, shorter flow times also result in additional unit sales and/or higher prices, which makes them interesting also from a broader management perspective.

Lower inventory results in lower working capital requirements as well as many quality advantages that we explore later in this book. A higher inventory also is directly related to longer flow times (explained below). Thus, a reduction in inventory also yields a reduction in flow time. As inventory is the most visible indication of a mismatch between supply and demand, we will now discuss it in greater detail.

2.3 Little's Law

Accountants view inventory as an asset, but from an operations perspective, inventory often should be viewed as a liability. This is not a snub on accountants; inventory *should* be an asset on a balance sheet, given how accountants define an asset. But in common speech, the word *asset* means "desirable thing to have" and the dictionary defines *liability* as "something that works to one's disadvantage." In this sense, inventory can clearly be a liability. This is most visible in a service process such as a hospital unit, where patients in the waiting room obviously cannot be counted toward the assets of the health care system.

Let's take another visit to the interventional radiology unit. Even without much medical expertise, we can quickly find out which of the patients are currently undergoing care from some resource and which are waiting for a resource to take care of them. Similarly, if we took a quick walk through a factory, we could identify which parts of the inventory serve as raw materials, which ones are work-in-process, and which ones have completed the production process and now take the form of finished goods inventory.

However, taking a single walk through the process—dishwasher factory or interventional radiology unit—will not leave us with a good understanding of the underlying operations. All it will give us is a snapshot of what the process looked like at one single moment in time. Unfortunately, it is this same snapshot approach that underlies most management (accounting) reports: balance sheets itemize inventory into three categories (raw materials, WIP, finished goods); hospital administrators typically distinguish between pre- and postoperative patients. But such snapshots do not tell us *why* these inventories exist in the first place! Thus, a static, snapshot approach neither helps us to analyze business processes (why is there inventory?) nor helps us to improve them (is this the right amount of inventory?).

Now, imagine that instead of our single visit to the hospital unit, we would be willing to stay for some longer period of time. We arrive early in the morning and make ourselves comfortable at the entrance of the unit. Knowing that there are no patients in the interventional radiology unit overnight, we then start recording any arrival or departure of patients. In other words, we collect data concerning the patient inflow and outflow.

At the end of our stay, we can plot a graph similar to Figure 2.7. The upper of the two curves illustrates the cumulative number of patients who have entered the unit. The curve begins at time zero (7:00) and with zero patients. If we had done the same exercise in a unit with overnight patients, we would have recorded our initial patient count there. The lower of the two curves indicates the cumulative number of patients who have left the unit. Figure 2.7 shows us that by noon, seven patients have arrived, of which five have left the unit again.

At any given moment in time, the *vertical distance* between the upper curve and the lower curve corresponds to the number of patients in the interventional radiology unit, or—abstractly speaking—the inventory level. Thus, although we have not been inside the interventional radiology unit this day, we are able to keep track of the inventory level by comparing the cumulative inflow and outflow. For example, the inventory at noon consisted of two patients.

We also can look at the *horizontal distance* between the two lines. If the patients leave the unit in the same order they entered it, the horizontal gap would measure the exact amount of time each patient spent in the interventional radiology unit. More generally, given that the length of stay might vary across patients and patients do not necessarily leave the unit in the exact same sequence in which they entered it, the average gap between the two lines provides the average length of stay.

Thus, Figure 2.7 includes all three of the basic process performance measures we discussed on the previous page: flow rate (the slope of the two graphs), inventory (the vertical distance between the two graphs), and flow time (the horizontal distance between the two graphs).

Based on either the graph or the patient log, we can now compute these performance measures for December 2. We already know that the flow rate was 11 patients/day.

Next, consider inventory. Inventory changes throughout the day, reflecting the differences between inflow and outflow of patients. A "brute force" approach to compute

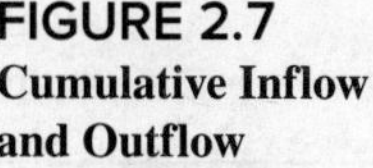

FIGURE 2.7
Cumulative Inflow and Outflow

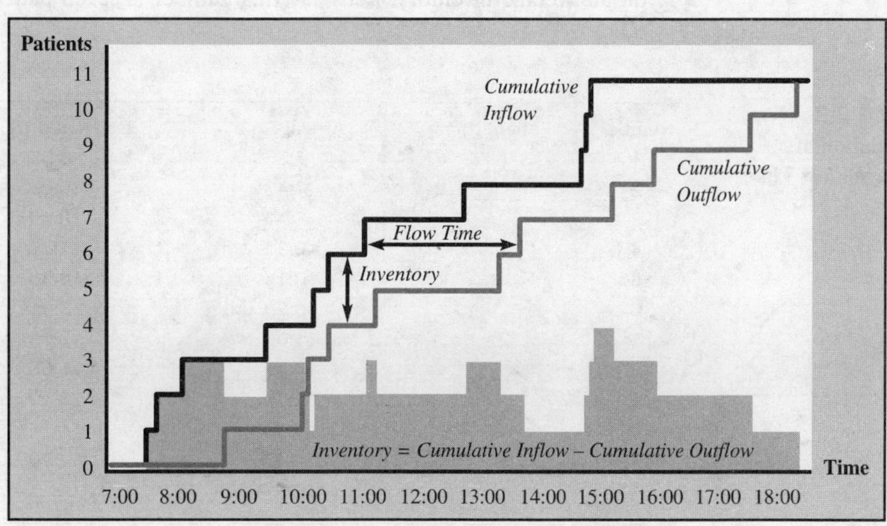

average inventory is to count the inventory at every moment in time throughout the day, say every five minutes, and then take the average. For December 2, this computation yields an average inventory of 2.076 patients.

Next, consider the flow time, the time a patient spends in the unit. To compute that information, we need to add to the patient log, Table 2.1, the time each patient left the interventional radiology unit. The difference between arrival time and departure time would be the flow time for a given patient, which in turn would allow us to compute the average flow time across patients. This is shown in Table 2.3 and is in many ways similar to the two graphs in Figure 2.7. We can easily compute that on December 2, the average flow time was 2 hours, 4 minutes, and 33 seconds, or 2.076 hours.

At this point, you might ask: "Does the average inventory always come out the same as the average flow time?" The answer to this question is a resounding *no.* However, the fact that the average inventory was 2.076 patients and the average flow time was 2.076 hours is no coincidence either.

To see how inventory and flow time relate to each other, let us review the three performance measures, flow rate, flow time, and inventory:

- Flow rate = 11 patients per day, which is equal to 1 patient per hour.
- Flow time = 2.076 hours.
- Inventory = 2.076 patients.

Thus, while inventory and flow time do not have to—and, in fact, rarely are—equal, they are linked in another form. We will now introduce this relationship as Little's Law (named after John D. C. Little).

$$\text{Average inventory} = \text{Average flow rate} \times \text{Average flow time} \qquad \text{(Little's Law)}$$

Many people think of this relationship as trivial. However, it is not. Its proof is rather complex for the general case (which includes—among other nasty things—variability) and by mathematical standards is very recent.

Little's Law is useful in finding the third performance measure when the other two are known. For example, if you want to find out how long patients in a radiology unit spend waiting for their chest X-ray, you could do the following:

1. Observe the inventory of patients at a couple of random points during the day, giving you an average inventory. Let's say this number is seven patients: four in the waiting

TABLE 2.3 Calculation of Average Flow Time

Number	Patient Name	Arrival Time	Departure Time	Flow Time
1		7:35	8:50	1:15
2		7:45	10:05	2:20
3		8:10	10:10	2:00
4		9:30	11:15	1:45
5		10:15	10:30	0:15
6		10:30	13:35	3:05
7		11:05	13:15	2:10
8		12:35	15:05	2:30
9		14:30	18:10	3:40
10		14:35	15:45	1:10
11		14:40	17:20	2:40
			Average	2:04:33

room, two already changed and waiting in front of the procedure room, and one in the procedure room.

2. Count the procedure slips or any other records showing how many patients were treated that day. This is the day's output. Let's say there were 60 patients over a period of 8 hours; we could say that we have a flow rate of 60/8 = 7.5 patients/hour.
3. Use Little's Law to compute Flow time = Inventory/Flow rate = 7/7.5 = 0.933 hour = 56 minutes. This tells us that, on average, it takes 56 minutes from the time a patient enters the radiology unit to the time his or her chest X-ray is completed. Note that this information would otherwise have to be computed by collecting additional data (e.g., see Table 2.3).

When does Little's Law hold? The short answer is *always.* For example, Little's Law does not depend on the sequence in which the flow units (e.g., patients) are served (remember FIFO and LIFO from your accounting class?). (However, the sequence could influence the flow time of a particular flow unit, e.g., the patient arriving first in the morning, but not the average flow time across all flow units.) Furthermore, Little's Law does not depend on randomness: it does not matter if there is variability in the number of patients or in how long treatment takes for each patient; all that matters is the average flow rate of patients and the average flow time.

In addition to the direct application of Little's Law, for example, in the computation of flow time, Little's Law is also underlying the computation of inventory costs as well as a concept known as inventory turns. This is discussed in the following section.

2.4 Inventory Turns and Inventory Costs

Using physical units as flow units (and, hence, as the inventory measure) is probably the most intuitive way to measure inventory. This could be vehicles at an auto retailer, patients in the hospital, or tons of oil in a refinery.

However, working with physical units is not necessarily the best method for obtaining an aggregate measure of inventory across different products: there is little value to saying you have 2,000 units of inventory if 1,000 of them are paper clips and the remaining 1,000 are computers. In such applications, inventory is often measured in some monetary unit, for example, $5 million worth of inventory.

Measuring inventory in a common monetary unit facilitates the aggregation of inventory across different products. This is why total U.S. inventory is reported in dollars. To illustrate the notion of monetary flow units, consider Kohl's Corp, a large U.S. retailer. Instead of thinking of Kohl's stores as sodas, toys, clothes, and bathroom tissues (physical units), we can think of its stores as processes transforming goods valued in monetary units into sales, which also can be evaluated in the form of monetary units.

As can easily be seen from Kohl's balance sheet, on January 31, 2016, the company held an inventory valued at $3.795 billion (see Table 2.4). Given that our flow unit now is the "individual dollar bill," we want to measure the flow rate through Kohl's operation.

The direct approach would be to take "revenue" as the resulting flow. Yet, this measure is inflated by Kohl's gross profit margin; that is, a dollar of sales is measured in revenue dollars, while a dollar of inventory is measured, given the present accounting practice, in a cost dollar. Thus, the appropriate measure for flow rate is the cost of goods sold, or COGS for short.

TABLE 2.4 Excerpts from Financial Statements of Kohl's and Walmart (All Numbers in Millions)

	2016
Kohl's	
Revenue	$ 18,686
Cost of Goods Sold	$ 11,944
Inventory	$ 3,795
Net Income	$ 556
Walmart	
Revenue	$482,130
Cost of Goods Sold	$360,984
Inventory	$ 44,469
Net Income	$ 14,694

Source: Taken from 10-K filings.

With these two measures—flow rate and inventory—we can apply Little's Law to compute what initially might seem a rather artificial measure: How long does the average flow unit (dollar bill) spend within the Kohl's system before being turned into sales, at which point the flow units will trigger a profit intake? This corresponds to the definition of flow time.

$$\text{Flow rate} = \text{Cost of goods sold} = \$11{,}944 \text{ million/year}$$
$$\text{Inventory} = \$3{,}795 \text{ million}$$

Hence, we can compute flow time via Little's Law as

$$\text{Flow time} = \frac{\text{Inventory}}{\text{Flow rate}}$$

$$= \$3{,}795 \text{ million}/\$11{,}944 \text{ million/year} = 0.3177 \text{ year} = 115.97 \text{ days}$$

Thus, we find that it takes Kohl's—on average—116 days to translate a dollar investment into a dollar of—hopefully profitable—revenues.

This calculation underlies the definition of another way of measuring inventory, namely in terms of *days of supply*. We could say that Kohl's has 116 days of inventory in their process. In other words, the average item we find at Kohl's spends 116 days in Kohl's supply chain.

Alternatively, we could say that Kohl's turns over its inventory 365 days/year/116 days = 3.15 times per year. This measure is called *inventory turns*. Inventory turns is a common benchmark in the retailing environment and other supply chain operations:

$$\text{Inventory turns} = \frac{1}{\text{Flow time}}$$

To illustrate this application of Little's Law further, consider Walmart, one of Kohl's competitors. Repeating the same calculations as outlined on the previous page, we find the following data about Walmart:

$$\begin{aligned}
\text{Cost of goods sold} &= \$360{,}984 \text{ million/year}\\
\text{Inventory} &= \$44{,}469 \text{ million}\\
\text{Flow time} &= \$44{,}469 \text{ million}/\$360{,}984 \text{ million/year}\\
&= 0.123 \text{ year} = 44.96 \text{ days}\\
\text{Inventory turns} &= 1/44.96 \text{ turns/day}\\
&= 365 \text{ days/year} \times 1/44.96 \text{ turns/day} = 8.12 \text{ turns per year}
\end{aligned}$$

TABLE 2.5
Inventory Turns and Margins for Selected Retail Segments

Retail Segment	Company	Annual Inventory Turns	Gross Margin
Apparel and accessory	GAP	5.40	36.3%
Catalog, mail-order	Lands End	2.34	43.3%
Department stores	Macy's	2.89	39.4%
Drug and proprietary stores	CVS	10.07	16.3%
Food stores	Kroger	11.40	22.4%
Hobby, toy/game stores	Toys R Us	3.00	35.6%
Home furniture/equipment	Bed Bath & Beyond	2.63	37.5%
Jewelry	Tiffany	0.70	62.2%
Radio, TV, consumer electronics	Best Buy	6.16	24.0%
Variety stores	Walmart	8.12	24.6%
e-Commerce	Amazon	7.70	35.1%

Thus, we find that Walmart is able to achieve substantially higher inventory turns than Kohl's. Table 2.5 summarizes inventory turn data for various segments of the retailing industry. Table 2.5 also provides information about gross margins in various retail settings (keep them in mind the next time you haggle for a new sofa or watch!).

Inventory requires substantial financial investments. Moreover, the inventory holding cost is substantially higher than the mere financial holding cost for a number of reasons:

- Inventory might become obsolete (think of the annual holding cost of a microprocessor).
- Inventory might physically perish (you don't want to think of the cost of holding fresh roses for a year).
- Inventory might disappear (also known as theft or shrinkage).
- Inventory requires storage space and other overhead cost (insurance, security, real estate, etc.).
- There are other less tangible costs of inventory that result from increased wait times (because of Little's Law, to be discussed in Chapter 9) and lower quality (to be discussed in Chapter 8).

Given an annual cost of inventory (e.g., 20 percent per year) and the inventory turn information as computed above, we can compute the per-unit inventory cost that a process (or a supply chain) incurs. To do this, we take the annual holding cost and divide it by the number of times the inventory turns in a year:

$$\text{Per-unit inventory costs} = \frac{\text{Annual inventory costs}}{\text{Annual inventory turns}}$$

For example, a company that works based on a 20 percent annual inventory cost and that turns its inventory six times per year incurs per-unit inventory costs of

$$\frac{20\%\text{ per year}}{6\text{ turns per year}} = 3.33\%$$

In the case of Kohl's (we earlier computed that the inventory turns 3.15 times per year), and assuming annual holding costs of 20 percent per year, this translates to inventory costs of about 6.35 percent of the cost of goods sold (20%/3.15 = 6.35). The calculations to obtain per unit inventory costs are summarized in Exhibit 2.1.

Exhibit 2.1

CALCULATING INVENTORY TURNS AND PER-UNIT INVENTORY COSTS

1. Look up the value of inventory from the balance sheet.
2. Look up the cost of goods sold (COGS) from the earnings statement; do *not* use sales!
3. Compute inventory turns as

$$\text{Inventory turns} = \frac{\text{COGS}}{\text{Inventory}}$$

4. Compute per-unit inventory costs as

$$\text{Per-unit inventory costs} = \frac{\text{Annual inventory costs}}{\text{Inventory turns}}$$

Note: The annual inventory cost needs to account for the cost of financing the inventory, the cost of depreciation, and other inventory-related costs the firm considers relevant (e.g., storage, theft).

To stay in the retailing context a little longer, consider a retailer of consumer electronics who has annual inventory costs of 30 percent (driven by financial costs and obsolescence). Assuming the retailer turns its inventory about six times per year (see Best Buy data in Table 2.5.), we obtain a per-unit inventory cost of 30%/6 = 5%. Consider a TV in the retailer's assortment that is on the shelf with a price tag of $300 and is procured by the retailer for $200. Based on our calculation, we know that the retailer incurs a $200 × 5% = $10 inventory cost for each such TV that is sold. To put this number into perspective, consider Figure 2.8.

Figure 2.8 plots the relationship between gross margin and inventory turns for consumer electronics retailers (based on Gaur, Fisher, and Raman 2005). Note that this graph does not imply causality in this relationship. That is, the model does not imply that if a firm increases its gross margin, its inventory turns will decline automatically. Instead, the way to look at Figure 2.8 is to think of gross margin for a given set of products as being fixed by the competitive environment. We can then make two interesting observations:

- A retailer can decide to specialize in products that turn very slowly to increase its margins. For example, Radio Shack is known for its high margins, as they carry many products in their assortment that turn only once or twice a year. In contrast, Best Buy is carrying largely very popular items, which exposes the company to stiffer competition and lower gross margins.
- For a given gross margin, we observe dramatic differences concerning inventory turns. For example, inventory turns vary between four and nine times for a 15 percent gross margin. Consider retailer A and assume that all retailers work with a 30 percent annual holding cost. Based on the annual inventory turns of 4.5, retailer A faces a 6.66 percent per-unit inventory cost. Now, compare this to competing retailer B, who turns its inventory eight times per year. Thus, retailer B operates with 3.75 percent per-unit inventory costs, almost a 3 percent cost advantage over retailer A. Given that net profits in this industry segment are around 2 percent of sales, such a cost advantage can make the difference between profits and bankruptcy.

FIGURE 2.8
Relationship between Inventory Turns and Gross Margin

Source: Based on Gaur, Fisher, and Raman 2005.

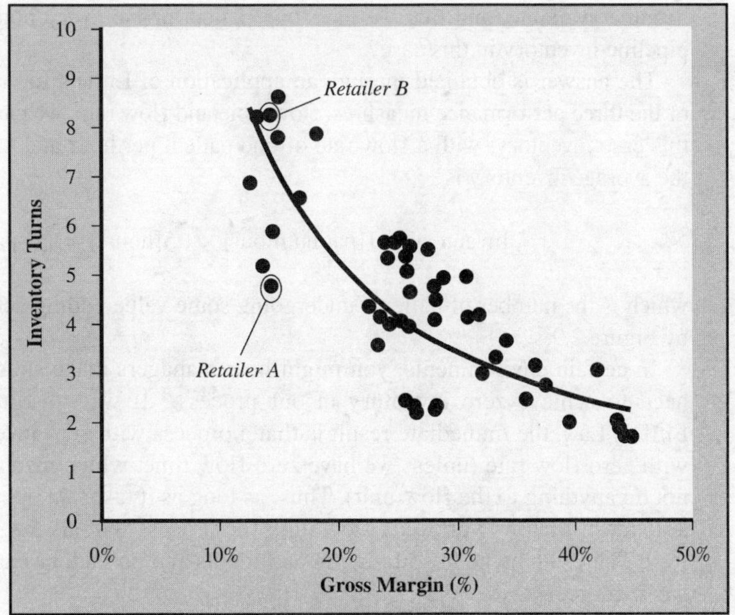

2.5 Five Reasons to Hold Inventory

While Little's Law allows us to compute the average inventory in the process (as long as we know flow time and flow rate), it offers no help in answering the question we raised previously: Why is there inventory in the process in the first place? To understand the need for inventory, we can no longer afford to take the black-box perspective and look at processes from the outside. Instead, we have to look at the process in much more detail.

As we saw from Figure 2.7, inventory reflected a deviation between the inflow into a process and its outflow. Ideally, from an operations perspective, we would like Figure 2.7 to take the shape of two identical, straight lines, representing process inflow and outflow. Unfortunately, such straight lines with zero distance between them rarely exist in the real world. De Groote (1994) discusses five reasons for holding inventory, that is, for having the inflow line differ from the outflow line: (1) the time a flow unit spends in the process, (2) seasonal demand, (3) economies of scale, (4) separation of steps in a process, and (5) stochastic demand. Depending on the reason for holding inventory, inventories are given different names: pipeline inventory, seasonal inventory, cycle inventory, decoupling inventory/ buffers, and safety inventory. It should be noted that these five reasons are not necessarily mutually exclusive and that, in practice, there typically exist more than one reason for holding inventory.

Pipeline Inventory

This first reason for inventory reflects the time a flow unit has to spend in the process in order to be transformed from input to output. Even with unlimited resources, patients still need to spend time in the interventional radiology unit; their flow time would be the length of the critical path. We refer to this basic inventory on which the process operates as *pipeline inventory*.

For the sake of simplicity, let's assume that every patient would have to spend exactly 1.5 hours in the interventional radiology unit, as opposed to waiting for a resource to become available, and that we have one patient arrive every hour. How do we find the pipeline inventory in this case?

The answer is obtained through an application of Little's Law. Because we know two of the three performance measures, flow time and flow rate, we can figure out the third, in this case inventory: with a flow rate of one patient per hour and a flow time of 1.5 hours, the average inventory is

$$\text{Inventory} = 1[\text{patient/hour}] \times 1.5[\text{hours}] = 1.5 \text{ patients}$$

which is the number of patients undergoing some value-adding activity. This is illustrated by Figure 2.9.

In certain environments, you might hear managers make statements of the type "we need to achieve zero inventory in our process." If we substitute Inventory = 0 into Little's Law, the immediate result is that a process with zero inventory is also a process with zero flow rate (unless we have zero flow time, which means that the process does not do anything to the flow unit). Thus, as long as it takes an operation even a minimum amount of time to work on a flow unit, the process will always exhibit pipeline inventory. There can be no hospital without patients and no factory can operate without some work in process!

Little's Law also points us toward the best way to reduce pipeline inventory. As reducing flow rate (and with it demand and profit) is typically not a desirable option, the *only* other way to reduce pipeline inventory is by reducing flow time.

Seasonal Inventory

Seasonal inventory occurs when capacity is rigid and demand is variable. Two examples illustrate this second reason for inventory. Campbell's Soup sells more chicken noodle soup in January than in any other month of the year—not primarily because of cold weather, but because Campbell's discounts chicken noodle soup in January. June is the next biggest sales month, because Campbell's increases its price in July.

So much soup is sold in January that Campbell's starts production several months in advance and builds inventory in anticipation of January sales. Campbell's could wait longer to start production and thereby not build as much inventory, but it would be too costly to assemble the needed capacity (equipment and labor) in the winter only to dismantle that capacity at the end of January when it is no longer needed.

In other words, as long as it is costly to add and subtract capacity, firms will desire to smooth production relative to sales, thereby creating the need for seasonal inventory.

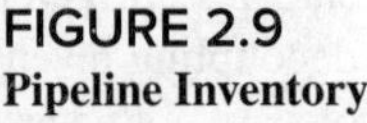
FIGURE 2.9
Pipeline Inventory

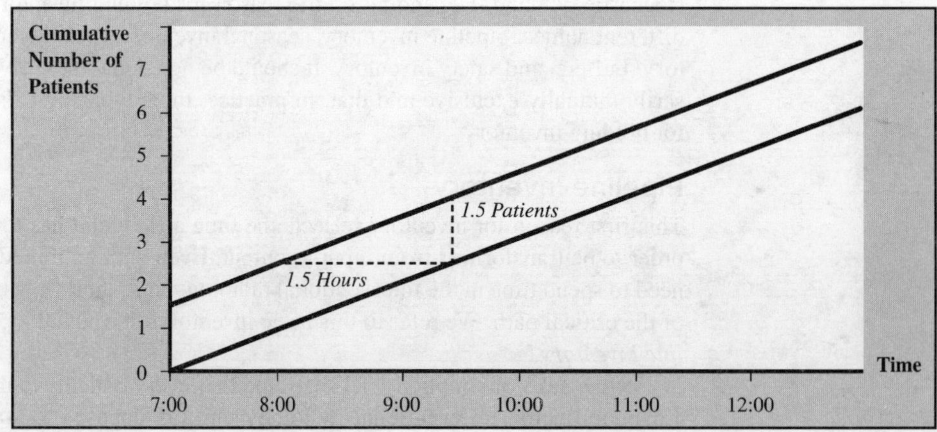

FIGURE 2.10
Seasonal Inventory—Sugar

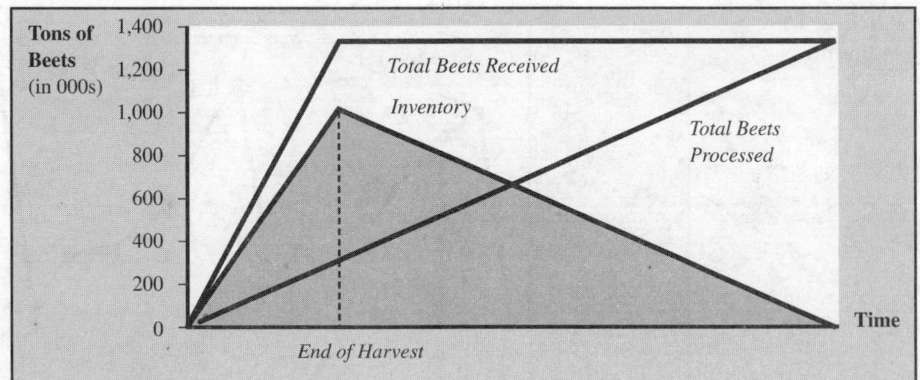

An extreme case of seasonal inventory can be found in the agricultural and food processing sector. Due to the nature of the harvesting season, the sugar farmers in the U.S. Midwest collect all raw material for their sugar production over a period of six weeks. At the end of the harvesting season, a large producer has accumulated—in the very meaning of the word—a pile of sugar beets, about 1 million tons, taking the form of a 67-acre sugar beets pile.

Given that food processing is a very capital-intense operation, the process is sized such that the 1.325 million tons of beets received and the almost 1 million tons of inventory that is built allow for a nonstop operation of the production plant until the beginning of the next harvesting season. Thus, as illustrated by Figure 2.10, the production, and hence the product outflow, is close to constant, while the product inflow is zero except for the harvesting season.

Cycle Inventory

Throughout this book, we will encounter many situations in which it is economical to process several flow units collectively at a given moment in time to take advantage of scale economies in operations.

The scale economics in transportation processes provide a good example for the third reason for inventory. Whether a truck is dispatched empty or full, the driver is paid a fixed amount and a sizeable portion of the wear and tear on the truck depends on the mileage driven, not on the load carried. In other words, each truck shipment incurs a fixed cost that is independent of the amount shipped. To mitigate the sting of that fixed cost, it is tempting to load the truck completely, thereby dividing the fixed cost across the largest number of units.

In many cases, this indeed may be a wise decision. But a truck often carries more product than can be immediately sold. Hence, it takes some time to sell off the entire truck delivery. During that interval of time, there will be inventory. This inventory is labeled *cycle inventory* as it reflects that the transportation process follows a certain shipment cycle (e.g., a shipment every week).

Figure 2.11 plots the inventory level of a simple tray that is required during the operation in the interventional radiology unit. As we can see, there exists a "lumpy" inflow of units, while the outflow is relatively smooth. The reason for this is that—due to the administrative efforts related to placing orders for the trays—the hospital places only one order per week.

The major difference between cycle inventory and seasonal inventory is that seasonal inventory is due to temporary imbalances in supply and demand due to variable demand (soup) or variable supply (beets) while cycle inventory is created due to a cost motivation.

FIGURE 2.11
Cycle Inventory

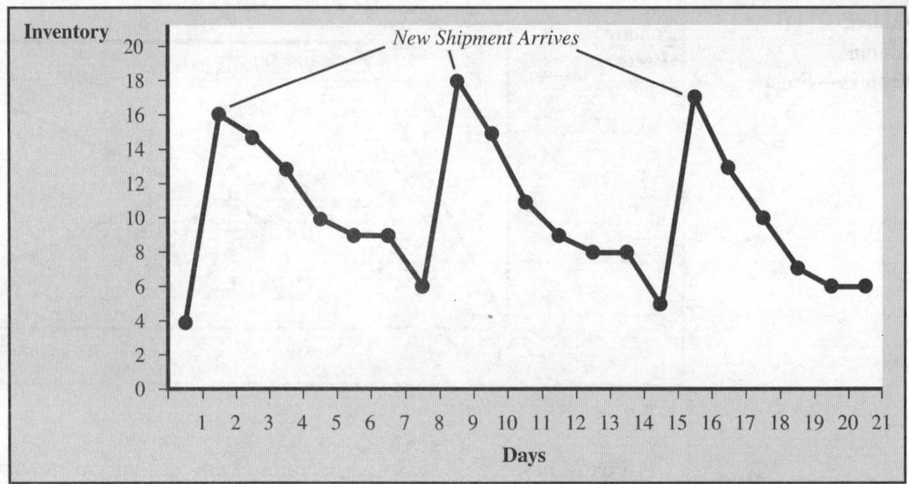

Decoupling Inventory/Buffers

Inventory between process steps can serve as buffers. An inventory buffer allows management to operate steps independently from each other. For example, consider two workers in a garment factory. Suppose the first worker sews the collar onto a shirt and the second sews the buttons. A buffer between them is a pile of shirts with collars but no buttons. Because of that buffer, the first worker can stop working (e.g., to take a break, repair the sewing machine, or change thread color) while the second worker keeps working. In other words, buffers can absorb variations in flow rates by acting as a source of supply for a downstream process step, even if the previous operation itself might not be able to create this supply at the given moment in time.

An automotive assembly line is another example of a production process that uses buffers to decouple the various stations involved with producing the vehicle. In the absence of such buffers, a disruption at any one station would lead to a disruption of all the other stations, upstream and downstream. Think of a bucket brigade to fight a fire: there are no buffers between firefighters in a bucket brigade, so nobody can take a break without stopping the entire process.

Safety Inventory

The final reason for inventory is probably the most obvious, but also the most challenging: stochastic demand. Stochastic demand refers to the fact that we need to distinguish between the predicted demand and the actually realized demand. In other words, we typically face variation in demand relative to our demand prediction. Note that this is different from variations in predictable demand, which is called *seasonality,* like a sales spike of Campbell's chicken noodle soup in January. Furthermore, stochastic demand can be present along with seasonal demand: January sales can be known to be higher than those for other months (seasonal demand) and there can be variation around that known forecast (stochastic demand).

Stochastic demand is an especially significant problem in retailing environments or at the finished goods level of manufacturers. Take a book retailer that must decide how many books to order of a given title. The book retailer has a forecast for demand, but forecasts are (at best) correct on average. Order too many books and the retailer is faced with leftover inventory. Order too few and valuable sales are lost. This trade-off can be managed, as we will discover in Chapter 14, but not eliminated (unless there are zero forecast errors).

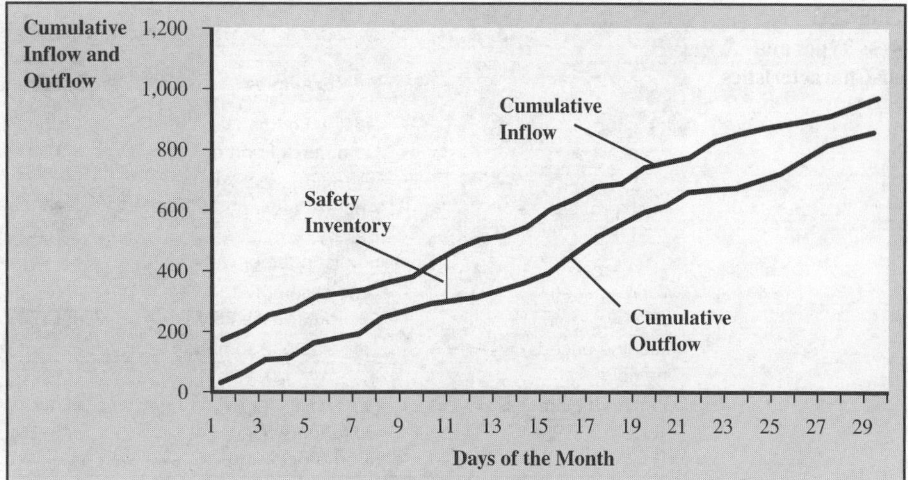

FIGURE 2.12
Safety Inventory at a Blood Bank

The resulting inventory thereby can be seen as a way to hedge against the underlying demand uncertainty. It might reflect a one-shot decision, for example, in the case of a book retailer selling short-life-cycle products such as newspapers or magazines. If we consider a title with a longer product life cycle (e.g., children's books), the book retailer will be able to replenish books more or less continuously over time.

Figure 2.12 shows the example of the blood bank in Presbyterian Hospital in Philadelphia. While the detailed inflow and consumption of blood units vary over the course of the month, the hospital always has a couple of days of blood in inventory. Given that blood perishes quickly, the hospital wants to keep only a small inventory at its facility, which it replenishes from the regional blood bank operated by the Red Cross.

2.6 The Product–Process Matrix

Processes leading to the supply of goods or services can take many different forms. Some processes are highly automated, while others are largely manual. Some processes resemble the legendary Ford assembly line, while others resemble more the workshop in your local bike store. Empirical research in operations management, which has looked at thousands of processes, has identified five "clusters" or types of processes. Within each of the five clusters, processes are very similar concerning variables such as the number of different product variants they offer or the production volume they provide. Table 2.6 describes these different types of processes.

By looking at the evolution of a number of industries, Hayes and Wheelwright (1979) observed an interesting pattern, which they referred to as the product–process matrix (see Figure 2.13). The product–process matrix stipulates that over its life cycle, a product typically is initially produced in a job shop process. As the production volume of the product increases, the production process for the product moves from the upper left of the matrix to the lower right.

For example, the first automobiles were produced using job shops, typically creating one product at a time. Most automobiles were unique; not only did they have different colors or add-ons, but they differed in size, geometry of the body, and many other aspects. Henry Ford's introduction of the assembly line corresponded to a major shift along the diagonal of the product–process matrix. Rather than producing a couple of products in a job shop, Ford produced thousands of vehicles on an assembly line.

TABLE 2.6
Process Types and Their Characteristics

	Examples	Number of Different Product Variants	Product Volume (Units/Year)
Job shop	• Design company • Commercial printer • Formula 1 race car	High (100+)	Low (1–100)
Batch process	• Apparel sewing • Bakery • Semiconductor wafers	Medium (10–100)	Medium (100–100k)
Worker-paced line flow	• Auto assembly • Computer assembly	Medium (1–50)	High (10k–1M)
Machine-paced line flow	• Large auto assembly	Low (1–10)	High (10k–1M)
Continuous process	• Paper mill • Oil refinery • Food processing	Low (1–10)	Very high

Note that the "off-diagonals" in the product–process matrix (the lower left and the upper right) are empty. This reflects that it is neither economical to produce very high volumes in a job shop (imagine if all of the millions of new vehicles sold in the United States every year were handcrafted in the same manner as Gottlieb Daimler created the first automobile) nor does it make sense to use an assembly line in order to produce only a handful of products a year.

We have to admit that few companies—if any—would be foolish enough to produce a high-volume product in a job shop. However, identifying a process type and looking at the product–process matrix is more than an academic exercise in industrial history. The usefulness of the product–process matrix lies in two different points:

1. Similar process types tend to have similar problems. For example, as we will discuss in Chapter 4, assembly lines tend to have the problem of line balancing (some workers working harder than others). Batch-flow processes tend to be slow in responding to

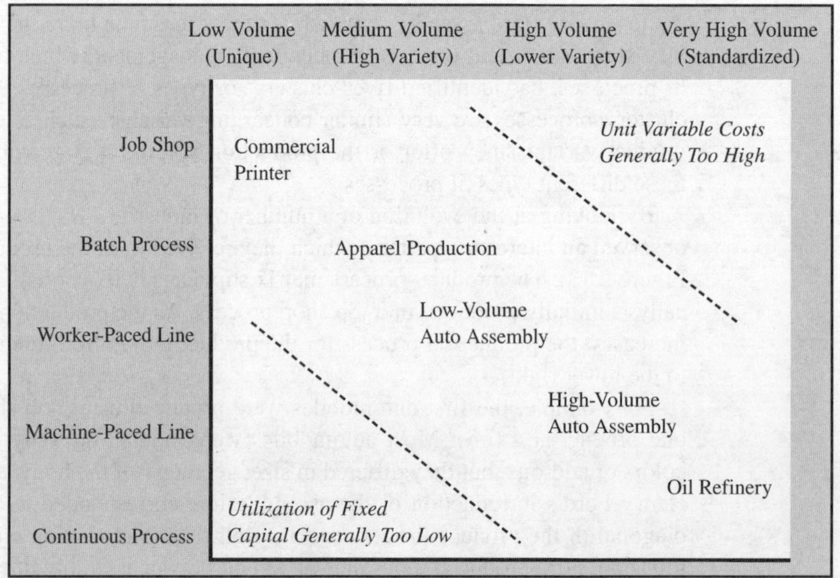

FIGURE 2.13
Product–Process Matrix

Source: Hayes and Wheelwright (1979).

customer demand (see Chapter 5). Thus, once you know a process type, you can quickly determine what type of problems the process is likely to face and what solution methods are most appropriate.

2. The "natural drift" of industries toward the lower right of Figure 2.13 enables you to predict how processes are likely to evolve in a particular industry. Consider, for example, the case of eye surgery. Up until the 1980s, corrective eye surgery was done in large hospitals. There, doctors would perform a large variety of very different eye-related cases. Fifteen years later, this situation had changed dramatically. Many highly specialized eye clinics have opened, most of them focusing on a limited set of procedures. These clinics achieve high volume and, because of the high volume and the lower variety of cases, can operate at much higher levels of efficiency.

2.7 Summary

In this chapter, we emphasized the importance of looking at the operations of a firm not just in terms of the products that the firm supplies, but also at the processes that generate the supply. Looking at processes is especially important with respect to demand–supply mismatches. From the perspective of the product, such mismatches take the form of waiting times; from the perspective of the process, they take the form of inventory.

For any process, we can define three fundamental performance measures: inventory, flow time, and flow rate. The three measures are related by Little's Law, which states that the average inventory is equal to the average flow time multiplied by the average flow rate.

Little's Law can be used to find any of the three performance measures, as long as the other two measures are known. This is specifically important with respect to flow time, which is in practice frequently difficult to observe directly.

A measure related to flow time is inventory turns. Inventory turns, measured by 1/(flow time), captures how fast the flow units are transformed from input to output. It is an important benchmark in many industries, especially retailing. Inventory turns are also the basis of computing the inventory costs associated with one unit of supply.

2.8 Further Reading

De Groote (1994) is a very elegant note describing the basic roles of inventory. This note, as well as many other notes and articles by de Groote, takes a very "lean" perspective to operations management, resembling much more the tradition of economics as opposed to engineering.

Gaur, Fisher, and Raman (2005) provide an extensive study of retailing performance. They present various operational measures, including inventory turns, and show how they relate to financial performance measures.

The Hayes and Wheelwright (1979) reference is widely recognized as a pioneering article linking operations aspects to business strategy. Subsequent work by Hayes, Wheelwright, and Clark (1988) established operations as a key source for a firm's competitive advantage.

2.9 Practice Problems

The following questions will help in testing your understanding of this chapter. After each question, we show the relevant section in parentheses [Section x].

Solutions to problems marked with an "*" are available in Appendix E. Video solutions to select problems are available in Connect.

Q2.1* **(Dell)** What percentage of cost of a Dell computer reflects inventory costs? Assume Dell's yearly inventory cost is 40 percent to account for the cost of capital for financing the inventory, the warehouse space, and the cost of obsolescence. In other words, Dell incurs a cost of $40 for a $100 component that is in the company's inventory for one entire year. In 2001, Dell's 10-k reports showed that the company had $400 million in inventory and COGS of $26,442 million. [2.4]

Q2.2 **(Airline)** Consider the baggage check-in of a small airline. Check-in data indicate that from 9 a.m. to 10 a.m., 255 passengers checked in. Moreover, based on counting the number of passengers waiting in line, airport management found that the average number of passengers waiting for check-in was 35. How long did the average passenger have to wait in line? [2.3]

Q2.3 **(Inventory Cost)** A manufacturing company producing medical devices reported $60,000,000 in sales over the last year. At the end of the same year, the company had $20,000,000 worth of inventory of ready-to-ship devices.

a. Assuming that units in inventory are valued (based on COGS) at $1,000 per unit and are sold for $2,000 per unit, how fast does the company turn its inventory? The company uses a 25 percent per year cost of inventory. That is, for the hypothetical case that one unit of $1,000 would sit exactly one year in inventory, the company charges its operations division a $250 inventory cost. [2.4]

b. What—in absolute terms—is the per unit inventory cost for a product that costs $1,000? [2.4]

Q2.4 **(Apparel Retailing)** A large catalog retailer of fashion apparel reported $100,000,000 in revenues over the last year. On average, over the same year, the company had $5,000,000 worth of inventory in their warehouses. Assume that units in inventory are valued based on cost of goods sold (COGS) and that the retailer has a 100 percent markup on all products.

a. How many times each year does the retailer turn its inventory? [2.4]

b. The company uses a 40 percent per year cost of inventory. That is, for the hypothetical case that one item of $100 COGS would sit exactly one year in inventory, the company charges itself a $40 inventory cost. What is the inventory cost for a $30 (COGS) item? You may assume that inventory turns are independent of the price. [2.4]

Q2.5 **(LaVilla)** LaVilla is a village in the Italian Alps. Given its enormous popularity among Swiss, German, Austrian, and Italian skiers, all of its beds are always booked in the winter season and there are, on average, 1,200 skiers in the village. On average, skiers stay in LaVilla for 10 days.

a. How many new skiers are arriving—on average—in LaVilla every day? [2.3]

b. A study done by the largest hotel in the village has shown that skiers spend on average $50 per person on the first day and $30 per person on each additional day in local restaurants. The study also forecasts that—due to increased hotel prices—the average length of stay for the 2003/2004 season will be reduced to 5 days. What will be the percentage change in revenues of local restaurants compared to last year (when skiers still stayed for 10 days)? Assume that hotels continue to be fully booked! [2.3]

Q2.6 **(Highway)** While driving home for the holidays, you can't seem to get Little's Law out of your mind. You note that your average speed of travel is about 60 miles per hour. Moreover, the traffic report from the WXPN traffic chopper states that there is an average of 24 cars going in your direction on a one-quarter mile part of the highway. What is the flow rate of the highway (going in your direction) in cars per hour? [2.3]

Q2.7 **(Industrial Baking Process)** Strohrmann, a large-scale bakery in Pennsylvania, is laying out a new production process for their packaged bread, which they sell to several grocery chains. It takes 12 minutes to bake the bread. How large an oven is required so that the company is able to produce 4,000 units of bread per hour (measured in the number of units that can be baked simultaneously)? [2.3]

Q2.8 **(Mt. Kinley Consulting)** Mt. Kinley is a strategy consulting firm that divides its consultants into three classes: associates, managers, and partners. The firm has been stable in size for the last 20 years, ignoring growth opportunities in the 90s, but also not suffering from a need to downsize in the recession at the beginning of the 21st century. Specifically, there have been—and are expected to be—200 associates, 60 managers, and 20 partners.

The work environment at Mt. Kinley is rather competitive. After four years of working as an associate, a consultant goes "either up or out," that is, becomes a manager or is dismissed from the company. Similarly, after six years, a manager either becomes a partner or is dismissed. The company recruits MBAs as associate consultants; no hires are made at the manager or partner level. A partner stays with the company for another 10 years (a total of 20 years with the company).

a. How many new MBA graduates does Mt. Kinley have to hire every year? [2.3]

b. What are the odds that a new hire at Mt. Kinley will become partner (as opposed to being dismissed after 4 years or 10 years)? [2.3]

Q2.9 **(Major U.S. Retailers)** The following table shows financial data (year 2004) for Costco Wholesale and Walmart, two major U.S. retailers.

	Costco	Walmart
	($ Millions)	($ Millions)
Inventories	$ 3,643	$ 29,447
Sales (net)	$48,106	$286,103
COGS	$41,651	$215,493

Source: Compustat, WRDS.

Assume that both companies have an average annual holding cost rate of 30 percent (i.e., it costs both retailers $3 to hold an item that they procured for $10 for one entire year).

a. How many days, on average, does a product stay in Costco's inventory before it is sold? Assume that stores are operated 365 days a year. [2.4]

b. How much lower is, on average, the inventory cost for Costco compared to Walmart of a household cleaner valued at $5 COGS? Assume that the unit cost of the household cleaner is the same for both companies and that the price and the inventory turns of an item are independent. [2.4]

Q2.10 **(McDonald's)** The following figures are taken from the 2003 financial statements of McDonald's and Wendy's.[1] Figures are in million dollars.

	McDonald's	Wendy's
Inventory	$ 129.4	$ 54.4
Revenue	17,140.5	3,148.9
Cost of goods sold	11,943.7	1,634.6
Gross profit	5,196.8	1,514.4

a. In 2003, what were McDonald's inventory turns? What were Wendy's inventory turns? [2.4]

b. Suppose it costs both McDonald's and Wendy's $3 (COGS) per their value meal offerings, each sold at the same price of $4. Assume that the cost of inventory for both companies is 30 percent a year. Approximately how much does McDonald's save in inventory cost *per value meal* compared to that of Wendy's? You may assume the inventory turns are independent of the price. [2.4]

Q2.11 **(BCH)** BCH, a large consulting firm in the United Kingdom, has a consulting staff consisting of 400 consultants at the rank of "associate." On average, a consultant remains at the

[1] Example adopted from an About.com article (http://beginnersinvest.about.com/cs/investinglessons/1/blles3mcwen.htm). Financial figures taken from Morningstar.com.

associate level for two years. After this time, 30 percent of the consultants are promoted to the rank of "engagement manager," and the other 70 percent have to leave the company.

In order to maintain the consulting staff at an average level of 400 associates, how many new consultants does BCH have to hire each year at the associate level? [2.3]

Q2.12 **(Kroger)** The following provides 2012 financial information for Kroger (in million $s):

	Kroger
Inventory	$ 6,244
Revenue	$ 95,751
Cost of goods sold	$ 76,858

a. In 2012, what were Kroger's inventory turns? [2.4]

If you would like to test your understanding of a specific section, here are the questions organized by section:

Section 2.3: Q2.2, Q2.5, Q2,6, Q2.7, Q2.8, and Q2.11

Section 2.4: Q2.1, Q2.3, Q2.4, Q2.9, Q2.10, and Q2.12

Chapter 3

Understanding the Supply Process: Evaluating Process Capacity

In the attempt to match supply with demand, an important measure is the maximum amount that a process can produce in a given unit of time, a measure referred to as the *process capacity*. To determine the process capacity of an operation, we need to analyze the operation in much greater detail compared to the previous chapter. Specifically, we need to understand the various activities involved in the operation and how these activities contribute toward fulfilling the overall demand.

In this chapter, you will learn how to perform a process analysis. Unlike Chapter 2, where we felt it was sufficient to treat the details of the operation as a black box and merely focus on the performance measures inventory, flow time, and flow rate, we now will focus on the underlying process in great detail.

Despite this increase in detail, this chapter (and this book) is not taking the perspective of an engineer. In fact, in this chapter, you will learn how to take a fairly technical and complex operation and simplify it to a level suitable for managerial analysis. This includes preparing a process flow diagram, finding the capacity and the bottleneck of the process, computing the utilization of various process steps, and computing a couple of other performance measures.

We will illustrate this new material with the Circored plant, a joint venture between the German engineering company Lurgi AG and the U.S. iron ore producer Cleveland Cliffs. The Circored plant converts iron ore (in the form of iron ore fines) into direct reduced iron (DRI) briquettes. Iron ore fines are shipped to the plant from mines in South America; the briquettes the process produces are shipped to various steel mills in the United States.

The example of the Circored process is particularly useful for our purposes in this chapter. The underlying process is complex and in many ways a masterpiece of process engineering (see Terwiesch and Loch [2002] for further details). At first sight, the process is so complex that it seems impossible to understand the underlying process behavior without a detailed background in engineering and metallurgy. This challenging setting allows us to demonstrate how process analysis can be used to "tame the beast" and create a managerially useful view of the process, avoiding any unnecessary technical details.

3.1 How to Draw a Process Flow Diagram

The best way to begin any analysis of an operation is by drawing a *process flow diagram.* A process flow diagram is a graphical way to describe the process and it will help us to structure the information that we collect during the case analysis or process improvement project. Before we turn to the question of how to draw a process flow diagram, first consider alternative approaches to how we could capture the relevant information about a process.

Looking at the plant from above (literally), we get a picture as is depicted in Figure 3.1. At the aggregate level, the plant consists of a large inventory of iron ore (input), the plant itself (the resource), and a large inventory of finished briquettes (output). In many ways, this corresponds to the black box approach to operations taken by economists and many other managerial disciplines.

In an attempt to understand the details of the underlying process, we could turn to the engineering specifications of the plant. Engineers are interested in a detailed description of the various steps involved in the overall process and how these steps are functioning. Such descriptions, typically referred to as specifications, were used in the actual construction of the plant. Figure 3.2 provides one of the numerous specification drawings for the Circored process.

Unfortunately, this attempt to increase our understanding of the Circored process is also only marginally successful. Like the photograph, this view of the process is also a rather static one: it emphasizes the equipment, yet provides us with little understanding of how the iron ore moves through the process. In many ways, this view of a process is similar to taking the architectural drawings of a hospital and hoping that this would lead to insights about what happens to the patients in this hospital.

In a third—and final—attempt to get our hands around this complex process, we change our perspective from the one of the visitor to the plant (photo in Figure 3.1) or the engineers who built the plant (drawing in Figure 3.2) to the perspective of the iron ore itself and

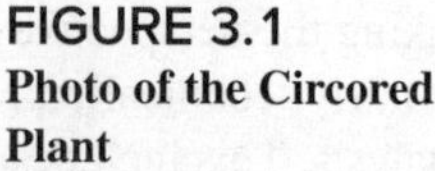

FIGURE 3.1
Photo of the Circored Plant

FIGURE 3.2 **Engineering Drawing**

Source: Terwiesch and Loch 2002.

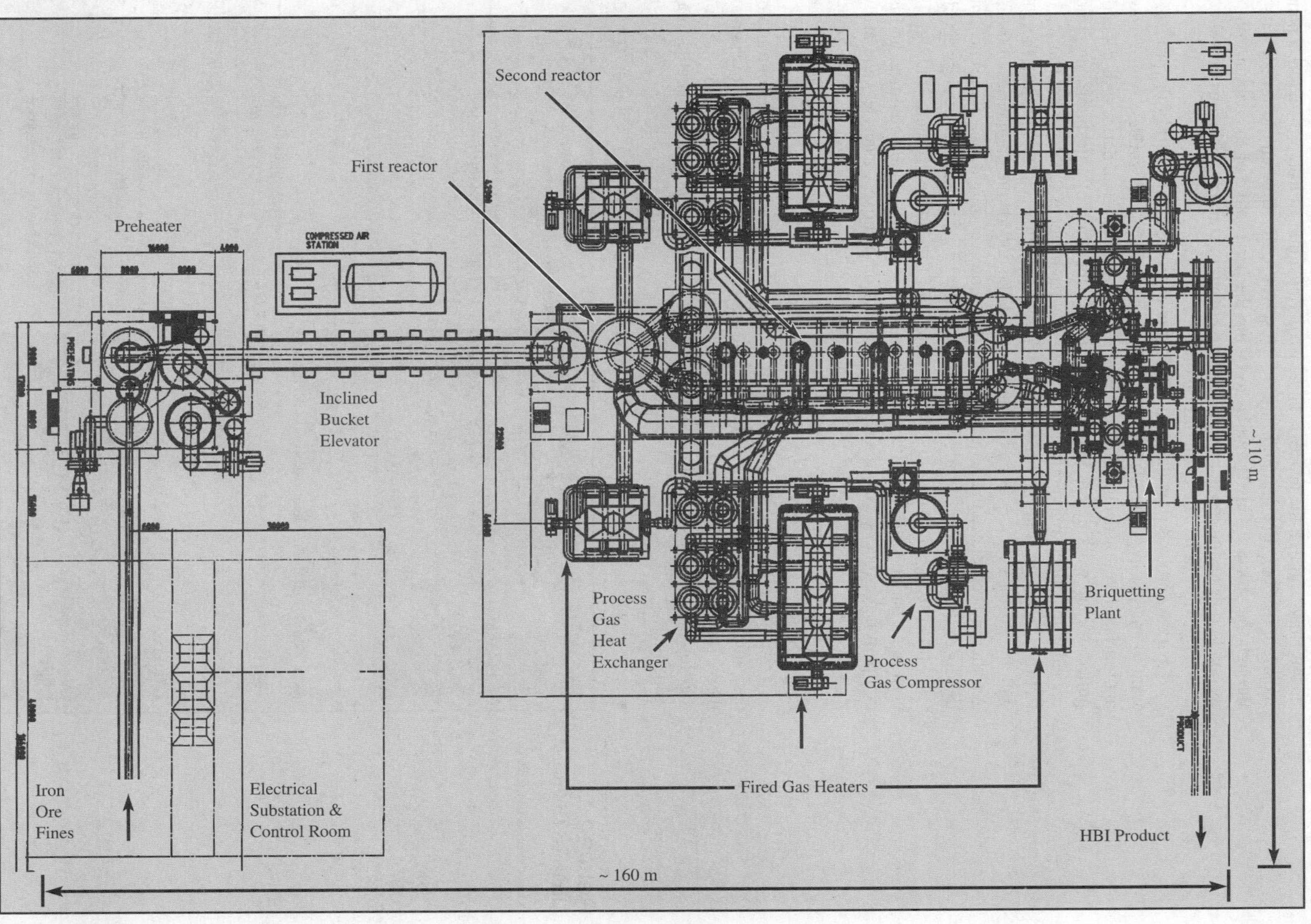

how it flows through the process. Thus, we define a unit of iron ore—a ton, a pound, or a molecule—as our flow unit and "attach" ourselves to this flow unit as it makes its journey through the process. This is similar to taking the perspective of the patient in a hospital, as opposed to taking the perspective of the hospital resources. For concreteness, we will define our flow unit to be a ton of iron ore.

To draw a process flow diagram, we first need to focus on a part of the process that we want to analyze in greater detail; that is, we need to define the *process boundaries* and an appropriate level of detail. The placement of the process boundaries will depend on the project we are working on. For example, in the operation of a hospital, one project concerned with patient waiting time might look at what happens to the patient waiting for a lab test (e.g., check-in, waiting time, encounter with the nurse). In this project, the encounter with the doctor who requested the lab test would be outside the boundaries of the analysis. Another project related to the quality of surgery, however, might look at the encounter with the doctor in great detail, while either ignoring the lab or treating it with less detail.

A process operates on flow units, which are the entities flowing through the process (e.g., patients in a hospital, cars in an auto plant, insurance claims at an insurance company). A process flow diagram is a collection of boxes, triangles, and arrows (see Figure 3.3). Boxes stand for process activities, where the operation adds value to the flow unit. Depending on the level of detail we choose, a process step (a box) can itself be a process.

Triangles represent waiting areas or *buffers* holding inventory. In contrast to a process step, inventories do not add value; thus, a flow unit does not have to spend time in them. However, as discussed in the previous chapter, there are numerous reasons why the flow unit might spend time in inventory even if it will not be augmented to a higher value there.

FIGURE 3.3
Elements of a Process

©Gerard Cachon/Terwiesch and Loch 2002.

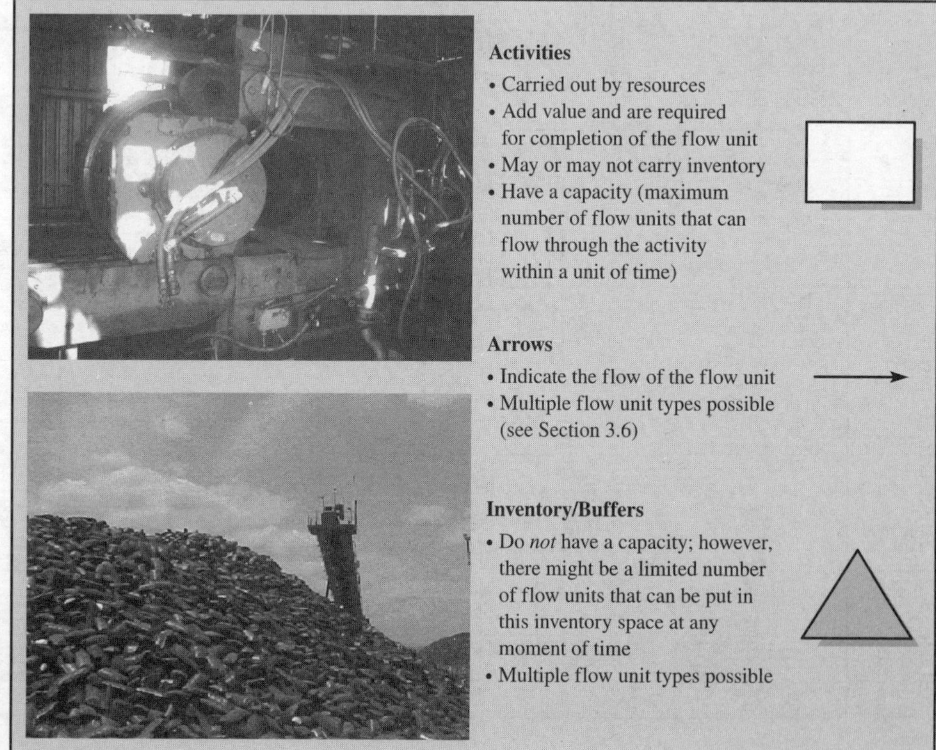

FIGURE 3.4
Process Flow Diagram, First Step

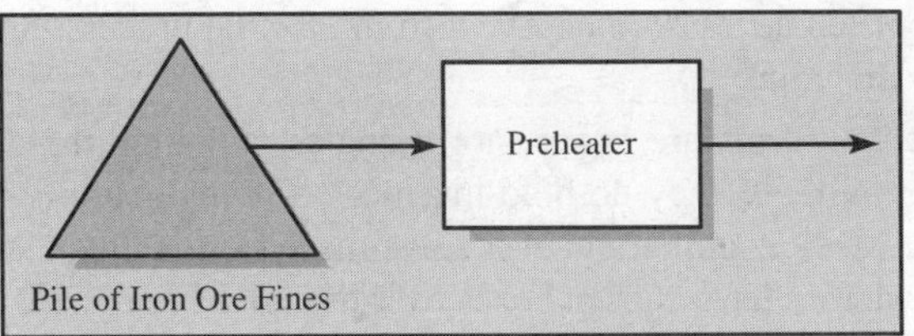

The arrows between boxes and triangles represent the route the flow unit takes through the process. If there are different flow units that take different routes through the process, it can be helpful to use different colors for the different routes. An example of this is given at the end of this chapter.

In the Circored plant, the first step the flow unit encounters in the process is the *preheater,* where the iron ore fines (which have a texture like large-grained sand) are dried and heated. The heating is achieved through an inflow of high-pressured air, which is blown into the preheater from the bottom. The high-speed air flow "fluidizes" the ore, meaning that the mixed air–ore mass (a "sandstorm") circulates through the system as if it was a fluid, while being heated to a temperature of approximately 850–900°C.

However, from a managerial perspective, we are not really concerned with the temperature in the preheater or the chemical reactions happening therein. For us, the preheater is a resource that receives iron ore from the initial inventory and processes it. In an attempt to take record of what the flow unit has experienced up to this point, we create a diagram similar to Figure 3.4.

From the preheater, a large bucket elevator transports the ore to the second process step, the *lock hoppers.* The lock hoppers consist of three large containers, separated by sets of double isolation valves. Their role is to allow the ore to transition from an oxygen-rich environment to a hydrogen atmosphere.

Following the lock hoppers, the ore enters the *circulating fluid bed reactor,* or *first reactor,* where the actual reduction process begins. The reduction process requires the ore to be in the reactor for 15 minutes, and the reactor can hold up to 28 tons of ore.

After this first reduction, the material flows into the *stationary fluid bed reactor,* or *second reactor.* This second reaction takes about four hours. The reactor is the size of a medium two-family home and contains 400 tons of the hot iron ore at any given moment in time. In the meantime, our diagram from Figure 3.4. has extended to something similar to Figure 3.5.

A couple of things are worth noting at this point:

- When creating Figure 3.5, we decided to omit the bucket elevator. There is no clear rule on when it is appropriate to omit a small step and when a step would have to be included in the process flow diagram. A reasonably good rule of thumb is to only include those process steps that are likely to affect the process flow or the economics of the process. The bucket elevator is cheap, the flow units spend little time on it, and this

FIGURE 3.5 **Process Flow Diagram (to Be Continued)**

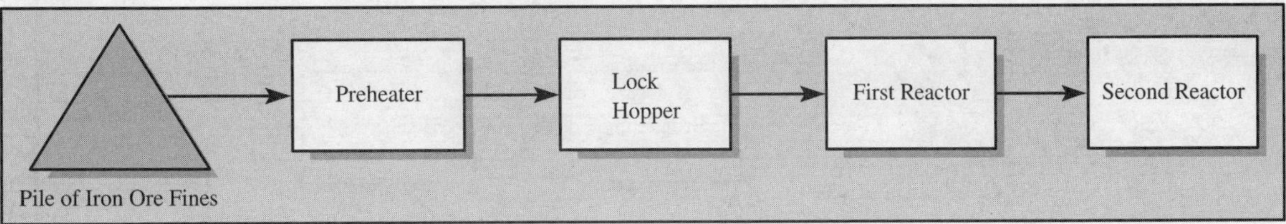

transportation step never becomes a constraint for the process. So it is not included in our process flow diagram.

• The reaction steps are boxes, not triangles, although there is a substantial amount of ore in them, that is, they do hold inventory. The reduction steps are necessary, value-adding steps. No flow unit could ever leave the system without spending time in the reactors. This is why we have chosen boxes over triangles here.

Following the second reactor, the reduced iron enters the *flash heater,* in which a stream of high-velocity hydrogen carries the DRI to the top of the plant while simultaneously reheating it to a temperature of 685°C.

After the flash heater, the DRI enters the *pressure let-down system (discharger).* As the material passes through the discharger, the hydrogen atmosphere is gradually replaced by inert nitrogen gas. Pressure and hydrogen are removed in a reversal of the lock hoppers at the beginning. Hydrogen gas sensors assure that material leaving this step is free of hydrogen gas and, hence, safe for briquetting.

Each of the three *briquetting* machines contains two wheels that turn against each other, each wheel having the negative of one-half of a briquette on its face. The DRI is poured onto the wheels from the top and is pressed into briquettes, or iron bars, which are then moved to a large pile of finished goods inventory.

This completes our journey of the flow unit through the plant. The resulting process flow diagram that captures what the flow unit has experienced in the process is summarized in Figure 3.6.

When drawing a process flow diagram, the sizes and the exact locations of the arrows, boxes, and triangles do not carry any special meaning. For example, in the context of Figure 3.6, we chose a "U-shaped" layout of the process flow diagram, as otherwise we would have had to publish this book in a larger format.

In the absence of any space constraints, the simplest way to draw a process flow diagram for a process such as Circored's is just as one long line. However, we should keep in mind that there are more complex processes; for example, a process with multiple flow units or a flow unit that visits one and the same resource multiple times. This will be discussed further at the end of the chapter.

Another alternative in drawing the process flow diagram is to stay much closer to the physical layout of the process. This way, the process flow diagram will look familiar for engineers and operators who typically work off the specification drawings (Figure 3.2) and it might help you to find your way around when you are visiting the "real" process. Such an approach is illustrated by Figure 3.7.

FIGURE 3.6 Completed Process Flow Diagram for the Circored Process

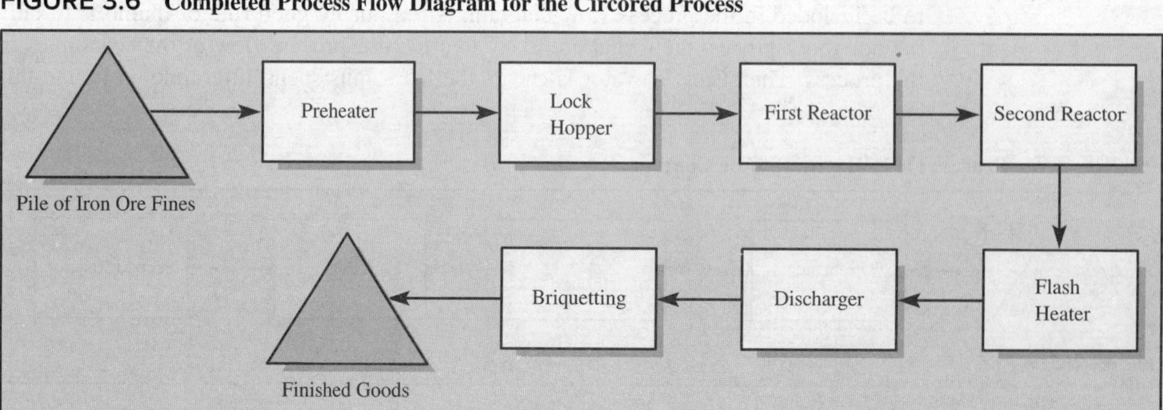

FIGURE 3.7 Completed Process Flow Diagram for the Circored Process

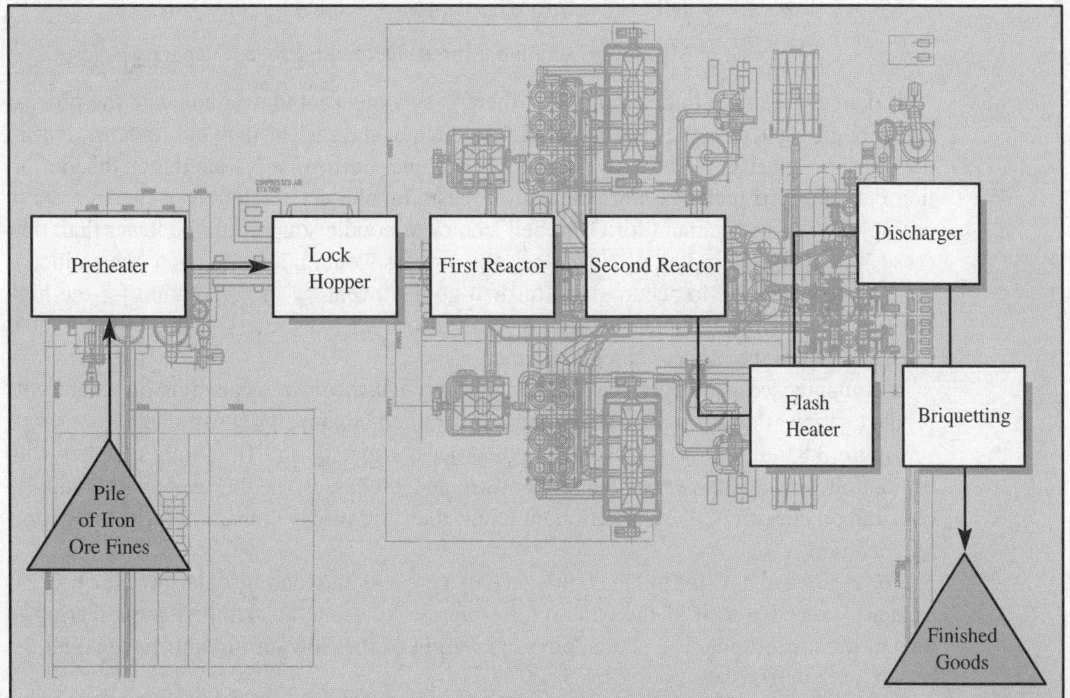

3.2 Bottleneck, Process Capacity, and Flow Rate (Throughput)

From a supply perspective, the most important question that arises is how much direct reduced iron the Circored process can supply in a given unit of time, say one day. This measure is the *capacity* of the process, which we also call the *process capacity*. Not only can capacity be measured at the level of the overall process, it also can be measured at the level of the individual resources that constitute the process. Just as we defined the process capacity, we define the capacity of a resource as the maximum amount the resource can produce in a given time unit.

Note that the process capacity measures how much the process *can* produce, opposed to how much the process actually *does* produce. For example, consider a day where—due to a breakdown or another external event—the process does not operate at all. Its capacity would be unaffected by this, yet the flow rate would reduce to zero. This is similar to your car, which might be able to drive at 130 miles per hour (capacity), but typically—or better, hopefully—only drives at 65 miles per hour (flow rate).

As the completion of a flow unit requires the flow unit to visit every one of the resources in the process, the overall process capacity is determined by the resource with the smallest capacity. We refer to that resource as the *bottleneck*. It provides the weakest link in the overall process chain, and, as we know, a chain is only as strong as its weakest link. More formally, we can write the process capacity as

$$\text{Process capacity} = \text{Minimum}\{\text{Capacity of resource } 1, \ldots, \text{Capacity of resource } n\}$$

where there are a total of n resources. How much the process actually does produce will depend not only on its capability to create supply (process capacity), but also on the demand for its output as well as the availability of its input. As with capacity, demand and the available input should be measured as rates, that is, as flow units per unit of time. For this process, our flow unit is one ton of ore, so we could define the available input and the demand in terms of tons of ore per hour.

The combination of available input, demand, and process capacity yields the rate at which our flow unit actually flows through the process, called the *flow rate:*

Flow rate = Minimum{Available input, Demand, Process capacity}

If demand is lower than supply (i.e., there is sufficient input available and the process has enough capacity), the process would produce at the rate of demand, independent of the process capacity. We refer to this case as *demand-constrained.* Note that in this definition demand also includes any potential requests for the accumulation of inventory. For example, while the demand for Campbell's chicken noodle soup might be lower than process capacity for the month of November, the process would not be demand-constrained if management decided to accumulate finished goods inventory in preparation for the high sales in the month of January. Thus, demand in our analysis refers to everything that is demanded from the process at a given time.

If demand exceeds supply, the process is *supply-constrained.* Depending on what limits product supply, the process is either input-constrained or capacity-constrained.

Figure 3.8 summarizes the concepts of process capacity and flow rate, together with the notion of demand- versus supply-constrained processes. In the case of the supply-constrained operation, there is sufficient input; thus, the supply constraint reflects a capacity constraint.

To understand how to find the bottleneck in a process and thereby determine the process capacity, consider each of the Circored resources. Note that all numbers are referring to tons of process output. The actual, physical weight of the flow unit might change over the course of the process.

Finding the bottleneck in many ways resembles the job of a detective in a crime story; each activity is a "suspect," in the sense that it could potentially constrain the overall supply of the process:

- The preheater can process 120 tons per hour.
- The lock hoppers can process 110 tons per hour.
- The analysis of the reaction steps is somewhat more complicated. We first observe that at any given moment of time, there can be, at maximum, 28 tons in the first reactor. Given that the iron ore needs to spend 15 minutes in the reactor, we can use Little's Law (see Chapter 2) to see that the maximum amount of ore that can flow through the reactor—and spend 15 minutes in the reactor—is

$$28 \text{ tons} = \text{Flow rate} \times 0.25 \text{ hour} \Rightarrow \text{Flow rate} = 112 \text{ tons/hour}$$

FIGURE 3.8 Supply-Constrained (left) and Demand-Constrained (right) Processes

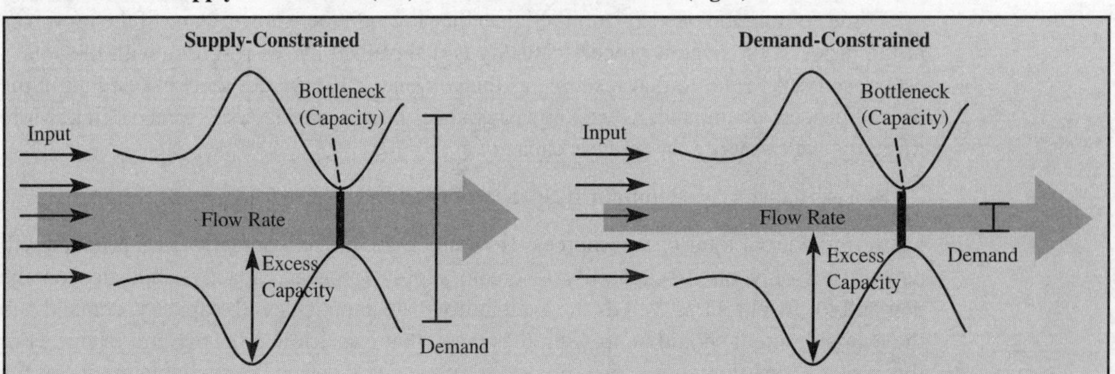

TABLE 3.1
Capacity Calculation

Process Step	Calculations	Capacity
Preheater		120 tons per hour
Lock hoppers		110 tons per hour
First reactor	Little's Law: Flow rate = 28 tons/0.25 hour	112 tons per hour
Second reactor	Little's Law: Flow rate = 400 tons/4 hours	100 tons per hour
Flash heater		135 tons per hour
Discharger		118 tons per hour
Briquetting machine	Consists of three machines: 3 × 55 tons per hour	165 tons per hour
Total process	Based on bottleneck, which is the second reactor	**100 tons per hour**

Thus, the capacity of the first reactor is 112 tons per hour. Note that a shorter reaction time in this case would translate to a higher capacity.

- We can apply a similar logic for the second reactor, which can hold up to 400 tons:

$$400 \text{ tons} = \text{Flow rate} \times 4 \text{ hours} \Rightarrow \text{Flow rate} = 100 \text{ tons/hour}$$

Thus, the capacity (the maximum possible flow rate through the resource) of the second reactor is 100 tons per hour.

- The flash heater can process 135 tons per hour.
- The discharger has a capacity of 118 tons per hour.
- Each of the three briquetting machines has a capacity of 55 tons per hour. As the briquetting machines collectively form one resource, the capacity at the briquetting machines is simply 3 × 55 tons per hour = 165 tons per hour.

The capacity of each process step is summarized in Table 3.1.

Following the logic outlined above, we can now identify the second reactor as the bottleneck of the Circored process. The overall process capacity is computed as the minimum of the capacities of each resource (all units are in tons per hour):

$$\text{Process capacity} = \text{Minimum}\,\{120, 110, 112, 100, 135, 118, 165\} = 100$$

3.3 How Long Does It Take to Produce a Certain Amount of Supply?

There are many situations where we need to compute the amount of time required to create a certain amount of supply. For example, in the Circored case, we might ask, "How long does it take for the plant to produce 10,000 tons?" Once we have determined the flow rate of the process, this calculation is fairly straightforward. Let *X* be the amount of supply we want to fulfill. Then,

$$\text{Time to fullfill } X \text{ units} = \frac{X}{\text{Flow rate}}$$

To answer our question,

$$\text{Time to produce 10,000 tons} = \frac{10{,}000 \text{ tons}}{100 \text{ tons/hour}} = 100 \text{ hours}$$

Note that this calculation assumes the process is already producing output, that is, the first unit in our 10,000 tons flows out of the process immediately. If the process started empty, it would take the first flow unit time to flow through the process. Chapter 4 provides the calculations for that case.

Note that in the previous equation we use flow rate, which in our case is capacity because the system is supply-constrained. However, if our system were demand-constrained, then the flow rate would equal the demand rate.

3.4 Process Utilization and Capacity Utilization

Given the first-of-its-kind nature of the Circored process, the first year of its operation proved to be extremely difficult. In addition to various technical difficulties, demand for the product (reduced iron) was not as high as it could be, as the plant's customers (steel mills) had to be convinced that the output created by the Circored process would be of the high quality required by the steel mills.

While abstracting from details such as scheduled maintenance and inspection times, the plant was designed to achieve a process capacity of 876,000 tons per year (100 tons per hour × 24 hours/day × 365 days/year, see above), the demand for iron ore briquettes was only 657,000 tons per year. Thus, there existed a mismatch between demand and potential supply (process capacity).

A common measure of performance that quantifies this mismatch is utilization. We define the *utilization* of a process as

$$\text{Utilization} = \frac{\text{Flow rate}}{\text{Capacity}}$$

Utilization is a measure of how much the process *actually produces* relative to how much it *could produce* if it were running at full speed (i.e., its capacity). This is in line with the example of a car driving at 65 miles per hour (flow rate), despite being able to drive at 130 miles per hour (capacity): the car utilizes 65/130 = 50 percent of its potential.

Utilization, just like capacity, can be defined at the process level or the resource level. For example, the utilization of the process is the flow rate divided by the capacity of the process. The utilization of a particular resource is the flow rate divided by that resource's capacity.

For the Circored case, the resulting utilization is

$$\text{Utilization} = \frac{657{,}000\,\text{tons per year}}{876{,}000\,\text{tons per year}} = 0.75 = 75\%$$

In general, there are several reasons why a process might not produce at 100 percent utilization:

- If demand is less than supply, the process typically will not run at full capacity, but only produce at the rate of demand.
- If there is insufficient supply of the input of a process, the process will not be able to operate at capacity.
- If one or several process steps only have a limited availability (e.g., maintenance and breakdowns), the process might operate at full capacity while it is running, but then go into periods of not producing any output while it is not running.

Given that the bottleneck is the resource with the lowest capacity and that the flow rate through all resources is identical, the bottleneck is the resource with the highest utilization.

In the case of the Circored plant, the corresponding utilizations are provided by Table 3.2. Note that all resources in a process with only one flow unit have the same flow rate, which is equal to the overall process flow rate. In this case, this is a flow rate of 657,000 tons per year.

TABLE 3.2 Utilization of the Circored Process Steps Including Downtime

Process Step	Calculations	Utilization
Preheater	657,000 tons/year/[120 tons/hour × 8,760 hours/year]	62.5%
Lock hoppers	657,000 tons/year/[110 tons/hour × 8,760 hours/year]	68.2%
First reactor	657,000 tons/year/[112 tons/hour × 8,760 hours/year]	66.9%
Second reactor	657,000 tons/year/[100 tons/hour × 8,760 hours/year]	75.0%
Flash heater	657,000 tons/year/[135 tons/hour × 8,760 hours/year]	55.6%
Discharger	657,000 tons/year/[118 tons/hour × 8,760 hours/year]	63.6%
Briquetting	657,000 tons/year/[165 tons/hour × 8,760 hours/year]	45.5%
Total process	657,000 tons/year/[100 tons/hour × 8,760 hours/year]	**75%**

Measuring the utilization of equipment is particularly common in capital-intensive industries. Given limited demand and availability problems, the bottleneck in the Circored process did not operate at 100 percent utilization. We can summarize our computations graphically, by drawing a utilization profile. This is illustrated by Figure 3.9.

Although utilization is commonly tracked, it is a performance measure that should be handled with some care. Specifically, it should be emphasized that the objective of most businesses is to maximize profit, not to maximize utilization. As can be seen in Figure 3.9, there are two reasons in the Circored case for why an individual resource might not achieve 100 percent utilization, thus exhibiting excess capacity.

- First, given that no resource can achieve a higher utilization than the bottleneck, every process step other than the bottleneck will have a utilization gap relative to the bottleneck.

FIGURE 3.9 Utilization Profile

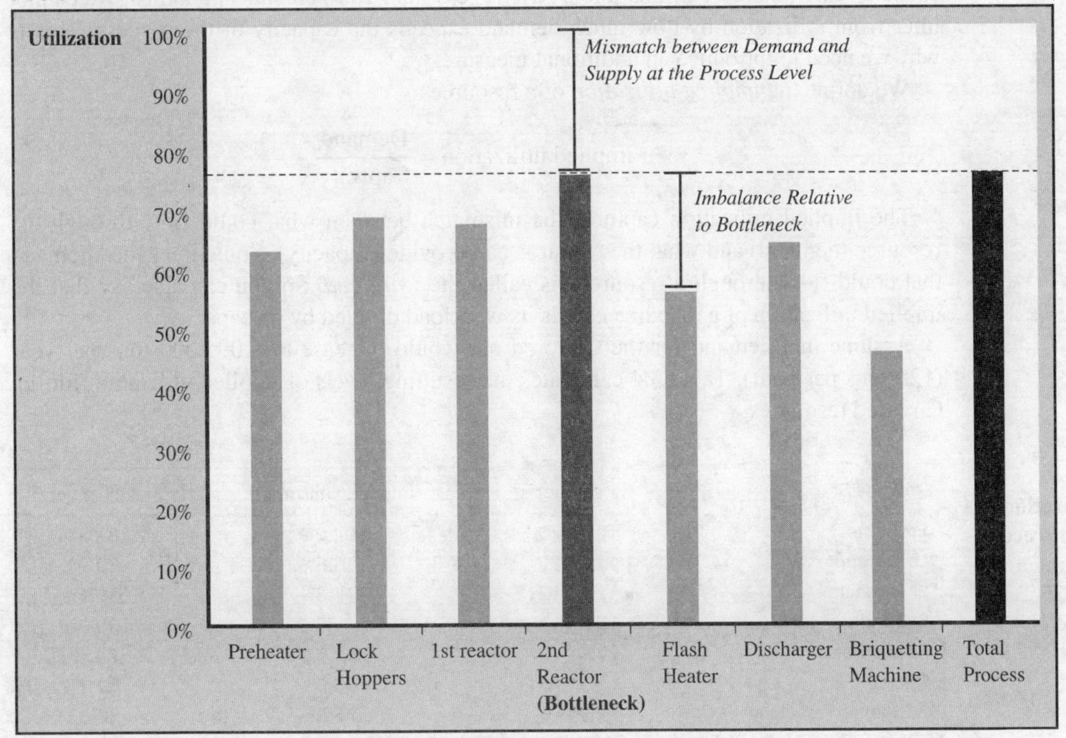

TABLE 3.3
Utilization of the Circored Process Steps Assuming Unlimited Demand and No Downtime

Process Step	Calculations	Utilization
Preheater	100/120	83.3%
Lock hoppers	100/110	90.9%
First reactor	100/112	89.3%
Second reactor	100/100	100.0%
Flash heater	100/135	74.1%
Discharger	100/118	84.7%
Briquetting machine	100/165	60.6%
Total process	**100/100**	**100%**

- Second, given that the process might not always be capacity-constrained, but rather be input- or demand-constrained, even the bottleneck might not be 100 percent utilized. In this case, every resource in the process has a "base level" of excess capacity, corresponding to the difference between the flow rate and the bottleneck capacity.

Note that the second reason disappears if there is sufficient market demand and full resource availability. In this case, only the bottleneck achieves a 100 percent utilization level. If the bottleneck in the Circored plant were utilized 100 percent, we would obtain an overall flow rate of 876,000 tons per year, or, equivalently 100 tons per hour. The resulting utilization levels in that case are summarized in Table 3.3.

3.5 Workload and Implied Utilization

Given the way we defined utilization (the ratio between flow rate and capacity), utilization can never exceed 100 percent. Thus, utilization only carries information about excess capacity, in which case utilization is strictly less than 100 percent. In contrast, we cannot infer from utilization by how much demand exceeds the capacity of the process. This is why we need to introduce an additional measure.

We define the *implied utilization* of a resource as

$$\text{Implied utilization} = \frac{\text{Demand}}{\text{Capacity}}$$

The implied utilization captures the mismatch between what could flow through the resource (demand) and what the resource can provide (capacity). Sometimes the "demand that could flow through a resource" is called the *workload*. So you can also say that the implied utilization of a resource equals its workload divided by its capacity.

Assume that demand for the Circored ore would increase to 1,095,000 tons per year (125 tons per hour). Table 3.4 calculates the resulting levels of implied utilization for the Circored resources.

TABLE 3.4
Implied Utilization of the Circored Process Steps Assuming a Demand of 125 Tons per Hour and No Downtime

Process Step	Calculations	Implied Utilization	Utilization
Preheater	125/120	104.2%	83.3%
Lock hoppers	125/110	113.6%	90.9%
First reactor	125/112	111.6%	89.3%
Second reactor	125/100	125%	100.0%
Flash heater	125/135	92.6%	74.1%
Discharger	125/118	105.9%	84.7%
Briquetting machine	125/165	75.8%	60.6%
Total process	**125/100**	**125%**	**100%**

Several points in the table deserve further discussion:

- Unlike utilization, implied utilization can exceed 100 percent. Any excess over 100 percent reflects that a resource does not have the capacity available to meet demand.
- The fact that a resource has an implied utilization above 100 percent does not make it the bottleneck. As we see in Table 3.4, it is possible to have several resources with an implied utilization above 100 percent. However, there is only one bottleneck in the process! This is the resource where the implied utilization is the highest. In the Circored case, this is—not surprisingly—the second reactor. Would it make sense to say that the process has several bottlenecks? No! Given that we can only operate the Circored process at a rate of 100 tons per hour (the capacity of the first reactor), we have ore flow through every resource of the process at a rate of 100 tons per hour. Thus, while several resources have an implied utilization above 100 percent, all resources other than the second reactor have excess capacity (their utilizations in Table 3.4 are below 100 percent). That is why we should not refer to them as bottlenecks.
- Having said this, it is important to keep in mind that in the case of a capacity expansion of the process, it might be worthwhile to add capacity to these other resources as well, not just to the bottleneck. In fact, depending on the margins we make and the cost of installing capacity, we could make a case to install additional capacity for all resources with an implied utilization above 100 percent. In other words, once we add capacity to the current bottleneck, our new process (with a new bottleneck) could still be capacity-constrained, justifying additional capacity to other resources.

3.6 Multiple Types of Flow Units

Choosing an appropriate flow unit is an essential step when preparing a process flow diagram. While, for the examples we have discussed so far, this looked relatively straightforward, there are many situations that you will encounter where this choice requires more care. The two most common complications are

- The flow of the unit moving through the process breaks up into multiple flows. For example, in an assembly environment, following an inspection step, good units continue to the next processing step, while bad units require rework.
- There are multiple types of flow units, representing, for example, different customer types. In an emergency room, life-threatening cases follow a different flow than less complicated cases.

The critical issue in choosing the flow unit is that you must be able to express all demands and capacities in terms of the chosen flow unit. For example, in the Circored process, we chose one ton of ore to be the flow unit. Thus, we had to express each resource's capacity and the demand in terms of tons of ore. Given that the process only makes ore, the choice of the flow unit was straightforward. However, consider the following example involving multiple product or customer types. An employment verification agency receives resumés from consulting firms and law firms with the request to validate information provided by their job candidates.

Figure 3.10 shows the process flow diagram for this agency. Note that while the three customer types share the first step and the last step in the process (filing and sending confirmation letter), they differ with respect to other steps:

- For internship positions, the agency provides information about the law school/business school the candidate is currently enrolled in as well as previous institutions of higher education and, to the extent possible, provides information about the applicant's course choices and honors.

FIGURE 3.10 Process Flow Diagram with Multiple Product Types

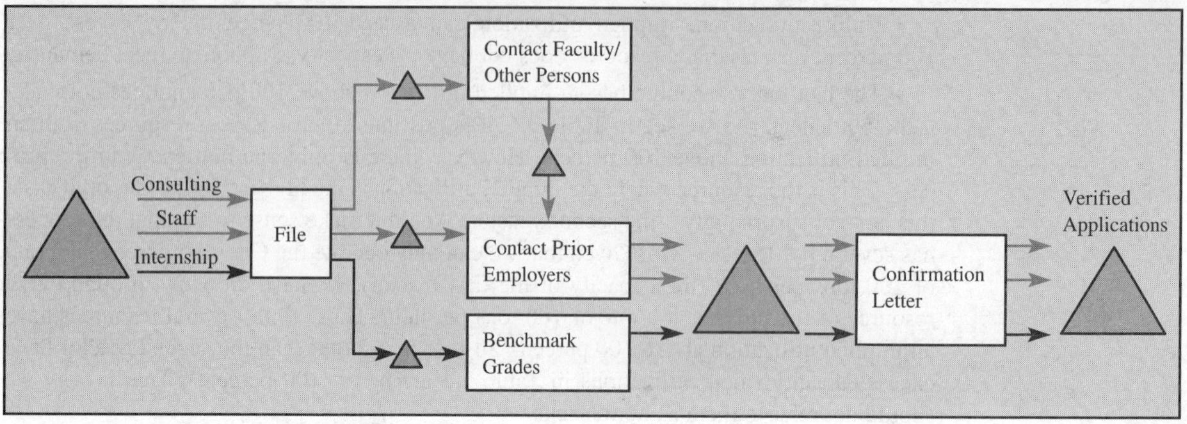

- For staff positions, the agency contacts previous employers and analyzes the letters of recommendation from those employers.
- For consulting/lawyer positions, the agency attempts to call former supervisors and/or colleagues in addition to contacting the previous employers and analyzes the letters of recommendation from those employers.

As far as demand, this process receives 3 consulting, 11 staff, and 4 internship applications per hour. Table 3.5 also provides the capacities of each activity, in applications per hour. Given that the workload on each activity as well as all of the capacities can be expressed in terms of "applications per hour," we can choose "one application" as our flow unit, despite the fact that there are multiple types of applications.

The next step in our process analysis is to find the bottleneck. In this setting this is complicated by the *product mix* (different types of customers flowing through one process). For example, the process step "contact persons" might have a very long processing time, resulting in a low capacity for this activity. However, if the workload on this activity (applications per hour) is also very low, then maybe this low capacity is not an issue.

To find the bottleneck and to determine capacity in a multiproduct situation, we need to compare each activity's capacity with its demand. The analysis is given in Table 3.5.

TABLE 3.5 Finding the Bottleneck in the Multiproduct Case

				Workload [Applications/Hour]				
	Processing Time	Number of Workers	Capacity	Consulting	Staff	Interns	Total	Implied Utilization
File	3 [min./appl.]	1	1/3 [appl./min.] = 20 [appl./hour]	3	11	4	18	18/20 = 90%
Contact persons	20 [min./appl.]	2	2/20 [appl./min.] = 6 [appl./hour]	3	0	0	3	3/6 = 50%
Contact employers	15 [min./appl.]	3	3/15 [appl./min.] = 12 [appl./hour]	3	11	0	14	14/12 = 117%
Grade/school analysis	8 [min./appl.]	2	2/8 [appl./min.] = 15 [appl./hour]	0	0	4	4	4/15 = 27%
Confirmation letter	2 [min./appl.]	1	1/2 [appl./min.] = 30 [appl./hour]	3	11	4	18	18/30 = 60%

To compute the demand on a given activity as shown in Table 3.5, it is important to remember that some activities (e.g., filing the applications) are requested by all product types, whereas others (e.g., contacting faculty and former colleagues) are requested by one product type. This is (hopefully) clear by looking at the process flow diagram.

To complete our analysis, divide each activity's demand by its capacity to yield each activity's implied utilization. This allows us to find the busiest resource. In this case, it is "contact prior employers," so this is our bottleneck. As the implied utilization is above 100 percent, the process is capacity-constrained.

The flow unit "one application" allowed us to evaluate the implied utilization of each activity in this process, but it is not the only approach. Alternatively, we could define the flow unit as "one minute of work." This might seem like an odd flow unit, but it has an advantage over "one application." Before explaining its advantage, let's figure out how to replicate our analysis of implied utilization with this new flow unit.

As before, we need to define our demands and our capacities in terms of our flow unit. In the case of capacity, each worker has "60 minutes of work" available per hour. (By definition, we all do!) So the capacity of an activity is (Number of workers) × 60 [minutes/hour]. For example "contact persons" has two workers. So its capacity is 2 × 60 = 120 minutes of work per hour. Each worker has 60 "minutes of work" available per hour, so two of them can deliver 120 minutes of work.

Now turn to the demands. There are 11 staff applications to be processed each hour and each takes 3 minutes. So the demand for staff applications is 11 × 3 = 33 minutes per hour. Now that we know how to express the demands and the capacities in terms of the "minutes of work," the implied utilization of each activity is again the ratio of the amount demanded from the activity to the activity's capacity. Table 3.6 summarizes these calculations. As we would expect, this method yields the same implied utilizations as the "one application" flow unit approach.

So if "one application" and "one minute of work" give us the same answer, how should we choose between these approaches? In this situation, you would work with the approach that you find most intuitive (which is probably "one application," at least initially) because they both allow us to evaluate the implied utilizations. However, the "one minute of work" approach is more robust. To explain why, suppose it took 3 minutes to file a staff application, 5 minutes to file a consulting application, and 2 minutes to file an internship application. In this case, we get into trouble if we define the flow unit to be "one application"—with that flow unit, we cannot express the capacity of the file activity! If we receive only internship applications, then filing could process 60/2 = 30 applications per hour. However, if we receive only consulting applications, then filing can only process 60/5 = 12 applications per hour. The number of applications per hour that filing can process depends on the mix of applications! The "minute of work" flow unit completely solves that problem—no matter what mix of applications is sent to filing, with one worker, filing has 60 minutes of work available per hour. Similarly, for a given mix of applications, we can also evaluate the workload on filing in terms of minutes of work (just as is done in Table 3.6.

To summarize, choose a flow unit that allows you to express all demands and capacities in terms of that flow unit. An advantage of the "minute of work" (or "hour of work," "day of work," etc.) approach is that it is possible to do this even if there are multiple types of products or customers flowing through the process.

So what is the next step in our process analysis? We have concluded that it is capacity-constrained because the implied utilization of "contact employers" is greater than 100 percent—it is the bottleneck. Given that it is the only activity with an implied utilization greater than 100 percent, if we are going to add capacity to this process, "contact

TABLE 3.6 Using "One Minute of Work" as the Flow Unit to Find the Bottleneck in the Multiproduct Case

	Processing Time	Number of Workers	Capacity	Workload [Minutes/Hour] Consulting	Staff	Interns	Total	Implied Utilization
File	3 [min./appl.]	1	60 [min./hour]	3 × 3	11 × 3	4 × 3	54	54/60 = 90%
Contact persons	20 [min./appl.]	2	120 [min./hour]	3 × 20	0	0	60	60/120 = 50%
Contact employers	15 [min./appl.]	3	180 [min./hour]	3 × 15	11 × 15	0	210	210/180 = 117%
Grade/school analysis	8 [min./appl.]	2	120 [min./hour]	0	0	4 × 8	32	32/120 = 27%
Confirmation letter	2 [min./appl.]	1	60 [min./hour]	3 × 2	11 × 2	4 × 2	36	36/60 = 60%

employers" should be the first candidate—in the current situation, they simply do not have enough capacity to handle the current mix of customers. Notice, if the mix of customers changes, this situation might change. For example, if we started to receive fewer staff applications (which have to flow through "contact employers") and more internship applications (which do not flow through "contact employers") then the workload on "contact employers" would decline, causing its implied utilization to fall as well. Naturally, shifts in the demands requested from a process can alter which resource in the process is the bottleneck.

Although we have been able to conclude something useful with our analysis, one should be cautious to not conclude too much when dealing with multiple types of products or customers. To illustrate some potential complications, consider the following example. At the international arrival area of a major U.S. airport, 15 passengers arrive per minute, 10 of whom are U.S. citizens or permanent residents and 5 are visitors.

The immigration process is organized as follows. Passengers disembark their aircraft and use escalators to arrive in the main immigration hall. The escalators can transport up to 100 passengers per minute. Following the escalators, passengers have to go through immigration. There exist separate immigration resources for U.S. citizens and permanent residents (they can handle 10 passengers per minute) and visitors (which can handle 3 visitors per minute). After immigration, all passengers pick up their luggage. Luggage handling (starting with getting the luggage off the plane and ending with moving the luggage onto the conveyor belts) has a capacity of 10 passengers per minute. Finally, all passengers go through customs, which has a capacity of 20 passengers per minute.

We calculate the implied utilization levels in Table 3.7. Notice when evaluating implied utilization we assume the demand on luggage handling is 10 U.S. citizens and 5 visitors even though we know (or discover via our calculations) that it is not possible for 15 passengers to arrive to luggage handling per minute (there is not enough capacity in immigration). We do this because we want to compare the potential demand on each resource with its capacity to assess its implied utilization. Consequently, we can evaluate each resource's implied utilization in isolation from the other resources.

Based on the values in Table 3.7, the bottleneck is immigration for visitors because it has the highest implied utilization. Furthermore, because its implied utilization is greater than 100 percent, the process is supply-constrained. Given that there is too little supply, we can expect queues to form. Eventually, those queues will clear because the

TABLE 3.7
Calculating Implied Utilization in Airport Example

Resource	Demand for U.S. Citizens and Permanent Residents [Pass./Min.]	Demand for Visitors [Pass./Min.]	Capacity [Pass./Min.]	Implied Utilization
Escalator	10	5	100	15/100 = 15%
Immigration—U.S. residents	10	0	10	10/10 = 100%
Immigration—visitors	0	5	3	5/3 = 167%
Luggage handling	10	5	10	15/10 = 150%
Customs	10	5	20	15/20 = 75%

demand rate of arriving passengers will at some point fall below capacity (otherwise, the queues will just continue to grow, which we know will not happen indefinitely at an airport). But during the times in which the arrival rates of passengers is higher than our capacity, where will the queues form? The answer to this question depends on how we prioritize work.

The escalator has plenty of capacity, so no priority decision needs to be made there. At immigration, there is enough capacity for 10 U.S. citizens and 3 visitors. So 13 passengers may be passed on to luggage handling, but luggage handling can accommodate only 10 passengers. Suppose we give priority to U.S. citizens. In that case, all of the U.S. citizens proceed through luggage handling without interruption, and a queue of visitors will form at the rate of 3 per minute. Of course, there will also be a queue of visitors in front of immigration, as it can handle only 3 per minute while 5 arrive per minute. With this priority scheme, the outflow from this process will be 10 U.S. citizens per minute. However, if we give visitors full priority at luggage handling, then a similar analysis reveals that a queue of U.S. citizens forms in front of luggage handling, and a queue of visitors forms in front of immigration. The outflow is 7 U.S. citizens and 3 visitors.

The operator of the process may complain that the ratio of U.S. citizens to visitors in the outflow (7 to 3) does not match the inflow ratio (2 to 1), even though visitors are given full priority. If we were to insist that those ratios match, then the best we could do is have an outflow of 6 U.S. citizens and 3 visitors—we cannot produce more than 3 visitors per minute given the capacity of immigration, so the 2 to 1 constraint implies that we can "produce" no more than 6 U.S. citizens per minute. Equity surely has a price in this case—we could have an output of 10 passengers per minute, but the equity constraint would limit us to 9 passengers per minute. To improve upon this output while maintaining the equity constraint, we should add more capacity at the bottleneck—immigration for visitors.

3.7 Summary

Figure 3.11 is a summary of the major steps graphically. Exhibits 3.1 and 3.2 summarize the steps required to do the corresponding calculations for a single flow unit and multiple flow units, respectively.

Exhibit 3.1

STEPS FOR BASIC PROCESS ANALYSIS WITH ONE TYPE OF FLOW UNIT

1. Find the capacity of every resource; if there are multiple resources performing the same activity, add their capacities together.
2. The resource with the lowest capacity is called the *bottleneck*. Its capacity determines the capacity of the entire process (*process capacity*).
3. The flow rate is found based on

$$\text{Flow rate} = \text{Minimum } \{\text{Available input, Demand, Process capacity}\}$$

4. We find the utilization of the process as

$$\text{Utilization} = \frac{\text{Flow rate}}{\text{Capacity}}$$

The utilization of each resource can be found similarly.

Any process analysis should begin with the creation of a process flow diagram. This is especially important for the case of multiple flow units, as their flows are typically more complex.

Next, we need to identify the bottleneck of the process. As long as there exists only one type of flow unit, this is simply the resource with the lowest capacity. However, for more general cases, we need to perform some extra analysis. Specifically, if there is a product mix, we have to compute the requested capacity (workload) at each resource and then compare it to the available capacity. This corresponds to computing the implied utilization, and we identify the bottleneck as the resource with the highest implied utilization.

Finally, once we have found the bottleneck, we can compute a variety of performance measures. As in the previous chapter, we are interested in finding the flow rate. The flow rate also allows us to compute the process utilization as well as the utilization profile across resources. Utilizations, while not necessarily a business goal by themselves, are important measures in many industries, especially capital-intensive industries.

FIGURE 3.11 Summary of Process Analysis

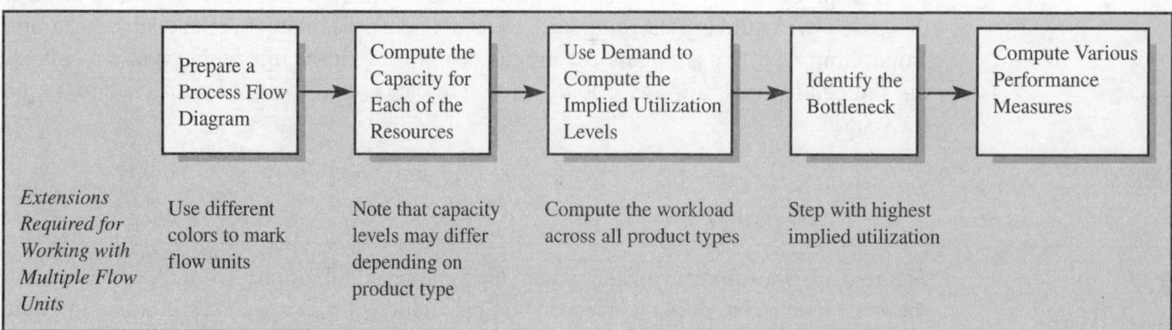

Exhibit 3.2

STEPS FOR BASIC PROCESS ANALYSIS WITH MULTIPLE TYPES OF FLOW UNITS

1. For each resource, compute the number of minutes that the resource can produce; this is 60 [min./hour] × Number of resources within the resource pool.
2. Create a process flow diagram, indicating how the flow units go through the process; use multiple colors to indicate the flow of the different flow units.
3. Create a table indicating how much workload each flow unit is consuming at each resource:
   - The rows of the table correspond to the resources in the process.
   - The columns of the table correspond to the different types of flow units.
   - Each cell of the table should contain one of the following:

   If flow unit does not visit the corresponding resource, 0; otherwise, demand per hour of the corresponding flow unit × processing time.
4. Add up the workload of each resource across all flow units.
5. Compute the implied utilization of each resource as

$$\text{Implied utilization} = \frac{\text{Result of step 4}}{\text{Result of step 1}}$$

The resource with the highest implied utilization is the bottleneck.

The preceding approach is based on Table 3.6; that is, the flow unit is "one minute of work."

3.8 Practice Problems

The following questions will help in testing your understanding of this chapter. After each question, we show the relevant section in parentheses [Section x].

Solutions to problems marked with an "*" are available in Appendix E. Video solutions to select problems are available in Connect.

Q3.1* **(Process Analysis with One Flow Unit)** Consider a process consisting of three resources:

Resource	Processing Time [Min./Unit]	Number of Workers
1	10	2
2	6	1
3	16	3

What is the bottleneck? What is the process capacity? What is the flow rate if demand is eight units per hour? [3.2] What is the utilization of each resource if demand is eight units per hour? [3.4]

Q3.2* **(Process Analysis with Multiple Flow Units)** Consider a process consisting of five resources that are operated eight hours per day. The process works on three different products, A, B, and C:

Resource	Number of Workers	Processing Time for A [Min./Unit]	Processing Time for B [Min./Unit]	Processing Time for C [Min./Unit]
1	2	5	5	5
2	2	3	4	5
3	1	15	0	0
4	1	0	3	3
5	2	6	6	6

Demand for the three different products is as follows: product A, 40 units per day; product B, 50 units per day; and product C, 60 units per day.

What is the bottleneck? What is the flow rate for each flow unit assuming that demand must be served in the mix described above (i.e., for every four units of A, there are five units of B and six units of C)? [3.6]

Q 3.3 **(Cranberries)** International Cranberry Uncooperative (ICU) is a competitor to the National Cranberry Cooperative (NCC). At ICU, barrels of cranberries arrive on trucks at a rate of 150 barrels per hour and are processed continuously at a rate of 100 barrels per hour. Trucks arrive at a uniform rate over eight hours, from 6:00 a.m. until 2:00 p.m. Assume the trucks are sufficiently small so that the delivery of cranberries can be treated as a continuous inflow. The first truck arrives at 6:00 a.m. and unloads immediately, so processing begins at 6:00 a.m. The bins at ICU can hold up to 200 barrels of cranberries before overflowing. If a truck arrives and the bins are full, the truck must wait until there is room in the bins.

a. What is the maximum number of barrels of cranberries that are waiting on the trucks at any given time? [3.3]
b. At what time do the trucks stop waiting? [3.3]
c. At what time do the bins become empty? [3.3]
d. ICU is considering using seasonal workers in addition to their regular workforce to help with the processing of cranberries. When the seasonal workers are working, the processing rate increases to 125 barrels per hour. The seasonal workers would start working at 10:00 a.m. and finish working when the trucks stop waiting. At what time would ICU finish processing the cranberries using these seasonal workers? [3.3]

Q3.4 **(Western Pennsylvania Milk Company)** The Western Pennsylvania Milk Company is producing milk at a fixed rate of 5,000 gallons/hour. The company's clients request 100,000 gallons of milk over the course of one day. This demand is spread out uniformly from 8 a.m. to 6 p.m. If there is no milk available, clients will wait until enough is produced to satisfy their requests.

The company starts producing at 8 a.m. with 25,000 gallons in finished goods inventory. At the end of the day, after all demand has been fulfilled, the plant keeps on producing until the finished goods inventory has been restored to 25,000 gallons.

When answering the following questions, treat trucks/milk as a continuous flow process. Begin by drawing a graph indicating how much milk is in inventory and how much milk is "back-ordered" over the course of the day.

a. At what time during the day will the clients have to start waiting for their requests to be filled? [3.3]
b. At what time will clients stop waiting? [3.3]
c. Assume that the milk is picked up in trucks that hold 1,250 gallons each. What is the maximum number of trucks that are waiting? [3.3]
d. Assume the plant is charged $50 per hour per waiting truck. What are the total waiting time charges on a day? [3.3]

Q3.5** **(Bagel Store)** Consider a bagel store selling three types of bagels that are produced according to the process flow diagram outlined below. We assume the demand is 180 bagels a day, of which there are 30 grilled veggie, 110 veggie only, and 40 cream cheese. Assume that the workday is 10 hours long and each resource is staffed with one worker.

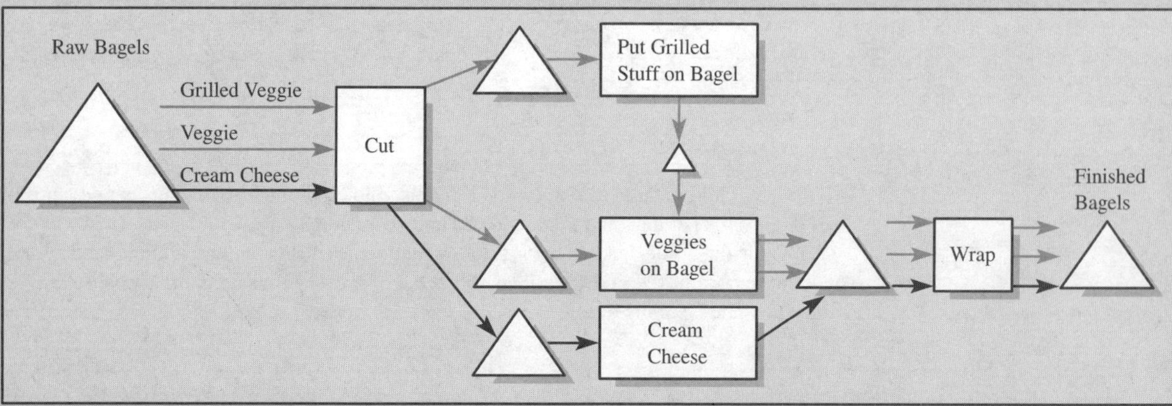

Moreover, we assume the following processing times:

	Cut	Grilled Stuff	Veggies	Cream Cheese	Wrap
Processing time	3 [min./bagel]	10 [min./bagel]	5 [min./bagel]	4 [min./bagel]	2 [min./bagel]

Processing times are independent of which bagel type is processed at a resource (for example, cutting a bagel takes the same time for a cream cheese bagel as for a veggie bagel).

a. Where in the process is the bottleneck? [3.6]

b. How many units can the process produce within one hour, assuming the product mix has to remain constant? [3.6]

Q3.6 **(Valley Forge Income Tax Advice)** VF is a small accounting firm supporting wealthy individuals in their preparation of annual income tax statements. Every December, VF sends out a short survey to their customers, asking for the information required for preparing the tax statements. Based on 24 years of experience, VF categorizes their cases into the following groups:

- Group 1 (new customers, easy): 15 percent of cases
- Group 2 (new customers, complex): 5 percent of cases
- Group 3 (repeat customers, easy): 50 percent of cases
- Group 4 (repeat customers, complex): 30 percent of cases

Here, "easy" versus "complex" refers to the complexity of the customer's earning situation.

In order to prepare the income tax statement, VF needs to complete the following set of activities. Processing times (and even which activities need to be carried out) depend on which group a tax statement falls into. All of the following processing times are expressed in minutes per income tax statement.

Group	Filing	Initial Meeting	Preparation	Review by Senior Accountant	Writing
1	20	30	120	20	50
2	40	90	300	60	80
3	20	No meeting	80	5	30
4	40	No meeting	200	30	60

The activities are carried out by the following three persons:

- Administrative support person: filing and writing.
- Senior accountant (who is also the owner): initial meeting, review by senior accountant.
- Junior accountant: preparation.

Assume that all three persons work eight hours per day and 20 days a month. For the following questions, assume the product mix as described above. Assume that there are 50 income tax statements arriving each month.

a. Which of the three persons is the bottleneck? [3.6]

b. What is the (implied) utilization of the senior accountant? The junior accountant? The administrative support person? [3.6]

c. You have been asked to analyze which of the four product groups is the most profitable. Which factors would influence the answer to this? [3.6]

d. How would the process capacity of VF change if a new word processing system would reduce the time to write the income tax statements by 50 percent? [3.6]

Q3.7 **(Car Wash Supply Process)** CC Car Wash specializes in car cleaning services. The services offered by the company, the exact service time, and the resources needed for each of them are described in the following table:

Service	Description	Processing Time	Resource Used
A. Wash	Exterior car washing and drying	10 min.	1 automated washing machine
B. Wax	Exterior car waxing	10 min.	1 automated waxing machine
C. Wheel cleaning	Detailed cleaning of all wheels	7 min.	1 employee
D. Interior cleaning	Detailed cleaning inside the car	20 min.	1 employee

The company offers the following packages to their customers:

- Package 1: Includes only car wash (service A).
- Package 2: Includes car wash and waxing (services A and B).
- Package 3: Car wash, waxing, and wheel cleaning (services A, B, and C).
- Package 4: All four services (A, B, C, and D).

Customers of CC Car Wash visit the station at a constant rate (you can ignore any effects of variability) of 40 customers per day. Of these customers, 40 percent buy Package 1, 15 percent buy Package 2, 15 percent buy Package 3, and 30 percent buy Package 4. The mix does not change over the course of the day. The store operates 12 hours a day.

a. What is the implied utilization of the employee doing the wheel cleaning service? [3.6]
b. Which resource has the highest implied utilization? [3.6]

For the next summer, CC Car Wash anticipates an increase in the demand to 80 customers per day. Together with this demand increase, there is expected to be a change in the mix of packages demanded: 30 percent of the customers ask for Package 1, 10 percent for Package 2, 10 percent for Package 3, and 50 percent for Package 4. The company will install an additional washing machine to do service A.

c. What will be the new bottleneck in the process? [3.6]
d. How many customers a day will not be served? Which customers are going to wait? Explain your reasoning! [3.6]

Q3.8 **(Starbucks)** After an "all night" study session the day before their last final exam, four students decide to stop for some much-needed coffee at the campus Starbucks. They arrive at 8:30 a.m. and are dismayed to find a rather long line.

Fortunately for the students, a Starbucks executive happens to be in line directly in front of them. From her, they learn the following facts about this Starbucks location:

I. There are three employee types:
   - There is a single cashier who takes all orders, prepares nonbeverage food items, grinds coffee, and pours drip coffee.
   - There is a single frozen drink maker who prepares blended and iced drinks.
   - There is a single espresso drink maker who prepares espressos, lattes, and steamed drinks.

II. There are typically four types of customers:
   - Drip coffee customers order only drip coffee. This requires 20 seconds of the cashier's time to pour the coffee.
   - Blended and iced drink customers order a drink that requires the use of the blender. These drinks take on average two minutes of work of the frozen drink maker.
   - Espresso drink customers order a beverage that uses espresso and/or steamed milk. On average, these drinks require one minute of work of the espresso drink maker.
   - Ground coffee customers buy one of Starbucks' many varieties of whole bean coffee and have it ground to their specification at the store. This requires a total of one minute of the cashier's time (20 seconds to pour the coffee and 40 seconds to grind the whole bean coffee).

III. The customers arrive uniformly at the following rates from 7 a.m. (when the store opens) until 10 a.m. (when the morning rush is over), with no customers arriving after 10 a.m.:

- Drip coffee customers: 25 per hour.
- Blended and iced drink customers: 20 per hour.
- Espresso drink customers: 70 per hour.
- Ground coffee customers: 5 per hour.

IV. Each customer spends, on average, 20 seconds with the cashier to order and pay.

V. Approximately 25 percent of all customers order food, which requires an additional 20 seconds of the cashier's time per transaction.

While waiting in line, the students reflect on these facts and they answer the following questions:

a. What is the implied utilization of the frozen drink maker? [3.6]

b. Which resource has the highest implied utilization? [3.6]

From their conversation with the executive, the students learn that Starbucks is considering a promotion on all scones (half price!), which marketing surveys predict will increase the percentage of customers ordering food to 30 percent (the overall arrival rates of customers will *not* change). However, the executive is worried about how this will affect the waiting times for customers.

c. How do the levels of implied utilization change as a response to this promotion? [3.6]

Q3.9 **(Paris Airport)** Kim Opim, an enthusiastic student, is on her flight over from Philadelphia (PHL) to Paris. Kim reflects upon how her educational experiences from her operations courses could help explain the long wait time that she experienced before she could enter the departure area of Terminal A at PHL. As an airline representative explained to Kim, there are four types of travelers in Terminal A:

- Experienced short-distance (short-distance international travel destinations are Mexico and various islands in the Atlantic) travelers: these passengers check in online and do not speak with any agent nor do they take any time at the kiosks.
- Experienced long-distance travelers: these passengers spend three minutes with an agent.
- Inexperienced short-distance travelers: these passengers spend two minutes at a kiosk; however, they do not require the attention of an agent.
- Inexperienced long-distance travelers: these passengers need to talk five minutes with an agent.

After a passenger checks in online, or talks with an agent, or uses a kiosk, the passenger must pass through security, where they need 0.5 minute independent of their type. From historical data, the airport is able to estimate the arrival rates of the different customer types at Terminal A of Philadelphia International:

- Experienced short-distance travelers: 100 per hour
- Experienced long-distance travelers: 80 per hour
- Inexperienced short-distance travelers: 80 per hour
- Inexperienced long-distance travelers: 40 per hour

At this terminal, there are four security check stations, six agents, and three electronic kiosks. Passengers arrive uniformly from 4 p.m. to 8 p.m., with the entire system empty prior to 4 p.m. (the "midafternoon lull") and no customers arrive after 8 p.m. All workers must stay on duty until the last passenger is entirely through the system (e.g., has passed through security).

a. What are the levels of implied utilization at each resource? [3.6]

b. At what time has the last passenger gone through the system? Note: If passengers of one type have to wait for a resource, passengers that do not require service at the resource can pass by the waiting passengers! [3.6]

c. Kim, an experienced long-distance traveler, arrived at 6 p.m. at the airport and attempted to move through the check-in process as quickly as she could. How long did she have to wait before she was checked at security? [3.6]

d. The airline considers showing an educational program that would provide information about the airport's check-in procedures. Passenger surveys indicate that 80 percent of the inexperienced passengers (short or long distance) would subsequently act as experienced passengers (i.e., the new arrival rates would be 164 experienced short-distance, 112 experienced long-distance, 16 inexperienced short-distance, and 8 inexperienced long-distance [passengers/hour]). At what time has the last passenger gone through the system? [3.6]

If you would like to test your understanding of a specific section, here are the questions organized by section:

Section 3.2: Q1

Section 3.3: Q3, Q4

Section 3.4: Q1

Section 3.6: Q2, Q5, Q6, Q7, Q8, Q9

You can view a video of how problems marked with a ** are solved by going on www.cachon-terwiesch.net and follow the links under 'Solved Practice Problems'

Chapter 

Estimating and Reducing Labor Costs

The objective of any process should be to create value (make profits), not to maximize the utilization of every resource involved in the process. In other words, we should not attempt to produce more than what is demanded from the market, or from the resource downstream in the process, just to increase the utilization measure. Yet, the underutilization of a resource, human labor or capital equipment alike, provides opportunities to improve the process. This improvement can take several forms, including

- If we can reduce the excess capacity at some process step, the overall process becomes more efficient (lower cost for the same output).
- If we can use capacity from underutilized process steps to increase the capacity at the bottleneck step, the overall process capacity increases. If the process is capacity-constrained, this leads to a higher flow rate.

In this chapter, we discuss how to achieve such process improvements. Specifically, we discuss the concept of line balancing, which strives to avoid mismatches between what is supplied by one process step and what is demanded from the following process step (referred to as the process step downstream). In this sense, line balancing attempts to match supply and demand within the process itself.

We use Novacruz Inc. to illustrate the concept of line balancing and to introduce a number of more general terms of process analysis. Novacruz is the producer of a high-end kick scooter, known as the Xootr (pronounced "zooter"), displayed in Figure 4.1.

4.1 Analyzing an Assembly Operation

With the increasing popularity of kick scooters in general, and the high-end market segment for kick scooters in particular, Novacruz faced a challenging situation in terms of organizing their production process. While the demand for their product was not much higher than 100 scooters per week in early March, it grew dramatically, soon reaching 1,200 units per week in the fall. This demand trajectory is illustrated in Figure 4.2.

First consider March, during which Novacruz faced a demand of 125 units per week. At this time, the assembly process was divided between three workers (resources) as illustrated by Figure 4.3.

The three workers performed the following activities. In the first activity, the first 30 of the overall 80 parts are assembled, including the fork, the steer support, and the t-handle.

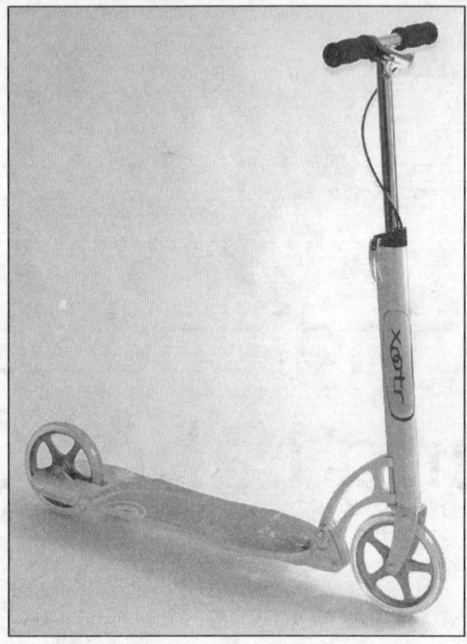

FIGURE 4.1
The Xootr by Novacruz

Given the complexity of this assembly operation, it takes about 13 minutes per scooter to complete this activity. We refer to the 13 minutes/unit as the *processing time*. Depending on the context, we will also refer to the processing time as the *activity time* or the *service time*. Note that in the current process, each activity is staffed with exactly one worker.

In the second activity, a worker assembles the wheel, the brake, and some other parts related to the steering mechanism. The second worker also assembles the deck. This step is somewhat faster and its processing time is 11 minutes per unit. The scooter is completed by the third worker, who wipes off the product, applies the decals and grip tape, and conducts the final functional test. The processing time is about 8 minutes per unit.

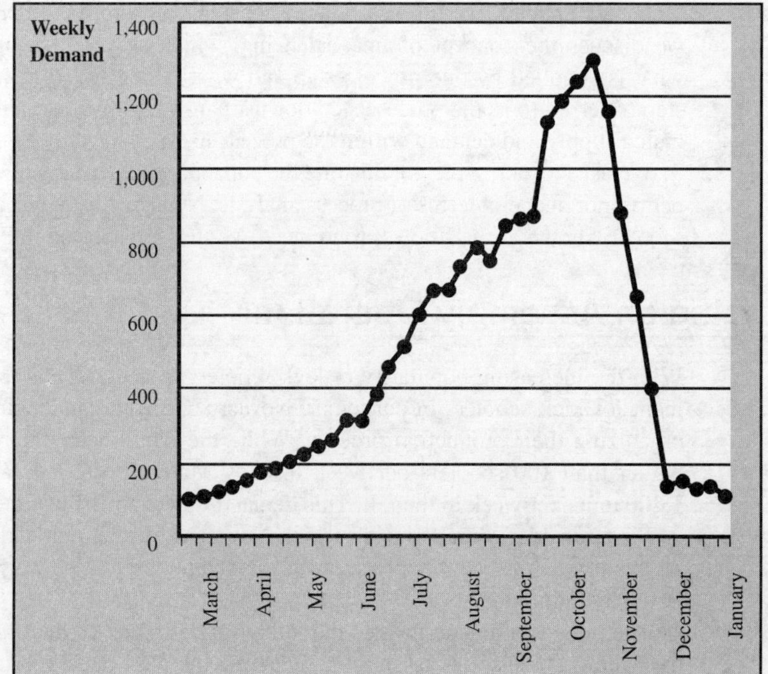

FIGURE 4.2
Lifecycle Demand Trajectory for Xootrs

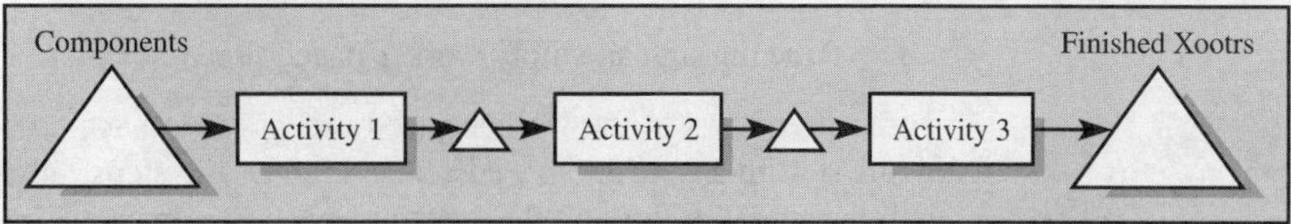

FIGURE 4.3
Current Process Layout

Left: ©Nathan Ulrich/Reprinted with permission from Xootr LLC. All rights reserved.
Right: ©Reprinted with permission from Xootr LLC. All rights reserved.

To determine the capacity of an individual resource or a group of resources performing the same activity, we write

$$\text{Capacity} = \frac{\text{Number of resources}}{\text{Processing time}}$$

This is intuitive, as the capacity grows proportionally with the number of workers.

For example, for the first activity, which is performed by one worker, we write

$$\text{Capacity} = \frac{1}{13 \text{ minutes/scooter}} = 0.0769 \text{ scooter/minute}$$

which we can rewrite as

$$0.0769 \text{ scooter/minute} \times 60 \text{ minutes/hour} = 4.6 \text{ scooters/hour}$$

Similarly, we can compute capacities of the second worker to be 5.45 scooters/hour and of the third worker to be 7.5 scooters/hour.

As we have done in the preceding chapter, we define the bottleneck as the resource with the lowest capacity. In this case, the bottleneck is the first resource, resulting in a process capacity of 4.6 scooters/hour.

4.2 Time to Process a Quantity *X* Starting with an Empty Process

Imagine Novacruz received a very important rush order of 100 scooters, which would be assigned highest priority. Assume further that this order arrives early in the morning and there are no scooters currently in inventory, neither between the resources (work-in-process, WIP) nor in the finished goods inventory (FGI). How long will it take to fulfill this order?

As we are facing a large order of scooters, we will attempt to move as many scooters through the system as possible. Therefore, we are capacity-constrained and the flow rate of the process is determined by the capacity of the bottleneck (one scooter every 13 minutes). The time between the completions of two subsequent flow units is called the *cycle time* of a process and will be defined more formally in the next section.

We cannot simply compute the time to produce 100 units as 100 units/0.0769 unit/minute = 1,300 minutes because that calculation assumes the system is producing at the bottleneck rate, one unit every 13 minutes. However, that is only the case once the system is "up and running." In other words, the first scooter of the day, assuming the system starts the day empty (with no work-in-process inventory), takes even longer than 13 minutes to complete. How much longer depends on how the line is paced.

The current system is called a *worker-paced line* because each worker is free to work at his or her own pace: if the first worker finishes before the next worker is ready to accept the parts, then the first worker puts the completed work in the inventory between them. Eventually the workers need to conform to the bottleneck rate; otherwise, the inventory before the bottleneck would grow too big for the available space. But that concern is not relevant for the first unit moving through the system, so the time to get the first scooter through the system is 13 + 11 + 8 = 32 minutes. More generally,

$$\text{Time through an empty worker-paced process} = \text{Sum of the processing times}$$

An alternative to the worker-paced process is a machine-paced process as depicted in Figure 4.4. In a machine-paced process, all of the steps must work at the same rate even with the first unit through the system. Hence, if a machine-paced process were used, then the first Xootr would be produced after 3 × 13 minutes, as the conveyor belt has the same speed at all three process steps (there is just one conveyor belt, which has to be paced to the slowest step). More generally,

$$\begin{aligned}&\text{Time through an empty machine-paced process}\\&= \text{Number of resources in sequence} \times \text{Processing time of the bottleneck step}\end{aligned}$$

Now return to our worker-paced process. After waiting 32 minutes for the first scooter, it only takes an additional 13 minutes until the second scooter is produced and from then onwards, we obtain an additional scooter every 13 minutes. Thus, scooter 1 is produced after 32 minutes, scooter 2 after 32 + 13 = 45 minutes, scooter 3 after 32 + (2 × 13) = 58 minutes, scooter 4 after 32 + (3 × 13) = 71 minutes, and so on.

More formally, we can write the following formula. The time it takes to finish *X* units starting with an empty system is

$$\begin{aligned}&\text{Time to finish } X \text{ units starting with an empty system}\\&= \text{Time through an empty process} + \frac{X - 1 \text{ unit}}{\text{Flow rate}}\end{aligned}$$

You may wonder whether it is always necessary to be so careful about the difference between the time to complete the first unit and all of the rest of the units. In this case, it is because the number of scooters is relatively small, so each one matters. But imagine a

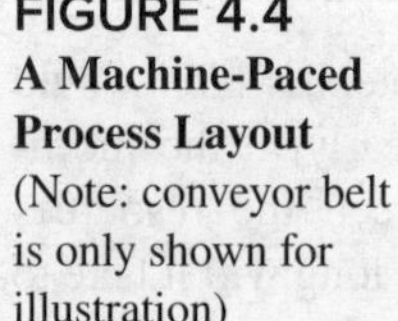

FIGURE 4.4
A Machine-Paced Process Layout
(Note: conveyor belt is only shown for illustration)

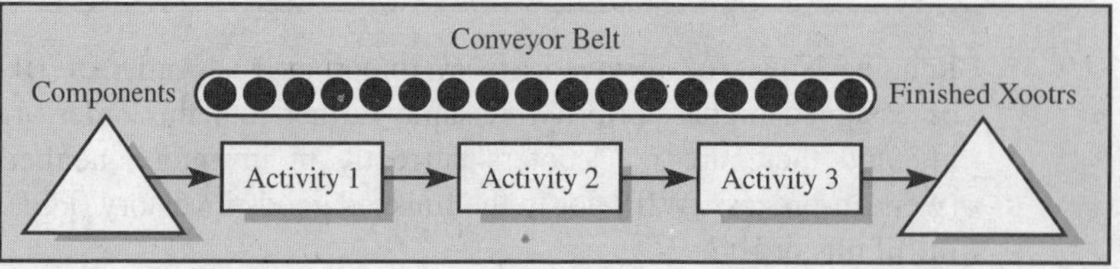

Exhibit 4.1

TIME TO PROCESS A QUANTITY X STARTING WITH AN EMPTY PROCESS

1. Find the time it takes the flow unit to go through the empty system:
   - In a worker-paced line, this is the sum of the processing times.
   - In a machine-paced line, this is the cycle time × the number of stations.
2. Compute the capacity of the process (see previous methods). Since we are producing X units as fast as we can, we are capacity-constrained; thus,

$$\text{Flow rate} = \text{Process capacity}$$

3. Time to finish X units

$$= \text{Time through empty process} + \frac{X - 1 \text{ unit}}{\text{Flow rate}}$$

Note: If the process is a continuous process, we can use X instead.

continuous-flow process such as a cranberry processing line. Suppose you want to know how long it takes to produce five tons of cranberries. Let's say a cranberry weighs one gram, so five tons equals five million cranberries. Now how long does it take to produce five million cranberries? Strictly speaking, we would look at the time it takes the first berry to flow through the system and then add the time for the residual 4,999,999 berries. However, for all computational purposes, five million minus one is still five million, so we can make our life a little easier by just ignoring this first berry:

$$\text{Time to finish } X \text{ units with a continuous-flow process}$$
$$= \text{Time through an empty process} + \frac{X \text{ units}}{\text{Flow rate}}$$

Exhibit 4.1 summarizes the calculations leading to the time it takes the process to produce X units starting with an empty system.

4.3 Labor Content and Idle Time

What is the role of labor cost in the production of the Xootr? Let's look first at how much actual labor is involved in the assembly of the Xootr. Toward this end, we define the *labor content* as the sum of the processing times of the three workers. In this case, we compute a labor content of

$$\begin{aligned}\text{Labor content} &= \text{Sum of processing times with labor}\\ &= 13 \text{ minutes/unit} + 11 \text{ minutes/unit} + 8 \text{ minutes/unit}\\ &= 32 \text{ minutes per unit}\end{aligned}$$

These 32 minutes per unit reflect how much labor is invested into the production of one scooter. We could visualize this measure as follows. Let's say there would be a slip of paper attached to a Xootr and each worker would write the amount of time spent working on the Xootr on this slip. The sum of all numbers entered on the slip is the labor content.

Assume that the average hourly rate of the assembly employees is \$12 per hour (and thus \$0.20 per minute). Would the resulting cost of labor then be 32 minutes/unit × \$0.20/minute = \$6.40/unit? The answer is a clear *no*! The reason for this is that the labor content is a measure that takes the perspective of the flow unit but does not reflect any information about how the process is actually operated.

Assume—for illustrative purposes—that we would hire an additional worker for the second activity. As worker 2 is not a constraint on the overall output of the process, this would probably not be a wise thing to do (and that is why we call it an illustrative example). How would the labor content change? Not at all! It would still require the same 32 minutes of labor to produce a scooter. However, we have just increased our daily wages by 33 percent, which should obviously be reflected in our cost of direct labor.

To correctly compute the cost of direct labor, we need to look at two measures:

- The number of scooters produced per unit of time (the flow rate).
- The amount of wages we pay for the same time period.

Above, we found that the process has a capacity of 4.6 scooters an hour, or 161 scooters per week (we assume the process operates 35 hours per week). Given that demand is currently 125 scooters per week (we are demand-constrained), our flow rate is at 125 scooters per week.

Now, we can compute the cost of direct labor as

$$\begin{aligned}\text{Cost of direct labor} &= \frac{\text{Total wages per unit of time}}{\text{Flow rate}}\\ &= \frac{\text{Wages per week}}{\text{Scooters produced per week}}\\ &= \frac{3 \times \$12/\text{h} \times 35\text{h/week}}{125\ \text{scooters/week}}\\ &= \frac{\$1{,}260/\text{week}}{125\ \text{scooters/week}} = \$10.08/\text{scooter}\end{aligned}$$

Why is this number so much higher than the number we computed based on the direct labor content? Because the workers are not working 100% of the time. The fraction of the time they are working, which is the *average labor utilization*, is

$$\begin{aligned}\text{Average labor utilization} &= \frac{\text{Labor content} \times \text{Flow rate}}{\text{Number of workers}}\\ &= \frac{(32\ \mathit{min}/60\ \mathit{min/hr}) \times 3.57\ \text{units/hr}}{3}\\ &= 63.5\%\end{aligned}$$

Note that we must be consistent with units in the above equation—if the flow rate is in units per hour then labor content must be in hours, not in minutes. To explain the equation, note that the numerator is the number of hours of labor that must be completed every hour: 3.57 units arrive every hour and they each need 32/60 hours of work. To make the numbers somewhat easier to work with, imagine a health clinic in which 4 patients arrive every hour and each needs 1/2 hour of attention from a physician. That would mean that the clinic needs to spend $4 \times 1/2 = 2$ hours of time with patients every hour. The denominator is the maximum number of hours of labor that could be provided: 3 workers are able to each give 1 hour of effort every hour, so in total they could all give 3 hours of work. If the health clinic has 3 physicians, then they too can give a total of 3 hours of work every hour. The ratio of the work demanded to the maximum that can be provided therefore is the fraction of time labor is working, which is the average labor utilization. With scooters it is 63.5%, and with the health clinic it is $2/3 = 67\%$.

Another way to think about labor utilization is through the time that workers are not working, what we will refer to as *idle time*. In this case, there are two sources of idle time:

- The process is never able to produce more than its bottleneck. In this case, this means one scooter every 13 minutes. However, if we consider worker 3, who only takes 8 minutes on a scooter, this translates into a 5-minute idle time for every scooter built.

- If the process is demand-constrained, even the bottleneck is not operating at its full capacity and, consequently also exhibits idle time. Given a demand rate of 125 scooters/week, that is, 3.57 scooters/hour or 1 scooter every 16.8 minutes, all three workers get an extra 3.8 minutes of idle time for every scooter they make.

This reflects the utilization profile and the sources of underutilization that we discussed in Chapter 3 with the Circored process.

Note that this calculation assumes the labor cost is fixed. If it were possible to shorten the workday from the current 7 hours of operations to 5 hours and 25 minutes (25 scooters a day × 1 scooter every 13 minutes), we would eliminate the second type of idle time.

More formally, define the following:

$$\text{Cycle time} = \frac{1}{\text{Flow rate}}$$

Cycle time provides an alternative measure of how fast the process is creating output. As we are producing one scooter every 16.8 minutes, the cycle time is 16.8 minutes. Similar to what we did intuitively above, we can now define the idle time for worker *i* as the following:

$$\text{Idle time for a single worker} = \text{Cycle time} - \text{Processing time of the single worker}$$

Note that this formula assumes that every activity is staffed with exactly one worker. The idle time measures how much unproductive time a worker has for every unit of output produced. These calculations are summarized by Table 4.1.

If we add up the idle time across all workers, we obtain the total idle time that is incurred for every scooter produced:

$$3.8 + 5.8 + 8.8 = 18.4 \text{ minutes/unit}$$

Now, apply the wage rate of \$12 per hour (\$0.20/minute × 18.4 minutes/unit) and, voilà, we obtain exactly the difference between the labor cost we initially expected based on the direct labor content alone (\$6.40 per unit) and the actual cost of direct labor computed above.

We can now use the information regarding idle time to evaluate

$$\text{Average labor utilization} = \frac{\text{Labor content}}{\text{Labor content} + \text{Sum of idle times across workers}}$$

$$= \frac{32[\text{minutes per unit}]}{32[\text{minutes per unit}] + 18.4[\text{minutes per unit}]} = 63.5\%$$

TABLE 4.1
Basic Calculations Related to Idle Time

	Worker 1	Worker 2	Worker 3
Processing time	13 minutes/unit	11 minutes/unit	8 minutes/unit
Capacity	$\frac{1}{13}$ unit/minute = 4.61 units/hour	$\frac{1}{11}$ unit/minute = 5.45 units/hour	$\frac{1}{8}$ unit/minute = 7.5 units/hour
Process capacity	Minimum {4.61 units/h, 5.45 units/h, 7.5 units/h} = 4.61 units/hour		
Flow rate	Demand = 125 units/week = 3.57 units/hour Flow rate = Minimum {demand, process capacity} = 3.57 units/hour		
Cycle time	1/3.57 hours/unit = 16.8 minutes/unit		
Idle time	16.8 minutes/unit − 13 minutes/unit = 3.8 minutes/unit	16.8 minutes/unit − 11 minutes/unit = 5.8 minutes/unit	16.8 minutes/unit − 8 minutes/unit = 8.8 minutes/unit
Utilization	3.57/4.61 = 77%	3.57/5.45 = 65.5%	3.57/7.5 = 47.6%

Exhibit 4.2

SUMMARY OF LABOR COST CALCULATIONS

1. Compute the capacity of all resources; the resource with the lowest capacity is the bottleneck (see previous methods) and determines the process capacity.
2. Compute Flow rate = Min{Available input, Demand, Process capacity}; then compute

$$\text{Cycle time} = \frac{1}{\text{Flow rate}}$$

3. Evaluate Total wages, which is the total wages (across all workers) that are paid per unit of time.
4. Cost of direct labor is

$$\text{Cost of direct labor} = \frac{\text{Total wages}}{\text{Flow rate}}$$

5. Average labor utilization is

$$\text{Average labor utilization} = \frac{\text{Labor content} \times \text{Flow rate}}{\text{Number of workers}}$$

6. Idle time across all workers at resource i

$$\text{Idle time across all workers at resource } i = \text{Cycle time} \times (\text{Number of workers at resource } i) - \text{Processing time at resource } i$$

7. Average labor utilization is also

$$\text{Average labor utilization} = \frac{\text{Labor content}}{\text{Labor content} + \text{Total idle time}}$$

An alternative way to compute the same number is by averaging the utilization level across the three workers:

$$\text{Average labor utilization} = \tfrac{1}{3} \times (\text{Utilization}_1 + \text{Utilization}_2 + \text{Utilization}_3) = 63.4\%$$

where Utilization_i denotes the utilization of the ith worker.

Exhibit 4.2 summarizes the calculations related to our analysis of labor costs. It includes the possibility that there are multiple workers performing the same activity.

4.4 Increasing Capacity by Line Balancing

Comparing the utilization levels in Table 4.1 reveals a strong imbalance between workers: while worker 1 is working 77 percent of the time, worker 3 is only active about half of the time (47.6 percent to be exact). Imbalances within a process provide micro-level mismatches between what could be supplied by one step and what is demanded by the following steps. *Line balancing* is the act of reducing such imbalances. It thereby provides the opportunity to

- Increase the efficiency of the process by better utilizing the various resources, in this case labor.
- Increase the capacity of the process (without adding more resources to it) by reallocating either workers from underutilized resources to the bottleneck or work from the bottleneck to underutilized resources.

While based on the present demand rate of 125 units per week and the assumption that all three workers are a fixed cost for 35 hours per week, line balancing would change neither the flow rate (process is demand-constrained) nor the cost of direct labor (assuming the 35 hours per week are fixed); this situation changes with the rapid demand growth experienced by Novacruz.

Consider now a week in May, by which, as indicated by Figure 4.2, the demand for the Xootr had reached a level of 200 units per week. Thus, instead of being demand-constrained, the process now is capacity-constrained, specifically, the process now is constrained by worker 1, who can produce one scooter every 13 minutes, while the market demands scooters at a rate of one scooter every 10.5 minutes (200 units/week/35 hours/week = 5.714 units/hour).

Given that worker 1 is the constraint on the system, all her idle time is now eliminated and her utilization has increased to 100 percent. Yet, workers 2 and 3 still have idle time:

- The flow rate by now has increased to one scooter every 13 minutes or $\frac{1}{13}$ unit per minute (equals $\frac{1}{13} \times 60 \times 35 = 161.5$ scooters per week) based on worker 1.
- Worker 2 has a capacity of one scooter every 11 minutes, that is, $\frac{1}{11}$ unit per minute. Her utilization is thus Flow rate/Capacity$_2 = \frac{1}{13} / \frac{1}{11} = \frac{11}{13} = 84.6\%$.
- Worker 3 has a capacity of one scooter every 8 minutes. Her utilization is thus $\frac{1}{13} / \frac{1}{8} = \frac{8}{13} = 61.5\%$.

Note that the increase in demand not only has increased the utilization levels across workers (the average utilization is now $\frac{1}{3} \times (100\% + 84.6\% + 61.5\%) = 82\%$), but also has reduced the cost of direct labor to

$$\begin{aligned}\text{Cost of direct labor} &= \frac{\text{Total wages per unit of time}}{\text{Flow rate per unit of time}} \\ &= \frac{\text{Wages per week}}{\text{Scooters produced per week}} \\ &= \frac{3 \times \$12/\text{hour} \times 35 \text{ hours/week}}{161.5 \text{ scooters/week}} \\ &= \frac{\$1{,}260/\text{week}}{161.5 \text{ scooters/week}} = \$7.80/\text{scooter}\end{aligned}$$

Now, back to the idea of line balancing. Line balancing attempts to evenly (fairly!) allocate the amount of work that is required to build a scooter across the three process steps.

In an ideal scenario, we could just take the amount of work that goes into building a scooter, which we referred to as the labor content (32 minutes/unit), and split it up evenly between the three workers. Thus, we would achieve a perfect line balance if each worker could take 32/3 minutes/unit; that is, each would have an identical processing time of 10.66 minutes/unit.

Unfortunately, in most processes, it is not possible to divide up the work that evenly. Specifically, the activities underlying a process typically consist of a collection of *tasks* that cannot easily be broken up. A closer analysis of the three activities in our case reveals the task structure shown in Table 4.2.

For example, consider the last task of worker 1 (assemble handle cap), which takes 118 seconds per unit. These 118 seconds per unit of work can only be moved to another worker in their entirety. Moreover, we cannot move this task around freely, as it obviously would not be feasible to move the "assemble handle cap" task to after the "seal carton" task.

TABLE 4.2
Task Durations

Worker	Tasks	Task Duration [seconds/unit]
Worker 1	Prepare cable	30
	Move cable	25
	Assemble washer	100
	Apply fork, threading cable end	66
	Assemble socket head screws	114
	Steer pin nut	49
	Brake shoe, spring, pivot bolt	66
	Insert front wheel	100
	Insert axle bolt	30
	Tighten axle bolt	43
	Tighten brake pivot bolt	51
	Assemble handle cap	118
		Total: 792
Worker 2	Assemble brake lever and cable	110
	Trim and cap cable	59
	Place first rib	33
	Insert axles and cleats	96
	Insert rear wheel	135
	Place second rib and deck	84
	Apply grip tape	56
	Insert deck fasteners	75
		Total: 648
Worker 3	Inspect and wipe off	95
	Apply decal and sticker	20
	Insert in bag	43
	Assemble carton	114
	Insert Xootr and manual	94
	Seal carton	84
		Total: 450

However, we could move the 118 seconds per unit from worker 1 to worker 2. In this case, worker 1 would now have a processing time of 674 seconds per unit and worker 2 (who would become the new bottleneck) would have a processing time of 766 seconds per unit. The overall process capacity is increased, we would produce more scooters, and the average labor utilization would move closer to 100 percent.

But can we do better? Within the scope of this book, we only consider cases where the sequence of tasks is given. Line balancing becomes more complicated if we can resequence some of the tasks. For example, there exists no technical reason why the second to last task of worker 2 (apply grip tape) could not be switched with the subsequent task (insert deck fasteners). There exist simple algorithms and heuristics that support line balancing in such more complex settings. Yet, their discussion would derail us from our focus on managerial issues.

But even if we restrict ourselves to line balancing solutions that keep the sequence of tasks unchanged, we can further improve upon the 766-second cycle time we outlined above. Remember that the "gold standard" of line balancing, the even distribution of the labor content across all resources, suggested a processing time of 10.66 minutes per unit, or 640 seconds per unit.

Moving the "assemble handle cap" task from worker 1 to worker 2 was clearly a substantial step in that direction. However, worker 2 has now 126 seconds per unit (766 seconds/unit − 640 seconds/unit) more than what would be a balanced workload. This situation can be improved if we take the worker's last two tasks (apply grip tape, insert deck fasteners) and move the corresponding 56 + 75 seconds/unit = 131 seconds/unit to worker 3.

The new processing times would be as follows:

- Worker 1: 674 seconds per unit (792 – 118 seconds/unit).
- Worker 2: 635 seconds per unit (648 + 118 – 56 – 75 seconds/unit).
- Worker 3: 581 seconds per unit (450 + 56 + 75 seconds/unit).

Are they optimal? No! We can repeat similar calculations and further move work from worker 1 to worker 2 (tighten brake pivot bolt, 51 seconds per unit) and from worker 2 to worker 3 (place second rib and deck, 84 seconds per unit). The resulting (final) processing times are now

- Worker 1: 623 seconds per unit (674 – 51 seconds/unit).
- Worker 2: 602 seconds per unit (635 + 51 – 84 seconds/unit).
- Worker 3: 665 seconds per unit (581 + 84 seconds/unit).

To make sure we have not "lost" any work on the way, we can add up the three new processing times and obtain the same labor content (1,890 seconds per unit) as before. The resulting labor utilization would be improved to

$$\text{Average labor utilization} = \text{Labor content} / (\text{Labor content} + \text{Total idle time})$$
$$= 1{,}890/(1{,}890 + 42 + 63 + 0) = 94.7\%$$

The process improvement we have implemented based on line balancing is sizeable in its economic impact. Based on the new bottleneck (worker 3), we see that we can produce one Xootr every 665 seconds, thereby having a process capacity of $\frac{1}{665}$ units/second × 3,600 seconds/hour × 35 hours/week = 189.5 units per week. Thus, compared to the unbalanced line (161.5 units per week), we have increased process capacity (and flow rate) by 17 percent (28 units) without having increased our weekly spending rate on labor. Moreover, we have reduced the cost of direct labor to $6.65/unit.

Figure 4.5 summarizes the idea of line balancing by contrasting cycle time and task allocation of the unbalanced line (before) and the balanced line (after).

4.5 Scale Up to Higher Volume

As indicated by Figure 4.2, demand for the Xootr increased dramatically within the next six months and, by July, had reached a level of 700 units per week. Thus, in order to maintain a reasonable match between supply and demand, Novacruz had to increase its process capacity (supply) further.

To increase process capacity for a worker-paced line, in this case from 189.5 units per week (see balanced line with three workers above) to 700 units per week, additional workers are needed. While the fundamental steps involved in building a Xootr remain unchanged, we have several options to lay out the new, high-volume process:

- Using the exact same layout and staffing plan, we could replicate the—now balanced—process and add another (and another, . . .) worker-paced line with three workers each.
- We could assign additional workers to the three process steps, which would increase the capacity of the steps and hence lead to a higher overall process capacity.
- We could divide up the work currently performed by three workers, thereby increasing the specialization of each step (and thus reducing processing times and hence increasing capacity).

FIGURE 4.5 Graphical Illustration of Line Balance

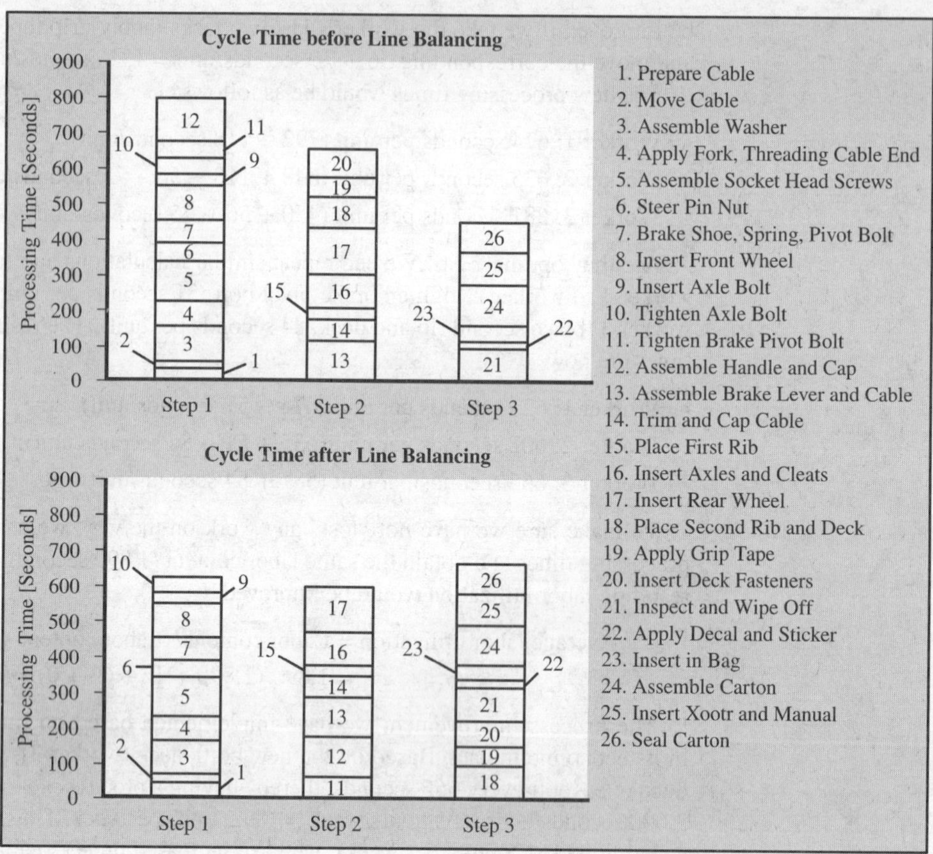

We will quickly go through the computations for all three approaches. The corresponding process flow diagrams are summarized in Figure 4.6.

Increasing Capacity by Replicating the Line

As the capacity of the entire operation grows linearly with the number of replications, we could simply add three replications of the process to obtain a new total capacity of 4×189.5 units/week = 758 units per week.

The advantage of this approach is that it would allow the organization to benefit from the knowledge it has gathered from their initial process layout. The downside of this approach is that it keeps the ratio of workers across the three process steps constant (in total, four people do step 1, four at step 2, and four at step 3), while this might not necessarily be the most efficient way of allocating workers to assembly tasks (it keeps the ratio between workers at each step fixed).

Alternatively, we could just add two replications and obtain a process capacity of 568.5 units per week and make up for the remaining 131.5 units (700 – 568.5 units/week) by adding overtime. Given that the 131.5 units to be produced in overtime would be spread over three lines, each line would have to produce 131.53/3 = 43.84 units per week corresponding to 8.1 hours of overtime per week (43.83 units/week/5.41 units/hour).

Under the assumption that we could use overtime, the average labor utilization would remain unchanged at 94.7 percent.

Increasing Capacity by Selectively Adding Workers

While the first approach assumed the number of workers at each process step to be the same, such a staffing might not necessarily be optimal. Specifically, we observe that (after the

FIGURE 4.6 Three Process Layouts for High-Volume Production

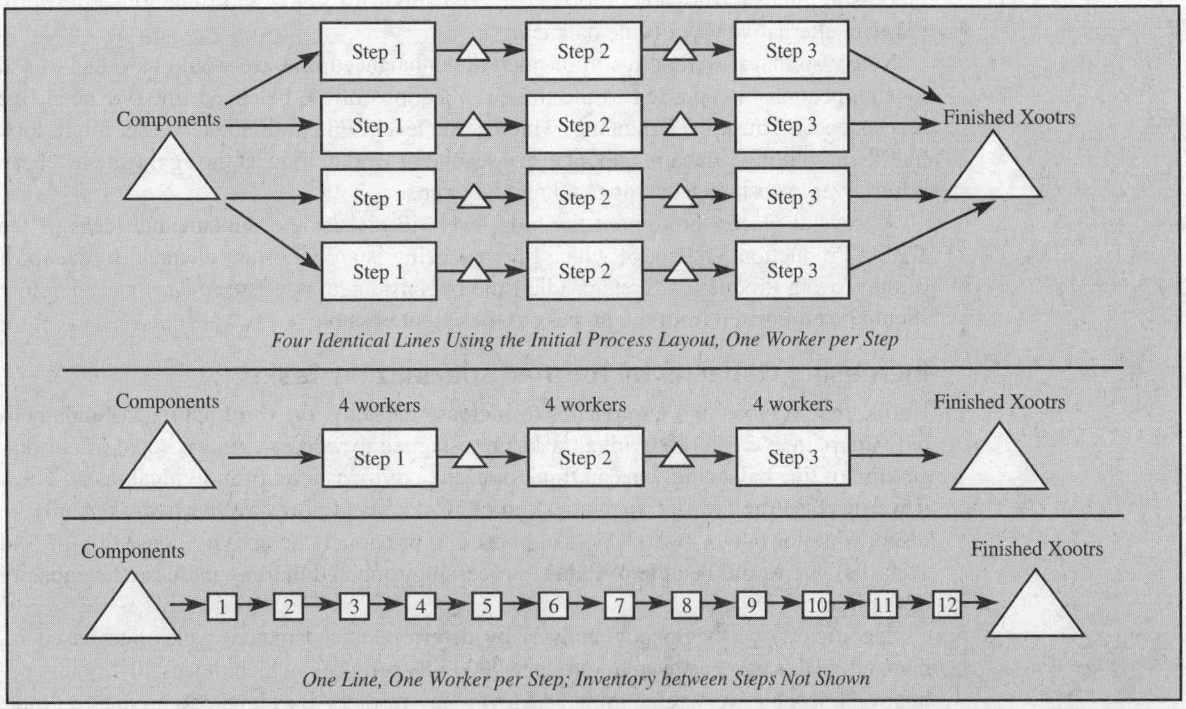

rebalancing) the third step is the bottleneck (processing time of 665 seconds per unit). Thus, we feel tempted to add over-proportionally more workers to this step than to the first two.

Given that we defined the capacity at each resource as the number of workers divided by the corresponding processing time, we can write the following:

$$\text{Requested capacity} = \frac{\text{Number of workers}}{\text{Activity time}}$$

For step 1, this calculation yields (700 units per week at 35 hours per week is 0.00555 unit per second):

$$0.00555 \text{ unit/second} = \frac{\text{Number of workers}}{623 \text{ seconds per unit}}$$

Thus, the number of workers required to meet the current demand is $0.00555 \times 623 = 3.46$ workers. Given that we cannot hire half a worker (and ignoring overtime for the moment), this means we have to hire four workers at step 1. In the same way, we find that we need to hire 3.34 workers at step 2 and 3.69 workers at step 3.

The fact that we need to hire a total of four workers for each of the three steps reflects the good balance that we have achieved above. If we would do a similar computation based on the initial numbers (792,648,450 seconds/unit for workers 1, 2, and 3, respectively; see Table 4.2), we would obtain the following:

- At step 1, we would hire 0.00555 unit/second = Number of workers/792 seconds/unit; therefore, Number of workers = 4.4.
- At step 2, we would hire 0.00555 unit/second = Number of workers/648 seconds/unit; therefore, Number of workers = 3.6.
- At step 3, we would hire 0.00555 unit/second = Number of workers/450 seconds/unit; therefore, Number of workers = 2.5.

Thus, we observe that a staffing that allocates extra resources to activities with longer processing times (five workers for step 1 versus four for step 2 and three for step 3) provides an alternative way of line balancing.

Note also that if we had just replicated the unbalanced line, we would have had to add four replications as opposed to the three replications of the balanced line (we need five times step 1). Thus, line balancing, which at the level of the individual worker might look like "hair-splitting," debating about every second of worker time, at the aggregate level can achieve very substantial savings in direct labor cost.

At several places throughout the book, we will discuss the fundamental ideas of the Toyota Production System, of which line balancing is an important element. In the spirit of the Toyota Production System, idle time is considered as waste (*muda*) and therefore should be eliminated from the process to the extent possible.

Increasing Capacity by Further Specializing Tasks

Unlike the previous two approaches to increase capacity, the third approach fundamentally alters the way the individual tasks are assigned to workers. As we noted in our discussion of line balancing, we can think of each activity as a set of individual tasks. Thus, if we increase the level of specialization of workers and now have each worker only be responsible for one or two tasks (as opposed to previously an activity consisting of 5 to 10 tasks), we would be able to reduce processing time and thereby increase the capacity of the line.

Specifically, we begin our analysis by determining a targeted cycle time based on demand: in this case, we want to produce 700 units per week, which means 20 scooters per hour or 1 scooter every three minutes. How many workers does it take to produce 1 Xootr every three minutes?

The answer to this question is actually rather complicated. The reason for this complication is as follows. We cannot compute the capacity of an individual worker without knowing which tasks this worker will be in charge of. At the same time, we cannot assign tasks to workers, as we do not know how many workers we have.

To break this circularity, we start our analysis with the staffing we have obtained under the previous approaches, that is, 12 workers for the entire line. Table 4.3 shows how we can assign the tasks required to build a Xootr across these 12 workers.

Following this approach, the amount of work an individual worker needs to master is reduced to a maximum of 180 seconds. We refer to this number as the *span of control*. Given that this span of control is much smaller than under the previous approaches (665 seconds), workers will be able to perform their tasks with significantly less training. Workers are also likely to improve upon their processing times more quickly as specialization can increase the rate of learning.

The downside of this approach is its negative effect on labor utilization. Consider what has happened to labor utilization:

$$\text{Average labor utilization} = \frac{\text{Labor content}}{\text{Labor content} + \text{Sum of idle time}}$$

$$= \frac{1890}{1{,}890 + 25 + 0 + 65 + 7 + 11 + 11 + 51 + 45 + 40 + 10 + 3 + 2} = 87.5\%$$

Note that average labor utilization was 94.7 percent (after balancing) with three workers. Thus, specialization (smaller spans of control) makes line balancing substantially more complicated. This is illustrated by Figure 4.7.

The reason for this decrease in labor utilization, and thus the poorer line balance, can be found in the granularity of the tasks. Since it is not possible to break up the individual tasks further, moving a task from one worker to the next becomes relatively more significant.

TABLE 4.3
Processing Times and Task Allocation under Increased Specialization

Worker	Tasks	Task Duration [seconds/unit]
Worker 1	Prepare cable	30
	Move cable	25
	Assemble washer	100
		Total: 155
Worker 2	Apply fork, threading cable end	66
	Assemble socket head screws	114
		Total: 180
Worker 3	Steer pin nut	49
	Brake shoe, spring, pivot bolt	66
		Total: 115
Worker 4	Insert front wheel	100
	Insert axle bolt	30
	Tighten axle bolt	43
		Total: 173
Worker 5	Tighten brake pivot bolt	51
	Assemble handle cap	118
		Total: 169
Worker 6	Assemble brake lever and cable	110
	Trim and cap cable	59
		Total: 169
Worker 7	Place first rib	33
	Insert axles and cleats	96
		Total: 129
Worker 8	Insert rear wheel	135
		Total: 135
Worker 9	Place second rib and deck	84
	Apply grip tape	56
		Total: 140
Worker 10	Insert deck fasteners	75
	Inspect and wipe off	95
		Total: 170
Worker 11	Apply decal and sticker	20
	Insert in bag	43
	Assemble carton	114
		Total: 177
Worker 12	Insert Xootr and manual	94
	Seal carton	84
		Total: 178
	Total labor content	1,890

For example, when we balanced the three-worker process, moving a 51-second-per-unit task to another step accounted for just 8 percent of the step's work (674 seconds per unit). In a 12-step process, however, moving the same 51-second-per-unit task is now relative to a 169-second-per-unit workload for the step, thereby accounting for 30 percent of work. For this reason, it is difficult to further improve the allocation of tasks to workers relative to what is shown in Figure 4.7.

The observation that line balancing becomes harder with an increase in specialization can best be understood if we "turn this reasoning on its head": line balancing becomes easier with a decrease in specialization. To see this, consider the case of having one

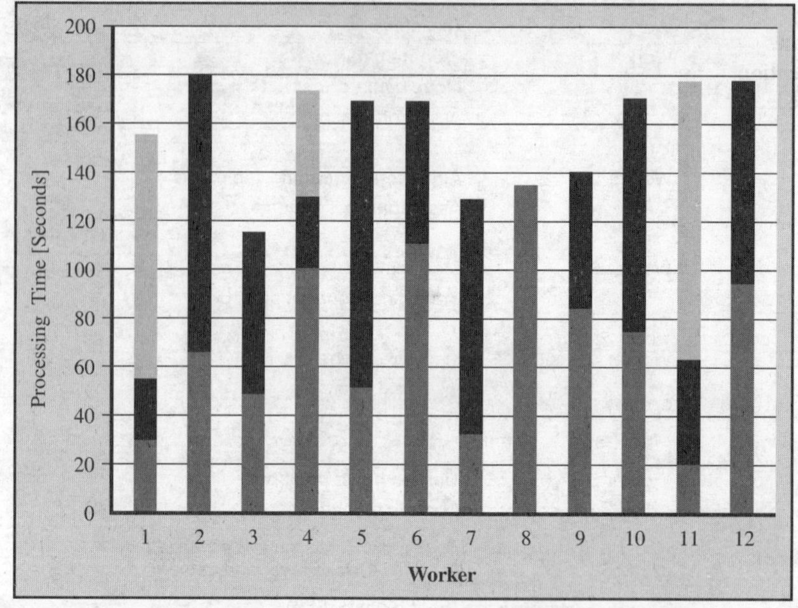

FIGURE 4.7
Line Balance in a Highly Specialized Line
(Different shades represent different tasks)

single worker do all the tasks in the process. The corresponding labor utilization would be 100 percent (assuming there is enough demand to keep at least one worker busy), as, by definition, this one person also would be the bottleneck.

The idea of having one resource perform all activities of the process is referred to as a work cell. The process flow diagram of a work cell is illustrated by Figure 4.8. Since the processing time at a work cell with one worker is the same as the labor content, we would have a capacity per work cell of $\frac{1}{1{,}890}$ unit per second = 1.9048 units per hour, or 66.67 units per week. Already 11 work cells would be able to fulfill the demand of 700 Xootrs per week. In other words, the improved balance that comes with a work cell would allow us to further improve efficiency.

Again, the downside of this approach is that it requires one worker to master a span of control of over 30 minutes, which requires a highly trained operator. Moreover, Novacruz found that working with the 12-person line and the corresponding increase in specialization led to a substantial reduction in processing times.

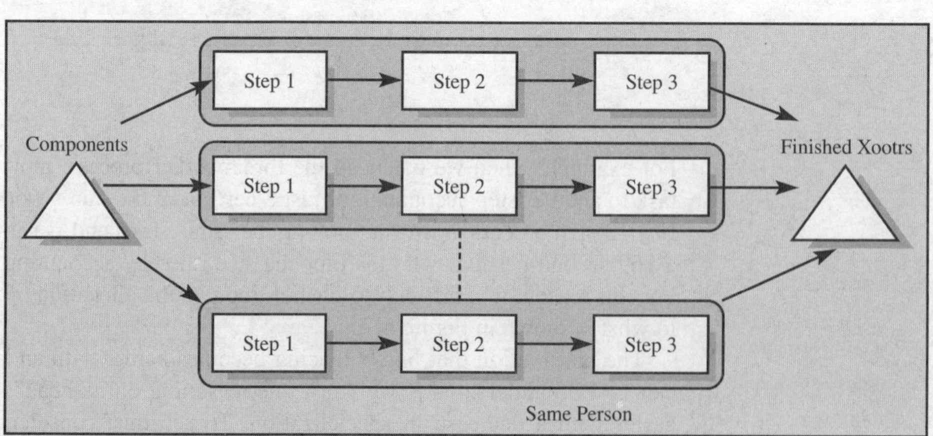

FIGURE 4.8
Parallel Work Cells
(Only three work cells are shown)

4.6 Summary

In this chapter, we introduced the concept of line balancing. Line balancing attempts to eliminate idle time from the process and thereby increase labor utilization. At first sight, line balancing seems to belong in the same category as "hair-splitting" and "penny-counting." However, it is important to understand the managerial role that line balancing plays in operations. Specifically, it is important to understand the following three managerial benefits:

- First of all, while it is always more tempting to talk about dollars rather than pennies, pennies do matter in many industries. Consider, for example, the computer industry. All PC manufacturers purchase from the same pool of suppliers of processors, disk drives, optical devices, and so forth. Thus, while the $10 of labor cost in a computer might seem small relative to the purchase price of the computer, those $10 are under our managerial control, while most of the other costs are dictated by the market environment.
- Second, in the spirit of the Toyota Production System (TPS), idle time is waste and thereby constitutes what in TPS is known as *muda*. The problem with *muda*/idle time is that it not only adds to the production costs, but has the potential to hide many other problems. For example, a worker might use idle time to finish or rework a task that she could not complete during the allocated processing time. While this does not lead to a direct, out-of-pocket cost, it avoids the root cause of the problem, which, when it surfaces, can be fixed.
- Third, while the $10 labor cost in the assembly operation of a PC manufacturer discussed above might seem like a low number, there is much more labor cost involved in the PC than $10. What appears as procurement cost for the PC maker is to some extent labor cost for the suppliers of the PC maker. If we "roll up" all operations throughout the value chain leading to a PC, we find that the cost of labor is rather substantial. This idea is illustrated in Figure 4.9 for the case of the automotive industry: while for a company like an automotive company assembly labor costs seem to be only a small element of costs, the 70 percent of costs that are procurement costs themselves include assembly labor costs from suppliers, subsuppliers, and so forth. If we look at all costs in the value chain (from an automotive company to their fifth-tier supplier), we see that about a quarter of costs in the automotive supply chain are a result of labor costs. A consequence of this observation is that it is not enough to improve our own operations

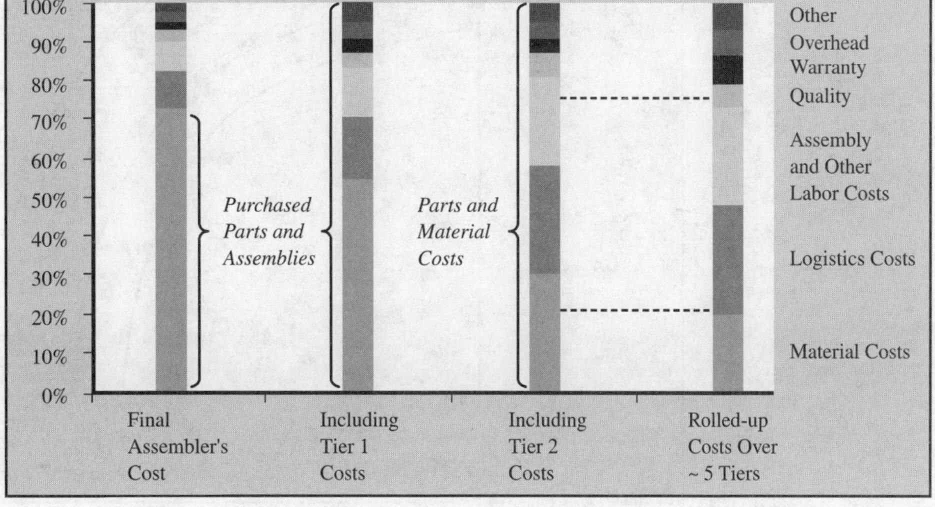

FIGURE 4.9
Sources of Cost in the Supply Chain

Source: Whitney 2004.

internally, but to spread such improvements throughout the supplier network, as this is where the biggest improvement opportunities are hidden. This concept of supplier development is another fundamental concept of the Toyota Production System.

In addition to these three factors, line balancing also illustrates an important—and from a managerial perspective very attractive—property of operations management. Line balancing improves per-unit labor cost (productivity) and does not require any financial investments in assets! To improve labor productivity, we would typically attempt to automate parts of the assembly, which would lower the per-unit labor cost, but at the same time require a higher investment of capital. Such an approach would be most likely if we operated in a high-wage location such as Germany or France. In contrast, we could try to operate the process with little or no automation but have a lot of labor time invested in the process. Such an approach would be more likely if we moved the process to a low-wage location such as China, Indonesia, or Taiwan.

This tension is illustrated by Figure 4.10. The horizontal axis of Figure 4.10 shows the return on the assets tied up in the manufacturing process. High returns are desirable, which could be achieved by using little automation and a lot of labor. The vertical axis shows the productivity of labor, which would be maximized if the process were highly automated. As can be seen in Figure 4.10, there exists a tension (trade-off) between the dimensions, visible in the form of an efficient frontier. Thus, changes with respect to the level of automation would move the process up or down the frontier. One dimension is traded against the other.

In contrast, the effect of line balancing in the context of Figure 4.10 is very different. Line balancing improves labor productivity without any additional investment. To the extent that line balancing allows the firm to eliminate some currently underutilized resources using production equipment, line balancing also reduces the required assets. Thus, what from a strategic perspective seems like a simple, one-dimensional positioning problem along the technology frontier now has an additional dimension. Rather than simply taking the current process as given and finding a good strategic position, the firm should attempt to improve its process capability and improve along both performance dimensions simultaneously.

FIGURE 4.10
Trade-off between Labor Productivity and Capital Investment

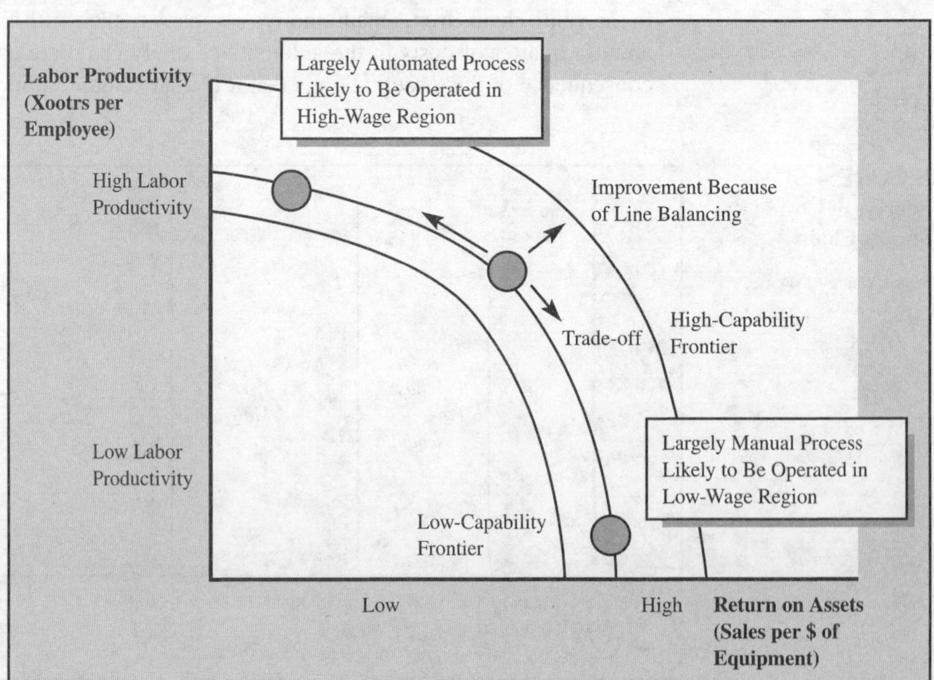

4.7 Further Reading

Bartholdi and Eisenstein (1996) develop the concept of a bucket brigade, which corresponds to a line operation that is self-balancing. In this concept, workers move between stations and follow relatively simple decision rules that determine which task should be performed next.

Whitney (2004) presents a systematic approach to design and production of mechanical assemblies. This book introduces mechanical and economic models of assemblies and assembly automation. The book takes a system view of assembly, including the notion of product architecture, feature-based design, computer models of assemblies, analysis of mechanical constraint, assembly sequence analysis, tolerances, system-level design for assembly and JIT methods, and economics of assembly automation.

4.8 Practice Problems

The following questions will help in testing your understanding of this chapter. After each question, we show the relevant section in parentheses [Section x].

Solutions to problems marked with an "*" are available in Appendix E. Video solutions to select problems are available in Connect.

Q4.1* **(Empty System, Labor Utilization)** Consider a process consisting of three resources in a worker-paced line and a wage rate of $10 per hour. Assume there is unlimited demand for the product.

Resource	Processing time (minutes)	Number of Workers
1	10	2
2	6	1
3	16	3

a. How long does it take the process to produce 100 units starting with an empty system? [4.2]

b. What is the average labor content? [4.3]

c. What is the average labor utilization? [4.3]

d. What is the cost of direct labor? [4.4]

Q4.2 **(Assign Tasks to Workers)** Consider the following six tasks that must be assigned to four workers on a conveyor-paced assembly line (i.e., a machine-paced line flow). Each worker must perform at least one task.

	Time to Complete Task (seconds)
Task 1	30
Task 2	25
Task 3	35
Task 4	40
Task 5	15
Task 6	30

The current conveyor-paced assembly line configuration assigns the workers in the following way:

- Worker 1: Task 1
- Worker 2: Task 2
- Worker 3: Tasks 3, 4
- Worker 4: Tasks 5, 6

a. What is the capacity of the current line? [4.1]

b. Now assume that tasks are allocated to maximize capacity of the line, subject to the conditions that (1) a worker can only perform two adjacent operations and (2) all tasks need to be done in their numerical order. What is the capacity of this line now? [4.4]

c. Now assume that tasks are allocated to maximize capacity of the line and that tasks can be performed in any order. What is the maximum capacity that can be achieved? [4.4]

Q4.3 **(PowerToys)** PowerToys Inc. produces a small remote-controlled toy truck on a conveyor belt with nine stations. Each station has, under the current process layout, one worker assigned to it. Stations and processing times are summarized in the following table:

Station	Task	Processing Times (seconds)
1	Mount battery units	75
2	Insert remote control receiver	85
3	Insert chip	90
4	Mount front axle	65
5	Mount back axle	70
6	Install electric motor	55
7	Connect motor to battery unit	80
8	Connect motor to rear axle	65
9	Mount plastic body	80

a. What is the bottleneck in this process? [4.1]

b. What is the capacity, in toy trucks per hour, of the assembly line? [4.1]

c. What is the direct labor cost for the toy truck with the current process if each worker receives $15/hour, expressed in dollars per toy truck? [4.4]

d. What would be the direct labor cost for the toy truck if work would be organized in a work cell; that is, one worker performs all tasks? Assume that the processing times would remain unchanged (i.e., there are no specialization gains). [4.5]

e. What is the utilization of the worker in station 2? [4.1]

Because of a drastically reduced forecast, the plant management has decided to cut staffing from nine to six workers per shift. Assume that (i) the nine tasks in the preceding table cannot be divided; (ii) the nine tasks are assigned to the six workers in the most efficient way possible; and (iii) if one worker is in charge of two tasks, the tasks have to be adjacent (i.e., one worker cannot work on tasks 1 and 3, unless the worker also does task 2).

f. How would you assign the nine tasks to the six workers? [4.4]

g. What is the new capacity of the line (in toy trucks per hour)? [4.4]

Q4.4 **(12 Tasks to 4 Workers)** Consider the following tasks that must be assigned to four workers on a conveyor-paced assembly line (i.e., a machine-paced line flow). Each worker must perform at least one task. There is unlimited demand.

	Time to Complete Task (seconds)
Task 1	30
Task 2	25
Task 3	15
Task 4	20
Task 5	15
Task 6	20
Task 7	50
Task 8	15
Task 9	20
Task 10	25
Task 11	15
Task 12	20

The current conveyor-paced assembly-line configuration assigns the workers in the following way:

- Worker 1: Tasks 1, 2, 3
- Worker 2: Tasks 4, 5, 6
- Worker 3: Tasks 7, 8, 9
- Worker 4: Tasks 10, 11, 12

a. What is the capacity of the current line? [4.1]

b. What is the direct labor content? [4.3]

c. What is the average labor utilization (do not consider any transient effects such as the line being emptied before breaks or shift changes)? [4.3]

d. How long would it take to produce 100 units, starting with an empty system? [4.2]

The firm is hiring a fifth worker. Assume that tasks are allocated to the five workers to maximize capacity of the line, subject to the conditions that (i) a worker can only perform adjacent operations and (ii) all tasks need to be done in their numerical order.

e. What is the capacity of this line now? [4.4]

Again, assume the firm has hired a fifth worker. Assume further that tasks are allocated to maximize capacity of the line and that tasks can be performed in any order.

f. What is the maximum capacity that can be achieved? [4.4]

g. What is the minimum number of workers that could produce at an hourly rate of 72 units? Assume the tasks can be allocated to workers as described in the beginning (i.e., tasks cannot be done in any order). [4.4]

Q4.5 **(Geneva Watch)** The Geneva Watch Corporation manufactures watches on a conveyor belt with six stations. One worker stands at each station and performs the following tasks:

Station	Tasks	Processing Time (seconds)
A: Preparation 1	Heat-stake lens to bezel	14
	Inspect bezel	26
	Clean switch holes	10
	Install set switch in bezel	18
	Total time for A	68
B: Preparation 2	Check switch travel	23
	Clean inside bezel	12
	Install module in bezel	25
	Total time for B	60
C: Battery installation	Install battery clip on module	20
	Heat-stake battery clip on module	15
	Install 2 batteries in module	22
	Check switch	13
	Total time for C	70
D: Band installation	Install band	45
	Inspect band	13
	Total time for D	58
E: Packaging preparation	Cosmetic inspection	20
	Final test	55
	Total time for E	75
F: Watch packaging	Place watch and cuff in display box	20
	Place cover in display box base	14
	Place owner's manual, box into tub	30
	Total time for F	64

These six workers begin their workday at 8:00 a.m. and work steadily until 4:00 p.m. At 4:00, no new watch parts are introduced into station A and the conveyor belt continues until all of the work-in-process inventory has been processed and leaves station F. Thus, each morning the workers begin with an empty system.

a. What is the bottleneck in this process? [4.1]

b. What is the capacity, in watches per hour, of the assembly line (ignore the time it takes for the first watch to come off the line)? [4.1]

c. What is the direct labor content for the processes on this conveyor belt? [4.3]

d. What is the utilization of the worker in station B (ignore the time it takes for the first watch to come off the line)? [4.1]

e. How many minutes of idle time will the worker in station C have in one hour (ignore the time it takes for the first watch to come off the line)? [4.3]

f. What time will it be (within one minute) when the assembly line has processed 193 watches on any given day? [4.2]

Q4.6 **(Yoggo Soft Drink)** A small, privately owned Asian company is producing a private-label soft drink, Yoggo. A machine-paced line puts the soft drinks into plastic bottles and then packages the bottles into boxes holding 10 bottles each. The machine-paced line is comprised of the following four steps: (1) the bottling machine takes 1 second to fill a bottle, (2) the lid machine takes 3 seconds to cover the bottle with a lid, (3) a labeling machine takes 5 seconds to apply a label to a bottle, and (4) the packaging machine takes 4 seconds to place a bottle into a box. When a box has been filled with 10 bottles, a worker tending the packaging machine removes the filled box and replaces it with an empty box. Assume that the time for the worker to remove a filled box and replace it with an empty box is negligible and hence does not affect the capacity of the line. At step 3 there are two labeling machines that each process alternating bottles; that is, the first machine processes bottles 1, 3, 5, . . . and the second machine processes bottles 2, 4, 6, ... Problem data are summarized in the table following.

Process Step	Number of Machines	Seconds per Bottle
Bottling	1	1
Applying a lid	1	3
Labeling	2	5
Packaging	1	4

a. What is the process capacity (bottles/hour) for the machine-paced line? [4.1]

b. What is the bottleneck in the process? [4.1]

c. If one more identical labeling machine is added to the process, how much is the increase in the process capacity going to be (in terms of bottles/hour)? [4.1]

d. What is the implied utilization of the packaging machine if the demand rate is 60 boxes/hour? Recall that a box consists of 10 bottles. [4.1]

Q4.7 **(Atlas Inc.)** Atlas Inc. is a toy bicycle manufacturing company producing a five-inch small version of the bike that Lance Armstrong rode to win his first Tour de France. The assembly line at Atlas Inc. consists of seven work stations, each performing a single step. Stations and processing times are summarized here:

- Step 1 (30 sec.): The plastic tube for the frame is cut to size.
- Step 2 (20 sec.): The tube is put together.
- Step 3 (35 sec.): The frame is glued together.
- Step 4 (25 sec.): The frame is cleaned.
- Step 5 (30 sec.): Paint is sprayed onto the frame.
- Step 6 (45 sec.): Wheels are assembled.
- Step 7 (40 sec.): All other parts are assembled to the frame.

Under the current process layout, workers are allocated to the stations as shown here:

- Worker 1: Steps 1, 2
- Worker 2: Steps 3, 4
- Worker 3: Step 5

- Worker 4: Step 6
- Worker 5: Step 7

a. What is the bottleneck in this process? [4.1]

b. What is the capacity of this assembly line, in finished units/hour? [4.1]

c. What is the utilization of Worker 4, ignoring the production of the first and last units? [4.1]

d. How long does it take to finish production of 100 units, starting with an empty process? [4.2]

e. What is the average labor utilization of the workers, ignoring the production of the first and last units? [4.3]

f. Assume the workers are paid $15 per hour. What is the cost of direct labor for the bicycle? [4.4]

g. Based on recommendations of a consultant, Atlas Inc. decides to reallocate the tasks among the workers to achieve maximum process capacity. Assume that if a worker is in charge of two tasks, then the tasks have to be adjacent to each other. Also, assume that the sequence of steps cannot be changed. What is the maximum possible capacity, in units per hour, that can be achieved by this reallocation? [4.4]

h. Again, assume a wage rate of $15 per hour. What would be the cost of direct labor if one single worker would perform all seven steps? You can ignore benefits of specialization, set-up times, or quality problems. [4.5]

i. On account of a reduced demand forecast, management has decided to let go of one worker. If work is to be allocated among the four workers such that (i) the tasks can't be divided, (ii) if one worker is in charge of two tasks, the tasks have to be adjacent, (iii) the tasks are assigned in the most efficient way and (iv) each step can only be carried out by one worker, what is the new capacity of the line (in finished units/hour)? [4.5]

Q4.8 **(Glove Design Challenge)** A manufacturer of women's designer gloves has employed a team of students to redesign her manufacturing unit. They gathered the following information. The manufacturing process consists of four activities: (1) fabric cutting; (2) dyeing; (3) stitching, done by specially designed machines; and (4) packaging. Processing times are shown below. Gloves are moved between activities by a conveyor belt that paces the flow of work (machine-paced line).

Process Step	Number of Machines	Minutes per Glove
Cutting	1	2
Dyeing	1	4
Stitching	1	3
Packaging	1	5

a. What is the process capacity in gloves/hour? [4.1]

b. Which one of the following statements is true? [4.1]

   i. The capacity of the process increases by reducing the dyeing time.

   ii. If stitching time increases to 5 minutes/glove, the capacity of the process remains unchanged, but "time through an empty machine-paced process" increases.

   iii. By reducing packaging time, the process capacity increases.

   iv. By reducing cutting time, the capacity of the process increases.

c. What is the implied utilization of the packaging machine if the demand rate is 10 gloves/hour? [4.1]

d. What is the flow time for a glove? [4.1]

Q4.9 **(Worker-Paced Line)**

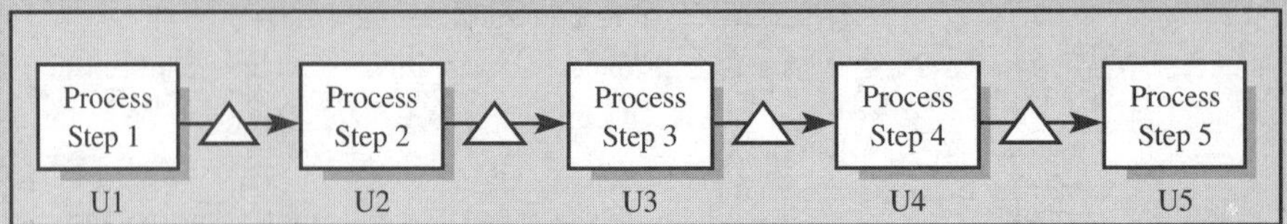

The accompanying diagram depicts a five-step, worker-paced headphone manufacturing plant. The headphones are meant to be used with iPods and DVD players. Step 1 involves a worker bending a metal strip into an arc shape. In step 2, the metal arc is fitted with a plastic sleeve. In step 3, the headphones are fitted at the end of the metal and plastic strips. In step 4, the wires are soldered into the headphones. Step 5 involves a specially designed packaging unit. After the plant has been operational for a couple of hours, the manager inspects the plant. He is particularly interested in cutting labor costs. He observes the following. The process is capacity-constrained and the entire process produces 36 units in one hour. U1 through U5 denote the utilization at steps 1 through 5 respectively. Currently, there is a single worker at each step and the utilizations are as follows: U1 = 4/30, U2 = 4/15, U3 = 4/5, U4 = 1, U5 = 2/5.

Answer the following questions based on the given data and information.

a. What is the capacity of step 5? [4.1]
b. Which step is the bottleneck? [4.1]
c. Which process step has the highest capacity? [4.1]
d. If the wage rate is $36 per hour per person, what is the direct labor cost per unit? [4.4]

If you would like to test your understanding of a specific section, here are the questions organized by section:

Section 4.1: Q4.2a, Q4.3abe, Q4.4a, Q4.5abd, Q4.6, Q4.7abc, Q4.8, Q4.9abc

Section 4.2: Q4.1a, Q4.4d, Q4.5f, Q4.7d

Section 4.3: Q4.1bc, Q4.4bc, Q4.5ce, Q4.7e

Section 4.4: Q4.1d, Q4.2bc, Q4.3cfg, Q4.4efg, Q4.7f, Q4.9d

Section 4.5: Q4.3d, Q4.7hi

Chapter 5

Batching and Other Flow Interruptions: Setup Times and the Economic Order Quantity Model

So far we have considered processes in which one flow unit consistently enters the process and one flow unit consistently exits the process at fixed intervals of time, called the process cycle time. For example, in the scooter example of Chapter 4, we establish a cycle time of three minutes, which allows for a production of 700 scooters per week.

In an ideal process, a cycle time of three minutes would imply that every resource receives one flow unit as an input each three-minute interval and creates one flow unit of output each three-minute interval. Such a smooth and constant flow of units is the dream of any operations manager, yet it is rarely feasible in practice. There are several reasons for why the smooth process flow is interrupted, the most important ones being setups and variability in processing times or quality levels. The focus of this chapter is on setups, which are an important characteristic of batch-flow operations.

To discuss setups, we return to the Xootr production process. In particular, we consider the computer numerically controlled (CNC) milling machine that is responsible for making two types of parts on each Xootr—the steer support and two ribs (see Figure 5.1). The steer support attaches the Xootr's deck to the steering column, and the ribs help the deck support the weight of the rider. Once the milling machine starts producing one of these parts, it can produce them reasonably quickly. However, a considerable setup time, or changeover time, is needed before the production of each part type can begin. Our primary objective is to understand how setups like these influence the three basic performance measures of a process: inventory, flow rate, and flow time.

FIGURE 5.1 Milling Machine (left) and Steer Support Parts (right)

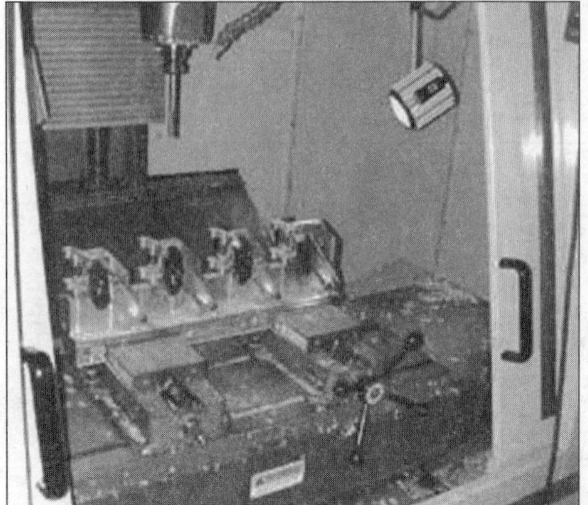

5.1 The Impact of Setups on Capacity

To evaluate the capacity of the milling machine, we need some more information. Specifically, once set up to produce a part, the milling machine can produce steer supports at the rate of one per minute and can produce ribs at the rate of two per minute. Recall, each Xootr needs one steer support and two ribs. Furthermore, one hour is needed to set up the milling machine to start producing steer supports and one hour is also needed to begin producing ribs. Although no parts are produced during those setup times, it is not quite correct to say that nothing is happening during those times either. The milling machine operator is busy calibrating the milling machine so that it can produce the desired part.

It makes intuitive sense that the following production process should be used with these two parts: set up the machine to make steer supports, make some steer supports, set up the machine to make ribs, make some ribs, and finally, repeat this sequence of setups and production runs. We call this repeating sequence a *production cycle*: one production cycle occurs immediately after another, and all productions cycles "look the same" in the sense that they have the same setups and production runs.

We call this a batch production process because parts are made in batches. Although it may be apparent by what is meant by a "batch," it is useful to provide a precise definition:

A *batch* is a collection of flow units.

Throughout our analysis, we assume that batches are produced in succession. That is, once the production of one batch is completed, the production of the next batch begins and all batches contain the same number and type of flow unit.

Given that a batch is a collection of flow units, we need to define our flow unit in the case of the Xootr. Each Xootr needs one steer support and two ribs, so let's say the flow unit is a "component set" and each component set is composed of those three parts. Hence, each production cycle produces a batch of component sets.

One might ask why we did not define the flow unit to be one of the two types of parts. For example, we could call the steering supports made in a production run a batch of steering supports. However, our interest is not specifically on the capacity to make steering

FIGURE 5.2 **The Impact of Setup Times on Capacity**

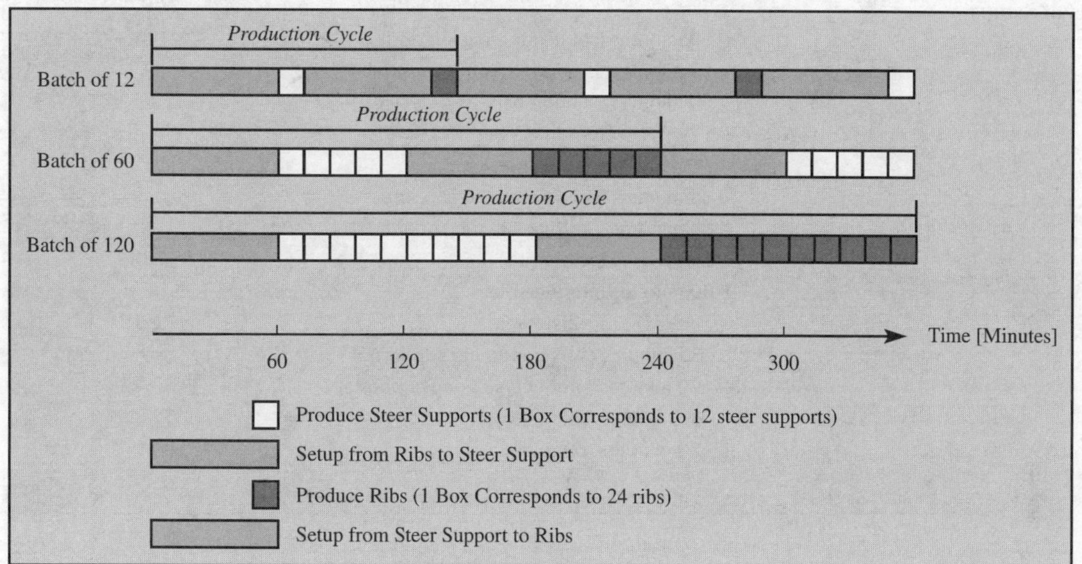

supports or ribs in isolation. We care about the capacity for component sets because one component set is needed for each Xootr. Thus, for the purpose of this analysis, it makes more sense to define the flow unit as a component set and to think in terms of a batch of component sets.

Because no output is produced while the resource is in setup mode, it is fairly intuitive that frequent setups lead to lower capacity. To understand how setups reduce the capacity of a process, consider Figure 5.2. As nothing is produced at a resource during setup, the more frequently a resource is set up, the lower its capacity. As discussed above, the milling machine underlying the example of Figure 5.2 has the following processing times/setup times:

- It takes one minute to produce one steer support unit (of which there is one per Xootr).
- It takes 60 minutes to change over the milling machine from producing steer supports to producing ribs (setup time).
- It takes 0.5 minute to produce one rib; because there are two ribs in a Xootr, this translates to one minute/per pair of ribs.
- Finally, it takes another 60 minutes to change over the milling machine back to producing steer supports.

Now consider the impact that varying the batch size has on capacity. Recall that we defined capacity as the maximum flow rate at which a process can operate. If we produce in small batches of 12 component sets per batch, we spend a total of two hours of setup time (one hour to set up the production for steer supports and one hour to set up the production of ribs) for every 12 component sets we produce. These two hours of setup time are lost from regular production.

The capacity of the resource can be increased by increasing the batch size. If the machine is set up every 60 units, the capacity-reducing impact of setup can be spread out over 60 units. This results in a higher capacity for the milling machine. Specifically, for a batch size of 60, the milling machine could produce at 0.25 component set per minute. Table 5.1 summarizes the capacity calculations for batch sizes of 12, 60, and 120.

TABLE 5.1
The Impact of Setups on Capacity

Batch Size	Time to Complete One Batch [minutes]	Capacity [units/minute]
12	60 minutes (set up steering support) + 12 minutes (produce steering supports) + 60 minutes (set up ribs) + 12 minutes (produce ribs) 144 minutes	12/144 = 0.0833
60	60 minutes (set up steering support) + 60 minutes (produce steering supports) + 60 minutes (set up ribs) + 60 minutes (produce ribs) 240 minutes	60/240 = 0.25
120	60 minutes (set up steering support) + 120 minutes (produce steering supports) + 60 minutes (set up ribs) + 120 minutes (produce ribs) 360 minutes	120/360 = 0.333

Generalizing the computations in Table 5.1, we can compute the capacity of a resource with setups as a function of the batch size:

$$\text{Capacity given batch size} = \frac{\text{Batch size}}{\text{Setup time} + \text{Batch size} \times \text{Processing time}}$$

Basically, the above equation is spreading the "unproductive" setup time over the members of a batch. To use the equation, we need to be precise about what we mean by batch size, the setup time, and processing time:

- The batch size is the number of flow units that are produced in one "cycle" (i.e., before the process repeats itself, see Figure 5.2).
- The setup time includes all setups in the production of the batch (i.e., all of the setups in the production cycle). In this case, this includes $S = 60$ minutes + 60 minutes = 120 minutes. It can also include any other nonproducing time associated with the production of the batch. For example, if the production of each batch requires a 10-minute worker break, then that would be included. Other "setup times" can include scheduled maintenance or forced idle time (time in which literally nothing is happening with the machine—it is neither producing nor being prepped to produce).
- The processing time includes all production time that is needed to produce one complete flow unit of output at the milling machine. In this case, this includes 1 minute/unit for the steer support as well as two times 0.5 minute/unit for the ribs. The processing time is thus $p = 1$ minute/unit + 2×0.5 minute/unit = 2 minutes/unit. Notice that the processing time is 2 minutes even though no single component set is actually produced over a single period of 2 minutes of length. Due to setups, the processing time for a component set is divided over two periods of one minute each, and those two periods can be separated by a considerable amount of time. Nevertheless, from the perspective of calculating the capacity of the milling machine when operated with a given batch size, it does not matter whether each component set is produced over a continuous period of time or disjointed periods of time. All that matters is that a total of 2 minutes is needed for each component set.

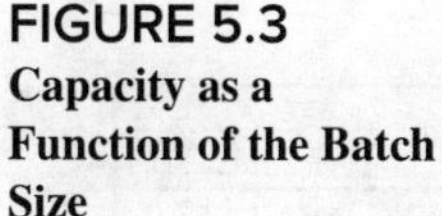

FIGURE 5.3
Capacity as a Function of the Batch Size

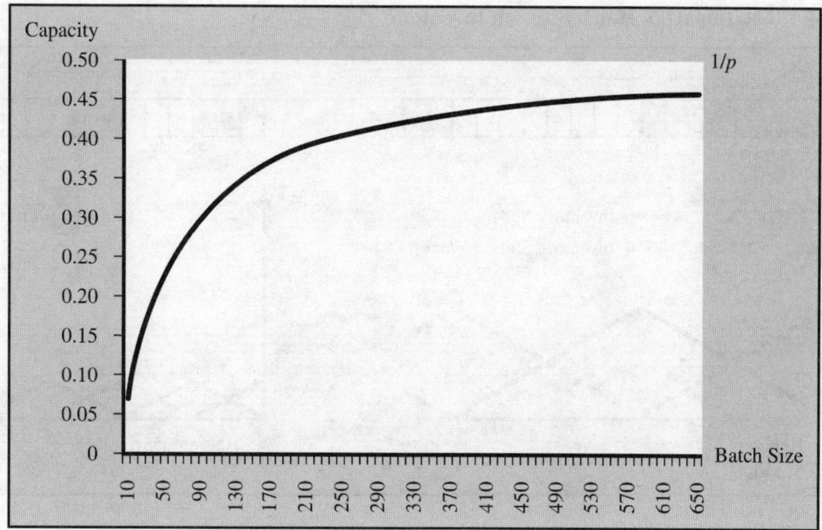

Given these definitions, say we operate with a batch size of 100 units. Our capacity in this case would be

$$\text{Capacity (for } B = 100) = \frac{\text{Batch size}}{\text{Setup time} + \text{Batch size} \times \text{Processing time}}$$

$$= \frac{100 \text{ units}}{120 \text{ minutes} + 100 \text{ units} \times 2 \text{ minutes/unit}}$$

$$= 0.3125 \text{ unit/minute}$$

No matter how large a batch size we choose, we never are able to produce faster than one unit every p units of time. Thus, $1/p$ can be thought of as the maximum capacity the process can achieve. This is illustrated in Figure 5.3.

5.2 Interaction between Batching and Inventory

Given the desirable effect that large batch sizes increase capacity, why not choose the largest possible batch size to maximize capacity? While large batch sizes are desirable from a capacity perspective, they typically require a higher level of inventory, either within the process or at the finished goods level. Holding the flow rate constant, we can infer from Little's Law that such a higher inventory level also leads to longer flow times. This is why batch-flow operations generally are not very fast in responding to customer orders (remember the last time you bought custom furniture?).

The interaction between batching and inventory is illustrated by the following example. Consider an auto manufacturer producing a sedan and a station wagon on the same assembly line. For simplicity, assume both models have the same demand rate, 400 cars per day each. The metal stamping steps in the process preceding final assembly are characterized by especially long setup times. Thus, to achieve a high level of capacity, the plant runs large production batches and produces sedans for eight weeks, then station wagons for eight weeks, and so on.

The production schedule results in lumpy output of sedans and station wagons, but customers demand sedans and station wagons at a constant rate (say). Hence, producing in large batches leads to a mismatch between the rate of supply and the rate of demand.

To make this schedule work, in addition to producing enough to cover demand over the eight weeks of production, the company needs to also produce enough cars to satisfy

FIGURE 5.4 **The Impact of Batch Sizes on Inventory**

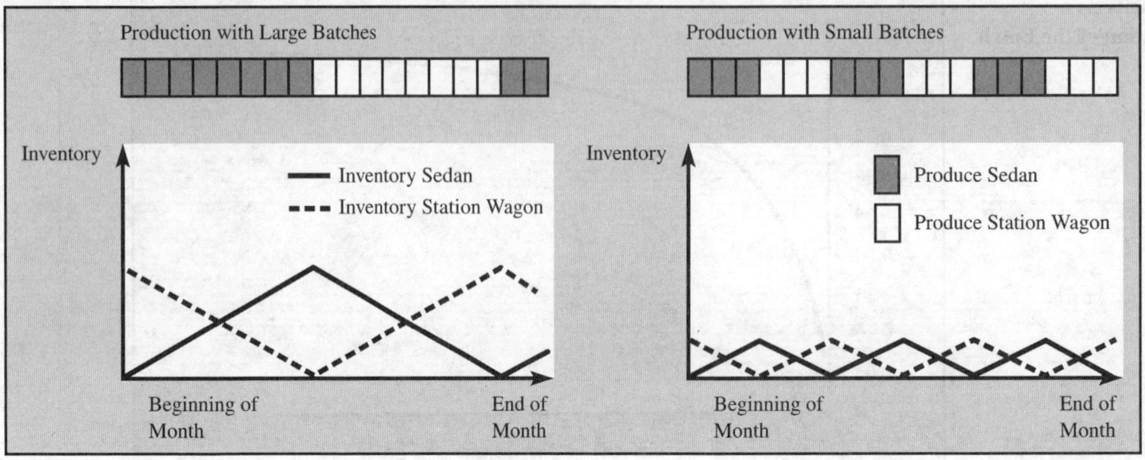

demand in the subsequent eight weeks while it is producing the other type of car. Assuming five days per week, that means that when sedan production finishes, there needs to be 400 cars per day × 5 days per week × 8 weeks = 16,000 sedans in inventory. Those 16,000 sedans are sold off at a constant rate of 2,000 cars per week for the eight weeks while station wagons are made. On average there are 8,000 sedans in inventory. The same applies to station wagons—when production of station wagons ends there needs to be 16,000 of them in inventory and they are then depleted over the subsequent eight weeks, leaving an average of 8,000 station wagons in inventory. This pattern of inventory rising and falling is illustrated by the left side of Figure 5.4.

Instead of producing one type of car for eight weeks before switching, the company may find that it is feasible to produce cars for three weeks before switching. Now at the end of each production run the company needs 400 cars per day × 5 days per week × 3 weeks = 6,000 cars to cover demand over the three weeks the other product is produced. That means that average inventory of each type is only 3,000 cars, which is dramatically lower than the inventory needed with the eight-week schedule. This is illustrated by the right side of Figure 5.4. Thus, smaller batches translate to lower inventory levels!

In the ideal case, which has been propagated by the Toyota Production Systems (see Chapter 8) under the word *heijunka* or *mixed-model* production, the company would alternate between producing one sedan and producing one station wagon, thereby producing in batch sizes of one. This way, a much better synchronization of the demand flow and the production flow is achieved and inventory basically eliminated.

Now let's turn our attention back to the milling machine at Nova Cruz. Similar to Figure 5.4, we can draw the inventory of components (ribs and steer supports) over the course of a production cycle. Remember that the assembly process following the milling machine requires a supply of one unit every three minutes. This one unit consists, from the view of the milling machine, of two ribs and a steer support unit. If we want to ensure a sufficient supply to keep the assembly process operating, we have to produce a sufficient number of ribs such that during the time we do not produce ribs (e.g., setup time and production of steer support) we do not run out of ribs. Say the milling machine operates with a batch size of 200 units, $B = 200$. In that case, the inventory of ribs changes as follows:

- During the production of ribs, inventory accumulates. As we produce one rib pair per minute, but assembly takes only one rib pair every three minutes, rib inventory accumulates at the rate of two rib pairs every three minutes, or 2/3 rib pairs per minute.

FIGURE 5.5 The Impact of Setup Times on Capacity

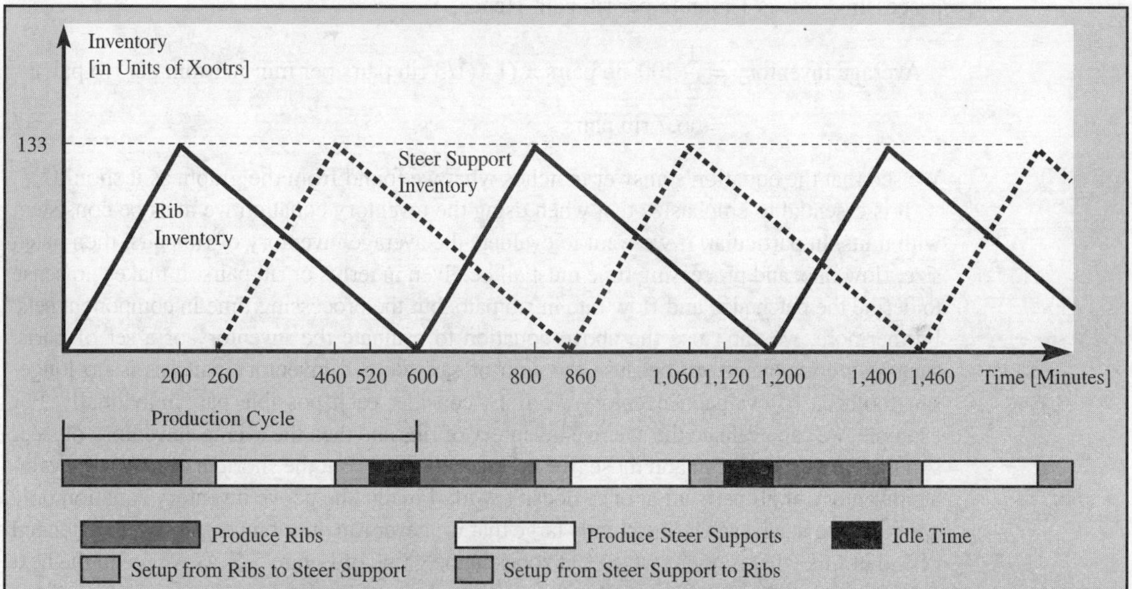

- The production of 200 rib pairs requires 200 minutes. Hence, the inventory of rib pairs at the end of the production run is 200 minutes × 2/3 rib pairs per minute = 133.3 rib pairs (i.e., 266 ribs).

The resulting production plan as well as the corresponding inventory levels are summarized by Figure 5.5. Notice that each production cycle takes 200 scooters × 3 minutes per scooter = 600 minutes, and this includes 80 minutes of idle time. Why is there idle time in the milling machine's production schedule? The answer is that without the idle time, the milling machine would produce too quickly given our batch size of 200 units. To explain, assembly takes 600 minutes to produce a batch of 200 scooters but the milling machine only needs 520 minutes to produce that batch of 600 scooters (120 minutes of setup and 400 minutes of production). Hence, if the milling machine produced one batch after another (without any idle time between them), it would produce 200 component sets every 520 minutes (or 200/520 = 0.3846 component set per minute), which is faster than assembly can use them (which is 1/3 component sets per minute). This analysis suggests that maybe we want to choose a different batch size, as we see in the next section.

Figure 5.5 helps us to visualize the pattern of inventory for both rib pairs and steer supports. We see that the inventory of rib pairs makes a "sawtooth" pattern over time, with a minimum of 0 and a maximum of 133.3. If we were to average over all of the inventory levels we would discover the average inventory to be 133.3/2 = 66.7. (The average across a triangle is half of its height.) But using a graph is not an efficient way to evaluate average inventory for each item in the production schedule. A better approach is to use the equation

$$\text{Average inventory} = \frac{1}{2}\,\text{Batch size}\,(1 - \text{Flow rate} \times \text{Processing time})$$

In our case the batch size is 200 rib pairs, the flow rate is 1/3 rib pairs per minute, and the processing time is 1 minute per rib pair. Hence,

$$\text{Average inventory} = \frac{1}{2}\,200 \text{ rib pairs} \times (1-(1/3 \text{ rib pairs per min} \times 1 \text{ min per rib pair})$$
$$= 66.7 \text{ rib pairs}$$

We see that the equation's answer matches what we found from the graph, as it should.

It is essential to emphasize that when using the inventory equation we must be consistent with units. In particular, if we want to evaluate the average inventory of rib pairs, then batch size, flow rate, and processing time must all be given in terms or rib pairs. It makes no sense to define the batch size and flow rate in rib pairs but the processing time in component sets. Furthermore, we can't use the above equation to evaluate the inventory of a set of parts, such as a component set, because the sum of saw-toothed inventory patterns is no longer saw-toothed. To evaluate inventory we must consider each possible part individually. For example, we can evaluate the average inventory of ribs and then the average inventory of steer supports and then we can add those two averages together. But the shortcut of trying to evaluate inventory of all parts all at once doesn't work. Finally, the above inventory equation only applies if the batch size is sufficiently large that we never run out of inventory for an extended period of time, that is, there are no flat zones in the graph of Figure 5.5. As we see in the next section, we will generally want to operate with such a sufficiently large batch size.

We can end this section by repeating the key observation that larger batches lead to more inventory, which is readily apparent in our average inventory equation. Thus, if we want to reduce inventory, we need to operate with smaller batches.

5.3 Choosing a Batch Size in the Presence of Setup Times

When choosing an appropriate batch size for a process flow, it is important to balance the conflicting objectives: capacity and inventory. Large batches lead to large inventory but more capacity; small batches lead to losses in capacity but less inventory.

To balance the conflict between our desire for more capacity and less inventory, we benefit from the following two observations:

- Capacity at the bottleneck step is extremely valuable (as long as the process is capacity-constrained; i.e., there is more demand than capacity) as it constrains the flow rate of the entire process.
- Capacity at a nonbottleneck step is free, as it does not provide a constraint on the current flow rate.

This has direct implications for choosing an appropriate batch size at a process step with setups.

- If the setup occurs at the bottleneck step (and the process is capacity-constrained), it is desirable to increase the batch size, as this results in a larger process capacity and, therefore, a higher flow rate.
- If the setup occurs at a nonbottleneck step (or the process is demand-constrained), it is desirable to decrease the batch size, as this decreases inventory as well as flow time.

The scooter example summarized by Figure 5.6 illustrates these two observations and how they help us in choosing a good batch size. Remember that B denotes the batch size, S the setup time, and p the per unit processing time.

FIGURE 5.6
Data from the Scooter Case about Setup Times and Batching

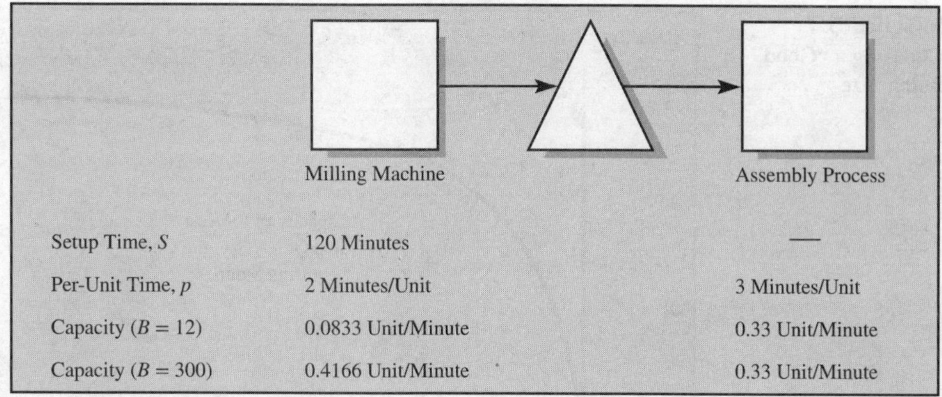

	Milling Machine	Assembly Process
Setup Time, S	120 Minutes	—
Per-Unit Time, p	2 Minutes/Unit	3 Minutes/Unit
Capacity ($B = 12$)	0.0833 Unit/Minute	0.33 Unit/Minute
Capacity ($B = 300$)	0.4166 Unit/Minute	0.33 Unit/Minute

The process flow diagram in Figure 5.6 consists of only two activities: the milling machine and the assembly operations. We can combine the assembly operations into one activity, as we know that its slowest step (bottleneck of assembly) can create one Xootr every three minutes, which is therefore assembly's *processing time*. The capacity of the assembly operation is 1/*Processing time,* so its capacity is $\frac{1}{3}$ unit per minute.

Let's evaluate this process with two different batch sizes. First, say $B = 12$. The capacity of the milling machine can be evaluated with the formula

$$\text{Capacity}\,(B) = \frac{\text{Batch size}}{\text{Setup time} + \text{Batch size} \times \text{Processing time}}$$

$$= \frac{B}{S + B \times p} = \frac{12}{120 + 12 \times 2} = 0.0833\,\text{unit/minute}$$

With $B = 12$ the milling machine is the bottleneck because its capacity (0.0833 unit/minute) is lower than the capacity of assembly (0.3333 unit/minute).

Next, consider what happens to the same calculations if we increase the batch size from 12 to 300. While this does not affect the capacity of the assembly operations, the capacity of the milling machine now becomes

$$\text{Capacity}\,(B) = \frac{B}{S + B \times p} = \frac{300}{120 + 300 \times 2} = 0.4166\,\text{unit/minute}$$

Thus, we observe that the location of the bottleneck has shifted from the milling machine to the assembly operation; with $B = 300$ the milling machine's capacity (0.4166 unit/minute) now exceeds assembly's capacity (0.3333 unit/minute). Just by modifying the batch size we can change which activity is the bottleneck! Now which of the two batch sizes is the "better" one, 12 or 300?

- The batch size of 300 is too large. A smaller batch size would reduce inventory but as long as assembly remains the bottleneck, the smaller batch size does not lower the process's flow rate.
- The batch size of 12 is probably too small. As long as demand is greater than 0.0833 unit per minute (the milling machine's capacity with $B = 12$), a larger batch size can increase the flow rate of the process. It would also increase inventory, but the higher flow rate almost surely justifies a bit more inventory.

As a batch size of 12 is too small and a batch size of 300 is too large, a good batch size is "somewhere in between." Specifically, we are interested in the smallest batch size that does not adversely affect process capacity.

FIGURE 5.7
Choosing a "Good" Batch Size

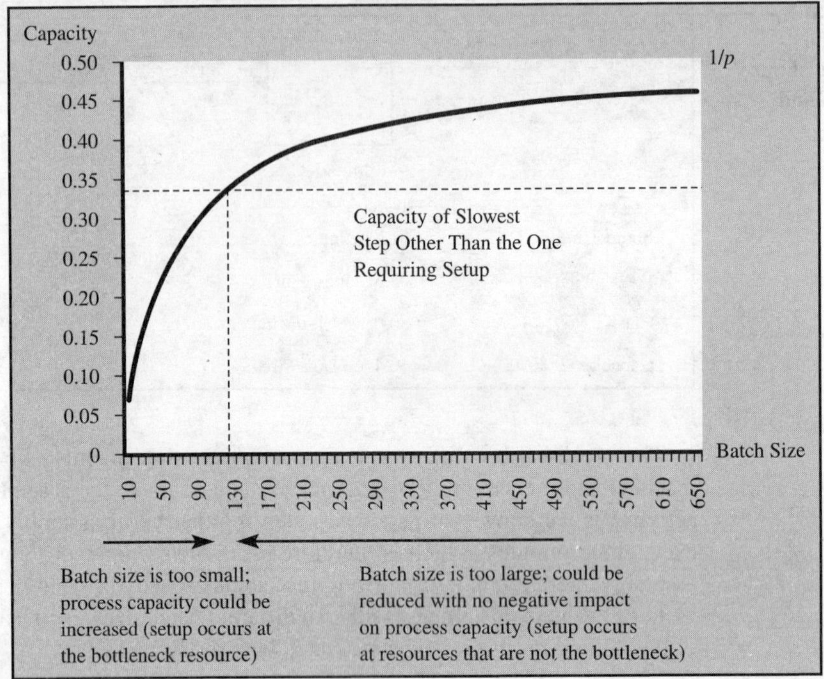

To find this number, we equate the capacity of the step with the setup (in this case, the milling machine) with the capacity of the step from the remaining process that has the smallest capacity (in this case, the assembly operations):

$$\frac{B}{120 + B \times 2} = \frac{1}{3}$$

and solve this equation for B:

$$\frac{B}{120 + B \times 2} = \frac{1}{3}$$

$$3 \times B = 120 + 2 \times B$$

$$B = 120$$

which gives us, in this case, $B = 120$. This algebraic approach is illustrated by Figure 5.7. If you feel uncomfortable with the algebra outlined above (i.e., solving the equation for the batch size B), or you want to program the method directly into Excel or another software package, you can use the following equation:

$$\text{Recommended batch size} = \frac{\text{Flow rate} \times \text{Setup time}}{1 - \text{Flow rate} \times \text{Processing time}}$$

which is equivalent to the analysis performed above. To see this, simply substitute Setup time = 120 minutes, Flow rate = 0.333 unit per minute, and Processing time = 2 minutes per unit and obtain

$$\text{Recommended batch size} = \frac{\text{Flow rate} \times \text{Setup time}}{1 - \text{Flow rate} \times \text{Processing time}} = \frac{0.333 \times 120}{1 - 0.333 \times 2} = 120$$

Figure 5.7 shows the capacity of the process step with the setup (the milling machine), which increases with the batch size B, and for very high values of batch size B approaches

Exhibit 5.1

FINDING A GOOD BATCH SIZE IN THE PRESENCE OF SETUP TIMES

1. Compute Flow rate = Minimum {Available input, Demand, Process capacity}.
2. Define the production cycle, which includes the processing and setups of all flow units in a batch. Let B be the number of units produced in the production cycle.
3. Compute the total time in a production cycle that the resource is in setup; setup times are those times that are independent of the batch size. Call this total the *Setup time.*
4. Compute the total time in a production cycle to process a single unit. If a single unit has multiple parts, then sum the times to process each of the parts. Call this total the *Processing time.*
5. Compute the capacity of the resource with setup for a given batch size:

$$\text{Capacity}(B) = \frac{B}{\text{Setup time} + B \times \text{Processing time}}$$

6. We are looking for the batch size that leads to the lowest level of inventory without affecting the flow rate; we find this by solving the equation

$$\text{Capacity}(B) = \text{Flow rate}$$

for the batch size B. This also can be done directly using the following formula:

$$\text{Recommended batch size} = \frac{\text{Flow rate} \times \text{Setup time}}{1 - \text{Flow rate} \times \text{Processing time}}$$

$1/p$ (similar to the graph in Figure 5.3). As the capacity of the assembly operation does not depend on the batch size, it corresponds to a constant (flat line).

The overall process capacity is—in the spirit of the bottleneck idea—the minimum of the two graphs. Thus, before the graphs intersect, the capacity is too low and flow rate is potentially given up. After the intersection point, the assembly operation is the bottleneck and any further increases in batch size yield no return. Exhibit 5.1 provides a summary of the computations leading to the recommended batch size in the presence of setup times.

5.4 Setup Times and Product Variety

As we have seen in the case of the Xootr production process, setup times often occur due to the need to change over production from one product to another. This raises the following question: What is the impact of product variety on a process with setup times? To explore this question, let's consider a simple process that makes two kinds of soup: chicken noodle and tomato.

Demand for chicken soup is 100 gallons per hour, while demand for tomato soup is 75 gallons per hour. Switching from one type of soup to another requires 30 minutes to clean the production equipment so that one flavor does not disrupt the flavor of the next soup. Once production begins, the process can make 300 gallons per hour of either type of soup. Given these parameters, let's evaluate a production cycle that minimizes inventory while satisfying demand.

We first need to define our flow unit. In this case, it is natural to let our flow unit be one gallon of soup. Hence, a production cycle of soup contains a certain number of gallons, some chicken and some tomato. In this case, a "batch" is the set of gallons produced in a production cycle. While the plant manager is likely to refer to batches of tomato soup and batches of chicken soup individually, and unlikely to refer to the batch that combines both flavors, we cannot analyze the production process of tomato soup in isolation from the production process of chicken soup. (For example, if we dedicate more time to tomato production, then we will have less time for chicken noodle production.) Because we are ultimately interested in our capacity to make soup, we focus our analysis at the level of the production cycle and refer to the entire production within that cycle as a "batch."

Our desired flow rate is 175 gallons per hour (the sum of demand for chicken and tomato), the setup time is 1 hour (30 minutes per soup and two types of soup) and the processing time is 1/300 hour per gallon. The batch size that minimizes inventory while still meeting our demand is then

$$\text{Recommended batch size} = \frac{\text{Flow rate} \times \text{Setup time}}{1 - \text{Flow rate} \times \text{Processing time}} = \frac{175 \times (2 \times 1/2)}{1 - 175 \times (1/300)}$$

$$= 420 \text{ gallons}$$

We should produce in proportion to demand (otherwise at least one of the flavors will have too much production and at least one will have too little), so of the 420 gallons, 420 × 100/(100 + 75) = 240 gallons should be chicken soup and the remainder, 420 – 240 = 180 gallons, should be tomato.

To evaluate the average inventory of chicken noodle soup, let's use the equation

$$\text{Average inventory} = \frac{1}{2} \text{ Batch Size} \times (1 - \text{Flow rate} \times \text{Processing time})$$

The flow unit is 1 gallon of chicken noodle soup, the batch size is 240 gallons, flow rate is 100 gallons per hour, and the processing time is 1/300 hours per gallon. Thus, average inventory of chicken noodle soup is 1/2 × 240 gallons × (1 – 100 gallons per hour × 1/300 hours per gallon) = 80 gallons.

To understand the impact of variety on this process, suppose we were to add a third kind of soup to our product offering, onion soup. Furthermore, with onion soup added to the mix, demand for chicken remains 100 gallons per hour, and demand for tomato continues to be 75 gallons per hour, while onion now generates 30 gallons of demand on its own. In some sense, this is an ideal case for adding variety—the new variant adds incrementally to demand without stealing any demand from the existing varieties.

The desired flow rate is now 100 + 75 + 30 = 205, the setup time is 1.5 hours (three setups per batch), and the inventory minimizing quantity for the production cycle is

$$\text{Recommended batch size} = \frac{\text{Flow rate} \times \text{Setup time}}{1 - \text{Flow rate} \times \text{Processing time}} = \frac{205 \times (3 \times 1/2)}{1 - 205 \times (1/300)}$$

$$= 971 \text{ gallons}$$

Again, we should produce in proportion to demand:

971 × (100/205) = 474 gallons of chicken,

971 × (75/205) = 355 gallons of tomato, and

971 × (30/205) = 142 gallons of onion.

What happened when we added to variety? In short, we need more inventory. With the batch size of 474 gallons, the average inventory of chicken noodle soup becomes 1/2 × 474 gallons × (1 – 100 gallons per hour × 1/300 hours per gallon) = 158 gallons. Because the batch size of chicken noodle soup nearly doubles (474/240 = 1.98), the average inventory of chicken noodle soup also nearly doubles.

Why did inventory of chicken soup increase when onion soup was added to the mix? Setup times are to blame. With more varieties in the production mix, the production process has to set up more often per production cycle. This reduces the capacity of the production cycle (no soup is made during a setup). To increase the capacity back to the desired flow rate (which is even higher now), we need to operate with larger batches (longer production cycles), and they lead to more inventory.

One may argue that the previous analysis is too optimistic—adding onion soup to the mix should steal some demand away from the other flavors. It turns out that our result is not sensitive to this assumption. To demonstrate, let's consider the opposite extreme—adding onion soup does not expand overall demand, it only steals demand from the other flavors. Specifically, the overall flow rate remains 175 gallons per hour, with or without onion soup. Furthermore, with onion soup, the demand rate for chicken, tomato, and onion are 80, 65, and 30 gallons per hour, respectively. The processing time is still 1/300 gallons per hour, and the setup time per batch is now 1.5 hours (three changeovers due to three types of soup). The batch size that minimizes our inventory while meeting our demand is

$$\text{Recommended batch size} = \frac{\text{Flow rate} \times \text{Setup time}}{1 - \text{Flow rate} \times \text{Processing time}} = \frac{175 \times (3 \times 1/2)}{1 - 175 \times (1/300)}$$
$$= 630\,\text{gallons}$$

The chicken noodle batch size is (80 gallons/175 gallons) × 630 gallons = 240 gallons. Average inventory is 1/2 × 240 gallons × (1 – 100 gallons per hour × 1/300 hours per gallon) = 96 gallons. Recall, with just the two flavors and a flow rate of 175 gallons of soup per hour, there are only 80 gallons of chicken noodle soup. So inventory does not increase as much in this case, but it still increases.

The conclusion from this investigation is that setup times and product variety do not mix very well. Consequently, there are two possible solutions to this challenge. The first is to offer only a limited amount of variety. That was Henry Ford's approach when he famously declared that "You can have any color Model-T you want, as long as it is black." While a convenient solution for a production manager, it is not necessarily the best strategy for satisfying demand in a competitive environment.

The other approach to the incompatibility of setups and variety is to work to eliminate setup times. This is the approach advocated by Shigeo Shingo, one of the most influential thought leaders in manufacturing. When he witnessed changeover times of more than an hour in an automobile plant, he responded with the quote, "The flow must go on," meaning that every effort must be made to ensure a smooth flow of production. One way to ensure a smooth flow is to eliminate or reduce setup times. Shigeo Shingo developed a powerful technique for doing exactly that, which we will revisit later in the chapter.

5.5 Setup Time Reduction

Despite improvement potential from the use of "good" batch sizes and smaller transfer batches, setups remain a source of disruption of a smooth process flow. For this reason, rather than taking setups as "God-given" constraints and finding ways to accommodate them, we should find ways that directly address the root cause of the disruption.

This is the basic idea underlying the single minute exchange of die (SMED) method. The creators of the SMED method referred to any setup exceeding 10 minutes as an unacceptable source of process flow disruption. The 10-minute rule is not necessarily meant to be taken literally: the method was developed in the automotive industry, where setup times used to take as much as four hours. The SMED method helps to define an aggressive, yet realistic setup time goal and to identify potential opportunities of setup time reduction.

The basic underlying idea of SMED is to carefully analyze all tasks that are part of the setup time and then divide those tasks into two groups, *internal setup* tasks and *external setup* tasks.

- Internal setup tasks are those tasks that can only be executed while the machine is stopped.
- External setup tasks are those tasks that can be done while the machine is still operating, meaning they can be done *before* the actual changeover occurs.

Experience shows that companies are biased toward using internal setups and that, even without making large investments, internal setups can be translated into external setups.

Similar to our discussion about choosing a good batch size, the biggest obstacles to overcome are ineffective cost accounting procedures. Consider, for example, the case of a simple heat treatment procedure in which flow units are moved on a tray and put into an oven. Loading and unloading of the tray is part of the setup time. The acquisition of an additional tray that can be loaded (or unloaded) while the other tray is still in process (before the setup) allows the company to convert internal setup tasks to external ones. Is this a worthwhile investment?

The answer is, as usual, it depends. SMED applied to nonbottleneck steps is not creating any process improvement at all. As discussed previously, nonbottleneck steps have excessive capacity and therefore setups are entirely free (except for the resulting increase in inventory). Thus, investing in any resource, technical or human, is not only wasteful, but it also takes scarce improvement capacity/funds away from more urgent projects. However, if the oven in the previous example were the bottleneck step, almost any investment in the acquisition of additional trays suddenly becomes a highly profitable investment.

The idea of internal and external setups as well as potential conversion from internal to external setups is best visible in car racing. Any pit stop is a significant disruption of the race car's flow toward the finish line. At any point and any moment in the race, an entire crew is prepared to take in the car, having prepared for any technical problem from tire changes to refueling. While the technical crew might appear idle and underutilized throughout most of the race, it is clear that any second they can reduce from the time the car is in the pit (internal setups) to a moment when the car is on the race track is a major gain (e.g., no race team would consider mounting tires on wheels during the race; they just put on entire wheels).

5.6 Balancing Setup Costs with Inventory Costs: The EOQ Model

Up to now, our focus has been on the role of setup times, as opposed to setup costs. Specifically, we have seen that setup time at the bottleneck leads to an overall reduction in process capacity. Assuming that the process is currently capacity-constrained, setup times thereby carry an opportunity cost reflecting the overall lower flow rate (sales).

Independent of such opportunity costs, setups frequently are associated with direct (out-of-pocket) costs. In these cases, we speak of setup costs (as opposed to setup times). Consider, for example, the following settings:

- The setup of a machine to process a certain part might require scrapping the first 10 parts that are produced after the setup. Thus, the material costs of these 10 parts constitute a setup cost.
- Assume that we are charged a per-time-unit usage fee for a particular resource (e.g., for the milling machine discussed above). Thus, every minute we use the resource, independent of whether we use it for setup or for real production, we have to pay for the resource. In this case, "time is money" and the setup time thereby translates directly into setup costs. However, as we will discuss below, one needs to be very careful when making the conversion from setup times to setup costs.
- When receiving shipments from a supplier, there frequently exists a fixed shipment cost as part of the procurement cost, which is independent of the purchased quantity. This is similar to the shipping charges that a consumer pays at a catalog or online retailer. Shipping costs are a form of setup costs.

All three settings reflect *economies of scale:* the more we order or produce as part of a batch, the more units there are in a batch over which we can spread out the setup costs.

If we can reduce per-unit costs by increasing the batch size, what keeps us from using infinite (or at least very large) batches? Similar to the case of setup times, we again need to balance our desire for large batches (fewer setups) with the cost of carrying a large amount of inventory.

In the following analysis, we need to distinguish between two cases:

- If the quantity we order is produced or delivered by an outside supplier, all units of a batch are likely to arrive at the same time.
- In other settings, the units of a batch might not all arrive at the same time. This is especially the case when we produce the batch internally.

Figure 5.8 illustrates the inventory levels for the two cases described above. The lower part of Figure 5.8 shows the case of the outside supplier and all units of a batch arriving at the same moment in time. The moment a shipment is received, the inventory level jumps up by the size of the shipment. It then falls up to the time of the next shipment.

The upper part of Figure 5.8 shows the case of units created by a resource with (finite) capacity. Thus, while we are producing, the inventory level increases. Once we stop production, the inventory level falls. Let us consider the case of an outside supplier first (lower part of Figure 5.8). Specifically, consider the case of the Xootr handle caps that Nova Cruz

FIGURE 5.8
Different Patterns of Inventory Levels

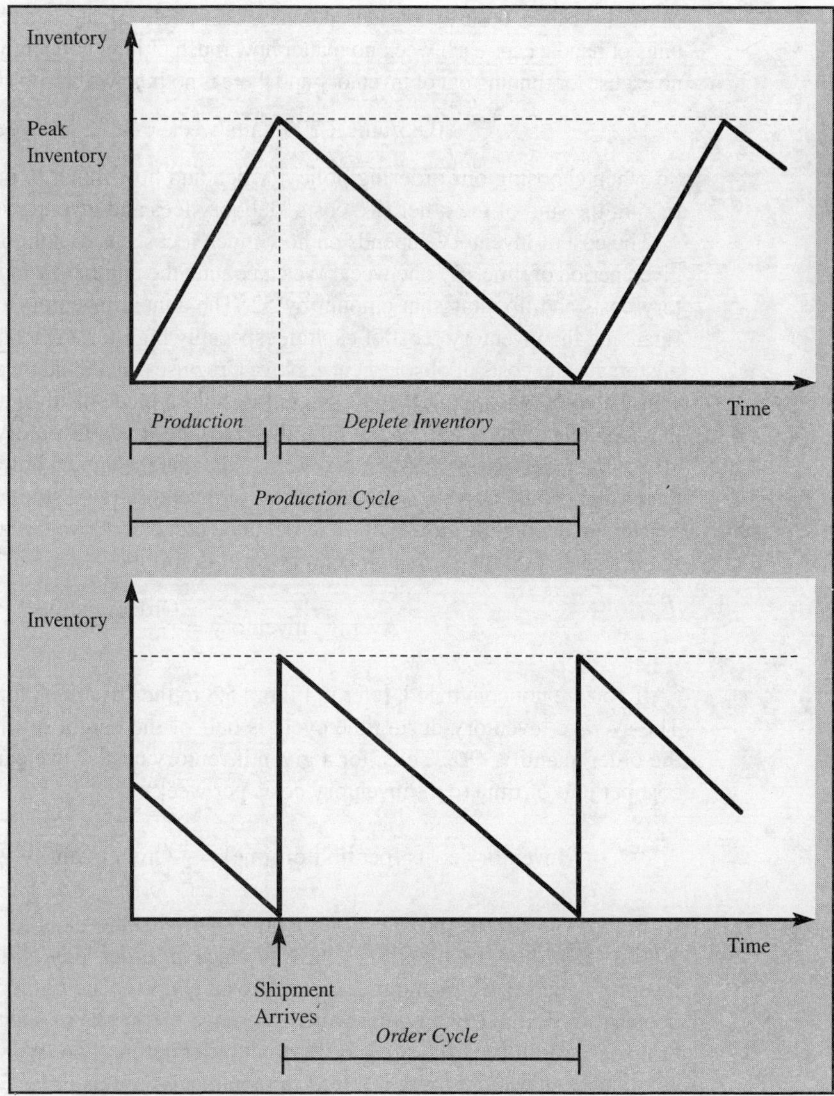

sources from a supplier in Taiwan for \$0.85 per unit. Note that the maximum inventory of handle caps occurs at the time we receive a shipment from Taiwan. The inventory is then depleted at the rate of the assembly operations, that is, at a flow rate, *R*, of 700 units (pairs of handle caps) per week, which is equal to one unit every three minutes.

For the following computations, we make a set of assumptions. We later show that these assumptions do not substantially alter the optimal decisions.

- We assume that production of Xootrs occurs at a constant rate of one unit every three minutes. We also assume our orders arrive on time from Taiwan. Under these two assumptions, we can deplete our inventory all the way to zero before receiving the next shipment.
- There is a fixed setup cost per order that is independent of the amount ordered. In the Xootr case, this largely consists of a \$300 customs fee.
- The purchase price is independent of the number of units we order, that is, there are no quantity discounts. We talk about quantity discounts in the next section.

The objective of our calculations is to minimize the cost of inventory and ordering with the constraint that we must never run out of inventory (i.e., we can keep the assembly operation running).

We have three costs to consider: purchase costs, delivery fees, and holding costs. We use 700 units of handle caps each week no matter how much or how frequently we order. Thus, we have no excuse for running out of inventory and there is nothing we can do about our purchase costs of

$$\$0.85/\text{unit} \times 700 \text{ units/week} = \$595 \text{ per week}$$

So when choosing our ordering policy (when and how much to order), we focus on minimizing the sum of the other two costs, delivery fees and inventory costs.

The cost of inventory depends on how much it costs us to hold one unit in inventory for a given period of time, say one week. We can obtain the number by looking at the annual inventory costs and dividing that amount by 52. The annual inventory costs need to account for financing the inventory (cost of capital, especially high for a start-up like Nova Cruz), costs of storage, and costs of obsolescence. Nova Cruz uses an annual inventory cost of 40 percent. Thus, it costs Nova Cruz 0.7692 percent to hold a piece of inventory for one week. Given that a handle cap costs \$0.85 per unit, this translates to an inventory cost of $h = 0.007692 \times \$0.85/\text{unit} = \$0.006538$ per unit per week. Note that the annual holding cost needs to include the cost of capital as well as any other cost of inventory (e.g., storage, theft, etc).

How many handle caps will there be, on average, in Nova Cruz's inventory? As we can see in Figure 5.8, the average inventory level is simply

$$\text{Average inventory} = \frac{\text{Order quantity}}{2}$$

If you are not convinced, refer in Figure 5.8 to the "triangle" formed by one order cycle. The average inventory during the cycle is half of the height of the triangle, which is half the order quantity, $Q/2$. Thus, for a given inventory cost, *h*, we can compute the inventory cost per unit of time (e.g., inventory costs per week):

$$\text{Inventory costs [per unit of time]} = \frac{1}{2}\,\text{Order quantity} \times h = \frac{1}{2}\,Q \times h$$

Before we turn to the question of how many handle caps to order at once, let's first ask ourselves how frequently we have to place an order. Say at time 0 we have *I* units in inventory and say we plan our next order to be *Q* units. The *I* units of inventory will satisfy demand until time I/R (in other words, we have I/R weeks of supply in inventory). At this time, our inventory will be zero if we don't order before then. We would then again receive an order of *Q* units (if there is a lead time in receiving this order, we simply would have to place this order earlier).

Do we gain anything by receiving the Q handle caps earlier than at the time when we have zero units in inventory? Not in this model: demand is satisfied whether we order earlier or not and the delivery fee is the same too. But we do lose something by ordering earlier: we incur holding costs per unit of time the Q units are held.

Given that we cannot save costs by choosing the order time intelligently, we must now work on the question of how much to order (the order quantity). Let's again assume that we order Q units with every order and let's consider just one order cycle. The order cycle begins when we order Q units and ends when the last unit is sold, Q/R time units later. For example, with $Q = 1{,}000$, an order cycle lasts 1,000 units/700 units per week = 1.43 weeks. We incur one ordering fee (setup costs), K, in that order cycle, so our setup costs per week are

$$\text{Setup costs [per unit of time]} = \frac{\text{Setup cost}}{\text{Length of order cycle}}$$

$$= \frac{K}{Q/R} = \frac{K \times R}{Q}$$

Let $C(Q)$ be the sum of our average delivery cost per unit time and our average holding cost per unit time (per week):

$$\text{Per unit of time cost } C(Q) = \text{Setup costs} + \text{Inventory costs}$$

$$= \frac{K \times R}{Q} + \frac{1}{2} \times h \times Q$$

Note that purchase costs are not included in $C(Q)$ for the reasons discussed earlier. From the above we see that the delivery fee per unit time decreases as Q increases: we amortize the delivery fee over more units. But as Q increases, we increase our holding costs.

Figure 5.9 graphs the weekly costs of delivery, the average weekly holding cost, and the total weekly cost, $C(Q)$. As we can see, there is a single order quantity Q that minimizes the total cost $C(Q)$. We call this quantity Q^*, the economic order quantity, or *EOQ* for short. Hence the name of the model.

FIGURE 5.9 **Inventory and Ordering Costs for Different Order Sizes**

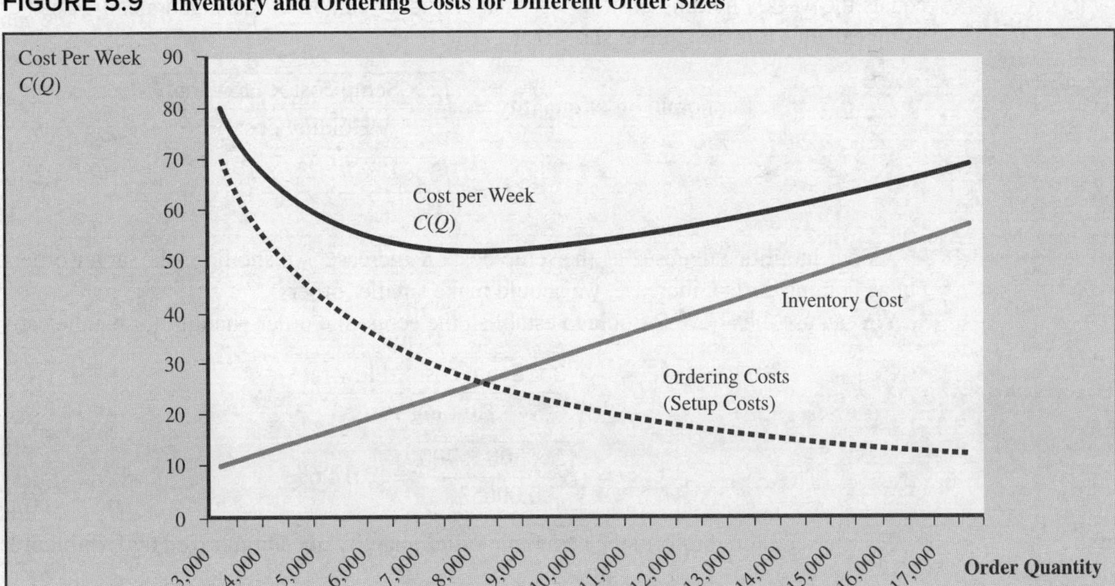

Exhibit 5.2

FINDING THE ECONOMIC ORDER QUANTITY

1. Verify the basic assumptions of the EOQ model:
   - Replenishment occurs instantaneously.
   - Demand is constant and not stochastic.
   - There is a fixed setup cost K independent of the order quantity.
2. Collect information on
   - Setup cost, K (only include out-of-pocket cost, not opportunity cost).
   - Flow rate, R.
   - Holding cost, h (not necessarily the yearly holding cost; needs to have the same time unit as the flow rate).
3. For a given order quantity Q, compute

$$\text{Inventory costs [per unit of time]} = \frac{1}{2} Q \times h$$

$$\text{Setup costs [per unit of time]} = \frac{K \times R}{Q}$$

4. The economic order quantity minimizes the sum of the inventory and the setup costs and is

$$Q^* = \sqrt{\frac{2 \times K \times R}{h}}$$

The resulting costs are

$$C(Q^*) = \sqrt{2 \times K \times R \times h}$$

From Figure 5.9 it appears that Q^* is the quantity at which the weekly delivery fee equals the weekly holding cost. In fact, that is true, as can be shown algebraically. Further, using calculus it is possible to show that

$$\text{Economic order quantity} = \sqrt{\frac{2 \times \text{Setup cost} \times \text{Flow rate}}{\text{Holding cost}}}$$

$$Q^* = \sqrt{\frac{2 \times K \times R}{h}}$$

As our intuition suggests, as the setup costs K increase, we should make larger orders, but as holding costs h increase, we should make smaller orders.

We can use the above formula to establish the economic order quantity for handle caps:

$$Q^* = \sqrt{\frac{2 \times \text{Setup cost} \times \text{Flow rate}}{\text{Holding cost}}}$$

$$= \sqrt{\frac{2 \times 300 \times 700}{0.006538}} = 8{,}014.69$$

The steps required to find the economic order quantity are summarized by Exhibit 5.2.

5.7 Observations Related to the Economic Order Quantity

If we always order the economic order quantity, our cost per unit of time, $C(Q^*)$, can be computed as

$$C(Q^*) = \frac{K \times R}{Q^*} + \frac{1}{2} \times h \times Q^* = \sqrt{2 \times K \times R \times h}$$

While we have done this analysis to minimize our average cost per unit of time, it should be clear that Q^* would minimize our average cost per unit (given that the rate of purchasing handle caps is fixed). The cost per unit can be computed as

$$\text{Cost per unit} = \frac{C(Q^*)}{R} = \sqrt{\frac{2 \times K \times h}{R}}$$

As we would expect, the per-unit cost is increasing with the ordering fee K as well as with our inventory costs. Interestingly, the per-unit cost is decreasing with the flow rate R. Thus, if we doubled our flow rate, our ordering costs increase by less than a factor of 2. In other words, there are economies of scale in the ordering process: the per-unit ordering cost is decreasing with the flow rate R. Put yet another way, an operation with setup and inventory holding costs becomes more efficient as the demand rate increases.

While we have focused our analysis on the time period when Nova Cruz experienced a demand of 700 units per week, the demand pattern changed drastically over the product life cycle of the Xootr. As discussed in Chapter 4, Nova Cruz experienced a substantial demand growth from 200 units per week to over 1,000 units per week. Table 5.2 shows how increases in demand rate impact the order quantity as well as the per-unit cost of the handle caps. We observe that, due to scale economies, ordering and inventory costs are decreasing with the flow rate R.

A nice property of the economic order quantity is that the cost function, $C(Q)$, is relatively flat around its minimum Q^* (see graph in Figure 5.9). This suggests that if we were to order Q units instead of Q^*, the resulting cost penalty would not be substantial as long as Q is reasonably close to Q^*. Suppose we order only half of the optimal order quantity, that is, we order $Q^*/2$. In that case, we have

$$C(Q^*/2) = \frac{K \times R}{Q^*/2} + \frac{1}{2} \times h \times Q^*/2 = \frac{5}{4} \times \sqrt{2 \times K \times R \times h} = \frac{5}{4} \times C(Q^*)$$

Thus, if we order only half as much as optimal (i.e., we order twice as frequently as optimal), then our costs increase only by 25 percent. The same holds if we order double the economic order quantity (i.e., we order half as frequently as optimal).

TABLE 5.2
Scale Economies in the EOQ Formula

Flow Rate, R	Economic Order Quantity, Q^*	Per-Unit Ordering and Inventory Cost, $C(Q^*)/R$	Ordering and Inventory Costs as a Percentage of Total Procurement Costs
200	4,284	0.14 [$/unit]	14.1%
400	6,058	0.10	10.4%
600	7,420	0.08	8.7%
800	8,568	0.07	7.6%
1,000	9,579	0.06	6.8%

This property has several important implications:

- Consider the optimal order quantity $Q^* = 8{,}014$ established above. However, now also assume that our supplier is only willing to deliver in predefined quantities (e.g., in multiples of 5,000). The robustness established above suggests that an order of 10,000 will only lead to a slight cost increase (increased costs can be computed as $C(Q = 10{,}000) =$ \$53.69, which is only 2.5 percent higher than the optimal costs).
- Sometimes, it can be difficult to obtain exact numbers for the various ingredients in the EOQ formula. Consider, for example, the ordering fee in the Nova Cruz case. While this fee of \$300 was primarily driven by the \$300 for customs, it also did include a shipping fee. The exact shipping fee in turn depends on the quantity shipped and we would need a more refined model to find the order quantity that accounts for this effect. Given the robustness of the EOQ model, however, we know that the model is "forgiving" with respect to small misspecifications of parameters.

A particularly useful application of the EOQ model relates to *quantity discounts*. When procuring inventory in a logistics or retail setting, we frequently are given the opportunity to benefit from quantity discounts. For example,

- We might be offered a discount for ordering a full truckload of supply.
- We might receive a free unit for every five units we order (just as in consumer retailing settings of "buy one, get one free").
- We might receive a discount for all units ordered over 100 units.
- We might receive a discount for the entire order if the order volume exceeds 50 units (or say \$2,000).

We can think of the extra procurement costs that we would incur from not taking advantage of the quantity discount—that is, that would result from ordering in smaller quantities—as a setup cost. Evaluating an order discount therefore boils down to a comparison between inventory costs and setup costs (savings in procurement costs), which we can do using the EOQ model.

If the order quantity we obtain from the EOQ model is sufficiently large to obtain the largest discount (the lowest per-unit procurement cost), then the discount has no impact on our order size. We go ahead and order the economic order quantity. The more interesting case occurs when the EOQ is less than the discount threshold. Then we must decide if we wish to order more than the economic order quantity to take advantage of the discount offered to us.

Let's consider one example to illustrate how to think about this issue. Suppose our supplier of handle caps gives us a discount of 5 percent off the entire order if the order exceeds 10,000 units. Recall that our economic order quantity was only 8,014. Thus, the question is "should we increase the order size to 10,000 units in order to get the 5 percent discount, yet incur higher inventory costs, or should we simply order 8,014 units?"

We surely will not order more than 10,000; any larger order does not generate additional purchase cost savings but does increase inventory costs. So we have two choices: either stick with the EOQ or increase our order to 10,000. If we order $Q^* = 8{,}014$ units, our total cost per unit time is

$$\begin{aligned} &700 \text{ units/week} \times \$0.85/\text{unit} + C(Q^*) \\ &= \$595/\text{week} + \$52.40/\text{week} \\ &= \$647.40/\text{week} \end{aligned}$$

Notice that we now include our purchase cost per unit time of 700 units/week × \$0.85/unit. The reason for this is that with the possibility of a quantity discount, our purchase cost now depends on the order quantity.

If we increase our order quantity to 10,000 units, our total cost per unit time would be

$$\begin{aligned} &700 \text{ units/week} \times \$0.85/\text{unit} \times 0.95 + C(10{,}000) \\ &\quad = \$565.25/\text{week} + \$52.06/\text{week} \\ &\quad = \$617.31/\text{week} \end{aligned}$$

where we have reduced the procurement cost by 5 percent (multiplied by 0.95) to reflect the quantity discount. (*Note:* The 5 percent discount also reduces the holding cost h in C.) Given that the cost per week is lower in the case of the increased order quantity, we want to take advantage of the quantity discount.

After analyzing the case of all flow units of one order (batch) arriving simultaneously, we now turn to the case of producing the corresponding units internally (upper part of Figure 5.8).

All computations we performed above can be easily transformed to this more general case (see, e.g., Nahmias 2005). Moreover, given the robustness of the economic order quantity, the EOQ model leads to reasonably good recommendations even if applied to production settings with setup costs. Hence, we will not discuss the analytical aspects of this. Instead, we want to step back for a moment and reflect on how the EOQ model relates to our discussion of setup times at the beginning of the chapter.

A common mistake is to rely too much on setup *costs* as opposed to setup *times.* For example, consider the case of Figure 5.6 and assume that the monthly capital cost for the milling machine is \$9,000, which corresponds to \$64 per hour (assuming four weeks of 35 hours each). Thus, when choosing the batch size, and focusing primarily on costs, Nova Cruz might shy away from frequent setups. Management might even consider using the economic order quantity established above and thereby quantify the impact of larger batches on inventory holding costs.

There are two major mistakes in this approach:

- This approach to choosing batch sizes ignores the fact that the investment in the machine is already sunk.
- Choosing the batch size based on cost ignores the effect setups have on process capacity. As long as setup costs are a reflection of the cost of capacity—as opposed to direct financial setup costs—they should be ignored when choosing the batch size. It is the overall process flow that matters, not an artificial local performance measure! From a capacity perspective, setups at nonbottleneck resources are free. And if the setups do occur at the bottleneck, the corresponding setup costs not only reflect the capacity costs of the local resource, but of the entire process!

Thus, when choosing batch sizes, it is important to distinguish between setup costs and setup times. If the motivation behind batching results from setup times (or opportunity costs of capacity), we should focus on optimizing the process flow. Section 5.3 provides the appropriate way to find a good batch size. If we face "true" setup costs (in the sense of out-of-pocket costs) and we only look at a single resource (as opposed to an entire process flow), the EOQ model can be used to find the optimal order quantity.

Finally, if we encounter a combination of setup times and (out-of-pocket) setup costs, we should use both approaches and compare the recommended batch sizes. If the batch size from the EOQ is sufficiently large so that the resource with the setup is not the bottleneck, minimizing costs is appropriate. If the batch size from the EOQ, however, makes the resource with the setups the bottleneck, we need to consider increasing the batch size beyond the EOQ recommendation.

5.8 Summary

Setups are interruptions of the supply process. These interruptions on the supply side lead to mismatches between supply and demand, visible in the form of inventory and—where this is not possible—lost throughput.

While in this chapter we have focused on inventory of components (handle caps), work-in-process (steer support parts), or finished goods (station wagons versus sedans, Figure 5.4), the supply–demand mismatch also can materialize in an inventory of waiting customer orders. For example, if the product we deliver is customized and built to the specifications of the customer, holding an inventory of finished goods is not possible. Similarly, if we are providing a substantial variety of products to the market, the risk of holding completed variants in finished goods inventory is large. Independent of the form of inventory, a large inventory corresponds to long flow times (Little's Law). For this reason, batch processes are typically associated with very long customer lead times.

In this chapter, we discussed tools to choose a batch size. We distinguished between setup times and setup costs. To the extent that a process faces setup times, we need to extend our process analysis to capture the negative impact that setups have on capacity. We then want to look for a batch size that is large enough to not make the process step with the setup the bottleneck, while being small enough to avoid excessive inventory.

To the extent that a process faces (out-of-pocket) setup costs, we need to balance these costs against the cost of inventory. We discussed the EOQ model for the case of supply arriving in one single quantity (sourcing from a supplier), as well as the case of internal production. Figure 5.10 provides a summary of the major steps you should take when analyzing processes with flow interruptions, including setup times, setup costs, or machine downtimes. There are countless extensions to the EOQ model to capture, among other things, quantity discounts, perishability, learning effects, inflation, and quality problems.

Our ability to choose a "good" batch size provides another example of process improvement. Consider a process with significant setup times at one resource. As a manager of this process, we need to balance the conflicting objectives of

- Fast response to customers (short flow times, which correspond, because of Little's Law, to low inventory levels), which results from using small batch sizes.
- Cost benefits that result from using large batch sizes. The reason for this is that large batch sizes enable a high throughput, which in turn allows the firm to spread out its fixed costs over a maximum number of flow units.

FIGURE 5.10 **Summary of Batching**

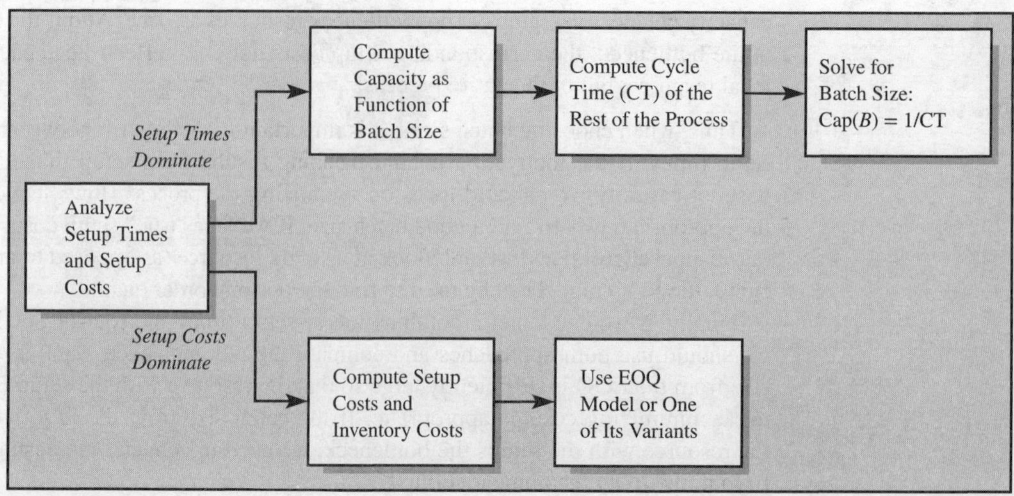

FIGURE 5.11
Choosing a Batch Size

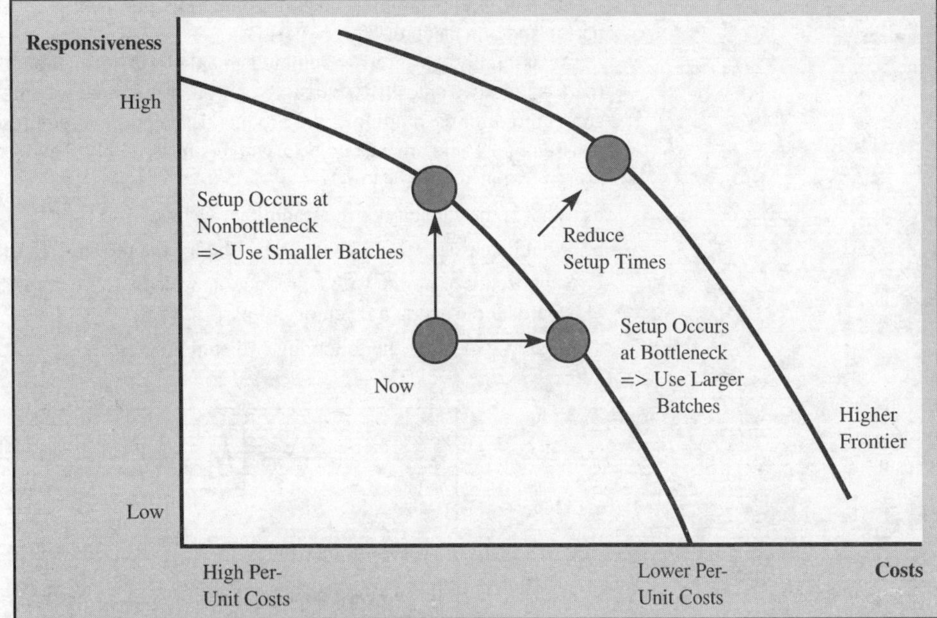

This tension is illustrated by Figure 5.11. Similar to the case of line balancing, we observe that adjustments in the batch size are not trading in one performance measure against the other, but allow us to improve by reducing current inefficiencies in the process.

Despite our ability to choose batch sizes that mitigate the tension between inventory (responsiveness) and costs, there ultimately is only one way to handle setups: eliminate them wherever possible or at least shorten them. Setups do not add value and are therefore wasteful.

Methods such as SMED are powerful tools that can reduce setup times substantially. Similarly, the need for transfer batches can be reduced by locating the process resources according to the flow of the process.

5.9 Further Reading

Nahmias (2005) is a widely used textbook in operations management that discusses, among other things, many variants of the EOQ model.

5.10 Practice Problems

The following questions will help in testing your understanding of this chapter. After each question, we show the relevant section in parentheses [Section x].

Solutions to problems marked with an "*" are available in Appendix E. Video solutions to select problems are available in Connect.

Q5.1* **(Window Boxes)** Metal window boxes are manufactured in two process steps: stamping and assembly. Each window box is made up of three pieces: a base (one part A) and two sides (two part Bs).

The parts are fabricated by a single stamping machine that requires a setup time of 120 minutes whenever switching between the two part types. Once the machine is set up, the processing time for each part A is one minute while the processing time for each part B is only 30 seconds.

Currently, the stamping machine rotates its production between one batch of 360 for part A and one batch of 720 for part B.

At assembly, parts are assembled manually to form the finished product. One base (part A) and two sides (two part Bs), as well as a number of small purchased components, are required for each unit of final product. Each product requires 27 minutes of labor time to assemble. There are currently 12 workers in assembly. There is sufficient demand to sell every box the system can make.

a. What is the capacity of the stamping machine? [5.1]

b. What batch size would you recommend for the process? [5.6]

c. Suppose they operate with a production cycle of 1,260 part As and 2,520 part Bs. What would be the average inventory of part A? [5.6]

Q5.2 **(Two-step)** Consider the following two-step process:

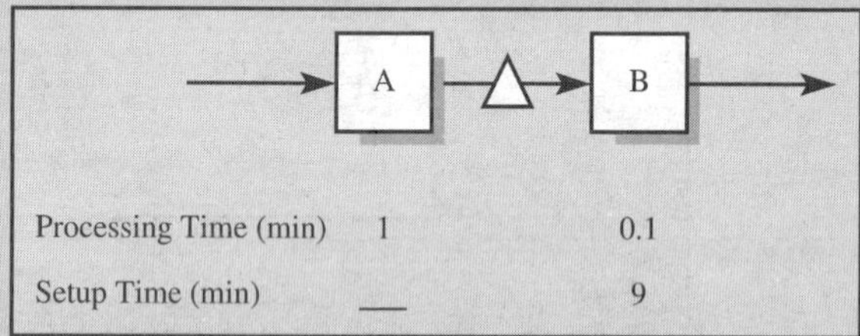

Step A has a processing time of 1 minute per unit, but no setup is required. Step B has a processing time of 0.1 minute per unit, but a setup time of 9 minutes is required per batch.

a. Suppose units are produced in batches of 5 (i.e., after each set of 5 units are produced, step B must incur a setup of 9 minutes). What is the capacity of the process (in units per minute)? [5.1]

b. Suppose they operate with a batch size of 15 and with this batch size step A is the bottleneck. What would be the average inventory after step B? [5.6]

c. What is the batch size that maximizes the flow rate of this process with minimal inventory? Assume there is ample demand. [5.6]

Q5.3 **(Simple Setup)** Consider the following batch flow process consisting of three process steps performed by three machines:

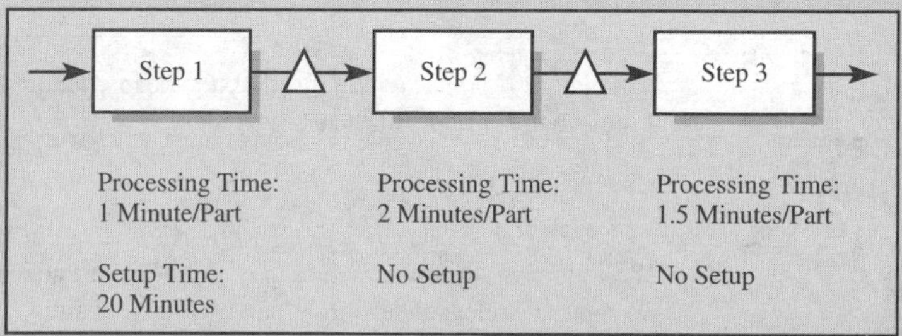

Work is processed in batches at each step. Before a batch is processed at step 1, the machine has to be set up. During a setup, the machine is unable to process any product.

a. Assume that the batch size is 50 parts. What is the capacity of the process? [5.1]

b. For a batch size of 10 parts, which step is the bottleneck for the process? [5.1]

c. What batch size would you choose? [5.6]

d. Suppose the batch size is 40 parts. What would be the average inventory after step 1? [5.6]

Q5.4 **(Setup Everywhere)** Consider the following batch-flow process consisting of three process steps performed by three machines:

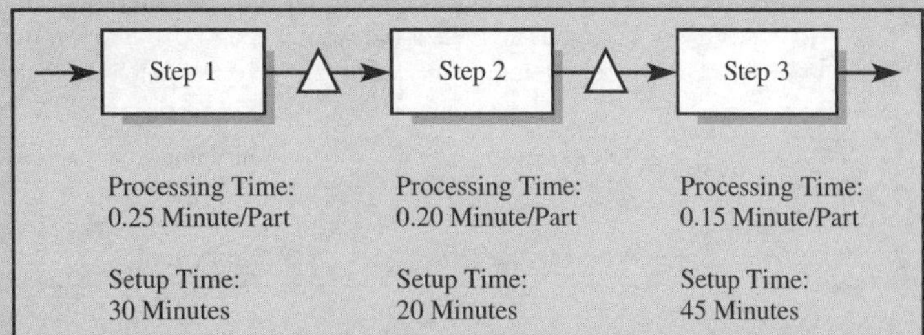

Work is processed in batches at each step. Before a batch is processed at a step, the machine at that step must be set up. (During a setup, the machine is unable to process any product.) Assume that there is a dedicated setup operator for each machine (i.e., there is always someone available to perform a setup at each machine.)

a. What is the capacity of step 1 if the batch size is 35 parts? [5.6]

b. For what batch sizes is step 1 (2, 3) the bottleneck? [5.6]

Q5.5 **(JCL Inc.)** JCL Inc. is a major chip manufacturing firm that sells its products to computer manufacturers like Dell, HP, and others. In simplified terms, chip making at JCL Inc. involves three basic operations: depositing, patterning, and etching.

- **Depositing:** Using chemical vapor deposition (CVD) technology, an insulating material is deposited on the wafer surface, forming a thin layer of solid material on the chip.
- **Patterning:** Photolithography projects a microscopic circuit pattern on the wafer surface, which has a light-sensitive chemical like the emulsion on photographic film. It is repeated many times as each layer of the chip is built.
- **Etching:** Etching removes selected material from the chip surface to create the device structures.

The following table lists the required processing times and setup times at each of the steps. Assume that the unit of production is a wafer, from which individual chips are cut at a later stage.

Note: A setup can only begin once the batch has arrived at the machine.

Process Step	1 Depositing	2 Patterning	3 Etching
Setup time	45 min.	30 min.	20 min.
Processing time	0.15 min./unit	0.25 min./unit	0.20 min./unit

a. What is the process capacity in units per hour with a batch size of 100 wafers? [5.1]

b. For what batch size is step 3 (etching) the bottleneck? [5.6]

c. Suppose JCL Inc. came up with a new technology that eliminated the setup time for step 1 (deposition), but increased the processing time to 0.45 minute/unit. What would be the batch size you would choose so as to maximize the overall capacity of the process? [5.6]

Q5.6 **(Kinga Doll Company)** Kinga Doll Company manufactures eight versions of its popular girl doll, Shari. The company operates on a 40-hour workweek. The eight versions differ in doll skin, hair, and eye color, enabling most children to have a doll with a similar appearance to them. It currently sells an average of 4,000 dolls (spread equally among its eight versions) per week to boutique toy retailers. In simplified terms, doll making at Kinga involves three basic operations: molding the body and hair, painting the face, and dressing the doll. Changing over between versions requires setup time at the molding and painting stations due to the different colors of plastic pellets, hair, and eye color paint required.

The table below lists the setup times for a batch and the processing times for each unit at each step. Unlimited space for buffer inventory exists between these steps.

Assume that (i) setups need to be completed first, (ii) a setup can only start once the batch has arrived at the resource, and (iii) all flow units of a batch need to be processed at a resource before any of the units of the batch can be moved to the next resource.

Process Step	1 Molding	2 Painting	3 Dressing
Setup time	15 min.	30 min.	No setup
Processing time	0.25 min./unit	0.15 min./unit	0.30 min./unit

a. What is the process capacity in units per hour with a batch size of 500 dolls? [5.1]
b. Which batch size would minimize inventory without decreasing the process capacity? [5.6]
c. Which batch size would minimize inventory without decreasing the current flow rate? [5.6]

Q5.7 **(PTests)** Precision Testing (PTests) does fluid testing for several local hospitals. Consider their urine testing process. Each sample requires 12 seconds to test, but after 300 samples, the equipment must be recalibrated. No samples can be tested during the recalibration process and that process takes 30 minutes.

a. What is PTests's maximum capacity to test urine samples (in samples per hour)? [5.1]
b. Suppose 2.5 urine samples need to be tested per minute. What is the smallest batch size (in samples) that ensures that the process is not supply constrained? (Note; A batch is the number of tests between calibrations.) [5.6]
c. PTests also needs to test blood samples. There are two kinds of tests that can be done—a "basic" test and a "complete" test. Basic tests require 15 seconds per sample, whereas "complete" tests require 1.5 minutes per sample. After 100 tests, the equipment needs to be cleaned and recalibrated, which takes 20 minutes. Suppose PTests runs the following cyclic schedule: 70 basic tests, 30 complete tests, recalibrate, and then repeat. With this schedule, how many *basic* tests can they complete per minute on average? [5.1]

Q5.8 **(Gelato)** Bruno Fruscalzo decided to set up a small production facility in Sydney to sell to local restaurants that want to offer gelato on their dessert menu. To start simple, he would offer only three flavors of gelato: fragola (strawberry), chocolato (chocolate), and bacio (chocolate with hazelnut). After a short time he found his demand and setup times to be

	Fragola	Chocolato	Bacio
Demand (kg/hour)	10	15	5
Setup time (hours)	3/4	1/2	1/6

Bruno first produces a batch of fragola, then a batch of chocolato, then a batch of bacio and then he repeats that sequence. For example, after producing bacio and before producing fragola, he needs 45 minutes to set up the ice cream machine, but he needs only 10 minutes to switch from chocolato to bacio. When running, his ice cream machine produces at the rate of 50 kg per hour no matter which flavor it is producing (and, of course, it can produce only one flavor at a time).

a. Suppose Bruno wants to minimize the amount of each flavor produced at one time while still satisfying the demand for each of the flavors. (He can choose a different quantity for each flavor.) If we define a batch to be the quantity produced in a single run of each flavor, how many kilograms should he produce in each batch? [5.6]
b. Given your answer in part (a), how many kilograms of fragola should he make with each batch? [5.6]
c. Given your answer in part (a), what is the average inventory of chocolato? (Assume production and demand occur at constant rates.) [5.6]

Q5.9 (**Carpets**) A carpet manufacturer makes four kinds of carpet on a machine. For simplicity, call these four types of carpet, A, B, C, and D. It takes 3 hours to switch production from one type of carpet to another. The demand rates (yards/hr) for the four types of carpet are as follows: 100, 80, 70, and 50. When producing, the machine can produce at the rate of 350 yards/hr. Batch sizes are chosen to minimize inventory while also satisfying the demand requirements. The manufacturer produces with a schedule that cycles through each of the four types, (e.g., A, B, C, D, A, B, . . .).

a. What batch size (yards) is chosen for carpet type A? [5.6]

b. Suppose they produce 16,800 yards of carpet A in each production cycle (and 50,400 yards of carpet in total within the production cycle). What would be the average inventory of carpet A? [5.6]

Q5.10* (**Cat Food**) Cat Lovers Inc. (CLI) is the distributor of a very popular blend of cat food that sells for $1.25 per can. CLI experiences demand of 500 cans per week on average. They order the cans of cat food from the Nutritious & Delicious Co. (N&D). N&D sells cans to CLI at $0.50 per can and charges a flat fee of $7 per order for shipping and handling.

CLI uses the economic order quantity as their fixed order size. Assume that the opportunity cost of capital and all other inventory cost is 15 percent annually and that there are 50 weeks in a year.

a. How many cans of cat food should CLI order at a time? [5.6]

b. What is CLI's total order cost for one year? [5.6]

c. What is CLI's total holding cost for one year? [5.6]

d. What is CLI's weekly inventory turns? [5.6]

Q5.11* (**Beer Distributor**) A beer distributor finds that it sells on average 100 cases a week of regular 12-oz. Budweiser. For this problem assume that demand occurs at a constant rate over a 50-week year. The distributor currently purchases beer every two weeks at a cost of $8 per case. The inventory-related holding cost (capital, insurance, etc.) for the distributor equals 25 percent of the dollar value of inventory per year. Each order placed with the supplier costs the distributor $10. This cost includes labor, forms, postage, and so forth.

a. Assume the distributor can choose any order quantity it wishes. What order quantity minimizes the distributor's total inventory-related costs (holding and ordering)? [5.6]

For the next three parts, assume the distributor selects the order quantity specified in part (a).

b. What are the distributor's inventory turns per year? [5.6]

c. What is the inventory-related cost per case of beer sold? [5.6]

d. Assume the brewer is willing to give a 5 percent quantity discount if the distributor orders 600 cases or more at a time. If the distributor is interested in minimizing its total cost (i.e., purchase and inventory-related costs), should the distributor begin ordering 600 or more cases at a time? [5.6]

Q5.12 (**Millennium Liquors**) Millennium Liquors is a wholesaler of sparkling wines. Their most popular product is the French Bete Noire. Weekly demand is for 45 cases. Assume demand occurs over 50 weeks per year. The wine is shipped directly from France. Millennium's annual cost of capital is 15 percent, which also includes all other inventory-related costs. Below are relevant data on the costs of shipping, placing orders, and refrigeration.

- Cost per case: $120
- Shipping cost (for any size shipment): $290
- Cost of labor to place and process an order: $10
- Fixed cost for refrigeration: $75/week

a. Calculate the weekly holding cost for one case of wine. [5.6]

b. Use the EOQ model to find the number of cases per order and the average number of orders per year. [5.6]

c. Currently orders are placed by calling France and then following up with a letter. Millennium and its supplier may switch to a simple ordering system using the Internet. The new system will require much less labor. What would be the impact of this system on the ordering pattern? [5.6]

Q5.13 **(Powered by Koffee)** Powered by Koffee (PBK) is a new campus coffee store. PBK uses 50 bags of whole bean coffee every month, and you may assume that demand is perfectly steady throughout the year.

PBK has signed a year-long contract to purchase its coffee from a local supplier, Phish Roasters, for a price of $25 per bag and an $85 fixed cost for every delivery independent of the order size. The holding cost due to storage is $1 per bag per month. PBK managers figure their cost of capital is approximately 2 percent per month.

a. What is the optimal order size, in bags? [5.6]

b. Given your answer in (a), how many times a year does PBK place orders? [5.6]

c. Given your answer in (a), how many months of supply of coffee does PBK have on average? [5.6]

d. On average, how many dollars per month does PBK spend to hold coffee (including cost of capital)? [5.6]

Suppose that a South American import/export company has offered PBK a deal for the next year. PBK can buy a year's worth of coffee directly from South America for $20 per bag and a fixed cost for delivery of $500. Assume the estimated cost for inspection and storage is $1 per bag per month and the cost of capital is approximately 2 percent per month.

e. Should PBK order from Phish Roasters or the South American import/export company? Quantitatively justify your answer. [5.6]

Chapter 

The Link between Operations and Finance

To the reader new to the area of operations management, the previous chapters might have appeared more technical than expected.[1] After all, most of the performance measures we used were concepts such as balancing the line to increase labor utilization, reducing inventories, improving flow time, and so on. But WHY do we have to worry about these measures? Do they really matter to our job? Or, asked differently, what is the objective of all this?

The objective of most incorporated organizations is to create economic value. Those who have money invested in the enterprise want to see a return on their money—a return that exceeds the return that they would get if they invested their money differently, for example, in a bond, a savings account, or a competing organization. Economic value is created whenever the return on invested capital (ROIC) in a corporation exceeds the cost of capital (the weighted average cost of capital, WACC, is an important concept from the field of corporate finance). This is visible in the basic value equation

$$\text{Economic value created} = \text{Invested capital} \times (\text{ROIC} - \text{WACC})$$

Since the cost of capital cannot be changed easily in the short term, our focus here is on the return on invested capital. More details about corporate valuation can be found in Koller, Goedhart, and Wessels (2010).

In this chapter, we show the link between the operational variables we have discussed previously (and that are discussed throughout this book) and ROIC. This is an ambitious task. In many organizations, not to mention business school courses, the topics of operations management and corporate finance are rather remote from each other.

Given this fundamental disconnect, managers and consultants often struggle with questions such as "What performance measures should we track?"; "How do operational performance measures impact the bottom line performance?"; or "How do we go about improving processes to achieve various operational performance improvements, including cost savings, lead-time reduction, or increases in product variety?"

[1] The authors thank Stephen Doig and Taylor Randall for their input to this chapter. They are especially grateful to Paul Downs for providing them with detailed data about his company.

The objective of this chapter is to provide readers with a set of tools that support them in analyzing the operational performance of a company and to guide them in increasing the overall value of the firm by improving its operations. We will do this in three steps. First, we introduce the ROIC tree, also known as the KPI tree (KPI stands for key performance indicators). Second, we show how to value operational improvement opportunities, that is, predicting by how much the ROIC improves if we improve our process along some of the operational measures defined elsewhere in the book. Third, we provide examples of KPI trees and look at how we can read financial statements to get a sense of the operational performance of a firm. The first two steps will be illustrated using the case of a small Pennsylvania furniture company, Paul Downs Cabinetmakers.

6.1 Paul Downs Cabinetmakers

Paul Downs started making furniture in 1986 in a small shop in Manayunk, Pennsylvania. (Manayunk, pronounced "Man-ee-yunk," is a hip neighborhood in Philadelphia.) Over the years, his business outgrew four shops and is now operating in a 33,000-square-foot facility in Bridgeport, Pennsylvania. The company focuses on high-end, residential furniture. Figure 6.1(a) shows one of their most popular dining table models.

Paul Downs's production facility includes machines and other wood-processing equipment valued at about $450,000. There is an annual depreciation associated with the machines (reflecting the duration of their useful life) of $80,000. Rents for the showroom and the factory amount to roughly $150,000 per year. Other indirect costs for the company are about $100,000 per year for marketing-related expenses, $180,000 for management and administration, and $60,000 for a highly skilled worker in charge of finishing furniture and conducting a quality inspection.

The company has two major types of inventory. There is about $20,000 tied up in raw materials. This is wood that is purchased from suppliers in large-order quantities (see Chapter 5 for further details on order quantities). When purchasing wood, Paul Downs needs to pay his suppliers roughly one month in advance of receiving the shipment. There is also about $50,000 of work-in-process inventory. This corresponds to furniture that is in the process of being completed.

Furniture production, especially in the high-end segment, is a very manual process and requires a highly skilled workforce. Paul employs 12 cabinetmakers (see Figure 6.1(b)), many of whom have been with his company for more than a decade. The cabinetmakers

FIGURE 6.1 **Finished Product and Work in Progress from Paul Downs's Production Facility**

(a)

(b)

work about 220 days in a year (on average about eight hours per day). The typical wage rate for a cabinetmaker is $20 per hour.

To finish a typical piece of furniture, a worker needs about 40 hours. This corresponds to our previous concept of a processing time. The work is organized in work cells. Instead of having the cabinetmakers specialize in one aspect of furniture making (e.g., cutting, sanding, or polishing), a cabinetmaker handles a job from beginning to end. Of their overall number of hours worked, cabinetmakers spend about 15 percent of their time building fixtures and setting up machines (more on setup times in the chapter on batching). Given the modern production equipment, a good part of this includes programming computer-controlled machines. Since the cabinetmakers are organized in work cells, it would be too expensive to equip each cell with all woodworking equipment; instead, the cabinetmakers share the most expensive tools. This leads to an occasional delay if multiple cabinetmakers need access to the same unit of equipment at the same time. Consequently, cabinetmakers spend about 10 percent of their time waiting for a particular resource to become available.

From a design perspective, a typical piece of furniture requires about 30 kg of wood. In addition to this wood, about 25 percent additional wood is needed to account for scrap losses, primarily in the cutting steps of a job. Wood costs about $10 per kg.

Purchasing high-end furniture is not cheap—customers pay about $3,000 for a dining table like the one shown in Figure 6.1(a). Typically, customers are expected to pay 50 percent of the price as a down payment. They then receive their furniture about three months later. This delay reflects the custom nature of the end product as well as the fact that Paul Downs's facility at the moment is fully utilized; that is, there is more demand than what can be processed by the factory.

6.2 Building an ROIC Tree

As the owner of the firm, Paul Downs is primarily interested in creating economic value and thus in increasing the ROIC of his firm. The problem with respect to increasing ROIC is that ROIC, in and of itself, is not a lever that is under direct managerial control. It can be computed at the end of a quarter or a year, but while a manager might go to work in the morning thinking, "Today, I will increase my ROIC by 5 percent," it is not at all clear how to achieve that objective. The idea behind building an ROIC tree is to cascade the high-level financial metric into its key operational ingredients, thereby revealing the levers a manager can use to improve ROIC. To use a metaphor from the sciences, to understand how a biological cell works, we need to explain the behavior of its component molecules.

Let's begin by writing down our overall goal, the ROIC:

$$\text{ROIC} = \frac{\text{Return}}{\text{Invested capital}}$$

Now, let's do a simple algebraic manipulation and write

$$\text{ROIC} = \frac{\text{Return}}{\text{Invested capital}} = \frac{\text{Return}}{\text{Revenue}} \times \frac{\text{Revenue}}{\text{Invested capital}}$$

The first ratio, Return/Revenue, is the company's margin. The second ratio, Revenue/Invested capital, is called the company's capital turns. Note that it resembles the measure of inventory turns that we introduced in Chapter 2. This simple, though elegant, way of decomposing the ROIC into margin and asset turns is often referred to as the DuPont model. DuPont was among the pioneers introducing financial performance measures to its business units.

Companies and industries differ widely with respect to how they achieve a specific ROIC. Some industries are asset-intensive: the capital turns are low, but their margins are significant. Others require little capital. Such industries are typically easier to enter for new competitors, leading to relatively thin margins.

Now, back to Paul Downs. As advisors to Paul, we can now help him improve his business by saying: "Paul, to improve your ROIC, you need to either increase your margin or turn your assets faster. . . ." It is unlikely that this advice would ensure our future career as management consultants.

Nevertheless, let's keep pushing the same logic further and now decompose margin and asset turns into their drivers. Consider margin first. Based on standard accounting logic, we can write the Return (profits) of the firm as

$$\text{Return} = \text{Revenue} - \text{Fixed costs} - \text{Production volume} \times \text{Variable costs}$$

Because this is not an accounting book, and to be consistent with our definitions throughout the book, let us use "Flow rate" instead of "Production volume." Given the above equation, and keeping in mind that Revenue = Flow rate × Price, we can rewrite the previous equation by dividing both sides by Revenue, which yields

$$\begin{aligned}\frac{\text{Return}}{\text{Revenue}} &= \frac{\text{Revenue}}{\text{Revenue}} - \frac{\text{Fixed costs}}{\text{Revenue}} - \frac{\text{Flow rate} \times \text{Variable costs}}{\text{Revenue}} \\ &= 1 - \frac{\text{Fixed costs}}{\text{Flow rate} \times \text{Price}} - \frac{\text{Flow rate} \times \text{Variable costs}}{\text{Flow rate} \times \text{Price}} \\ &= 1 - \frac{\text{Fixed costs}}{\text{Flow rate} \times \text{Price}} - \frac{\text{Variable costs}}{\text{Price}}\end{aligned}$$

Using a similar logic as we used for margin, we can write asset turns as

$$\frac{\text{Revenue}}{\text{Invested capital}} = \frac{\text{Flow rate} \times \text{Price}}{\text{Invested capital}}$$

Our overall ROIC equation can now be written as

$$\text{ROIC} = \left[1 - \frac{\text{Fixed costs}}{\text{Flow rate} \times \text{Price}} - \frac{\text{Variable costs}}{\text{Price}}\right] \times \frac{\text{Flow rate} \times \text{Price}}{\text{Invested capital}}$$

Because ultimately, we want to be able to express the ROIC as a function of its atomic ingredients such as wage rates, processing times, idle times, and so forth, we need to continue this process further. To avoid an explosion of mathematical equations, we prefer to write them in tree forms (see Figure 6.2).

Now, consider the four variables that we discovered as drivers of margins in greater detail: Flow rate, Fixed costs, Variable costs, and Price.

To focus our analysis on the operations aspects of this case, we assume Price has already been established—in other words, we do not consider Price to be one of our potential levers. Of course, we could take our operations-focused analysis and modify it appropriately to conduct a similar marketing-focused analysis that concentrates on the pricing decision. In general though, we caution the reader not to "build a machine with too many moving parts"—especially at the start of a project, looking at an operation in detail, one simply needs to make some assumptions. Otherwise, one runs the risk of getting lost in the complexity.

Next, consider the variable costs. In our example, the variable costs are driven primarily by the consumption of wood. In some cases, one also could consider the cost of labor as a variable cost (especially if workers get paid part of their salary on a piece-rate basis).

FIGURE 6.2
ROIC Tree

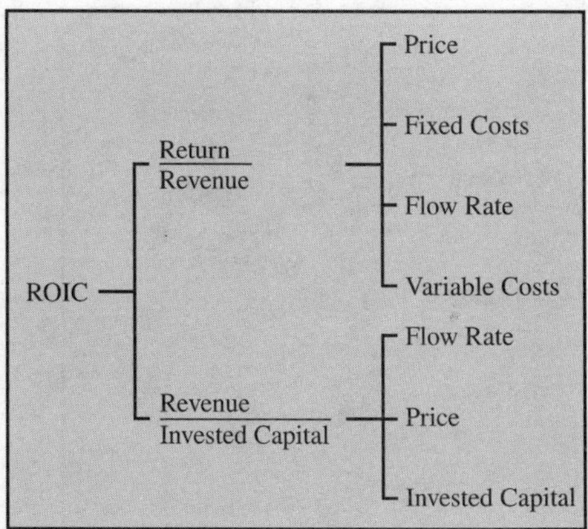

Yet, in our case, the number of cabinetmakers, as well as their hourly wages, is given and thus constitutes a fixed cost. Focusing on wood expenses, we can write the variable costs of a piece of furniture as

$$\text{Variable cost} = \text{Price of wood} \times \text{Wood per table}$$
$$= \text{Price of wood} \times (\text{Wood in final table} + \text{Cutting loss})$$

Now, let us turn our attention to Flow rate. Recall from our earlier definition that

$$\text{Flow rate} = \text{Min}\{\text{Demand, Process capacity}\}$$

Because we assume that there is enough demand at the moment, Flow rate is determined by Process capacity. But what determines capacity in this case? The main constraint on this operation is the work of the cabinetmakers. The number of units of furniture that we can produce per year depends on

- The number of available worker hours, which is determined by the number of cabinetmakers multiplied by the hours each cabinetmaker works per year.
- The time a worker needs for a piece of furniture, which is determined by the amount of time it takes a cabinetmaker to wait for a machine to become available, the time to set up the machine, and the actual time to do the work.

Figure 6.3 summarizes these calculations in tree format. The figure also shows how we can make the tree more informative by adding the corresponding mathematical symbols into it.

FIGURE 6.3
The Drivers of Process Capacity

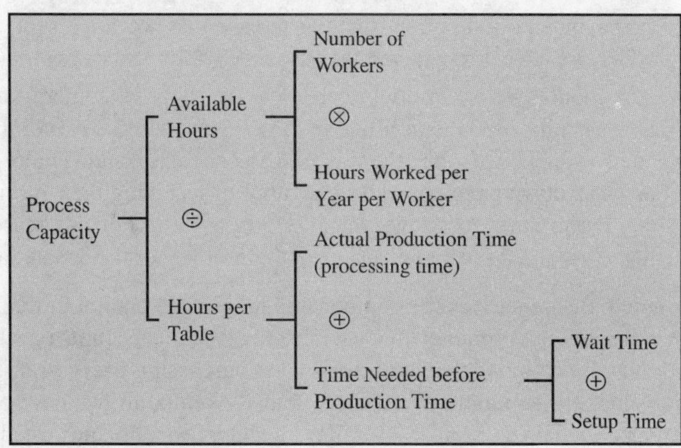

FIGURE 6.4
ROIC Tree for Fixed Costs

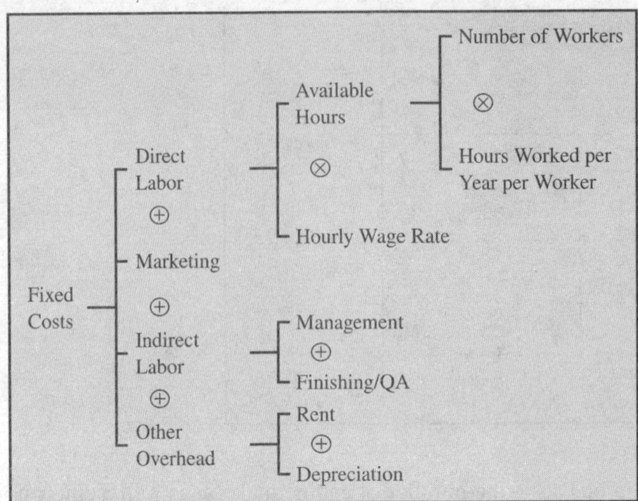

Finally, let us consider the Fixed costs. They include expenses for marketing, the labor expenses for overhead (inspection, administration), rent, depreciation, and the cost of the workforce. Figure 6.4 summarizes the main components.

It should be noted that one should be very careful how to measure depreciation. It is important to distinguish between the loss of value of a machine (e.g., a reduction in its useful life) and the depreciation as it is calculated for tax purposes. Following the standard practice of valuation and corporate finance, our emphasis is on the former view of depreciation. Note further that we do not include taxes in our analysis here (i.e., we compute the pretax ROIC).

Combining our previous work, we now can extend Figure 6.2 to a more complete picture of ROIC drivers as shown in Figure 6.5. Note that, based on this extended tree, we now have achieved an important part of our objective for this chapter—we have created a direct linkage between the ROIC and "down-to-earth" operational variables such as idle time, setup time, processing time, and flow rate.

To complete our ROIC tree, we now need to turn to the asset-turn branch of the tree and explore it to the same level of detail as we have explored the margin branch. Because we can take the Flow rate (and the Price) from our previous analysis, what is left to be done is a refined analysis of the invested capital. Capital is invested in plant, property, and equipment (PP&E) as well as in three forms of working capital:

- Inventory includes the inventory of raw materials (wood) as well as all work-in-process inventory (WIP), that is, a pile of semi-finished pieces of furniture.
- Prepayments to suppliers include money that we have sent to our suppliers but for which we have not received the associated shipment of raw materials.
- Any money we are waiting to receive from our customers for products that we have already shipped to them. While in most businesses this part of the balance sheet requires an investment in capital, the situation, in our case, is much more favorable. As customers pay us a down payment well in advance of receiving their furniture, this line item actually corresponds to an inexpensive form of cash. For this reason, we should label this item "unearned revenues" so as not to upset any of the accountants in our readership.

Figure 6.6 summarizes the components in invested capital in tree format. When we compute the amount of money that we need to invest in accounts payable, we first need to find out how much money we spend on wood purchasing every year. Because we have to pay our supplier one month in advance, at any given point, we have one-twelfth of the yearly payment tied up as capital. A similar logic applies to the unearned revenues.

FIGURE 6.5 **Expanded ROIC Tree**

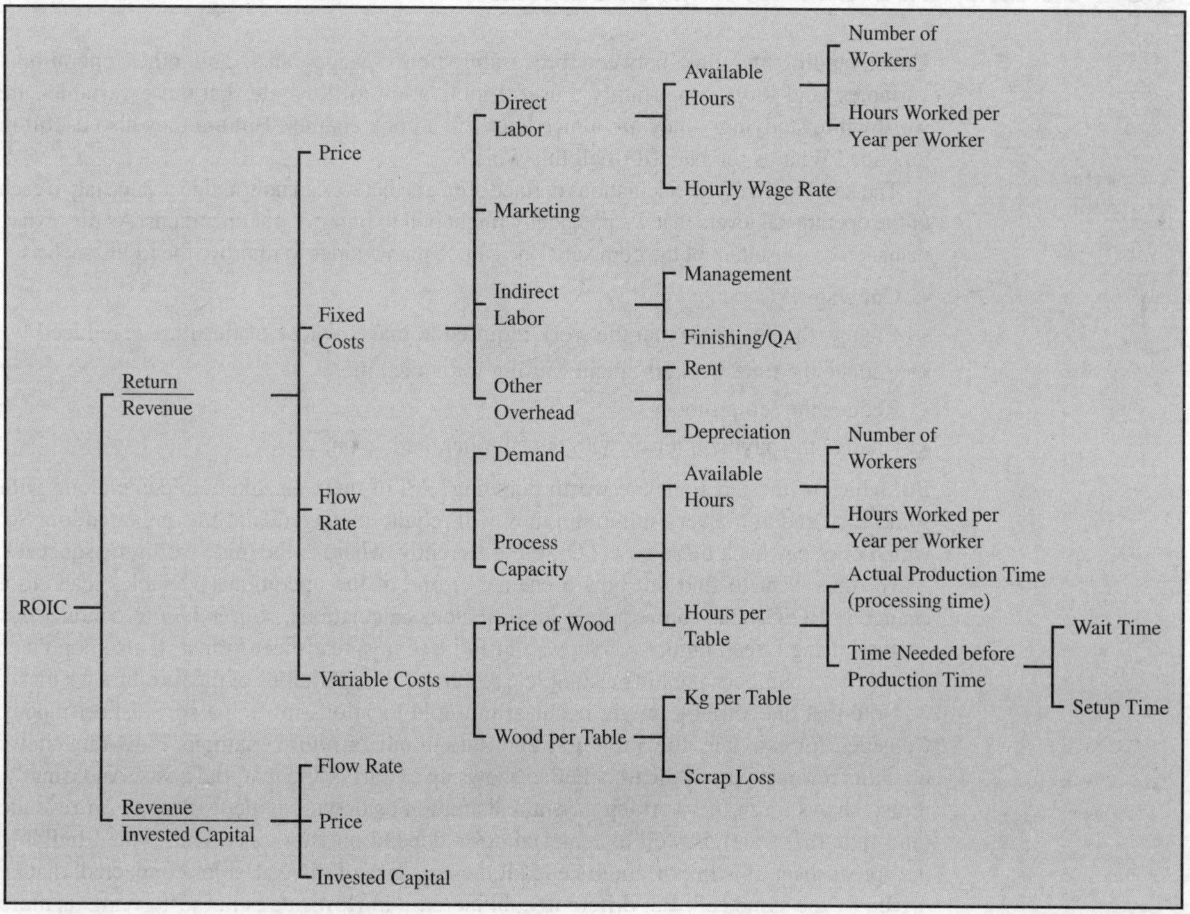

- ROIC
  - Return / Revenue
    - Price
    - Fixed Costs
      - Direct Labor
        - Available Hours
          - Number of Workers
          - Hours Worked per Year per Worker
        - Hourly Wage Rate
      - Marketing
      - Indirect Labor
        - Management
        - Finishing/QA
      - Other Overhead
        - Rent
        - Depreciation
    - Flow Rate
      - Demand
      - Process Capacity
        - Available Hours
          - Number of Workers
          - Hours Worked per Year per Worker
        - Hours per Table
          - Actual Production Time (processing time)
          - Time Needed before Production Time
            - Wait Time
            - Setup Time
    - Variable Costs
      - Price of Wood
      - Wood per Table
        - Kg per Table
        - Scrap Loss
  - Revenue / Invested Capital
    - Flow Rate
    - Price
    - Invested Capital

This completes the development of the ROIC tree. We now have expressed our key financial performance measure, ROIC, as a function of detailed operational variables. We have explained the behavior of the cell by looking at its molecules and ultimately at its atoms.

FIGURE 6.6
ROIC Tree for Invested Capital

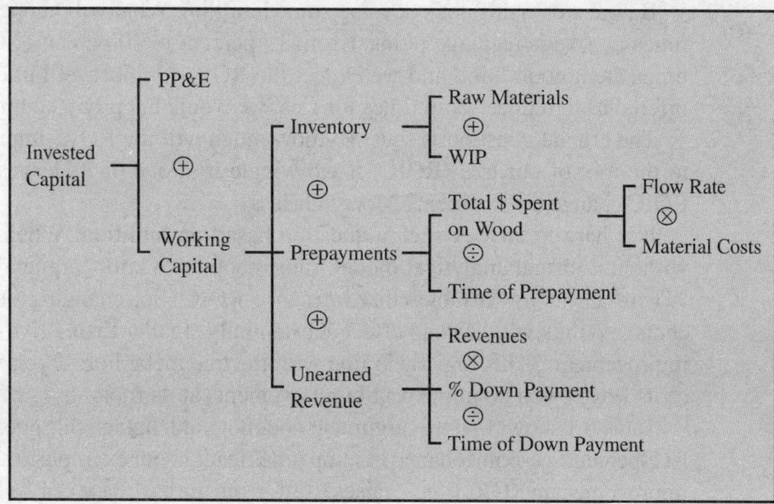

6.3 Valuing Operational Improvements

Understanding the link between processing times, wage rates, and other operational variables, and ROIC is certainly a useful motivation to illustrate that these variables are worthwhile studying—they are a nice teaser in a book chapter. But are they also useful in practice? What is the benefit of all this work?

The key benefit of the calculations defined above is that we can now assign a value tag to each of the operational levers that we potentially might pull to improve our operations. As the owner, manager, or consultant of the company, one can do many things to improve the ROIC such as

- Cut wages.
- Change the design so that the work required to make a piece of furniture is reduced.
- Reduce the time workers spend waiting for a machine.
- Reduce the setup times.
- Change the payment terms with the supplier, and so on.

But which of these actions are worth pursuing? All of them are likely to come along with some cost, and at the very minimum they will require management time and attention. So, which ones pay back these costs? Or, put differently, where is the juice worth the squeeze?

We thus want to find out how a change in one of the operational variables leads to a change in ROIC. This can require a lot of tedious calculations, so it is best to conduct this analysis using Excel. Figure 6.7 shows our full tree in spreadsheet format. It also populates the tree with numbers, creating a complete picture of the operations of the furniture we make.

Note that one variable might occur at multiple locations in such a spreadsheet model. Consider, for example, the variable Flow Rate in our furniture example. Flow rate shows up in the revenue part of the tree. It also shows up as part of the material costs. And, finally, it also shows up in the working capital calculation as down payments depend on revenue (and thus flow rate) as well as material costs depend on flow rate. Thus, when building the spreadsheet, it is important to keep all these usages of one variables connected, that is, driven by the same cell. Put differently, an increase in flow rate is not just giving us more revenue. It also creates more material costs, it adds working capital by increasing the down payments, and it reduces our working capital by adding to the prepaid expenses.

Once we are equipped with such a spreadsheet model, we can easily find the impact of an operational variable by changing the corresponding cell and observing the change in the cell corresponding to the ROIC.

Before we do this, let's develop some intuition. What will happen if we reduce the setup times by five percentage points (from 15 percent to 10 percent)? Of course, shorter setup times are a good thing and we expect the ROIC to improve. Put differently, if somebody offered us to reduce setup times for free, we would happily take him or her up on the offer.

The crucial question is thus: By how much will the ROIC improve? What will happen to the root of our tree (ROIC) if we wiggle it at one of its leaves (setup time)? Will the ROIC change by 1 percent? More? Or less?

It is hard to answer such a question based on intuition. When asked to make a guess without a formal analytical model, most people we know argue along the following line: "There are many variables that influence ROIC. So, changing one of them by five percentage points will have an effect substantially smaller than a five-percentage-point ROIC improvement." This logic is in line with the tree metaphor: if you wiggle a tree at any one of its leaves, you do not expect big movements at its roots.

Table 6.1 shows that this argument does not hold. In fact, this guess is well off the mark. A five-percentage-point change in setup times leads in our example to an 18.8-percentage-point improvement in ROIC (i.e., it raises ROIC from the base case of 12.3 percent to 31.1 percent).

FIGURE 6.7 ROIC Tree in Excel

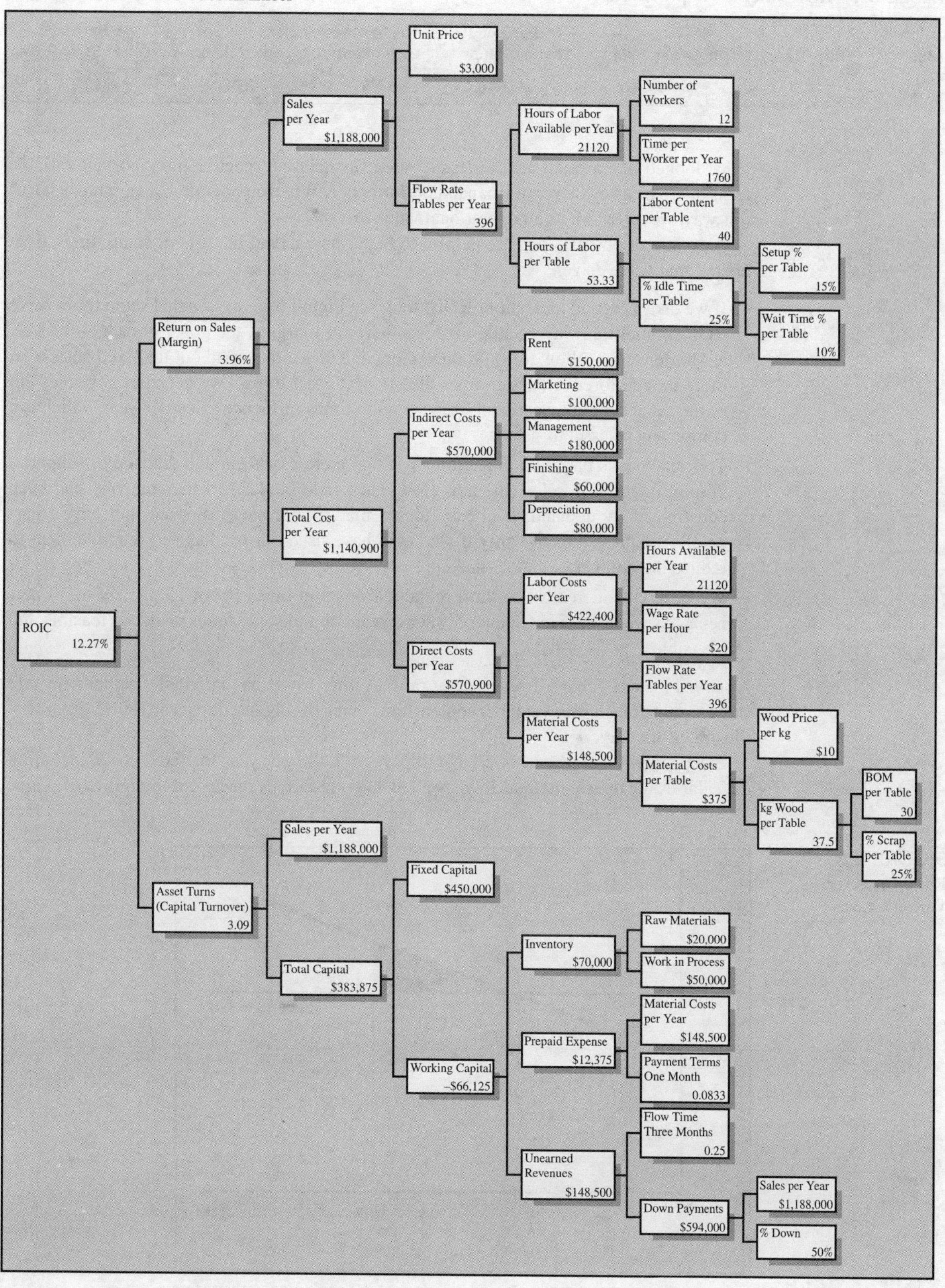

TABLE 6.1 ROIC after the Improvement

Scenario	Base Case	$1/hr Lower Wages	5 Percent Shorter Setups	$10k per Year Lower Rent	2 hr/Table Lower Labor Content	5 Percent Lower Scrap Rate
ROIC [%]	12.3	17.7	31.1	14.8	27.0	13.8

What looked like a small and, at least from a financial perspective, unimportant variable turns out to be a key driver of financial performance. When an operational variable behaves this way, we refer to it as an operational value driver.

A couple of observations are helpful to better understand the role of setup times as an operational value driver.

- If we take a second look at our ROIC tree (see Figure 6.7), we see that setup times drive ROIC in multiple ways. Setup time is a driver of margins, the upper branch of the tree, as shorter setups allow us to produce more and hence to spread out the fixed costs over more units. Moreover, setup times also impact asset turns—we get more revenues out of the same capital investment because setup times influence sales-per-year, which is a component of asset turns.
- This analysis is based on the assumption that there exists enough demand to support a 26-unit increase in sales (the new flow rate would be 422). If the company had been constrained by demand, it is easy to see that shorter setup times would have (marginally) improved ROIC only if we could have used our productivity improvement to reduce the number of cabinetmakers.
- We have considered a one-third reduction in setup times (from 15 percent to 10 percent). As we discuss in Chapter 5, such a reduction in setup times is indeed feasible and plausible.

A second look at Table 6.1 reveals that process improvements that yield a higher flow rate (lower setup times and lower labor content) are having the biggest impact on ROIC. Figure 6.8 illustrates this logic.

Independent of flow rate, we have to pay $992,400 per year for fixed costs, including the salaries for the cabinetmakers as well as the other items discussed in Figure 6.4. Once

FIGURE 6.8
Fixed Costs versus Variable Costs

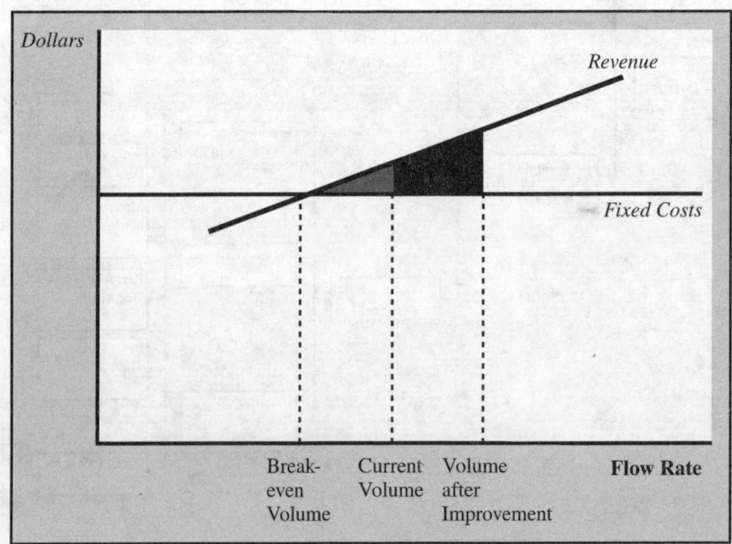

Exhibit 6.1

HOW TO CREATE AN ROIC TREE

1. Start with the objective (ROIC) on one side of the tree.
2. Decompose a variable into its components.
   - Example: ROIC = Income/Invested Capital
   - Relationships of variables can be a + b, a − b, a/b, or a × b.
3. Decide which branches of the tree have an impact and are important.
   - What are the main cost drivers (80/20 rule)?
   - What are the strategic levers of the company?
   - Which inputs are most likely to change?
4. Expand important branches (return to step 2).
5. End with measures that can be tied to operational strategy.
6. Populate the tree with actual numbers.
7. Reflect on the tree to see if it makes sense.
   - Benchmark performance.
   - Perform sensitivity analysis.

these fixed costs are covered (i.e., we exceed the break-even volume), every additional unit of flow rate leads to a $2,625 ($3,000 price minus $375 for wood consumption) increase in profit. As can be seen by the shaded area in Figure 6.8, the small increase in flow rate leads to a big increase in profits. This logic is true for all high fixed-cost operations such as hotels, airlines, and many other services.

Exhibit 6.1 summarizes the key steps of building an ROIC tree and evaluating potential operational improvements. Such a tree is a powerful starting point for consultants entering a new engagement looking at their client's operations, for a general manager who wants to have a comprehensive understanding of what drives value in his/her business, and for private equity investors that intend to quickly increase the value of a firm by fixing parts of its operation.

6.4 Analyzing Operations Based on Financial Data

In the previous section, we have looked at a relatively small business and built an ROIC tree that was grounded in a detailed understanding of the company's operations. Alternatively, we can start the analysis based on publicly available data (most often, this would be the case for larger firms). In this section, we use the example of the airline industry to illustrate the usefulness of the ROIC tree method.

The first step in our analysis is to identify firms in an industry that have demonstrated and sustained superior financial performance. In the case of the U.S. airline industry, the prime candidate for a success story is clearly Southwest Airlines.

Second, we build an ROIC tree as we did in the Paul Downs case. When analyzing an airline, the following bits of airline vocabulary are helpful:

- Instead of thinking of an airline selling tickets, it is easier to think of an airline selling *revenue passenger miles* (RPMs). An RPM corresponds to transporting a paying customer for one mile. A flight from Philadelphia to Boston, for example, with

200 passengers would correspond to 447 miles × 200 paying passengers = 89,400 RPMs. By focusing on RPM, we avoid some of the problems associated with comparisons between airlines that have different route structures. Furthermore, as we will see, variable costs for an airline are generally tied to the number of miles flown, so it is also convenient to express revenue on a per-mile basis.

- The capacity of an airline is determined by the number and the sizes of its aircraft. This leads to a measure known as the *available seat miles* (ASMs). One ASM corresponds to one airline seat (with or without a passenger in it) flying for one mile.
- Airlines only make money if they can turn their ASMs into RPMs: a seat with a paying customer is good; an empty seat is not. The ratio RPM/ASM is called the *load factor*—it strongly resembles our definition of utilization as it looks at how many revenue passenger miles the airline creates relative to how much it could create if every seat were filled. Clearly, the load factor must always be less than one—other than small infants sitting on a parent's lap, airlines do not allow two paying customers to occupy the same seat.

Figure 6.9 summarizes a simplified version of an ROIC tree for an airline. There exist, of course, many more levels of details that could be analyzed, including aspects of fleet age

FIGURE 6.9
ROIC Tree for a Generic Airline (profit corresponds to pretax income)

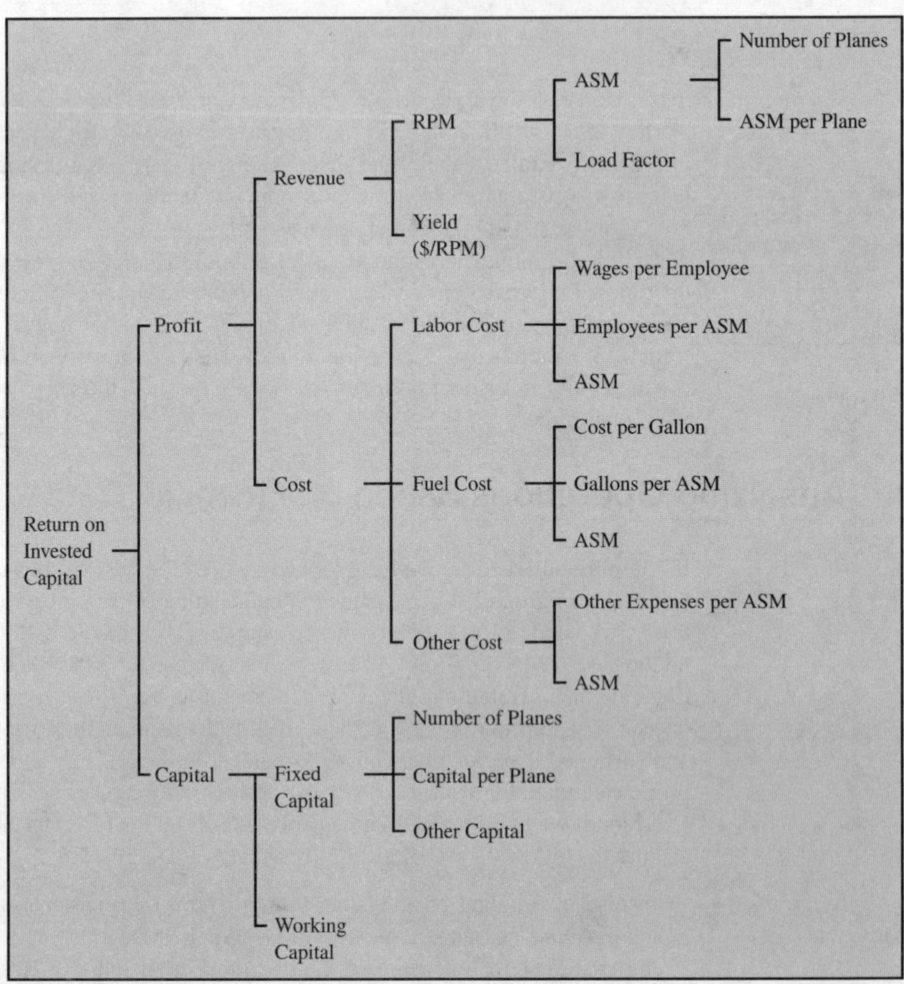

and composition, size of flight crews, the percentage of flying time of an aircraft, and so on. But since we are growing this tree from the left to the right, any additional level of detail could be simply tagged on to our analysis in Figure 6.9.

As a third step, we want to explore why the financially high-performing firm is doing better than its peers. A good diagnostic tool toward this end is the following method we call productivity ratios. We can write productivity as

$$\text{Productivity} = \frac{\text{Revenue}}{\text{Cost}}$$

and we can write labor productivity as

$$\text{Labor productivity} = \frac{\text{Revenue}}{\text{Labor cost}}$$

and see that Southwest's labor is substantially more productive than labor at Delta or United. The Southwest labor productivity ratio is 2606.0, which is almost 10 percent higher than the ones for United and Delta. The following calculations are illustrated with data from the year 2016. We use Southwest as a reference point, as the airline has managed to be profitable quarter after quarter, even including the most difficult times of airline operations that followed the September 11, 2001, terrorist attacks.

But where does the productivity advantage come from? Are Southwest employees serving more customers? Do they make less money? From the ratio alone, we cannot tell. For this reason, we will rewrite the productivity measure as follows:

$$\text{Productivity} = \frac{\text{Revenue}}{\text{Cost}} = \frac{\text{Revenue}}{\text{Flow rate}} \times \frac{\text{Flow rate}}{\text{Resource}} \times \frac{\text{Resource}}{\text{Cost}}$$

Or, applied to labor productivity in airlines,

$$\text{Labor productivity} = \frac{\text{Revenue}}{\text{Labor cost}} = \underbrace{\frac{\text{Revenue}}{\text{RPM}}}_{\text{Yield}} \times \underbrace{\frac{\text{RPM}}{\text{ASM}} \times \frac{\text{ASM}}{\text{Employees}}}_{\text{Efficiency}} \times \underbrace{\frac{\text{Employees}}{\text{Labor costs}}}_{\text{Cost}}$$

It is helpful to break up this expanded productivity calculation into three pieces:

- Yields: the operational yield (Revenue/Flow rate) measures how much money the firm can squeeze out of its output, the flow rate. This measure is largely driven by the firm's pricing power.
- Efficiency: the transformation efficiency (Flow rate/Resource) measures how many resources we need to support the flow rate. This number is determined by how we utilize our resources. It captures the resource utilization (in our case, the load factor) as well as the inherent processing times at each resource (how many available seat miles can a single employee serve?).
- Cost: the cost of resources (Resource/Cost) measures how much of a resource we can get per $1 spent. The reciprocal of this measure is simply the cost of that resource, for example, the average yearly salary of an employee.

Now, let's see what these productivity ratios tell us about Southwest's source of higher labor productivity. Table 6.2 summarizes our results.

The results of our diagnostics might be surprising to you. Though Southwest has a history of being a low-cost carrier, it now obtains the same yield as Delta and United.

TABLE 6.2 Comparison between US Airways and Southwest

Airline	Operational Yield [$/RPM]	Load Factor [%]	ASM per Employee	Number of Employees/Million US$ of Labor Costs	Overall Labor Productivity
Delta	0.14	0.85	2682.7	7.42	2419.2
South-west	0.15	0.84	2912.7	7.15	2606.0
United	0.14	0.83	2529.5	8.32	2364.7

Source: 2016 MIT Airline data.

Interestingly, all three airlines operate at roughly the same load factor. Let's turn to the last two ratios:

- A Southwest employee is able to support almost 10 percent more ASMs compared to United and Delta employees (2912.7 as opposed to 2682.7 and 2529.5). This advantage used to be substantially larger (up to around 30 percent just five years ago), but most airlines have recently managed to catch up and close the gap to Southwest.
- Southwest employees earn substantially higher wages than their counterparts at United and Delta. Their higher productivity is not just good for the business, it also has helped the workforce to command higher salaries.

Unlike the analysis that we did in the Paul Downs case, the approach introduced in this section is much more of a top-down analysis. Before entering the details of the operations, we start out our analysis by broadly analyzing financial data.

In general, the top-down approach is most useful when analyzing competing organizations or when there simply are limited data available about operational details; thus, when the analysis happens from "the outside in." In contrast, it should be emphasized that for the management within an operation, a more detailed analysis is needed, as we conducted in the Paul Downs case.

6.5 Summary

In this chapter, we have provided a link between the operations of a company and its financial performance. This link can be studied at the micro level, as we have done in the Paul Downs case, or it can be done starting with the financial statements, as we have done in the airline case. Either way, operational variables are key drivers of a company's financial performance. Value creation takes place in the operations of a company and so, to increase the economic value of a company, a detailed analysis of operations is a must.

6.6 Further Reading

Koller, Goedhart, and Wessels (2010) is an excellent book on topics related to valuation and corporate finance. Compared to most other finance books, it is very hands-on and does not shy away from the operational details of business.

Cannon, Randall, and Terwiesch (2007) study the empirical relationship between operational variables and future financial performance in the airline industry.

6.7 Practice Problems

The following questions will help in testing your understanding of this chapter. After each question, we show the relevant section in parentheses [Section x].

Solutions to problems marked with an "*" are available in Appendix E. Video solutions to select problems are available in Connect.

Q6.1* **(Crazy Cab)** Crazy Cab is a small taxi cab company operating in a large metropolitan area. The company operates 20 cabs. Each cab is worth about $20k. The metropolitan area also requires that each cab carry a medallion (a type of license). Medallions are currently traded at $50k. Cab drivers make $8 per hour and are available at every time of the day. The average cab is used for 40 trips per day. The average trip is three miles in length. Passengers have to pay $2 as a fixed fee and $2 per mile they are transported. Fuel and other costs, such as maintenance, are $0.20 per mile. The cab drives about 40 percent of the distance without a paying passenger in it (e.g. , returning from a drop-off location, picking up a passenger, etc.)

a. Draw an ROIC tree for the cab company. [6.2]

b. Populate the tree with numbers. Make assumptions to explore operational variables in as much detail as possible (e.g., assumptions about gas prices, gas consumption, etc.). [6.2]

c. Which of the variables would you classify as operational value drivers? [6.3]

d. Analyze the labor efficiency and the efficiency of using the fleet of cabs using productivity ratios. [6.4]

Q6.2 **(Penne Pesto)** Penne Pesto is a small restaurant in the financial district of San Francisco. Customers order from a variety of pasta dishes. The restaurant has 50 seats and is always full during the four hours in the evening. It is not possible to make reservations at Penne; most guests show up spontaneously on their way home from work. If there is no available seat, guests simply move on to another place.

On average, a guest spends 50 minutes in the restaurant, which includes 5 minutes until the guest is seated and the waiter has taken the order, an additional 10 minutes until the food is served, 30 minutes to eat, and 5 minutes to handle the check-out (including waiting for the check, paying, and leaving). It takes the restaurant another 10 minutes to clean the table and have it be ready for the next guests (of which there are always plenty). The average guest leaves $20 at Penne, including food, drink, and tip (all tips are collected by the restaurant; employees get a fixed salary).

The restaurant has 10 waiters and 10 kitchen employees, each earning $90 per evening (including any preparation, the 4 hours the restaurant is open, and clean-up). The average order costs $5.50 in materials, including $4.50 for the food and $1 for the average drink. In addition to labor costs, fixed costs for the restaurant include $500 per day of rent and $500 per day for other overhead costs.

The restaurant is open 365 days a year and is full to the last seat even on weekends and holidays. There is about $200,000 of capital tied up in the restaurant, largely consisting of furniture, decoration, and equipment.

a. How many guests will the restaurant serve in one evening? [6.2]

b. What is the return on invested capital (ROIC) for the owner of the restaurant? [6.2]

c. Assume that you could improve the productivity of the kitchen employees and free up one person who would be helping to clean up the table. This would reduce the clean-up to 5 minutes instead of 10 minutes. What would be the new ROIC? [6.3]

d. What would be the new ROIC if overhead charges could be reduced by $100 per day? [6.3]

Q6.3 **(Philly Air)** PhillyAir Inc. offers low cost air travel between Philadelphia and Atlantic City. Philly Air's invested capital is $5,000,000, corresponding to the investment in the two planes the company owns. Each of the two planes can carry 50 passengers. Each plane does 12 daily trips from Philadelphia to Atlantic City and 12 from Atlantic City to Philadelphia. The price is $100 for each one-way ticket. The current load factor is 70 percent (i.e., 35 seats are sold on the average flight). The annual cost of operating the service and running the business is $60,000,000 (including all costs, such as labor, fuel, marketing, gate fees, landing fees, maintenance, etc.). The company operates 365 days a year.

a. Draw an ROIC (return on invested capital) tree for the company that incorporates all of the above information. [6.2]

b. What is the current ROIC? [6.2]

c. What is the minimum load factor at which the company breaks even? [6.3]

d. What load factor would the company have to achieve so that it obtained a 10 percentage-point increase in the ROIC (e.g., an ROIC increasing from 5 percent to 15 percent)? [6.3]

Q6.4 **(Oscar's Office Building)** Oscar is considering getting into the real estate business. He's looking at buying an existing office building for $1.8 million in cash. He wants to estimate what his return on invested capital (ROIC) will be on an annual basis. The building has 14,000 square feet of rentable space. He'd like to set the rent at $4.00 per square foot per month. However, he knows that demand depends on price. He estimates that the percentage of the building he can fill roughly follows the equation

$$\% \text{ Occupied} = 2 - 0.3 \times \text{Rent}$$

(rent is in dollars per square foot per month)

So, at $4.00, Oscar thinks he can fill about 80 percent of the office space.

Oscar considers two categories of costs: variable costs, which are a function of the square feet occupied, and fixed costs. Fixed costs will be $8,000 per month and include such items as insurance, maintenance, and security. Variable costs cover such things as electricity and heat and run $1.25 per month for each square foot occupied.

a. Draw an ROIC (return on invested capital) tree for the company. [6.2]

b. What is the ROIC? [6.2]

c. What would be the new ROIC be if Oscar decides to charge rent of $5.00 per square foot per month? [6.3]

Q6.5 **(OPIM Bus Inc.)** OPIM Bus Inc. offers low-cost bus transportation between Philadelphia and Bryn Mawr. The invested capital is $500,000, corresponding to the investment in the two vehicles it owns. Each of the two buses can carry 50 passengers. Each bus does 12 daily trips from Philadelphia to Bryn Mawr and 12 from Bryn Mawr to Philadelphia. The price is $10 for each one-way ticket. The current load factor is 70 percent (i.e., 35 seats are sold on average). The annual cost of operating the service and running the business is $6 million. The company operates 365 days a year.

a. Draw an ROIC (return on invested capital) tree for the company. [6.2]

b. What is the current ROIC? [6.2]

c. What is the minimum load factor at which the company breaks even? [6.3]

d. What load factor would the company have to achieve so that it obtained a 10 percentage-point increase in the ROIC (e.g., an ROIC increasing from 5 percent to 15 percent)? [6.3]

If you would like to test your understanding of a specific section, here are the questions organized by section:

Section 6.2: Q6.1ab, Q6.2ab, Q6.3ab, Q6.4ab, Q6.5ab

Section 6.3: Q6.1c, Q6.2cd, Q6.3cd, Q6.4c, Q6.5cd

Section 6.4: Q6.1d

Chapter 7

Quality and Statistical Process Control

Many production and service processes suffer from quality problems. Airlines lose baggage, computer manufacturers ship laptops with defective disk drives, pharmacies distribute the wrong medications to patients, and postal services lose or misdeliver articles by mail. In addition to these quality problems directly visible to us as consumers, many quality problems remain hidden to us, because they are detected and corrected within the boundaries of the process, oftentimes leading to substantially increased production costs. The purpose of this chapter is to better understand what quality problems are, why they occur, and how operations can be improved to reduce the frequency of such problems.

As we will see in this chapter, variation is the root cause of all quality problems. Without variation, a process would either always function as desired, in which case we would not need a chapter on quality, or it would never function as desired, in which case it would be unlikely that the operation would be in business to begin with. Given the importance of variation in influencing quality, this chapter will oftentimes use tools and frameworks taken from the field of statistics.

To see the effect that variation has on quality, consider the following examples:

- European Union commission regulation No 1677/88 states that cucumbers are allowed a bend of 10 millimeters per 10 centimeters of length. Cucumbers that bend more than this do not qualify as Class I or "extra class." Class II cucumbers are allowed to bend twice as much. In other words, the commission acknowledges that cucumbers come in different shapes and sizes, reflecting the variation inherent in an agricultural production process. Moreover, according to the EU bureaucrats, there exists an ideal cucumber shape in the form of a straight line, and the more a cucumber bends, the less desirable it is.
- In the fall of 2013, publicly traded electronics retailer Tweeter saw its (extremely low) share prices rise by 1400 percent in a single day. Why? Some investors apparently confused the shares of Tweeter with the shares of Twitter, which was in the process of launching an initial public offering. While there always existed some variation in the frequency of Tweeter share trades, trades for Tweeter shares increased from a typical volume of 29,000 shares per day to 14.4 million shares per day. Once Twitter changed its ticker symbol from TWTRQ to THEGQ, Tweeter shares dropped to their previous level within a matter of hours.
- In the hospital associated with the medical school of Münster, Germany, an interning medical school student injected the medication prepared in a syringe into a baby's IV instead of delivering the medication orally as intended. The syringe design was the

same for medications given orally and for medications to be delivered via an IV. Using one common syringe had previously worked countless times without leading to a mistake. This time, it did not—the baby tragically died the same day.

- Quality problems caused an even bigger loss of lives in the accident of the MS *Estonia.* On September 28, 1994, the MS *Estonia,* a cruise ferry, headed out from Tallin (in Estonia) into the Baltic Sea. That day, the sea was rough and the ship's cargo was distributed with a slight imbalance. However, the MS *Estonia* had mastered rough weather many times without problems, and it is rare for a ferry to find a perfect load distribution. Yet, this day, the many variables that influenced the safety of the ferry were lined up badly. The MS *Estonia* sank, causing over 800 fatalities in one of the most tragic maritime disasters since the sinking of the *Titanic.*

From the almost comical cucumber regulations of the EU and the funny confusion of Twitter with Tweeter to the tragic loss of lives in the cases of the German hospital and the MS *Estonia,* understanding the roles that variation plays in these settings is critical for analyzing and improving operations.

7.1 The Statistical Process Control Framework

Variation exists everywhere. At the risk of being overly poetic for a business textbook, let us observe that no two snowflakes are identical. The same holds for any two cucumbers. Nature itself creates randomness and so the size and curvature of every cucumber differs. Some of this variation in cucumber shape and size is entirely random. Even if we would grow 50 cucumbers in the same soil, water them with the same frequency, and expose them to the same sunlight, we would still not get 50 identical cucumbers. We refer to this natural form of variation as *natural variation* or *common cause variation*.

Common cause variation also exists in medicine. Two babies are given the same medication under the same medical circumstances. Yet, their reactions might differ. The death of the baby in Münster, however, was not a result of common cause variation. The medical student made a mistake and delivered the medication to the baby by injecting it into the IV, which led to a much faster diffusion of the medication into the baby's body relative to oral delivery. This was not nature's randomness at work. There exists a simple explanation for the variation in how quickly the medication diffused. In this case, we speak of an *assignable cause variation*.

Common cause variation and assignable cause variation impact the performance of a process. At an abstract level, we can think of the outcome associated with a process as depicted in Figure 7.1. The management and the operators of the process influence a number of *input variables*. For trading a share of Twitter (or Tweeter for that matter), these input variables are the choice of which share to buy, how many shares to buy, and what price to pay per share. Few operations, however, are so simple and have so few input variables as electronic trading. Growing cucumbers, while arguably also a rather simple task, already has many more variables, including irrigation settings, fertilizer usage, light exposure, usage of pesticides, and so on. The list of input variables for health care services or the operation of a boat or airplane is much longer.

Input variables are not the only things that affect the outcome of the process. There typically exist a number of *environmental variables* that also matter. For example, in the case of the MS *Estonia,* we can think about the weather and the sea as such environmental variables. In contrast to input variables, environmental variables are not directly under the control of the operation. They simply happen and, in most cases, negatively impact quality. High-tech production processes such as the production of semiconductors are so vulnerable that even minor environmental variables such as small dust particles or miniscule vibrations of the equipment can ruin a large percentage of the production output.

FIGURE 7.1
Framework of Quality

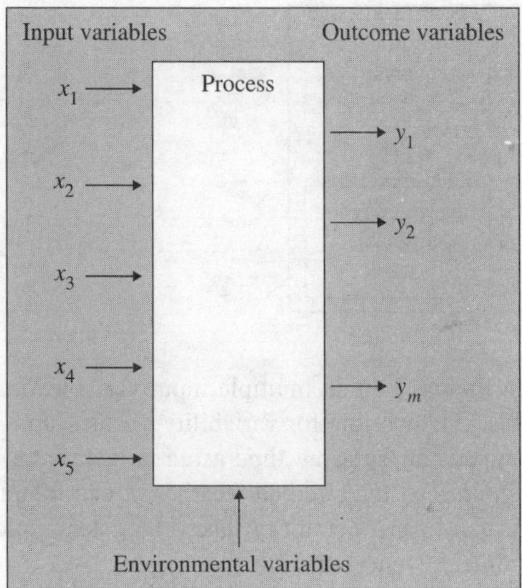

The output of the process can be measured using a number of *outcome variables*. Outcome variables might be the curvature of a cucumber or the degree to which a boat leans over to one side or the other. Whether or not the outcome variables lead to a *defective* unit or not depends on a *set of specifications*. We define the specifications as a set of acceptable values for the outcome variable. In the case of cucumbers, the specifications define the curvature.

Sometimes, as in the case with the cucumber, it is possible to define a defect using a mathematical definition based on the outcome variables ("A cucumber is defective if its curvature exceeds 10 mm in 10 cm"). At other times, it might be hard to formally define such mathematical criteria. We know that the medical student delivering the medication via an IV committed a mistake and hence created a defect, but it would not help much to create a mathematical formulation of this situation.

Figure 7.1 illustrates the relationship between input variables, environmental variables, outcomes, and defects. Based on this framework, we make the following comments:

- In order for a defect to happen, we need to have some variation in outcome. But for a variation in outcome to happen, we need to have some variation either in the input variables or in the environmental variables. So when diagnosing a defect, we need to find the input or environmental variable(s) that caused that defect. We refer to that variable or these variables as the *root cause* for the defect.
- Even in a well-managed operation, input variables and environmental variables will always be subject to some common cause variation. The goal of management ought to be to keep that variation small and design the process so that this variation does not translate in large variations in outcome variables and ultimately defects.
- Just as we need to avoid that common cause variation in input and environmental variables leads to a large common cause variation in outcome variables, we need to avoid that an assignable cause variation in an input variable leads to a defect. We define a process as *robust* if it is able to tolerate (common or assignable cause) variation in input or environmental variables without leading to a large amount of variation in outcome variables and ultimately to defects. For example, the process of medication delivery via a common syringe in the German hospital was not robust with respect to inexperienced care providers. A different process design in which syringes used for oral medication delivery would be incompatible with IV delivery would have been a more robust process.

FIGURE 7.2
Framework for Statistical Process Control

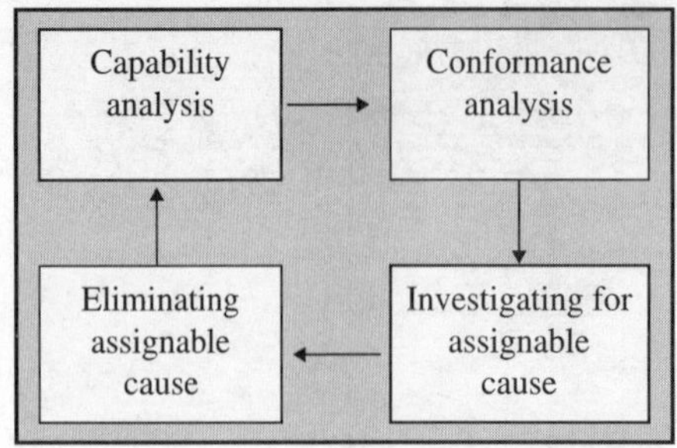

- We also observe in Figure 7.1 that multiple input variables impact the outcome variable. Because of this, it is possible for variability to stack up—sometimes, an unlucky realization of x_1 happens at the same time as an unlucky realization of x_2. A process such as the MS *Estonia* can tolerate bad weather, it can tolerate imbalances in cargo distribution, and it can tolerate operator mistakes. Disasters typically happen when multiple statistically unlikely events coincide.

As managers of operations, our goal is to understand quality problems and reduce their frequency of occurrence by redesigning the process and by addressing the underlying root causes. Figure 7.2 summarizes the approach that we will take in this chapter to achieve this goal. Given the previously mentioned emphasis on variation and statistical analysis, this approach is known as *statistical process control (SPC).*

It includes the following four steps:

1. Measuring the current amount of outcome variation in the process and comparing how this variation relates to the outcome specifications and thus the likelihood of making a defect. This determines the capability of the process.
2. Monitoring this process and identifying instances in which the outcome variation is *abnormal,* suggesting the occurrence of some assignable cause variation in input or environmental variables. In other words, we monitor the process and determine if the presently observed variation conforms to the usual patterns of variation (in which case we are dealing with common cause variation). In the cases in which the presently observed variation does not conform to historical data, we expect an assignable cause to have occurred.
3. Investigating the root cause of an assignable cause variation by finding the input or environmental variable(s) that caused the variation.
4. Avoiding the recurrence in the future of similar assignable cause variations and/or changing the process so that it is sufficiently robust to not have its quality be affected by such events in the future.

The following sections will elaborate on these four steps in greater detail.

7.2 Capability Analysis

Achieving consistency by controlling variation is critical for achieving high quality. This is true in operations management, but also applies to other aspects of our lives. Consider the following example from the world of sports. In target shooting, a shooter aims at a target similar to what is shown in Figure 7.3. The figure compares the results of three shooters, each of whom fired six shots at the target. Assume for the moment that each hit in the black area in the center of the target is worth one point. Note that all three shooters hit, on average, the center point (bull's-eye). Note further that shooters 2 and 3 both managed to get six points. Who, in your view, is the best target shooter?

FIGURE 7.3 **Six Shots Fired at a Target by Three Different Shooters (from left to right: shooters 1 to 3)**

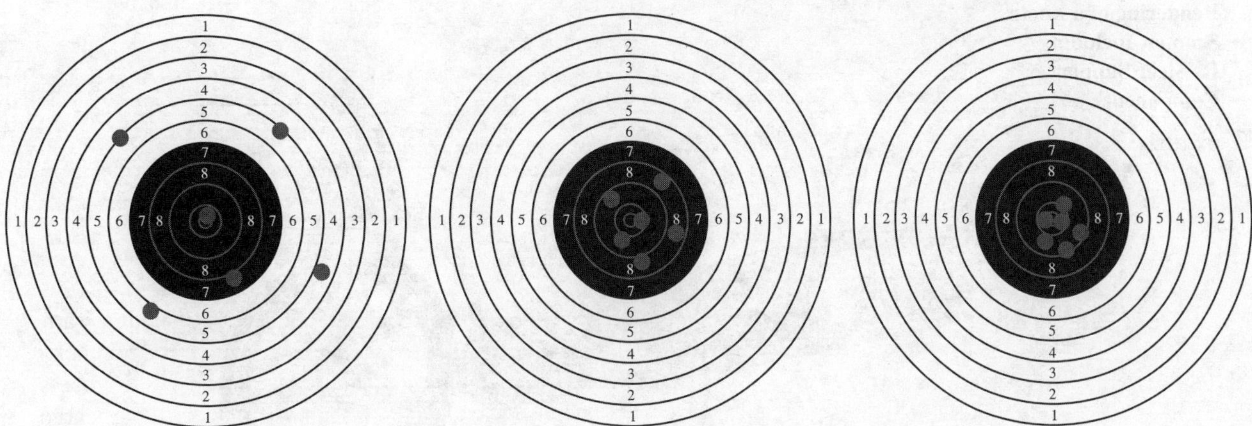

Let's start looking at the results of shooter 1. A target shooter who misses the target by two feet to the left, only to then "compensate" by shooting the next shot two feet to the right, might be right on average, but nevertheless is a bad target shooter. Next, consider shooters 2 and 3. Both of them managed to get six points (recall that we award one point to every shot in the black area). Yet, intuitively, we would label shooter 3 as being the better shooter.

The example of the target shooters illustrates two important lessons about measuring variation in a process. First, when we measure the capability of the shooter, it is not the average location of the shot that matters (all three, on average, hit a bull's-eye). Instead, it is the spread of shots over the target that makes us call one shooter better than the other. Second, we can infer more from six shots about a shooter's capability than just counting how many shots are "in" versus "out." By carefully measuring the exact position of each shot relative to the ideal point (the bull's-eye), we gain additional information. Imagine we would want to extrapolate and predict how many shots out of 100 shots would be on target. A naïve analysis would argue that shooters 2 and 3 both got 100 percent of their shots on target and so are likely to not make mistakes in the future either. However, knowing that shooter 2 had a number of "near misses" (i.e., shots close to the edge of the black circle) makes us wonder if this shooter really would be able to hit the black area 100 times in a row.

Determining a Capability Index

From the shooting range, back to the world of operations management. Consider the production of kick scooters at Xootr LLC, a product that has achieved a number of design awards (see Figure 7.4; also see earlier chapters for details about the Xootr production process). In the production of the steer support for the Xootr, the component is obtained via extrusion from aluminum and subsequent refinement at a computer-controlled machine tool (CNC machine).

Figure 7.5 shows the engineering drawing for the component. Despite the fact that every steer support component is refined by the CNC machine, there still exists some variation with respect to the exact geometry of the output. This variation is the result of many causes, including input variables (such as raw materials, the way the component is placed in the machine, an occasional mistake in programming the CNC machine) and environmental variables (such as the temperature of the room at the time of the processing).

FIGURE 7.4
Rendering of a Xootr Scooter, Including Its Steer Support Component

©Xootr LLC

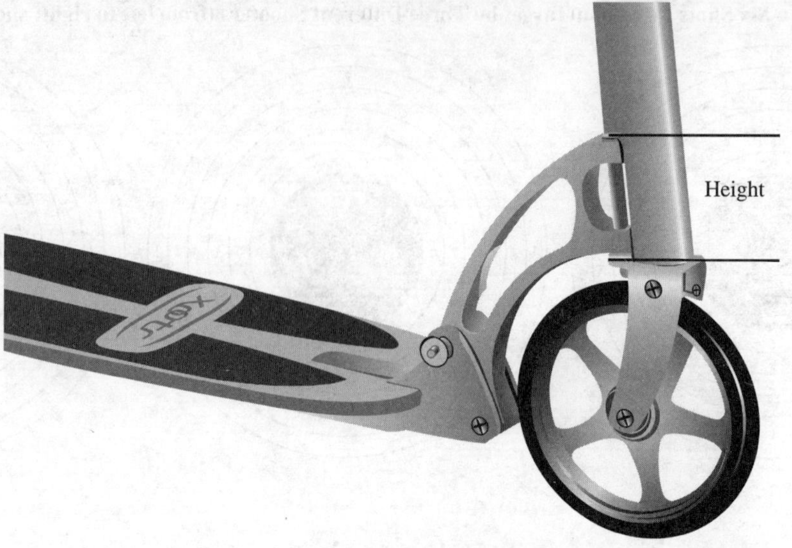

According to the design of the product, the ideal steer support would measure 79.950 mm in height. This is the bull's-eye for Xootr's production process. The engineering drawing specifies that the height must fall between 79.900 mm and 80.000 mm. If the height is less than 79.900 mm, the part may rattle excessively because it fits loosely. If the height is

FIGURE 7.5 **Engineering Drawing of the Steer Support Unit**

©Xootr LLC

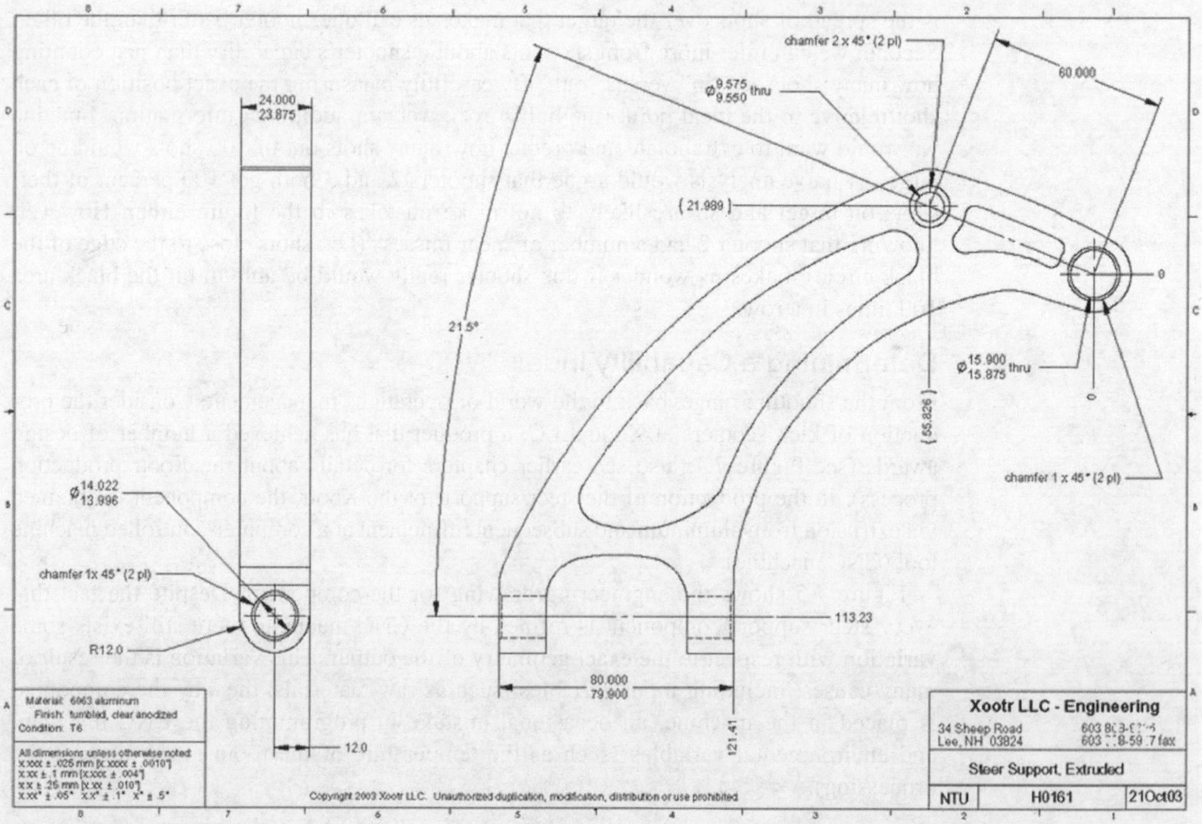

greater than 80.000 mm, then the part may not fit in the available gap in the handle assembly. We refer to 79.900 mm as the *lower specification limit (LSL)* and to 80.000 mm as the *upper specification limit (USL)*. The specification limits determine which units are acceptable and which ones are defective. They correspond to the black circle that determined whether or not a shot was on target in Figure 7.3.

Given that variation of the steer support's height can cause quality problems, the engineers of the company (Xootr LLC) monitor the height very carefully. Every day, a sample of components is taken and measured accurately. This sample allows the engineers to estimate the current amount of variation in the steer support production. It is common in statistics to measure variation using the standard deviation, oftentimes abbreviated by using the Greek letter sigma (σ). Given that we estimate this standard deviation on a (small) sample, we refer to the estimated variation in the process as sigma-hat ($\hat{\sigma}$).

But given an estimated amount of variation in the process, ($\hat{\sigma}$), what is the likelihood that the process produces a defect? The answer to this question depends on

- The tightness of the design specification, which we can quantify as the difference between the upper specification level and lower specification level (USL – LSL).
- The amount of variation in the current process, which is captured by the estimated standard deviation sigma-hat.

Thus, the capability of the process in meeting a given set of design specifications—that is, the likelihood of a defect—depends on the magnitude of variability in the process, sigma-hat, relative to the tolerance levels, USL – LSL. We can combine these two measures into a single score, which is frequently referred to as the *process capability index:*

$$C_p = \frac{\text{USL} - \text{LSL}}{6\hat{\sigma}}$$

The process capability index, C_p, measures the allowable tolerance relative to the actual variation of the process. Both numerator and denominator are expressed in the same units (millimeters in the case of Xootr) and thus C_p itself is unitless. To interpret C_p, consider a $C_p = 1$. For this to happen, the tolerance interval, USL – LSL, has to be six times as large as the estimated standard deviation, sigma-hat. In other words, for a $C_p = 1$, it is possible to fit six times the standard deviation of the variation into the tolerance interval. We know from statistics that the average of a sample tends to be distributed according to a normal distribution. If we assume that the mean (the average) of that normal distribution is in the middle of the tolerance interval (79.5 mm in the case of Xootr), then a C_p value of 1 implies that we can go three standard deviations from that center point to either side before hitting the specification limit. For this reason, we label a process with a $C_p = 1$ as a "three-sigma process."

Figure 7.6 compares two different values of C_p for a given set of design specifications. The upper part of the figure depicts a three-sigma process. We thus know that it's $C_p = 1$. In the lower part of the figure, the specification limits are the same, but the standard deviation, labeled σ_B, of the process is much smaller. We can afford moving six standard deviations to either side of the mean before hitting the specification limit. In other words, in such a *six-sigma process*, the tolerance interval is 12 standard deviations σ_B wide. The capability index is thus

$$C_p = \frac{\text{USL} - \text{LSL}}{6\hat{\sigma}} = \frac{12\hat{\sigma}}{6\hat{\sigma}} = 2$$

The likelihood of a defect (statistically spoken, this is the probability mass of the bell-shaped density function outside the tolerance interval) is much smaller compared to the upper case.

FIGURE 7.6
Comparing a Three-Sigma Process with a Six-Sigma Process

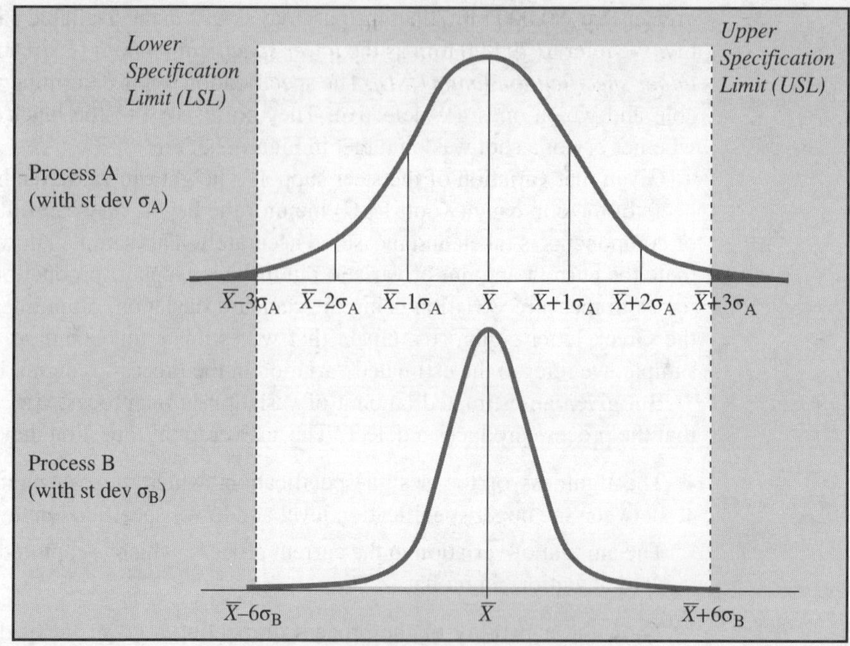

For the steer support component, Xootr engineers estimated a standard deviation of 0.017291 mm. This lets us compute the process capability measure as follows:

$$C_p = \frac{\text{USL} - \text{LSL}}{6\hat{\sigma}} = \frac{80.000 - 79.900}{6 \times 0.017291} = 0.963889$$

Predicting the Probability of a Defect

Knowing the mean, the standard deviation, and the specification limits of a process, and relying on the fact that the process follows a normal distribution, enables us to predict the probability of future defects. To compute this *defect probability,* we perform the following calculations:

Step 1: Find the probability that a unit falls below the lower specification limit, LSL. This can be achieved by entering NORM.DIST(LSL, Mean, Standard Deviation, 1) into Excel. NORM.DIST returns the value of the cumulative normal distribution. Mathematically, this is the area under the probability density function (the bell-shaped curve associated with the normal distribution) to the left of the LSL. In our Xootr calculations, this gives us

Probability{part too small} = NORM.DIST(79.9, 79.95, 0.017291, 1) = 0.001915954

Step 2: Find the probability that a unit falls above the USL. Do this by entering 1 – NORM.DIST(USL, Mean, Standard Deviation, 1) into Excel. Mathematically, this is the area under the probability density function to the right of the USL.

Probability{part too big} = 1 – NORM.DIST(80, 79.95, 0.017291, 1) = 0.001915954

Note that the results of steps 1 and 2 are identical. This is because, in our case, the mean of the distribution is right in the middle of the tolerance interval. This is not always the case, so we encourage you to do steps 1 and 2 as opposed to simply doing step 1 and then assuming that the probability that the part being too big is the same as the probability of the part being too small.

Step 3: Add the results of step 1 and step 2 to get the defect probability (because a unit is either too big or too small, the probability that it is defective is simply the sum of the two probabilities):

$$\text{Probability}\{\text{part defective}\} = 0.001915954 + 0.001915954 = 0.003831908$$

In addition to obtaining the defect probability, it is also common to express the number of units expected to be defective out of one million units (also referred to as *parts per million*, or ppm for short). To obtain the ppm number, simply multiply the defect probability by 1,000,000. In the case of Xootr's steer support part, we get

$$\text{PPM} = \text{Probability }\{\text{part defective}\} \times 1{,}000{,}000 = 0.003831908 \times 1{,}000{,}000 = 3831.9$$

As we have seen from the preceding calculations, it is possible to translate the number of standard deviations between the mean of the distribution and the specification limit into a defect probability. This is really a matter of applying the statistical calculations of the normal distribution. Table 7.1 shows the defect probabilities and the PPM number for a generic process depending on how many standard deviations fit between the mean and the specification limit.

TABLE 7.1 **The Relationship between the Standard Deviations That Fit between Mean and Specification Limit and the Defect Probability**

Sigma	Capability Index	Probability Too Small	Probability Too Large	Prob(Defect)	PPM
1	0.333333333	0.1586552539	0.1586552539	0.31731050786	317310.5
1.2	0.4	0.1150696702	0.1150696702	0.23013934044	230139.3
1.4	0.466666667	0.0807566592	0.0807566592	0.16151331847	161513.3
1.6	0.533333333	0.0547992917	0.0547992917	0.10959858340	109598.6
1.8	0.6	0.0359303191	0.0359303191	0.07186063823	71860.64
2	0.666666667	0.0227501319	0.0227501319	0.04550026390	45500.26
2.2	0.733333333	0.0139034475	0.0139034475	0.02780689503	27806.9
2.4	0.8	0.0081975359	0.0081975359	0.01639507185	16395.07
2.6	0.866666667	0.0046611880	0.0046611880	0.00932237605	9322.376
2.8	0.933333333	0.0025551303	0.0025551303	0.00511026066	5110.261
3	1	0.0013498980	0.0013498980	0.00269979606	2699.796
3.2	1.066666667	0.0006871379	0.0006871379	0.00137427588	1374.276
3.4	1.133333333	0.0003369293	0.0003369293	0.00067385853	673.8585
3.6	1.2	0.0001591086	0.0001591086	0.00031821718	318.2172
3.8	1.266666667	0.0000723480	0.0000723480	0.00014469609	144.6961
4	1.333333333	0.0000316712	0.0000316712	0.00006334248	63.34248
4.2	1.4	0.0000133457	0.0000133457	0.00002669150	26.6915
4.4	1.466666667	0.0000054125	0.0000054125	0.00001082509	10.82509
4.6	1.533333333	0.0000021125	0.0000021125	0.00000422491	4.224909
4.8	1.6	0.0000007933	0.0000007933	0.00000158666	1.586656
5	1.666666667	0.0000002867	0.0000002867	0.00000057330	0.573303
5.2	1.733333333	0.0000000996	0.0000000996	0.00000019929	0.199289
5.4	1.8	0.0000000333	0.0000000333	0.00000006664	0.066641
5.6	1.866666667	0.0000000107	0.0000000107	0.00000002144	0.021435
5.8	1.933333333	0.0000000033	0.0000000033	0.00000000663	0.006631
6	2	0.0000000010	0.0000000010	0.00000000197	0.001973

A capability index of $C_p = 1$ (i.e., a three-sigma process) is defective with a probability of 0.002699796. It thus is not defective with a probability of 0.997300204. Consequently, it would have 2700 defects per 1,000,000 units (2699.796 to be exact).

Traditionally, quality experts have recommended a minimum process capability index of 1.33. However, many organizations, as part of their **six-sigma program,** now postulate that all efforts should be made to obtain a process capability C_p of 2.0 at every individual step. This is statistically equivalent to requiring that the USL is six standard deviations above the mean and the LSL is six standard deviations below the mean. This explains the name "six-sigma."

A six-sigma process makes a defect with a probability of 0.00000000197, which corresponds to about two defects in a billion units. This number seems almost ridiculously small. Why not settle for less? Why was the previously mentioned quality target of $C_p = 1.33$ corresponding to a defect probability of 0.000063342 not good enough?

This is indeed a tricky question. Let us first point out that the concept of "good enough" is misleading. Every defect is one too many, especially if you recall the third and fourth examples at the beginning of the chapter. Second, one has to understand that processes often consist of many steps, each having the potential of being defective. The Xootr does not only consist of a steer support part, but has many other parts as well. Complex assemblies such as computers, phones, or cars have hundreds of subassemblies and components in them. The final product only functions correctly if all of them work correctly. Consider a product with 200 subassemblies and components, each of them having a probability of 0.01 percent of going defective. Hence, the probability of producing each unit correctly is $1 - 0.0001 = 0.9999$. The probability that the resulting output functions correctly is then given by $0.9999^{200} = 0.980198$, which is a 2 percent defect probability. In other words, in complex systems in which many things have to function correctly, even extremely low defect probabilities at the subassembly or component level can lead to significant amounts of defects.

Setting a Variance Reduction Target

Our previous analysis started out with the empirically observed variation in the process (in the form of the standard deviation estimate, sigma-hat) and we computed the defect probability. We can also do these calculations starting with a desired (targeted) defect probability and then compute the allowable standard deviation in the process. Assume, for example, that Xootr LLC's management would want to tighten the quality standards. Instead of allowing the present defect frequency of 0.003831908 (i.e., 3831.9 ppm), imagine the new goal would be set to 10 ppm. To what level would Xootr LLC have to reduce the standard deviation in the steer support parts so that this goal is met?

We can see from Table 7.1 that obtaining 10 ppm corresponds to a capability score $C_p = 1.4667$. For this, we simply go down the rightmost column in the table until we find the closest ppm number and then look up the capability index in the second-to-the-left column. Using the definition of the capability score, we thus obtain the following equation:

$$C_p = \frac{\text{USL} - \text{LSL}}{6\hat{\sigma}} \Leftrightarrow 1.4667 = \frac{80.000 - 79.900}{6 \times \hat{\sigma}}$$

Though the sigma is in the denominator, this equation is a linear equation in sigma. Rearranging terms, we obtain the *target variation* as

$$\hat{\sigma} = \frac{\text{USL} - \text{LSL}}{6C_p} = \frac{80.000 - 79.900}{6 \times 1.4667} = 0.011364$$

Put differently, if the Xootr engineers are able to reduce the standard deviation they have in the steer support part from its current value of 0.017291 to 0.011364, they will be able to improve their capability score from 0.964 to roughly 1.4667 and reduce their ppm from 3831.9 to 10.

Process Capability Summary and Extensions

In this section on capability analysis, you have learned to use the specification limits of a process alongside its estimated standard deviation and compute the process capability as well as its defect rate. Notice the strong resemblance to the earlier example of the target shooter. You might sample 10 steer support parts and not observe a single defective unit (all measurements fall within the specification limits). Would this make you comfortable in having zero defects in a million parts? To extrapolate to a larger sample, we have to use more information than just the binary classification into defects and good units. Just like we measured the capability of the target shooter by looking at how far his shots are away from the bull's-eye, we look at the variation of the measurements and see how many standard deviations of "wiggle room" we have before we hit the specification limits on either side. We have also seen how one can start with a targeted number of defects and then calculate how much variation is allowed in the process. Clearly, defects and variation go hand-in-hand.

In our analysis, we assumed that the process has an upper specification limit and a lower specification limit, with the mean of the collected data being right in the middle. These assumptions might not always be in line with what you observe in practice:

- In some cases, there exists only one specification limit. Imagine you want to track the call waiting time in a call center and measure to what extent customers are served in a given wait time or sooner. In this case, it would not make sense to call a wait time that is exceptionally short a defect. So, we might set our lower specification limit at zero.
- The mean of the distribution is unlikely to always be in the middle of the tolerance interval. We needed to make this midpoint assumption to generate the data in Table 7.1 and when we searched for the allowable level of sigma. All other calculations did not rely on this assumption. You first compute the probability that the unit is below the lower specification limit, then the probability that the unit is above the upper specification limit, and then add up the two.

7.3 Conformance Analysis

Now that we have measured the capability of the process and understand how much variation exists in the process at a given point in time, we are well positioned to monitor the process on an ongoing basis. Specifically, when we observe variation in the process, we want to decide if that variation is normal, in which case it most likely reflects the common cause variation in the process, or if it is abnormal, indicating the presence of an assignable cause.

Control charts plot data over time in a graph similar to what is shown in Figure 7.7. The *x*-axis of the control chart captures the various time periods at which samples from the process are taken. For the *y*-axis, we plot the mean of each sample. Such control charts are often called $\overline{X}$ charts (pronounced ***X-bar charts***, which captures that ***X-bar*** typically denotes the mean of a sample). $\overline{X}$ charts can be used to document trends over time and to identify unexpected drifts (e.g., resulting from the wear of a tool) or jumps (e.g., resulting from a new person operating a process step), corresponding to assignable causes of variation.

More formally, we define the mean of a sample consisting of *n* units, *X*-bar, as

$$\overline{X} = \frac{x_1 + x_2 + \cdots + x_n}{n}$$

FIGURE 7.7
Example of a Generic Control Chart

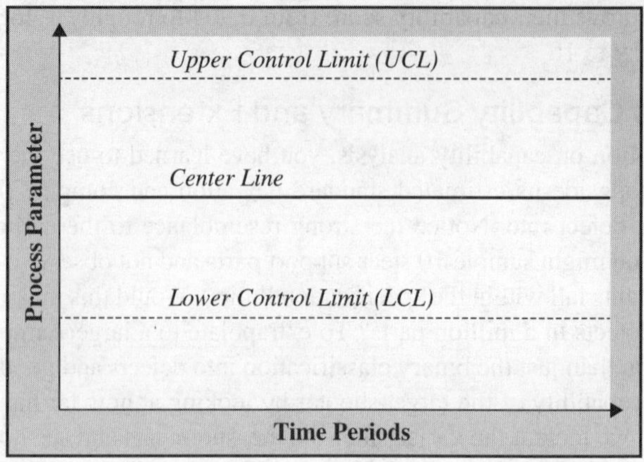

As we are plotting the realizations of $\overline{X}$, we want to know if the sample we obtained was a sample that was in line with past process outcomes. For this, we visually inspect whether the value we enter for a period (say the sample mean for day 11) is above an upper limit, which is also known as the *upper control limit (UCL)* or below a lower limit, which is also known as the *lower control limit (LCL)*.

Consider the data related to the height of the steer support component displayed in Table 7.2 collected by the Xootr engineers in the same way as the data for our capability analysis. The data show five observations for each day over a 25-day period. Based on the preceding definitions of $\overline{X}$, we can compute the mean for each day, which is shown in the last column. For example, for day 14, $\overline{X}$ is computed as

$$\overline{X} = \frac{79.973 + 79.986 + 79.942 + 79.978 + 79.979}{5} = 79.972$$

After computing the mean for every period, we proceed to compute the average across all days. The average $\overline{X}$ across all $\overline{X}$ is called $\overline{\overline{X}}$ (pronounced "***X-double-bar***" or "X-*bar-bar*"), reflecting that it is an average across averages. As we can see at the bottom of Table 7.2, we have

$$\overline{\overline{X}} = 79.951$$

In creating the $\overline{X}$ chart, we use the computed value of $\overline{\overline{X}}$ as a center line and plot the values of $\overline{X}$ for each day in the sample.

Once we have the *x*-axis (time periods), the *y*-axis (the mean), the samples for each period, and the center line, the last information missing is the control limits. Recall the idea behind the control limits. We would like to infer from a sample mean *X*-bar that lies above the upper control limit or below the lower control limit that the sample was abnormal. Now, any inference that we make with statistical data is subject to noise and so we can only make such a statement with a limited amount of statistical confidence. The data that we sample from the process are noisy and the estimates for *X*-bar are at best right, on average.

We estimate the standard deviation for the entire sample by using Excel's STDEV.S procedure. So, we compute the *estimated standard deviation of all parts* as

$$\text{Standard deviation for all parts} = \text{STDEV.S}(\text{Day1}_{\text{Part1}}, \ldots, \text{Day1}_{\text{Part}n}, \ldots, \text{Day}m_{\text{Part1}}, \ldots, \text{Day}m_{\text{Part}n})$$

In the above example, the estimated standard deviation for all parts is

$$\text{Standard deviation for all parts} = 0.017846388$$

TABLE 7.2
Measurements of the Steer Support Dimension in Groups of Five Observations

Period	x_1	x_2	x_3	x_4	x_5	Mean
1	79.941	79.961	79.987	79.940	79.956	79.957
2	79.953	79.942	79.962	79.956	79.944	79.951
3	79.926	79.986	79.958	79.964	79.950	79.957
4	79.960	79.970	79.945	79.967	79.967	79.962
5	79.947	79.933	79.932	79.963	79.954	79.946
6	79.950	79.955	79.967	79.928	79.963	79.953
7	79.971	79.960	79.941	79.962	79.918	79.950
8	79.970	79.952	79.946	79.928	79.970	79.953
9	79.960	79.957	79.944	79.945	79.948	79.951
10	79.936	79.945	79.961	79.958	79.947	79.949
11	79.911	79.954	79.968	79.947	79.918	79.940
12	79.950	79.955	79.992	79.964	79.940	79.960
13	79.952	79.945	79.955	79.945	79.952	79.950
14	79.973	79.986	79.942	79.978	79.979	79.972
15	79.931	79.962	79.935	79.953	79.937	79.944
16	79.966	79.943	79.919	79.958	79.923	79.942
17	79.960	79.941	80.003	79.951	79.956	79.962
18	79.954	79.958	79.992	79.935	79.953	79.959
19	79.910	79.950	79.947	79.915	79.994	79.943
20	79.948	79.946	79.943	79.935	79.920	79.939
21	79.917	79.949	79.957	79.971	79.968	79.952
22	79.973	79.959	79.971	79.947	79.949	79.960
23	79.920	79.961	79.937	79.935	79.934	79.937
24	79.937	79.934	79.931	79.934	79.964	79.940
25	79.945	79.954	79.957	79.935	79.961	79.950
					Average	79.951

Each day, we collect a sample and so when we estimate the sample mean, *X*-bar, we have to acknowledge that it is noisy. Moreover, we know that it gets less noisy the bigger our daily sample size. For a given sample of measurements, we know that the *estimated standard deviation for* **X**-*bar* (the estimated standard deviation of that sample mean) can be estimated by

$$\text{Estimated standard deviation}(X\text{-bar}) = \frac{\text{Standard deviation of all parts}}{\sqrt{n}}$$

For the Xootr case, we compute the estimated standard deviation (ESD):

$$\text{Estimated standard deviation(X-bar)} = \frac{\text{Standard deviation of all parts}}{\sqrt{n}}$$

$$= \frac{0.017846388}{\sqrt{5}} = 0.007981147$$

We call the process out of control if the sample is three standard deviations above or below the long-term mean. This leads to the following control limit calculations:

1. Compute the upper control limit for $\overline{X}$ as

   $$\text{UCL} = \overline{\overline{X}} + [3 \times \text{ESD(X-bar)}] = 79.951 + (3 \times 0.007981147) = 79.9749$$

2. Compute the lower control limit for $\overline{X}$ as

   $$\text{LCL} = \overline{\overline{X}} - [3 \times \text{ESD(X-bar)}] = 79.951 - (3 \times 0.007981147) = 79.9271$$

A process that is behaving in line with historical data will have the estimated sample mean fall between the LCL and the UCL in 99.7 percent of the cases. This is the same logic that was underlying our capability calculations and the derivation of the probability that an outcome would hit the specification limits, which are three standard deviations above the mean.

The control charts obtained this way allow for a visual assessment of the variation of the process. The definition of control limits implies that 99.7 percent of the sample points are expected to fall between the upper and lower control limits. Thus, if any point falls outside the control limits, we can claim with a 99.7 percent confidence level that the process has gone "out of control"—that is, that an assignable cause has occurred.

In addition to inspecting if sample means are outside the three-sigma confidence interval (i.e., below the LCL or above the UCL), we can look for other patterns in the control chart that are statistically unlikely to occur. For example, we can look for a sequence of sample means that are above or below the center line. For example, it is unlikely that we will see a sequence of eight subsequent points above (or below) the center line. Because each point has an equal probability of being above or below the center line, we can compute the likelihood of eight points to the same side simply as $(0.5)^8 = 0.004$, which corresponds to a very unlikely event. Thus, we can also treat such a pattern as a warning sign justifying further investigation.

Figure 7.8 shows the control charts for the Xootr. We observe that the production process for the steer support is well in control. There seems to be an inherent randomness in the exact size of the component. Yet, there is no systemic pattern, such as a drift or a sudden jump outside the control limits. The process behaves in line with its historical variation—it is in control.

Note that the fact that the process is in control does not rule out that we produce defects. In fact, it is important to not confuse the concepts of control limits and specification limits:

- The control limits measure to what extent the process is behaving the same way it did in the past.
- The specification limits measure to what extent the process meets the specifications of the customer.

So it is possible that the outcome of the process is within the control limits but outside the specification limits. In this case, the process capability is low and defects occur regularly as a result of common cause variation. Vice versa, it is possible that the outcome is outside the control limits but within the specification limits. A very high capability process has very tight control limits. Even a very small assignable cause variation would make the process outcome jump outside the control limits; nevertheless, that corresponding unit does not necessarily have to be a defect, especially not if the specification interval is relatively wide.

FIGURE 7.8
The *X*-bar Chart for the Steer Support Part

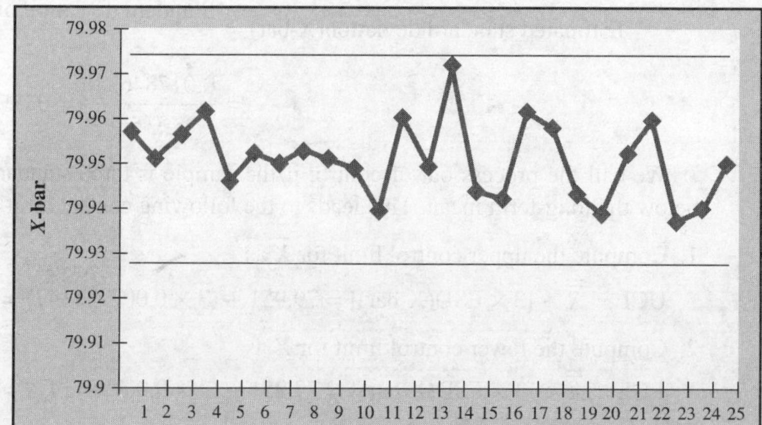

7.4 Investigating Assignable Causes

Earlier on in this chapter, we discussed how the outcome of a process and thus its occurrence of defects are driven by a set of input variables and environmental variables (see Figure 7.1). By definition, we know that a defect occurrence reflects some abnormal variation in the outcome variable. And such abnormal variation in the outcome variable must be the result of some abnormal variation in input variables or in environmental variables. So once our control chart has alerted us that some assignable cause variation has occurred in the outcome variable, it is our job to look for what input or environmental variables led to this result. We investigate the root cause for the abnormal variation.

The first step in our exploration of root causes is to create a more careful diagram illustrating the relationship between the outcome variable and the various input and environmental variables. An example of such a diagram is shown in Figure 7.9. Such diagrams—also known as *fishbone diagrams* (reflecting their resemblance to fish bones), *cause–effect diagrams,* or *Ishikawa diagrams* (in honor of Kaoru Ishikawa, a Japanese quality scholar)—graphically represent the input and environmental variables that are causally related to a specific outcome, such as an increase in variation or a shift in the mean.

When drawing a fishbone diagram, we typically start with a horizontal arrow that points at the name of the outcome variable we want to analyze. Diagonal lines than lead to this arrow representing main causes. Smaller arrows then lead to these causality lines creating a fishbone-like shape. Diagonal lines can capture both input variables and environmental variables. Ishikawa diagrams are simple yet powerful problem-solving tools that can be used to structure brainstorming sessions and to visualize the causal structure of a complex system.

A related tool that also helps in developing causal models is known as the "*Five Whys*." The tool is prominently used in Toyota's organization when workers search for the root cause of a quality problem. The basic idea of the "Five Whys" is to continually question ("Why did this happen?") whether a potential cause is truly the root cause or is merely a symptom of a deeper problem. Consider the example of a student arriving late to class. A quick analysis might ask, "Why did the student come late?" and in response learn that the student wanted to grab a coffee. Argued this way, "grabbing coffee" appears as the root cause for the lateness. However, the "Five Whys" framework digs deeper:

- Why did it take the student so long to grab coffee? Because the coffee shop is far from the classrooms.
- Why does the student go to the coffee shop far away from the classrooms instead of going to the one in the building? Because there the coffee is better and cheaper.

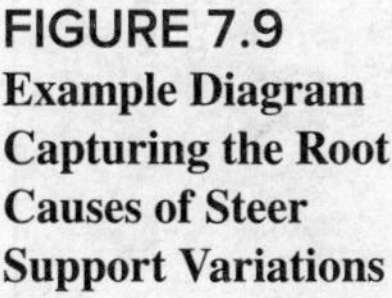

FIGURE 7.9
Example Diagram Capturing the Root Causes of Steer Support Variations

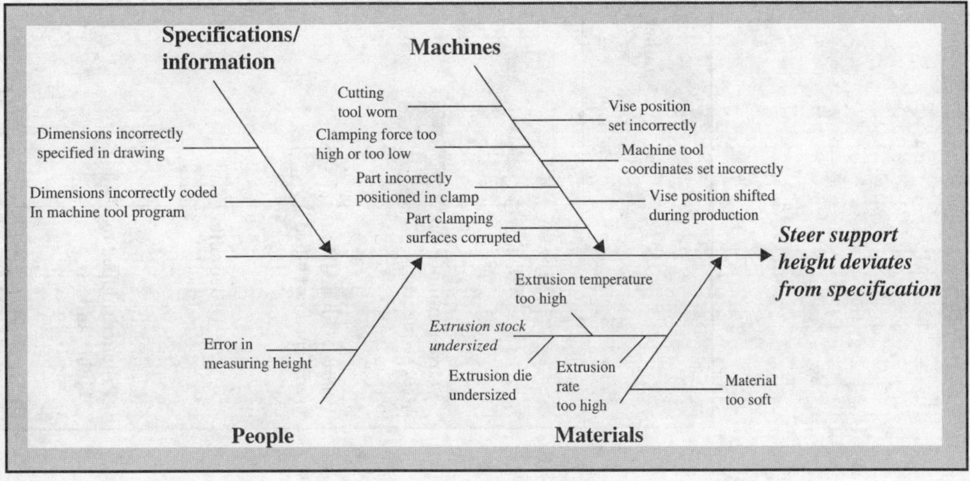

- Why is the coffee shop in the building offering bad coffee at high prices? Because they have a local monopoly and don't really respond to customer needs.
- Why does the coffee shop in the building have a local monopoly? Because the university decided to sell the rights to coffee sales to a third party.

Notice what happened as we asked "Why?" five times. First, we really get to the underlying root causes as opposed to just dealing with the symptoms of the problem. Second, observe how the responsible party for the problem has shifted from the student (who wanted coffee) to the university (that sold the rights to sell coffee to a third party).

Given the multiple potential root causes of a defect, it is frequently desirable to find which of these root causes accounts for the majority of the problems. The *Pareto diagram* is a graphical way to identify the most important causes of process defects. To create a Pareto diagram, we need to collect data on the number of defect occurrences as well as the associated defect types. We can then plot simple bars with heights indicating the relative occurrences of the defect types. It is also common to plot the cumulative contribution of the defect types. An example of a Pareto diagram is shown in Figure 7.10. The figure categorizes defects related to customer orders at Xootr LLC.

The Pareto principle was postulated by J. M. Juran. Juran observed that managers spent too much time trying to fix "small" problems, while not paying enough attention to "big" problems. The Pareto principle, also referred to as the 80–20 rule, postulates that

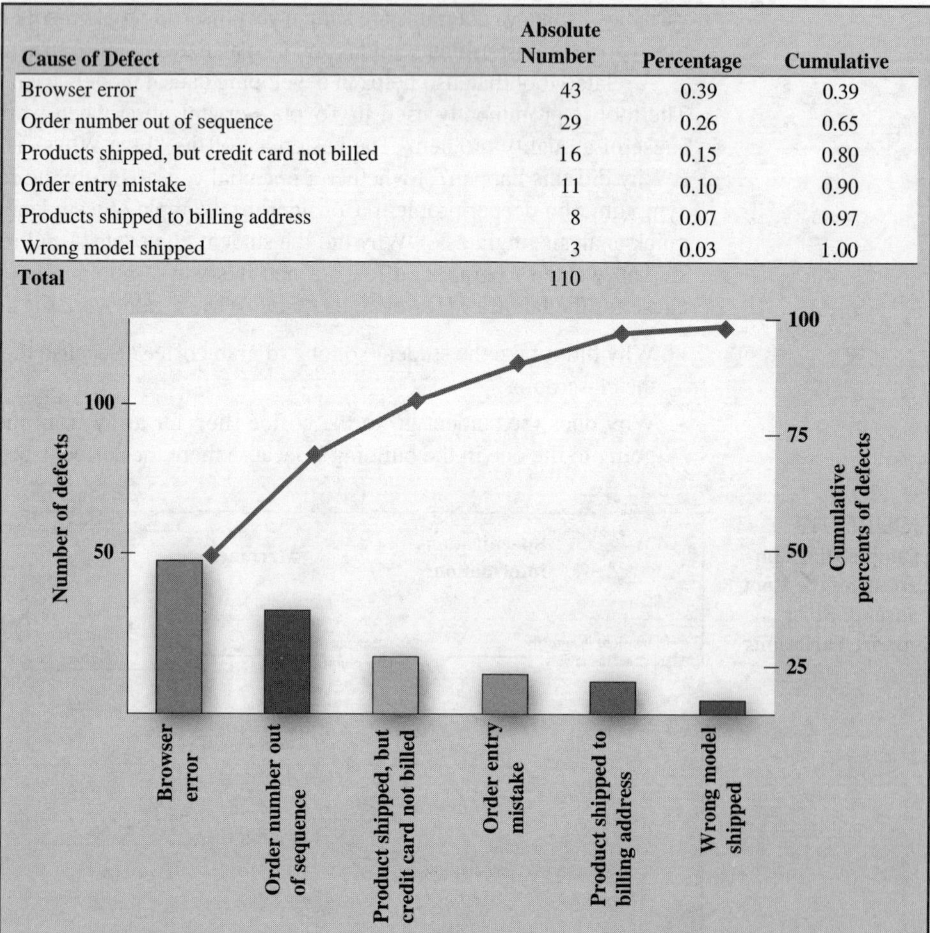

Cause of Defect	Absolute Number	Percentage	Cumulative
Browser error	43	0.39	0.39
Order number out of sequence	29	0.26	0.65
Products shipped, but credit card not billed	16	0.15	0.80
Order entry mistake	11	0.10	0.90
Products shipped to billing address	8	0.07	0.97
Wrong model shipped	3	0.03	1.00
Total	110		

FIGURE 7.10 Root Causes for Various Defects in Order Handling at Xootr

20 percent of the causes account for 80 percent of the problems. In the context of quality, the Pareto principle implies that a few defect types account for the majority of defects.

7.5 Defects with Binary Outcomes: *p*-Charts

When constructing an *X*-bar chart, we are able to measure an outcome variable on a single dimension and then use the interval between the lower control limit and the upper control limit to determine if a unit is defective or not. Now that we are dealing with discrete outcomes, this no longer works. All we can do is to distinguish defective and nondefective flow units.

So, when we now take a sample of units from the process, the only information we have on each unit is whether it is classified as a good unit or as a defective unit. We can then compute the percentage of flow units in the sample that are defective. And, similar to what we did with the *X*-bar charts, we can then track this percentage over time. This is the idea behind creating a **p-*chart*,** also known as an *attribute-based control chart*.

Sample sizes for *p*-charts tend to be larger, typically ranging from 50 to 200 for each period. Larger sample sizes are needed in particular if defects are relatively rare events. If you have a 1 percent defect probability, chances are that you would not find any defects with a sample size as low as 5 or 10. Samples are collected in each period, just as in the case of *X*-bar control charts. Within each sample, we evaluate the percentage of defective items. Let p denote this percentage (that's why we call them *p*-charts). We then compute the average percentage of defects over all samples, which we call $\overline{p}$. This "average across averages" is the center line in our attribute control chart, just as we used *X*-double-bar as the center line for variable control charts.

To compute the control limits, we first need to obtain an estimate of the standard deviation of defects. This estimate is given by the following equation:

$$\text{Estimated standard deviation} = \sqrt{\frac{\overline{p}\,(1 - \overline{p})}{\text{Sample size}}}$$

We then compute the upper and lower control limits:

$$\text{UCL} = \overline{p} + (3 \times \text{Estimated standard deviation})$$

$$\text{LCL} = \overline{p} - (3 \times \text{Estimated standard deviation})$$

Thus, we again set control limits such that the process is allowed to vary three standard deviations in each direction from the mean. Note that in the case when the lower control limit determined earlier is negative, we use the 0 line as the LCL.

Once we have created the center line and the lower and upper control limits, we use the *p*-chart in exactly the same way we use the *X*-bar chart. Every time period, we plot the percentage of defective items in the *p*-chart. If that percentage goes above the upper control limit, we expect some (negative) assignable cause to be at work. If that percentage goes below the lower control limit, we expect some (positive) assignable cause variation to be at work (after all, the percentage of defects in this case has gone down).

7.6 Impact of Yields and Defects on Process Flow

Defects, as described in previous sections, have a profound impact on the process flow. In this section, we discuss processes consisting of a sequence of process steps, of which at least one step suffers from detectable quality problems. In other words, there exists at least one step at which units are separated into "good units" and "defective units." Whereas good items can continue processing at the next operation, defective units either have to be *reworked* or are *eliminated from the process* (known as scrapped in the manufacturing context).

- In the case of the Xootr, the company scraps all steer support parts that do not meet the specifications as discussed previously.
- In contrast, Xootr LLC reworks Xootrs that require adjustments in the brake assembly. These Xootrs are rerouted to a separate operator in charge of rework. This (highly skilled) operator disassembles the brake (typically scrapping the brake cable) and adjusts the brake as needed, thereby creating a sellable Xootr.

The following examples help illustrate that the ideas of rework and flow unit elimination are by no means restricted to manufacturing:

- Following heart surgery, patients typically spend time recovering in the intensive care unit. While most patients can then be moved to a regular unit (and ultimately be sent home), some patients are readmitted to the intensive care unit in case of complications. From the perspective of the ICU, patients who have been discharged to regular units but then are readmitted to the ICU constitute rework.
- The recruitment process of large firms, most prominently the one of consulting companies, also exhibits a large percentage of flow units that are eliminated before the end of the process. For every offer made, consulting firms process hundreds of resumés and interview dozens of job candidates (possibly staged in several rounds). Typically, job candidates are eliminated from the applicant pool—rework (a job candidate asked to repeat her first-round interviews) is very rare.
- Pharmaceutical development analyzes thousands of chemical compounds for every new drug that enters the market. The initial set of compounds is reduced through a series of tests, many of which are very costly. After a test, some units are allowed to proceed to the next phase, while others are eliminated from the set of potential compounds for the clinical indication the company is looking for.

We define the *yield* of a resource as

$$\text{Yield of resource} = \frac{\text{Flow rate of units processed successfully at the resource}}{\text{Flow rate}}$$

$$= 1 - \frac{\text{Flow rate of defects at the resource}}{\text{Flow rate}}$$

Thus, the yield of a resource measures the percentage of good units that are processed at this resource. Similarly, we can define yields at the level of the overall process:

$$\text{Process yield} = \frac{\text{Flow rate of units processed successfully}}{\text{Flow rate}} = 1 - \frac{\text{Flow rate of defects}}{\text{Flow rate}}$$

Obviously, the words *defects* and *rework* sound harsh in some of the examples described above, especially if we are dealing with human flow units. However, the following concepts and calculations apply equally well for disk drives that have to be reworked because they did not meet the specifications of final tests and patients that have to be readmitted to intensive care because they did not recover as quickly as required to safely stay in a regular hospital unit.

It also should be pointed out that a defect does not always reflect the failure of a process step, but can reflect inherent randomness (common cause variation) in the process or differences with respect to the flow units at the beginning of the process. For example, dismissing a chemical compound as a potential cure for a given disease does not imply that previous development steps did not do their job correctly. Instead, the development steps have simply revealed a (previously unknown) undesirable property of the chemical compound. Similarly, it lies in the nature of a recruiting process that its yield (percentage of applications resulting in a job) is well below 100 percent.

Rework

Rework means that some steps prior to the detection of the problem must be redone, or some additional process steps are required to transform a defective unit into a good unit. Two examples of rework are shown in Figure 7.11 (inventory locations are left out for simplicity).

In the upper part of the figure, defective units are taken out of the regular process and moved to a separate rework operation. This is common in many production processes such as in the Xootr example discussed above. If the rework step is always able to turn a defective unit into a good unit, the process yield would return to 100 percent. In the lower part of the figure, defective units are reworked by the same resource that previously processed the unit. The readmission of a patient to the intensive care unit corresponds to such a case.

Rework changes the utilization profile of the process. Compared to the case of no defects, rework means that a resource has additional work flowing to it, which in turn increases utilization. As a consequence, rework can potentially change the location of the bottleneck.

Thus, when analyzing the influence of yields (and rework) on process capacity, we need to distinguish between bottleneck and nonbottleneck resources. If rework involves only nonbottleneck machines with a large amount of idle time, it has a negligible effect on the overall process capacity (note that it will still have cost implications, reflecting costs of material and extra labor at the rework step).

In many cases, however, rework is severe enough to make a resource a bottleneck (or, even worse, rework needs to be carried out on the bottleneck). As the capacity of the bottleneck equals the capacity of the overall process, all capacity invested in rework at the bottleneck is lost from the perspective of the overall process.

Eliminating Flow Units from the Process

In many cases, it is not possible or not economical to rework a flow unit and thereby transform a defective unit into a good unit. Once the Xootr machine has produced a defective steer support unit, it is almost impossible to rework this unit into a nondefective unit. Instead, despite an approximate material cost of $12 for the unit, the company scraps the unit and produces a replacement for it.

FIGURE 7.11
Two Processes with Rework

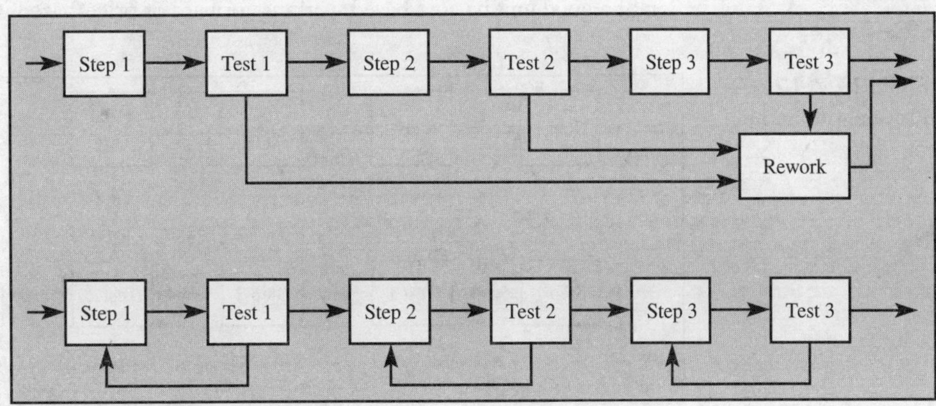

Similarly, a consulting firm searching for a new hire will prefer to simply reject the application, instead of investing in training to improve the job candidate's skills. If defective units are eliminated from the process, final output of good units is correspondingly reduced.

Strictly speaking, eliminating flow units from the process is a special form of rework, where all operations between the step where the defective unit leaves the process and the beginning of the process have to be reworked. Given that all operations up to the point of defect detection have to be reworked, the earlier we can detect and eliminate the corresponding flow unit, the less we waste capacity. This wasted capacity reflects that more units need to be started in the process than are finished. For example, to get 100 good units at the end of the process, we have to start with

$$\text{Number of units started to get 100 good units} = 100/\text{Process yield}$$

at the beginning of the process.

Two examples of processes in which defective units are eliminated are shown in Figure 7.12. In the upper part of the figure, defects are only detected at the end, and thereby have wasted capacity of every resource in the process. In the lower part of the figure, a test is conducted after every process step, which allows for the early elimination of defective parts, leading to less wasted capacity.

In a process in which defective units are eliminated, we can write the process yield as

$$\text{Process yield} = y_1 \times y_2 \times \cdots \times y_m$$

where m is the number of resources in the sequence and y_i is the yield of the ith resource.

Cost Economics and Location of Test Points

In addition to their effect on capacity, yields determine the value that a good unit has at various stages in the process. What is the value of a good unit in the process? The answer to this question will differ depending on whether we are capacity constrained or whether we are constrained by demand.

Consider the demand-constrained case first. At the beginning of the process, the value of a good item equals its input cost (the cost of raw material in the case of production). The value of a good unit increases as it moves through the process, even if no additional material is being added. Again, let y_n be the yield at the nth stage. The value leaving resource n is approximately $1/y_n$ times the sum of the value entering stage n plus any variable costs we incur at stage n.

The capacity-constrained case is fundamentally different. At the end of the process, the marginal extra revenue of the unit determines the value of a good unit. Yet, at the beginning of the process, the value of a good unit still equals its input costs. So should the valuation of a good unit be cost-based working forward or price-based working backwards? The

FIGURE 7.12
Process with Scrap

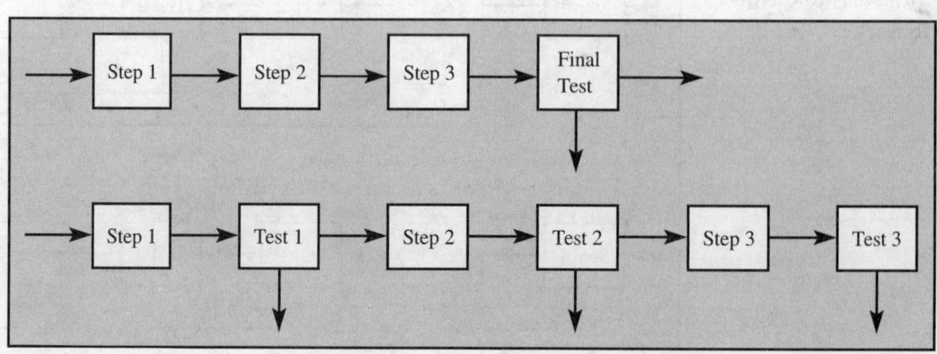

discontinuity between these two approaches comes at the bottleneck operation. After the bottleneck, value is based on selling price; before the bottleneck, it is based on cost.

For example, assume that Xootr LLC is currently demand-constrained and we want to value a flow unit as it moves through the process. We should do this using a cost-based calculation, as—independent of a defect in this flow unit—we will achieve the same sales rate (i.e., we fulfill demand). In contrast, if Xootr LLC is capacity-constrained, we have to factor in the marginal extra revenue for those flow units that have already passed the bottleneck.

As a consequence of this, the costs that arise with detecting a defect dramatically increase as a flow unit moves through the process to market. Consider the case of a nonreworkable defect occurring at a prebottleneck resource, as depicted in Figure 7.13. If the defect is detected before the bottleneck, the costs of this defect are simply the costs of the materials that went into the unit up to the detection of the defect. However, if the defect is detected after the bottleneck and the process is currently capacity-constrained, the unit is almost as valuable as a complete unit. In the extreme case, if the defect is detected on the market, we are likely to incur major costs related to warranty, field repair, liability, and so forth. For this reason, in a capacity-constrained process, it is essential to have an inspection step prior to the bottleneck.

At a more conceptual level, Figure 7.13 relates to an idea referred to as *quality at the source,* an element of the Toyota Production System emphasizing that defects should be detected right when and where they occur, as opposed to being detected in a remote final inspection step. In addition to the cost benefits discussed above, another advantage of quality at the source is that the correction of the root cause that led to the defect is typically much easier to identify at the place and time when the defect is made. While a worker in charge of a process step that leads to a defect is likely to remember the context of the defect, figuring out what went wrong with a unit at a final inspection step is typically much harder.

Defects and Variability

Quality losses and yield-related problems not only change the capacity profile of a process, but they also cause variability. A yield of 90 percent means not that every tenth flow unit is defective, but that there is a 10 percent probability of a defect occurring. Thus, yield losses increase variability, which reduces capacity.

Consider again the process flow diagram in the lower part of Figure 7.11, that is, a process where defective units are immediately reworked by repeating the operation. Even if the actual activity time is deterministic, yield losses force items into multiple visits at the same resource, and thus make the effective activity time for a *good* item a random variable.

Capacity losses due to variability can be partially compensated by allowing inventory after each operation with yields below 100 percent. The larger these buffers, the more the capacity-reducing impact of variability is reduced. However, additional inventory increases costs and flow times; it also can hurt the detection and solution of quality problems.

FIGURE 7.13
Cost of a Defect as a Function of Its Detection Location, Assuming a Capacity-Constrained Process

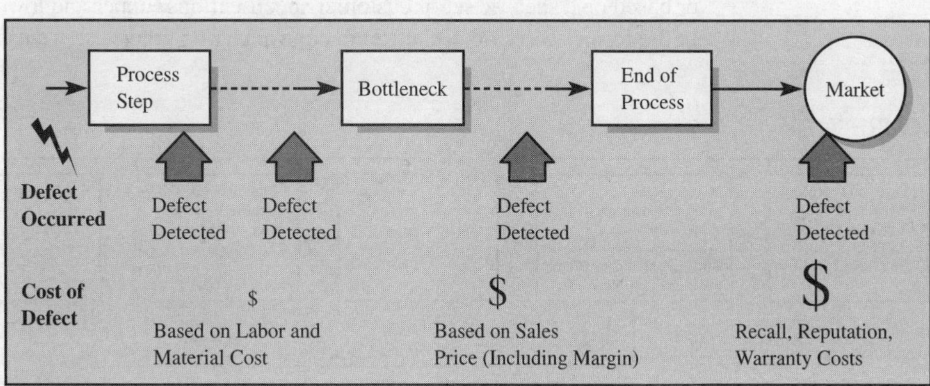

7.7 A Process for Improvement

The strength of the statistical process control techniques discussed in this chapter results from their combination of collecting actual data with using professional analysis techniques.

The importance of data collection cannot be overemphasized. In many industries, collecting data about process performance is the exception rather than the norm. Once you have collected data, process improvement meetings turn fact-based and objective as opposed to being largely subjective. While most manufacturing facilities by now routinely collect data about their processes, most service processes are lagging behind. Only in the last couple of years have service providers in banking or health care started to systematically track process data. This is somewhat surprising given that services are often blessed with loads of data because of their electronic workflow management systems.

But a successful process improvement project needs more than data. It is important to statistically analyze data. Otherwise, every small, random change in the process (including common cause variation) is interpreted as meaningful and acted upon. The tools outlined above help to separate the important from the unimportant.

In addition to statistical tools, it is also essential to have a clear action plan on how to organize a project aiming at process improvement. A well-executed process improvement project tends to go through the following steps:

- You sense a problem and explore it broadly.
- You formulate a specific problem to work on/state a specific improvement theme.
- You collect data and analyze the situation.
- You find the root causes.
- You plan a solution and implement it.
- You evaluate the effects of the solution.
- You standardize the process to include the new solution if it is good.
- Then you take on the next problem.

Figure 7.14 summarizes the tools introduced in this chapter by outlining a systematic process to achieve quality improvement.

The focus of the improvement project is guided by where defects are most costly and hence improvements have the biggest economic impact. Typically, this involves the bottleneck resource. We then collect data and analyze it, determining process capabilities and exact yields. This helps us understand the impact of defects on the process flow and ultimately on the economics of the process.

We have a choice between thinking of defects in a binary way (defect versus no defect) or based on a specific set of customer specifications (upper and lower specification limits). In the former case, we use attribute control charts; otherwise we use regular control charts

FIGURE 7.14

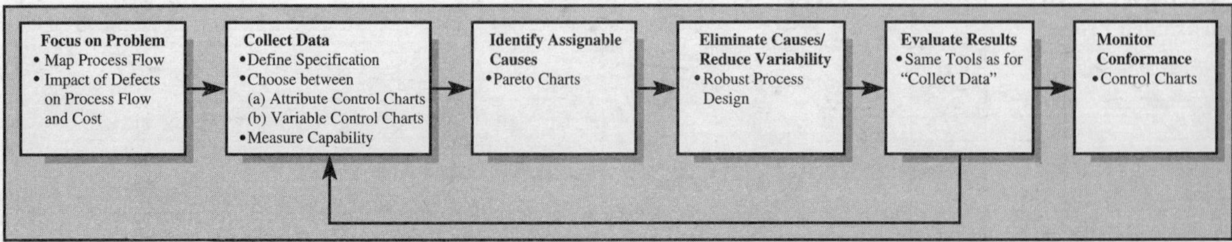

as introduced previously in this chapter. This analysis lets us determine our current process capability. By classifying the defects and assigning them to causes (Pareto analysis), we also can find out the most significant root causes.

We then either eliminate these root causes or, using the robust process design logic, attempt to minimize their sensitivity to variation in process parameters. The resulting improved process is monitored and analyzed in the same way as previously, which either confirms or disconfirms the usefulness of our action. This is an iterative process, reflecting that there are multiple (potentially interacting) causes and a potentially limited understanding of the process.

Finally, control charts help with respect to standardizing a solution and in determining the degree of conformance with the new process design. They will also alert us of an emergence of any new assignable causes.

7.8 Further Reading

Wadsworth, Stephens, and Godfrey (1986) provide an excellent overview of various control charting methods. Their book also includes several examples of implementation. Breyfogle (1999) provides a detailed overview of many tools and definitions underlying six sigma. Interested readers also should look at the initial Motorola document about six sigma, which is summarized in Motorola (1987).

Six-sigma training is often done using a catapult to help illustrate that it often is better to consistently hit a spot that is slightly off target as opposed to occasionally hitting the target, yet hit a wide range of different points as well. See www.xpult.com for more details on six sigma and catapults.

More details on quality can be found in the earlier work by Juran (1951) or the more recent work Juran (1989).

Bohn and Terwiesch (1999) provide a framework for analyzing the economics of yield-driven processes, which we used as the foundation for the discussion of rework and scrap.

Ulrich and Eppinger (2011) is an excellent source for more details about robust process design and the design of experiments to improve products and processes.

Finally, the small booklet "Memory Jogger" is a highly effective manual for the quality improvement tools discussed in this chapter and beyond.

7.9 Practice Problems

The following questions will help in testing your understanding of this chapter. After each question, we show the relevant section in parentheses [Section x].

Q7.1 **(Pizza)** In the production of pizza, which of the following four variables is not an input variable? [7.1]

a. The amount of dough prepared for the pizza
b. The temperature of the oven
c. The type of cheese on the pizza
d. The time that the customer leaves the pizza in the refrigerator

Q7.2 **(MakeStuff)** John is a newly minted quality engineer at MakeStuff Inc. His boss, intending to promote higher quality in the company, tells him to increase the process capability index of their main product. John decides to simply increase the upper specification limit and reduce the lower specification limit.

Choose the correct sentence [7.2]:

A. The process capability index does not increase, because the variation in the process is unchanged.
B. The process capability index does not increase, because the process capability index would only change if the control limits were changed.
C. The process capability index does increase, though one might question if the underlying process is really better.

D. The process capability index does increase, which is why the process quality is reduced.

E. More data is needed to answer the question.

Q7.3 **(Precision Machining)** For a key joint, a precision machining process has a lower specification limit of a width of 0.99 mm and an upper specification limit of 1.01 mm. The standard deviation is 0.005 mm and the mean is 1 mm.

a. What is the process capability index for the bottle filling process? [7.2]

b. The company now wants to reduce its defect probability and operate a "six sigma process." To what level would they have to reduce the standard deviation in the process to meet this target? [7.2]

Q7.4 **(Vetro Inc)** Vetro Inc. is a glass manufacturer that produces glasses of every shape and type. Recently it signed a contract to supply round glasses to Switch, a Swiss watch manufacturer. The specifications require the diameter to be between 4.96 cm and 5.04 cm. With the current production process, Vetro Inc. manages to produce glasses whose diameter is, on average, equal to 5 cm; however, a closer inspection reveals some variability in the process, with the diameter of the glass being normally distributed with standard deviation equal to 0.01cm.

1. What is the capability index (score) of Vetro Inc.? [7.2]
2. What is the maximum standard deviation allowed for the process to meet the rigorous six-sigma standards? [7.2]

Q7.5 **(CycloCross)** A company making tires for bikes is concerned about the exact width of their cyclocross tires. The company has a lower specification limit of 22.8 mm and an upper specification limit of 23.2 mm. The standard deviation is 0.25 mm and the mean is 23 mm.

a. What is the process capability index for the process? [7.2]

b. The company now wants to reduce its defect probability and run a "six-sigma process." To what level would they have to reduce the standard deviation in the process to meet this target? [7.2]

Q7.6 **(Quality check)** Once the raw materials are collected, a single flow unit manufacturing process comprises three sequential steps:

- Step 1 consumes large amounts of an expensive paint
- Step 2 is the bottleneck
- Step 3 has a large amount of idle time

There exists a 20 percent chance at each step to produce a defect, and raw materials have a 20 percent chance to have a defect. However, defects are not immediately observable. A defect reduces the value of the final product to zero; that is, a product with just one defect has no value and must be discarded. Consider the following statements.

The process presently is capacity constrained. Which of the following statements best captures good advice on where to locate a single inspection point? [7.6]

A. The only inspection point should be before step 1.

B. If the focus is on cost savings of the expensive paint, the inspection should occur before step 1. If the focus is on flow rate, the inspection point should be before step 2.

C. If the focus is on cost savings of the expensive paint, the inspection should occur before step 2. If the focus is on flow rate, the inspection point should be before step 3.

D. The only inspection point should be before step 3.

If you would like to test your understanding of a specific section, here are the questions organized by section:

Section 7.1: Q7.1

Section 7.2: Q7.2, Q7.3a, Q7.3b, Q7.4a, Q7.4b, Q7.5a, Q7.5b

Section 7.6: Q7.6

Chapter 

Lean Operations and the Toyota Production System

Toyota is frequently associated with high quality as well as overall operational excellence, and, as we will discuss in this chapter, there are good reasons for this association—Toyota has enjoyed decades of economic success while changing the history of operations management.

- Various elements of the company's famous Toyota Production System (TPS) are covered throughout this book, but in this chapter we will review and summarize the components of TPS, as well as a few that have not been discussed in earlier chapters.
- We also will illustrate how the various elements of TPS are intertwined, thereby making it difficult to adapt some elements while not adapting others.

As we will discuss, one of the key objectives of TPS is the elimination of "waste" from processes such as idle time, unnecessary inventory, defects, and so forth. As a result, people often refer to (parts of) TPS as "lean operations." The expression "lean operations" has been especially popular in service industries.

8.1 The History of Toyota

To appreciate the elegance and success of the Toyota Production System, it is helpful to go back in time and compare the history of the Toyota Motor Company with the history of the Ford Motor Corporation.

Inspired by moving conveyor belts at slaughterhouses, Henry Ford pioneered the use of the assembly line in automobile production. The well-known Model T was the first mass-produced vehicle that was put together on an assembly line using interchangeable parts. Working with interchangeable parts allowed Ford to standardize assembly tasks, which had two important benefits. First, it dramatically reduced variability, and thereby increased quality. Second, it streamlined the production process, thereby making both manual and automated assembly tasks faster.

With the luxury of hindsight, it is fair to say that Ford's focus was on running his automotive production process with the goal of utilizing his expensive production equipment as much as possible, thereby allowing him to crunch out the maximum number of vehicles. Ford soon reached an unmatched production scale—in the early days of the Model T, 9 out of 10 automotive vehicles in the world were produced by Ford! Benefiting from his scale economies, Ford drove the price of a Model T down, which made it affordable to the American middle class, an enormous market that was well suited to be served by mass production.

The Toyota Motor Corporation grew out of Toyota Industries, a manufacturer of automated looms, just prior to World War II. Toyota supported the Japanese army by supplying it with military trucks. Given the shortages of most supplies in Japan at that time, Toyota trucks were equipped with only one headlight and had an extremely simplistic design. As we will see, both the heritage as a loom maker as well as the simplicity of its first vehicle product had consequences for the future development of Toyota.

Following the war, shortages in Japan were even more severe. There existed virtually no domestic market for vehicles and little cash for the acquisition of expensive production equipment. The United States had an active role in the recovery process of Japan and so it is not surprising that the American production system had a strong influence on the young automaker. Toyota's early vehicles were in part produced using secondhand U.S. equipment and also otherwise had significant resemblances with the U.S. brands of Dodge and Chevrolet.

As inspiring as the Western industrial engineering must have been to Toyota, replicating it was out of the question. Mass production, with its emphasis on scale economies and large investments in machinery, did not fit Toyota's environment of a small domestic market and little cash.

Out of this challenging environment of scarcity, Toyota's management created the various elements of a system that we now refer to as the Toyota Production System (TPS). TPS was not invented overnight—it is the outcome of a long evolution that made Toyota the most successful automaker in the world and the gold standard for operations management.

But enough about Toyota—this chapter is not about Toyota, but it is about TPS. Many other industries are implementing TPS, with examples ranging from health care to banking. You can use TPS in your organization, whether you work for Toyota or for the German government. And, even Toyota does not always follow TPS. Thus, the power of TPS does not depend on Toyota's position in the ranking of the world's top automakers.

8.2 TPS Framework

While TPS is frequently associated with certain buzzwords such as JIT, kanban, and kaizen, one should not assume that simply implementing any of these concepts would lead to the level of operational excellence at Toyota. TPS is not a set of off-the-shelf solutions for various operational problems, but instead a complex configuration of various routines ranging from human resource management to the management of production processes.

Figure 8.1 summarizes the architecture of TPS. At the top, we have the principle of waste reduction. Below, we have a set of methods that help support the goal of waste reduction. These methods can be grouped into JIT methods (JIT stands for just-in-time) and quality improvement methods. There exist strong interdependencies among the various methods. We will discuss some of these interdependencies throughout this chapter, especially the interaction between JIT and quality.

Collectively, these methods help the organization to attack the various sources of waste that we will define in the next section. Among them are overproduction, waiting, transport, overprocessing, and inventory, all of which reflect a mismatch between supply and demand. So the first set of methods that we will discuss (Section 8.4) relate to synchronizing the production flow with demand. Output should be produced exactly when the customer wants it and in the quantity demanded. In other words, it should be produced just in time.

FIGURE 8.1 The Basic Architecture of TPS
(The numbers in the black circles correspond to the related section numbers of this chapter.)

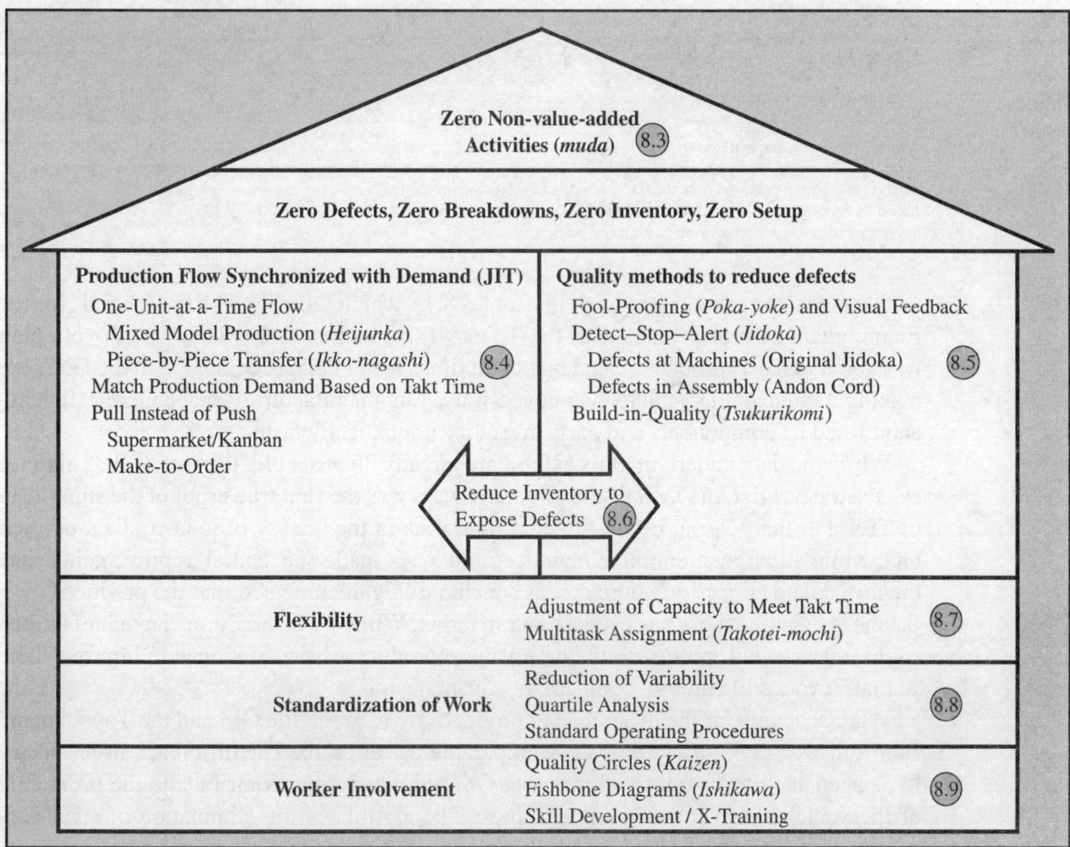

If we want to obtain a flow rate of the process that reliably matches demand while also following the just-in-time idea, we have to operate a process with no defects and no breakdowns.

Toyota's strong emphasis on quality lets the company overcome the buffer-or-suffer tension: by producing with zero defects and zero breakdowns, the company neither has to suffer (sacrifice flow rate) nor to buffer (hold inventory). For this reason, and the fact that defects are associated with the waste of rework, quality management is the second pillar around which TPS is built.

Both JIT and quality management require some foundational methods such as the standardization of work (which eliminates variability), the flexibility to scale up and down process capacity in response to fluctuations in demand, and a set of human resource management practices.

8.3 The Seven Sources of Waste

In the late 1980s, a research consortium known as the International Motor Vehicle Program (IMVP) conducted a global benchmarking of automotive plants. The study compared quality and productivity data from plants in Asia, Europe, and North America. The results were a clear indication of how far Toyota already had journeyed in redesigning the historical concept of mass production.

TABLE 8.1
General Motors Framingham Assembly Plant versus Toyota Takaoka Assembly Plant
(Based on 1986 benchmarking data from the IMVP Assembly Plant Survey.)

	GM Framingham	Toyota Takaoka
Gross Assembly Hours per Car	40.7	18
Assembly Defects per 100 Cars	130	45
Assembly Space per Car	8.1	4.8
Inventories of Parts (average)	2 weeks	2 hours

Source: Womack, Jones, and Roos (1991).
Notes: Gross assembly hours per car are calculated by dividing total hours of effort in the plant by the total number of cars produced.
Defects per car were estimated from the JD Power Initial Quality Survey for 1987.
Assembly Space per Car is square feet per vehicle per year, corrected for vehicle size.
Inventories of Parts are a rough average for major parts.

Consider the data displayed in Table 8.1, which compares the General Motors Framingham assembly plant with the Toyota Takaoka assembly plant. The Toyota plant was about twice as productive and had three times fewer defects compared to the GM plant making a comparable vehicle. Moreover, it used its manufacturing space more efficiently and turned its components and parts inventory dramatically faster.

While the data underlying this exhibit are already 30 years old, they are still of high relevance today. First, the IMVP study in many ways was the first true proof of the superiority of TPS. For that reason, it constituted a milestone in the history of industrialization. Second, while all large automotive manufacturers have made substantial improvements since the initial data collection, more recent benchmarking documented that the productivity of Japanese manufacturers has been a moving target. While U.S. and European manufacturers could improve their productivity, the Japanese producers have continued to improve theirs so that Toyota still enjoys a competitive advantage today.

What accounts for the difference in productivity between the GM and the Toyota plant? Both processes end up with a very comparable car after all. The difference in productivity is accounted for by all the things that GM did that did not contribute to the production of the vehicle: non–value-added activities. TPS postulates the elimination of such non–value-added activities, which are also referred to as *muda*.

There are different types of muda. According to T. Ohno, one of the thought leaders with respect to TPS, there are seven sources of waste:

1. Overproduction. Producing too much, too soon, leads to additional waste in the forms of material handling, storage, and transportation. The Toyota Production System seeks to produce only what the customer wants and when the customer wants it.
2. Waiting. In the spirit of "matching supply with demand," there exist two types of waiting. In some cases, a resource waits for flow units, leading to idle time at the resource. Utilization measures the amount of waiting of this type—a low utilization indicates the resource is waiting for flow units to work on. In other cases, flow units wait for resources to become available. As a consequence, the flow time is longer than the value-added time. A good measure for this second type of waiting is the percentage of flow time that is value-added time.
3. Transport. Internal transport, be it carrying around half-finished computers, wheeling patients through the hospital, or carrying around folders with insurance claims, corresponds to the third source of waste. Processes should be laid out such that the physical layout reflects the process flow to minimize the distances flow units must travel through a process.
4. Overprocessing. A close analysis of activity times reveals that workers often spend more time on a flow unit than necessary. A worker might excessively polish the surface of a piece of metal he just processed or a doctor might ask a patient the same questions that a nurse has asked five minutes earlier.

5. Inventory. In the spirit of matching supply with demand, any accumulation of inventory has the potential to be wasteful. Inventory is closely related to overproduction and often indicates that the JIT methods have not (yet) been implemented correctly. Not only is inventory often non–value-adding, it often hides other problems in the process as it leads to long information turnaround times and eases the pressure to find and eliminate underlying root causes (see Section 8.6 for more details).
6. Rework. A famous saying in the Toyota Production System and the associated quality movement has been "Do it right the first time." As we have discussed in the previous chapter, rework increases variability and consumes capacity from resources. Not only does rework exist in manufacturing plants, it is also (unfortunately) common in service operations. For example, hospitals all too frequently repeat X-rays because of poor image quality or readmit patients to the intensive care unit.
7. Motion. There are many ways to perform a particular task such as the tightening of a screw on the assembly line or the movement of a patient from a wheelchair into a hospital bed. But, according to the early pioneers of the industrial revolution, including Frederick Taylor and Frank and Lillian Gilbreth, there is only one "right way." Every task should be carefully analyzed and should be optimized using a set of tools that today is known as ergonomics. To do otherwise is wasteful.

Just as we have seen in the context of line balancing, the objective of waste reduction is to maximize the percentage of time a resource is engaged in value-adding activity by reducing the non–value-added (wasteful) activities as much as possible.

At this point, a clarification of wording is in order. TPS's objective is to achieve zero waste, including zero inventory and zero defects. However, this objective is more an aspirational one than it is a numerical one. Consider the objective of zero inventory and recall from Little's Law: Inventory = Flow rate × Flow time. Thus, unless we are able to produce at the speed of light (flow time equal to zero), the only way to achieve zero inventory is by operating at zero flow rate—arguably, not a desirable outcome. So, of course, Toyota's factories don't operate at zero inventory, but they operate at a low level of inventory and keep on decreasing this low level. The same holds for zero defects. Defects happen in each of Toyota's assembly plants many, many times a shift. But they happen less often than elsewhere and are always thought of as a potential for process improvement.

It is important to emphasize that the concept of waste is not unique to manufacturing. Consider, for example, the day of a nurse in a large hospital. In an ideal world, a nurse is there to care for patients. Independent of managed care, this is both the ambition of the nurse and the desire of the patient. However, if one carefully analyzes the workday of most nurses, a rather different picture emerges. Most nurses spend less than half of their time helping patients and waste the other time running around in the hospital, doing paperwork, searching for medical supplies, coordinating with doctors and the hospital administration, and so on. (See Tucker [2004] for an excellent description of nursing work from an operations management perspective.) This waste is frustrating for the nurse, leads to poor care for the patient, and is expensive for the health care provider.

Once we have reduced waste, we can perform the same work, yet at lower costs. In a process that is currently capacity constrained, waste reduction is also a way to increase output (flow rate) and hence revenues. As we have discussed in Chapter 6, the economic impact of these improvements can be dramatic.

A useful way to analyze and describe the effects of waste is the Overall Equipment Effectiveness (OEE) framework, used by McKinsey and other consulting firms. The objective of the framework is to identify what percentage of a resource's time is true, value-added time and what percentage is wasted. This provides a good estimate for the potential for process improvement before engaging in waste reduction.

As illustrated by Figure 8.2, we start the OEE analysis by documenting the total available time of the resource. From this total time (100 percent), some time is wasted on machine breakdowns (or, in the case of human resources, absenteeism) and setup times, leading to an available time that is substantially less than the total planned time (in this case, only 55 percent of the total planned time is available for production). However, not all of the remaining 55 percent is value-added time. Because of poor process balance, the resource is likely to be occasionally idle. Also, the resource might not operate at an optimum speed, as the activity time includes some waste and some incidental work that does not add direct customer value. In the case of Figure 8.2, 82 percent of the available time is used for operation, which leaves a total of 45 percent (= 55% × 82%). If one then factors in a further waste of capacity resulting from defects, rework, and start-ups (67 percent), we see that only 30 percent (55% × 82% × 67%) of the available capacity is used to really add value!

The following two examples illustrate the usefulness of the OEE framework in non-manufacturing settings. They also illustrate that wasting as much as half of the capacity of an expensive resource is much more common than one might expect:

- In the loan underwriting process of a major consumer bank, a recent case study documented that a large fraction of the underwriting capacity is not used productively. Unproductive time included (a) working on loans that are unlikely to be accepted by customers because the bank has already taken too long to get a response back to the customer, (b) idle time, (c) processing loans that resources preceding underwriting already could have rejected because of an obviously low creditworthiness of the application, (d) incidental activities of paper handling, and (e) attempting to reach customers on the phone but failing to do so. The study estimates that only 40 percent of the underwriting capacity is used in a value-adding way.
- In the operating rooms of a major hospital, the capacity is left unused because of (a) gaps in the schedule, (b) procedure cancellation, (c) room cleaning time, (d) patient preparation time, and (e) procedure delays because of the doctor or the anesthesiologist arriving late. After completing waste identification, the hospital concluded that only 60 percent of its operating room time was used productively. One might argue that patient preparation is a rather necessary and hence value-adding step prior to surgery.

FIGURE 8.2
The Overall Equipment Effectiveness Framework

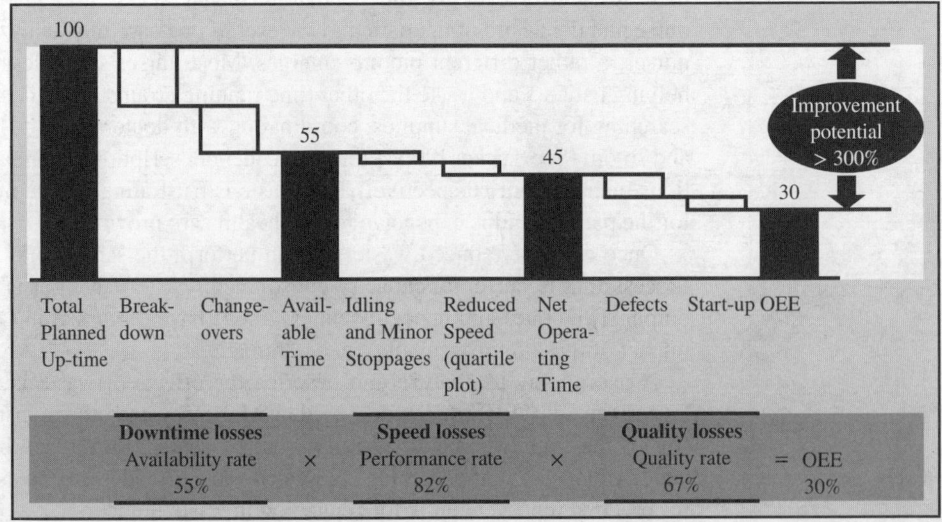

Yet, it is not clear that this step has to happen in the operating room. In fact, some hospitals are now using the tools of setup time reduction discussed in Chapter 5 and preparing the patient for surgery outside of the operating room so that the changeover from one surgical procedure to another is reduced.

8.4 JIT: Matching Supply with Demand

Just-in-time (JIT) is about matching supply with demand. The goal is to create a supply process that forms a smooth flow with its demand, thereby giving customers exactly what they need, when they need it.

In this section, we discuss three steps toward achieving a JIT process. The three steps build on each other and hence should be taken in the order they are presented. They presume that the process is already in-control (see Chapter 7) using standardized tasks and is able to achieve reliable quality:

1. Achieve a *one-unit-at-a-time* flow.
2. Produce at the rate of customer demand.
3. Implement a *pull system* using *kanban* or *make-to-order production*.

Achieve One-Unit-at-a-Time Flow

Compare the following two technologies that move people from one level of a building to another: an escalator and an elevator. Most of us associate plenty of waiting with elevators—we wait for the elevator to arrive and we wait stuck between dozens of people as the elevator stops at seemingly every floor. Escalators, in contrast, keep people moving toward their destination, no waiting and no jamming of people.

People waiting for and standing in elevators are like batches in a production setting. Chapter 5 already has discussed the concepts of SMED, the reduction of setup times that makes small production batches economically possible. In TPS, production plans are designed to avoid large batches of the same variant. Instead, product variants are mixed together on the assembly line (mixed-model production, which is also known as *heijunka*), as discussed in Chapter 5.

In addition to reducing setup times, we also should attempt to create a physical layout for our resources that closely mirrors the process flow. In other words, two resources that are close to each other in the process flow diagram also should be co-located in physical space. This avoids unnecessary transports and reduces the need to form transport batches. This way flow units can flow one unit at a time from one resource to the next (*ikko-nagashi*).

Produce at the Rate of Customer Demand

Once we have created a one-unit-at-a-time flow, we should make sure that our flow rate is in line with demand. Historically, most large-scale operations have operated their processes based on forecasts. Using planning software (often referred to as MRP, for materials requirement planning, and ERP, for enterprise resource planning), work schedules were created for the various subprocesses required to create the final product.

Forecasting is a topic for itself (see Chapter 13), but most forecasts have the negative property of not being right. So at the end of a planning period (e.g., one month), the ERP system would update its next production plan, taking the amount of inventory in the process into account. This way, in the long run, production more or less matches demand. Yet, in the day-to-day operations, extensive periods of substantial inventories or customer back orders exist.

TPS aims at reducing finished goods inventory by operating its production process in synchronization with customer orders. This is true for both the overall number of vehicles produced as well as with respect to the mix of vehicles across various models.

We translate customer demand into production rate (flow rate) using the concept of takt time. Takt time is derived from the German word *takt,* which stands for "tact" or "clock." Just like an orchestra needs to follow a common tact imposed by the conductor, a JIT process should follow the tact imposed by demand. Takt time calculations are identical to what we have seen with demand rate and flow rate calculations in earlier chapters.

Implement Pull Systems

The synchronization with the aggregate level of demand through takt time is an important step toward the implementation of JIT. However, inventory not only exists at the finished-goods level, but also throughout the process (work-in-process inventory). Some parts of the process are likely to be worker paced with some (hopefully modest) amount of inventory between resources. We now have to design a coordination system that coordinates these resources by controlling the amount of inventory in the process. We do this by implementing a pull system.

In a pull system, the resource farthest downstream (i.e., closest to the market) is paced by market demand. In addition to its own production, it also relays the demand information to the next station upstream, thus ensuring that the upstream resource also is paced by demand. If the last resource assembles two electronics components into a computer, it relays the demand for two such components to the next resource upstream. This way, the external demand is transferred step-by-step through the process, leading to an information flow moving in the opposite direction relative to the physical flow of the flow units.

Such a demand-driven pull system is in contrast to a *push system* where flow units are allowed to enter the process independent of the current amount of inventory in process. Especially if the first resources in the process have low levels of utilization—and are thereby likely to flood the downstream with inventory—push systems can lead to substantial inventory in the process.

To implement a pull system, TPS advocates two forms of process control:

- In kanban-based pull (also known as fill-up or supermarket pull), the upstream replenishes what demand has withdrawn from the downstream.
- Make-to-order refers to the release of work into a system only when a customer order has been received for that unit.

Consider the kanban system first. *Kanban* refers to a production and inventory control system in which production instructions and parts delivery instructions are triggered by the consumption of parts at the downstream step (Fujimoto 1999).

In a kanban system, standardized returnable parts containers circulate between the upstream and the downstream resources. The upstream resource is authorized to produce a unit when it receives an empty container. In other words, the arrival of an empty container triggers a production order. The term *kanban* refers to the card that is attached to each container. Consequently, kanban cards are frequently called work authorization forms.

A simplified description of a kanban system is provided by Figure 8.3. A downstream resource (right) consumes some input component that it receives from its upstream resource (left). The downstream resource empties containers of these input components—the downstream resource literally takes the part out of the container for its own use, thereby creating an empty container, which in turn, as already mentioned, triggers a production order for the upstream resource. Thus, the use of kanban cards between all resources in the process provides an effective and easy-to-implement mechanism for tying the demand of

FIGURE 8.3
The Operation of a Kanban System

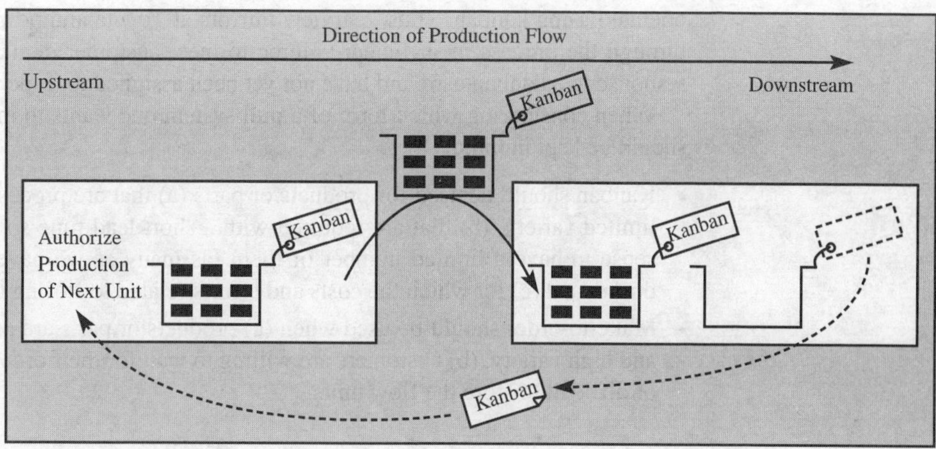

the process (downstream) with the production of the resources (upstream). They therefore enforce a match between supply and demand.

The main advantage of a kanban system is that there can never be more inventory between two resources than what has been authorized by the kanban cards—the upstream resource can only produce when it has an empty container, so production stops when all of the containers are full, thereby limiting the inventory to the number of containers. In contrast, with a push system, the upstream resource continues to produce as long as it has work. For example, suppose the upstream resource is a lathe that produces the legs for a wood chair. With a push system, the lathe keeps producing legs as long as it has blocks of wood to work on. With a kanban system, the lathe produces a set of chair legs only if it has an empty kanban. Hence, with a kanban system, the lathe stops working only when it runs out of kanbans, whereas with a push system the lathe stops working only when it runs out of raw materials. The distinction can lead to very different behavior. In a push system, inventory can simply "happen" to management because there is theoretically no limit to the amount of inventory that can pile up after a resource (e.g., think of the plant manager walking through the process and saying, "Wow, we have a lot of inventory at this step today"). In contrast, in a kanban system the amount of inventory becomes a managerial decision variable—the maximum inventory is controlled via the number of kanban cards in the process.

As an alternative to a kanban system, we also can implement a pull system using a make-to-order process. As is suggested by the term "make-to-order," resources in such a process only operate after having received an explicit customer order. Typically, the products corresponding to these orders then flow through the process on a first-in, first-out (FIFO) basis. Each flow unit in the make-to-order process is thereby explicitly assigned to one specific customer order. Consider the example of a rearview mirror production in an auto plant to see the difference between kanban and make-to-order. When the operator in charge of producing the interior rearview mirror at the plant receives the work authorization through the kanban card, it has not yet been determined which customer order will be filled with this mirror. All that is known is that there are—at the aggregate—a sufficient number of customer orders such that production of this mirror is warranted. Most likely, the final assembly line of the same auto plant (including the mounting of the rearview mirror) will be operated in a make-to-order manner, that is, the operator putting in the mirror can see that it will end up in the car of Mr. Smith.

Many organizations use both forms of pull systems. Consider computer maker Dell. Dell's computers are configured in work cells. Processes supplying components are often operated using kanban. Thus, rearview mirrors at Toyota and power supplies at Dell flow through the process in sufficient volume to meet customer demand, yet are produced in response to a kanban card and have not yet been assigned to a specific order.

When considering which form of a pull system one wants to implement, the following should be kept in mind:

- Kanban should be used for products or parts (a) that are processed in high volume and limited variety, (b) that are required with a short lead time so that it makes economic sense to have a limited number of them (as many as we have kanban cards) preproduced, and (c) for which the costs and efforts related to storing the components are low.
- Make-to-order should be used when (a) products or parts are processed in low volume and high variety, (b) customers are willing to wait for their order, and (c) it is expensive or difficult to store the flow units.

8.5 Quality Management

If we operate with no buffers and want to avoid the waste of rework, operating at zero defects is a must. To achieve zero defects, TPS relies on defect prevention, rapid defect detection, and a strong worker responsibility with respect to quality.

Defects can be prevented by "fool-proofing" many assembly operations, that is, by making mistakes in assembly operations physically impossible (*poka-yoke*). Components are designed in a way that there exists one single way of assembling them.

If, despite defect prevention, a problem occurs, TPS attempts to discover and isolate this problem as quickly as possible. This is achieved through the *jidoka* concept. The idea of jidoka is to stop the process immediately whenever a defect is detected and to alert the line supervisor. This idea goes back to the roots of Toyota as a maker of automated looms. Just like an automated loom should stop operating in the case of a broken thread, a defective machine should shut itself off automatically in the presence of a defect.

Shutting down the machine forces a human intervention in the process, which in turn triggers process improvement (Fujimoto 1999). The jidoka concept has been generalized to include any mechanism that stops production in response to quality problems, not just for automated machines. The most well-known form of jidoka is the *Andon cord,* a cord running adjacent to assembly lines that enables workers to stop production if they detect a defect. Just like the jidoka automatic shut-down of machines, this procedure dramatizes manufacturing problems and acts as a pressure for process improvements.

A worker pulling the Andon cord upon detecting a quality problem is in sharp contrast to Henry Ford's historical assembly line that would leave the detection of defects to a final inspection step. In TPS, "the next step is the customer" and every resource should only let those flow units move downstream that have been inspected and evaluated as good parts. Hence, quality inspection is "built-in" (*tsukurikomi*) and happens at every step in the line, as opposed to relying on a final inspection step alone.

The idea of detect–stop–alert that underlies the jidoka principle is not just a necessity to make progress toward implementing the zero inventory principle. Jidoka also benefits from the zero inventory principle, as large amounts of work-in-process inventory achieve the opposite of jidoka: they delay the detection of a problem, thereby keeping a defective process running and hiding the defect from the eyes of management. This shows how the various TPS principles and methods are interrelated, mutually strengthening each other.

To see how work-in-process inventory is at odds with the idea of jidoka, consider a sequence of two resources in a process, as outlined in Figure 8.4. Assume the activity times at both resources are equal to one minute per unit. Assume further that the upstream

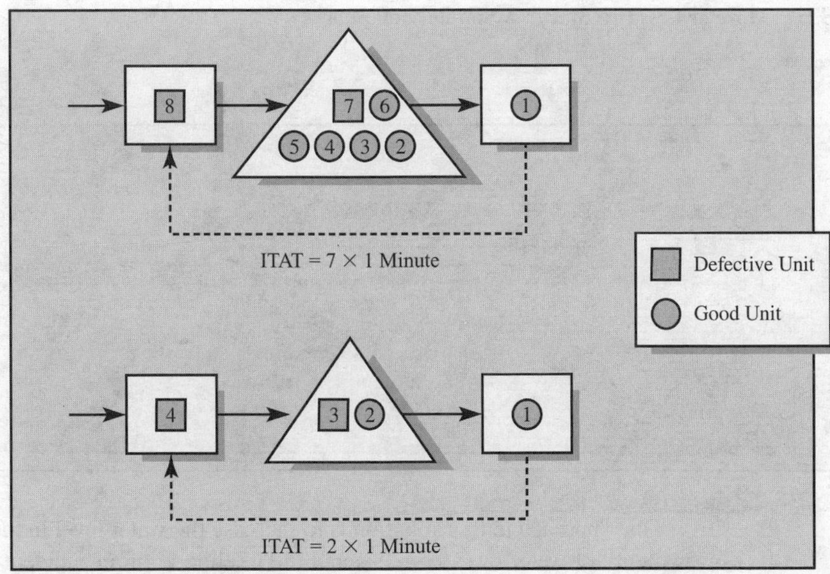

FIGURE 8.4
Information Turnaround Time and Its Relationship with Buffer Size

resource (on the left) suffers quality problems and—at some random point in time—starts producing bad output. In Figure 8.4, this is illustrated by the resource producing squares instead of circles. How long will it take until a quality problem is discovered? If there is a large buffer between the two resources (upper part of Figure 8.4), the downstream resource will continue to receive good units from the buffer. In this example, it will take seven minutes before the downstream resource detects the defective flow unit. This gives the upstream resource seven minutes to continue producing defective parts that need to be either scrapped or reworked.

Thus, the time between when the problem occurred at the upstream resource and the time it is detected at the downstream resource depends on the size of the buffer between the two resources. This is a direct consequence of Little's Law. We refer to the time between creating a defect and receiving the feedback about the defect as the *information turnaround time (ITAT)*. Note that we assume in this example that the defect is detected in the next resource downstream. The impact of inventory on quality is much worse if defects only get detected at the end of the process (e.g., at a final inspection step). In this case, the ITAT is driven by all inventory downstream from the resource producing the defect. This motivates the built-in inspection we mentioned above.

8.6 Exposing Problems through Inventory Reduction

Our discussion on quality reveals that inventory covers up problems. So to improve a process, we need to turn the "inventory hiding quality problems" effect on its head: we want to reduce inventory to expose defects and then fix the underlying root cause of the defect.

Recall that in a kanban system, the number of kanban cards—and hence the amount of inventory in the process—is under managerial control. So we can use the kanban system to gradually reduce inventory and thereby expose quality problems. The kanban system and its approach to buffers can be illustrated with the following metaphor. Consider a boat sailing on a canal that has numerous rocks in it. The freight of the boat is very valuable, so the company operating the canal wants to make sure that the boat never hits a rock. Figure 8.5 illustrates this metaphor.

FIGURE 8.5 More or Less Inventory? A Simple Metaphor

Source: Stevenson 2006.

One approach to this situation is to increase the water level in the canal. This way, there is plenty of water over the rocks and the likelihood of an accident is low. In a production setting, the rocks correspond to quality problems (defects), setup times, blocking or starving, breakdowns, or other problems in the process and the ship hitting a rock corresponds to lost throughput. The amount of water corresponds to the amount of inventory in the process (i.e., the number of kanban cards), which brings us back to our previous "buffer-or-suffer" discussion.

An alternative way of approaching the problem is this: instead of covering the rocks with water, we also could consider reducing the water level in the canal (reduce the number of kanban cards). This way, the highest rocks are exposed (i.e., we observe a process problem), which provides us with the opportunity of removing them from the canal. Once this has been accomplished, the water level is lowered again, until—step by step—all rocks are removed from the canal. Despite potential short-term losses in throughput, the advantage of this approach is that it moves the process to a better frontier (i.e., it is better along multiple dimensions).

This approach to inventory reduction is outlined in Figure 8.6. We observe that we first need to accept a short-term loss in throughput reflecting the reduction of inventory (we stay on the efficient frontier, as we now have less inventory). Once the inventory level is lowered, we are able to identify the most prominent problems in the process (rocks in the water). Once identified, these problems are solved and thereby the process moves to a more desirable frontier.

Both in the metaphor and in our ITAT discussion above, inventory is the key impediment to learning and process improvement. Since with kanban cards, management is in control of the inventory level, it can proactively manage the tension between the short-term need of a high throughput and the long-term objective of improving the process.

8.7 Flexibility

Given that there typically exist fluctuations in demand from the end market, TPS attempts to create processes with sufficient flexibility to meet such fluctuations. Since forecasts are more reliable at the aggregate level (across models or components, see discussion of pooling in later chapters), TPS requests workers to be skilled in handling multiple machines.

- When production volume has to be decreased for a product because of low demand, TPS attempts to assign some workers to processes creating other products and to have

FIGURE 8.6
Tension between Flow Rate and Inventory Levels/ITAT

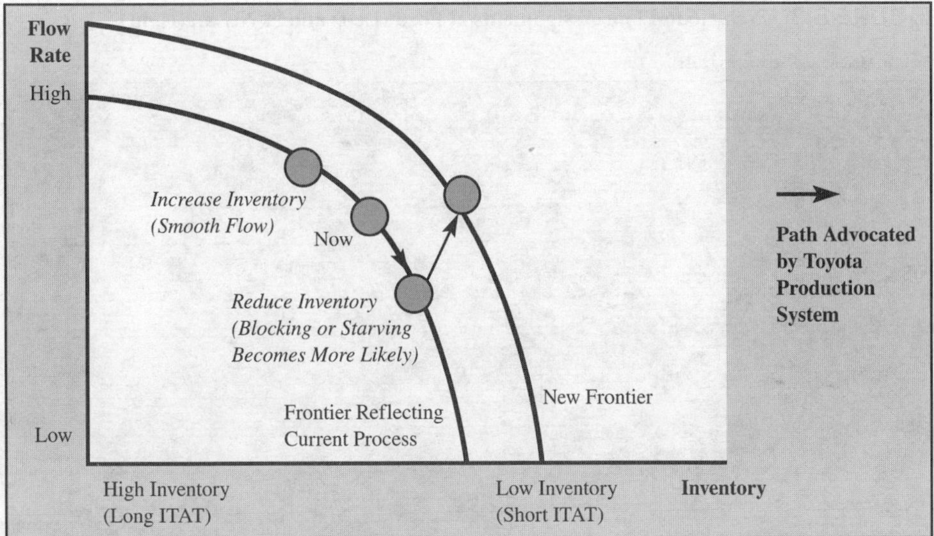

the remaining workers handle multiple machines simultaneously for the process with the low-demand product.

- When production volume has to be increased for a product because of high demand, TPS often uses a second pool of workers (temporary workers) to help out with production. Unlike the first pool of full-time employees (typically with lifetime employment guarantee and a broad skill set), these workers are less skilled and can only handle very specific tasks.

Consider the six-step operation shown in Figure 8.7. Assume all activities have an activity time of one minute per unit. If demand is low (right), we avoid idle time (low average labor utilization) by running the process with only three operators (typically, full-time employees). In this case, each operator is in charge of two minutes of work, so we would achieve a flow rate of 0.5 unit per minute. If demand is high (left in the Figure 8.7), we assign one worker to each step, that is, we bring in additional (most likely temporary) workers. Now, the flow rate can be increased to one unit per minute.

This requires that the operators are skilled in multiple assembly tasks. Good training, job rotation, skill-based payment, and well-documented standard operating procedures are essential requirements for this. This flexibility also requires that we have a multitiered workforce consisting of highly skilled full-time employees and a pool of temporary workers (who do not need such a broad skill base) that can be called upon when demand is high.

Such multitask flexibility of workers also can help decrease idle time in cases of activities that require some worker involvement but are otherwise largely automated. In these

FIGURE 8.7 **Multitask Flexibility**
(Note: The figure assumes a 1 minute/unit activity time at each station.)

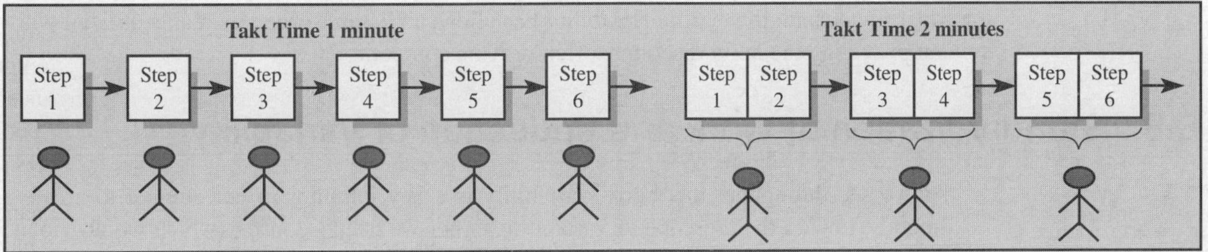

FIGURE 8.8 Vehicle-to-Plant Assignments at Ford (Left) and at Nissan (right)

Source: Moreno and Terwiesch (2011).

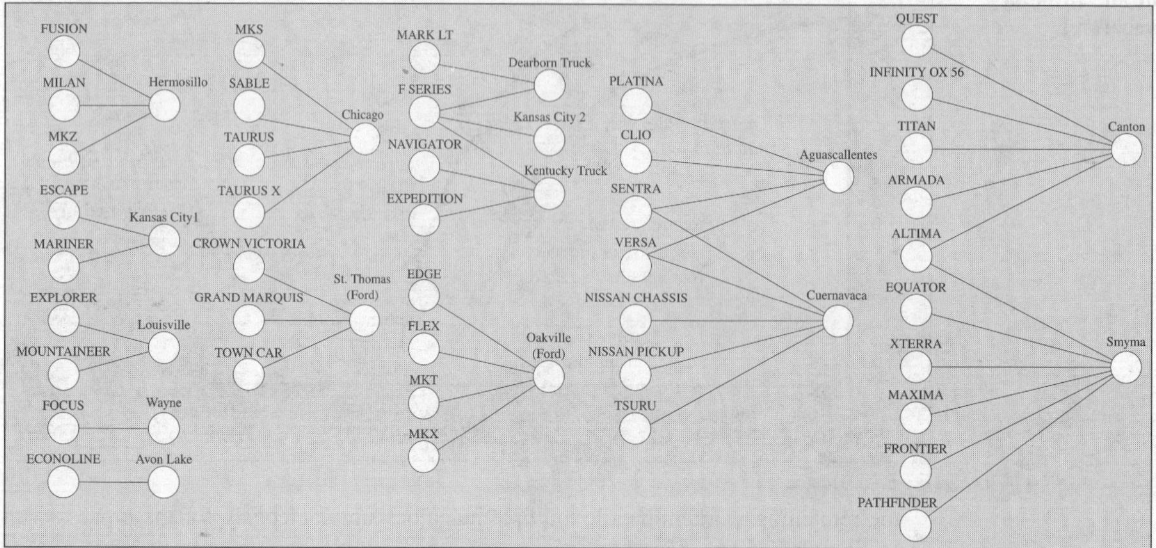

cases, a worker can load one machine and while this machine operates, the worker—instead of being idle—operates another machine along the process flow (*takotei-mochi*). This is facilitated if the process flow is arranged in a U-shaped manner, in which case a worker can share tasks not only with the upstream and the downstream resource, but also with another set of tasks in the process. Another important form of flexibility relates to the ability of one plant to produce more than one vehicle model. Consider the data displayed in Figure 8.8. The left part of the figure shows how Ford's vehicles are allocated to Ford's production plants. As we can see, many vehicles are dedicated to one plant and many of the plants can only produce a small set of vehicles. Consequently, if demand increases relative to the plant's capacity, that plant is unlikely to have sufficient capacity to fulfill it. If demand decreases, the plant is likely to have excess capacity.

In an ideal world, the company would be able to make every model in every plant. This way, high demand from one model would cancel out with low demand from another one, leading to better plant utilization and more sales. However, such capacity pooling would require the plants to be perfectly flexible—requiring substantial investments in production tools and worker skills. An interesting alternative to such perfect flexibility is the concept of partial flexibility, also referred to as *chaining*. The idea of chaining is that every car can be made in two plants and that the vehicle-to-plant assignment creates a chain that connects as many vehicles and plants as possible. As we will see in Chapter 17, such partial flexibility results in almost the same benefits of full flexibility, yet at dramatically lower costs. The right side of Figure 8.8 shows the vehicle-to-plant assignment of Nissan (North America) and provides an illustrative example of partial flexibility. In an environment of volatile demand, this partial flexibility has allowed Nissan to keep its plants utilized without providing the hefty discounts offered by its competitors.

8.8 Standardization of Work and Reduction of Variability

As we see throughout this book, variability is a key inhibitor in our attempt to create a smooth flow. In the presence of variability, either we need to buffer (which would violate the zero inventory philosophy) or we suffer occasional losses in throughput (which would

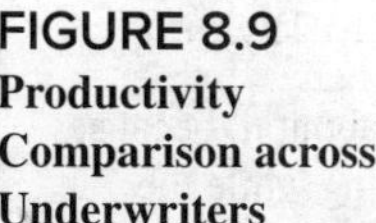

FIGURE 8.9
Productivity Comparison across Underwriters

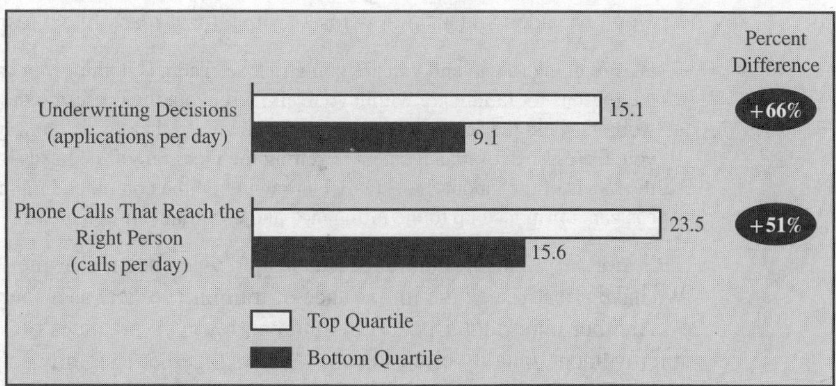

violate the principle of providing the customer with the requested product when demanded). For this reason, the Toyota Production System explicitly embraces the concepts of variability measurement, control, and reduction discussed in Chapter 7.

The need for stability in a JIT process and the vulnerability of an unbuffered process were visible in the computer industry following the 1999 Taiwanese earthquake. Several of the Taiwanese factories that were producing key components for computer manufacturers around the world were forced to shut down their production due to the earthquake. Such an unpredicted shutdown was more disruptive for computer manufacturers with JIT supply chains than those with substantial buffers (e.g., in the form of warehouses) in their supply chains.

Besides earthquakes, variability occurs because of quality defects (see above) or because of differences in activity times for the same or for different operators. Figure 8.9 shows performance data from a large consumer loan processing organization. The figure compares the performance of the top-quartile operator (i.e., the operator who has 25 percent of the other operators achieving a higher performance and 75 percent of the operators achieving a lower performance) with the bottom quartile operator (the one who has 75 percent of the operators achieving a higher performance). As we can see, there can exist dramatic differences in the productivity across employees.

A quartile analysis is a good way to identify the presence of large differences across operators and to estimate the improvement potential. For example, we could estimate what would happen to process capacity if all operators would be trained so that they achieve a performance in line with the current top-quartile performance.

8.9 Human Resource Practices

We have seen seven sources of waste, but the Toyota Production System also refers to an eighth source—the waste of the human intellect. For this reason, a visitor to an operation that follows the Toyota Production System philosophy often encounters signs with expressions like "In our company, we all have two jobs: (1) to do our job and (2) to improve it."

To illustrate different philosophies toward workers, consider the following two quotes. The first one comes from the legendary book *Principles of Scientific Management* written by Frederick Taylor, which still makes an interesting read almost a century after its first appearance (once you have read the quote below, you will at least enjoy Taylor's candid writing style). The second quote comes from Konosuka Matsushita, the former chairman of Panasonic.

Let us look at Taylor's opinion first and consider his description of pig iron shoveling, an activity that Taylor studied extensively in his research. Taylor writes: "This work is so crude and elementary that the writer firmly believes that it would be possible to train an intelligent gorilla so as to become a more efficient pig-iron handler than any man can be."

Now, consider Matsushita, whose quote almost reads like a response to Taylor:

> We are going to win and you are going to lose. There is nothing you can do about it, because the reasons for failure are within yourself. With you, the bosses do the thinking while the workers wield the screw drivers. You are convinced that this is the way to run a business. For you, the essence of management is getting the ideas out of the heads of the bosses and in to the hands of the labour. [. . .] Only by drawing on the combined brainpower of all its employees can a firm face up to the turbulence and constraints of today's environment.

TPS, not surprisingly, embraces Matsushita's perspective of the "combined brainpower." We have already seen the importance of training workers as a source of flexibility.

Another important aspect of the human resource practices of Toyota relates to process improvement. Quality circles bring workers together to jointly solve production problems and to continuously improve the process (*kaizen*). Problem solving is very data driven and follows a standardized process, including control charts, fishbone (Ishikawa) diagrams, the "Five Whys," and other problem-solving tools. Thus, not only do we standardize the production process, we also standardize the process of improvement.

Ishikawa diagrams (also known as *fishbone diagrams* or cause–effect diagrams) graphically represent variables that are causally related to a specific outcome, such as an increase in variation or a shift in the mean. When drawing a fishbone diagram, we typically start with a horizontal arrow that points at the name of the outcome variable we want to analyze. Diagonal lines then lead to this arrow representing main causes. Smaller arrows then lead to these causality lines, creating a fishbone-like shape. An example of this is given by Figure 8.10. Ishikawa diagrams are simple yet powerful problem-solving tools that can be used to structure brainstorming sessions and to visualize the causal structure of a complex system.

FIGURE 8.10 **Example of an Ishikawa Diagram**

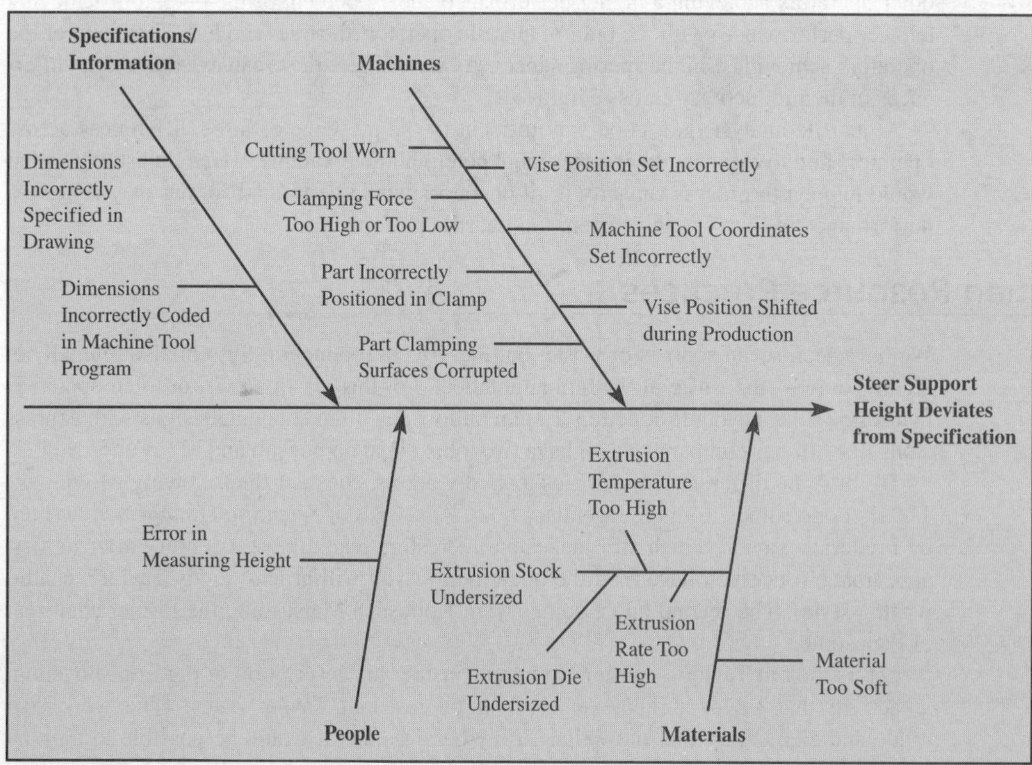

A related tool that also helps in developing causal models is known as the "Five Whys." The tool is prominently used in Toyota's organization when workers search for the root cause of a quality problem. The basic idea of the "Five Whys" is to continually question ("Why did this happen?") whether a potential cause is truly the root cause or is merely a symptom of a deeper problem.

In addition to these operational principles, TPS includes a range of human resource management practices, including stable employment ("lifetime employment") for the core workers combined with the recruitment of temporary workers; a strong emphasis on skill development, which is rewarded financially through skill-based salaries; and various other aspects relating to leadership and people management.

8.10 Lean Transformation

How do you turn around an existing operation to achieve operational excellence as we have discussed it above? Clearly, even an operations management textbook has to acknowledge that there is more to a successful operational turnaround than the application of a set of tools.

McKinsey, as a consulting firm with a substantial part of its revenues resulting from operations work, refers to the set of activities required to improve the operations of a client as a *lean transformation.* There exist three aspects to such a lean transformation: the operating system, a management infrastructure, and the mind-sets and behaviors of the employees involved.

With the operating system, the firm refers to various aspects of process management as we have discussed in this chapter and throughout this book: an emphasis on flow, matching supply with demand, and a close eye on the variability of the process.

But technical solutions alone are not enough. So the operating system needs to be complemented by a management infrastructure. A central piece of this infrastructure is performance measurement. Just as we discussed in Chapter 6, defining finance-level performance measures and then cascading them into the operations is a key struggle for many companies. Moreover, the performance measures should be tracked over time and be made transparent throughout the organization. The operator needs to understand which performance measures he or she is supposed to achieve and how these measures contribute to the bigger picture. Management infrastructure also includes the development of operator skills and the establishment of formal problem-solving processes.

Finally, the mind-set of those involved in working in the process is central to the success of a lean transformation. A nurse might get frustrated from operating in an environment of waste that is keeping him or her from spending time with patients. Yet, the nurse, in all likelihood, also will be frustrated by the implementation of a new care process that an outsider imposes on his or her ward. Change management is a topic well beyond the scope of this book: open communication with everyone involved in the process, collecting and discussing process data, and using some of the tools discussed in Chapter 7 as well as with respect to kaizen can help make the transformation a success.

8.11 Further Reading

Readers who want to learn more about TPS are referred to excellent reading, such as Fujimoto (1999) or Ohno (1988), from which many of definitions in this chapter are taken.

Fujimoto (1999) describes the evolution of the Toyota Production System. While not a primary focus of the book, it also provides excellent descriptions of the main elements of the Toyota Production System. The results of the benchmarking studies are reported in Womack, Jones, and Roos (1991) and Holweg and Pil (2004).

Bohn and Jaikumar (1992) is a classic reading that challenges the traditional, optimization-focused paradigm of operations management. Their work stipulates that companies should not focus on optimizing decisions for their existing business processes, but rather should create new processes that can operate at higher levels of performance.

Drew, McCallum, and Roggenhofer (2004) describe the "Journey to Lean," a description of the steps constituting a lean transformation as described by a group of McKinsey consultants.

Tucker (2004) provides a study of TPS-like activities from the perspective of nurses who encounter quality problems in their daily work. Moreno and Terwiesch discuss flexibility strategies in the U.S. automotive industry and analyze if and to what extent firms with flexible production systems are able to achieve higher plant utilization and lower price discounts.

The Wikipedia entries for Toyota, Ford, Industrial Revolution, Gilbreth, and Taylor are also interesting summaries and were helpful in compiling the historical reviews presented in this chapter.

8.12 Practice Problems

The following questions will help in testing your understanding of this chapter. After each question, we show the relevant section in parentheses [Section x].

Q8.1 **(Waste)** An employee in a restaurant spends his time on the following: waiting for a customer order, taking the order, forwarding the order to the kitchen, waiting for the kitchen to confirm the order, bringing the food to the customer, serving the customer, and collecting the payment. Which of these time commitments are waste, which are non–value-added work, and which are value-added work? [8.3]

Q8.2 **(Push)** A production process has two machines. The first machine has a capacity of 100 units per hour and the second machine has a capacity of 60 units per hour. Demand for the process is 100 units per hour.

a. In a push process, what would be the utilization of the first machine? What would happen to the inventory of the process? [8.4]

b. How would the situation change with a pull system? [8.4]

Q8.3 **(Three Step)** Consider a worker-paced line with three process steps, each of which is staffed with one worker. The sequence of the three steps does not matter for the completion of the product. Currently, the three steps are operated in the following sequence.

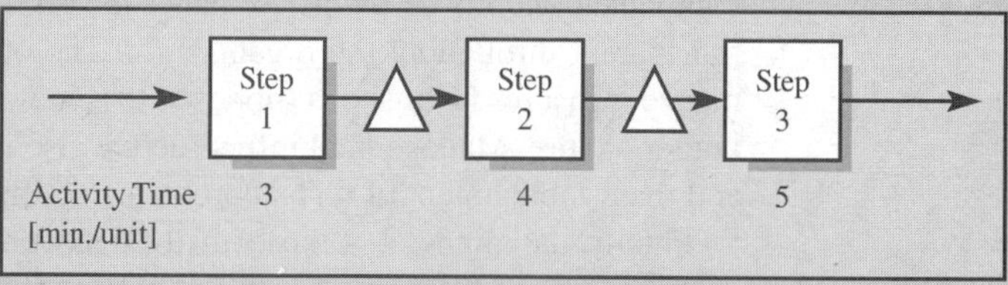

a. What would happen to the inventory in the process if the process were operated as a push system? [8.4]

b. How would you implement a pull system? [8.4]

Q8.4 **(Heijunka)** If you were to implement *heijunka* at a production facility, which of the following tasks would you prioritize? [8.4]

a. Encourage feedback among workers so as to introduce kaizen teams.

b. Reduce setup and changeover times at the different stations.

c. Reduce the number of Kanban cards.

d. Introduce jidoka if not present.

e. Train the design team following the teachings of poka-yoke.

f. Increase the storage space for finished products.

Q8.5 **(ITAT)** Consider the following two production processes making an electronic component for a navigation system. Both processes consist of 20 stations and operate at a cycle time of 1 minute/unit. Their most error prone operation is step 9.

Process 1: Has a final inspection at the end of the process and has about 300 units of inventory between step 9 and the inspection.

Process 2: Has each worker check the work of the previous steps and about 50 units of inventory between step 9 and the end of the process, roughly equally distributed across the remainder of the process.

What would be the information turnaround time for a defect made at station 9? [8.4]

Q8.6 **(Jidoka)** In the Toyota Production System, *jidoka* refers to [8.4]

a. Level production, where different models are produced alongside each other on the assembly line.
b. Continuous improvement, where workers organize meetings to discuss ways of improving the production process.
c. The inventory retrieval system where parts are replenished only when they are needed.
d. The aggressive reduction of changeover and setup times.
e. Continuous line-balancing to maximize utilization.
f. The cross-training of workers for a wide range of skills.
g. None of the above.

Q8.7 **(Kanban)** What is the relationship between the number of Kanban cards in a process and the inventory level? Pick one of the following answers [8.4].

A. There can never be more inventory in the process than what was authorized via Kanban cards.
B. The inventory of the process grows with the square root of the number of Kanban cards.
C. The inventory of the process is reduced by adding more Kanban cards.
D. There is no relationship between the two.

If you would like to test your understanding of a specific section, here are the questions organized by section:

Section 8.3: Q8.1

Section 8.4: Q8.2, Q8.3ab, Q8.4, Q8.7

Section 8.5: Q8.5, Q8.6

Chapter 9

Variability and Its Impact on Process Performance: Waiting Time Problems

For consumers, one of the most visible—and probably annoying—forms of supply–demand mismatches is waiting time. As consumers, we seem to spend a significant portion of our life waiting in line, be it in physical lines (supermarkets, check-in at airports) or in "virtual" lines (listening to music in a call center, waiting for a response e-mail).

It is important to distinguish between different types of waiting time:

- Waiting time predictably occurs when the expected demand rate exceeds the expected supply rate for some limited period of time. This happens especially in cases of constant capacity levels and demand that exhibits seasonality. This leads to implied utilization levels of over 100 percent for some time period. Queues forming at the gate of an airport after the flight is announced are an example of such queues.
- As we will see in the next section, in the presence of variability, queues also can arise if the implied utilization is below 100 percent. Such queues can thereby be fully attributed to the presence of variability, as there exists, on average, enough capacity to meet demand.

While the difference between these two types of waiting time probably does not matter much to the customer, it is of great importance from the perspective of operations management. The root cause for the first type of waiting time is a capacity problem; variability is only a secondary effect. Thus, when analyzing this type of a problem, we first should use the tools outlined in Chapters 3 and 4 instead of focusing on variability.

The root cause of the second type of waiting time is variability. This makes waiting time unpredictable, both from the perspective of the customer as well as from the perspective of the operation. Sometimes, it is the customer (demand) waiting for service (supply) and, sometimes, it is the other way around. Demand just never seems to match supply in these settings.

Analyzing waiting times and linking these waiting times to variability require the introduction of new analytical tools, which we present in this chapter. We will discuss the tools for analyzing waiting times based on the example of An-ser Services, a call-center operation in

Wisconsin that specializes in providing answering services for financial services, insurance companies, and medical practices. Specifically, the objective of this chapter is to

- Predict waiting times and derive some performance metrics capturing the service quality provided to the customer.
- Recommend ways of reducing waiting time by choosing appropriate capacity levels, redesigning the service system, and outlining opportunities to reduce variability.

9.1 Motivating Example: A Somewhat Unrealistic Call Center

For illustrative purposes, consider a call center with just one employee from 7 a.m. to 8 a.m. Based on prior observations, the call-center management estimates that, on average, a call takes 4 minutes to complete (e.g., giving someone driving directions) and there are, on average, 12 calls arriving in a 60-minute period, that is, on average, one call every 5 minutes.

What will be the average waiting time for a customer before talking to a customer service representative? From a somewhat naïve perspective, there should be no waiting time at all. Since the call center has a capacity of serving 60/4 = 15 calls per hour and calls arrive at a rate of 12 calls per hour, supply of capacity clearly exceeds demand. If anything, there seems to be excess service capacity in the call center since its utilization, which we defined previously (Chapter 3) as the ratio between flow rate and capacity, and can be computed as

$$\text{Utilization} = \frac{\text{Flow rate}}{\text{Capacity}} = \frac{12 \text{ calls per hour}}{15 \text{ calls per hour}} = 80\%$$

First, consider the arrivals and processing times as depicted in Figure 9.1. A call arrives exactly every 5 minutes and then takes exactly 4 minutes to be served. This is probably the weirdest call center that you have ever seen! No need to worry, we will return to "real operations" momentarily, but the following thought experiment will help you grasp how variability can lead to waiting time.

Despite its almost robotlike processing times and the apparently very disciplined customer service representative ("sorry, 4 minutes are over; thanks for your call"), this call center has one major advantage: no incoming call ever has to wait.

FIGURE 9.1
A Somewhat Odd Service Process

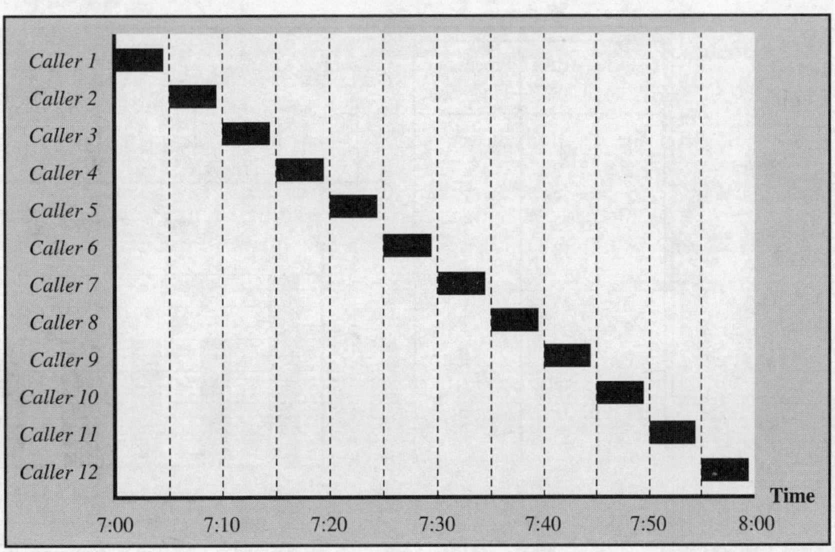

Assuming that calls arrive like kick scooters at an assembly line and are then treated by customer service representatives that act like robots reflects a common mistake managers make when calculating process performance. These calculations look at the process at an aggregate level and consider how much capacity is available over the entire hour (day, month, quarter), yet ignore how the requests for service are spaced out within the hour.

If we look at the call center on a minute-by-minute basis, a different picture emerges. Specifically, we observe that calls do not arrive like kick scooters appear at the end of the assembly line, but instead follow a much less systematic pattern, which is illustrated by Figure 9.2.

Moreover, a minute-by-minute analysis also reveals that the actual service durations also vary across calls. As Figure 9.2 shows, while the average processing time is 4 minutes, there exist large variations across calls, and the actual processing times range from 2 minutes to 7 minutes.

Now, consider how the hour from 7:00 a.m. to 8:00 a.m. unfolds. As can be seen in Figure 9.2, the first call comes in at 7:00 a.m. This call will be served without waiting time, and it takes the customer service representative 5 minutes to complete the call. The following 2 minutes are idle time from the perspective of the call center (7:05–7:07). At 7:07, the second call comes in, requiring a 6-minute processing time. Again, the second caller does not have to wait and will leave the system at 7:13. However, while the second caller is being served, at 7:09 the third caller arrives and now needs to wait until 7:13 before beginning the service.

Figure 9.3 shows the waiting time and processing time for each of the 12 customers calling between 7:00 a.m. and 8:00 a.m. Specifically, we observe that

- Most customers do have to wait a considerable amount of time (up to 10 minutes) before being served. This waiting occurs, although, on average, there is plenty of capacity in the call center.
- The call center is not able to provide a consistent service quality, as some customers are waiting, while others are not.
- Despite long waiting times and—because of Little's Law—long queues (see lower part of Figure 9.3), the customer service representative incurs idle time repeatedly over the time period from 7 a.m. to 8 a.m.

Why does variability not average out over time? The reason for this is as follows. In the call center example, the customer service representative can only serve a customer if

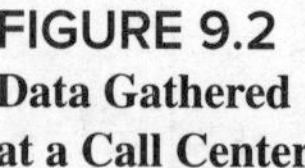

FIGURE 9.2
Data Gathered at a Call Center

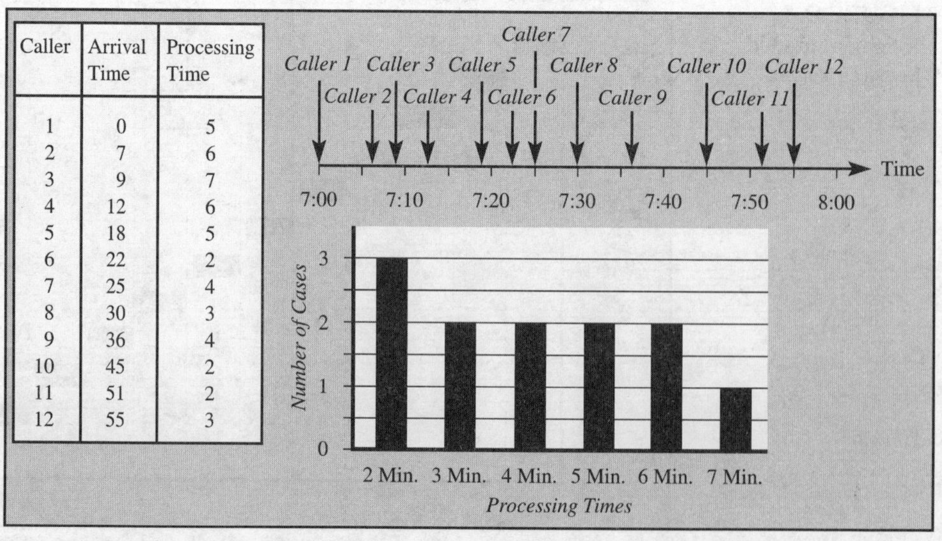

Caller	Arrival Time	Processing Time
1	0	5
2	7	6
3	9	7
4	12	6
5	18	5
6	22	2
7	25	4
8	30	3
9	36	4
10	45	2
11	51	2
12	55	3

FIGURE 9.3
Detailed Analysis of Call Center

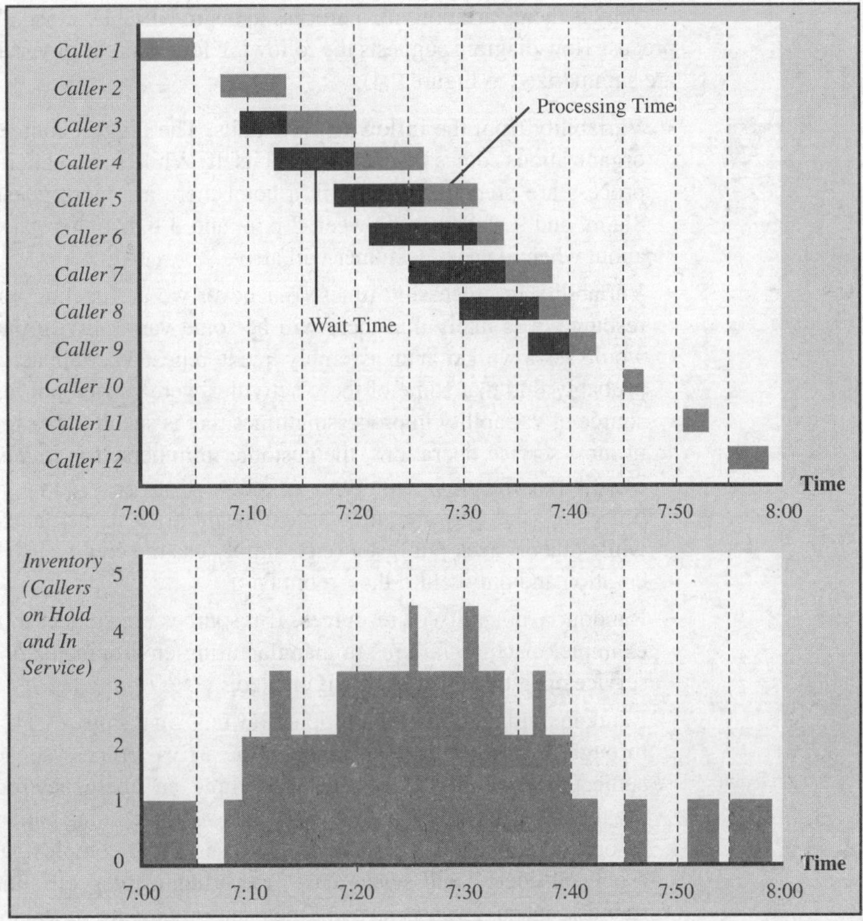

there is capacity *and* demand at the same moment in time. Therefore, capacity can never "run ahead" of demand. However, demand can "run ahead" of capacity, in which case the queue builds up. The idea that inventory can be used to decouple the supply process from demand, thereby restoring the flow rate to the level achievable in the absence of variability, is another version of the "buffer or suffer" principle that we already encountered in the batching chapter. Thus, if a service organization attempts to achieve the flow-rate levels feasible based on averages, long waiting times will result (unfortunately, in those cases, it is the customer who gets "buffered" and "suffers").

Taking the perspective of a manager attempting to match supply and demand, our objectives have not changed. We are still interested in calculating the three fundamental performance measures of an operation: inventory, flow rate, and flow time. Yet, as the above example illustrated, we realize that the process analysis tools we have discussed up to this point in the book need to be extended to appropriately deal with variability.

9.2 Variability: Where It Comes From and How It Can Be Measured

As a first step toward restoring our ability to understand a process's basic performance measures in the presence of variability, we take a more detailed look at the concept of variability itself. Specifically, we are interested in the sources of variability and how to measure variability.

Why is there variability in a process to begin with? Drawing a simple (the most simple) process flow diagram suggests the following four sources of variability (these four sources are summarized in Figure 9.4):

- Variability from the inflow of flow units. The biggest source of variability in service organizations comes from the market itself. While some patterns of the customer-arrival process are predictable (e.g., in a hotel there are more guests checking out between 8 a.m. and 9 a.m. than between 2 p.m. and 3 p.m.), there always remains uncertainty about when the next customer will arrive.
- Variability in processing times. Whenever we are dealing with human operators at a resource, it is likely that there will be some variability in their behavior. Thus, if we would ask a worker at an assembly line to repeat a certain activity 100 times, we would probably find that some of these activities were carried out faster than others. Another source of variability in processing times that is specific to a service environment is that in most service operations, the customer him/herself is involved in many of the tasks constituting the processing time. At a hotel front desk, some guests might require extra time (e.g., the guest requires an explanation for items appearing on his or her bill), while others check out faster (e.g., simply use the credit card that they used for the reservation and only return their room key).
- Random availability of resources. If resources are subject to random breakdowns, for example, machine failures in manufacturing environments or operator absenteeism in service operations, variability is created.
- Random routing in case of multiple flow units in the process. If the path a flow unit takes through the process is itself random, the arrival process at each individual resource is subject to variability. Consider, for example, an emergency room in a hospital. Following the initial screening at the admissions step, incoming patients are routed to different resources. A nurse might handle easy cases, more complex cases might be handled by a general doctor, and severe cases are brought to specific units in the hospital (e.g., trauma center). Even if arrival times and processing times are deterministic, this random routing alone is sufficient to introduce variability.

In general, any form of variability is measured based on the standard deviation. In our case of the call center, we could measure the variability of call durations based on collecting

FIGURE 9.4
Variability and Where It Comes From

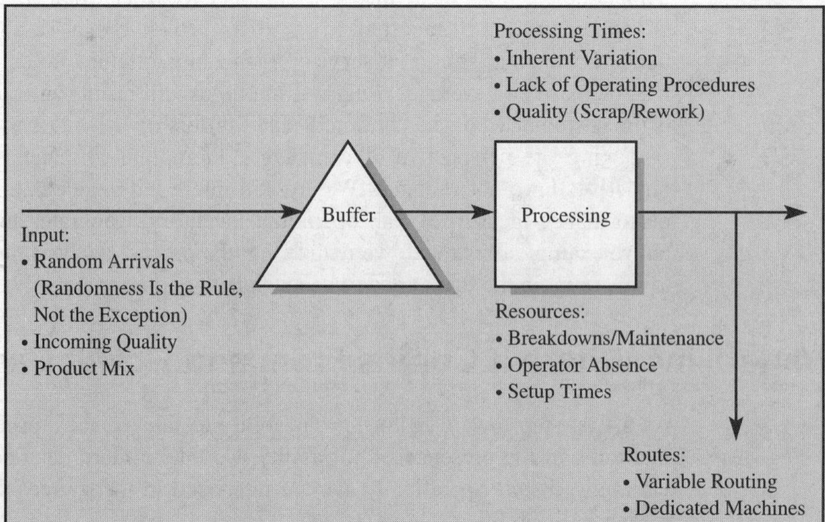

some data and then computing the corresponding standard deviation. The problem with this approach is that the standard deviation provides an *absolute* measure of variability. Does a standard deviation of 5 minutes indicate a high variability? A 5-minute standard deviation for call durations (processing times) in the context of a call center seems like a large number. In the context of a 2-hour surgery in a trauma center, a 5-minute standard deviation seems small.

For this reason, it is more appropriate to measure variability in *relative* terms. Specifically, we define the *coefficient of variation* of a random variable as

$$\text{Coefficient of variation} = \text{CV} = \frac{\text{Standard deviation}}{\text{Mean}}$$

As both the standard deviation and the mean have the same measurement units, the coefficient of variation is a unitless measure.

9.3 Analyzing an Arrival Process

Any process analysis we perform is only as good as the information we feed into our analysis. For this reason, Sections 9.3 and 9.4 focus on data collection and data analysis for the upcoming mathematical models. As a manager intending to apply some of the following tools, this data analysis is essential. You also should take a look at the forecasting chapter in this book. However, as a student with only a couple of hours left to the final exam, you might be better off jumping straight to Section 9.5.

Of particular importance when dealing with variability problems is an accurate representation of the demand, which determines the timing of customer arrivals.

Assume we got up early and visited the call center of An-ser; say we arrived at their offices at 6:00 a.m. and we took detailed notes of what takes place over the coming hour. We would hardly have had the time to settle down when the first call comes in. One of the An-ser staff takes the call immediately. Twenty-three seconds later, the second call comes in; another 1:24 minutes later, the third call; and so on.

We define the time at which An-ser receives a call as the *arrival time*. Let AT_i denote the arrival time of the *i*th call. Moreover, we define the time between two consecutive arrivals as the *interarrival time*, IA. Thus, $\text{IA}_i = \text{AT}_{i+1} - \text{AT}_i$. Figure 9.5 illustrates these two definitions.

If we continue this data collection, we accumulate a fair number of arrival times. Such data are automatically recorded in call centers, so we could simply download a file that looks like Table 9.1.

Before we can move forward and introduce a mathematical model that predicts the effects of variability, we have to invest in some simple, yet important, data analysis. A major

FIGURE 9.5 The Concept of Interarrival Times

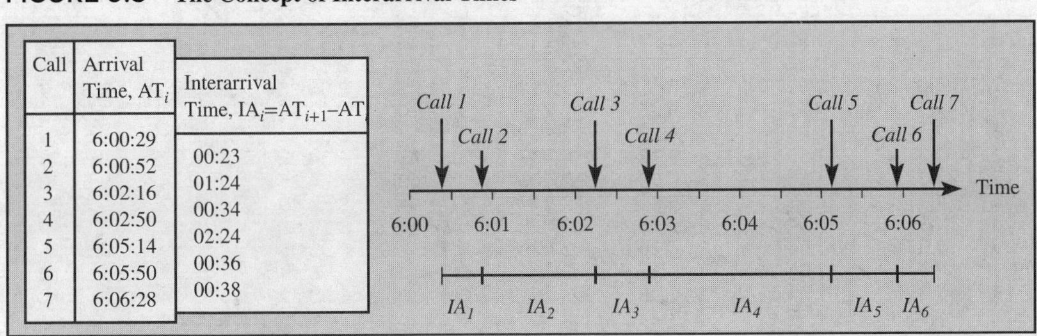

Call	Arrival Time, AT_i	Interarrival Time, $\text{IA}_i=\text{AT}_{i+1}-\text{AT}_i$
1	6:00:29	00:23
2	6:00:52	01:24
3	6:02:16	00:34
4	6:02:50	02:24
5	6:05:14	00:36
6	6:05:50	00:38
7	6:06:28	

TABLE 9.1 Call Arrivals at An-ser on April 2, from 6:00 a.m. to 10:00 a.m.

6:00:29	6:52:39	7:17:57	7:33:51	7:56:16	8:17:33	8:28:11	8:39:25	8:55:56	9:21:58
6:00:52	6:53:06	7:18:10	7:34:05	7:56:24	8:17:42	8:28:12	8:39:47	8:56:17	9:22:02
6:02:16	6:53:07	7:18:17	7:34:19	7:56:24	8:17:50	8:28:13	8:39:51	8:57:42	9:22:02
6:02:50	6:53:24	7:18:38	7:34:51	7:57:39	8:17:52	8:28:17	8:40:02	8:58:45	9:22:30
6:05:14	6:53:25	7:18:54	7:35:10	7:57:51	8:17:54	8:28:43	8:40:09	8:58:49	9:23:13
6:05:50	6:54:18	7:19:04	7:35:13	7:57:55	8:18:03	8:28:59	8:40:23	8:58:49	9:23:29
6:06:28	6:54:24	7:19:40	7:35:21	7:58:26	8:18:12	8:29:06	8:40:34	8:59:32	9:23:45
6:07:37	6:54:36	7:19:41	7:35:44	7:58:41	8:18:21	8:29:34	8:40:35	8:59:38	9:24:10
6:08:05	6:55:06	7:20:10	7:35:59	7:59:12	8:18:23	8:29:38	8:40:46	8:59:45	9:24:30
6:10:16	6:55:19	7:20:11	7:36:37	7:59:20	8:18:34	8:29:40	8:40:51	9:00:14	9:24:42
6:12:13	6:55:31	7:20:26	7:36:45	7:59:22	8:18:46	8:29:45	8:40:58	9:00:52	9:25:07
6:12:48	6:57:25	7:20:27	7:37:07	7:59:22	8:18:53	8:29:46	8:41:12	9:00:53	9:25:15
6:14:04	6:57:38	7:20:38	7:37:14	7:59:36	8:18:54	8:29:47	8:41:26	9:01:09	9:26:03
6:14:16	6:57:44	7:20:52	7:38:01	7:59:50	8:18:58	8:29:47	8:41:32	9:01:31	9:26:04
6:14:28	6:58:16	7:20:59	7:38:03	7:59:54	8:19:20	8:29:54	8:41:49	9:01:55	9:26:23
6:17:51	6:58:34	7:21:11	7:38:05	8:01:22	8:19:25	8:30:00	8:42:23	9:02:25	9:26:34
6:18:19	6:59:41	7:21:14	7:38:18	8:01:42	8:19:28	8:30:01	8:42:51	9:02:30	9:27:02
6:19:11	7:00:50	7:21:46	7:39:00	8:01:56	8:20:09	8:30:08	8:42:53	9:02:38	9:27:04
6:20:48	7:00:54	7:21:56	7:39:17	8:02:08	8:20:23	8:30:23	8:43:24	9:02:51	9:27:27
6:23:33	7:01:08	7:21:58	7:39:35	8:02:26	8:20:27	8:30:23	8:43:28	9:03:29	9:28:25
6:24:25	7:01:31	7:23:03	7:40:06	8:02:29	8:20:44	8:30:31	8:43:47	9:03:33	9:28:37
6:25:08	7:01:39	7:23:16	7:40:23	8:02:39	8:20:54	8:31:02	8:44:23	9:03:38	9:29:09
6:25:19	7:01:56	7:23:19	7:41:34	8:02:47	8:21:12	8:31:11	8:44:49	9:03:51	9:29:15
6:25:27	7:04:52	7:23:48	7:42:20	8:02:52	8:21:12	8:31:19	8:45:05	9:04:11	9:29:52
6:25:38	7:04:54	7:24:01	7:42:33	8:03:06	8:21:25	8:31:20	8:45:10	9:04:33	9:30:47
6:25:48	7:05:37	7:24:09	7:42:51	8:03:58	8:21:28	8:31:22	8:45:28	9:04:42	9:30:58
6:26:05	7:05:39	7:24:45	7:42:57	8:04:07	8:21:43	8:31:23	8:45:31	9:04:44	9:30:59
6:26:59	7:05:42	7:24:56	7:43:23	8:04:27	8:21:44	8:31:27	8:45:32	9:04:44	9:31:03
6:27:37	7:06:37	7:25:01	7:43:34	8:05:53	8:21:53	8:31:45	8:45:39	9:05:22	9:31:55
6:27:46	7:06:46	7:25:03	7:43:43	8:05:54	8:22:19	8:32:05	8:46:24	9:06:01	9:33:08
6:29:32	7:07:11	7:25:18	7:43:44	8:06:43	8:22:44	8:32:13	8:46:27	9:06:12	9:33:45
6:29:52	7:07:24	7:25:39	7:43:57	8:06:47	8:23:00	8:32:19	8:46:40	9:06:14	9:34:07
6:30:26	7:07:46	7:25:40	7:43:57	8:07:07	8:23:02	8:32:59	8:46:41	9:06:41	9:35:15
6:30:32	7:09:17	7:25:46	7:45:07	8:07:43	8:23:12	8:33:02	8:47:00	9:06:44	9:35:40
6:30:41	7:09:34	7:25:48	7:45:32	8:08:28	8:23:30	8:33:27	8:47:04	9:06:48	9:36:17
6:30:53	7:09:38	7:26:30	7:46:22	8:08:31	8:24:04	8:33:30	8:47:06	9:06:55	9:36:37
6:30:56	7:09:53	7:26:38	7:46:38	8:09:05	8:24:17	8:33:40	8:47:15	9:06:59	9:37:23
6:31:04	7:09:59	7:26:49	7:46:48	8:09:15	8:24:19	8:33:47	8:47:27	9:08:03	9:37:37
6:31:45	7:10:29	7:27:30	7:47:00	8:09:48	8:24:26	8:34:19	8:47:40	9:08:33	9:37:38
6:33:49	7:10:37	7:27:36	7:47:15	8:09:57	8:24:39	8:34:20	8:47:46	9:09:32	9:37:42
6:34:03	7:10:54	7:27:50	7:47:53	8:10:39	8:24:48	8:35:01	8:47:53	9:10:32	9:39:03
6:34:15	7:11:07	7:27:50	7:48:01	8:11:16	8:25:03	8:35:07	8:48:27	9:10:46	9:39:10
6:36:07	7:11:30	7:27:56	7:48:14	8:11:30	8:25:04	8:35:25	8:48:48	9:10:53	9:41:37
6:36:12	7:12:02	7:28:01	7:48:14	8:11:38	8:25:07	8:35:29	8:49:14	9:11:32	9:42:58
6:37:21	7:12:08	7:28:17	7:48:50	8:11:49	8:25:16	8:36:13	8:49:19	9:11:37	9:43:27
6:37:23	7:12:18	7:28:25	7:49:00	8:12:00	8:25:22	8:36:14	8:49:20	9:11:50	9:43:37
6:37:57	7:12:18	7:28:26	7:49:04	8:12:07	8:25:31	8:36:23	8:49:40	9:12:02	9:44:09
6:38:20	7:12:26	7:28:47	7:49:48	8:12:17	8:25:32	8:36:23	8:50:19	9:13:19	9:44:21
6:40:06	7:13:16	7:28:54	7:49:50	8:12:40	8:25:32	8:36:29	8:50:38	9:14:00	9:44:32
6:40:11	7:13:21	7:29:09	7:49:59	8:12:41	8:25:45	8:36:35	8:52:11	9:14:04	9:44:37
6:40:59	7:13:22	7:29:27	7:50:13	8:12:42	8:25:48	8:36:37	8:52:29	9:14:07	9:44:44
6:42:17	7:14:04	7:30:02	7:50:27	8:12:47	8:25:49	8:37:05	8:52:40	9:15:15	9:45:10
6:43:01	7:14:07	7:30:07	7:51:07	8:13:40	8:26:01	8:37:11	8:52:41	9:15:26	9:46:15
6:43:05	7:14:49	7:30:13	7:51:31	8:13:41	8:26:04	8:37:12	8:52:43	9:15:27	9:46:44
6:43:57	7:15:19	7:30:50	7:51:40	8:13:52	8:26:11	8:37:35	8:53:03	9:15:36	9:49:48
6:44:02	7:15:38	7:30:55	7:52:05	8:14:04	8:26:15	8:37:44	8:53:08	9:15:40	9:50:19
6:45:04	7:15:41	7:31:24	7:52:25	8:14:41	8:26:28	8:38:01	8:53:19	9:15:40	9:52:53
6:46:13	7:15:57	7:31:35	7:52:32	8:15:15	8:26:28	8:38:02	8:53:30	9:15:40	9:53:13
6:47:01	7:16:28	7:31:41	7:53:10	8:15:25	8:26:37	8:38:10	8:53:32	9:15:41	9:53:15
6:47:10	7:16:36	7:31:45	7:53:18	8:15:39	8:26:58	8:38:15	8:53:44	9:15:46	9:53:50
6:47:35	7:16:40	7:31:46	7:53:19	8:15:48	8:27:07	8:38:39	8:54:25	9:16:12	9:54:24
6:49:23	7:16:45	7:32:13	7:53:51	8:16:09	8:27:09	8:38:40	8:54:28	9:16:34	9:54:48
6:50:54	7:16:50	7:32:16	7:53:52	8:16:10	8:27:17	8:38:44	8:54:49	9:18:02	9:54:51
6:51:04	7:17:08	7:32:16	7:54:04	8:16:18	8:27:26	8:38:49	8:55:05	9:18:06	9:56:40
6:51:17	7:17:09	7:32:34	7:54:16	8:16:26	8:27:29	8:38:57	8:55:05	9:20:19	9:58:25
6:51:48	7:17:09	7:32:34	7:54:26	8:16:39	8:27:35	8:39:07	8:55:14	9:20:42	9:59:19
6:52:17	7:17:19	7:32:57	7:54:51	8:17:16	8:27:54	8:39:20	8:55:22	9:20:44	
6:52:17	7:17:22	7:33:13	7:55:13	8:17:24	8:27:57	8:39:20	8:55:25	9:20:54	
6:52:31	7:17:22	7:33:36	7:55:35	8:17:28	8:27:59	8:39:21	8:55:50	9:21:55	

risk related to any mathematical model or computer simulation is that these tools always provide us with a number (or a set of numbers), independent of the accuracy, with which the inputs we enter into the equation reflect the real world.

Answering the following two questions before proceeding to any other computations improves the predictions of our models substantially.

- Is the arrival process *stationary;* that is, is the expected number of customers arriving in a certain time interval constant over the period we are interested in?
- Are the interarrival times *exponentially distributed,* and therefore form a so-called *Poisson* arrival process?

We now define the concepts of stationary arrivals and exponentially distributed interarrival times. We also describe how these two questions can be answered, both in general as well as in the specific setting of the call center described previously. We also discuss the importance of these two questions and their impact on the calculations in this and the next chapter.

Stationary Arrivals

Consider the call arrival pattern displayed in Table 9.1. How tempting it is to put these data into a spreadsheet, compute the mean and the standard deviation of the interarrival times over that time period, and end the analysis of the arrival pattern at this point, assuming that the mean and the standard deviation capture the entire behavior of the arrival process. Five minutes with Excel, and we could be done!

However, a simple graphical analysis (Figure 9.6) of the data reveals that there is more going on in the arrival process than two numbers can capture. As we can see graphically in Figure 9.6, the average number of customers calling within a certain time interval (e.g., 15 minutes) is not constant over the day.

To capture such changes in arrival processes, we introduce the following definitions:

- An arrival process is said to be *stationary* if, for any time interval (e.g., an hour), the expected number of arrivals in this time interval only depends on the length of the time interval, not on the starting time of the interval (i.e., we can move a time interval of a fixed length back and forth on a time line without changing the expected number of arrivals). In the context of Figure 9.6, we see that the arrival process is not stationary. For example, if we take a 3-hour interval, we see that there are many more customers arriving from 6 a.m. to 9 a.m. than there are from 1 a.m. to 4 a.m.
- An arrival process exhibits *seasonality* if it is not stationary.

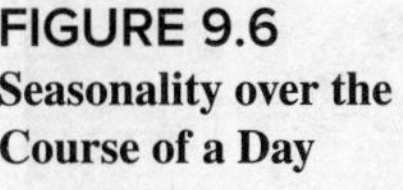
FIGURE 9.6
Seasonality over the Course of a Day

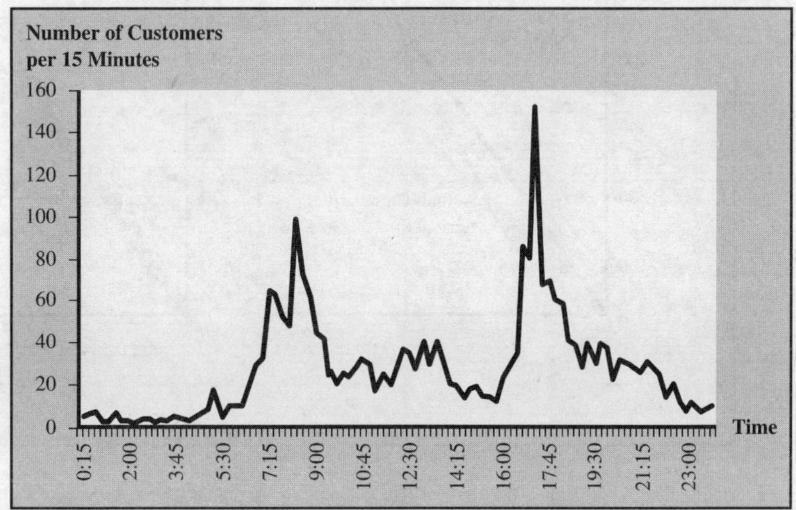

When analyzing an arrival process, it is important that we distinguish between changes in demand (e.g., the number of calls in 15 minutes) that are a result of variability and changes in demand that are a result of seasonality. Both variability and seasonality are unpleasant from an operations perspective. However, the effect of seasonality alone can be perfectly predicted *ex ante,* while this is not possible for the case of variability (we might know the expected number of callers for a day, but the actual number is a realization of a random variable).

Based on the data at hand, we observe that the arrival process is not stationary over a period of several hours. In general, a simple analysis determines whether a process is stationary.

- Sort all arrival times so that they are increasing in time (label them as $AT_1 \ldots AT_n$).
- Plot a graph with (x AT_i; $y = i$) as illustrated by Figure 9.7.
- Add a straight line from the lower left (first arrival) to the upper right (last arrival).

If the underlying arrival process is stationary, there will be no significant deviation between the graph you plotted and the straight line. In this case, however, in Figure 9.7 (left) we observe several deviations between the straight line and the arrival data. Specifically, we observe that for the first hour, fewer calls come in compared to the average arrival rate from 6 a.m. to 10 a.m. In contrast, around 8:30 a.m., the arrival rate becomes much higher than the average. Thus, our analysis indicates that the arrival process we face is not stationary.

When facing nonstationary arrival processes, the best way to proceed is to divide up the day (the week, the month) into smaller time intervals and have a separate arrival rate for each interval. If we then look at the arrival process within the smaller intervals—in our case, we use 15-minute intervals—we find that the seasonality within the interval is relatively low. In other words, within the interval, we come relatively close to a stationary arrival stream. The stationary behavior of the interarrivals within a 15-minute interval is illustrated by Figure 9.7 (right).

FIGURE 9.7
Test for Stationary Arrivals

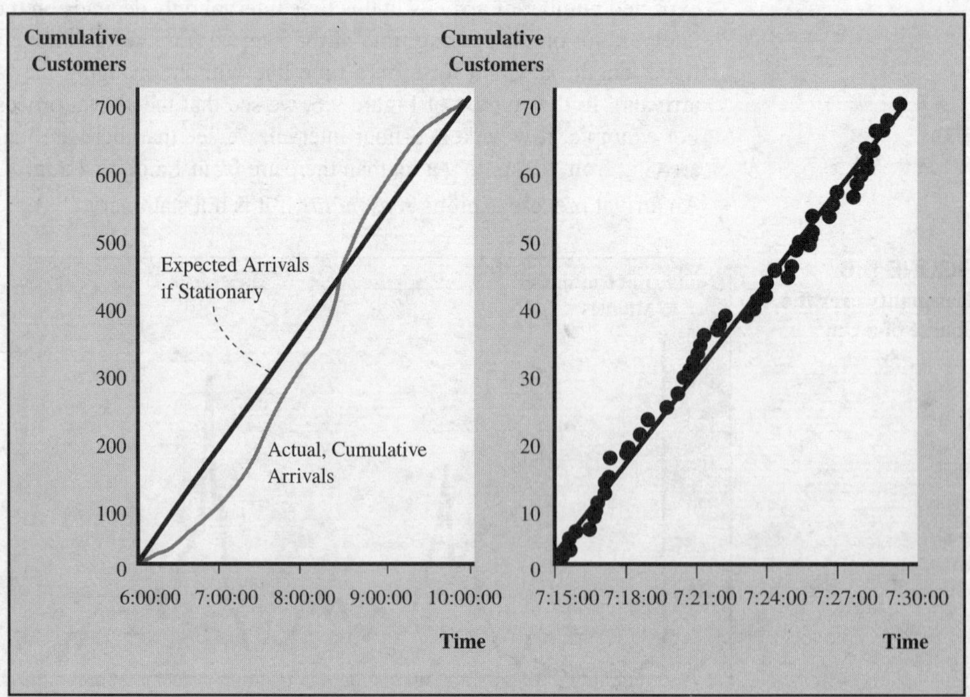

Figure 9.7 (left) is interesting to compare with Figure 9.7 (right): the arrival process behaves as stationary "at the micro-level" of a 15-minute interval, yet exhibits strong seasonality over the course of the entire day, as we observed in Figure 9.6. Note that the peaks in Figure 9.6 correspond to those time slots where the line of "actual, cumulative arrivals" in Figure 9.7 grows faster than the straight line "predicted arrivals."

In most cases in practice, the context explains this type of seasonality. For example, in the case of An-ser, the spike in arrivals corresponds to people beginning their day, expecting that the company they want to call (e.g., a doctor's office) is already "up and running." However, since many of these firms are not handling calls before 9 a.m., the resulting call stream is channeled to the answering service.

Exponential Interarrival Times

Interarrival times commonly are distributed following an *exponential distribution*. If IA is a random interarrival time and the interarrival process follows an exponential distribution, we have

$$\text{Probability } \{\text{IA} \leq t\} = 1 - e^{-\frac{t}{a}}$$

where a is the average interarrival time as defined above. Exponential functions are frequently used to model interarrival time in theory as well as practice, both because of their good fit with empirical data as well as their analytical convenience. If an arrival process has indeed exponential interarrival times, we refer to it as a *Poisson arrival process*.

It can be shown analytically that customers arriving independently from each other at the process (e.g., customers calling into a call center) form a demand pattern with exponential interarrival times. The shape of the cumulative distribution function for the exponential distribution is given in Figure 9.8. The average interarrival time is in minutes. An important property of the exponential distribution is that the standard deviation is also equal to the average, a.

FIGURE 9.8 **Distribution Function of the Exponential Distribution (left) and an Example of a Histogram (right)**

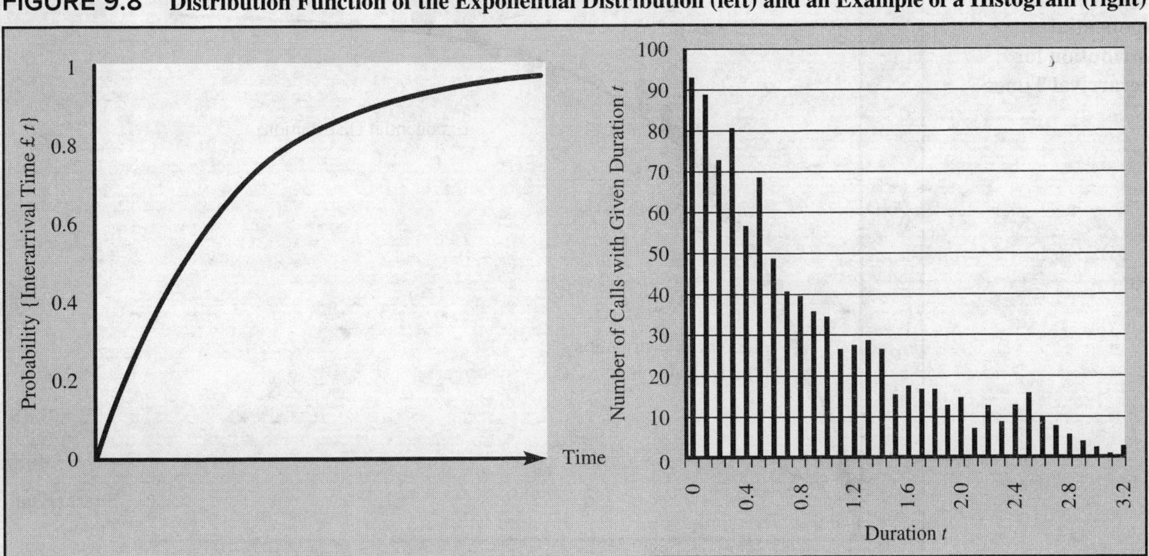

Another important property of the exponential distribution is known as the *memoryless property*. The memoryless property simply states that the number of arrivals in the next time slot (e.g., 1 minute) is independent of when the last arrival has occurred.

To illustrate this property, consider the situation of an emergency room. Assume that, on average, a patient arrives every 10 minutes and no patients have arrived for the last 20 minutes. Does the fact that no patients have arrived in the last 20 minutes increase or decrease the probability that a patient arrives in the next 10 minutes? For an arrival process with exponential interarrival times, the answer is *no*.

Intuitively, we feel that this is a reasonable assumption in many settings. Consider, again, an emergency room. Given that the population of potential patients for the ER is extremely large (including all healthy people outside the hospital), we can treat new patients as arriving independently from each other (the fact that Joan Wiley fell off her mountain bike has nothing to do with the fact that Joe Hoop broke his ankle when playing basketball).

Because it is very important to determine if our interarrival times are exponentially distributed, we now introduce the following four-step diagnostic procedure:

1. Compute the interarrival times $IA_1 \ldots IA_n$.
2. Sort the interarrival times in increasing order; let a_i denote the ith smallest interarrival time (a_1 is the smallest interarrival time; a_n is the largest).
3. Plot pairs ($x = a_i$, $y = i/n$). The resulting graph is called an empirical distribution function.
4. Compare the graph with an exponential distribution with "appropriately chosen parameter." To find the best value for the parameter, we set the parameter of the exponential distribution equal to the average interarrival time we obtain from our data. If a few observations from the sample are substantially remote from the resulting curve, we might adjust the parameter for the exponential distribution "manually" to improve fit.

Figure 9.9 illustrates the outcome of this process. If the underlying distribution is indeed exponential, the resulting graph will resemble the analytical distribution as in the case of

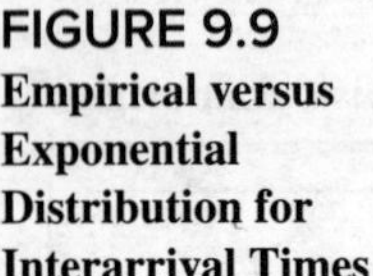
FIGURE 9.9 **Empirical versus Exponential Distribution for Interarrival Times**

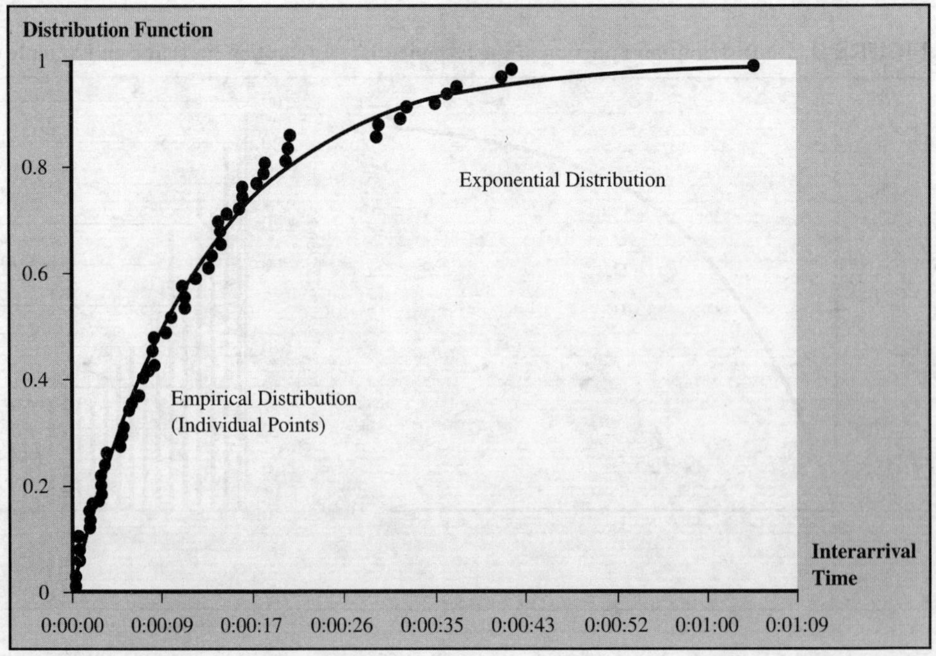

FIGURE 9.10
How to Analyze a Demand/Arrival Process

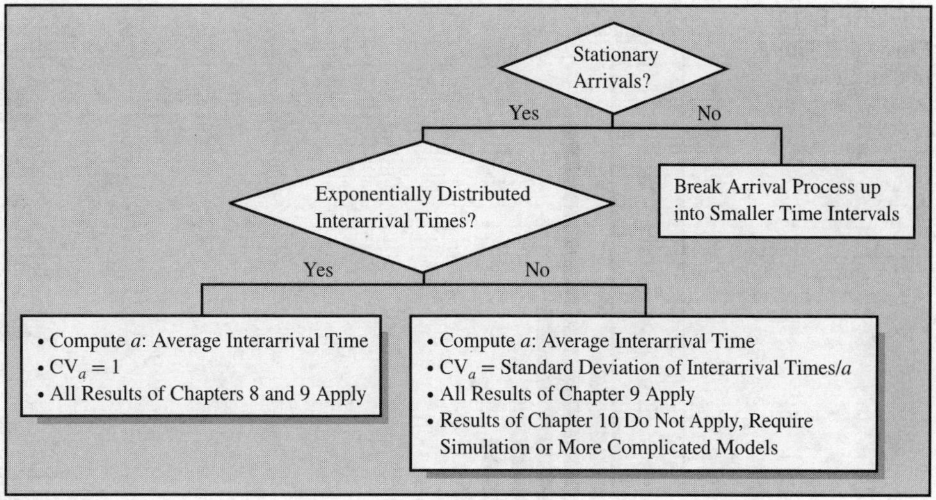

Figure 9.9. Note that this procedure of assessing the goodness of fit works also for any other distribution function.

Nonexponential Interarrival Times

In some cases, we might find that the interarrival times are not exponentially distributed. For example, we might encounter a situation where arrivals are scheduled (e.g., every hour), which typically leads to a lower amount of variability in the arrival process.

While in the case of the exponential distribution the mean interarrival time is equal to the standard deviation of interarrival times and, thus, one parameter is sufficient to characterize the entire arrival process, we need more parameters to describe the arrival process if interarrival times are not exponentially distributed.

Following our earlier definition of the coefficient of variation, we can measure the variability of an arrival (demand) process as

$$\text{CV}_a = \frac{\text{Standard deviation of interarrival time}}{\text{Average interarrival time}}$$

Given that for the exponential distribution the mean is equal to the standard deviation, its coefficient of variation is equal to 1.

Summary: Analyzing an Arrival Process

Figure 9.10 provides a summary of the steps required to analyze an arrival process. It also shows what to do if any of the assumptions required for other models are violated.

9.4 Processing Time Variability

Just as exact arrival time of an individual call is difficult to predict, so is the actual duration of the call. Thus, service processes also have a considerable amount of variability from the supply side. Figure 9.11 provides a summary of call durations for the case of the An-ser call center. From the perspective of the customer service representative, these call durations are the processing times. As mentioned previously, we will use the words *processing time, service time,* and *activity time* interchangeably.

FIGURE 9.11
Processing Times in Call Center

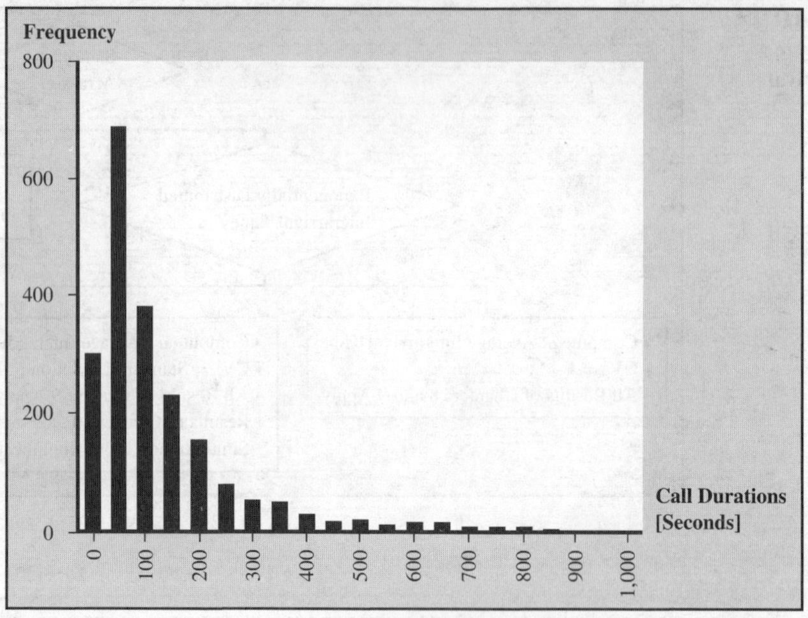

We observe that the variability in processing times is substantial. While some calls were completed in less than a minute, others took more than 10 minutes! Thus, in addition to the variability of demand, variability also is created within the process.

There have been reports of numerous different shapes of processing time distributions. For the purposes of this book, we focus entirely on their mean and standard deviation. In other words, when we collect data, we do not explicitly model the distribution of the processing times, but assume that the mean and standard deviation capture all the relevant information. This information is sufficient for all computations in Chapters 9 and 10.

Based on the data summarized in Figure 9.11, we compute the mean processing time as 120 seconds and the corresponding standard deviation as 150 seconds. As we have done with the interarrival times, we can now define the coefficient of variation, which we obtain by

$$CV_p = \frac{\text{Standard deviation of processing time}}{\text{Average processing time}}$$

Here, the subscript p indicates that the CV measures the variability in the processing times. As with the arrival process, we need to be careful not to confuse variability with seasonality. Seasonality in processing times refers to known patterns of call durations as a function of the day of the week or the time of the day (as Figure 9.12 shows, calls take significantly longer on weekends than during the week). Call durations also differ depending on the time of the day.

The models we are about to introduce require a stationary service process (in the case of seasonality in the service process, just divide up the time line into smaller intervals, similar to what we did with the arrival process) but do not require any other properties (e.g., exponential distribution of processing time). Thus, the standard deviation and mean of the processing time are all we need to know.

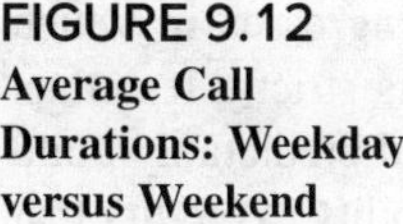

FIGURE 9.12
Average Call Durations: Weekday versus Weekend

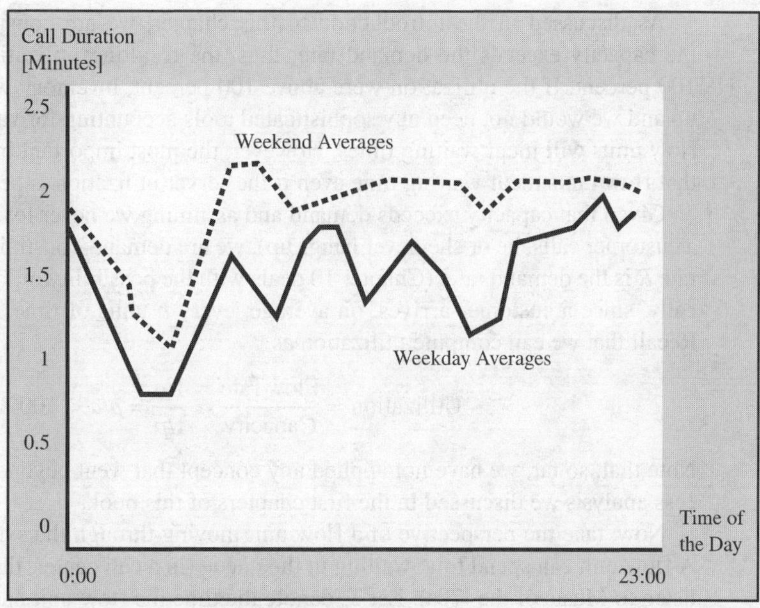

9.5 Predicting the Average Waiting Time for the Case of One Resource

Based on our measures of variability, we now introduce a simple formula that restores our ability to predict the basic process performance measures: inventory, flow rate, and flow time.

In this chapter, we restrict ourselves to the most basic process diagram, consisting of one buffer with unlimited space and one single resource. This process layout corresponds to the call center example discussed above. Figure 9.13 shows the process flow diagram for this simple system.

Flow units arrive to the system following a demand pattern that exhibits variability. On average, a flow unit arrives every *a* time units. We labeled *a* as the average interarrival time. This average reflects the mean of interarrival times IA_1 to IA_n. After computing the standard deviation of the IA_1 to IA_n interarrival times, we can compute the coefficient of variation CV_a of the arrival process as discussed previously.

Assume that it takes on average *p* units of time to serve a flow unit. Similar to the arrival process, we can define p_1 to p_n as the empirically observed processing times and compute the coefficient of variation for the processing times, CV_p, accordingly. Given that there is only one single resource serving the arriving flow units, the capacity of the server can be written as $1/p$.

FIGURE 9.13
A Simple Process with One Queue and One Server

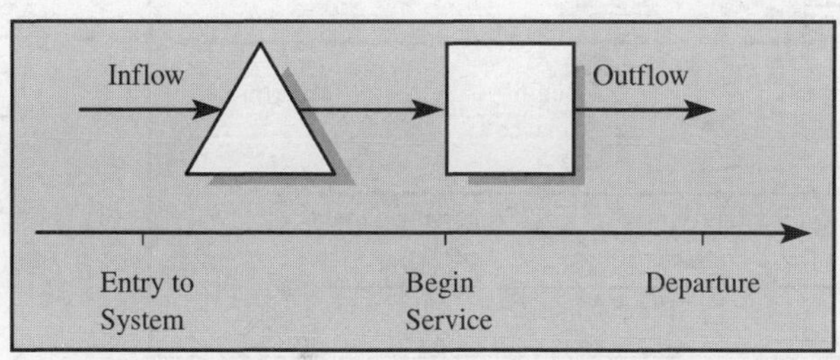

As discussed in the introduction to this chapter, we are considering cases in which the capacity exceeds the demand rate; thus, the resulting utilization is strictly less than 100 percent. If the utilization were above 100 percent, inventory would predictably build up and we would not need any sophisticated tools accounting for variability to predict that flow units will incur waiting times. However, the most important insight of this chapter is that flow units incur waiting time even if the server utilization is below 100 percent.

Given that capacity exceeds demand and assuming we never lose a customer (i.e., once a customer calls, he or she never hangs up), we are demand-constrained and, thus, the flow rate R is the demand rate. (Chapter 10 deals with the possibility of lost customers.) Specifically, since a customer arrives, on average, every a units of time, the flow rate $R = 1/a$. Recall that we can compute utilization as

$$\text{Utilization} = \frac{\text{Flow rate}}{\text{Capacity}} = \frac{1/a}{1/p} = p/a < 100\%$$

Note that, so far, we have not applied any concept that went beyond the deterministic process analysis we discussed in the first chapters of this book.

Now, take the perspective of a flow unit moving through the system (see Figure 9.14). A flow unit can spend time waiting in the queue (in a call center, this is the time when you listen to Music of the '70s). Let T_q denote the time the flow unit has to spend in the queue waiting for the service to begin. The subscript q denotes that this is only the time the flow unit waits in the queue. Thus, T_q does *not* include the actual processing time, which we defined as p. Based on the waiting time in the queue T_q and the average processing time p, we can compute the flow time (the time the flow unit will spend in the system) as

$$\text{Flow time} = \text{Time in queue} + \text{Processing time}$$
$$T = T_q + p$$

Instead of taking the perspective of the flow unit, we also can look at the system as a whole, wondering how many flow units will be in the queue and how many will be in service. Let I_q be defined as the inventory (number of flow units) that are in the queue and I_p be the number of flow units in process. Since the inventory in the queue I_q and the inventory in process I_p are the only places we can find inventory, we can compute the overall inventory in the system as $I = I_q + I_p$.

As long as there exists only one resource, I_p is a number between zero and one: sometimes there is a flow unit in service ($I_p = 1$); sometimes there is not ($I_p = 0$). The probability that at a random moment in time the server is actually busy, working on a flow unit, corresponds to the utilization. For example, if the utilization of the process is 30 percent,

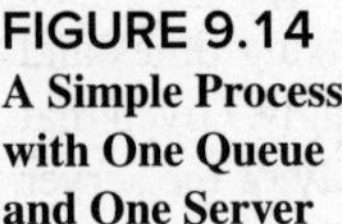

FIGURE 9.14
A Simple Process with One Queue and One Server

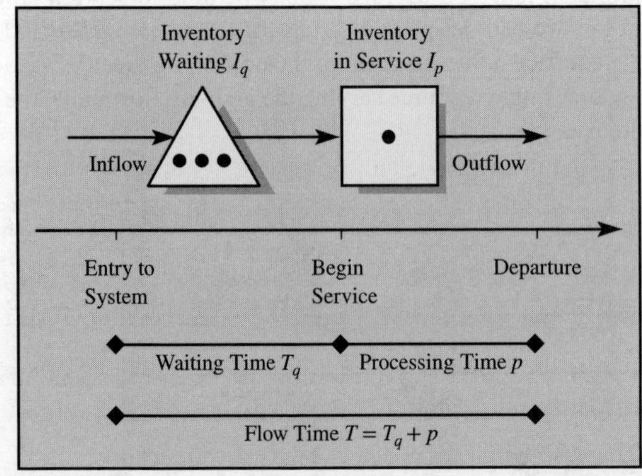

there exists a .3 probability that at a random moment in time the server is busy. Alternatively, we can say that over the 60 minutes in an hour, the server is busy for

$$.3 \times 60[\text{minutes/hour}] = 18 \text{ minutes}$$

While the inventory in service I_p and the processing time p are relatively easy to compute, this is unfortunately not the case for the inventory in the queue I_q or the waiting time in the queue T_q.

Based on the processing time p, the utilization, and the variability as measured by the coefficients of variation for the interarrival time CV_a and the processing time CV_p, we can compute the average waiting time in the queue using the following formula:

$$\text{Time in queue} = \text{Processing time} \times \left(\frac{\text{Utilization}}{1 - \text{Utilization}}\right) \times \left(\frac{CV_a^2 + CV_p^2}{2}\right)$$

The formula does not require that the processing times or the interarrival times follow a specific distribution. Yet, for the case of nonexponential interarrival times, the formula only approximates the expected time in the queue, as opposed to being 100 percent exact. The formula should be used only for the case of a stationary process (see Section 9.3 for the definition of a stationary process as well as for what to do if the process is not stationary).

The above equation states that the waiting time in the queue is the product of three factors:

- The waiting time is expressed as multiples of the processing time. However, it is important to keep in mind that the processing time also directly influences the utilization (as Utilization = Processing time/Interarrival time). Thus, one should not think of the waiting time as increasing linearly with the processing time.
- The second factor captures the utilization effect. Note that the utilization has to be less than 100 percent. If the utilization is equal to or greater than 100 percent, the queue continues to grow. This is not driven by variability, but simply by not having the requested capacity. We observe that the utilization factor is nonlinear and becomes larger and larger as the utilization level is increased closer to 100 percent. For example, for Utilization = 0.8, the utilization factor is 0.8/(1 – 0.8) = 4; for Utilization = 0.9, it is 0.9/(1 – 0.9) = 9; and for Utilization = 0.95, it grows to 0.95/(1 – 0.95) = 19.
- The third factor captures the amount of variability in the system, measured by the average of the squared coefficient of variation of interarrival times CV_a and processing times CV_p. Since CV_a and CV_p affect neither the average processing time p nor the utilization u, we observe that the waiting time grows with the variability in the system.

The best way to familiarize ourselves with this newly introduced formula is to apply it and "see it in action." Toward that end, consider the case of the An-ser call center at 2:00 a.m. in the morning. An-ser is a relatively small call center and they receive very few calls at this time of the day (see Section 9.3 for detailed arrival information), so at 2:00 a.m., there is only one person handling incoming calls.

From the data we collected in the call center, we can quickly compute that the average processing time at An-ser at this time of the day is around 90 seconds. Given that we found in the previous section that the processing time does depend on the time of the day, it is important that we use the processing time data representative for these early morning hours: Processing time p = 90 seconds.

Based on the empirical processing times we collected in Section 9.4, we now compute the standard deviation of the processing time to be 120 seconds. Hence, the coefficient of variation for the processing time is

$$CV_p = 120 \text{ seconds}/90 \text{ seconds} = 1.3333$$

From the arrival data we collected (see Figure 9.6), we know that at 2:00 a.m. there are 3 calls arriving in a 15-minute interval. Thus, the interarrival time is a = 5 minutes = 300 seconds. Given the processing time and the interarrival time, we can now compute the utilization as

$$\text{Utilization} = \text{Processing time/Interarrival time}(= p/a)$$
$$= 90 \text{ seconds}/300 \text{ seconds} = 0.3$$

Concerning the coefficient of variation of the interarrival time, we can take one of two approaches. First, we could take the observed interarrival times and compute the standard deviation empirically. Alternatively, we could view the arrival process during the time period as random. Given the good fit between the data we collected and the exponential distribution (see Figure 9.9), we assume that arrivals follow a Poisson process (interarrival times are exponentially distributed). This implies a coefficient of variation of

$$CV_a = 1$$

Substituting these values into the waiting time formula yields

$$\text{Time in queue} = \text{Processing time} \times \left(\frac{\text{Utilization}}{1 - \text{Utilization}}\right) \times \left(\frac{CV_a^2 + CV_p^2}{2}\right)$$
$$= 90 \times \frac{0.3}{1 - 0.3} \times \frac{1^2 + 1.3333^2}{2}$$
$$= 53.57 \text{ seconds}$$

Note that this result captures the average waiting time of a customer before getting served. To obtain the customer's total time spent for the call, including waiting time and processing time, we need to add the processing time p for the actual service. Thus, the flow time can be computed as

$$T = T_q + p = 53.57 \text{ seconds} + 90 \text{ seconds} = 143.57 \text{ seconds}$$

It is important to point out that the value 53.57 seconds provides the average waiting time. The actual waiting times experienced by individual customers vary. Some customers get lucky and receive service immediately; others have to wait much longer than 53.57 seconds. This is discussed further below.

Waiting times computed based on the methodology outlined above need to be seen as long-run averages. This has the following two practical implications:

- If the system would start empty (e.g., in a hospital lab, where there are no patients before the opening of the waiting room), the first couple of patients are less likely to experience significant waiting time. This effect is transient: Once a sufficient number of patients have arrived, the system reaches a "steady state." Note that given the 24-hour operation of An-ser, this is not an issue in this specific case.
- If we observe the system for a given time interval, it is unlikely that the average waiting time we observe within this interval is exactly the average we computed. However, the longer we observe the system, the more likely the expected waiting time T_q will indeed coincide with the empirical average. This resembles a casino, which cannot predict how much money a specific guest will win (or typically lose) in an evening, yet can well predict the economics of the entire guest population over the course of a year.

Now that we have accounted for the waiting time T_q (or the flow time T), we are able to compute the resulting inventory. With $1/a$ being our flow rate, we can use Little's Law to compute the average inventory I as

$$I = R \times T = \frac{1}{a} \times (T_q + p)$$

$$= 1/300 \times (53.57 + 90) = 0.479$$

Thus, there is, on average, about half a customer in the system (it is 2:00 a.m. after all . . .). This inventory includes the two subsets we defined as inventory in the queue (I_q) and inventory in process (I_p):

- I_q can be obtained by applying Little's Law, but this time, rather than applying Little's Law to the entire system (the waiting line and the server), we apply it only to the waiting line in isolation. If we think of the waiting line as a mini process in itself (the corresponding process flow diagram consists only of one triangle), we obtain a flow time of T_q. Hence,

$$I_q = 1/a \times T_q = 1/300 \times 53.57 = 0.179$$

- At any given moment in time, we also can look at the number of customers that are currently talking to the customer service representative. Since we assumed there would only be one representative at this time of the day, there will never be more than one caller at this stage. However, there are moments in time when no caller is served, as the utilization of the employee is well below 100 percent. The average number of callers in service can thus be computed as

$$I_p = \text{Probability}\{0 \text{ callers talking to representative}\} \times 0$$
$$+ \text{Probability}\{1 \text{ caller talking to representative}\} \times 1$$
$$I_p = (1 - u) \times 0 + u \times 1 = u$$

In this case, we obtain $I_p = 0.3$.

9.6 Predicting the Average Waiting Time for the Case of Multiple Resources

After analyzing waiting time in the presence of variability for an extremely simple process, consisting of just one buffer and one resource, we now turn to more complicated operations. Specifically, we analyze a waiting time model of a process consisting of one waiting area (queue) and a process step performed by multiple, identical resources.

We continue our example of the call center. However, now we consider time slots at busier times over the course of the day, when there are many more customer representatives on duty in the An-ser call center. The basic process layout is illustrated in Figure 9.15.

Let m be the number of parallel servers we have available. Given that we have m servers working in parallel, we now face a situation where the average processing time is likely to be much longer than the average interarrival time. Taken together, the m resources have a capacity of m/p, while the demand rate continues to be given by $1/a$. We can compute the utilization u of the service process as

$$\text{Utilization} = \frac{\text{Flow rate}}{\text{Capacity}} = \frac{1/\text{Interarrival time}}{(\text{Number of resources/Processing time})}$$

$$= \frac{1/a}{m/p} = \frac{p}{a \times m}$$

FIGURE 9.15
A Process with One Queue and Multiple, Parallel Servers (m = 5)

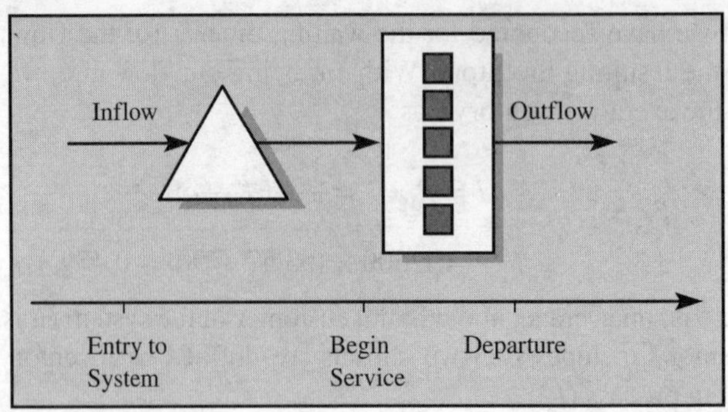

Similar to the case with one single resource, we are only interested in the cases of utilization levels below 100 percent.

The flow unit will initially spend T_q units of time waiting for service. It then moves to the next available resource, where it spends p units of time for service. As before, the total flow time is the sum of waiting time and processing time:

$$\text{Flow time} = \text{Waiting time in queue} + \text{Processing time}$$
$$T = T_q + p$$

Based on the processing time p, the utilization u, the coefficients of variation for both service (CV_p) and arrival process (CV_a) as well as the number of resources in the system (m), we can compute the average waiting time T_q using the following formula:[1]

$$\text{Time in queue} = \left(\frac{\text{Processing time}}{m}\right) \times \left(\frac{\text{Utilization}^{\sqrt{2(m+1)}-1}}{1 - \text{Utilization}}\right) \times \left(\frac{CV_a^2 + CV_p^2}{2}\right)$$

As in the case of one single resource, the waiting time is expressed as the product of the processing time, a utilization factor, and a variability factor. We also observe that for the special case of $m = 1$, the above formula is exactly the same as the waiting time formula for a single resource. Note that all other performance measures, including the flow time (T), the inventory in the system (I), and the inventory in the queue (I_q), can be computed as discussed before.

While the above expression does not necessarily seem an inviting equation to use, it can be programmed without much effort into a spreadsheet. Furthermore, it provides the average waiting time for a system that otherwise could only be analyzed with much more sophisticated software packages.

Unlike the waiting time formula for the single resource case, which provides an exact quantification of waiting times as long as the interarrival times follow an exponential distribution, the waiting time formula for multiple resources is an approximation. The formula works well for most settings we encounter, specifically if the ratio of utilization u to the number of servers m is large (u/m is high).

Now that we have computed waiting time, we can again use Little's Law to compute the average number of flow units in the waiting area I_q, the average number of flow units in service I_p, and the average number of flow units in the entire system $I = I_p + I_q$. Figure 9.16 summarizes the key performance measures.

[1] Hopp and Spearman (1996); the formula initially had been proposed by Sakasegawa (1977) and used successfully by Whitt (1983). For $m = 1$, the formula is exactly the same as in the previous section. The formula is an approximation for $m > 1$. An exact expression for this case does not exist.

FIGURE 9.16
Summary of Key Performance Measures

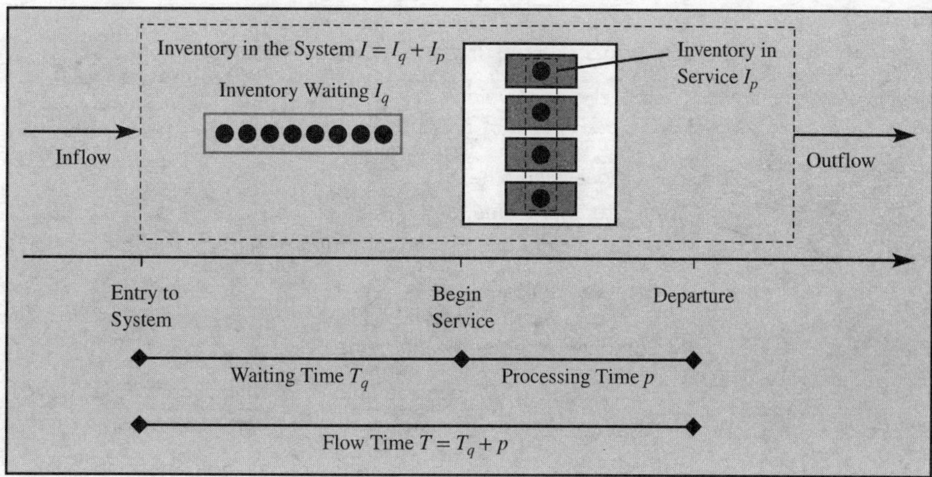

Note that in the presence of multiple resources serving flow units, there can be more than one flow unit in service simultaneously. If u is the utilization of the process, it is also the utilization of each of the m resources, as they process demand at the same rate. We can compute the expected number of flow units at any of the m resources *in isolation* as

$$u \times 1 + (1 - u) \times 0 = u$$

Adding up across the m resources then yields

$$\text{Inventory in process} = \text{Number of resources} \times \text{Utilization}$$
$$I_p = m \times u$$

We illustrate the methodology using the case of An-ser services. Assuming we would work with a staff of 10 customer service representatives (CSRs) for the 8:00 a.m. to 8:15 a.m. time slot, we can compute the utilization as follows:

$$\text{Utilization } u = \frac{p}{a \times m} = \frac{90[\text{seconds/call}]}{11.39 \times 10[\text{seconds/call}]} = 0.79$$

where we obtained the interarrival time of 11.39 seconds between calls by dividing the length of the time interval (15 minutes = 900 seconds) by the number of calls received over the interval (79 calls). This now allows us to compute the average waiting time as

$$T_q = \left(\frac{p}{m}\right) \times \left(\frac{u^{\sqrt{2(m+1)}-1}}{1-u}\right) \times \left(\frac{CV_a^2 + CV_p^2}{2}\right)$$
$$= \left(\frac{90}{10}\right) \times \left(\frac{0.79^{\sqrt{2(10+1)}-1}}{1-0.79}\right) \times \left(\frac{1 + 1.3333^2}{2}\right) = 24.94 \text{ seconds}$$

The most important calculations related to waiting times caused by variability are summarized in Exhibit 9.1.

Exhibit 9.1

SUMMARY OF WAITING TIME CALCULATIONS

1. Collect the following data:
   - Number of servers, m
   - Processing time, p
   - Interarrival time, a
   - Coefficient of variation for interarrival (CV_a) and processing time (CV_p)
2. Compute utilization: $u = \dfrac{p}{a \times m}$
3. Compute expected waiting time:

$$T_q = \left(\frac{\text{Processing time}}{m}\right) \times \left(\frac{\text{Utilization}^{\sqrt{2(m+1)}-1}}{1 - \text{Utilization}}\right) \times \left(\frac{CV_a^2 + CV_p^2}{2}\right)$$

4. Based on T_q, we can compute the remaining performance measures as

$$\text{Flow time } T = T_q + p$$
$$\text{Inventory in service } I_p = m \times u$$
$$\text{Inventory in the queue } I_q = T_q / a$$
$$\text{Inventory in the system } I = I_p + I_q$$

9.7 Service Levels in Waiting Time Problems

So far, we have focused our attention on the average waiting time in the process. However, a customer requesting service from our process is not interested in the average time he or she waits in queue or the average total time to complete his or her request (waiting time T_q and flow time T respectively), but in the wait times that he or she experiences personally.

Consider, for example, a caller who has just waited for 15 minutes listening to music while on hold. This caller is likely to be unsatisfied about the long wait time. Moreover, the response from the customer service representative of the type "we are sorry for your delay, but our average waiting time is only 4 minutes" is unlikely to reduce this dissatisfaction.

Thus, from a managerial perspective, we not only need to analyze the average wait time, but also the likelihood that the wait time exceeds a certain *target wait time* (*TWT*). More formally, we can define the *service level* for a given target wait time as the percentage of customers that will begin service in the TWT or less units of waiting time:

$$\text{Service level} = \text{Probability}\{\text{Waiting time} \leq \text{TWT}\}$$

This service level provides us with a way to measure to what extent the service is able to respond to demand within a consistent waiting time. A service level of 95 percent for a target waiting time of TWT = 2 minutes means that 95 percent of the customers are served in less than 2 minutes of waiting time.

Figure 9.17 shows the empirical distribution function (see Section 9.3 on how to create this graph) for waiting times at the An-ser call center for a selected time slot. Based on the graph, we can distinguish between two groups of customers. About 65 percent of the customers did not have to wait at all and received immediate service. The remaining 35 percent of the customers experienced a waiting time that strongly resembles an exponential distribution.

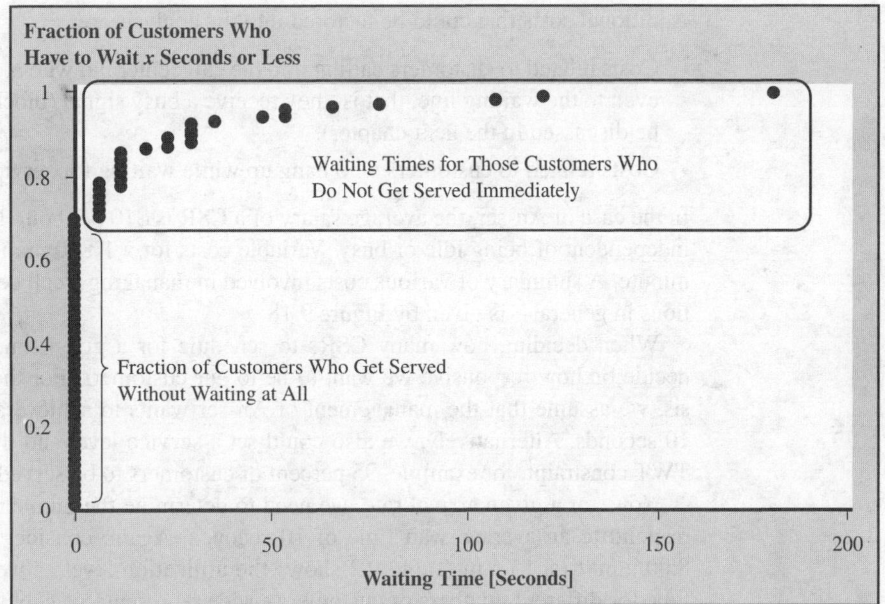

FIGURE 9.17 **Empirical Distribution of Waiting Times at An-ser**

We observe that the average waiting time for the entire calling population (not just the ones who had to wait) was, for this specific sample, about 10 seconds. For a target wait time TWT = 30 seconds, we find a service level of 90 percent; that is, 90 percent of the callers had to wait 30 seconds or less.

Service levels as defined above are a common performance measure for service operations in practice. They are used internally by the firm in charge of delivering a certain service. They also are used frequently by firms that want to outsource a service, such as a call center, as a way to contract (and track) the responsiveness of their service provider.

There is no universal rule of what service level is right for a given service operation. For example, responding to large public pressure, the German railway system (Deutsche Bundesbahn) introduced a policy that 80 percent of the calls to their customer complaint number should be handled within 20 seconds. Previously, only 30 percent of the calls were handled within 20 seconds. How fast you respond to calls depends on your market position and the importance of the incoming calls for your business. A service level that worked for the German railway system (30 percent within 20 seconds) is likely to be unacceptable in other, more competitive environments.

9.8 Economic Implications: Generating a Staffing Plan

So far, we have focused purely on analyzing the call center for a given number of customer service representatives (CSRs) on duty and predicted the resulting waiting times. This raises the managerial question of how many CSRs An-ser should have at work at any given moment in time over the day. The more CSRs we schedule, the shorter the waiting time, but the more we need to pay in terms of wages.

When making this trade-off, we need to balance the following two costs:

- Cost of waiting, reflecting increased line charges for 1-800 numbers and customer dissatisfaction (line charges are incurred for the actual talk time as well as for the time the customer is on hold).
- Cost of service, resulting from the number of CSRs available.

Additional costs that could be factored into the analysis are

- Costs related to customers calling into the call center but who are not able to gain access even to the waiting line, that is, they receive a busy signal (blocked customers; this will be discussed in the next chapter).
- Costs related to customers who hang up while waiting for service.

In the case of An-ser, the average salary of a CSR is $10 per hour. Note that CSRs are paid independent of being idle or busy. Variable costs for a 1-800 number are about $0.05 per minute. A summary of various costs involved in managing a call center—or service operations in general—is given by Figure 9.18.

When deciding how many CSRs to schedule for a given time slot, we first need to decide on how responsive we want to be to our customers. For the purpose of our analysis, we assume that the management of An-ser wants to achieve an average wait time of 10 seconds. Alternatively, we also could set a service level and then staff according to a TWT constraint, for example, 95 percent of customers to be served in 20 seconds or less.

Now, for a given arrival rate, we need to determine the number of CSRs that will correspond to an average wait time of 10 seconds. Again, consider the time interval from 8:00 a.m. to 8:15 a.m. Table 9.2 shows the utilization level as well as the expected wait time for different numbers of customer service representatives. Note that using fewer than 8 servers would lead to a utilization above one, which would mean that queues would build up independent of variability, which is surely not acceptable.

Table 9.2 indicates that adding CSRs leads to a reduction in waiting time. For example, while a staff of 8 CSRs would correspond to an average waiting time of about 20 minutes, the average waiting time falls below 10 seconds once a twelfth CSR has been added. Thus, working with 12 CSRs allows An-ser to meet its target of an average wait time of 10 seconds. In this case, the actual service would be even better and we expect the average wait time for this specific time slot to be 5.50 seconds.

Providing a good service level does come at the cost of increased labor. The more CSRs are scheduled to serve, the lower is their utilization. In Chapter 4 we defined the cost of direct labor as

$$\text{Cost of direct labor} = \frac{\text{Total wages per unit of time}}{\text{Flow rate per unit of time}}$$

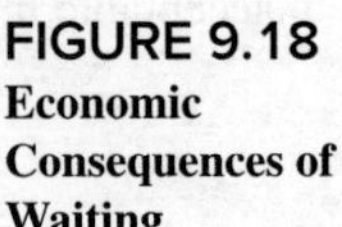

FIGURE 9.18 Economic Consequences of Waiting

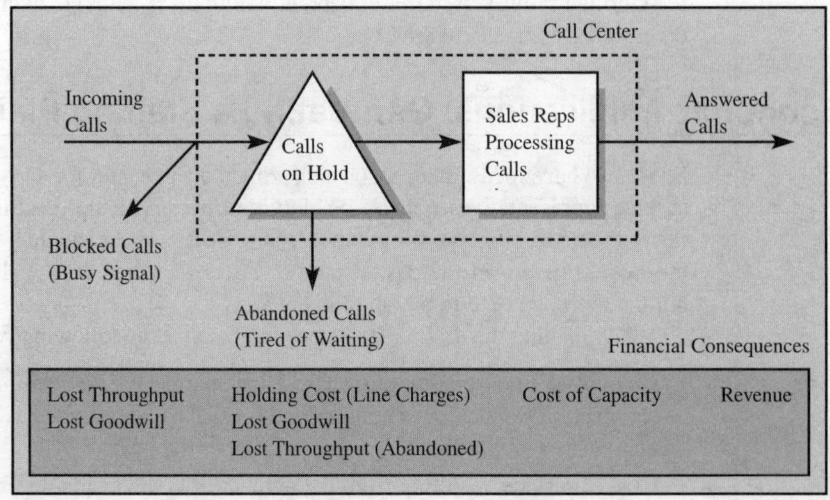

TABLE 9.2
Determining the Number of CSRs to Support Target Wait Time

Number of CSRs, m	Utilization $u = p/(a \times m)$	Expected Wait Time T_q [seconds] Based on Waiting Time Formula
8	0.99	1221.23
9	0.88	72.43
10	0.79	24.98
11	0.72	11.11
12	0.66	5.50
13	0.61	2.89
14	0.56	1.58

where the total wages per unit of time are determined by the number of CSRs m times their wage rate (in our case, \$10 per hour or 16.66 cents per minute) and the flow rate is determined by the arrival rate. Therefore,

$$\text{Cost of direct labor} = \frac{m \times 16.66 \text{ cents/minute}}{1/a} = a \times m \times 16.66 \text{ cents/minute}$$

An alternative way of writing the cost of labor uses the definition of utilization ($u = p/(a \times m)$). Thus, in the above equation, we can substitute p/u for $a \times m$ and obtain

$$\text{Cost of direct labor} = \frac{p \times 16.66 \text{ cents/minute}}{u}$$

This way of writing the cost of direct labor has a very intuitive interpretation: The actual processing time p is inflated by a factor of 1/Utilization to appropriately account for idle time. For example, if utilization were 50 percent, we are charged \$1 of idle time penalty for every \$1 we spend on labor productively. In our case, the utilization is 66 percent; thus, the cost of direct labor is

$$\text{Cost of direct labor} = \frac{1.5 \text{ minutes/call} \times 16.66 \text{ cents/minute}}{0.66} = 38 \text{ cents/call}$$

This computation allows us to extend Table 9.2 to include the cost implications of the various staffing scenarios (our calculations do not consider any cost of lost goodwill). Specifically, we are interested in the impact of staffing on the cost of direct labor per call as well as in the cost of line charges.

Not surprisingly, we can see in Table 9.3 that moving from a very high level of utilization of close to 99 percent (using 8 CSRs) to a more responsive service level, for example, as provided by 12 CSRs, leads to a significant increase in labor cost.

TABLE 9.3
Economic Implications of Various Staffing Levels

Number of Servers	Utilization	Cost of Labor per Call	Cost of Line Charges per Call	Total Cost per Call
8	0.988	0.2531	1.0927	1.3458
9	0.878	0.2848	0.1354	0.4201
10	0.790	0.3164	0.0958	0.4122
11	0.718	0.3480	0.0843	0.4323
12	0.658	0.3797	0.0796	0.4593
13	0.608	0.4113	0.0774	0.4887
14	0.564	0.4429	0.0763	0.5193
15	0.527	0.4746	0.0757	0.5503

At the same time, though, line charges drop from over $1 per call to almost $0.075 per call. Note that $0.075 per call is the minimum charge that can be achieved based on staffing changes, as it corresponds to the pure talk time.

Adding line charges and the cost of direct labor allows us to obtain total costs. In Table 9.3, we observe that total costs are minimized when we have 10 CSRs in service.

However, we need to be careful in labeling this point as the optimal staffing level, as the total cost number is a purely internal measure and does not take into account any information about the customer's cost of waiting. For this reason, when deciding on an appropriate staffing level, it is important to set acceptable service levels for waiting times as done in Table 9.2 and then staffing up to meet these service levels (opposed to minimizing internal costs).

If we repeat the analysis that we have conducted for the 8:00 a.m. to 8:15 a.m. time slot over the 24 hours of the day, we obtain a staffing plan. The staffing plan accounts for both the seasonality observed throughout the day as well as the variability and the resulting need for extra capacity. This is illustrated by Figure 9.19.

When we face a nonstationary arrival process as in this case, a common problem is to decide into how many intervals one should break up the time line to have close to a stationary arrival process within a time interval (in this case, 15 minutes). While we cannot go into the theory behind this topic, the basic intuition is this: It is important that the time intervals are large enough so that

- We have enough data to come up with reliable estimates for the arrival rate of the interval (e.g., if we had worked with 30-second intervals, our estimates for the number of calls arriving within a 30-second time interval would have been less reliable).
- Over the course of an interval, the queue needs sufficient time to reach a "steady state"; this is achieved if we have a relatively large number of arrivals and service completions within the duration of a time interval (more than 10).

In practice, finding a staffing plan can be somewhat more complicated, as it needs to account for

- Breaks for the operators.
- Length of work period. It is typically not possible to request an operator to show up for work for only a one-hour time slot. Either one has to provide longer periods of time or one would have to temporarily route calls to other members of the organization (supervisor, back-office employees).

Despite these additional complications, the analysis outlined above captures the most important elements typical for making supply related decisions in service environments.

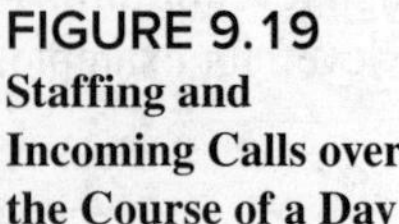

FIGURE 9.19
Staffing and Incoming Calls over the Course of a Day

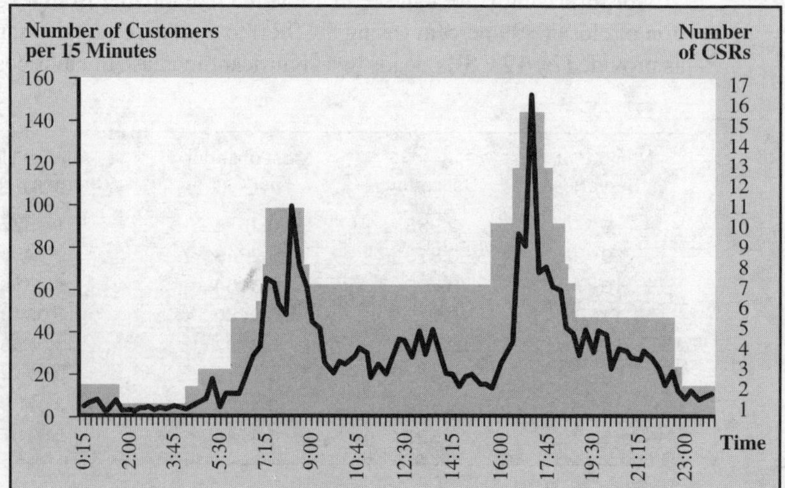

9.9 Impact of Pooling: Economies of Scale

Consider a process that currently corresponds to two (m) demand arrival processes that are processed by two (m) identical servers. If demand cannot be processed immediately, the flow unit waits in front of the server where it initially arrived. An example of such a system is provided in Figure 9.20 (left).

Here is an interesting question: Does combining the two systems into a single system with one waiting area and two (m) identical servers lead to lower average waiting times? We refer to such a combination of multiple resources into one "mega-resource" as *pooling*.

Consider, for example, two small food services at an airport. For simplicity, assume that both of them have a customer arrival stream with an average interarrival time a of 4 minutes and a coefficient of variation equal to one. The processing time p is three minutes per customer and the coefficient of variation for the service process also is equal to one. Consequently, both food services face a utilization of $p/a = 0.75$.

Using our waiting time formula, we compute the average waiting time as

$$T_q = \text{Processing time} \times \left(\frac{\text{Utilization}}{1 - \text{Utilization}}\right) \times \left(\frac{\text{CV}_a^2 + \text{CV}_p^2}{2}\right)$$
$$= 3 \times \left(\frac{0.75}{1 - 0.75}\right) \times \left(\frac{1+1}{2}\right)$$
$$= 3 \times (0.75/0.25) = 9 \text{ minutes}$$

Now compare this with the case in which we combine the capacity of both food services to serve the demand of both services. The capacity of the pooled process has increased by a factor of two and now is $\frac{2}{3}$ unit per minute. However, the demand rate also has doubled: If there was one customer every four minutes arriving for service 1 and one customer every four minutes arriving for service 2, the pooled service experiences an arrival rate of one customer every $a = 2$ minutes (i.e., two customers every four minutes is the same as one customer every two minutes).We can compute the utilization of the pooled process as

$$u = \frac{p}{a \times m}$$
$$= 3/(2 \times 2) = 0.75$$

Observe that the utilization has not changed compared to having two independent services. Combining two processes with a utilization of 75 percent leads to a pooled system with a 75 percent utilization. However, a different picture emerges when we look at the

FIGURE 9.20
The Concept of Pooling

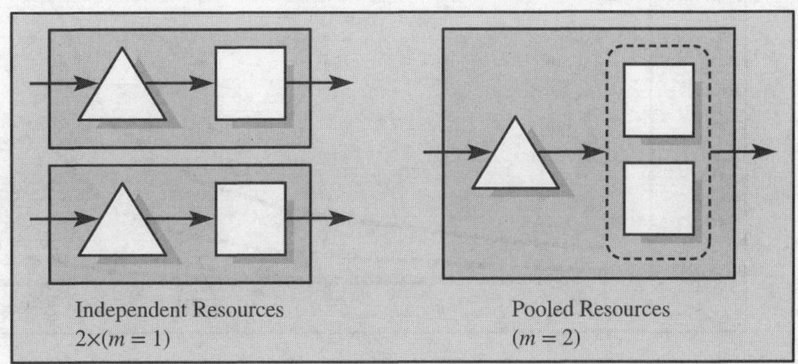

waiting time of the pooled system. Using the waiting time formula for multiple resources, we can write

$$T_q = \left(\frac{\text{Processing time}}{m}\right) \times \left(\frac{\text{Utilization}^{\sqrt{2(m+1)}-1}}{1 - \text{Utilization}}\right) \times \left(\frac{\text{CV}_a^2 + \text{CV}_p^2}{2}\right)$$

$$= \left(\frac{3}{2}\right) \times \left(\frac{0.75^{\sqrt{2(2+1)}-1}}{1 - 0.75}\right) \times \left(\frac{1+1}{2}\right) = 3.95 \text{ minutes}$$

In other words, the pooled process on the right of Figure 9.20 can serve the same number of customers using the same processing time (and thereby having the same utilization), but in only *half* the waiting time!

While short of being a formal proof, the intuition for this result is as follows. The pooled process uses the available capacity more effectively, as it prevents the case that one resource is idle while the other faces a backlog of work (waiting flow units). Thus, pooling identical resources balances the load for the servers, leading to shorter waiting times. This behavior is illustrated in Figure 9.21.

Figure 9.21 illustrates that for a given level of utilization, the waiting time decreases with the number of servers in the resource pool. This is especially important for higher levels of utilization. While for a system with one single server waiting times tend to "go through the roof" once the utilization exceeds 85 percent, a process consisting of 10 identical servers can still provide reasonable service even at utilizations approaching 95 percent.

Given that a pooled system provides better service than individual processes, a service organization can benefit from pooling identical branches or work groups in one of two forms:

- The operation can use pooling to reduce customer waiting time without having to staff extra workers.
- The operation can reduce the number of workers while maintaining the same responsiveness.

These economic benefits of pooling can be illustrated nicely within the context of the Anser case discussed above. In our analysis leading to Table 9.2, we assumed that there would be 79 calls arriving per 15-minute time interval and found that we would need 12 CSRs to serve customers with an average waiting time of 10 seconds or less.

FIGURE 9.21
How Pooling Can Reduce Waiting Time

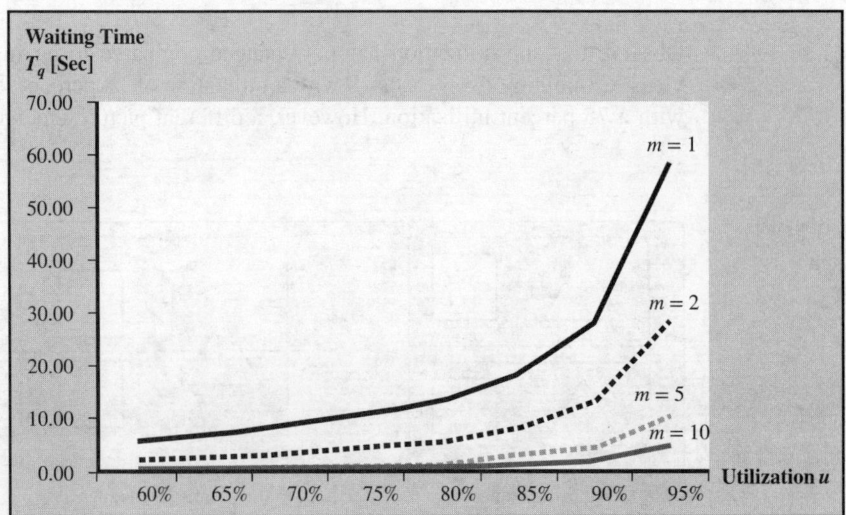

Assume we could pool An-ser's call center with a call center of comparable size; that is, we would move all CSRs to one location and merge both call centers' customer populations. Note that this would not necessarily require the two call centers to "move in" with each other; they could be physically separate as long as the calls are routed through one joint network.

Without any consolidation, merging the two call centers would lead to double the number of CSRs and double the demand, meaning 158 calls per 15-minute interval. What would be the average waiting time in the pooled call center? Or, alternatively, if we maintained an average waiting time of 10 seconds or less, how much could we reduce our staffing level? Table 9.4 provides the answers to these questions.

First, consider the row of 24 CSRs, corresponding to pooling the entire staff of the two call centers. Note specifically that the utilization of the pooled call center is not any different from what it was in Table 9.2. We have doubled the number of CSRs, but we also have doubled the number of calls (and thus cut the interarrival time by half). With 24 CSRs, we expect an average waiting time of 1.2 seconds (compared to almost 6 seconds before).

Alternatively, we could take the increased efficiency benefits resulting from pooling by reducing our labor cost. We also observe from Table 9.4 that a staff of 20 CSRs would be able to answer calls with an average wait time of 10 seconds. Thus, we could increase utilization to almost 80 percent, which would lower our cost of direct labor from $0.3797 to $0.3165. Given an annual call volume of about 700,000 calls, such a saving would be of significant impact for the bottom line.

Despite the nice property of pooled systems outlined above, pooling should not be seen as a silver bullet. Specifically, pooling benefits are much lower than expected (and potentially negative) in the following situations:

- Pooling benefits are significantly lower when the systems that are pooled are not truly independent. Consider, for example, the idea of pooling waiting lines before cash registers in supermarkets, similar to what is done at airport check-ins. In this case, the individual queues are unlikely to be independent, as customers in the current, nonpooled layout will intelligently route themselves to the queue with the shortest waiting line. Pooling in this case will have little, if any, effect on waiting times.

TABLE 9.4
Pooling Two Call Centers

Number of CSRs	Utilization	Expected Wait Time [seconds]	Labor Cost per Call	Line Cost per Call	Total Cost
16	0.988	588.15	0.2532	0.5651	0.8183
17	0.929	72.24	0.2690	0.1352	0.4042
18	0.878	28.98	0.2848	0.0992	0.3840
19	0.832	14.63	0.3006	0.0872	0.3878
20	0.790	8.18	0.3165	0.0818	0.3983
21	0.752	4.84	0.3323	0.0790	0.4113
22	0.718	2.97	0.3481	0.0775	0.4256
23	0.687	1.87	0.3639	0.0766	0.4405
24	0.658	1.20	0.3797	0.0760	0.4558
25	0.632	0.79	0.3956	0.0757	0.4712
26	0.608	0.52	0.4114	0.0754	0.4868
27	0.585	0.35	0.4272	0.0753	0.5025
28	0.564	0.23	0.4430	0.0752	0.5182
29	0.545	0.16	0.4589	0.0751	0.5340
30	0.527	0.11	0.4747	0.0751	0.5498

- Similar to the concept of line balancing we introduced earlier in this book, pooling typically requires the service workforce to have a broader range of skills (potentially leading to higher wage rates). For example, an operator sufficiently skilled that she can take orders for hiking and running shoes, as well as provide answering services for a local hospital, will likely demand a higher wage rate than someone who is just trained to do one of these tasks.
- In many service environments, customers value being treated consistently by the same person. Pooling several lawyers in a law firm might be desirable from a waiting-time perspective but ignores the customer desire to deal with one point of contact in the law firm.
- Similarly, pooling can introduce additional setups. In the law-firm example, a lawyer unfamiliar with the situation of a certain client might need a longer time to provide some quick advice on the case and this extra setup time mitigates the operational benefits from pooling.
- Pooling can backfire if it combines different customer classes because this might actually increase the variability of the service process. Consider two clerks working in a retail bank, one of them currently in charge of simple transactions (e.g., processing time of 2 minutes per customer), while the other one is in charge of more complex cases (e.g., processing time of 10 minutes). Pooling these two clerks makes the service process more variable and might actually increase waiting time.

9.10 Reducing Variability

In this chapter, we have provided some new methods to evaluate the key performance measures of flow rate, flow time, and inventory in the presence of variability. We also have seen that variability is the enemy of all operations (none of the performance measures improves as variability increases). Thus, in addition to just taking variability as given and adjusting our models to deal with variability, we should always think about ways to reduce variability.

Ways to Reduce Arrival Variability

One—somewhat obvious—way of achieving a match between supply and demand is by "massaging" demand such that it corresponds exactly to the supply process. This is basically the idea of *appointment systems* (also referred to as reservation systems in some industries).

Appointment systems have the potential to reduce the variability in the arrival process as they encourage customers to arrive at the rate of service (more on the topic of appointments in Chapter 11). However, one should not overlook the problems associated with appointment systems, which include

- Appointment systems do not eliminate arrival variability. Customers do not perfectly arrive at the scheduled time (and some might not arrive at all, "no-shows"). Consequently, any good appointment system needs ways to handle these cases (e.g., extra charge or extra waiting time for customers arriving late). However, such actions are typically very difficult to implement, due to what is perceived to be "fair" and/or "acceptable," or because variability in processing times prevents service providers from always keeping on schedule (and if the doctor has the right to be late, why not the patient?).
- What portion of the available capacity should be reserved in advance. Unfortunately, the customers arriving at the last minute are frequently the most important ones: emergency operations in a hospital do not come through an appointment system and business travelers paying 5 to 10 times the fare of low-price tickets are not willing to book in advance (this topic is further explored in Chapter 18).

The most important limitation, however, is that appointment systems might reduce the variability of the arrival process as seen by the operation, but they do not reduce the variability of the true underlying demand. Consider, for example, the appointment system of a dental office. While the system (hopefully) reduces the time the patient has to wait before seeing the dentist on the day of the appointment, this wait time is not the only performance measure that counts, as the patient might already have waited for three months between requesting to see the dentist and the day of the appointment. Thus, appointment systems potentially hide a much larger supply–demand mismatch and, consequently, any good implementation of an appointment system includes a continuous measurement of both of the following:

- The inventory of customers who have an appointment and are now waiting for the day they are scheduled to go to the dentist.
- The inventory of customers who wait for an appointment in the waiting room of the dentist.

In addition to the concept of appointment systems, we can attempt to influence the customer arrival process (though, for reasons similar to the ones discussed, not the true underlying demand pattern) by providing incentives for customers to avoid peak hours. Frequently observed methods to achieve this include

- Early-bird specials at restaurants or bars.
- Price discounts for hotels during off-peak days (or seasons).
- Price discounts in transportation (air travel, highway tolls) depending on the time of service.
- Pricing of air travel depending on the capacity that is already reserved.

It is important to point out that, strictly speaking, the first three items do not reduce variability; they level expected demand and thereby reduce seasonality (remember that the difference between the two is that seasonality is a pattern known already *ex ante*).

Ways to Reduce Processing Time Variability

In addition to reducing variability by changing the behavior of our customers, we also should consider how to reduce internal variability. However, when attempting to standardize activities (reducing the coefficient of variation of the processing times) or shorten processing times, we need to find a balance between operational efficiency (call durations) and the quality of service experienced by the customer (perceived courtesy).

Figure 9.22 compares five of An-ser's operators for a specific call service along these two dimensions. We observe that operators NN, BK, and BJ are achieving relatively short call durations while being perceived as friendly by the customers (based on recorded calls). Operator KB has shorter call durations, yet also scores lower on courtesy. Finally, operator NJ has the longest call durations and is rated medium concerning courtesy.

Based on Figure 9.22, we can make several interesting observations. First, observe that there seems to exist a frontier capturing the inherent trade-off between call duration and courtesy. Once call durations for this service go below 2.5 minutes, courtesy seems hard to maintain. Second, observe that operator NJ is away from this frontier, as he is neither overly friendly nor fast. Remarkably, this operator also has the highest variability in call durations, which suggests that he is not properly following the operating procedures in place (this is not visible in the graph).

To reduce the inefficiencies of operators away from the frontier (such as NJ), call centers invest heavily in training and technology. For example, technology allows operators to receive real-time instruction of certain text blocks that they can use in their interaction with the customer (scripting). Similarly, some call centers have instituted training programs in which operators listen to audio recordings of other operators or have operators

FIGURE 9.22 Operator Performance Concerning Call Duration and Courtesy

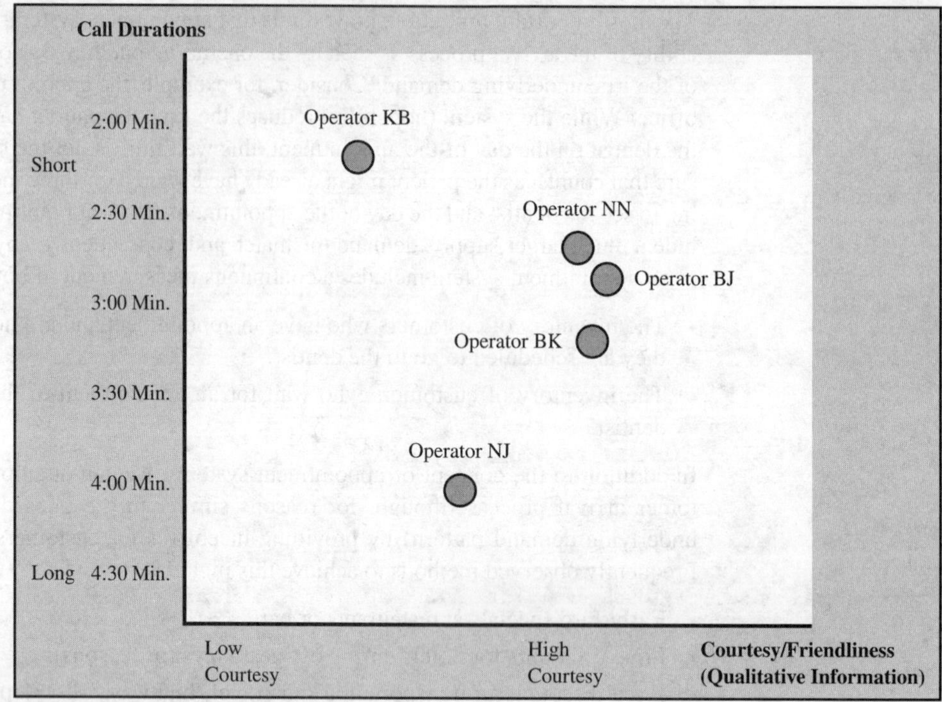

call other operators with specific service requests. Such steps reduce both the variability of processing times as well as their means and, therefore, represent substantial improvements in operational performance.

There are other improvement opportunities geared primarily toward reducing the variability of the processing times:

- Although in a service environment (or in a make-to-order production setting) the operator needs to acknowledge the idiosyncrasy of each customer, the operator still can follow a consistent process. For example, a travel agent in a call center might use predefined text blocks (scripts) for his or her interaction with the customer (welcome statement, first question, potential up-sell at the end of the conversation). This approach allowed operators NN, BK, and BJ in Figure 9.22 to be fast and friendly. Thus, being knowledgeable about the process (when to say what) is equally important as being knowledgeable about the product (what to say).
- Processing times in a service environment—unlike processing times in a manufacturing context—are not under the complete control of the resource. The customer him/herself plays a crucial part in the activity at the resource, which automatically introduces a certain amount of variability (e.g., having the customer provide his or her credit card number, having the customer bag the groceries, etc.). What is the consequence of this? At least from a variability perspective, the answer is clear: Reduce the involvement of the customer during the service at a scarce resource wherever possible (note that if the customer involvement does not occur at a scarce resource, having the customer be involved and thereby do part of the work might be very desirable, e.g., in a self-service setting).
- Variability in processing times frequently reflects quality problems. In manufacturing environments, this could include reworking a unit that initially did not meet specifications. However, rework also occurs in service organizations (e.g., a patient who is released from the intensive care unit but later on readmitted to intensive care can be thought of as rework).

9.11 Summary

In this chapter, we have analyzed the impact of variability on waiting times. As we expected from our more qualitative discussion of variability in the beginning of this chapter, variability causes waiting times, even if the underlying process operates at a utilization level of less than 100 percent. In this chapter, we have outlined a set of tools that allows us to quantify this waiting time, with respect to both the average waiting time (and flow time) as well as the service level experienced by the customer.

There exists an inherent tension between resource utilization (and thereby cost of labor) and responsiveness: Adding service capacity leads to shorter waiting times but higher costs of labor (see Figure 9.23). Waiting times grow steeply with utilization levels. Thus, any responsive process requires excess capacity. Given that capacity is costly, it is important that only as much capacity is installed as is needed to meet the service objective in place for the process. In this chapter, we have outlined a method that allows a service operation to find the point on the frontier that best supports their business objectives (service levels).

However, our results should be seen not only as a way to predict/quantify the waiting time problem. They also outline opportunities for improving the process. Improvement opportunities can be broken up into capacity-related opportunities and system-design-related opportunities, as summarized below.

Capacity-Related Improvements

Operations benefit from flexibility in capacity, as this allows management to adjust staffing levels to predicted demand. For example, the extent to which a hospital is able to have more doctors on duty at peak flu season is crucial in conducting the staffing calculations outlined in this chapter. A different form of flexibility is given by the operation's ability to increase capacity in the case of unpredicted demand. For example, the extent to which a bank can use supervisors and front-desk personnel to help with unexpected spikes in inbound calls can make a big difference in call center waiting times. This leads to the following two improvement opportunities:

FIGURE 9.23
Balancing Efficiency with Responsiveness

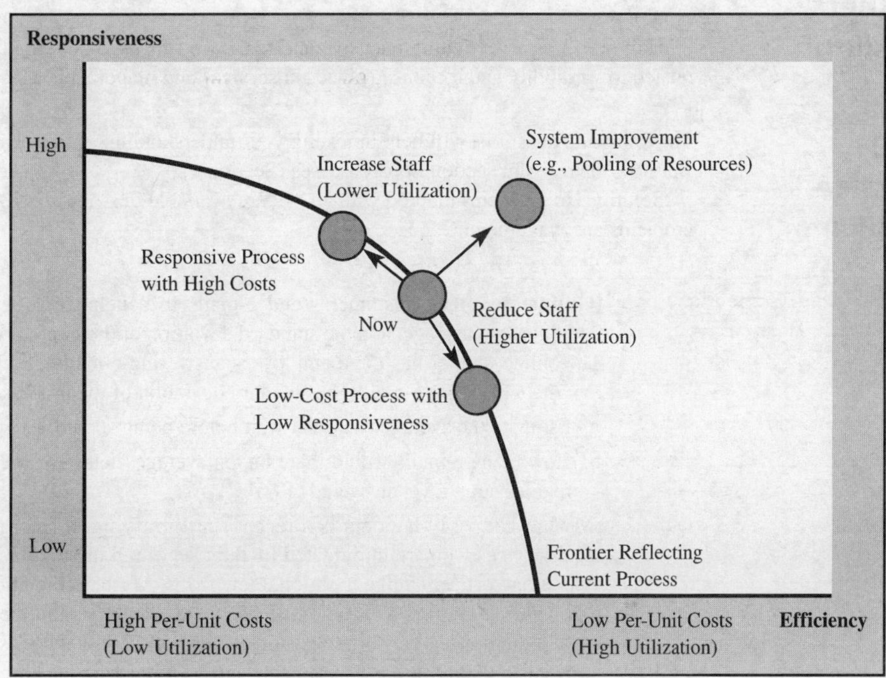

- Demand (and sometimes supply) can exhibit seasonality over the course of the day. In such cases, the waiting time analysis should be done for individual time intervals over which the process behaves relatively stationary. System performance can be increased to the extent the organization is able to provide time-varying capacity levels that mirror the seasonality of demand (e.g., Figure 9.19).
- In the presence of variability, a responsive process cannot avoid excess capacity, and thereby will automatically face a significant amount of idle time. In many operations, this idle time can be used productively for tasks that are not (or at least are less) time critical. Such work is referred to as background work. For example, operators in a call center can engage in outbound calls during times of underutilization.

System-Design-Related Improvements

Whenever we face a trade-off between two conflicting performance measures, in this case between responsiveness and efficiency, finding the right balance between the measures is important. However, at least equally important is the attempt to improve the underlying process, shifting the frontier and allowing for higher responsiveness and lower cost (see Figure 9.23). In the context of services suffering from variability-induced waiting times, the following improvement opportunities should be considered:

- By combining similar resources into one joint resource pool (pooling resources), we are able to either reduce wait times for the same amount of capacity or reduce capacity for the same service level. Processes that face variability thereby exhibit very strong scale economies.
- Variability is not exogenous and we should remember to reduce variability wherever possible.

9.12 Further Reading

Gans, Koole, and Mandelbaum (2003) is an overview on call-center management from a queuing theory perspective. Further quantitative tools on queueing can be found in Hillier and Lieberman (2002).

Hall (1997) is a very comprehensive and real-world-focused book that provides numerous tools related to variability and its consequences in services and manufacturing.

9.13 Practice Problems

The following questions will help in testing your understanding of this chapter. After each question, we show the relevant section in parentheses [Section x].

Solutions to problems marked with an "*" are available in Appendix E. Video solutions to select problems are available in Connect.

Q9.1* **(Online Retailer)** Customers send e-mails to a help desk of an online retailer every 2 minutes, on average, and the standard deviation of the interarrival time is also 2 minutes. The online retailer has three employees answering e-mails. It takes on average 4 minutes to write a response e-mail. The standard deviation of the processing times is 2 minutes.

a. Estimate the average customer wait before being served. [9.5]

b. How many e-mails would there be, on average, that have been submitted to the online retailer but not yet answered? [9.5]

Q9.2 **(My-law.com)** My-law.com is a recent start-up trying to cater to customers in search of legal services who are intimidated by the idea of talking to a lawyer or simply too lazy to enter a law office. Unlike traditional law firms, My-law.com allows for extensive interaction between lawyers and their customers via telephone and the Internet. This process is used in the upfront part of the customer interaction, largely consisting of answering some basic customer questions prior to entering a formal relationship.

In order to allow customers to interact with the firm's lawyers, customers are encouraged to send e-mails to my-lawyer@My-law.com. From there, the incoming e-mails are distributed to the lawyer who is currently "on call." Given the broad skills of the lawyers, each lawyer can respond to each incoming request.

E-mails arrive from 8 a.m. to 6 p.m. at a rate of 10 e-mails per hour (coefficient of variation for the arrivals is 1). At each moment in time, there is exactly one lawyer "on call," that is, sitting at his or her desk waiting for incoming e-mails. It takes the lawyer, on average, 5 minutes to write the response e-mail. The standard deviation of this is 4 minutes.

a. What is the average time a customer has to wait for the response to his/her e-mail, ignoring any transmission times? *Note:* This includes the time it takes the lawyer to start writing the e-mail *and* the actual writing time. [9.6]

b. How many e-mails will a lawyer have received at the end of a 10-hour day? [9.6]

c. When not responding to e-mails, the lawyer on call is encouraged to actively pursue cases that potentially could lead to large settlements. How much time in a 10-hour day can a My-law.com lawyer dedicate to this activity (assume the lawyer can instantly switch between e-mails and work on a settlement)? [9.6]

To increase the responsiveness of the firm, the board of My-law.com proposes a new operating policy. Under the new policy, the response would be highly standardized, reducing the standard deviation for writing the response e-mail to 0.5 minute. The average writing time would remain unchanged.

d. How would the amount of time a lawyer can dedicate to the search for large settlement cases change with this new operating policy? [9.6]

e. How would the average time a customer has to wait for the response to his/her e-mail change? *Note:* This includes the time until the lawyer starts writing the e-mail *and* the actual writing time. [9.6]

Q9.3 **(Car Rental Company)** The airport branch of a car rental company maintains a fleet of 50 SUVs. The interarrival time between requests for an SUV is 2.4 hours, on average, with a standard deviation of 2.4 hours. There is no indication of a systematic arrival pattern over the course of a day. Assume that, if all SUVs are rented, customers are willing to wait until there is an SUV available. An SUV is rented, on average, for 3 days, with a standard deviation of 1 day.

a. What is the average number of SUVs parked in the company's lot? [9.6]

b. Through a marketing survey, the company has discovered that if it reduces its daily rental price of $80 by $25, the average demand would increase to 12 rental requests per day and the average rental duration will become 4 days. Is this price decrease warranted? Provide an analysis! [9.6]

c. What is the average time a customer has to wait to rent an SUV? Please use the initial parameters rather than the information in part (b). [9.6]

d. How would the waiting time change if the company decides to limit all SUV rentals to *exactly* 4 days? Assume that if such a restriction is imposed, the average interarrival time will increase to 3 hours, with the standard deviation changing to 3 hours. [9.6]

Q9.4 **(Tom Opim)** The following situation refers to Tom Opim, a first-year MBA student. In order to pay the rent, Tom decides to take a job in the computer department of a local department store. His only responsibility is to answer telephone calls to the department, most of which are inquiries about store hours and product availability. As Tom is the only person answering calls, the manager of the store is concerned about queuing problems.

Currently, the computer department receives an average of one call every 3 minutes, with a standard deviation in this interarrival time of 3 minutes.

Tom requires an average of 2 minutes to handle a call. The standard deviation in this processing time is 1 minute.

The telephone company charges $5.00 per hour for the telephone lines whenever they are in use (either while a customer is in conversation with Tom or while waiting to be helped).

Assume that there are no limits on the number of customers that can be on hold and that customers do not hang up even if forced to wait a long time.

a. For one of his courses, Tom has to read a book (*The Pole,* by E. Silvermouse). He can read 1 page per minute. Tom's boss has agreed that Tom could use his idle time for studying, as long as he drops the book as soon as a call comes in. How many pages can Tom read during an 8-hour shift? [9.5]

b. How long does a customer have to wait, on average, before talking to Tom? [9.5]

c. What is the average total cost of telephone lines over an 8-hour shift? Note that the department store is billed whenever a line is in use, including when a line is used to put customers on hold. [9.5]

Q9.5 **(Atlantic Video)** Atlantic Video, a small video rental store in Philadelphia, is open 24 hours a day, and—due to its proximity to a major business school—experiences customers arriving around the clock. A recent analysis done by the store manager indicates that there are 30 customers arriving every hour, with a standard deviation of interarrival times of 2 minutes. This arrival pattern is consistent and is independent of the time of day. The checkout is currently operated by one employee, who needs on average 1.7 minutes to check out a customer. The standard deviation of this checkout time is 3 minutes, primarily as a result of customers taking home different numbers of videos.

a. If you assume that every customer rents at least one video (i.e., has to go to the checkout), what is the average time a customer has to wait in line before getting served by the checkout employee, not including the actual checkout time (within 1 minute)? [9.5]

b. If there are no customers requiring checkout, the employee is sorting returned videos, of which there are always plenty waiting to be sorted. How many videos can the employee sort over an 8-hour shift (assume no breaks) if it takes exactly 1.5 minutes to sort a single video? [9.5]

c. What is the average number of customers who are at the checkout desk, either waiting or currently being served (within 1 customer)? [9.5]

d. Now assume *for this question only* that 10 percent of the customers do not rent a video at all and therefore do not have to go through checkout. What is the average time a customer has to wait in line before getting served by the checkout employee, not including the actual checkout time (within 1 minute)? Assume that the coefficient of variation for the arrival process remains the same as before. [9.5]

e. As a special service, the store offers free popcorn and sodas for customers waiting in line at the checkout desk. (*Note:* The person who is currently being served is too busy with paying to eat or drink.) The store owner estimates that every minute of customer waiting time costs the store 75 cents because of the consumed food. What is the optimal number of employees at checkout? Assume an hourly wage rate of $10 per hour. [9.8]

Q9.6 **(RentAPhone)** RentAPhone is a new service company that provides European mobile phones to American visitors to Europe. The company currently has 80 phones available at Charles de Gaulle Airport in Paris. There are, on average, 25 customers per day requesting a phone. These requests arrive uniformly throughout the 24 hours the store is open. (*Note:* This means customers arrive at a faster rate than 1 customer per hour.) The corresponding coefficient of variation is 1.

Customers keep their phones on average 72 hours. The standard deviation of this time is 100 hours.

Given that RentAPhone currently does not have a competitor in France providing equally good service, customers are willing to wait for the telephones. Yet, during the waiting period, customers are provided a free calling card. Based on prior experience, RentAPhone found that the company incurred a cost of $1 per hour per waiting customer, independent of day or night.

a. What is the average number of telephones the company has in its store? [9.6]

b. How long does a customer, on average, have to wait for the phone? [9.6]

c. What are the total monthly (30 days) expenses for telephone cards? [9.6]

d. Assume RentAPhone could buy additional phones at $1,000 per unit. Is it worth it to buy one additional phone? Why? [9.8]

e. How would waiting time change if the company decides to limit all rentals to *exactly* 72 hours? Assume that if such a restriction is imposed, the number of customers requesting a phone would be reduced to 20 customers per day. [9.6]

Q9.7 **(Webflux Inc.)** Webflux is an Internet-based DVD rental business specializing in hard-to-find, obscure films. Its operating model is as follows. When a customer finds a film on the Webflux website and decides to watch it, she puts it in the virtual shopping cart. If a DVD is available, it is shipped immediately (assume it can be shipped during weekends and holidays, too). If not available, the film remains in the customer's shopping cart until a rented DVD is returned to Webflux, at which point it is shipped to the customer if she is next in line to receive it. Webflux maintains an internal queue for each film and a returned DVD is shipped to the first customer in the queue (first-in, first-out).

Webflux has one copy of the 1990 film *Sundown, the Vampire in Retreat,* starring David Carradine and Bruce Campbell. The average time between requests for the DVD is 10 days, with a coefficient of variation of 1. On average, a customer keeps the DVD for 5 days before returning it. It also takes 1 day to ship the DVD to the customer and 1 day to ship it from the customer back to Webflux. The standard deviation of the time between shipping the DVD out from Webflux and receiving it back is 7 days (i.e., it takes on average 7 days to (a) ship it, (b) have it with the customer, and (c) ship it back); hence, the coefficient of variation of this time is 1.

a. What is the average time that a customer has to wait to receive *Sundown, the Vampire in Retreat* DVD after the request? Recall it takes 1 day for a shipped DVD to arrive at a customer address (i.e., in your answer, you have to include the 1-day shipping time). [9.5]

b. On average, how many customers are in Webflux's internal queue for *Sundown*? Assume customers do not cancel their items in their shopping carts. [9.5]

Thanks to David Carradine's renewed fame after the recent success of *Kill Bill Vol. I* and *II* which he starred in, the demand for *Sundown* has spiked. Now the average interarrival time for the DVD requests at Webflux is 3 days. Other numbers (coefficient of variation, time in a customer's possession, shipping time) remain unchanged. *For the following question only,* assume sales are lost for customers who encounter stockouts; that is, those who cannot find a DVD on the Webflux website simply navigate away without putting it in the shopping cart.

c. To satisfy the increased demand, Webflux is considering acquiring a second copy of the *Sundown* DVD. If Webflux owns a total of two copies of *Sundown* DVDs (whether in Webflux's internal stock, in a customer's possession, or in transit), what percentage of the customers are turned away because of a stockout? (*Note:* To answer this question, you will need material from the next chapter.) [9.8]

Q9.8 **(Security Walking Escorts)** A university offers a walking escort service to increase security around campus. The system consists of specially trained uniformed professional security officers that accompany students from one campus location to another. The service is operated 24 hours a day, seven days a week. Students request a walking escort by phone. Requests for escorts are received, on average, every 5 minutes with a coefficient of variation of 1. After receiving a request, the dispatcher contacts an available escort (via a mobile phone), who immediately proceeds to pick up the student and walk her/him to her/his destination. If there are no escorts available (that is, they are all either walking a student to her/his destination or walking to pick up a student), the dispatcher puts the request in a queue until an escort becomes available. An escort takes, on average, 25 minutes for picking up a student and taking her/him to her/his desired location (the coefficient of variation of this time is also 1). Currently, the university has 8 security officers who work as walking escorts.

a. How many security officers are, on average, available to satisfy a new request? [9.6]

b. How much time does it take—on average—from the moment a student calls for an escort to the moment the student arrives at her/his destination? [9.6]

For the next two questions, consider the following scenario. During the period of final exams, the number of requests for escort services increases to 19.2 per hour (one request every 3.125 minutes). The coefficient of variation of the time between successive requests equals 1. However, if a student requesting an escort finds out from the dispatcher that her/his request would have to be put in the queue (i.e., all security officers are busy walking other students), the student cancels the request and proceeds to walk on her/his own.

c. How many students per hour who called to request an escort end up canceling their request and go walking on their own? (*Note:* To answer this question, you will need material from the next chapter.) [9.6]

d. University security regulations require that at least 80 percent of the students' calls to request walking escorts have to be satisfied. What is the minimum number of security officers that are needed in order to comply with this regulation? [9.8]

Q9.9 **(Mango Electronics Inc.)** Mango Electronics Inc. is a *Fortune* 500 company that develops and markets innovative consumer electronics products. The development process proceeds as follows.

Mango researches new technologies to address unmet market needs. Patents are filed for products that have the requisite market potential. Patents are granted for a period of 20 years starting from the date of issue. After receiving a patent, the patented technologies are then developed into marketable products at five independent development centers. Each product is only developed at one center. Each center has all the requisite skills to bring any of the products to market (a center works on one product at a time). On average, Mango files a patent every 7 months (with standard deviation of 7 months). The average development process lasts 28 months (with standard deviation of 56 months).

a. What is the utilization of Mango's development facilities? [9.6]

b. How long does it take an average technology to go from filing a patent to being launched in the market as a commercial product? [9.6]

c. How many years of patent life are left for an average product launched by Mango Electronics? [9.6]

If you would like to test your understanding of a specific section, here are the questions organized by section:

Section 9.5: Q9.1ab, Q9.4abc, Q9.5abcd, Q9.7ab

Section 9.6: Q9.2abcde, Q9.3abcd, Q9.6abce, Q9.8abc, Q9.9abc

Section 9.8: Q9.5e, Q9.6d, Q9.7c, Q9.8d

Chapter 10

The Impact of Variability on Process Performance: Throughput Losses

After having analyzed waiting times caused by variability, we now turn to a second undesirable impact variability has on process performance: *throughput loss*. Throughput losses occur in the following cases, both of which differ from the case of flow units patiently waiting for service discussed in the previous chapter:

- There is a limited buffer size and demand arriving when this buffer is full is lost.
- Flow units are impatient and unwilling or unable to spend too much time waiting for service, which leads to flow units leaving the buffer before being served.

Analyzing processes with throughput losses is significantly more complicated compared to the case of patient customers discussed in the previous chapter. For this reason, we focus our analysis on the simplest case of throughput loss, which assumes that the buffer size is zero, that is, there is no buffer. We will introduce a set of analytical tools and discuss their application to time-critical emergency care provided by hospitals, especially trauma centers. In these settings, waiting times are not permissible and, when a trauma center is fully utilized, incoming ambulances are diverted to other hospitals.

There exist more general models of variability that allow for buffer sizes larger than zero, yet due to their complexity, we only discuss those models conceptually. Again, we start the chapter with a small motivating example.

10.1 Motivating Examples: Why Averages Do Not Work

Consider a street vendor who sells custom-made sandwiches from his truck parked along the sidewalk. Demand for these sandwiches is, on average, one sandwich in a five-minute time slot. However, the actual demand varies, and thus sometimes no customer places an order, while at other times the owner of the truck faces one or two orders. Customers are not willing to wait for sandwiches and leave to go to other street vendors if they cannot be served immediately.

TABLE 10.1 Street Vendor Example of Variability

Scenario	Demand	Capacity	Flow Rate
A	0	0	0
B	0	1	0
C	0	2	0
D	1	0	0
E	1	1	1
F	1	2	1
G	2	0	0
H	2	1	1
I	2	2	2
Average	1	1	$\frac{5}{9}$

The capacity leading to the supply of sandwiches over a five-minute time slot also varies and can take the values 0, 1, or 2 with equal probabilities (the variability of capacity might reflect different order sizes or operator absenteeism). The average capacity therefore is one, just as is the average demand.

From an aggregate planning perspective, demand and supply seem to match, and on average, the truck should be selling at a flow rate of one sandwich every five minutes:

$$\text{Flow rate} = \text{Minimum}\{\text{Demand, Capacity}\} = \text{Minimum}\{1, 1\} = 1$$

Now, consider an analysis that is conducted at the more detailed level. If we consider the potential outcomes of both the demand and the supply processes, we face nine possible scenarios, which are summarized in Table 10.1.

Consider each of the nine scenarios. But instead of averaging demand and capacity and then computing the resulting flow rate (as done above, leading to a predicted flow rate of one), we compute the flow rate for each of the nine scenarios and then take the average across scenarios. The last column in Table 10.1 provides the corresponding calculations.

Note that for the first three scenarios (Demand = 0), we are not selling a single sandwich. However, if we look at the last three scenarios (Demand = 2), we cannot make up for this loss, as we are constrained by capacity. Thus, even while demand is booming (Demand = 2), we are selling on average one sandwich every five minutes.

If we look at the average flow rate that is obtained this way, we observe that close to half of the sales we expected to make based on our aggregate analysis do not materialize! The explanation for this is as follows: In order to sell a sandwich, the street vendor needed demand (a customer) and supply (the capacity to make a sandwich) at the same moment in time. Flow rate could have been improved if the street vendor could have moved some supply to inventory and thereby stored it for periods of time in which demand exceeded supply, or, vice versa, if the street vendor could have moved some demand to a backlog of waiting customers and thereby stored demand for periods of time in which supply exceeded demand: another example of the "buffer or suffer" principle.

10.2 Ambulance Diversion

Now, let's move from analyzing a "cooked-up" food-truck to a problem of much larger importance, with respect to both its realism as well as its relevance. Over the last couple of years, reports have shown a substantial increase in visits to emergency departments. At the same time many hospitals, in response to increasing cost pressure, have downsized important resources that are part of the emergency care process. This has led to a decrease in the number of hours hospitals are "open" for emergency patients arriving by helicopter or ambulance.

Under U.S. federal law, all hospitals that participate in Medicare are required to screen—and, if an emergency condition is present, stabilize—any patient who comes to the emergency department, regardless of the individual's ability to pay. Under certain circumstances where a hospital lacks staffing or facilities to accept additional emergency patients, the hospital may place itself on "diversion status" and direct en route ambulances to other hospitals.

In total, the General Accounting Office estimates that about 2 of every 3 hospitals went on diversion at least once during the year. Moreover, the study estimates that about 2 in every 10 of these hospitals were on diversion for more than 10 percent of the time, and about 1 in every 10 was on diversion for more than 20 percent of the time—or about five hours per day.

We focus our analysis on trauma cases, that is, the most severe and also the most urgent type of emergency care. A triage system evaluates the patients while they are in the ambulance/helicopter and directs the arrival to the emergency department (less severe cases) or the trauma center (severe cases). Thus, the trauma center only receives patients who have had a severe trauma.

10.3 Throughput Loss for a Simple Process

Consider the following situation of a trauma center in a hospital in the Northeastern United States. Incoming patients are moved into one of three trauma bays. On average, patients spend two hours in the trauma bay. During that time, the patients are diagnosed and, if possible, stabilized. The most severe cases, which are difficult or impossible to stabilize, spend very little time in a trauma bay and are moved directly to the operating room.

Given the severe conditions of patients coming into the trauma center, any delay of care can have fatal consequences for the patient. Thus, having patients wait for service is not an option in this setting. If, as a result of either frequent arrivals or long service times, all three trauma bays are utilized, the trauma center has to move to the ambulance diversion status defined above.

We model the trauma center as a process flow diagram consisting of no buffer and multiple parallel resources (see Figure 10.1). Given that we have three trauma bays (and corresponding staff) available, there can be a maximum of three patients in the process. Once all three bays are in use, the trauma center informs the regional emergency system that it has to go on diversion status; that is, any patients needing trauma services at that time are transported to other hospitals in the region.

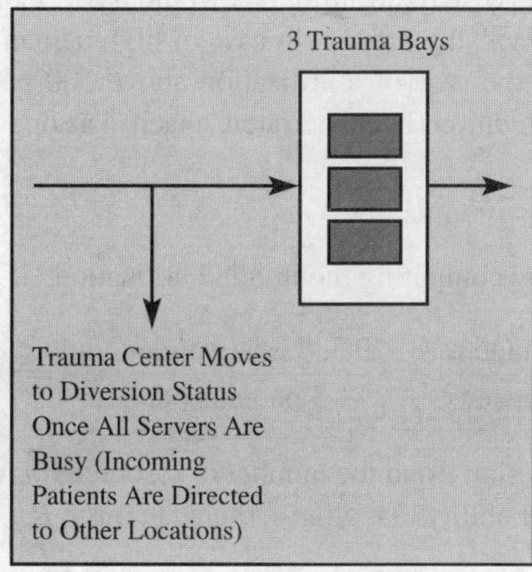

FIGURE 10.1 Process Flow Diagram for Trauma Center

The trauma center we analyze handles about 2,000 cases per year. For our analysis, we focus on the late evening hours, during which, on average, a new patient arrives every three hours. In addition to traffic rush hour, the late evening hours are among the busiest for the trauma center, as many of the incoming cases are results of vehicle accidents (alcohol-induced car accidents tend to happen in the evening) and victims of violence (especially in the summer months, many violent crimes occur in the evening hours).

Thus, we have a new patient every $a = 3$ hours and it takes, on average, $p = 2$ hours of time to get the patient out of the trauma center. In our analysis, we assume that the trauma bays are the resources and that there is sufficient staff to operate all three bays simultaneously, if the need arises.

Given that there are three trauma bays available, the capacity of the trauma center is

$$\text{Capacity} = \frac{\text{Number of resources}}{\text{Processing time}} = \frac{3}{2 \text{ hours/patient}}$$
$$= 1.5 \text{ patients per hour}$$

Since incoming patients arrive randomly, we use exponential interarrival times and consequently face a coefficient of variation of CV_a equal to one. The coefficient of variation of the service time in this case turns out to be above one (many medical settings are known to have extremely high variability). However, as we will see below, the following computations do not depend on the service time variability and apply to any service time distribution.

We are interested in analyzing the following performance measures:

- What percent of the time will the trauma center have to go on diversion status? Similarly, how many patients are diverted because all three trauma bays are utilized?
- What is the flow rate through the trauma center, that is, how many patients are treated every unit of time (e.g., every day)?

The most difficult, yet also most important step in our analysis is computing the probability with which the process contains m patients, P_m. This probability is of special importance, as once m patients are in the trauma center, the trauma center needs to divert any incoming requests until it has discharged a patient. The probability of having all m servers busy, P_m, depends on two variables:

- The *implied utilization*. Given that some patients are not admitted to the process (and thereby do not contribute to throughput), we no longer need to impose the condition that the capacity exceeds the demand rate ($1/a$). This assumption was necessary in the previous chapter, as otherwise the waiting line would have "exploded." In a system that automatically "shuts down" the process in case of high demand, this does not happen. Hence, u now includes the case of a utilization above 100 percent, which is why we speak of the implied utilization (Demand rate/Capacity) as opposed to utilization (Flow rate/Capacity).
- The number of resources (trauma bays) m.

We begin our analysis by computing the implied utilization:

$$u = \frac{\text{Demand rate}}{\text{Capacity}} = \frac{0.3333 \text{ patient per hour}}{1.5 \text{ patients per hour}} = 0.2222$$

Based on the implied utilization u and the number of resources m, we can use the following method to compute the probability that all m servers are busy, P_m. Define $r = u \times m = p/a$. Thus, $r = 0.67$.

TABLE 10.2
Finding the Probability $P_m(r)$ Using the Erlang Loss Table from Appendix B

	Erlang Loss Table						
				m			
		1	2	3	4	5	6...
	0.10	0.0909	0.0045	0.0002	0.0000	0.0000	0.0000
	0.20	0.1667	0.0164	0.0011	0.0001	0.0000	0.0000
	0.25	0.2000	0.0244	0.0020	0.0001	0.0000	0.0000
	0.30	0.2308	0.0335	0.0033	0.0003	0.0000	0.0000
r	0.33	0.2500	0.0400	0.0044	0.0004	0.0000	0.0000
	0.40	0.2857	0.0541	0.0072	0.0007	0.0001	0.0000
	0.50	0.3333	0.0769	0.0127	0.0016	0.0002	0.0000
	0.60	0.3750	0.1011	0.0198	0.0030	0.0004	0.0000
	0.67	0.4000	0.1176	0.0255	0.0042	0.0006	0.0001
	0.70	0.4118	0.1260	0.0286	0.0050	0.0007	0.0001
	0.75	0.4286	0.1385	0.0335	0.0062	0.0009	0.0001
	...						

We can then use the *Erlang loss formula* table (Appendix B) to look up the probability that all *m* resources are utilized and hence a newly arriving flow unit has to be rejected. First, we find the corresponding row heading in the table ($r = 0.67$) indicating the ratio of processing time to interarrival time (see Table 10.2). Second, we find the column heading ($m = 3$) indicating the number of resources. The intersection of that row with that column is

$$\text{Probability}\{\text{all } m \text{ servers busy}\} = \text{P}_m(r) = 0.0255 \quad \text{(Erlang loss formula)}$$

Thus, we find that our trauma center, on average, will be on diversion for 2.5 percent of the time, which corresponds to about 0.6 hour per day and about 18 hours per month.

A couple of remarks are in order to explain the impact of the processing time-to-interarrival-time ratio *r* and the number of resources *m* on the probability that all servers are utilized:

- The probability $P_m(r)$ and hence the analysis do not require the coefficient of variation for the service process. The analysis only applies to the (realistic) case of exponentially distributed interarrival times; therefore, we implicitly assume that the coefficient of variation for the arrival process is equal to one.
- The formula underlying the table in Appendix B is attributed to the work of Agner Krarup Erlang, a Danish engineer who invented many (if not most) of the models that we use in this chapter and the previous chapter for his employer, the Copenhagen Telephone Exchange. In this context, the arrivals were incoming calls for which there was either a telephone line available or not (in which case the calls were lost, which is why the formula is also known as the *Erlang loss formula*).
- At the beginning of Appendix B, we provide the formula that underlies the Erlang loss formula table. We can use the formula directly to compute the probability $P_m(r)$ for a given processing-time-to-interarrival-time ratio *r* and the number of resources *m*.

In addition to the probability that all resources are utilized, we also can compute the number of patients that will have to be diverted. Since demand for trauma care continues at a rate of $1/a$ independent of the diversion status of the trauma center, we obtain our flow rate as

$$\begin{aligned}\text{Flow rate} &= \text{Demand rate} \times \text{Probability that not all servers are busy}\\ &= 1/a \times (1 - P_m) = \tfrac{1}{3} \times 0.975 = 0.325 \text{ patient per hour}\end{aligned}$$

Similarly, we find that we divert $\frac{1}{3} \times 0.025 = 0.0083$ patient per hour = 0.2 patient per day.

The case of the trauma center provides another example of how variability needs to be accommodated in a process by putting excess capacity in place. A utilization level of 22 percent in an environment of high fixed costs seems like the nightmare of any administrator. Yet, from the perspective of a person in charge of creating a responsive process, absolute utilization numbers should always be treated with care: The role of the trauma center is not to maximize utilization; it is to help people in need and ultimately save lives.

One main advantage of the formula outlined above is that we can quickly evaluate how changes in the process affect ambulance diversion. For example, we can compute the probability of diversion that would result from an increased utilization. Such a calculation would be important, both to predict diversion frequencies, as well as to predict flow rate (e.g., number of patients served per month).

Consider, for example, a utilization of 50 percent. Such a case could result from a substantial increase in arrival rate (e.g., consider the case that a major trauma center in the area closes because of the financial problems of its hospital).

Based on the increased implied utilization, $u = 0.5$, and the same number of trauma bays, $m = 3$, we compute $r = u \times m = 1.5$. We then use the Erlang loss formula table to look up the probability $P_m(r)$ that all m servers are utilized:

$$P_3(1.5) = 0.1343$$

Thus, this scenario of increased utilization would lead to ambulance diversion more than 13 percent of the time, corresponding to close to 100 hours of diversion every month.

Figure 10.2 shows the relationship between the level of implied utilization and the probability that the process cannot accept any further incoming arrivals. As we can see, similar to waiting time problems, there exist significant scale economies in loss systems: While a 50 percent utilization would lead to a diversion probability of 30 percent with one server ($m = 1$), it only leads to a 13 percent diversion probability with three servers and less than 2 percent for 10 servers.

Exhibit 10.1 summarizes the computations required for the Erlang loss formula.

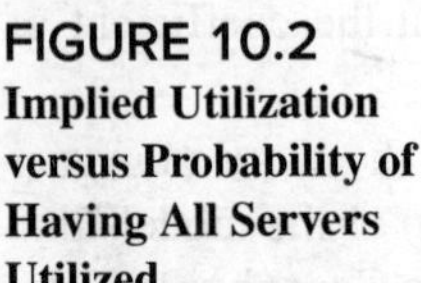

FIGURE 10.2
Implied Utilization versus Probability of Having All Servers Utilized

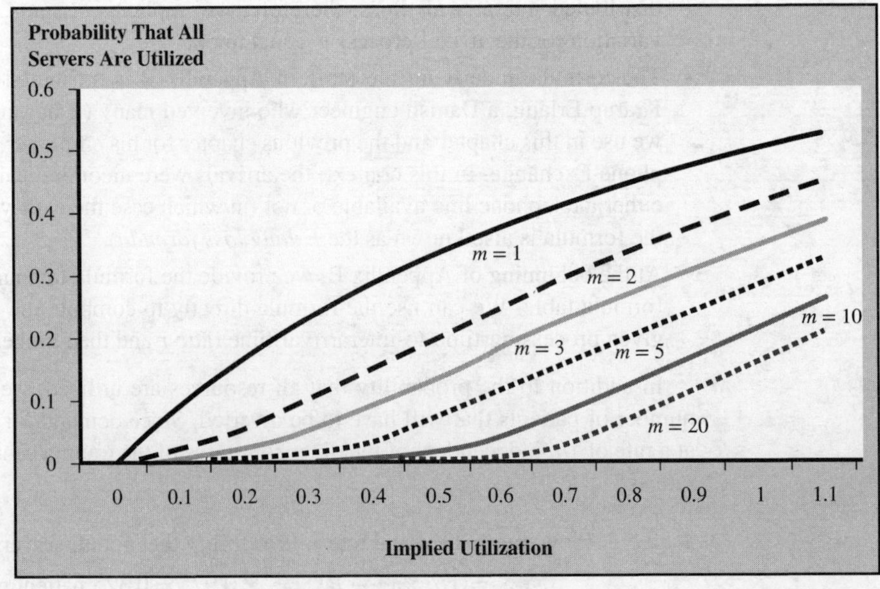

Exhibit 10.1

USING THE ERLANG LOSS FORMULA

1. Define $r = \frac{p}{a}$ where p is the processing time and a is the interarrival time
2. Use the Erlang loss formula table in Appendix B to look up the probability that all servers are busy:

$$\text{Probability \{all } m \text{ servers are busy\}} = P_m(r)$$

3. Compute flow rate based on

$$\text{Flow rate} = \text{Demand rate} \times \text{Probability that not all servers are busy}$$
$$R = 1/a \times (1 - P_m)$$

4. Compute lost customers as

$$\text{Customers lost} = \text{Demand rate} \times \text{Probability that all servers are busy}$$
$$= 1/a \times P_m$$

10.4 Customer Impatience and Throughput Loss

In the previous chapter, we analyzed a process in which flow units patiently waited in a queue until it was their turn to be served. In contrast, in the case of the trauma center, we have analyzed a process in which flow units never waited but, when all servers were busy, were turned immediately into lost flow units (were routed to other hospitals).

These two cases, a waiting problem on one side and a loss problem on the other side, are important, yet they also are extreme cases concerning the impact of variability on process performance. Many interesting applications that you might encounter are somewhere in between these two extremes. Without going into a detailed analysis, it is important that we at least discuss these intermediate cases at the conceptual level.

The first important intermediate case is a waiting problem in which there is a buffer that allows a limited number of flow units to wait for service. The limit of the buffer size might represent one of these situations:

- In a call center, there exist a maximum number of calls that can be on hold simultaneously; customers calling in when all these lines are in use receive a busy signal (i.e., they don't even get to listen to the '70s music!). Similarly, if one thinks of a queue in front of a drive-through restaurant, there exist a maximum number of cars that can fit in the queue; once this maximum is reached, cars can no longer line up.
- Given that, as a result of Little's Law, the number of customers in the queue can be translated into an expected wait time, a limit on the queue size might simply represent a maximum amount of time customers would be willing to wait. For example, customers looking at a queue in front of a movie theater might simply decide that the expected wait time is not justified by the movie they expect to see.

Although we will not discuss them in this book, there exist mathematical models to analyze this type of problem and for a given maximum size of the buffer, we can compute the usual performance measures, inventory, flow rate, and wait time (see, e.g., Hillier and Liebermann (2002)).

For the case of a single server, Figure 10.3 shows the relationship between the number of available buffers and the probability that all buffers are full; that is, the probability that the process can no longer accept incoming customers. As we can see, this probability

FIGURE 10.3
Impact of Buffer Size on the Probability P_m for Various Levels of Implied Utilization as well as on the Throughput of the Process in the Case of One Single Server

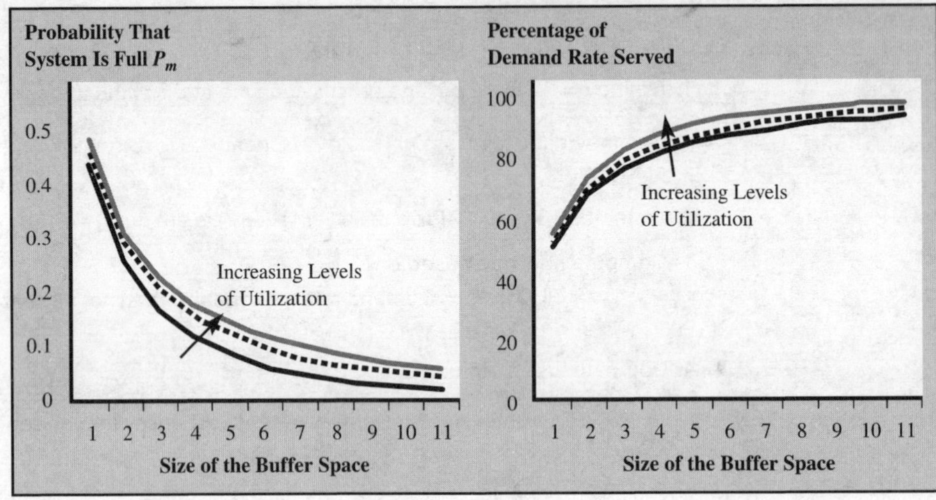

is quickly decreasing as we add more and more buffer space. Note that the graph shifts up as we increase the level of utilization, which corresponds to the intuition from earlier chapters.

Since we can compute the throughput of the system as

$$(1 - \text{Probability that all buffers are full}) \times \text{Demand rate}$$

we also can interpret Figure 10.3 as the throughput loss. The right part of Figure 10.3 shows the impact of buffer size on throughput. Even for a single server and a utilization of 90 percent, we need more than 10 buffers to come close to restoring the throughput we would expect in the absence of variability.

The second intermediate case between a waiting problem and a loss problem resembles the first case but is different in the sense that customers always enter the system (as opposed to not even joining the queue), but then leave the queue unserved as they become tired of waiting. The technical term for this is "customers *abandon* the queue" or the customers *balk*. This case is very common in call centers that have very long wait times. However, for call centers with high service levels for short target wait times, such as in the case of the An-ser call center discussed in the previous chapter, there are very few abandonment cases (this is why we could safely ignore customers abandoning the queue for our analysis).

Figure 10.4 shows an example of call center data (collected by Gans, Koole, and Mandelbaum (2003)) in a setting with long waiting times. The horizontal axis shows how long customers had to wait before talking to an agent. The vertical axis represents the percentage of customers hanging up without being served. We observe that the longer customers have to wait, the larger the proportion of customers lost due to customer impatience.

There are three types of improvement opportunities for the two intermediate cases, limited buffer space and abandoning customers:

- Reduce wait times. Similar to our prior analysis, anything we can do to reduce wait times (intelligently choose capacity, reduce variability, etc.) helps reduce throughput losses resulting from customer impatience.
- Increase the maximum number of flow units that can be in the buffer. This can be achieved by either altering the actual buffer (adding more space, buying more telephone lines) or increasing the customers' willingness to tolerate waiting.
- Avoid customers leaving that have already waited. Having customers wait and then leave is even worse than having customers leave immediately, so it is important to

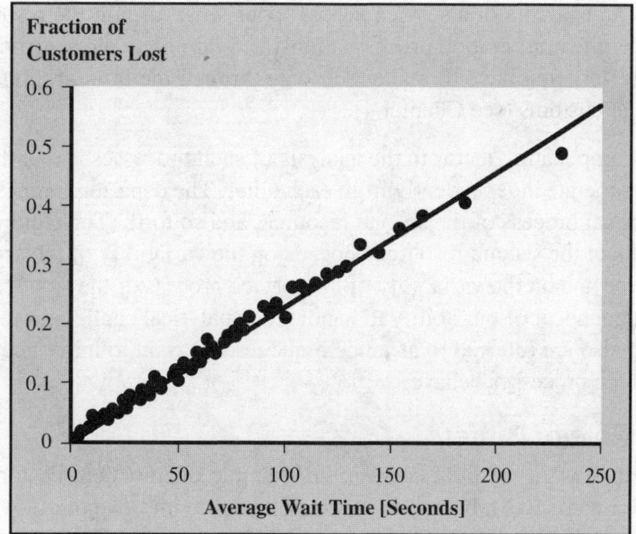

FIGURE 10.4 **Impact of Waiting Time on Customer Loss**

Source: Gans, Koole, and Mandelbaum, 2003.

avoid this case as much as possible. One way of achieving this is to reduce the perceived waiting duration by giving customers meaningful tasks to do (e.g., key in some information, help reduce the actual service time) or by creating an environment where waiting is not too painful (two generations of operations managers were told to install mirrors in front of elevators, so we are not going to repeat this suggestion). Obviously, mirrors at elevators and playing music in call centers alone do not solve the problem entirely; however, these are changes that are typically relatively inexpensive to implement. A more meaningful (and also low-cost) measure would be to communicate the expected waiting time upfront to the customer (e.g., as done in some call centers or in Disney's theme parks). This way, customers have expectations concerning the wait time and can make a decision whether or not to line up for this service (Disney case) or can even attempt to run other errands while waiting for service (call center case).

10.5 Several Resources with Variability in Sequence

After having analyzed variability and its impact on process performance for the case of very simple processes consisting of just one resource, we now extend our analysis to more complicated process flow diagrams.

Specifically, we analyze a sequence of resources as described in the process flow diagram in Figure 10.5. Such processes are very common, both in manufacturing and service environments:

- The kick-scooter assembly process that we analyzed in Chapter 4 consists (ignoring variability) of multiple resources in sequence.

FIGURE 10.5 **A Serial Queuing System with Three Resources**

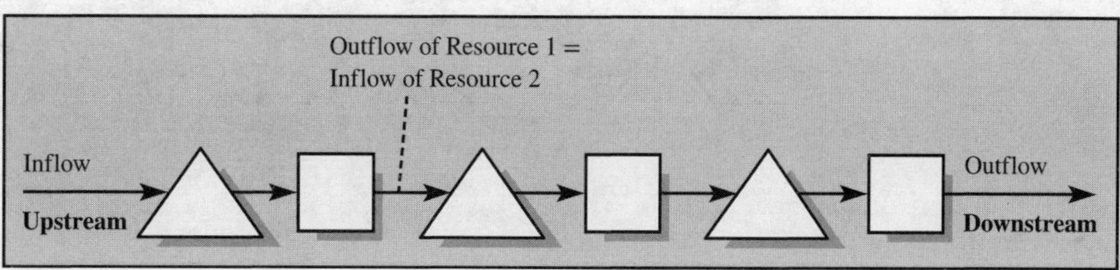

- As an example of a service process consisting of multiple resources in sequence, consider the immigration process at most U.S. airports. When arriving in the United States, travelers first have to make their way through the immigration authority and then line up at customs (see Chapter 4).

A complicating factor in the analysis of such processes is that the subsequent resources do not operate independently from each other: The departure process of the first resource is the arrival process of the second resource, and so forth. Thus, the variability of the arrival process of the second resource depends on the variability of the arrival process of the first resource and on the variability of the service process of the first resource. What a mess!

Independent of our ability to handle the analytical challenges related to such processes, which also are referred to as tandem queues, we want to introduce some basic intuition of how such processes behave.

The Role of Buffers

Similar to what we have seen in the example of impatient customers and limited buffer space (Figure 10.3), buffers have the potential to improve the flow rate through a process. While, in the case of a single resource, buffers increase flow rate as they reduce the probability that incoming units are denied access to the system, the impact of buffers in *tandem queues* is somewhat more complicated. When looking at a tandem queue, we can identify two events that lead to reductions in flow rate (see Figure 10.6):

- A resource is *blocked* if it is unable to release the flow unit it has just completed as there is no buffer space available at the next resource downstream.
- A resource is *starved* if it is idle and the buffer feeding the resource is empty.

In the trauma center example discussed at the beginning of the chapter, blocking is the most important root cause of ambulance diversion. The actual time the trauma surgeon needs to care for a patient in the trauma bay is only, on average, one hour. However, on average, patients spend one additional hour in the trauma bay waiting for a bed in the intensive care unit (ICU) to become available. Since, during this time, the trauma bay cannot be used for newly arriving patients, a full ICU "backs up" and blocks the trauma center. The study of the General Accounting Office on emergency department crowding and ambulance diversion, mentioned above, pointed to the availability of ICU beds as the single largest source leading to ambulance diversion.

FIGURE 10.6
The Concepts of Blocking and Starving

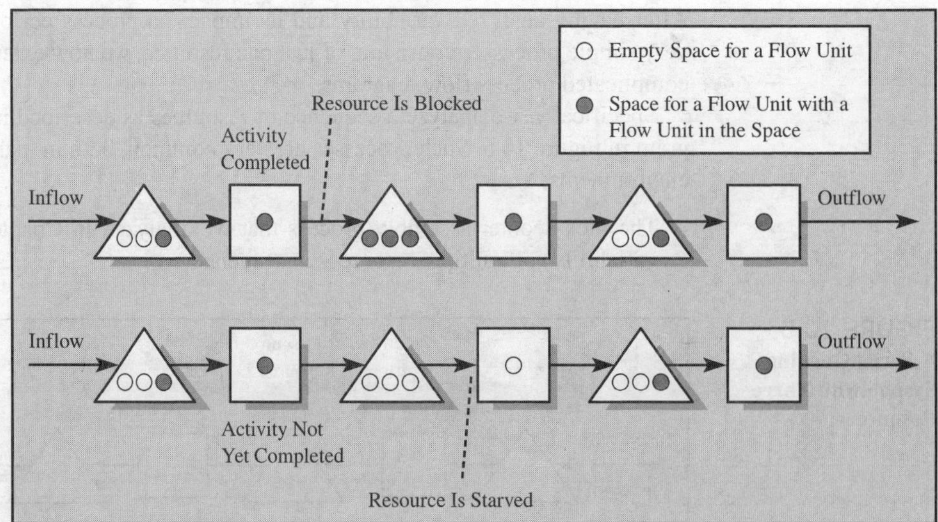

It is important to understand that the effects of blocking can snowball from one resource to additional resources upstream. This can be illustrated in the hospital setting outlined above. Consider a patient who is ready to be discharged from a general care unit at 11 a.m. However, as the patient wants to be picked up by a family member, the patient can only leave at 5 p.m. Consequently, the unit cannot make the bed available to newly arriving patients, including those who come from the ICU. This, in turn, can lead to a patient in the ICU who is ready to be discharged but now needs to wait in an ICU bed. And, yes, you guessed right, this in turn can lead to a patient in the trauma center, who could be moved to the ICU, but now has to stay in the trauma bay. Thus, in a process with limited buffer space, all resources are dependent on another. This is why we defined buffers that help management to relax these dependencies as *decoupling inventory* (Chapter 2).

Blocking and starving can be easily avoided by adding buffers. The buffers would have to contain a sufficient number of flow units so as to avoid starvation of the downstream resource. At the same time, the buffer should have enough space to prevent the resource upstream from ever being blocked. Several hospitals have recently experimented with introducing discharge rooms for patients who are ready to go home from a general care unit: Even a buffer at the end of the process (healthy patient) will reduce the probability that an incoming trauma patient has to be diverted because of a fully utilized trauma center.

In addition to the probability of not being able to admit newly arriving flow units, an important performance measure for our process continues to be the flow rate. Figure 10.7 uses simulation to compare four process layouts of three resources with variability. This situation corresponds to a worker-paced line, with one worker at every resource. The processing times are exponentially distributed with means of 6.5 minutes/unit, 7 minutes/unit, and 6 minutes/unit, respectively.

Based on averages, we would expect the process to produce one unit of output every 7 minutes. However, in the absence of any buffer space, the process only produces at a rate of one unit every 11.5 minutes (upper left). The process does not realize its full capacity, as the bottleneck is frequently blocked (station 2 has completed a flow unit but cannot forward it to station 3) or starved (station 2 wants to initiate production of the next flow unit but does not receive any input from upstream).

FIGURE 10.7 **Flow Rate Compared at Four Configurations of a Queuing System (cycle times computed using simulation)**

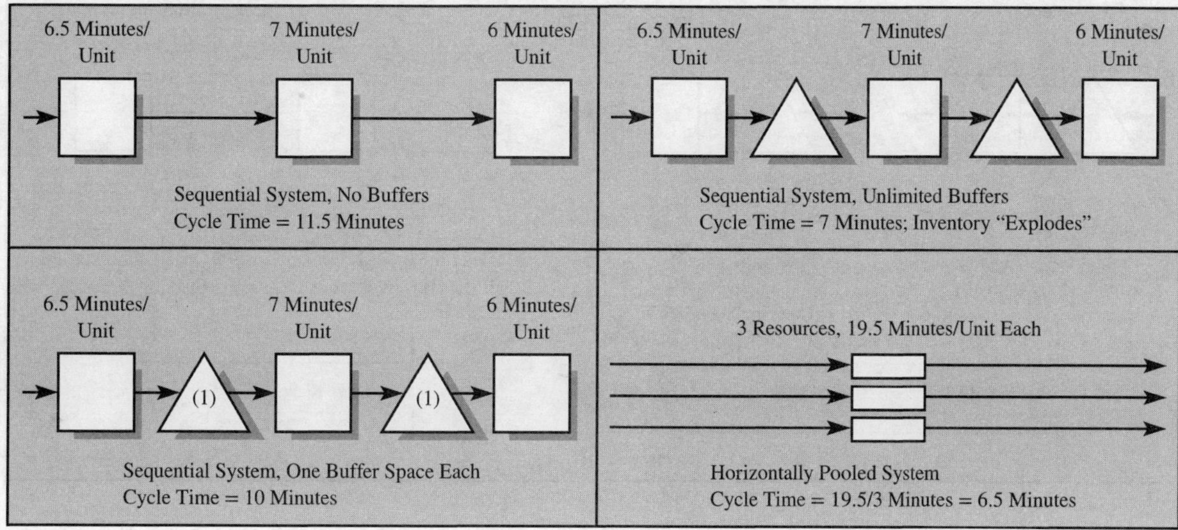

If we introduce buffers to this process, the flow rate improves. Even just allowing for one unit in buffer before and after the bottleneck increases the output to one unit every 10 minutes (lower left). If we put no limits on buffers, the process is able to produce the expected flow rate of one unit every 7 minutes (upper right). Yet, we also observe that the buffer between the first and the second steps will grow very rapidly.

Finally, the lower-right part of Figure 10.7 outlines an alternative way to restore the flow rate, different from the concept of "buffer or suffer" (in fact, the flow rate is even a little larger than in the case of the upper right). By combining the three activities into one activity, we eliminate starving and blocking entirely. This concept is called *horizontal pooling*, as it resembles the concept of pooling identical activities and their previously separate arrival streams that we discussed in the previous chapter. Observe further the similarities between horizontal pooling and the concept of a work cell discussed in Chapter 4.

Given the cost of inventory as well as its detrimental impact on quality discussed in Chapter 7, we need to be careful in choosing where and how much inventory (buffer space) we allow in the process. Since the bottleneck is the constraint limiting the flow rate through the process (assuming sufficient demand), we want to avoid the bottleneck being either starved or blocked. Consequently, buffers are especially helpful right before and right after the bottleneck.

10.6 Summary

Variability not only impacts inventory and wait time but potentially also leads to losses in throughput. In this chapter, we have presented and analyzed the simplest case of such loss systems, consisting of multiple parallel resources with no buffer. The key computations for this case can be done based on the Erlang loss formula.

We then extended our discussion to the case in which customers potentially wait for service but are sufficiently impatient that a loss in throughput can still occur.

Figure 10.8 shows an overview of the various types of scenarios we discussed and, at least partially, analyzed. On the very left of the figure is the waiting problem of the previous chapter; on the very right is the no-buffer loss system (Erlang loss system) presented

FIGURE 10.8 Different Types of Variability Problems

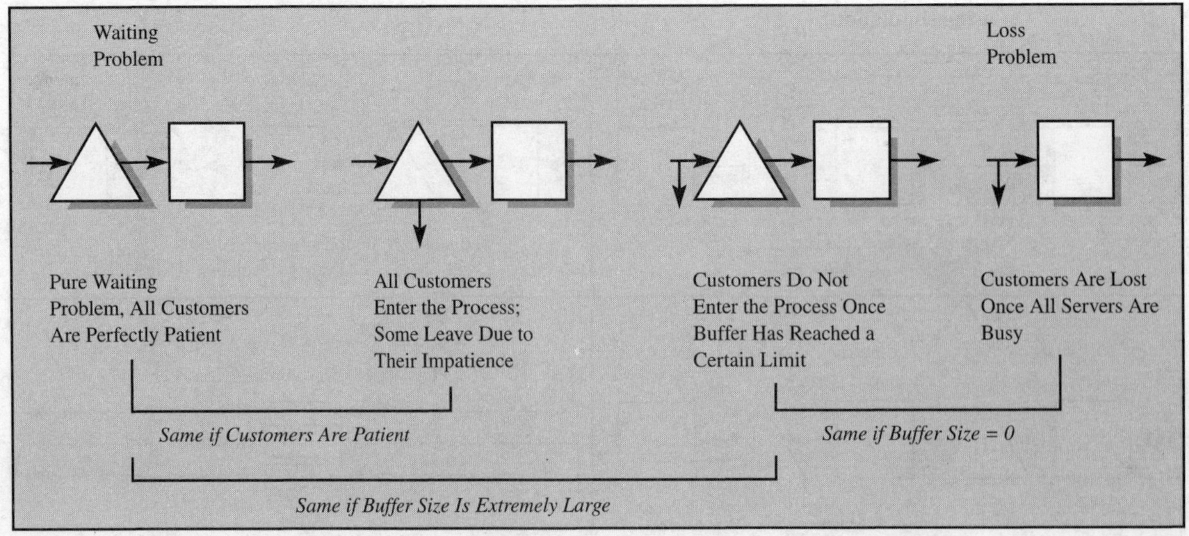

at the beginning of this chapter. In between are the intermediate cases of impatient customers. Observe that the four process types share a lot of similarities. For example, a wait system with limited, but large, buffer size is likely to behave very similarly to a pure waiting problem. Similarly, as the buffer size approaches zero, the system behavior approaches the one of the pure loss system. Finally, we also looked at the case of several resources in series, forming a sequence of queues.

From a managerial perspective, the primary objective continues to be to reduce variability wherever possible. All concepts we discussed in the waiting time chapter still apply, including the ideas to reduce the variability of service times through standardization and training.

However, since we cannot reduce variability entirely, it is important that we create processes that are robust enough so that they can accommodate as much of the remaining variability as possible. The following should be kept in mind to address throughput loss problems resulting from variability:

- *Use Buffers.* Nowhere else in this book is the concept of "buffer or suffer" so visible as in this chapter. To protect process resources, most importantly the bottleneck, from variability, we need to add buffers to avoid throughput losses of the magnitude in the example of Figure 10.7. In a sequence of resources, buffers are needed right before and right after the bottleneck to avoid the bottleneck either starving or becoming blocked.
- *Keep track of demand.* A major challenge in managing capacity-related decisions in a process with customer loss is to collect *real* demand information, which is required to compute the implied utilization level. Why is this difficult? The moment our process becomes sufficiently full that we cannot admit any new flow units (all trauma bays are utilized, all lines are busy in the call center), we lose demand, and, even worse, we do not even know how much demand we lose (i.e., we also lose the demand information). A common mistake that can be observed in practice is that managers use flow rate (sales) and utilization (Flow rate/Capacity) when determining if they need additional capacity. As we have discussed previously, utilization is by definition less than 100 percent. Consequently, the utilization measure always gives the impression that there is sufficient capacity in place. The metric that really matters is demand divided by capacity (implied utilization), as this reveals what sales could be if there were sufficient capacity.
- *Use background work.* Similar to what we discussed with respect to waiting time problems, we typically cannot afford to run a process at the low levels of utilization discussed in the trauma care setting. Instead, we can use less time-critical work to use potential idle time in a productive manner. However, a word of caution is in order. To qualify as background work, this work should not interfere with the time-critical work. Thus, it must be possible to interrupt or delay the processing of a unit of background work. Moreover, we have to ensure that background work does not compete for the same resource as time-critical work further downstream. For example, it has been reported that elective surgery (at first sight a great case of background work for a hospital) can lead to ambulance diversion, as it competes with trauma care patients for ICU capacity.

10.7 Further Reading

Gans, Koole, and Mandelbaum (2003), referenced in the previous chapter, is also a great reading with respect to customer loss patterns. Again, we refer the interested readers to Hillier and Lieberman (2002) and Hall (1997) for additional quantitative methods.

10.8 Practice Problems

The following questions will help in testing your understanding of this chapter. In this chapter, all questions relate to the calculations introduced in Section 10.3.

Solutions to problems marked with an "*" are available in Appendix E. Video solutions to select problems are available in Connect.

Q10.1* **(Loss System)** Flow units arrive at a demand rate of 55 units per hour. It takes, on average, six minutes to serve a flow unit. Service is provided by seven servers.

a. What is the probability that all seven servers are utilized?

b. How many units are served every hour?

c. How many units are lost every hour?

Q10.2 **(Home Security)** A friend of yours approaches you with the business idea of a private home security service. This private home security service guarantees to either dispatch one of their own five guards immediately if one of their customers sends in an alarm or, in the case that all five guards are responding to other calls, direct the alarm to the local police. The company receives 12 calls per hour, evenly distributed over the course of the day.

The local police charges the home security company $500 for every call that the police responds to. It takes a guard, on average, 90 minutes to respond to an alarm.

a. What fraction of the time are incoming alarms directed to the police?

b. How much does the home security company have to pay the local police every month?

Q10.3 **(Video Store)** A small video store has nine copies of the DVD *Captain Underpants, The Movie* in its store. There are 15 customers every day who request this movie for their children. If the movie is not on the shelf, they leave and go to a competing store. Customers arrive evenly distributed over 24 hours.

The average rental duration is 36 hours.

a. What is the likelihood that a customer going to the video store will find the movie available?

b. Assume each rental is $5. How much revenue does the store make per day from the movie?

c. Assume each child that is not able to obtain the movie will receive a $1 bill. How much money would the store have to give out to children requesting *Captain Underpants* every day?

d. Assume the demand for the movie will stay the same for another six months. What would be the payback time (not considering interest rates) for purchasing an additional copy of the movie at $50? Consider the extra revenues related to question b and the potential cost savings (question c).

Q10.4 **(Gas Station)** Consider the situation of Mr. R. B. Cheney, who owns a large gas station on a highway in Vermont. In the afternoon hours, there are, on average, 1,000 cars per hour passing by the gas station, of which 2 percent would be willing to stop for refueling. However, since there are several other gas stations with similar prices on the highway, potential customers are not willing to wait and bypass Cheney's gas station.

The gas station has six spots that can be used for filling up vehicles and it takes a car, on average, five minutes to free up the spot again (includes filling up and any potential delay caused by the customer going inside the gas station).

a. What is the probability that all six spots are taken?

b. How many customers are served every hour?

Q10.5 **(Two Workstations)** Suppose a process contains two workstations that operate with no buffer between them.

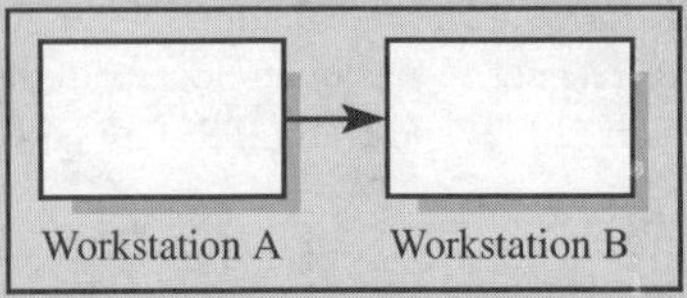

Now consider the three possible scenarios below:

Scenario	Processing Time of Workstation A	Processing Time of Workstation B
Scenario 1	5 minutes	5 minutes
Scenario 2	5 minutes	4 minutes or 6 minutes equally likely
Scenario 3	5 minutes	3 minutes or 5 minutes equally likely

a. Which of the three scenarios will have, on average, the highest flow rate?

b. Which of the three scenarios will have, on average, the lowest flow time?

Q10.6 **(XTremely Fast Service Inc.)** XTremely Fast Service Inc. is a call center with several business units. One of its business units, Fabulous 4, currently staffs four operators who work eight hours per day Monday through Friday. They provide customer support for a mail-order catalog company. Assume customers call Fabulous 4 during business hours and that—on average—a call arrives every three minutes (standard deviation of the interarrival time is equal to three minutes). You do *not* have to consider any seasonality in this call arrival pattern. If all four staff members are busy, the customer is rerouted to another business unit instead of being put on hold. Suppose the processing time for each call is five minutes on average.

a. What is the probability that an incoming call is *not* processed by Fabulous 4?

b. Suppose that Fabulous 4 receives $1 for each customer that it processes. What is Fabulous 4's daily revenue?

c. Suppose Fabulous 4 pays $5 for every call that gets routed to another business unit. What is its daily transfer payment to the other business unit?

Q10.7 **(Gotham City Ambulance Services)** Gotham City Ambulance Services (GCAS) owns eight ambulances. On average, emergencies are reported to GCAS every 15 minutes (with a coefficient of variation of 1, no seasonality exists). If GCAS has available ambulances, it immediately dispatches one. If there are no ambulances available, the incident is served by the emergency services at a neighboring community. You can assume that in the neighboring community, there is always an ambulance available. On average, an ambulance and its crew are engaged for 1.5 hours (with a coefficient of variation of 1.5) on every call. GCAS operates 24 hours a day.

a. What fraction of the emergencies reported to GCAS are handled by the emergency services at the neighboring community?

b. How many emergencies are served by GCAS during an average 24-hour day?

c. GCAS updated the operating procedures for its staff. This led to a reduction in the coefficient of variation of the time spent on each trip by its staff from 1.5 to 1.25. How will this training program affect the number of emergencies attended to by the GCAS?

d. New regulations require that every emergency service respond to at least 95 percent of all incidents reported in its area of service. Does GCAS need to buy more ambulances to meet this requirement? If yes, how many ambulances will be required? (Assume that the mean time spent on each trip cannot be changed.)

Chapter 11

Scheduling to Prioritize Demand

If you need a surgical operation and you live in England, you can rest assured that the British government sets targets for how long patients should wait for various procedures. For example, a hospital might be required to schedule 90 percent of its patients within 18 weeks. While that might seem like a reasonable goal, it still gives hospitals considerable latitude with respect to how they actually schedule surgeries. Naturally, some surgeries need to be done without much delay: If Uncle Bruce is having a heart attack, he needs stents inserted into his arteries immediately. But there is much more flexibility with other surgeries, such as a knee replacement: Although Aunt Janet would prefer to have her knee fixed this week, she can get about with some care and her cane.

In this chapter, we explore the practice of *scheduling*, the process of deciding what work to assign to which resources and when to assign the work. For example, the work could be "a knee replacement," the resource could be "an orthopedist" or an "operating room," and the when could be "May 19 at 8:00 a.m."

We begin by exploring the breadth of situations in which scheduling is required. Clearly, scheduling is relevant in health care, but it is relevant even more broadly. In fact, some form of scheduling probably applies in all operations. Next, we study how to schedule work in the simplest of situations with just one resource. For example, say you are an underwriter of mortgages and you must decide which of the 10 mortgage applications on your desk you should work on next. You could use the intuitive "first-come-first-served" rule (FCFS)—just line up the applications as they arrive and process them in that order. But as we will discover, there can be reasons to do something other than FCFS.

Sticking with a single resource, we then complicate our scheduling task in four different ways. First, how should you schedule when different types of work have different priorities in terms of their need to be completed quickly. Second, we consider scheduling work that has due dates. Third, we consider how to schedule in complex processes with many types of jobs and servers. Fourth, we investigate scheduling via a reservation or appointment system. You might assume that not much thought is needed to design an appointment system—just determine the time slots and then let customers select which one they want. While you could do that, we will learn that an effective appointment system must carefully balance several important trade-offs.

11.1 Scheduling Timeline and Applications

Though it has already been mentioned, it bears repeating, a common thread in all scheduling applications is the matching of demand to resources: When will a particular resource be used to process a particular demand? Given the emphasis it puts on time, scheduling can occur over substantially different time horizons, from immediate decisions to decisions spanning a decade, as described in Table 11.1.

Not only does scheduling occur over a large span of different time horizons, it is not surprising that scheduling is implemented in a wide spectrum of operations. A few are mentioned below.

Project management. Large, one-time projects require a vast array of activities and resources that must be coordinated; that is, scheduled. For example, the development of healthcare.gov for the Affordable Health Care Act required extensive integration of numerous different databases and software systems managed by both private enterprises and government agencies. The Channel Tunnel was a huge public infrastructure project that cost about $7 billion (in 1985 prices) and required six years to build. Scheduling is critical for the success of projects, which is why we devote an entire chapter to it.

Manufacturing. An automobile assembly line usually produces different versions of the same model. Every fourth car coming down the line might be a hatchback (rather than a sedan) and every tenth car might have a sunroof. Scheduling the manufacturing sequence of vehicles influences how well the line is balanced, as well as the variability of requests from suppliers for parts. Speaking of which, most manufacturing operations require a *materials requirement planning (MRP)* system. An MRP system contains a *bill of materials* database, which is a listing of all of the parts of every product made—the bill of materials for a car would include thousands of different components. Using the bill of materials and the production schedule, the MRP system evaluates how many of each part are needed and when they are needed. It then schedules deliveries of those parts to ensure that they arrive early enough for assembly, but not so early that too much inventory accumulates.

Service scheduling. If you reserve a mid-sized vehicle from a car rental agency, the company needs to decide (schedule) the particular car in its fleet that it will use to serve you. And if you call a small bed and breakfast (B&B) to request a room for Saturday night, it must decide if it is willing to offer you a room for that evening—if it gives you the room for just Saturday, it might not be able to sell a reservation to someone else who wants a room for Friday and Saturday. Scheduling decisions like these are often grouped under the heading of *revenue management*: the practice of trying to maximize the revenue generated from a set of fixed assets (like cars in a rental fleet, rooms in a hotel, or tables in a restaurant). We explore revenue management in greater detail in Chapter 18.

TABLE 11.1 Different Time Horizons for Scheduling

Time Period	Examples
Long: 1 year or more	An airline schedules the delivery of new aircraft over the next decade. A sports league schedules next year's matches between teams.
Medium: 1 month to 1 year	Scheduled shutdowns of a nuclear power plant for maintenance. The number of temporary workers to hire for the fourth quarter.
Short: 1 minute to 1 month	Which patient to treat next in the emergency room. Which caller to respond to in a call center. Workforce scheduling for next week.

Transportation scheduling. As a customer, you probably look at posted schedules whenever you fly, take a train, or ride a bus. Somebody had to develop those schedules—and he or she had to make many more decisions than you might see. For example, an airline not only decides when it will offer a flight between two cities, it also must decide which plane will fly that route and which gate the plane will use at the airport. The flight controller needs to decide when the plane is cleared for landing or takeoff and on which runway.

Patient scheduling. Patients with chronic conditions often need to make regular visits to a health care facility for treatment. For example, radiotherapy for oncology patients is often performed over multiple sessions over a long duration of time. Because this equipment is very expensive, the hospital wants to ensure that it is highly utilized. At the same time, however, each patient requires a regimen of procedures that need to be performed at precise intervals—not too close to each other, but also not too far apart. The challenge for a scheduling system is to balance the desire for high utilization with the goal to maximize the effectiveness of treatment.

Workforce scheduling. Some people are fortunate enough to have a job with regular hours. But many jobs involve irregular hours that can change from week to week as needs change. This is relatively common in retail, but nurses and airline crews are often scheduled on a week-to-week basis as well.

Tournament scheduling. Scheduling a season for a professional sports league is a huge challenge, primarily because there are many constraints and objectives that need to be satisfied. For example, leagues want teams to play both home and away games throughout the season—a schedule is unacceptable if one team plays at home for the first half of the season and then away for the second half. Leagues also want to minimize travel, both for cost and for the well-being of the players: Imagine playing a game on the East Coast of the United States on Thursday, then a West Coast game on Friday, and then back to the East Coast for a game on Saturday.

The preceding examples reveal several common themes. For one, scheduling can be immensely complex primarily because of the staggering number of possible combinations for many real-life problems. Second, although scheduling applies in diverse settings, the objectives across the systems are similar: to ensure that resources are highly utilized and demand is served in a timely manner.

11.2 Resource Scheduling—Shortest Processing Time

Consider a loan underwriting process at Capital One. Underwriters are responsible for deciding which loans to fund and which to deny. Capital One has eight underwriters in one of its offices and each underwriter takes, on average, 40 minutes to process a loan.

While an underwriter takes 40 minutes, on average, to process a loan, there naturally is some variation in the processing times. In addition, it is also likely that an underwriter can quickly ascertain the needed time for a loan when he or she first looks at the loan. Say one of the underwriters, Annick Gallino, currently has five loans on her desk, which we label A, B, C, D, and E, but she hasn't started to process any of them. In the language of scheduling, each loan is called a *job*—a job is a flow unit that requires processing from one or more resources. Table 11.2 lists the jobs and Annick's estimates for each job's processing time. Annick quickly determines each job's processing time by looking at a few key pieces of information in the application. Let's assume (i) Annick has enough experience that her estimates are accurate, (ii) each of the jobs has equal priority (they are all equally valuable to complete quickly), and (iii) there are no due dates (ideally each job is finished as soon as possible). We'll later discuss how to handle situations in which those three assumptions do not apply.

TABLE 11.2 Processing Time for Five Loans, Which Arrived in Alphabetical Sequence (i.e., A arrived first, E arrived last)

Job	A	B	C	D	E
Processing time (minutes)	45	20	65	30	40

The average processing time across the five jobs on Annick's desk is indeed 40 minutes. However, not all of the jobs are the same. Loan B looks relatively simple, requiring only 20 minutes of time to process. In contrast, loan C is more involved because it requires 65 minutes.

With 200 minutes of work on her desk, Annick should get busy processing some loans. But in which order should she work on these loans? *First-come-first-served (FCFS)* is an intuitive sequence. With FCFS, the resource (Annick) works on jobs in the sequence in which they arrive, which in this case is in alphabetical order (i.e., A arrived first, E arrived last). But is this the best way to sequence the jobs? To answer that question, we need to decide how to measure "best"; that is, we need some performance measures.

Performance Measures

Chapter 2 highlights three key process performance metrics: inventory, flow rate, and flow time. To refresh your memory:

- *Inventory, I,* is the average number of flow units in the system over an interval of time.
- *Flow rate, R,* is the average rate at which flow units enter or exit the system.
- *Flow time, T,* is the average time a flow unit (i.e., a job) spends in the system.

All three are relevant in a scheduling application, but according to Little's Law (see Chapter 2), we only need to track two of them—once you know two of the metrics, you can evaluate the third using the following equivalent equations:

$$I = R \times T$$

$$R = \frac{I}{T}$$

$$T = \frac{I}{R}$$

In the case of Annick, we know that she has 200 minutes of work ahead of her no matter how she sequences the various jobs. Thus, after 200 minutes she will have completed five jobs. This means that her flow rate over the next 200 minutes, *R,* is 5 jobs/200 min = 0.025 job per min. While the flow rate is independent of the sequence, we will soon see that the flow time does depend on the chosen schedule for processing the jobs. Given that *R* is fixed and *T* depends on the chosen schedule, *I* also depends on the chosen schedule.

The measures of inventory, flow rate, and flow time are all based on averages. There is no doubt that average performance is relevant and important. But a manager may also be interested in outlier performance. Take the example from the beginning of the chapter: In England, hospitals are required to schedule 90 percent of surgeries within 18 weeks. That performance measure focuses on ensuring that bad outcomes (patients who have to wait more than 18 weeks) are infrequent (less than 10 percent of surgeries). Although a target like "*X* percent of jobs are completed in *T* units of time" is intuitively reasonable, it also suffers from a potential limitation: It gives the scheduler an incentive to strategically manipulate the schedule. For example, if a patient's surgery cannot be scheduled within 18 weeks, then the scheduler no longer has an incentive to schedule the surgery "as soon as possible"—from the perspective of the target, a surgery scheduled for week 19 is not any worse than the same surgery scheduled for week 30 in the sense that neither situation contributes toward the goal of 90 percent of surgeries within 18 weeks. However, from the perspective of an average waiting time, 19 weeks is still 11 weeks less of a delay than 30 weeks. Put another way, average performance measures always have an incentive to reduce the time a job is in the system, no matter how long it has been in the system. Thus, doing well, on average, also tends to avoid bad outlier outcomes. For that reason, we focus on average performance measures.

First-Come-First-Served vs. Shortest Processing Time

First-come-first-served is the natural way to sequence jobs. It doesn't require much thinking on the part of the resource (just do the jobs in the order they arrive) and it seems fair (more on that later). But it isn't the only way to sequence the jobs. Let's focus on one particular alternative, the *shortest-processing-time (SPT)* rule—with SPT, jobs are sequenced in increasing order of processing times. For example, from the data in Table 11.2, Annick would process job B first (it has the shortest processing time, 20 minutes), then D, E, A, and finally C (it has the longest processing time, 65 minutes). If additional jobs were to arrive before these five are completed, then the new jobs would be placed in their proper place in the "to be completed" queue so that processing times are always sequenced in increasing order.

So which is better, FCFS (A, B, C, D, E) or SPT (B, D, E, A, C)? As already mentioned, no matter what the sequence, Annick takes 200 minutes to complete all five jobs. (This assumes that no other job arrives in the next 200 minutes with a processing time that is less than 65 minutes, which we assume for simplicity.) Given that the two sequences require the same total amount of time, you might assume that the sequence doesn't matter all that much for the various performance measures. While you are correct with respect to the flow rate, you are wrong with respect to the flow time and inventory.

Figure 11.1 illustrates Gantt charts for FCFS and SPT sequencing. Time is shown on the horizontal axis and each job is displayed in the time interval it is processed. It is customary to show each job on a different row, which helps to highlight the time each job waits and when it is completed.

Let's now evaluate the flow times for each job with each sequencing rule. With FCFS, job A goes first and has a flow time equal to its processing time, 45 minutes, because it

FIGURE 11.1
Two Different Approaches to Sequencing Five Jobs (A, B, C, D, E): first-come-first-served (top) and shortest processing time (bottom)

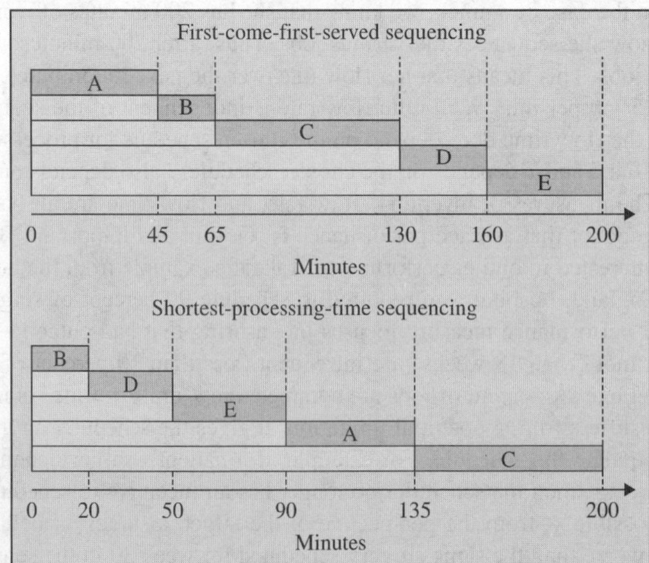

doesn't wait. Job B is next, with a flow time of 65 minutes: Job B waits 45 minutes for A to be completed and then is processed in 20 minutes. The other flow times are 130 minutes for job C (65 minutes waiting, 65 minutes processing), 160 minutes for job D (130 minutes waiting, 30 minutes processing), and finally 200 minutes for job E (160 minutes waiting, 40 minutes processing). The average flow time among these jobs is

$$\frac{45 + 65 + 130 + 160 + 200}{5} = 120 \text{ minutes}$$

With SPT, the flow times are 20, 50, 90, 135, and 200 (see Figure 11.1). The average flow time is

$$\frac{20 + 50 + 90 + 135 + 200}{5} = 99 \text{ minutes}$$

Although the flow time of the last job is the same with either sequencing (200 minutes), the average flow times are indeed different. Even though SPT does exactly the same amount of work as FCFS and it works at the same speed (the processing times are not different), each job, on average, spends 21 minutes less in the system with SPT relative to FCFS $(120 - 99 = 21)$!

To understand why SPT is more effective than FCFS (in terms of flow), note that the early jobs all impose waiting times on the jobs that come afterward. For example, job A is first with FCFS and it requires 45 minutes to process. This means that if A were to go first, then 45 minutes is added to the flow time of each of the four other jobs. In contrast, with SPT, the first job, B, only requires 20 minutes to process. So job B only adds 20 minutes to the flow time of the other four jobs. Clearly, the choice of the first job to process makes a big difference because it causes a delay in all of the other jobs. In contrast, the last job processed doesn't add flow time to any of the other jobs. So you want the shortest-processing-time job to go first (because it imposes the least cost on the other jobs) and the longest-processing-time job to go last (because it doesn't make any other job wait). That is precisely what SPT does!

Jobs spend less time in the system with SPT than with FCFS, but that doesn't mean the system has more capacity with SPT. Jobs flow at the same rate with either system—the flow rate, R, is 0.025 job per minute with SPT and FCFS. This is initially confusing: How is it that jobs spend less time in the system with SPT, but they flow at the same rate? The answer is that the average inventory in the system, I, is less with SPT than with FCFS. To be specific, with FCFS the average number of jobs in the system is

$$I = R \times T = 0.025 \text{ job per min} \times 120 \text{ min} = 3 \text{ jobs}$$

whereas with SPT the average number of jobs in the system is

$$I = R \times T = 0.025 \text{ job per min} \times 99 \text{ min} = 2.5 \text{ jobs}$$

SPT looks great relative to FCFS in this particular instance, when Annick has these five jobs on her desk. But is this just a special case? It isn't. No matter how many jobs need to be processed or what their processing times are, SPT always beats FCFS in terms of average flow time. Because the flow rate is constant, SPT also always beats FCFS in terms of average inventory.

Although our example illustrates how SPT can do better than FCFS, it is also possible that SPT can do much better than FCFS. To explain, suppose the jobs arrive in the following order: C, A, E, D, B. In other words, the jobs arrive in descending order of processing time: The longest job arrives first and the shortest job arrives last. That sequence is the complete opposite of SPT and is sometimes called the *longest-processing-time (LPT)* rule.

If we draw a Gantt chart (as in Figure 11.1) for the LPT sequence and then evaluate the average flow time, we get

$$\frac{65 + 110 + 150 + 180 + 200}{5} = 141 \text{ minutes}$$

Wow! FCFS could actually generate an average flow time that is 42 minutes (141 − 99) longer than SPT—that is a 42 percent increase in average flow time across all of the jobs (not just one of the jobs). Again, this gap occurs without changing the total amount of work done or the flow rate of jobs.

FCFS can be pretty bad, but in fairness to FCFS, it is really bad only in the special case in which the jobs arrive (by chance) in descending order of processing time. To understand SPT's real advantage, we should consider all possible arrival sequences and see how much better SPT is on average. To do that, we can use a discrete event simulator.

The simulation is done in four steps:

1. Generate a bunch of different processing times. For this simulation there are 25,000 processing times. A histogram of those processing times is displayed in Figure 11.2. To help visualize this process, imagine we create a bag containing 25,000 balls, each with a processing time written on it.
2. Randomly choose a sequence of processing times from the sample to simulate the jobs that are on an underwriter's desk ready to be processed. This is like reaching into our "bag" and grabbing five balls, one at a time, to construct a sequence of jobs like that displayed in the top panel of Figure 11.1.
3. Evaluate the average flow time using the FCFS rule, as well as the SPT rule. As in Figure 11.1, the average flow times are likely to be different.
4. Repeat steps 2 and 3 many times and then average the flow times obtained with those iterations. In this case, we did 2,500 iterations. Note: All of the 25,000 processing times are used only when there are 10 jobs waiting to be processed—2,500 iterations × 10 jobs = 25,000 processing times.

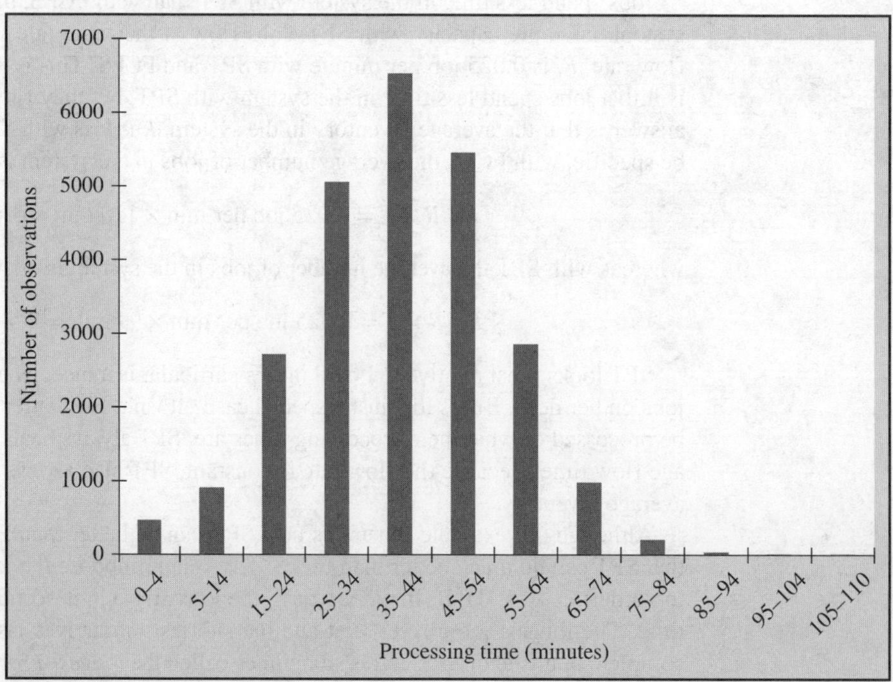

FIGURE 11.2 Histogram of 25,000 Processing Times. The Average Processing Time Is 40 Minutes and the Standard Deviation Is 15 Minutes.

Figure 11.3 displays the results from the discrete event simulation for different values for the number of jobs waiting to be processed. In the example displayed in Figure 11.1, there are five jobs waiting to be processed. In that particular example, the average flow times are 99 and 120 minutes for SPT and FCFS, respectively. According to Figure 11.3, across a large sample of different sequences with five jobs, the average flow times are 103 minutes for SPT and 120 minutes for FCFS. Thus, the example shown in Figure 11.1 is reasonably representative of the difference one might expect in performance between SPT and FCFS with five jobs.

Figure 11.3 reveals one additional important finding. The gap between FCFS and SPT grows as the number of jobs in the queue grows. If there are only two jobs in the queue, then, by a 50/50 chance, FCFS might sequence the jobs exactly the same way as SPT. Hence, FCFS does okay when there are only two jobs in the queue—the flow times are 55 and 59 minutes for SPT and FCFS, respectively. However, when there are 10 jobs in the queue, the average flow time for SPT is 182 minutes, but the average flow time for FCFS is 37 minutes higher (219 minutes)! We can conclude that it is most important to use SPT instead of FCFS when it is likely that there will be many jobs in the system. And when is that likely? The system is likely to have more jobs when the system's utilization is very high. When demand is close to capacity, using SPT instead of FCFS can make a big difference in terms of flow time and inventory.

So SPT always gives a lower flow time than FCFS and the gap between the two is largest when there are many jobs waiting for service. This makes SPT look very good. And,

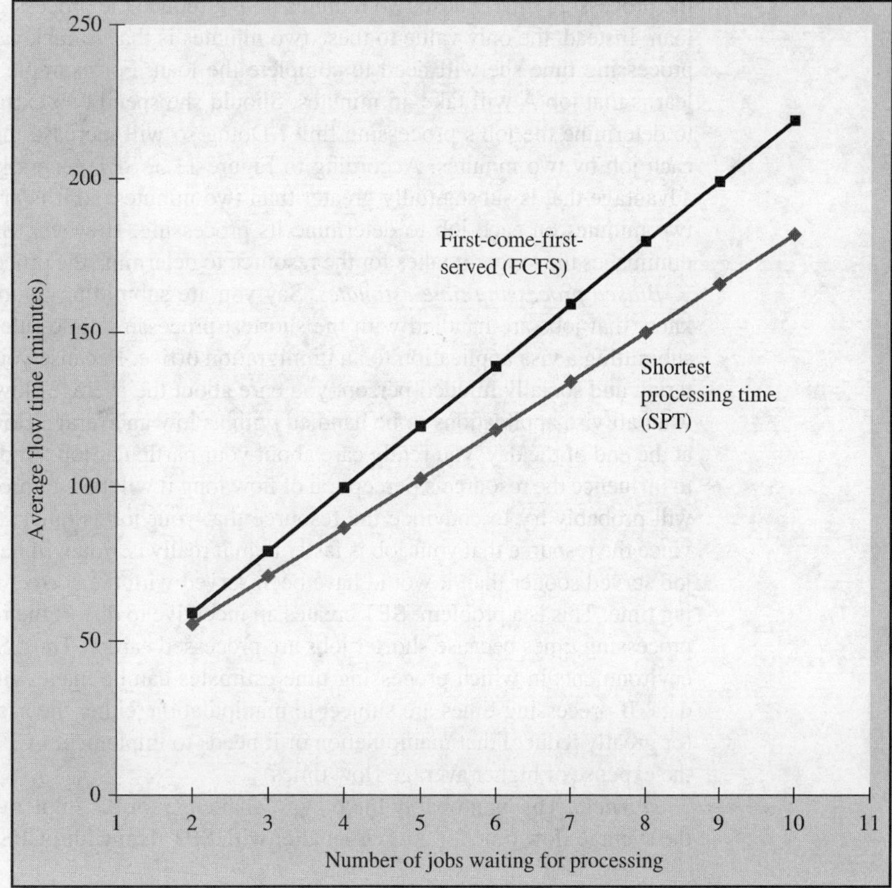

FIGURE 11.3
Discrete Event Simulation Results for the Average Flow Time with First-Come-First-Served or Shortest-Processing-Time Sequencing as a Function of the Number of Jobs in the Queue Waiting for Processing; 2,500 Samples Are Generated for Each Value for the Number of Jobs Waiting for Processing

in fact, it has been proven to be the very best sequencing rule: If you want to minimize the average flow time (and in turn the average inventory of jobs in the system), you cannot do any better than SPT!

Limitations of Shortest Processing Time

With so much going for it, why wouldn't a manager always use SPT? There are three reasons why you might choose FCFS rather than SPT: (i) it takes too long to determine the processing time of the jobs; (ii) the estimates of the processing times may be biased; and/or (iii) SPT raises concerns of fairness—it does not treat all jobs equally. Let's discuss each reason.

Delay to determine processing times. In one extreme, when a job arrives, it is possible to immediately determine its processing time with high accuracy and nearly no cost. For example, if a data packet arrives to a telecommunications server, the time to process the packet might be a function of the amount of data in the packet, which might be trivial to observe. Or a translator might know how long it will take to translate a document merely by the number of pages in the document. These situations are ideal for SPT because SPT doesn't lose any time in determining the best sequence. At the other extreme, it is also possible that the only way to know the processing time for a job is to actually do the job. In those situations, SPT provides no benefit relative to FCFS: If you have to complete the job to know how long it will take to do the job, then you cannot do any better than FCFS sequencing. As with all extremes, there are plenty of cases in the middle, situations in which it takes some time merely to learn how long it will take to process a job. For example, suppose Annick needs two minutes to look over a loan application to determine the processing time. These two minutes do not reduce the processing time to complete the loan. Instead, the only value to these two minutes is that Annick can figure out how much processing time she will need to complete the loan. For example, after two minutes she learns that job A will take 45 minutes. Should she spend two extra minutes for every job to determine the job's processing time? Doing so will increase the average flow time of each job by two minutes. According to Figure 11.3, SPT generally provides a flow time advantage that is substantially greater than two minutes, so it is probably worth spending two minutes on each job to determine its processing. However, SPT's advantage clearly diminishes the longer it takes for the resource to determine the processing time of each job.

Biased processing time estimates. Say you are submitting a job to a resource and you know that jobs are handled with the shortest-processing-time rule. For instance, you are submitting a visa application to an immigration office. Because you are probably an egalitarian and socially minded person, you care about the average flow time of all jobs—you want all visa applications to be handled with as low an average flow time as possible. But at the end of the day, you really care about your particular job. And if you have any ability to influence the resource's perception of how long it will take to process your job, then you will probably try to convince the resource that your job is quick. If you indeed can convince the resource that your job is faster than it really is, you will have managed to get your job served sooner than it would have been served with the correct estimate of its processing time. This is a problem: SPT creates an incentive to distort the resource's perception of processing times because shorter jobs are processed earlier. Thus, SPT is most suitable for environments in which processing time estimates can be made with objective (unbiased) data. If processing times are subject to manipulation, either the system needs to eliminate (or greatly reduce) that manipulation or it needs to implement FCFS to avoid this issue (at the expense of higher average flow times).

Fairness. This is probably the biggest challenge for the implementation of SPT. While the average flow time for a job is smaller with SPT than with FCFS, this doesn't mean it is lower for all jobs. Return to the discrete event simulator for the loans processed by Annick. Figure 11.4 displays the average time a job waits before it begins its processing as a function of the job's processing time when there are five jobs to be processed (as in our earlier example). With FCFS, every job basically waits 80 minutes before it begins processing, no matter if it is a small job (10 minutes) or a large job (80 minutes). (The flow times of these jobs are different because the flow time includes the processing time, and the processing time for a small job is different than for a large job.) The same is clearly not true with SPT. SPT puts small jobs at the front of the queue and large jobs at the back of the queue. Hence, small jobs wait less time to begin processing, while a large job might spend a considerable amount of time waiting. For example, a 10-minute job is likely to be the smallest job, so it spends essentially no time waiting before it begins processing. However, an 80-minute job is likely to be the last of five jobs, so its flow time is essentially 160 minutes—it must wait for four jobs to be completed, which takes, on average, 4×40 minutes = 160 minutes. Thus, if it is important to treat all jobs equally, FCFS is the better approach. This is most likely an issue when people are able to observe the flow times of the other jobs. However, equality definitely comes at a cost: To treat all jobs equally means that, on average, a job spends more time in the system.

One reason to not avoid using SPT is uncertainty in the processing time estimates. For example, say job X might take between 20 and 50 minutes, while job Y might take between 40 and 70 minutes. It is possible that job X takes longer than job Y, but it is more likely that job X will take less time to process. Hence, job X should be processed first to minimize average flow time. In general, if there is some uncertainty in the processing time estimates, SPT is still effective and it works merely by sorting the jobs in increasing order by their expected processing times.

FIGURE 11.4
Average Time a Job Waits before Beginning to be Processed as a Function of a Job's Processing Time When There Are Five Jobs to be Processed. The Average Processing Time Is 40 Minutes.

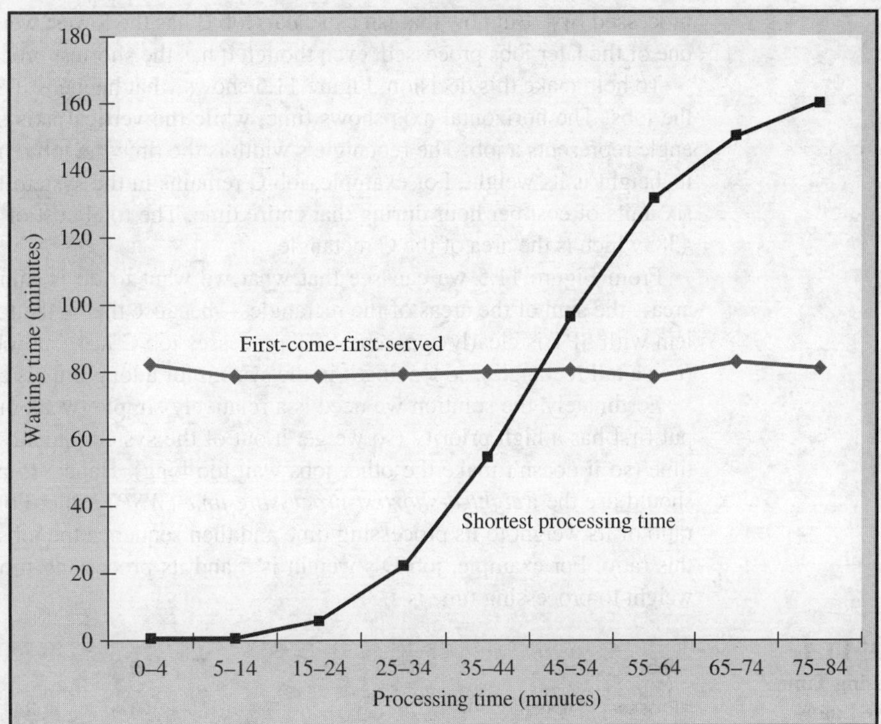

11.3 Resource Scheduling with Priorities—Weighted Shortest Processing Time

If you want to minimize the average flow time across all jobs, use the shortest processing time to schedule resources. But is that still true if it costs more to have some jobs wait than others? As you might expect, it isn't. But neither do we have to completely throw away SPT.

Consider the situation displayed in Table 11.3. There are five jobs to process on a single resource. They vary in processing times, from 6 hours to 24 hours. They also vary in terms of the cost they incur for each unit of time they remain in the system, which is listed as the "weight" of the job. There are several interpretations for this weight:

- The weight of a job could be a literal cost, as in $0.10 per hour, like an inventory holding cost.
- Customers differ in the profit they bring to the firm—some customers are highly profitable, whereas others are less so. For example, banks love customers who maintain large deposits and never use tellers or call the customer service center for assistance. In contrast, customers are not so profitable if they have a low balance, bounce checks, and frequently request personal assistance. Thus, more profitable customers may be assigned a higher weight.
- Customers differ in their sensitivity to delays. It is costly to lose a customer, but some customers are more patient than others. Hence, a higher weight could be assigned to the more impatient customers.
- The server might have different priorities for serving customers. For example, in health care, priorities are assigned to patients based on the severity of their needs for fast service.

The scheduling decision certainly becomes more complex when jobs have different priorities. If they all had the same priority, we could use SPT and job B would surely be processed first. But now that isn't so clear. Job B has the lowest weight. So should job B be one of the later jobs processed, even though it has the shortest processing time?

To help make this decision, Figure 11.5 shows what happens if SPT is used to schedule the jobs. The horizontal axis shows time, while the vertical axis shows costs. Each rectangle represents a job: The rectangle's width is the time the job remains in the system and its height is its weight. For example, job C remains in the system for 73 hours and incurs six units of cost per hour during that entire time. The total cost of job C is then $73 \times 6 = 438$, which is the area of the C rectangle.

From Figure 11.5 we can see that what we want to do is minimize the total shaded area—the sum of the areas of the rectangles—because that is the total cost. And the problem with SPT is clearly apparent: SPT processes job C last, but job C has a lot of weight (i.e., a tall rectangle), so leaving it in the system for a long time is costly.

Fortunately, the solution we need is a relatively simple tweak on SPT. The ideal job to put first has a high priority (so we get it out of the system quickly) and a low processing time (so it doesn't make the other jobs wait too long). Hence, to minimize total cost, we should use the *weighted-shortest-processing-time (WSPT)* rule: For each job, evaluate the ratio of its weight to its processing time and then sequence the jobs in decreasing order of this ratio. For example, job D's weight is 5 and its processing time is 15, so the ratio of weight to processing time is 1/3.

TABLE 11.3 Processing Time for Five Loans

Job	A	B	C	D	E
Processing time (hours)	10	6	24	15	18
Weight/priority (cost per unit of time)	2	1	6	5	2

FIGURE 11.5
Costs and Times to Process Five Jobs in SPT Order

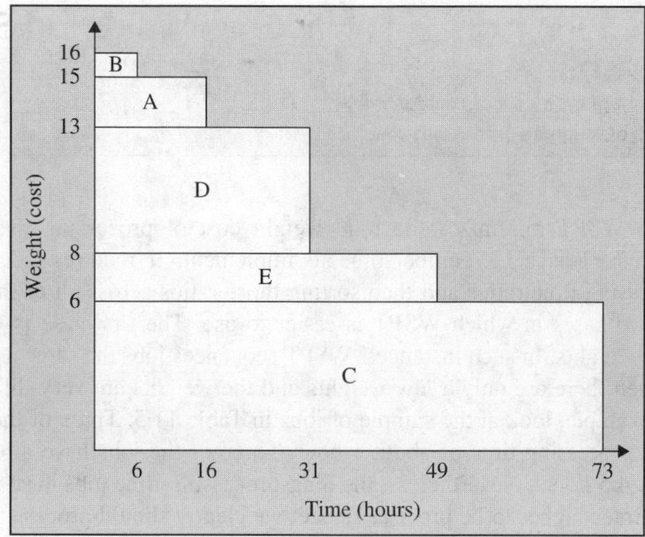

Table 11.4 displays the jobs in decreasing order of their weighted processing times. According to WSPT, job C should be one of the earlier jobs—the second job to be precise. And job B, despite having the shortest processing time, is processed second to last because it has the lowest weight.

Figure 11.6 displays the five jobs in WSPT order. Comparing Figure 11.5 to Figure 11.6, you probably can notice that the total shaded area has indeed decreased by using WSPT. In fact, the total cost decreases from 729 with SPT to 608 with WSPT—a 17 percent reduction in cost! (In case you are curious, FCFS yields a total cost of 697, which is less than with SPT—by chance, FCFS does a better job of accounting for the job's priorities than SPT.)

TABLE 11.4
Jobs Sequenced by Weighted Shortest Processing Time

Job	D	C	A	B	E
Processing time (hours)	15	24	10	6	18
Weight/priority (cost per unit of time)	5	6	2	1	2
Ratio of weight to processing time	1/3	1/4	1/5	1/6	1/9

FIGURE 11.6
Costs and Time to Process Five Jobs in WSPT Order

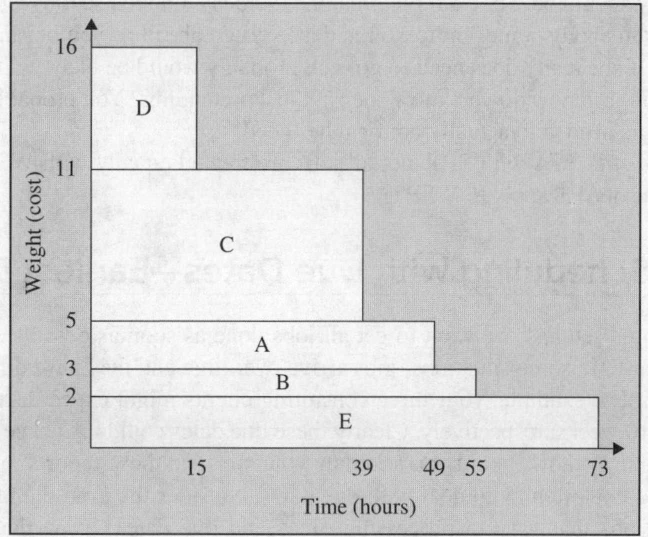

TABLE 11.5
Six Jobs That Differ in Processing Times and Priority

Job	A	B	C	D	E	F
Processing time (hours)	1	1.5	0.75	5	4	4.5
Weight/priority (cost per unit of time)	1	1	1	100	100	100
Ratio of weight to processing time	1	2/3	4/3	20	25	16.7

So WSPT minimizes the total weight cost of processing the jobs, which is great. But WSPT is a bit cumbersome to implement. It requires calculating the weight-to-processing-time ratios and then sorting those ratios across all of the jobs. However, there are two cases in which WSPT is easier to use. The first case is when all jobs have the same weights. In such instances, WSPT sequences jobs the same as SPT. The second case is when there are only a few weights and the weights are very different from each other. For example, look at the sample of jobs in Table 11.5. Three of the jobs have a relatively short processing time of about 1 hour. Three of the jobs have a long processing time of about 4.5 hours. Nevertheless, the long-processing-time jobs have a much higher priority, 100 times higher to be precise. Hence, we clearly should process the higher-priority jobs first, no matter their particular processing time.

Emergency rooms tend to operate with a strict priority scheme. Patients are first assigned an *Emergency Severity Index (ESI)* score between 1 and 5: 1—resuscitation, 2—emergent, 3—urgent, 4—less urgent, and 5—nonurgent. A patient's ESI score influences the type of care received. For example, ESI 1 and 2 patients are immediately sent into treatment, whereas ESI 3, 4, and 5 patients can safely wait. The emergency room is one service provider where you really don't want to be the one with the highest priority.

Like SPT, WSPT can be implemented if uncertainty remains in the processing time estimates—just use the expected processing time to implement the rule. Also like SPT, there are some situations that make WSPT less attractive, such as the following:

Delay to determine priority or processing time. WSPT is less attractive if it takes a long time to determine the flow unit's priority or processing time. However, if jobs can have a wide range of priorities (as in an emergency room), then the time to do this activity might be needed even if it is longer than desirable.

Biased priority or processing time estimates. With SPT, the user can only bias the perception of the processing time. But with WSPT, the user can also get better service than he or she deserves if the user can convince the resource that his or her priority is higher than it really should be. For example, imagine there is a line to use the restroom and you are next, but somebody comes up to you and asks to go ahead of you because she "really needs to go." If she really does need to go, you probably would be okay with letting her cut in front of you. But how do you know she isn't just pretending? You probably would not want to do what is needed to actually confirm her need!

Fairness. As with SPT, not all jobs are treated equally with WSPT. All of the fairness issues of SPT apply to WSPT.

11.4 Resource Scheduling with Due Dates—Earliest Due Date

In some settings, we want to get all jobs done as soon as possible. But that is not always the case. In some situations, jobs arrive over time and they have due dates associated with them. For example, your three consulting clients might expect a report from you in 6, 9, and 10 weeks, respectively. Clearly these due dates could influence which report you work on first. So how should you schedule your work on those reports?

To explore how to deal with due dates, consider the example in Table 11.6. There are five jobs that vary in processing times and due dates. In particular, they are arranged

TABLE 11.6
Five Projects with Due Dates

Job	A	B	C	D	E
Processing time (days)	2	4	6	8	10
Due date (days from today)	20	18	16	14	12

in increasing order of processing time and decreasing order of due dates. This special (i.e., contrived) structure helps us illustrate why due dates present a challenge for scheduling.

Before we actually start sequencing jobs, let's think about the performance measures we could use. In the example with no due dates, it is reasonable to measure the average flow time of jobs and the average number of jobs in the system (the inventory). But other metrics may come to mind, such as the following:

- *Percent on time*. This is the fraction of jobs that are completed on or before their due date.
- *Lateness*. The lateness of a job is the difference between its completion time and its due date. For example, if a job is due on day 10 and it is completed on day 12, then it is late 12 – 10 = 2 days. Lateness can also be negative. For example, if the job is due on day 10, but it is completed on day 7, then it is –3 days "late," which means it is three days early. It might seem odd to have a negative lateness, which means the job is early, but this is a relatively common definition of lateness, so we'll stick with it.
- *Tardiness*. If a job is completed after its due date, then the tardiness of a job is the difference between its completion time and its due date. If the job is completed before its due date (i.e., it is early), then its tardiness is 0. In some sense, the tardiness measure makes more sense than lateness because a job never has negative tardiness.

Related to the percent on time, if you prefer, we could measure the percent of tardy jobs (i.e., the fraction of jobs completed beyond the due date). Lateness and tardiness are measures that apply to individual jobs. It is useful to aggregate these measures over many jobs by taking their average (e.g., the average lateness) or evaluating their maximum value (e.g., the maximum tardiness).

Now return to the set of jobs listed in Table 11.6. We could use shortest processing time to schedule the jobs, but that rule completely ignores the due dates. For example, if we use SPT on the jobs in Table 11.6, then the first job we do has the latest due date and the last job we do has the earliest due date. That is a rather odd way of dealing with due dates.

Because SPT ignores due dates, maybe we should develop a sequencing rule that explicitly accounts for them. You probably can quickly develop several ways to handle due dates, and maybe you would even consider the simple *earliest-due-date (EDD)* rule: Process the jobs in increasing order of due dates. In the special case of the projects in Table 11.6, the EDD rule sequences the jobs in exactly the opposite order of SPT! Note, while SPT ignores due dates, EDD ignores processing times! So which does better? The answer is "it depends." To see why, let's evaluate several performance measures for both SPT and EDD.

Table 11.7 shows the flow times for each of the jobs in Table 11.6 using the SPT rule. For example, job A is completed within 2 days and then job B is completed on day 6: The flow time for a job is the sum of its processing time and the processing times of the jobs completed before it. With SPT, the average lateness is –2, meaning that, on average, jobs are completed 2 days before their due date. But the maximum lateness is 18 days. In terms of on-time performance, three of the jobs, or 60 percent, are not tardy.

Table 11.8 shows the results for EDD. In many ways, EDD does worse than SPT. We know that the average flow time with EDD is higher (22 days versus 14 days) because SPT minimizes average flow time. What is somewhat surprising is that EDD does worse than SPT even on some of the measures that focus on due dates, such as the average lateness

TABLE 11.7 Performance Measures for Shortest Processing Time

Job	Processing Time (days)	Due Date (days)	Flow Time	Lateness	Tardiness	Tardy
A	2	20	2	–18	0	0
B	4	18	6	–12	0	0
C	6	16	12	–4	0	0
D	8	14	20	6	6	1
E	10	12	30	18	18	1
Average			14	–2	4.8	0.4
Maximum				18	18	1

TABLE 11.8 Performance Measures for Earliest Due Date

Job	Processing Time (days)	Due Date (days)	Flow Time	Lateness	Tardiness	Tardy
E	10	12	10	–2	0	0
D	8	14	18	4	4	1
C	6	16	24	8	8	1
B	4	18	28	10	10	1
A	2	20	30	10	10	1
Average			22	6	6.4	0.8
Maximum				10	10	1

TABLE 11.9 Performance Measure Comparison between Shortest Processing Time (SPT) and Earliest Due Date (EDD)

Performance Measure	Recommendation
Average flow time, average lateness	SPT minimizes both.
Maximum lateness or tardiness	EDD minimizes both.
Average tardiness	SPT is often better, but not always better than EDD.
Percent on time	SPT is often better, but not always better than EDD.

(6 days versus –2 days), average tardiness (6.4 days versus 4.8 days), or the percent on time (20 percent versus 60 percent). The one metric that EDD does well with is the maximum tardiness (10 days versus 18 days).

The results in Tables 11.7 and 11.8 provide one snapshot of the comparison between SPT and EDD. Nevertheless, the results are consistent with findings from detailed studies that compare the two approaches, which are summarized in Table 11.9.

In sum, it is actually pretty hard to beat SPT even if due dates are important and even though SPT ignores them. The main advantage of SPT is that it keeps the average flow time as low as possible, which is valuable whether or not there are due dates. However, if there is a strong preference for avoiding very late jobs, then EDD might be the best approach because it minimizes the maximum lateness/tardiness among the jobs. But this is a conservative approach: By avoiding very late jobs, EDD might make all jobs, on average, a bit later than SPT.

11.5 Theory of Constraints

Scheduling jobs on a single resource is complex, but scheduling jobs across multiple resources can be mind-boggling. Take, for instance, a semiconductor manufacturing process. Roughly speaking, making a semiconductor starts with a wafer of silicon, which then goes through a series of steps, as shown in Figure 11.7, that can include (i) deposition, (ii) lithography, (iii) etching, and (iv) testing. Each step usually includes a number of machines, wafers frequently recirculate through steps (e.g., a single wafer can pass through

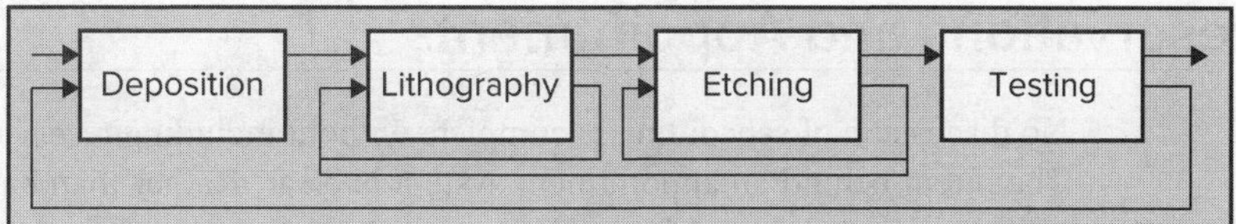

FIGURE 11.7
A Semiconductor Manufacturing Process

lithography and etching several times), different types of wafers have different processing times at the various steps, and many of the steps include setup times that depend on the particular type of semiconductor being made. A typical semiconductor manufacturing facility has hundreds, if not thousands, of jobs in process, all with different due date requirements and revenue potential. Finally, each piece of equipment can cost several million dollars and the total cost of a modern semiconductor facility can be more than $1 billion, sometimes more than several billion. With such a large capital investment, it is of utmost importance to maximize flow rate, which generally means ensuring high utilization.

Even in processes that are simpler than semiconductor manufacturing, there can be essentially a limitless number of different schedules for moving flow units through the process. So how is a manager to choose among them if it might not even be possible to count all of them? One effective approach is to "see through" the complexity by simplifying the analysis. This is the idea behind the *theory of constraints*. The theory of constraints states that the flow rate of a process is primarily dictated by the flow rate through the bottleneck resource, so all managerial attention should be placed on the bottleneck. In other words, the main constraint on a system is the bottleneck. Consequently, all a manager needs to do to maximize the flow rate through the process is to ensure that the flow rate through the bottleneck is as high as it can be. In particular, a manager should not pay much attention to nonbottleneck resources because idle time on those resources does not constrain the overall flow through the process, and therefore should not be a concern.

The first step in the application of the theory of constraints is to identify the bottleneck. The bottleneck is the resource with the highest implied utilization (the ratio of demand to capacity). Next, care should be taken to ensure that the flow rate through the bottleneck is maximized, which also maximizes the utilization of the bottleneck. For example, if the bottleneck involves setups, then batch sizes should be sufficiently large to avoid adding too much unproductive time. Finally, it is critical to schedule work through the process so that the bottleneck is never blocked or starved. Hence, jobs should be scheduled on nonbottleneck steps to ensure that there is always a buffer of work in front of the bottleneck (to prevent starving) and sufficient space after the bottleneck (to prevent blocking). Interestingly, this might require a combination of sequencing rules. In general, the jobs in the buffers before the bottleneck and after the bottleneck should be scheduled with SPT to minimize the average inventory in those buffers. But there are times in which the scheduling rule should actually switch to longest processing time (LPT)! For example, suppose the buffer after the bottleneck is starting to get full. In that case, the bottleneck is at risk of getting blocked. If the bottleneck switches to LPT, then it reduces the chance that it will be blocked because LPT temporarily slows down the inflow of jobs into the buffer after the bottleneck. Alternatively, suppose the buffer before the bottleneck is nearly empty. An empty buffer in front of the bottleneck risks starving the bottleneck. Hence, the bottleneck should switch to LPT to give the upstream resources an opportunity to increase the jobs in front of the bottleneck.

At a higher level, the theory of constraints recognizes that limited managerial time is another constraint on a system. Consequently, that time should best be used by focusing it on the part of the process that has the greatest influence over its overall performance (i.e., the bottleneck).

11.6 Reservations and Appointments

No discussion of scheduling is complete without including reservations and appointments. The intent behind an appointment system is clear: Rather than have people arrive as they want, which can create long queues or idle servers, use appointments to add predictability and smoothness to the arrival process. Consider the process flow for a physician, as shown in Figure 11.8. Unlike most process flow diagrams, Figure 11.8 shows two places for "inventory" next to each other: Patients can wait for the doctor either at home or at the doctor's office. All else being equal, patients obviously prefer waiting at home than at the doctor's office.

Before proceeding further, let's be clear that using an appointment system does not actually increase the capacity of the system. If the flow rate of patients wanting to see a doctor is larger than the doctor's capacity, then the number of patients waiting grows very large, whether an appointment system is used or not. This can indeed be a source of irritation: Patients might call their doctor only to learn that the next available appointment is months away. The primary solution for that problem is to add capacity to the system.

So an appointment system deals with matching supply with demand when there is sufficient capacity. Each person (or job) is scheduled to arrive just as the previous person finishes service. This way, in theory, the server is never idle and jobs never wait. However, there are several complications that challenge an appointment system: (1) processing times are not perfectly predictable, so it is not clear when the next person should arrive for her appointment, and (2) people don't always arrive for their appointment—that is, demand, even scheduled demand, is not perfectly predictable.

To explore the design challenges of an appointment system, let's make the example of the doctor's office concrete. Suppose we are scheduling appointments for a primary care physician. Each patient requires, on average, 20 minutes of the doctor's time, but the actual time for each patient varies uniformly between 10 minutes and 30 minutes. For simplicity, let's say the doctor only sees patients—she doesn't eat lunch, have other paperwork to attend to, or even need a bathroom break. Finally, the doctor starts seeing patients at 8:00 a.m. and wants to treat 20 patients during the day. How should we set the appointment times?

As usual, before making appointment decisions, we need to be clear about the performance measures we care about:

- Utilization of the resource (the physician).
- Average flow time for each flow unit (the patients).

Utilization measures how well we are using our resource's time. Given a fixed physician salary, a more highly utilized physician either works fewer hours to treat the same number of patients or treats more patients per hour worked. The average flow time measures how well we are using our flow units' time. It might not be possible to put a credible cost on patient time, but they will be happier with the service they receive if they spend less time in the doctor's office. Clearly, we want utilization to be as high as possible and flow time to be as low as possible.

FIGURE 11.8
Process Flow Diagram for a Doctor

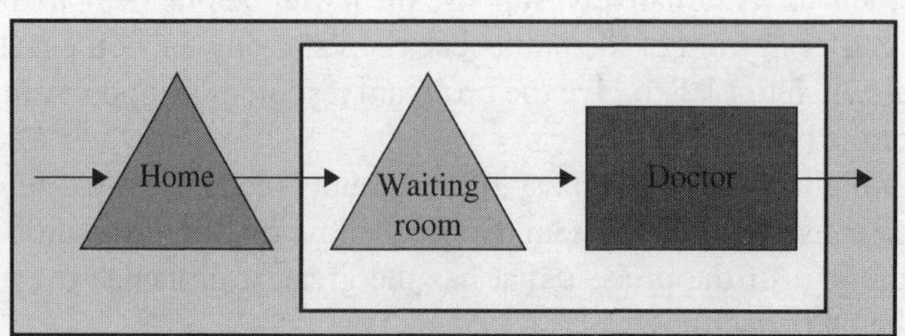

Scheduling Appointments with Uncertain Processing Times

Let's choose an appointment schedule for the physician, assuming her patients are very responsible—they always arrive at their set appointment time. One natural choice is to schedule patients to arrive every 20 minutes because that is how long the doctor sees each patient, on average. Table 11.10 shows the results for one possible day—the processing times are randomly generated, assuming each processing time between 10 and 30 minutes is equally likely. (This is another discrete event simulator.) For example, the first patient spends 18 minutes with the physician, while the second patient spends 11 minutes. Because the first patient is finished before the second patient arrives, the physician has 2 minutes of idle time before treating the second patient and then 9 minutes of idle time before treating the third patient. Unfortunately, patient six requires 29 minutes, which means patient seven must wait 9 minutes before seeing the doctor, leading to a total flow time of 38 minutes (9 minutes waiting and 29 minutes seeing the doctor).

The fourth column of Table 11.11 summarizes the results from the data in Table 11.10. The average flow time is the average of the times in the Patient Flow Time column in Table 11.10. The average processing time is also the average of the actual processing times shown in Table 11.10. Notice that the average processing time is slightly less than the expected value, 18.35 versus 20 minutes. This is just by chance.

To evaluate the total work time for the physician, note that the physician starts at 8:00 and finishes with the last patient at 14:37, which is 397 minutes or 6.62 hours. The total time to process a set of jobs (in this case, 20 patients) is also called the *makespan*. The makespan can never be smaller than the sum of the processing times, but it can be larger if the resource has some idle time.

With an average processing time of 18.35 minutes, a physician's capacity is 1/Processing time, which is 0.0545 patient per minute or 3.27 patients per hour. The flow rate is

TABLE 11.10 **Simulation Results for One Day Treating 20 Patients with 20-Minute Intervals between Appointments**

Patient	Scheduled	Processing Time (min)	Start Time	End Time	Patient Flow Time (min)	Physician Idle Time (min)
1	8:00	18	8:00	8:18	18	0
2	8:20	11	8:20	8:31	11	2
3	8:40	18	8:40	8:58	18	9
4	9:00	20	9:00	9:20	20	2
5	9:20	10	9:20	9:30	10	0
6	9:40	29	9:40	10:09	29	10
7	10:00	29	10:09	10:38	38	0
8	10:20	18	10:38	10:56	36	0
9	10:40	16	10:56	11:12	32	0
10	11:00	21	11:12	11:33	33	0
11	11:20	15	11:33	11:48	28	0
12	11:40	18	11:48	12:06	26	0
13	12:00	18	12:06	12:24	24	0
14	12:20	13	12:24	12:37	17	0
15	12:40	16	12:40	12:56	16	3
16	13:00	30	13:00	13:30	30	4
17	13:20	16	13:30	13:46	26	0
18	13:40	18	13:46	14:04	24	0
19	14:00	19	14:04	14:23	23	0
20	14:20	14	14:23	14:37	17	0

the number of patients served (20) divided by the time to serve them (6.62 hours), or 3.02 patients per hour. Finally, utilization is the flow rate divided by capacity, which is 92 percent.

A 92 percent utilization for the physician and only 5.45 minutes of waiting, on average, for patients (23.80 – 18.35) seems reasonable. But Table 11.11 also reveals what happens with a shorter (15-minute) or longer (25-minute) interval between appointments.

Patients get great service when there are 25 minutes between appointments! In that case, they wait, on average, a grand total of 0.9 minute to see the physician. However, this great service comes at a price. The poor physician's utilization has dropped to 75 percent and instead of working 6.62 hours to treat 20 patients, she must spend 8.15 hours. That means that moving from 20-minute intervals to 25-minute intervals saved 20 patients a total of 91 minutes waiting (= 20 × (5.45 – 0.90)), but the physician has about 1.5 hours added on to her day (= 8.15 – 6.62). This is a reasonable trade-off if physician time is cheap relative to patient waiting time, but a terrible trade-off if physician time is expensive relative to patient waiting time.

TABLE 11.11 Performance Measure Results with Appointments Spaced Out at Different Intervals

		Interval between Appointments (min)		
Calculation	Measure	15	20	25
a	Average flow time (min)	51.1	23.80	19.25
b	Average processing time (min)	18.35	18.35	18.35
c	Number of patients	20	20	20
d	Makespan (hr)	6.13	6.62	8.15
$e = 60/b$	Capacity (patients/hr)	3.27	3.27	3.27
$f = c/d$	Flow rate (patients/hr)	3.26	3.02	2.45
$g = f/e$	Utilization	1.00	0.92	0.75
$h = a - b$	Average waiting time (min)	32.75	5.45	0.90

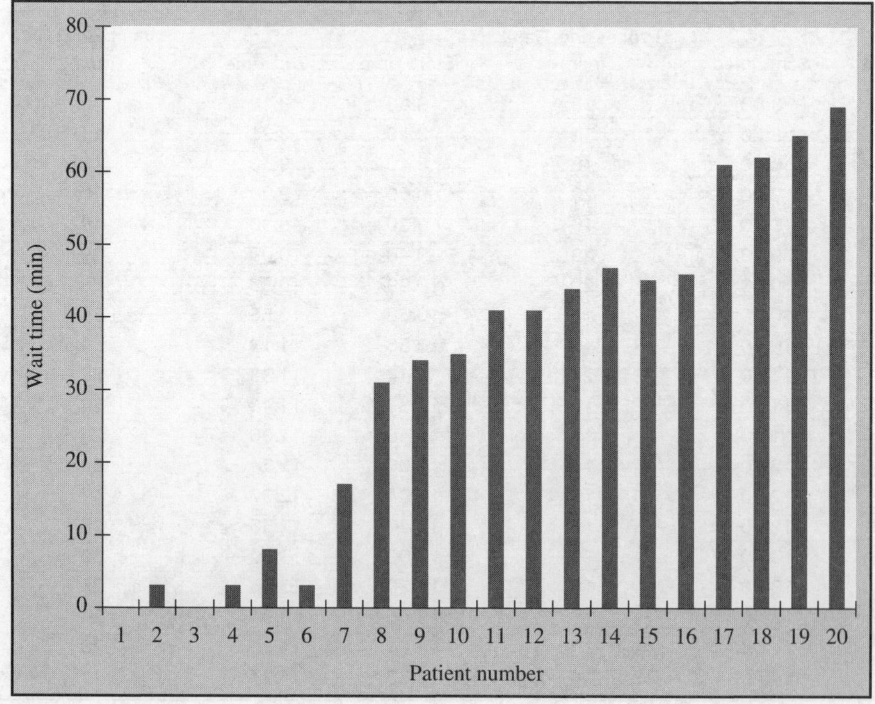

FIGURE 11.9 Wait Time for Each of the 20 Patients When the Appointment Interval Is 15 Minutes

The other extreme displayed in Table 11.11 is a 15-minute interval. Now patients are arriving faster than the physician can treat them, on average. As you might expect, this keeps the physician occupied—her utilization is now 100 percent—but patients must wait a considerable amount of time—the average waiting time is 32.75 minutes. Waiting about one-half hour might not seem like a disaster, but remember that that is an average. Some patients have to wait much longer. Figure 11.9 displays the waiting time for each of the 20 patients. The last four patients scheduled have to wait more than an hour each, which is about twice the average wait. This is one reason why you want to grab an early morning appointment rather than one in the afternoon.

A scheduling system that schedules more flow units (patients) than can be handled by the resource (physician) in a period of time is said to be *overbooking*—deliberately scheduling more work than can be handled to try to maintain a high utilization for the resource. See Chapter 18 for a broader discussion of overbooking.

No-Shows

Looking at the results in Table 11.11, it seems like the 20-minute interval might be a good compromise between making patients wait for the doctor (a short appointment interval) or making the doctor wait for patients (a long interval). But there is one key assumption that needs to be revisited: Patients don't always arrive for their appointments. In fact, the rate of *no-shows,* patients who do not arrive for their appointment, can be as high as 20 to 30 percent in many physician offices.

To see the impact of no-shows, let's assume that about 20 percent of the patients do not arrive for their scheduled appointment. Nevertheless, the physician still wants to treat 20 patients during the day. Consequently, let's say the physician schedules 25 appointments with the hope of having 20 patients treated. Table 11.12 displays one possible outcome. Notice that the processing times in Table 11.12 are identical to the processing times in Table 11.10. The only difference between the results in the two tables is that 20 percent of the patients in Table 11.12 are no-shows.

Table 11.13 evaluates the performance measures when there are 20 percent no-shows. Comparing Table 11.11 to Table 11.13, we can see that no-shows are not good for the efficient use of the physician's time. For each of the appointment intervals, the physician's utilization decreases when no-shows are possible. However, no-shows seem to help reduce average waiting times: If some patients don't show up for their appointment, then the patients that do show up don't have to wait as long. Thus, it is not immediately obvious that no-shows are bad.

Figure 11.10 makes it clear that no-shows are positively and unambiguously not helpful. The figure plots the trade-off between utilization and average waiting time. Each observation in each curve corresponds to a particular appointment interval. For example, a 24-minute appointment interval with 20 percent no-shows has a utilization of about 62 percent and an average waiting time of 1.25 minutes, whereas with an 18-minute appointment interval and all patients arriving (0 percent no-shows), the utilization is 97 percent and the waiting time is 14 minutes. The key finding from the figure is that the trade-off curve moves up and to the left as patients become more likely to not show up for their appointment. This is simply not good. For example, suppose the office wants to keep the average patient waiting time to under 5 minutes. If all patients show up for their appointment, then the physician's utilization can be above 90 percent (the 0 percent no-shows curve crosses the horizontal 5-minute waiting line at about 91 percent utilization). But if 20 percent of patients are no-shows, then the physician's utilization is likely to drop to around 75 percent (the 20 percent no-shows curve crosses the horizontal 5-minute waiting line at about 75 percent utilization). Holding the physician's salary fixed, a drop in utilization translates into a higher cost to serve each patient.

TABLE 11.12 Simulation Results for One Day Treating 20 Patients with 20-Minute Intervals between Appointments and Five No-Show Patients

Patient	Scheduled	Status	Processing Time (min)	Start Time	End Time	Patient Flow Time (min)	Physician Idle Time (min)
1	8:00		18	8:00	8:18	18	0
2	8:15	No-show					
3	8:30		18	8:40	8:58	18	22
4	8:45		20	9:00	9:20	20	2
5	9:00		10	9:20	9:30	10	0
6	9:15		29	9:40	10:09	29	10
7	9:30		29	10:09	10:38	38	0
8	9:45		18	10:38	10:56	36	0
9	10:00		16	10:56	11:12	32	0
10	10:15		21	11:12	11:33	33	0
11	10:30		15	11:33	11:48	28	0
12	10:45		18	11:48	12:06	26	0
13	11:00		18	12:06	12:24	24	0
14	11:15	No-show					
15	11:30		16	12:40	12:56	16	16
16	11:45		30	13:00	13:30	30	4
17	12:00		16	13:30	13:46	26	0
18	12:15	No-show					
19	12:30	No-show					
20	12:45		14	14:20	14:34	14	34
21	13:00	No-show					
22	13:15		11	15:00	15:11	11	26
23	13:30		13	15:20	15:33	13	9
24	13:45		18	15:40	15:58	18	7
25	14:00		19	16:00	16:19	19	2

TABLE 11.13 Performance Measure Results with Appointments Spaced Out at Different Intervals and 20 Percent of Patients Do Not Arrive for Their Appointment

		Interval between Appointments (min)		
Calculation	Measure	15	20	25
a	Average flow time (min)	38.10	22.95	19.25
b	Average processing time (min)	18.35	18.35	18.35
c	Number of patients	20	20	20
d	Total work time (hr)	6.37	8.22	10.32
$e = 60/b$	Capacity (patients/hr)	3.27	3.27	3.27
$f = c/d$	Flow rate (patients/hr)	3.14	2.43	1.94
$g = f/e$	Utilization	0.96	0.74	0.59
$h = a - b$	Average waiting time (min)	19.75	4.60	0.90

If Figure 11.10 looks familiar, then you have probably read Chapter 9, Variability and Its Impact on Process Performance. In Chapter 9, Figure 9.2 shows the trade-off between utilization and time in queue in a system with random processing times, random interarrival times, and no appointments. Even though those systems are not exactly the same as the doctor's office with appointments, the fundamental trade-off between utilization and flow time continues to be true.

FIGURE 11.10
The Trade-Off between Utilization and Average Waiting Time in Two Cases: (i) all customers arrive for their appointments (black square markers) and (ii) 20 percent of customers are no-shows (gray diamond markers). Numbers next to markers indicate the interval length between appointments (in minutes).

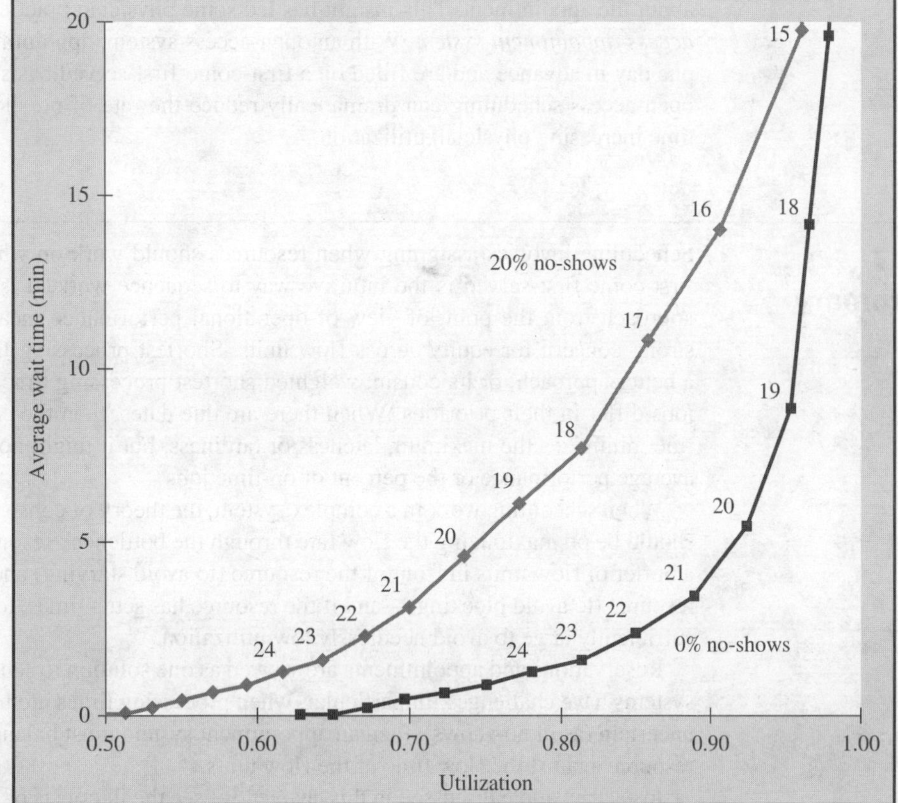

So we see that appointment systems are not the perfect panacea for all operational ills. Variable processing times create uncertainty. Appointment no-shows create uncertainty. Managing this uncertainty requires a trade-off between physician utilization and patient waiting. Either the physician waits for patients (long intervals between appointments) or patients wait for the physician (short intervals between appointments). This trade-off cannot be avoided and it certainly becomes worse as more uncertainty is added to the system.

Beyond choosing the appropriate point on the trade-off curve, is there something that can be done to improve the situation? As with most cases in operations, the obvious solution is to reduce the variability that is causing the problem!

The first issue to tackle is the variability in processing times. This can be addressed by adopting standardized procedures, better and quicker training of new staff, and an effort by physicians to avoid cases taking longer than necessary (e.g., learn how to politely move on when dealing with a chatty patient).

The second issue to tackle is no-shows. Several techniques have been adopted. For example, the physician's office could contact the patient the day before his or her appointment to remind the patient. A more heavy-handed approach is to actually charge the patient if he or she does not arrive for the scheduled appointment. In some cases, this may be difficult to do and it surely risks creating ill will with the patient. Furthermore, even though it removes some of the sting from the physician's office because it collects some revenue, the absence of a patient still can create some physician idle time, which is not ideal. Finally, it has been noticed that the likelihood a patient doesn't arrive for an appointment depends heavily on how long ago the patient made the appointment. If the patient called two months ago to make the appointment, then he or she might be more likely to forget about the appointment. This insight has led some physician practices to move to an *open-access appointment system*. With an open-access system, appointments are only available one day in advance and are filled on a first-come-first-served basis. It has been found that open-access scheduling can dramatically reduce the rate of no-shows, while at the same time increasing physician utilization.

11.7 Summary

Scheduling involves assigning when resources should work on which demand. Although first-come-first-served is the intuitive way to sequence work, it is generally not the best approach from the point of view of operational performance measures unless there is a strong concern for equity across flow units. Shortest processing time (SPT) is generally a better approach, or its cousin, weighted shortest processing time (WSPT), can be when jobs differ in their priorities. When there are due dates, then the earliest-due-date (EDD) rule minimizes the maximum lateness or tardiness, but it might not do as well as SPT on average performance or the percent of on-time jobs.

When scheduling work in a complex system, the theory of constraints suggests the focus should be on maximizing the flow rate through the bottleneck resource—to ensure there is a buffer of flow units in front of the resource (to avoid starving) and ample space after the resource (to avoid blocking)—and if the resource has setup times, to make sure batches are sufficiently large to avoid needlessly low utilization.

Reservations and appointments are viewed as one solution to scheduling, but even those systems have challenges. In particular, when processing times are uncertain or arrivals are uncertain (as in no-shows), then an appointment system must balance the utilization of the resource against the flow time of the flow units.

In each example discussed in this chapter, we see the ill effects of the three system inhibitors: variability, waste, and inflexibility. Variability comes in the form of arrival time uncertainty and processing time uncertainty. Waste manifests itself in ways that contribute to longer processing times, such as poorly trained service providers. And the lack of flexibility to increase and decrease staffing on a moment's notice is a key reason why scheduling is needed.

11.8 Further Reading

Cox, Eliyahu, and Goldratt (1986) is a classic in operations management—who knew an interesting and entertaining book could be written about operations management!? That book, and a follow on by Goldratt (1990), presents the Theory of Constraints.

For a comprehensive treatment of the topic of scheduling, see Pinedo (2009).

Cox, Jeff, and Eliyahu M. Goldratt. *The Goal: A Process of Ongoing Improvement.* Great Barrington, MA: North River Press, 1986.

Goldratt, Eliyahu M. *Essays on the Theory of Constraints.* Great Barrington, MA: North River Press, 1990.

Pinedo, Michael. *Planning and Scheduling in Manufacturing and Services.* New York: Springer-Verlag, 2009.

11.9 Practice Problems

The following questions will help in testing your understanding of this chapter. After each question, we show the relevant section in parentheses [Section x].

Solutions to problems marked with an "*" are available in Appendix E. Video solutions to select problems are available in Connect.

Q11.1* There are 10 jobs waiting to be processed at a resource. The total processing time across those jobs is 200 minutes. During the period of time in which those jobs are processed, what is the flow rate through the resource (jobs per hour)? [11.2]

Q11.2 An architect has five projects to complete. She estimates that three of the projects will require one week to complete and the other two will require three weeks and four weeks. During the time these projects are completed (and assuming no other projects are worked on during this time), what is the architect's flow rate (projects per week)? [11.2]

TABLE 11.14
Processing Time for Six Jobs

Job	A	B	C	D	E	F
Processing time (minutes)	5	11	8	2	1	9

Q11.3* Consider the jobs displayed in Table 11.14. Assume shortest processing time is used to sequence the jobs.

a. Which job is the fourth to be processed? [11.2]
b. What is the flow time of job F (in minutes)? [11.2]
c. What is the flow rate of jobs (jobs per minute)? [11.2]
d. What is the average flow time of jobs in the system? [11.2]
e. What is the average inventory of jobs in the system? [11.2]

TABLE 11.15
Processing Time for Eight Projects, Displayed in the Sequence They Arrived

Project	P1	P2	P3	P4	P5	P6	P7	P8
Processing time (hours)	4	1	2	3	6	5	1	0.5

Q11.4 Given the projects displayed in Table 11.15, assume FCFS is used to sequence the jobs.

a. What is the average flow rate of the projects (in projects per hour)? [11.2]
b. What is the average flow time of the projects (in hours)? [11.2]
c. What is the average inventory of the projects (in projects)? [11.2]

Q11.5* Assume the jobs displayed in Table 11.16 need to be processed on a single resource and are sequenced with the WSPT rule.

a. Which job would be processed second? [11.3]

TABLE 11.16
Processing Times and Weights for Five Jobs

Job	A	B	C	D	E
Processing time (minutes)	1	4	2	3	5
Weight	1.5	1	1.25	0.5	2

b. What is the average flow rate of the jobs (in jobs per minute)? [11.3]
c. What is the average flow time of the jobs (in minutes)? [11.3]
d. What is the average inventory of the jobs? [11.3]

Q11.6 Assume the jobs displayed in Table 11.17 need to be processed on a single resource and are sequenced with the WSPT rule. Which job would be processed third? [11.3]

TABLE 11.17
Processing Times and Weights for Four Jobs

Job	A	B	C	D
Processing time (minutes)	15	5	25	30
Weight	5	10	1	15

Q11.7 There are five planes ready for departure at an airport. The number of passengers on each plane is displayed in Table 11.18. Each plane requires 10 minutes to taxi to the runway and 2 minutes to take off (i.e., there needs to be 2 minutes between departures). If the air traffic controller wants to minimize the weighted average number of passengers waiting for departure (i.e., weighted by the number of passengers on the plane), in what sequence should the planes take off? [11.3]

TABLE 11.18 Number of Passengers on Five Planes Ready for Departure

Plane	A	B	C	D	E
Passengers	150	50	400	200	250

a. A, B, C, D, E
b. B, A, D, E, C
c. C, B, E, A, D
d. C, E, D, A, B
e. It doesn't matter what sequence they depart in because they have equal processing times.

TABLE 11.19 Processing Times and Due Dates for Five Jobs

Job	A	B	C	D	E
Processing time (days)	10	25	40	5	20
Due date (days)	100	40	75	55	30

Q11.8* If the jobs displayed in Table 11.19 are processed using the earliest-due-date rule,
a. What would be the lateness of job C? [11.4]
b. What would be the lateness of job E? [11.4]
c. What would be the tardiness of job D? [11.4]
d. What is the maximum tardiness? [11.4]

TABLE 11.20 Processing Times and Due Dates for Five Jobs

Job	A	B	C	D	E
Processing time (weeks)	2	0.5	1	3	1.5
Due date (weeks)	3	6	4	5	2

Q11.9 If the jobs displayed in Table 11.20 are processed using the earliest-due-date rule,
a. What would be the lateness of job B? [11.4]
b. What would be the tardiness of job E? [11.4]
c. What is the maximum tardiness? [11.4]
d. What is the average flow time? [11.4]

Chapter 12

Project Management

In the previous chapters, we established the process view of the organization.[1] Processes are all about repetition—we don't perform an operation once, we perform it over and over again. This process management view fits many, if not most, operations problems well. Mining and production plants, back-offices of insurances or banks, hospitals, and call centers are all about repetition, and many flow units journey through the corresponding processes on a daily basis.

There are, however, a number of operations for which the repetition-based approach of process management is less appropriate. Consider, for example, a major construction project, the development of a new product, or the planning of a wedding party. In these situations, your primary concern is about planning the completion of one flow unit, and typically, you would like to see this completion to happen sooner rather than later.

Whether you care about the completion of one or many flow units often depends on which role you play in an operation. While most of us think about one wedding (at a time) and thus should think of a wedding event as a project, a wedding planner organizes numerous weddings and thus should think of weddings as flow units in a process. Similarly, a developer working on the launch of a new product or the construction worker building a new office complex are likely to think about their work as a project, while many echelons up in the organization, the vice president of product development or the owner of a real estate development company think about these projects as flow units in a big process.

We define a *project* as a temporary (and thus nonrepetitive) operation. Projects have a limited time frame, have one or more specific objectives, a temporary organizational structure, and thus often are operated in a more ad hoc, improvised management style. In this chapter, you will learn the basics of project management, including

- Mapping out the various activities that need to be completed as part of the project.
- Computing the completion time of the project based on the critical path.
- Accelerating a project to achieve an earlier completion time.
- Understanding the types of uncertainty a project faces and how to deal with them.

12.1 Motivating Example

Unmanned aerial vehicles (UAVs) are aircraft that are flown without a human being on board. They are either controlled remotely or have built-in navigation intelligence to determine their direction. Most of their applications lie in the military arena, but UAVs can also be used for scientific exploration or search-and-rescue operations (see Figure 12.1). In the

[1] The authors gratefully acknowledge the help of Christoph Loch and Stylios Kavadias, whose case study on the Dragonfly UAV is the basis for the motivating example in this chapter.

FIGURE 12.1
UAV Offered by Boeing

Source: U.S. Air Force

last few years, UAVs, which are now most often referred to as "drones," have also entered the consumer product space and can be purchased for a few hundred dollars.

We use the example of the development of a UAV to illustrate several tools and techniques of project management. In particular, we look at the decision situation of a developer who has just completed a prototype UAV and now is putting together a more detailed proposal for commercial development (see Kavadias, Loch, and De Meyer for further details. The authors gratefully acknowledge the help of Christoph Loch and Stylios Kavadias, whose case study on the Dragonfly UAV is the basis for the chapter). Table 12.1 lists the activities that need to be done to complete the proposal. Note that this entirely captures the work required for the proposal, not the actual development itself.

A quick (and rather naïve) view of Table 12.1 is that the total time to complete the proposal will be 9 + 3 + 11 + 7 + 8 + 6 + 21 + 10 + 15 + 5 = 95 days. Alternatively, one might (equally naïvely) claim, the proposal development should take 21 days, the duration of the longest activity.

Both of these views omit an important aspect of the nature of project management. Some, but not all, of the activities are dependent on each other. For example, activity A_3 (aerodynamics analysis) requires the completion of activity A_2 (prepare and discuss surface models). Such dependencies are also referred to as precedence relationships. They can be summarized in a dependency matrix as shown in Table 12.2. In the dependency

TABLE 12.1
Activities for the UAV Proposal Development

Activity	Description	Expected Duration (days)
A_1	Prepare preliminary functional and operability requirements, and create preliminary design configuration	9
A_2	Prepare and discuss surface models	3
A_3	Perform aerodynamics analysis and evaluation	11
A_4	Create initial structural geometry, and prepare notes for finite element structural simulation	7
A_5	Develop structural design conditions	8
A_6	Perform weights and inertia analyses	6
A_7	Perform structure and compatibility analyses and evaluation	21
A_8	Develop balanced free-body diagrams and external applied loads	10
A_9	Establish internal load distributions, evaluate structural strength stiffness; preliminary manufacturing planning and analysis	15
A_{10}	Prepare proposal	5

TABLE 12.2 Dependency Matrix for the UAV

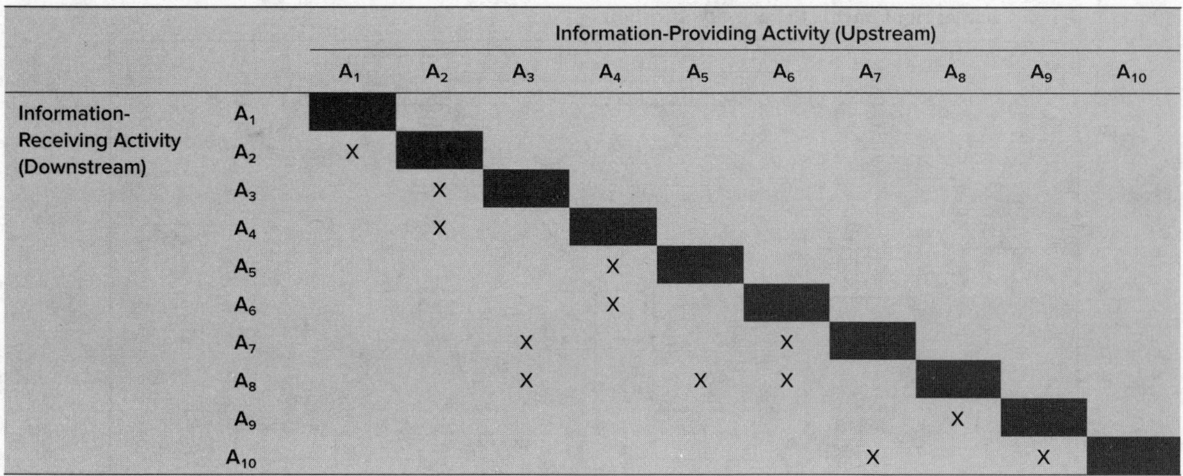

		Information-Providing Activity (Upstream)									
		A_1	A_2	A_3	A_4	A_5	A_6	A_7	A_8	A_9	A_{10}
Information-Receiving Activity (Downstream)	A_1										
	A_2	X									
	A_3		X								
	A_4		X								
	A_5				X						
	A_6				X						
	A_7			X			X				
	A_8			X		X	X				
	A_9								X		
	A_{10}							X		X	

matrix, each column represents an activity that provides information, and each row indicates an activity that receives information. An entry in column i and row j suggests that the activity in the i-th column (A_i) provides information to the activity in the j-th row (A_j). We also say that A_i precedes A_j or that A_j is dependent of A_i. Dependent activities require information or physical outputs from the input providing activities. The dependency matrix implicitly suggests a sequencing of the activities and thus dictates the flow of the project. The project will start with activity A_1, because it does not have any input providing activities. It will end with activity A_{10}. Similar to process flow terminology, people often refer to a preceding activity as "upstream" and the dependent activity as "downstream."

12.2 Critical Path Method

There exist multiple approaches to represent project information as displayed in Tables 12.1 and 12.2. In the *activity-on-node (AON) representation*, nodes correspond to project activities and arrows correspond to precedence relationships (with an arrow going from the input providing activity to the corresponding dependent activity). In this chapter, we focus on the AON representation because it is similar to the process flow diagrams that we discuss in the other chapters of this book.

To create an AON representation of a project, we start with the activity that requires no input, in our case that is activity A_1. We then work our way through the dependency matrix, mimicking the evolution of the project:

1. We create a node in the form of a box for the activity, including its name as well as its expected duration.
2. After creating the node for the activity, we consider the activity as done. Thus, all information provided by the activity to its dependent activities is now available. We can draw a line through the corresponding column, and draw an arrow out of the activity for each dependency (for each "X").
3. Next, we look for any other activity in the dependency matrix that has all its information providing activities completed and go back to step 1 until we have worked ourselves to the last activity.

FIGURE 12.2 **Activity on Node (AON) Representation of the UAV Project. Left part of the box is the activity name; right part is the activity duration**

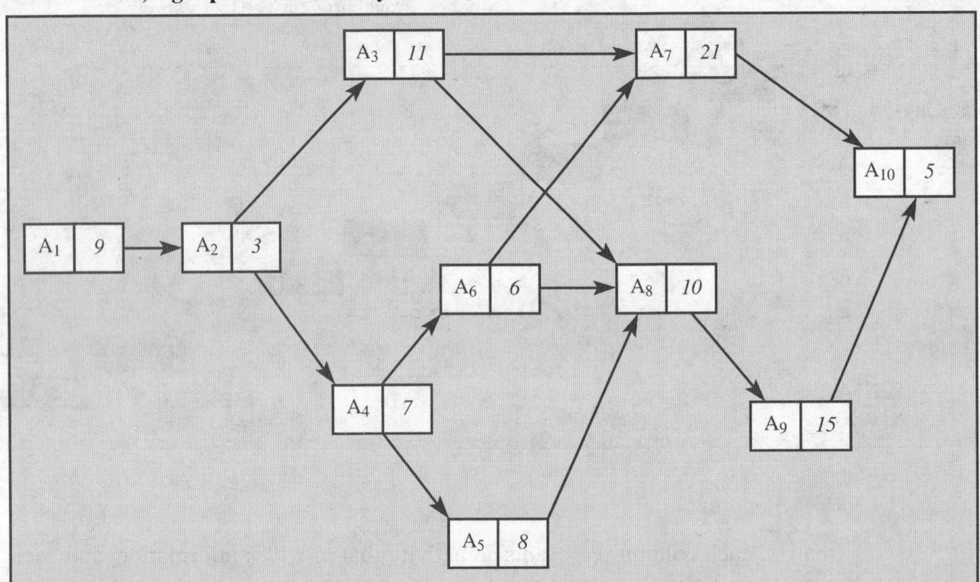

If we repeatedly execute these three steps, we obtain a graph as shown in Figure 12.2. This graph provides a practical and visual way to illustrate the evolution of the project. It resembles the process flow diagram introduced in Chapter 3.

12.3 Computing Project Completion Time

Despite the similarity between the process flow diagram and the AON representation, we should remember the fundamental difference between process management and project management. In process management, we directed our attention to the resource that had the lowest capacity, the bottleneck. If each activity in the process flow diagram was staffed by one worker (or machine), the bottleneck was the activity with the longest activity time.

What matters for the completion time of the project, however, is not the individual activity times, but the completion time of the entire project. This completion time requires ALL activities to be completed. In fact, we will see that in the UAV project, the activity with the longest duration (A_7) will not constrain the duration of the overall project.

So, how long then will the project in Figure 12.2 take? This turns out to be a tricky question. It is intuitive that the project can be carried out in less than $9 + 3 + 11 + 7 + 8 + 6 + 21 + 10 + 15 + 5 = 95$ days (the sum of the activity times). Some activities can be carried out in parallel and so the 10 activities do not create a 10-person relay race. On the other hand, the degree to which we can execute the activities in parallel is limited by the dependency matrix. For example, activity A_3 requires the completion of activity A_2, which, in turn, requires the completion of activity A_1. Things get even more convoluted as we consider activity A_7. For it to be complete, A_3 and A_6 have to be complete. A_3, in turn, requires completion of A_2 and A_1, while A_6 requires completion of A_4, which, once again, requires completion of A_2 and A_1. What a mess!

To correctly compute the completion time of the project, a more structured approach is needed. This approach is based on considering all possible paths through the network in Figure 12.2. A path is a sequence of nodes (activities) and (directional) arrows. For example, the sequence A_1, A_2, A_3, A_7, A_{10} is a path. Every path can be assigned a duration by simply adding up the durations of the activities that constitute the path. The duration of the path A_1, A_2, A_3, A_7, A_{10} is $9 + 3 + 11 + 21 + 5 = 49$ days.

The number of paths through the AON representation depends on the shape of the dependency matrix. In the easiest case, every activity would just have one information-providing activity and one dependent activity. In such a (relay race) project, the dependency matrix had just one entry per row and one entry per column. The duration of the project would be the sum of the activity times. Every time one activity provides information to multiple activities, the number of paths is increased.

In the UAV project and its project graph shown in Figure 12.2, we can identify the following paths connecting the first activity (A_1) with the last activity (A_{10}):

$$A_1 - A_2 - A_3 - A_7 - A_{10} \text{ with a duration of } 9 + 3 + 11 + 21 + 5 = 49 \text{ days}$$

$$A_1 - A_2 - A_3 - A_8 - A_9 - A_{10} \text{ with a duration of } 9 + 3 + 11 + 10 + 15 + 5 = 53 \text{ days}$$

$$A_1 - A_2 - A_4 - A_6 - A_7 - A_{10} \text{ with a duration of } 9 + 3 + 7 + 6 + 21 + 5 = 51 \text{ days}$$

$$A_1 - A_2 - A_4 - A_6 - A_8 - A_9 - A_{10} \text{ with a duration of } 9 + 3 + 7 + 6 + 10 + 15 + 5 = 55 \text{ days}$$

$$A_1 - A_2 - A_4 - A_5 - A_8 - A_9 - A_{10} \text{ with a duration of } 9 + 3 + 7 + 8 + 10 + 15 + 5 = 57 \text{ days}$$

The path with the longest duration is called the critical path. Its duration determines the duration of the overall project. In our case, the critical path is $A_1 - A_2 - A_4 - A_5 - A_8 - A_9 - A_{10}$ and the resulting project duration is 57 days. Note that A_7, the activity with the longest duration, is not on the *critical path.*

12.4 Finding the Critical Path and Creating a Gantt Chart

The exercise of identifying every possible path through the project graph along with its duration is a rather tedious exercise. The more activities and the more dependency relationships we have, the greater the number of paths we have to evaluate before we find the one we truly care about, the *critical path*.

Fortunately, there is a simpler way to compute the project duration. The idea behind this easier way is to compute the earliest possible start time for each activity. For each activity, we can find the *earliest start time (EST)* by looking at the earliest time all information providing activities have been completed. The earliest start time of the first activity is time zero. The *earliest completion time (ECT)* of an activity is the earliest start time plus the activity duration. We then work our way through the project graph, activity by activity, starting from the first activity and going all the way to the last.

More formally, we can define the following algorithm to compute the earliest completion time of the project. The approach is similar to our method of coming up with the graphical representation of the project graph:

1. Start with the activity that has no information-providing activity and label that activity as the start. The earliest start time of that activity is defined as 0. The earliest completion time is the duration of this activity.
2. Identify all activities that can be initiated at this point (i.e., have all information-providing activities complete). For a given such activity i, compute the earliest start time as

$$\text{EST}(A_i) = \text{Max}\{\text{ECT}(A_j)\}, \text{ where } A_j \text{ are all activities providing input to } A_i$$

3. Compute the earliest completion time of A_i as

$$\text{ECT}(A_i) = \text{EST}(A_i) + \text{Duration}(A_i)$$

4. Consider activity i as completed, and identify any further activities that now can be initiated. Go back to step 2.

TABLE 12.3 Computing the Completion Time of a Project (table is created row by row, starting with the first activity)

Activity	Earliest Start Time (EST)	Expected Duration (days)	Earliest Completion Time (ECT)
A_1	0	9	9
A_2	$ECT(A_1) = 9$	3	12
A_3	$ECT(A_2) = 12$	11	23
A_4	$ECT(A_2) = 12$	7	19
A_5	$ECT(A_4) = 19$	8	27
A_6	$ECT(A_4) = 19$	6	25
A_7	$Max\{ECT(A_3), ECT(A_6)\} = Max\{23,25\} = 25$	21	46
A_8	$Max\{ECT(A_3), ECT(A_5), ECT(A_6)\} = Max\{23, 27, 25\} = 27$	10	37
A_9	$ECT(A_8) = 37$	15	52
A_{10}	$ECT(A_9) = 52$	5	57

This algorithm is illustrated in Table 12.3. The table is created from the top to the bottom, one activity at a time. As you construct a given row i, you have to ask yourself, "What activities provide information to i? What activities does i depend on?" You can see this by reading row i in the dependency matrix, or you can see this in the project graph.

Based on the earliest start and earliest completion time, we can create a Gantt chart for the project. The *Gantt chart* is basically a timeline with the activities included as bars. Gantt charts are probably the most commonly used visualization for project time lines. Note that unlike the AON representation, the Gantt chart itself does not capture the dependencies of the activities. Based on the previously explained computations of the earliest start and completion times, we have already ensured that activities only get initiated when all required information is available.

The Gantt chart for the UAV project is shown in Figure 12.3.

12.5 Computing Slack Time

It lies in the nature of the critical path that any delay in activities on the critical path will immediately cause a delay in the overall project. For example, a one-day delay in activity A_9 will automatically delay the overall project by one day. However, this is not true for

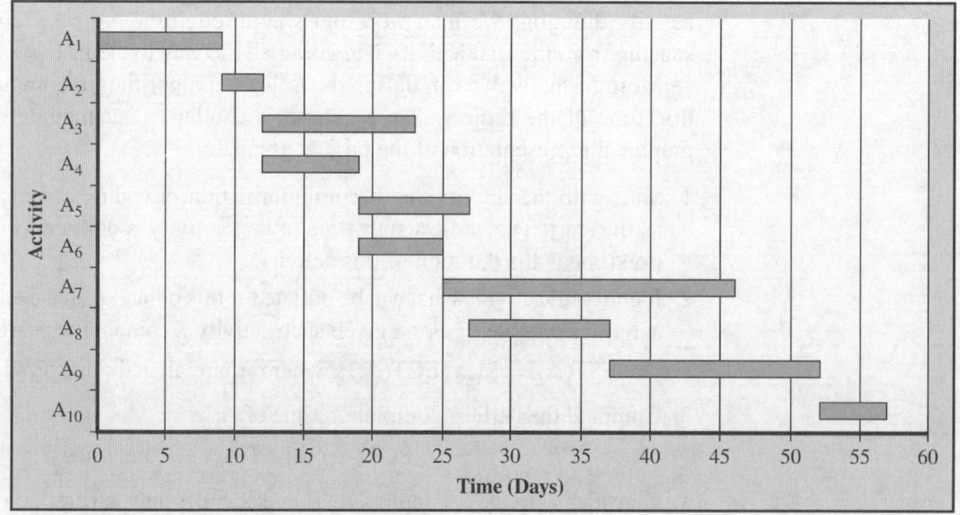

FIGURE 12.3 Gantt Chart for the UAV Project

activities that are not part of the critical path. We can delay activity A_7 even by several days (six to be exact) without affecting the overall completion of the project. In other words, activity A_7 has some built in "wiggle room." The technical term for this wiggle room is *slack time*. It is the amount of time an activity can be delayed without affecting the overall completion time of the project.

The slack time of an activity is determined based on an additional set of calculations known as the late start schedule. So far, we have computed the earliest start time (EST) and earliest completion time (ECT) of each activity by going through the project from beginning to end. We now compute the *latest start time (LST)* and *latest completion time (LCT)* for each activity such that the project still completes on time. We do this by beginning with the last activity and working our way backward through the project until we reach the beginning. Thus, we start with the last activity (A_{10}) and end with the first activity (A_1).

So, let's start with the last activity. Assuming we want to complete the project as early as possible, we define the LCT of the last activity as being the same as its ECT:

$$\text{LCT(Last activity)} = \text{ECT(Last activity)}$$
$$\text{LCT}(A_{10}) = \text{ECT}(A_{10}) = 57$$

There exist some cases in which an early completion is not desired—instead, there exists a target time at which the project should be complete. In this case, we can define the LCT of the last activity as the target date.

The latest start time of the last activity is simply the latest completion time minus the duration of the last activity:

$$\text{LST(Last activity)} = \text{LCT(Last activity)} - \text{Duration(Last activity)}$$
$$\text{LST}(A_{10}) = \text{LCT}(A_{10}) - 5 = 57 - 5 = 52$$

More generally, we define the LCT for an activity as the smallest (earliest) LST value of all activities that are depending on it and the LST as the LCT minus the duration. Consider activity A_9, which only has A_{10} as a dependent activity. Thus, we can define

$$\text{LCT}(A_9) = \text{LST}(A_{10}) = 52$$
$$\text{LST}(A_9) = \text{LCT}(A_9) - \text{Duration}(A_9) = 52 - 15 = 37$$

In the same manner, we compute

$$\text{LCT}(A_8) = \text{LST}(A_9) = 37$$
$$\text{LST}(A_8) = \text{LCT}(A_8) - \text{Duration}(A_8) = 37 - 10 = 27$$

Next, consider activity A_7, the activity we previously observed to have some slack time.

$$\text{LCT}(A_7) = \text{LST}(A_{10}) = 52$$
$$\text{LST}(A_7) = \text{LCT}(A_7) - \text{Duration}(A_7) = 52 - 21 = 31$$

Note the difference between the earliest start time of A_7, which was 25, and the latest start time of A_7, which we just found to be 31. In other words, we can delay the start of A_7 by six days without affecting the overall completion time of the project.

Based on this observation, we define the slack of an activity as

$$\text{Slack time} = \text{Latest start time} - \text{Earliest start time}$$

In the same way, we can compute the other information of the late schedule. This information is shown in Table 12.4. Note that the columns LST and LCT are computed by going backward through the project graph; thus, we start with the rows at the bottom of the table and work our way up. As expected, the slack time of all activities on the critical path is zero.

TABLE 12.4 Computation of Slack Time

Activity	EST	Duration	ECT	LCT	LST = LCT – Duration	Slack = LST – EST
A_1	0	9	9	$LST(A_2) = 9$	$9 - 9 = 0$	0
A_2	9	3	12	$Min\{LST(A_3), LST(A_4)\}$ $= Min\{16, 12\} = 12$	$12 - 3 = 9$	0
A_3	12	11	23	$Min\{LST(A_7), LST(A_8)\}$ $= Min\{31, 27\} = 27$	$27 - 11 = 16$	$27 - 23 = 4$
A_4	12	7	19	$Min\{LST(A_5), LST(A_6)\}$ $= Min\{19, 21\} = 19$	$19 - 7 = 12$	0
A_5	19	8	27	$LST(A_8) = 27$	$27 - 8 = 19$	0
A_6	19	6	25	$Min\{LST(A_7), LST(A_8)\}$ $= Min\{31, 27\} = 27$	$27 - 6 = 21$	$27 - 25 = 2$
A_7	25	21	46	$LST(A_{10}) = 52$	$52 - 21 = 31$	$52 - 46 = 6$
A_8	27	10	37	$LST(A_9) = 37$	$37 - 10 = 27$	0
A_9	37	15	52	$LST(A_{10}) = 52$	$52 - 15 = 37$	0
A_{10}	52	5	57	57	$57 - 5 = 52$	0

What is the benefit of knowing how much slack time there is associated with an activity? The main benefit from knowing the slack time information is as follows:

- *Potentially delay the start of the activity:* To the extent that we can delay the start of an activity without delaying the overall project, we might prefer a later start over an earlier start. Because activities are often associated with direct expenses, simple discounted cash flow calculations suggest that the start times be delayed wherever possible.
- *Accommodate the availability of resources:* Internal or external resources might not always be available when we need them. Slack time provides us with a way to adjust our schedule (as shown in the Gantt chart) without compromising the completion time of the overall project.

Exhibit 12.1 summarizes the steps to plan the time line of a project and to identify the critical path as well as the slack times of the activities. Based on this information, we can augment the initial project graph and present all information we computed for each activity in a graphical format, similar to what is shown in Figure 12.2. This representation, as shown in Figure 12.4, is the output of many commercial software packages dealing with project management as well as a set of consulting tools.

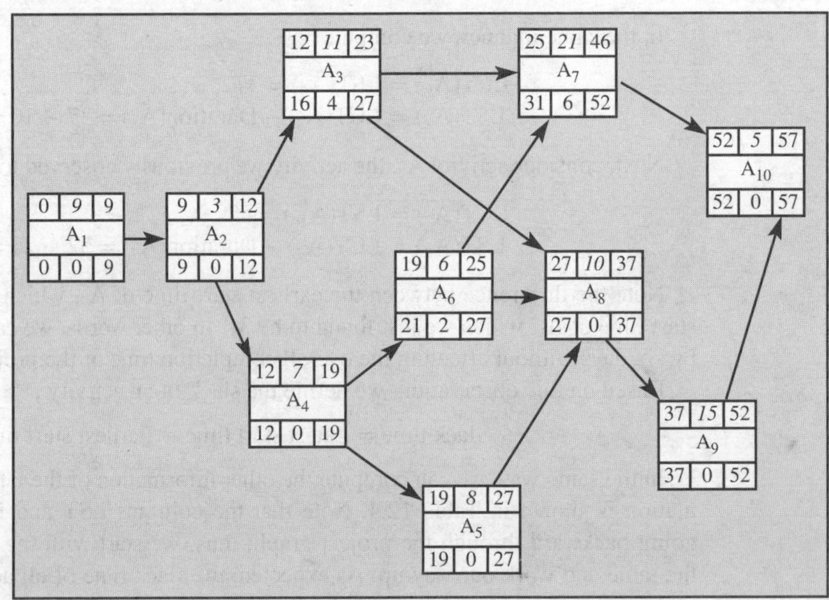

FIGURE 12.4 Augmented Project Graph. The top row includes the earliest start time, the duration, and the earliest completion time. The middle row is the activity name. The bottom row is the latest start time, the slack, and the latest completion time.

Exhibit 12.1

SUMMARY OF CALCULATIONS FOR A CRITICAL PATH ANALYSIS

1. Identify all activities that constitute the project.
2. Determine the dependencies among the activities by either creating a dependency matrix or by creating the project graph. Make sure there exists no circularity in the dependencies (i.e., the dependency matrix only has entries to the lower left of the diagonal and the project graph does not contain any loops).
3. Compute the earliest start time (EST) and the earliest completion time (ECT) by working forward through the project graph (from start to end).

$$\text{EST}(A_i) = \text{Max}\{\text{ECT}(A_j)\}, \text{ where } A_j \text{ are all activities providing input to } A_i$$

$$\text{ECT}(A_i) = \text{EST}(A_i) + \text{Duration}(A_i)$$

4. Compute the latest start time (LST) and the latest completion time (LCT) by working backward through the project graph (from end to start)

$$\text{LCT}(A_i) = \text{Min}\{\text{LST}(A_j)\}, \text{ where } A_j \text{ are all activities receiving input from } A_i$$

$$\text{LST}(A_i) = \text{LCT}(A_i) - \text{Duration}(A_i)$$

5. Compute the slack of an activity as

$$\text{Slack}(A_i) = \text{LST}(A_i) - \text{EST}(A_i)$$

6. Create the critical path by highlighting all activities with zero slack.

Note that all of these computations assume that there exists no uncertainty in the activity durations (and dependencies). Uncertainty is the subject of the next section.

12.6 Dealing with Uncertainty

Given our definition of projects as temporary operations that deal with nonroutine work, projects often face a significant amount of uncertainty at their outset. Incorporating this uncertainty into the project plan is thus a central concern of project management.

How much uncertainty a project is exposed to depends on the nature of a project and its environment. Launching a new entrepreneurial venture is likely to be associated with more uncertainty than the construction of a residential building. We find it helpful to distinguish among four project management frameworks that we present in increasing order of the level of uncertainty they are suited for.

Random Activity Times

So far, we have behaved as if all activity times in the project were deterministic—that is, they could be predicted with certainty. However, it lies in the nature of many project activities that their duration can vary considerably. Often, project managers are asked to come up with a best-case, an expected-case, and a worst-case scenario for the duration of each activity.

With that information in mind, it is possible to compute the variance of an activity time as well as the probability of meeting a certain due date. This is similar to the logic of uncertain activity times in waiting models that we explore in some later chapters. Figure 12.5 shows the activity durations for a sample of cardiac surgeries in the operating room of a large hospital. We observe that there exists a considerable amount of

FIGURE 12.5 Procedure Durations in the Operating Room for Open Heart Surgery

Source: Data taken from Olivares et al.

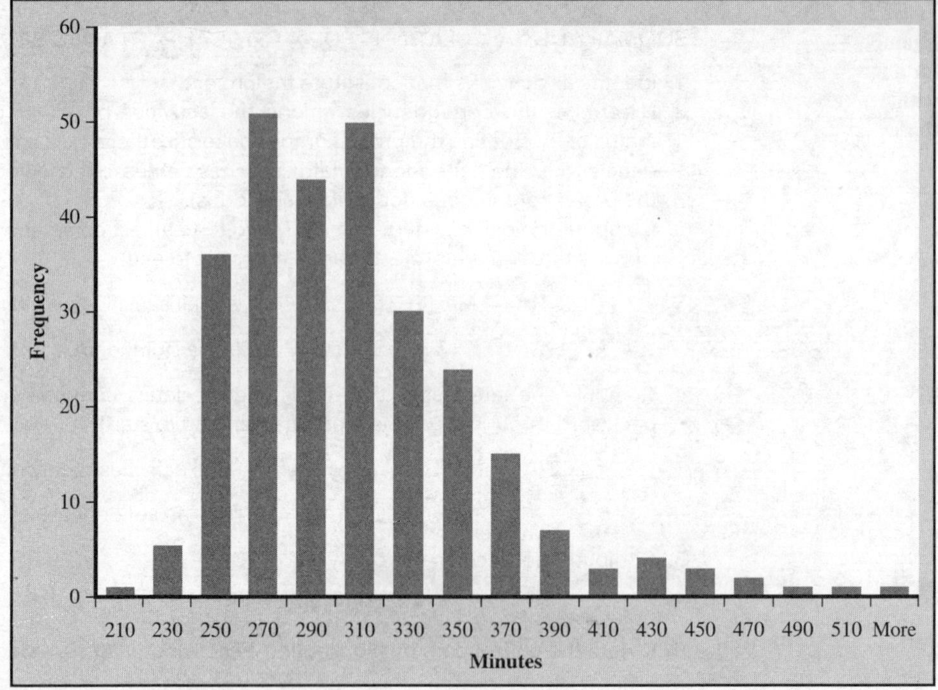

procedure variation. Moreover, we observe that the distribution is not symmetric: Activity durations that are more than double the mean duration can happen—the distribution has a "long tail."

When facing uncertainty in the activity time durations, it is important to understand that uncertainty in activity duration is a bad thing because it, on average, will lead to a later completion time of the project. It is a misconception that uncertainties in activity times will cancel each other out, just as the statement, "Put your head in the freezer and your feet in the oven and the average temperature you are exposed to is just about right," makes little sense. In a similar manner, variation in activity duration will not cancel out. When some activities are completed early and others are completed late, the overall impact on the project duration is almost always undesirable.

To see this, consider the simple project graph displayed in Figure 12.6. On the left side of the figure, we have a project with deterministic activity times. Given the activity durations of 5 days for A_1, 4 days for A_2, and 6 days for A_3, as well as the dependency structure shown by the project graph, the critical path of this project is $A_1 - A_3$ and the completion time is 11. Now, consider the activity times on the ride side of the figure. A_1 now has a completion time of 3 days with a 50 percent probability and 7 days with a 50 percent probability and A_2 has a completion time of 2 days with a 50 percent probability and 6 days with a 50 percent probability.

FIGURE 12.6 Simple Example of a Project with Uncertainty in the Activity Duration

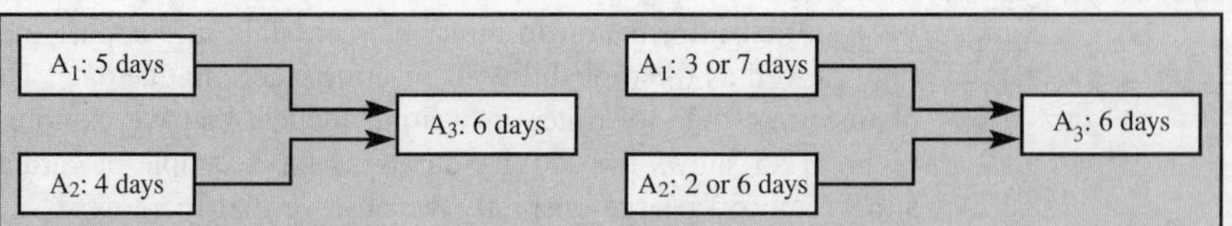

TABLE 12.5
Example Calculations for a Small Project with Three Activities (based on Figure 12.6)

Scenario	Probability	Explanation	Start of A_3	Completion
A_1 late and A_2 late	0.25	A_1 would take 7 days (during which time, the 6 days of A_2 will also be completed)	7	13
A_1 early, A_2 late	0.25	A_2 would take 6 days (during which time, the 3 days of A_1 would also be completed)	6	12
A_1 late, A_2 early	0.25	A_1 would take 7 days (during which time, the 2 days of A_2 would also be completed)	7	13
A_1 early and A_2 early	0.25	A_1 would take 3 days (during which time, the 2 days of A_2 would also be completed)	3	9

Note that in expectation (on average) the completion times of A_1 and A_2 have not changed. But the expected completion time of the project has. To see this, consider the calculations displayed in Table 12.5.

Observe that the expected completion time is

$$0.25 \times 13 \text{ days} + 0.25 \times 12 \text{ days} + 0.25 \times 13 \text{ days} + 0.25 \times 9 \text{ days} = 11.75 \text{ days}$$

almost one day (0.75 day, to be exact) longer than in the deterministic base case. Note that this relies on a rather optimistic assumption in the case that both activities are completed early: we implicitly assume that A_3 has the flexibility of starting earlier than planned, when both A_1 and A_2 are completed early. If we cannot benefit from the early completion of activities, the overall penalty we incur from uncertainty would be even higher.

In the first three scenarios, we are slower than the deterministic completion time of 11 days. Only in the last case are we faster. Thus, we are not just exposed to the risk of the project running later than in the deterministic case, but we will be running later on average.

The reason for this effect is that the critical path of the project can potentially shift. In other words, an activity not on the critical path might delay the overall project because of a longer than expected duration. While A_2 was not on the critical path in the deterministic base case, we saw that it was holding up the project (and thus was on the critical path) in the second scenario analyzed earlier. Unfortunately, many books and software packages ignore this effect and pretend that the variance of the overall project duration can be directly computed from the variances of the activity times on the critical path. This is simply incorrect—a rigorous evaluation of the overall project duration almost always requires some Monte Carlo simulation.

Beyond avoiding this simple, yet very common mistake, correctly estimating the duration of the activity is a challenge. Estimates of activity durations are often inflated, especially when working with internal resources: Because nobody on the team wants to be blamed for potential schedule overruns, it is common to quote excessively long estimates of activity durations (the estimates are "padded"). This is especially common if there exists no threat of substitution for a resource, as is common with resources internal to the organization (e.g., the IT department). Resources simply declare that it takes 10 days to complete the activity, even if their true forecast for the completion is 5 days. After all, what would be the incentive for the resource to commit to an aggressive schedule? Once the project gets under way, the schedule looks very tight. However, if one truly observes the execution of the project, most activities make little progress, and the corresponding resources are either idle or working on other projects, even if they are associated with the critical path.

Obtaining honest (unbiased) activity durations is thus essential. One technique is to compare actual activity durations with their forecasts.

However, estimates of activity durations can also be underestimated, especially when working with external resources: If contractors for a project are asked to submit a time estimate, they have a substantial incentive to underestimate the project completion time because this increases their likelihood of being selected for the project. Once on the job, however, they know that they cannot be easily kicked out of the project should their activity run late. For example, consider the OR data from Figure 12.5 discussed earlier. If we compare the actual time taken in the OR with the time estimates made initially when the OR was booked, it turns out that, on average, procedures take 10 percent longer than initially forecasted. The reason for this is that doctors often want to get a particular slot on the OR schedule—and they know that they are more likely to get a slot in the near future if their procedure time is short. However, they also know that once they have started the procedure, there exists no way to penalize them for a schedule overrun. With this in mind, they simply promise overly optimistic activity durations. Again, obtaining unbiased activity durations is important. Project contracts, and especially late completion penalties, are also an instrument to consider when working with external parties.

Potential Iteration/Rework Loops

The previously introduced dependency matrix (see Table 12.2) had an important property—all dependencies were on the lower left of the diagonal. In other words, there existed a one-way path from the beginning of the project to the end.

In practice, however, projects often require iteration. In fact, the previously discussed UAV project commonly (in about 3 out of 10 cases) iterates between activities A_4 and A_9. Such iterations are typical for product development and innovation projects where problem solving can be a more organic, iterative process. It is often referred to as rework.

In general, such *rework loops* are more likely to happen in high-uncertainty environments. For example, a development team for an Internet platform might want to adjust its business plan after having launched a beta prototype, creating a rework loop. In contrast, we hope that the architect in charge of a major construction project does not want to revisit her drawings after the first tenants moved into the building. Consequently, project planning tools such as Gantt charts and the critical path method are more valuable for low-uncertainty projects, and they can provide a false sense of planning accuracy when applied in high-uncertainty environments.

Several tools exist for modeling and analyzing projects with iteration. We restrict ourselves to the main insight from this line of research. The presence of iteration loops typically dominates the effect of uncertain activity duration. In other words, when faced with the potential of some activities taking longer than expected and an unexpected iteration requiring reworking one or multiple previously completed activities, a project manager should focus on the threat of the iteration because it has a stronger effect on the overall completion time.

Decision Tree/Milestones/Exit Option

The previous two types of uncertainty reflected the question, "When will the project be completed?" Activities might take a little longer (uncertain activity times) or sometimes might even have to be repeated (rework loops), but in the end, we always complete the project.

Often, however, a more fundamental question is of essence to the project manager: "Will we complete this project at all, or should we terminate the project?" Such uncertainty is common in many innovation settings, include venture capital–funded projects or pharmaceutical research and development (R&D). For example, only a small fraction of

R&D projects that enter phase 1 clinical trials will be launched in the market. More than 80 percent of the projects will be canceled along the way.

Project management techniques as reviewed earlier are inappropriate for handling this type of uncertainty. The threat of terminating the project because of new market data (market uncertainty) or new technical data (technological uncertainty) looms so large that it trumps the previously discussed types of uncertainty.

Decision trees map out the potential scenarios that can occur once the uncertainty is resolved and the potential set of actions that can be taken in each scenario are determined. A key insight that can be derived from such models is the observation that it is often substantially cheaper to exit a project early, instead of letting costs escalate and then exiting the project later on at higher costs. The project management implication of this is that it is very desirable to move activities that resolve this type of uncertainty (feasibility studies, market research) to the early part of the project.

Unknown Unknowns

When Christopher Columbus set out to find a new way to sail to India, he (most likely) did not set up a project plan. Even for modern time explorers, be it in sailing or in business, there exist situations where the amount of uncertainty we face is simply too large to make any careful planning process meaningful. In such settings, we face so much uncertainty that we don't even know what we don't know. We face *unknown unknowns*, also referred to as *unk-unks*.

It lies in the nature of many high-uncertainty projects that they will not be completed. In that sense, a timely abandonment often is the goal as it avoids an escalation in costs. Often, a useful exercise is to simply list all variables in the project that are currently not known and to look for activities that would help resolve these unknowns. At any moment in time, the project manager should then attempt to spend as little as possible to learn enough to decide whether or not to move forward with the project. This technique, also referred to as *discovery-driven planning*, will help resolve some uncertainties and potentially identify new ones.

Exhibit 12.2 summarizes these levels of project uncertainty. The main point is that different project management tools apply to different projects, depending on the amount of uncertainty they face. It is neither advisable to use a high-uncertainty tool (such as decision trees) for a low-uncertainty project (why would you want to evaluate an exit option every day in an ongoing construction project?) nor vice versa (why try to find and optimize the critical path if you do not even know if you are in business next quarter?).

12.7 How to Accelerate Projects

Project managers typically pursue a combination of three objectives: project completion time, project cost (budget), and the quality of the accomplished work. Sometimes, these objectives are in conflict with another. This then creates a trade-off among the three dimensions, similar to what we have seen in other chapters of this book (e.g., the trade-off between call center responsiveness and efficiency in Chapter 1).

Consider the development of the UAV discussed earlier. Most likely, more time would allow the developers to put together an even more convincing proposal. Similarly, if budget would not be a constraint, it might be possible to outsource at least some work, which, if it shortens the duration of a critical path activity, would lead to an earlier project completion time.

Beyond trading off one goal against another goal, we can also try to "break the trade-off" and just be smarter about how we manage the project. The following provides a set of

Exhibit 12.2

SUMMARY OF DIFFERENT UNCERTAINTY LEVELS IN A PROJECT

Certainty	Low uncertainty project such as construction projects or routine development projects	Calculate critical path use slack to optimize timing
Uncertainty in activity duration	Projects with minor uncertainties about activity durations and or resource availability	Monte Carlo Analysis–watch for changes in critical path
Potential iteration	Potentially iterative projects that include one or multiple rework loops	Rework loops
Potential termination	Multiple scenarios exist, one or more of them require termination of the project	Decision trees
Unk-Unks	High levels of uncertainty and a dynamic environment; chaos	Discovery driven planning

inexpensive actions a project manager can take to accelerate the completion time of the project without necessarily sacrificing the quality of the accomplished work or the project budget:

- *Start the project early:* The last day before the project's due date is typically a day of stress and busyness. In contrast, the first day of the project is typically characterized by little action. This effect is similar to the "term paper syndrome" well familiar to most students. It reflects human optimism and overconfidence in the ability to complete work in the future. At the risk of stating the obvious—a day at the beginning of the project is equally long as a day at the end of the project—why do little or no work on the former and jam all the work into the latter?
- *Manage the project scope:* One of the most common causes of delay in projects is that the amount of work that is part of the project changes over the course of the project. Features are added and engineering change orders requested. If such changes occur late in the project, they often cause significant project delays and budget overruns for relatively little increased quality. For this reason, it is advisable to finalize the scope of the project early on.
- *Crash activities:* Often, an increase in spending allows for a faster completion time of a project. Contractors are willing to work overtime for a premium, and expensive equipment might help further shorten activity duration. However, the reverse is not always true. Projects that take excessively long are not necessarily cheaper. Because typically there are some fixed costs associated with a project, a project that drags on forever might actually be also very expensive.
- *Overlap critical path activities:* A central assumption underlying the dependency matrix shown in Table 12.2 has been that an activity that is dependent on an information-providing activity needs to wait until that activity is completed. However, it is often possible to allow the dependent activity to start early, relying on preliminary information from the information-providing activity. For example, it seems plausible that the activity "Building design" should be completed before starting the activity "Building construction."

However, does this imply that all of the design has to be completed? Or, maybe, would it be possible to begin digging the foundation of the building while the designers are still finalizing the shape of the windows? By identifying the exact dependencies among activities, it is often possible to provide the dependent activity with a head start.

12.8 Literature/ Further Reading

Loch et al. (2006) provide a comprehensive framework of managing projects with uncertainty. The authors use many illustrative examples and target experienced project managers as their audience.

Terwiesch and Ulrich (2009) deal with far-horizon innovation projects as well as multiple challenges associated with financial evaluations of innovation projects.

Ulrich and Eppinger (2011) is the classic textbook for product development and includes an easy-to-follow introductory chapter on project management and project organization.

12.9 Practice Problems

The following questions will help in testing your understanding of this chapter. After each question, we show the relevant section in parentheses [Section x].

Solutions to problems marked with an "*" are available in Appendix E. Video solutions to select problems are available in Connect.

Q12.1* **(Venture Fair)** In order to participate at a venture fair, Team TerraZ is preparing a project plan for their new-product offering. The team plans to spend 3 days on ideation. Once ideation is complete, the team aims to interview 20 potential customers (6 days) and to engage in a careful analysis of competing products (12 days). Following the customer interviews, the team expects to spend 10 days on careful user observation and 4 days on sending out e-mail surveys. These two activities are independent from each other, but both require that the interviews be completed. With the input from the customer observation and the e-mail surveys, the team then plans to spend 5 days on putting together the target specifications for the product. This activity also requires the analysis of competing products to be complete.

After the target specifications, the team aims to create a product design, which will take 10 days. With the product design complete, they plan to get price quotes (6 days) and build a prototype (4 days) that they then want to test out with some customers (5 days). Once the prototype has been tested and the price quotes are in, they can put together their information material for the venture fair (3 days).

a. Create a dependency matrix for the activities described, and build a project graph. [12.1]
b. Find the critical path. What is the latest time the team can start working, assuming the venture fair is scheduled for April 18? [12.4]

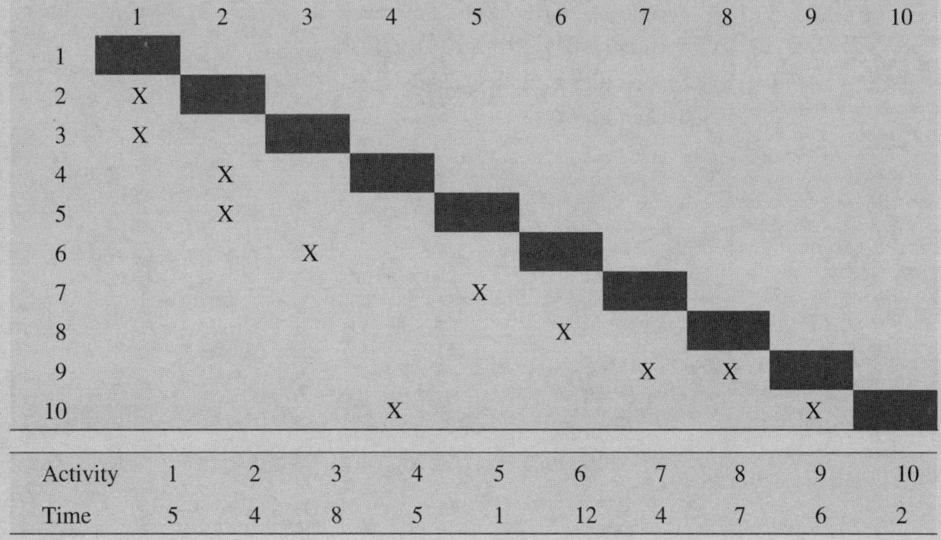

	1	2	3	4	5	6	7	8	9	10
1										
2	X									
3	X									
4		X								
5		X								
6			X							
7					X					
8						X				
9							X	X		
10				X					X	

Activity	1	2	3	4	5	6	7	8	9	10
Time	5	4	8	5	1	12	4	7	6	2

Q12.2 **(10 Activities)** Consider the dependency matrix and the activity durations provided above.

a. Build a project graph, visually depicting the evolution of this project. [12.2]

b. Find the critical path. What is the earliest time that the project can be completed? [12.4]

c. For each activity, compute the late start, the late completion, and the slack time. [12.5]

Q12.3 **(Graduation Party)** Thierry, Ute, and Vishal are getting ready for their last period in the MBA program. Following the final exams, they intend to throw a big party with many of their friends from back home. Presently, they have identified the following set of activities that need to be completed. They decide to not do any work on preparing the party until all final exams are over. Moreover, they aim to go on a 3-day beach vacation as early as possible, but not before all party planning activities are completed.

On June 10, they will enter the final exam week, which will take 5 days. They then want to arrange for live music (which will take 5 days), evaluate a number of potential party sites (6 days), and prepare a guest list, which includes inviting their friends and receiving the RSVPs (7 days). They want to visit their two most promising party sites, which they expect to take 4 days. However, this can only be done once they have completed the list of party sites. Once they have finished the guest list and received the RSVPs, they want to book hotel rooms for their friends and create a customized T-shirt with their names on it as well as the name of the guest. Hotel room reservation (3 days) and T-shirt creation (6 days) are independent from each other, but both of them require the guest list to be complete. Once they have picked the party site, they want to have a meeting on site with an event planner, which they expect to take 4 days. And then, once all work is completed, they plan to take off to the beach.

a. Create a dependency matrix for the activities described. [12.1]

b. Build a project graph, visually depicting the evolution of this project. [12.2]

c. Find the critical path. What is the earliest time that the three can go to the beach? [12.4]

d. For each activity, compute the late start, the late completion, and the slack time. [12.5]

Q12.4 **(Three Activities with Uncertainty)** A small project consists of three activities: A, B, and C. To start activity C, both activities A and B need to be complete. Activity A takes 3 days with a probability of 50 percent and 5 days with a probability of 50 percent, and so does Activity B. Activity C takes 1 day. What is the expected completion time of the project? [12.6]

If you would like to test your understanding of a specific section, here are the questions organized by section:

Section 12.1: Q12.1a, Q12.3a

Section 12.2: Q12.2a, Q12.3b

Section 12.4: Q12.1b, Q12.2b, Q12.3c

Section 12.5: Q12.2c, Q12.3d

Section 12.6: Q12.4

Chapter 13

Forecasting

Imagine you had a crystal ball—a crystal ball that would show you the future. What type of things would you look for in the crystal ball? Next week's winning lottery numbers? The stock market data for next year? Being able to foresee the future is an ancient dream of mankind. And being able to predict the future and to forecast what will happen would come with substantial economic advantages.

This chapter is about forecasting future events. In particular, we want to forecast the future demand for the products or services we supply. And we should break the bad news right at the beginning of the chapter: We cannot offer you a crystal ball. To the best of our knowledge (and we are pretty confident on this one), there exists no such thing. But the absence of crystal balls does not mean we cannot make good forecasts. We might not be able to make perfect forecasts, but, as we will see, a little bit of intelligence goes a long way.

Forecasting how much customers like our products or services in the future is hard. In fact, it is very hard, as the following two examples from history illustrate:

- Thomas Watson, legendary CEO of IBM, forecasted the demand for computers. He predicted that the world market demand for computers would be—five. Yes, you read correctly, not 5 million—5 computers. In his defense, he made this forecast in the 1950s—we weren't even born back then.
- In the 1960s, the managers at Decca Recording were offered the opportunity to publish the music of a Liverpool guitar band. Decca's forecast for sales of this band was pessimistic—"guitar groups are on the way out" was the management consensus. Unfortunately for Decca, the band that they rejected was the Beatles, a band that subsequently went on to become one of the most successful music bands in history.

In defense of Watson and the folks at Decca Recording, forecasting something radically new, something for which no prior history existed, is particularly challenging. Such forecasting problems are typical in business when it comes to predicting the sales of a new product or service before launch. The focus of this chapter is about forecasting in business settings for which we already have some data from past transactions.

Consider the following situation. Every year, millions of Americans are impacted by the flu. You might have had that experience yourself and so you know this is no fun. Especially as far as infants, the elderly, and other vulnerable population groups are concerned, the flu can be a matter of life or death. During flu season, patients with the flu flood the emergency departments of hospitals and demand medical services. Patients suffering from the flu also come to pharmacies and demand pharmaceutical products such as TamiFlu (a drug that helps to ease flu-related symptoms). So, forecasting the number of patients with the flu is critical.

Figure 13.1 shows the data for the number of patients visiting hospitals with the flu over the time period from 2009 to 2014. Imagine you were in charge of forecasting the number

FIGURE 13.1
Flu Data from 2009 to 2014

(Source: CDC)

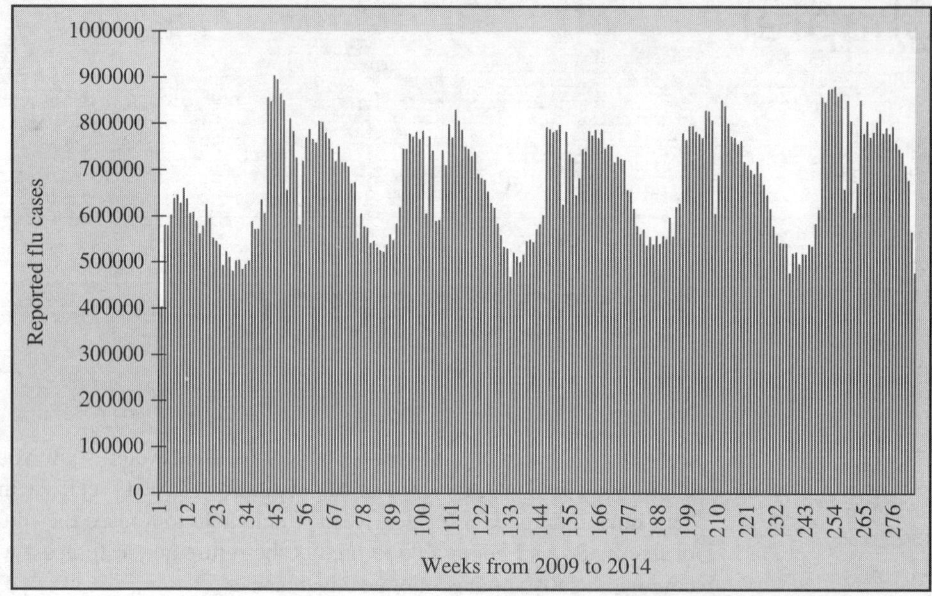

of flu cases, be it for a hospital or a pharmaceutical company. Can you perfectly predict the number of flu patients in 2015? Perfect forecasts are typically impossible. Each year is different and, short of crystal balls, every forecast will be wrong. But just "eyeballing" the data, you have some idea about the future. And this is the intuition you need for this chapter.

This chapter helps you forecast future demand. We proceed using the following steps:

- We first outline a framework for forecasting. We introduce some terminology, describe different forecasting methods (not including the acquisition of a crystal ball), and overview forecasting problems in business.
- We then discuss what makes a forecast a good forecast, defining a number of quality metrics that can be used when comparing forecasts with reality.
- Next, we introduce a simple set of forecasting methods, including naïve forecasts, moving average, and exponential smoothing.
- The next two sections then introduce more advanced forecasts that allow you to deal with seasonality and trends.
- The final section discusses the use of expert panels and points to some organizational challenges when dealing with subjective forecasts.

13.1 Forecasting Framework

Forecasting is the process of creating statements about outcomes of variables that presently are uncertain and will only be realized in the future. *Demand forecasting* is thus the process of creating statements about future realizations of demand.

During the FIFA soccer world cup 2010, zookeepers in a German zoo made international headlines because they were able to forecast the outcomes of all matches of the German team, including Germany's loss in the semifinals against Spain. How did they do this? The zoo had an octopus by the name of Paul. Before each match of the German national team, the zookeepers offered Paul food in two boxes that were colored with the flags of the opposing teams. Depending on which box Paul would go to first, the zookeepers made their forecast.

FIGURE 13.2
Forecasting Framework

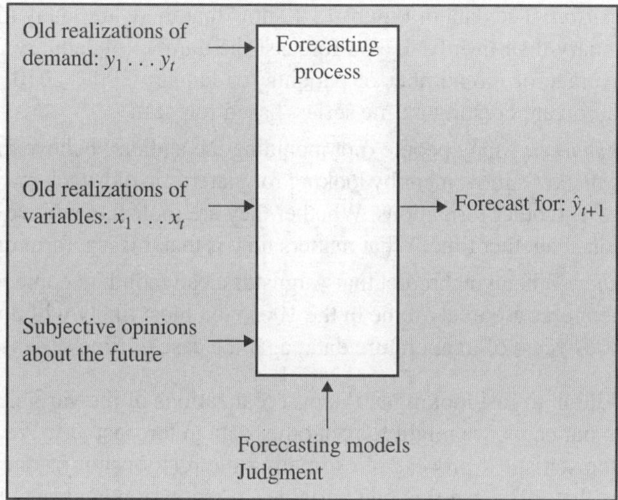

Does watching an octopus having lunch qualify as forecasting? We argue it does. Let's revisit our definition. Forecasting is the process of creating statements about outcomes of variables that are presently uncertain and will only be realized in the future:

- The zookeepers clearly had a process in place because they had marked the food boxes and had agreed on how to interpret Paul's behavior.
- The outcomes of the matches were uncertain at the time of Paul's food choice.
- The outcomes of the matches were realized in the future.

So, all considered, watching Paul pick the box with a Spanish flag on it and declaring that Spain would win against Germany squarely qualifies as forecasting.

We find it helpful to formalize the process of demand forecasting a little further. Let y_t be the demand in period *t,* where a period can be a day, a week, or a month, or any other unit of time. We want to forecast the demand in the next period and potentially beyond. So we want to say something about y_{t+1} before being able to observe it. It is common to use a "^" symbol as a sign that a value for a variable is a forecast, as opposed to being its true realized value. So, y_{t+1} is the demand for period $t + 1$, while $\hat{y}_{t+1}$ is the forecasted value (pronounced $y\ t + 1$ hat) for period $t + 1$ before y_{t+1} itself is known.

So, when we forecast, we want to say something about $\hat{y}_{t+1}$, while we are still at time *t* or before. By definition, at time *t,* we only have data about demand and about any other variable from period *t* and before. Consider Figure 13.2, which provides a high-level framework for the forecasting process. The output of the process, as already mentioned, is the demand forecast for period $t + 1$, $\hat{y}_{t+1}$.

The inputs to this process can be broken up into three groups: old realizations of demand, old realizations of other variables, and subjective opinions about the future. Consider old realizations of demand first. When we forecast demand for period $t + 1$, we know the demand for previous periods. We define *time series analysis* as the process of analyzing the old (demand) data $y_1 \dots y_t$. A *time series–based forecast* is a forecast that is obtained based on nothing but old demand data. We can think of time series–based forecasting as a form of *extrapolation;* that is, of estimating a value beyond the range of the original observations assuming that some patterns in the data observed so far will also prevail in the future. Here are some examples for time series–based forecasting:

- *Soccer:* If you forecast a team's victory on nothing but the outcomes of past matches ("Brazil will win because they have won the last 10 matches"), you are extrapolating a time series.

- *Flu season:* The data in Figure 13.1 show that there are many more flu-related patients in January than in July. If you forecast the number of January 2015 patients by taking the average of the number of patients for January 2009, 2010, 2011, 2012, 2013, and 2014, you are creating a time series–based forecast.
- *Stock market:* Many people (not including the authors) believe that they can forecast the stock market's movement by looking for patterns in old stock market data, such as trends, cycles, and other formations. Whether they are foolish to believe so or not is worth a discussion at another time. What matters now is that this is a form of time series analysis.
- *Weather:* When you predict that August is a bad month to come to Philadelphia, because temperatures are likely to be in the 100s, you most likely will do so based on looking at previous years of temperature data; again, a case of time series–based forecasting.

In addition to just looking at the past realizations of the variable we try to forecast (old y_t data in our case), we might look at other data to forecast $\hat{y}_{t+1}$. We define *regression analysis* as the statistical process of estimating the relationship of one variable with multiple variables that influence this one variable. In regression analysis, we call the one variable that we try to understand the *dependent variable* (also called the *outcome variable*) and the other variables influencing the dependent variable the *independent variables*. So, in the context of forecasting, we can look at many other independent variables influencing our forecast for the dependent variable. Again, looking at examples helps:

- *Soccer:* Chances are that when you predict the outcome of your favorite team's next match, you would not just look at how often the team has won recently, you would also look at who the opponent is and how they have recently been scoring. You might also factor in that the top player is injured or that the next game is a home game. In other words, you are looking at many other variables. And, yes, looking at the movements of an octopus having lunch also corresponds to considering an additional variable.
- *Flu season:* When forecasting the number of flu patients, it is informative to not just look at the number of patients in past months, but to also consider other data. These include the amount of vaccination and flu data from other countries. Researchers forecasting flu outbreaks have also analyzed to what extent the number of times "flu" is entered into Google is a good predictor of how many patients will seek medical help for flu-related symptoms (the evidence for the predictive power in this case is mixed).
- *Stock market:* In addition to the stock market values from the past, economists consider variables such as growth rates, recent monetary policy decisions, earnings announcements, and many more.
- *Weather:* You might think that August is hot in Philadelphia, but when you see the wind change and a cold front moving in, you might want to update your forecast.

Determining the effects of playing a home game on winning, of Google search terms on flu patients, of unemployment data on stock market prices, or of cold fronts on future temperatures—all of this is the domain of regression analysis.

An implicit risk in forecasting based on old data, be it in the form of time series–based forecasting or regression analysis, is that these techniques assume that the future will behave according to the past. In contrast, an informed expert might have a "gut feel" that something will happen that cannot be explained by past data. Whether or not we should trust such experts is a topic for discussion further on in this chapter. For now, what matters is that such subjective opinions can also be considered when determining a forecast. So, the third set of variables determining a forecast in Figure 13.2 is subjective.

In the remainder of this chapter, we mostly focus on time series–based forecasts. In the last section, we discuss how to deal with subjective opinions. However, this chapter does not cover regression analysis. Not that we don't feel regression analysis is important, we simply think it deserves the proper treatment in a statistics book, as opposed to being covered in passing in an operations book.

The three different types of input variables discussed in conjunction with Figure 13.2 also point to different methods and organizational processes of generating forecasts. We find it helpful to distinguish between:

- *Automated forecasting*: When weather.com makes a prediction for the temperature in Manhattan tomorrow at 9 a.m., it cannot convene an expert panel of meteorologists. Most forecasts in business need to be made millions of times, so they have to be done cheaply, which typically means without human involvement. How many cheeseburgers will customers order in an hour at a particular McDonald's? How many rental cars will be needed on a particular day at a particular airport? Forecasts of these types are created by computers, typically with no human intervention. You might have heard buzzwords such as machine learning and Big Data; both of these stand for sophisticated versions of regression analysis in which computers find out what variables best help make a good prediction.
- *Expert panel forecasting*: When McDonald's needs to make a forecast for corporate sales, however, there is so much at stake that the costs of generating the forecast simply matter less. So, for forecasts where there is a lot at stake, automated forecasting is typically augmented by expert panels. On such panels, a group of managers share their subjective opinions and try to reach a consensus about a demand forecast.

After discussing how to generate a forecast, consider the question of what to do with the forecast after it has been generated. We find it helpful to distinguish between three types of forecasting applications in business. These three types can be categorized based on the time horizons that they consider:

- *Short-term forecasts* are used to support decisions that are made for short time periods ranging from the daily level to the monthly level. In extreme cases, forecasts might even be made at the hourly level. These forecasts are used to help decisions related to staffing (restaurants have more servers at lunch than in the afternoon) and short-term pricing. They can also be used to predict waiting times and help with scheduling decisions. In the flu example, this corresponds to making a forecast for tomorrow or the next week so that an appropriate number of nurses can be scheduled.
- *Mid-term forecasts* are forecasts that are made from the monthly level to the yearly level. They drive capacity-related decisions (recruiting, acquisition of machinery), but also are used for financial planning. In the flu example, this corresponds to making a forecast for the entire flu season so that the right number of nurses can be recruited or the right number of flu vaccines/medications can be produced.
- *Long-term forecasts* are forecasts that are made over multiple years. These forecasts help with strategic decisions such as entering new markets, launching new products or services, expanding capacity by investing in new facilities, or closing facilities. In the flu example, we might think of the decision of drug store giant CVS to launch its MinuteClinic (a walk-in medical service) as one that was made after forecasting many years of data.

We find this distinction between the three horizons helpful, though we admit it is not always possible to draw clear lines between these three categories. One reason this distinction is nevertheless useful relates to the forecasting methodology. Short-term forecasts tend to be automated forecasts, relying primarily on extrapolation of old data and regression analysis. Long-term forecasts, in contrast, tend to be based on a combination of old realizations of demand data, independent variables, and expert opinions. They thus are typically created by expert panels.

13.2 Evaluating the Quality of a Forecast

Imagine you work for an emergency department that wants to get ready for the flu season. You are asked to forecast the number of flu cases showing up to the emergency department over the course of the next four weeks. Before you start looking at any old data, you decide to seek advice from some experts, so you go to four doctors, who give you their forecasts for the next four weeks (Table 13.1).

Which forecast should you use? Which forecast is the best one? Clearly, this cannot be answered BEFORE we have seen the true demand; that is, the number of flu-related patients who actually show up to the ED over these four weeks. But, as we will now show, determining the best forecast is even difficult AFTER we have seen the true demand.

Table 13.2 repeats the four forecasts of our docs, but it also shows the true number of patients who came to the ED. To determine which forecast is best, we must first define what we mean by best. As is apparent from the preceding text, none of the four forecasts is right every single time, and so all of them are wrong to some extent. We thus have to define the extent to which a forecast is wrong. This can be done in multiple ways.

We define the *forecast error* for period t as the difference between the forecast for period t and the actual value for period t:

$$\text{Forecast error in } t = \text{Forecast for } t - \text{Actual value for } t$$

For doctor 1, we compute the forecast errors, oftentimes abbreviated FE, for the four periods as

$$\text{Forecast error in week 1} = \text{Forecast for week 1} - \text{Actual value for week 1} = 70 - 38 = 32$$

$$\text{Forecast error in week 2} = \text{Forecast for week 2} - \text{Actual value for week 2} = 55 - 49 = 6$$

$$\text{Forecast error in week 3} = \text{Forecast for week 3} - \text{Actual value for week 3} = 40 - 59 = -19$$

$$\text{Forecast error in week 4} = \text{Forecast for week 4} - \text{Actual value for week 4} = 80 - 44 = 36$$

So, the forecast errors for doctor 1 are $FE_1 = 32$, $FE_2 = 6$, $FE_3 = -19$, and $FE_4 = 36$. But how do we interpret these forecast errors? Consider the information displayed by Table 13.3. The table shows the forecast errors for doctor 1 and for doctor 2 over the four weeks, along with their initial forecasts and the true number of patients who showed up. Which of the two doctors does a better job at forecasting?

A first way to measure the quality of a forecast is to see if it is right, on average. We define a forecast as an *unbiased forecast* if the forecast is, on average, correct. This is equivalent to having the average forecast error be zero. Doctor 2 is sometimes forecasting on the high side, sometimes on the low side, but, on average, she is right. So, her forecast is unbiased. This is consistent with the average of her forecast errors being equal to zero. Doctor 1, in contrast, seems to be mostly forecasting on the high side. His average forecast error is 13.75. We don't know why: Maybe the doctor feels stressed out and overworked and so always believes that there are many patients out there. But always forecasting too

TABLE 13.1 Four Forecasts for the Number of Flu-Related Patients Coming to the Emergency Department in the Next Four Weeks

	Doc 1	Doc 2	Doc 3	Doc 4
Week 1	70	50	29	43
Week 2	55	32	52	44
Week 3	40	48	62	54
Week 4	80	60	47	49

TABLE 13.2
Four Forecasts for the Number of Flu-Related Patients Coming to the Emergency Department in the Next Four Weeks and the True Demand Data

	Doc 1	Doc 2	Doc 3	Doc 4	True Demand
Week 1	70	50	29	43	38
Week 2	55	32	52	44	49
Week 3	40	48	62	54	59
Week 2	80	60	47	49	44

TABLE 13.3
Comparison of Doctor 1 and Doctor 2

	Forecast Doc 1	Forecast Doc 2	True Demand	FE Doc 1	FE Doc 2
Week 1	70	50	38	32	12
Week 2	55	32	49	6	−17
Week 3	40	48	59	−19	−11
Week 4	80	60	44	36	16
Average	61.25	47.5	47.5	13.75	0

much is not a good thing. We define a forecast that is wrong, on average, as a *biased forecast*.

Next, compare doctor 2 with doctor 3. As we can see in Table 13.4, both of them are giving us an unbiased forecast. They are both right, on average. Does this mean that they are equally good at forecasting?

Though both of the doctors have a forecast that is correct, on average, most of us would agree that doctor 3 is doing a better job forecasting. This points to an important principle of forecasting. In forecasting, it is not the average alone that determines the quality of a forecast. Yes, being wrong, on average, is a bad thing. But if you forecast too much for today and too little for tomorrow, that does not make you a good forecaster. Imagine the weather forecaster who announces a snowstorm with freezing temperatures today and a heat wave tomorrow, when in reality both days are mild. Being right, on average, can still create a bad forecast.

To capture this intuition, we need to create another measure of forecast quality that goes beyond simply averaging out the forecast errors. A commonly used metric is the *mean squared error (MSE)*, which simply takes the average of the squared forecast errors:

$$\text{MSE} = \frac{\sum_{t=1}^{N} \text{FE}_t^2}{N}$$

Instead of adding up the forecast errors, FE, and then averaging them, the idea behind the mean squared errors is to first square the errors and then average them. Why would one want to do this? Because by squaring the numbers, a negative forecast error is turned into a positive number. And, thus, a negative forecast error and a positive forecast error combined will no longer cancel each other out. This is shown in Table 13.5. Observe that

TABLE 13.4
Comparison of Doctor 2 and Doctor 3

	Forecast Doc 2	Forecast Doc 3	True Demand	FE Doc 2	FE Doc 3
Week 1	50	29	38	12	−9
Week 2	32	52	49	−17	3
Week 3	48	62	59	−11	3
Week 4	60	47	44	16	3
Average	47.5	47.5	47.5	0	0

TABLE 13.5 Comparison of Doctor 2 and Doctor 3

	Forecast Doc 2	Forecast Doc 3	True Demand	FE Doc 2	FE Doc 3	FE_t^2 Doc 2	FE_t^2 Doc 3	$\|FE_t\|$ Doc 2	$\|FE_t\|$ Doc 3
Week 1	50	29	38	12	−9	144	81	12	9
Week 2	32	52	49	−17	3	289	9	17	3
Week 3	48	62	59	−11	3	121	9	11	3
Week 4	60	47	44	16	3	256	9	16	3
Average	47.5	47.5	47.5	0	0	202.5	27	14	4.5

doctor 2 has a much higher mean squared error than doctor 3, confirming our intuition that doctor 3 does a better job at forecasting.

Now, you might say that squaring the forecast errors is a really complicated way of turning a negative number into a positive number. Why would one not simply take the absolute values of the forecast errors and average those out. You are right, you can do this. We define the *mean absolute error (MAE)* as the average of the absolute values of the forecast errors. Often, this is also referred to as the mean absolute deviation (MAD). This is shown in the last two columns of Table 13.5.

$$\text{MAE} = \frac{\sum_{t=1}^{N} |\text{FE}_t|}{N}$$

This new measure also confirms our intuition. The forecasts of doctor 3 are better than the forecasts of doctor 2, no matter if we look at the MSE or the MAE.

One other way in which we can aggregate forecast errors is called the mean absolute percentage error (MAPE). This measure does not look at the forecast errors in absolute terms, but in relative terms. This is achieved by dividing the forecast errors by the actual demand y_t. So we get

$$\text{MAPE} = \frac{\sum_{t=1}^{N} \left|\frac{\text{FE}_t}{y_t}\right|}{N}$$

So, what constitutes a good forecast? The answer to this question is more complicated than we would like. In general, we like the forecast to have the following properties:

- The forecast should be unbiased; that is, be correct on average.
- The forecast should come close to the real outcomes as measured by the mean squared error (MSE) or the mean absolute error (MAE).

Sometimes, these two properties are in conflict with each other. We might prefer a forecast with a small bias if that comes with a dramatically lower value of MSE or MAE. Note further that MSE and MAE do not always agree on which forecast is better. Consider the data displayed by Table 13.6. Note that doctor 4 has the lower mean squared error while doctor 3 has the lower mean absolute error.

TABLE 13.6 Comparison of Doctor 3 and Doctor 4

	Forecast Doc 3	Forecast Doc 4	True Demand	FE Doc 3	FE Doc 4	FE_t^2 Doc 3	FE_t^2 Doc 4	$\|FE_t\|$ Doc 3	$\|FE_t\|$ Doc 4
Week 1	29	43	38	−9	5	81	25	9	5
Week 2	52	44	49	3	−5	9	25	3	5
Week 3	62	54	59	3	−5	9	25	3	5
Week 4	47	49	44	3	5	9	25	3	5
Average	47.5	47.5	47.5	0	0	27	25	4.5	5

Which forecast is better? That really depends on what you are looking for. When evaluating the mean squared errors, we notice that this score can be heavily influenced by one single mistake. Take the case of doctor 3. The reason why doctor 3 did so poorly on the MSE score is that for week 1, her forecast error was −9. Now, squaring (−9) leads to a big number (81, to be exact), which is so large that the next three very good forecasts are not compensating for this mistake. So, the MSE value penalizes a forecaster for one large mistake, while the MAE views each deviation as equally bad.

Which measure of forecast quality you use is really up to you. The key, however, is that you use a metric and assess the quality of old forecasts. This first and foremost requires that you keep data from your old forecasts. Many companies have a hard time doing so, because those who came up with the forecasts don't want to be reminded how wrong they were. Yet, keeping old forecasting data is extremely informative in detecting systematic deviations between forecasts and reality. So, keeping old forecasts and then analyzing these data, no matter which forecast quality measure you use, already gets you 90 percent of the way.

13.3 Eliminating Noise from Old Data

Now that we know how to evaluate the quality of a forecaster by comparing some old forecasts with the true outcomes of the forecasted variables, we can turn to the question of how to create a forecast. As mentioned earlier, we restrict our discussion in this chapter to time series–based forecasting. In other words, we will try to obtain a forecast, $\hat{y}_{t+1}$, by looking at old data $y_1 \ldots y_t$. We now introduce three simple methods that accomplish this: the naïve forecasting model, moving averages, and exponential smoothing. We illustrate all three methods using the flu-related data shown in Figure 13.3. The figure shows the number of flu-related patients in the first 10 weeks for the year 2014 for the average U.S. hospital. Our goal is, using this information, to forecast the number of cases in week 11.

Naïve Model

Because our focus is on time series–based forecasting, we look at old data (number of flu cases from previous weeks) to predict new data (number of flu cases for next week). So,

FIGURE 13.3 **Number of Flu-Related Patients in the First 10 Weeks of 2014**

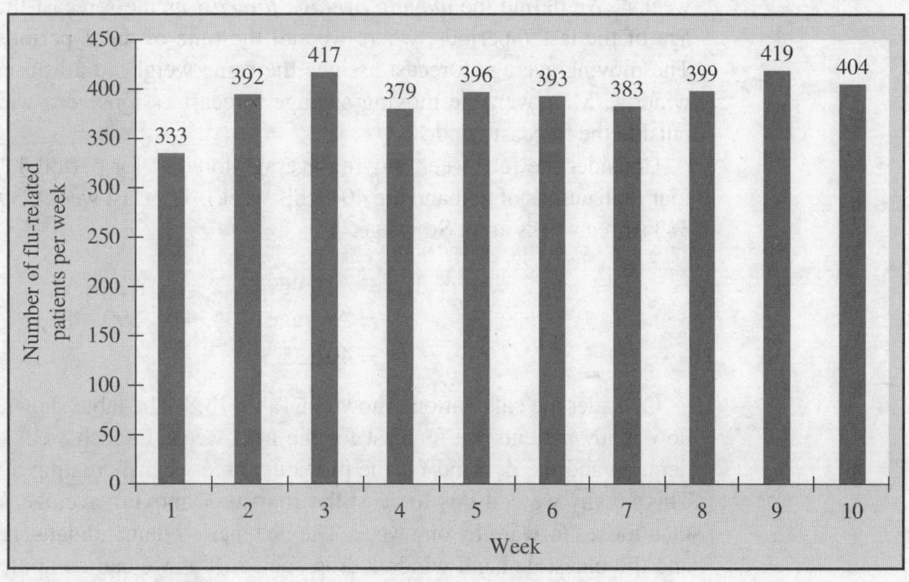

TABLE 13.7
The Naïve Forecasting Method

Week	Patients per Week	Forecast for Next Week
1	333	333
2	392	392
3	417	417
4	379	379
5	396	396
6	393	393
7	383	383
8	399	399
9	419	419
10	404	404

the simplest way of forecasting the demand for the next period is to assume that it is the same as in the last period. More formally, we define

$$\hat{y}_{t+1} = y_t$$

Applied to our flu example, this implies that we predict demand for week 11 to be 404 because

$$\hat{y}_{11} = y_{10} = 404$$

We call this method of creating a forecast for the next period by just using the last realized value the *naïve forecasting method*, as shown in Table 13.7. This method is extremely simple to use. Its main downside is that it ignores all other old data. As a result, the forecast is subject to a lot of *statistical noise*. We define the statistical noise in the demand for a process as the amount of demand that is purely a result of randomness (good or bad luck) and that could not have been forecasted even with the best forecasting methods.

Moving Averages

The best way to take care of statistical noise in data is by taking averages. Maybe last week was special. So, how about we look at the average of the last three weeks? Or the last six weeks? We define the *moving average forecast* as the forecast that is based on the average of the last T periods, where we call the time of the T periods the **forecast window.** The moving average forecast assigns the same weight to all observations in the forecast window. Moreover, the moving average forecast assigns zero weight to all observations outside the forecast window.

Consider the four-week moving average forecast for period 11. At period 11, the last four realizations of demand are 404 (this week), 419 (last week), 399 (two weeks ago), and 383 (three weeks ago). So we get

$$\begin{aligned}\hat{y}_{t+1} &= \text{Average}\ (y_t,\ y_{t-1},\ y_{t-2},\ y_{t-3}) \\ &= \text{Average}\ (404,\ 419,\ 399,\ 383) \\ &= 401.25\end{aligned}$$

Consider the calculations shown in Table 13.8. The table shows, starting with period 5, how many patients we forecast for the next week. In each week, we look at the current demand and the demand for the previous three weeks, creating a window of four weeks. This is why we call this forecast the four-week moving average. The four-week window then moves forward by one week. The new period demand data are entered in the window and the oldest demand window drops out. Just as we can compute the four-week moving

TABLE 13.8
The Moving Average Forecasting Method

Week	Patients per Hospital	1 Week Ago	2 Weeks Ago	3 Weeks Ago	Forecast for Next Week
1	333				
2	392	333			
3	417	392	333		
4	379	417	392	333	380.25
5	396	379	417	392	396
6	393	396	379	417	396.25
7	383	393	396	379	387.75
8	399	383	393	396	392.75
9	419	399	383	393	398.5
10	404	419	399	383	401.25

average, we can compute the two-week, three-week, five-week, six-week, and so on, moving averages. Note that the one-week moving average forecast corresponds to the naïve forecast, because it would just take the average over one (the last) week.

By taking the moving averages, we reduce the effect of the statistical noise. The bigger the window over which we compute the moving averages, the stronger the effect of noise reduction. This begs the question of why not take the average over a large—a really large—window. Can we take a 30-week moving average? The answer to this question is a simple YES, we can. But do we want to?

Recall from our definition of the moving average forecasting method that each week in the forecasting window has an equal weight assigned to it. So, the question this boils down to is: Do we really believe that the demand from 30 weeks ago has as much information in it about the next week as the demand from last week? If the answer to this question is YES, we indeed should use the 30-week moving average. More likely, however, you might argue that the older a demand (the longer ago it happened), the less of an impact it should have on the forecast for the next week. This is exactly the intuition behind our next forecasting method.

Exponential Smoothing Method

The moving average forecasting method implicitly assigns an equal weight to each time period in the window. In contrast, every period outside the window is entirely ignored. For example, when we took the four-week moving average, the current (period t), last ($t - 1$), last but one ($t - 2$), and last but two ($t - 3$) periods all have the same influence on our forecast. In contrast, all periods prior to this have absolutely no influence. Put differently, an old demand value is either in the forecast window or it is out.

The idea of **exponential smoothing** is to put more weight on recent data and less weight on older data. We simply take a weighted average between the current demand and the old demand forecast.

The method works as follows:

$$\begin{matrix}\text{Next period}\\ \text{demand forecast}\end{matrix} = \left[\alpha \times \begin{matrix}\text{Current}\\ \text{demand}\end{matrix}\right] + \left[\left(1 - \alpha\right) \times \begin{matrix}\text{Last period}\\ \text{demand forecast}\end{matrix}\right]$$

Or, put more formally,

$$\hat{y}_{t+1} = (\alpha \times y_t) + (1 - \alpha) \times \hat{y}_t$$

where α is called the *smoothing parameter,* which is a number between zero and one. If α is small (say 0.1), we put little weight on the current demand and thus a lot of weight on old data. In contrast, if α is large (say 0.9), we put a lot of weight on the current demand and thus only a little weight on the old demand. In the extreme case of $\alpha = 1$, we are back to the naïve forecast.

Consider how we would forecast the number of flu cases for week 11. Let's assume a smoothing parameter of $\alpha = 0.1$ and let's assume that the forecast for week 10 was 370. We can compute the new forecast for week 11 as

$$\hat{y}_{t+1} = (\alpha \times y_t) + (1 - \alpha) \times \hat{y}_t$$
$$\hat{y}_{t+1} = (0.1 \times 404) + [(1 - 0.1) \times 370]$$
$$= 373.4$$

Note that this forecast for week 11 is much lower than what we had computed with the naïve forecasting method and the four-week moving average. The reason for this is simply that with $\alpha = 0.1$, we put a lot of weight on the old data. And, as you could see in Figure 13.3, the first-week demand was only 333 patients. This one single period has a very strong influence if we have such a small smoothing parameter. Table 13.9 (left) shows the application of the exponential smoothing for $\alpha = 0.1$. Table 13.9 (right) shows the same calculations, this time with a smoothing parameter of $\alpha = 0.4$.

In this case, as we forecast demand for week 11, we have an old forecast of 402.55 and a realized demand for week 10 of 404. The forecast for week 11 is thus computed as

$$\hat{y}_{t+1} = (\alpha \times y_t) + (1 - \alpha) \times \hat{y}_t$$
$$\hat{y}_{t+1} = (0.4 \times 404) + [(1 - 0.4) \times 402.549]$$
$$= 403.129$$

There exists no general theory for finding the optimal smoothing parameter, but we encourage you to consider the following observations when choosing α:

- *Fit with historical data:* In the previous section, we explained how to evaluate the quality of a forecast and/or a forecaster. You can think of each possible value of α as its own

TABLE 13.9 The Exponential Smoothing Method with $\alpha = 0.1$ (left) and $\alpha = 0.4$ (right)

$\alpha = 0.1$				$\alpha = 0.4$			
Week	Patients per Week	Old Forecast	New Forecast	Week	Patients per Week	Old Forecast	New Forecast
1	333	333	333	1	333	333	333
2	392	333	338.9	2	392	333	356.6
3	417	338.9	346.71	3	417	356.6	380.76
4	379	346.71	349.939	4	379	380.76	380.056
5	396	349.939	354.545	5	396	380.056	386.434
6	393	354.545	358.391	6	393	386.434	389.060
7	383	358.391	360.852	7	383	389.060	386.636
8	399	360.852	364.666	8	399	386.636	391.582
9	419	364.666	370.100	9	419	391.582	402.549
10	404	370.100	373.490	10	404	402.549	403.129

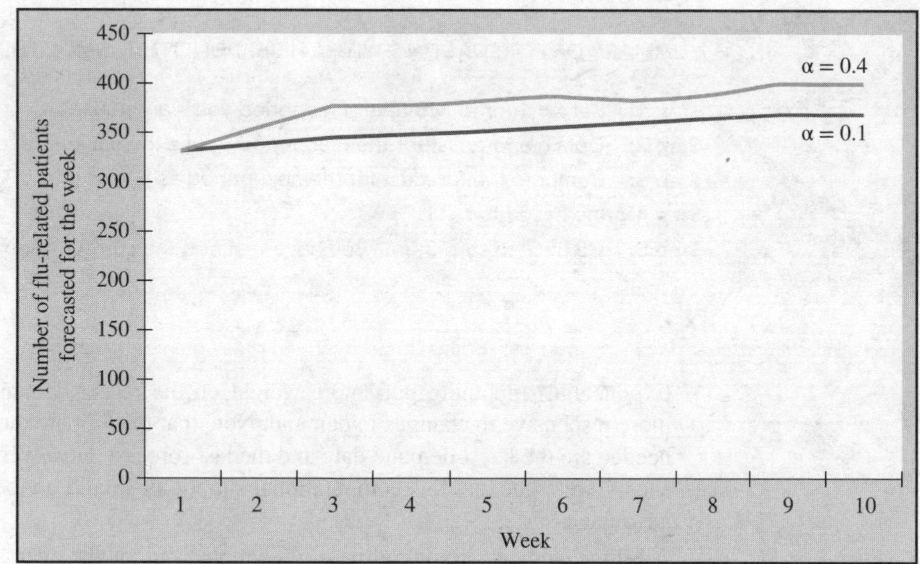

FIGURE 13.4
Comparison of Two Exponential Smoothing Forecasts, Using Different Values of the Smoothing Parameter α

set of forecasts. We can then use historical data and compare the mean squared errors or the mean absolute errors for different values of α.

- *Importance of new information:* Note that the higher smoothing parameter puts a much larger weight on the more recent data. In a fast-changing world, this favors higher values of α, corresponding to a range of $0.2 < \alpha < 0.4$. If one wants to be more conservative and thus assign a larger weight to old data, one ought to choose smaller values of α, such that $0.05 < \alpha < 0.2$.

Figure 13.4 shows the effect of using two different smoothing parameters. Observe that the line for the lower value of α (with $\alpha = 0.1$) is much "smoother"; that is, it does not change as much from one period to the next as the line with $\alpha = 0.4$.

Another practical question is how to get started with the exponential smoothing method. After all, the method assumes that you have had an exponentially smoothed forecast in the last period. To come up with the first (initial forecast), we suggest you use the naïve forecasting method; that is, simply use the last available demand data. Note that the longer ago the initial period is, the lower the importance of the initial forecast. Especially for larger values of α, the old data matter less and less as time progresses.

Exhibit 13.1 summarizes the previously discussed approach of exponential smoothing.

Comparison of Methods

So far, we have introduced three methods of forecasting based on time series analysis: the naïve method, moving averages, and exponential smoothing. Before we turn to more sophisticated methods, let's pause for a moment and reflect upon the strengths and weaknesses of these approaches:

- The naïve method is very vulnerable to noise. One period of exceptionally high (or low) demand data will likely make the next period forecast highly incorrect. We see no reason to use this method in practice.
- Moving averages take care of statistical noise by averaging it out. One has to choose the length of the window over which the average is taken. All periods in the forecast window are weighted equally when computing the new forecast.

Exhibit 13.1

SUMMARY OF FORECASTING WITH THE EXPONENTIAL SMOOTHING METHOD

Step 1: Set $t = 1$ (or to whatever first period you want to use).
Step 2: Obtain a forecast for the first period $\hat{y}_t$; use the naïve forecasting method for this.
Step 3: Compute the forecast for the next period as $\hat{y}_{t+1} = (\alpha \times y_t) + (1 - \alpha) \times \hat{y}_t$
Step 4: Increase t to $t + 1$.
Step 5: Go back to step 3 until you have reached the current period.

- Exponential smoothing puts more weight on the recent demand data. This makes it more responsive to changes in demand. Note that to compute the new forecast, all data needed are the latest demand data and the last forecast. However, in a world of spreadsheets, we argue that this computational simplicity should not be seen as too big of an advantage.
- All three methods are data-driven. As simple (and maybe even simplistic, see the previous point) as they might be, they help establish a managerial discipline of collecting data, and they also support a statistical analysis of old forecast errors.

All three methods fail to detect systemic variation in the data. Patterns such as long-term trends (for example, the demand rate going up over time) or seasonal variation (more patients suffering from the flu in January than in June) are not captured in any of these methods. More advanced methods are needed, as we will explore in the next two sections.

13.4 Time Series Analysis—Trends

Given the way they are constructed, all of the three previously introduced forecasting methods (naïve method, moving averages, and exponential smoothing) are backward looking. The next period's demand is forecasted by taking old demand realizations and then somehow finding a "compromise" between these values. As a result, none of these methods is able to create a forecast that is higher than any of the previously realized demand values or that is lower than any of the previously realized demand values.

Many demand rates in practice, however, are characterized by long-term trends. In these cases, it oftentimes is entirely plausible to expect the next period demand to exceed (or fall short of) any realization of past demand. Consider the following three examples captured in Figure 13.5:

- The social network site Facebook had only a couple of million users in 2006. However, by 2013, the number of users had reached 1 billion.
- From 2006 to 2013, demand for motor vehicles in China was growing by over 10 percent each year, making each new year a record in sales.
- Trends don't only go up. Consider the circulation of newspapers in the United Kingdom. Year after year, the number has been shrinking.

Facebook users, vehicle demand in China, or newspapers—all three examples have in common that there seems to exist a long-term trend. We define a *trend* as a continuing increase or decrease in a variable that is consistent over a long period of time. When you have to forecast the number of Facebook users in 2010 for 2011, would you really want to take an average over the last three years? Or would it make more sense to extrapolate the trend going forward?

FIGURE 13.5 **Examples of Demand Trajectories Including a Long-Term Trend**

(Sources: http://en.wikipedia.org/wiki/Facebook, http://www.shanghaijungle.com/news/China-Auto-Sales-Rise-9, http://blogs.spectator.co.uk/coffeehouse/2013/06/david-dinsmore-is-the-new-editor-of-the-sun)

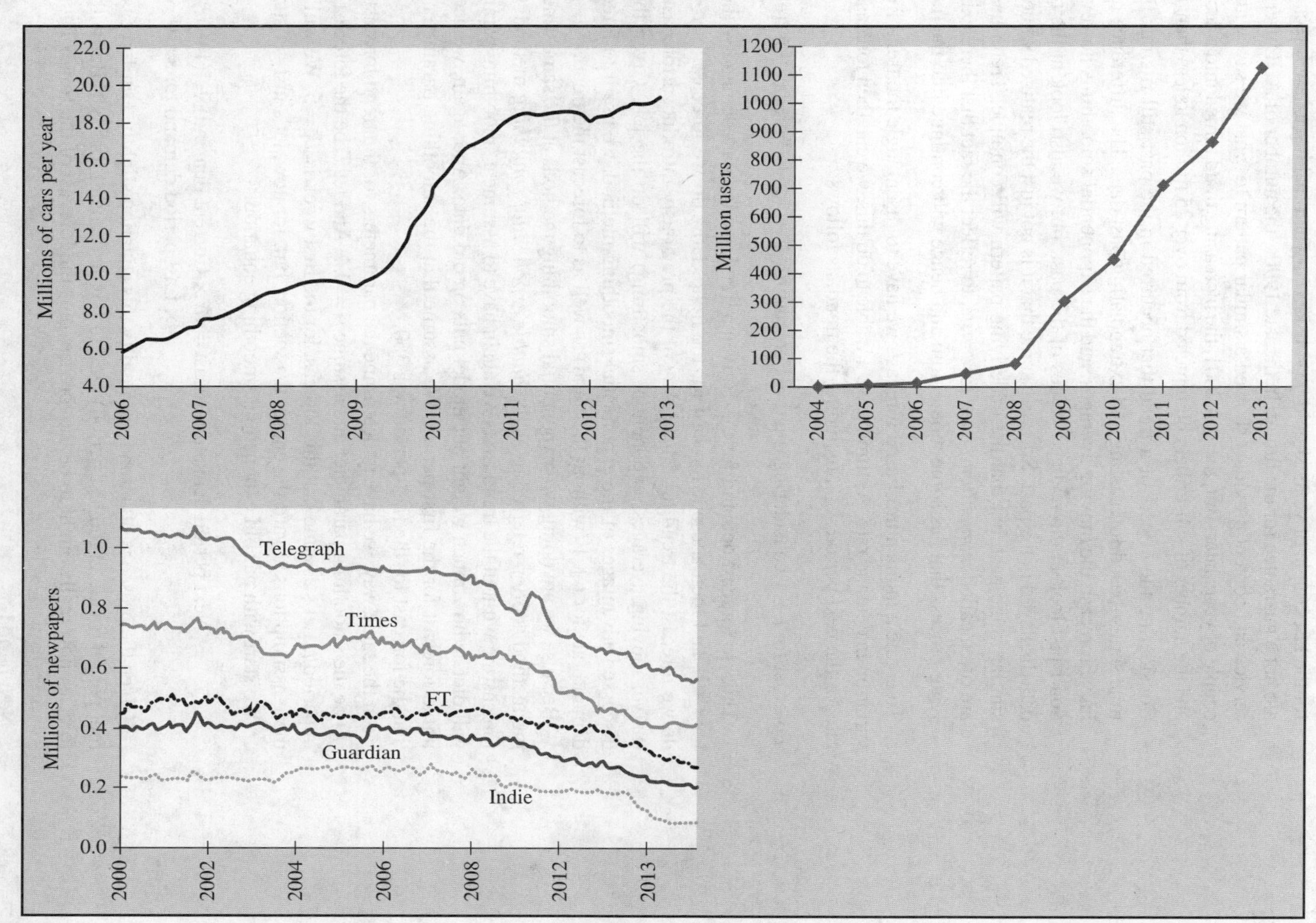

We now introduce a method that extends our previous forecasting methods to business settings characterized by a long-term trend. We should preface this extension with two remarks:

- Trends are statistically observed patterns in old data. The fact that a trend has been present for the last couple of years should be considered when making a new forecast. But trends are not a guarantee for the future. In the late 1990s, the number of AOL users (an Internet service and content provider) showed a similar pattern to what we saw with Facebook a couple of years later. But, then, in 2001, the increasing trend turned into a decreasing trend and the number of subscribers plummeted from over 25 million to less than 10 million.
- Considering the effects of a trend that occurred in the past still fits our framework of time series–based forecasting and extrapolating past data. The difference relative to the naïve forecast, the moving averages, and the exponential smoothing, however, is that we don't just look at the realized values of the past, but we also look at the trend that the data displayed in the past. So, we assume that it is not just the realized values that will be similar to the past, but that the underlying pattern will continue. Trend-based forecasts are often called *momentum-based forecasts*, to reflect the fact that there exists an underlying process that has some momentum and hence will continue into the future.

To create a momentum-based forecast, we have to disentangle the trend from the other variation in demand rate. Assuming we are able to do this, we can then forecast the demand rate for the next period, $\hat{y}_{t+1}$, including the trend, as follows:

$$\text{Forecast for } t + 1 \text{ considering trend} = \text{Forecast for } (t + 1) + \text{Forecast for trend in } (t + 1)$$

Thus, to forecast demand for $t + 1$ given a trend, we forecast demand without the trend for $t + 1$ and then add our forecast for the trend. How do we forecast for $t + 1$ and how do we forecast the trend for $t + 1$? Any of the previously introduced forecasting methods (naïve, moving averages, exponential smoothing) will do the job. Given the previously discussed advantages of the exponential smoothing method, we use it to forecast both the demand rate for $t + 1$ (without the trend) as well as to forecast the trend.

Because we are doing two exponential smoothing methods at the same time, the following method is often referred to as the *double exponential smoothing* method. Consider the forecasting without the trend first. We again have to assume a smoothing parameter, α, that will dictate how much weight our model puts on old data. And, again, we need to have an initial forecast for the first period. We assume that the smoothing parameter $\alpha = 0.2$ and that the forecast for the first period was 360.

In the same way, we have to determine the parameters for the trend forecasting. Let beta (β) be the smoothing parameter and assume $\beta = 0.4$. And let T_t be the forecast for the trend in period t. Let's assume that this forecast for the first week is $T_1 = 5$. We will comment on these assumptions toward the end of the section, but, for now, let's just get started.

We start with our old exponential smoothing equation:

$$\text{Next period demand forecast} = (\alpha \times \text{Current demand}) + [(1 - \alpha) \times \text{Last period demand forecast}]$$

Given the presence of a trend, we modify this equation slightly. Our forecast for the current period (made in the last period) used to be the demand forecast. But with a trend, the forecast now really ought to be the forecast plus the forecast of the trend. Thus, we write

$$\begin{matrix}\text{Next period} \\ \text{demand} \\ \text{forecast}\end{matrix} = \underbrace{(\alpha \times \text{Current demand}) + \left[(1 - \alpha) \times \begin{matrix}\text{Last period} \\ \text{demand forecast}\end{matrix}\right]}_{\text{Smoothed demand forecast}} + \underbrace{\begin{matrix}\text{Forecast} \\ \text{for trend}\end{matrix}}_{\text{Added trend}}$$

And, to keep an up-to-date forecast of the trend, we forecast the trend using the exponential smoothing method:

$$\text{Trend forecast} = (\beta \times \text{Current trend}) + [(1 - \beta) \times \text{Old trend forecast}]$$

The current realization of the trend is the difference between the old and the new demand forecasts. We can rewrite this to

$$\text{Trend forecast} = [\beta \times (\text{New demand forecast} - \text{Old demand forecast})] + [(1 - \beta) \times \text{Old trend forecast}]$$

So, as we obtain new data for period *t,* we create a new forecast for period $t + 1$ by

- Exponentially smoothing the demand forecast and then forecasting the next period demand as the smoothed demand rate plus our forecast for the trend.
- Exponentially smoothing the trend forecast and then updating our trend forecast for the next period.

This is why we called this method the double exponential smoothing method.

More formally, define the following:

y_t: realized demand in period t

$\hat{y}_{t+1}$: forecasted demand for period $t + 1$ obtained via exponential smoothing using smoothing parameter α

$\hat{T}_t$: forecasted trend for period $t + 1$ obtained via exponential smoothing using smoothing parameter β

With this notation, we write the demand rate exponential smoothing as

$$\hat{y}_{t+1} = (\alpha \times y_t) + [(1 - \alpha) \times \hat{y}_t] + \hat{T}_t$$

and the exponentially smoothed trend as

$$\hat{T}_{t+1} = [\beta \times (\hat{y}_{t+1} - \hat{y}_t)] + (1 - \beta)\,\hat{T}_t$$

where $(\hat{y}_{t+1} - \hat{y}_t)$ can be thought of as our latest estimate of our trend.

Let's illustrate this method with some more flu data, specifically the data shown in Table 13.10. It is week 1 and we want to make a forecast for week 2. Recall that we assumed a smoothing parameter $\alpha = 0.2$, a forecast for the first period of 360, a trend smoothing parameter $\beta = 0.4$, and an initial trend forecast of $\hat{T} = 5$.

With this information, we can compute the smoothed demand forecast:

$$\begin{aligned}\hat{y}_{t+1} &= (\alpha \times y_t) + [(1 - \alpha) \times \hat{y}_t] + \hat{T}_t \\ &= (0.2 \times 377) + [(1 - 0.2) \times 360] + 5 \\ &= 368.4\end{aligned}$$

TABLE 13.10 Number of Flu Patients at the Beginning of the 2013 Flu Season

Week	Patients
1	377
2	402
3	409
4	413
5	428
6	409
7	446
8	458
9	462

TABLE 13.11 Trend Forecast with the Double Exponential Smoothing Method

Week	Patients	Forecast for Next Period ($\alpha = 0.2$)	Trend Forecast ($\beta = 0.4$)
		360.000	5.000
1	377	368.400	6.360
2	402	381.480	9.048
3	409	396.032	11.250
4	413	410.675	12.607
5	428	426.747	13.993
6	409	437.191	12.573
7	446	451.526	13.278
8	458	466.099	13.796
9	462	479.075	13.468

and the exponentially smoothed trend as

$$\begin{aligned}\hat{T}_{t+1} &= [\beta \times (\hat{y}_{t+1} - \hat{y}_t)] + (1 - \beta) \times \hat{T}_t \\ &= [0.4 \times (368.4 - 360)] + [(1 - 0.4) \times 5] \\ &= 6.36\end{aligned}$$

Table 13.11 shows all calculations for the next periods.

Figure 13.6 compares the realized value of the demand with the forecasted demand. Unlike the realized demand data, the forecasted data do not show the many ups and downs—instead, it is steadily increasing over time. This is a result of smoothing. The first smoothing reduces any ups and downs. The second smoothing makes sure that the trend is relatively steady, creating almost a constant increase from one period to the next.

Exhibit 13.2 summarizes the previously discussed approach dealing with trends in forecasting.

A couple of comments are in order about the double exponential smoothing method:

- The double exponential smoothing method is an additive method. Every period, we add the forecasted (smoothed) trend to our demand forecast. Often, however, trends are

FIGURE 13.6 Trend Forecast with the Double Exponential Smoothing Method

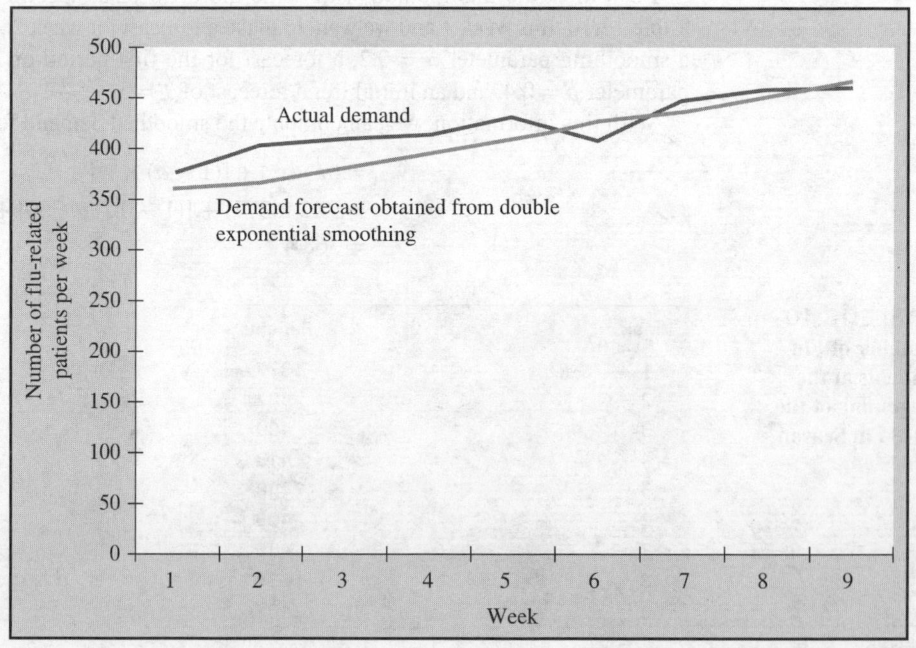

Exhibit 13.2

SUMMARY OF FORECASTING ADJUSTING FOR TRENDS: THE DOUBLE EXPONENTIAL SMOOTHING METHOD

Step 1: Set $t = 1$ (or to whatever first period you want to use).

Step 2: Obtain a forecast for the first period $\hat{y}_t$ and a forecast for the first trend $\hat{T}_t$. Use the naïve forecast in the first period.

Step 3: Compute the smoothed forecast for the next period as

$$\hat{y}_{t+1} = (\alpha \times y_t) + [(1 - \alpha) \times \hat{y}_t] + \hat{T}_t$$

Step 4: Compute the smoothed forecast for the trend as

$$\hat{T}_{t+1} = [\beta \times (\hat{y}_{t+1} - \hat{y}_t)] + (1 - \beta) \times \hat{T}_t$$

Step 5: Increase t to $t + 1$.

Step 6: Go back to step 3 until you have reached the current period.

not additive, but multiplicative in nature. Facebook did not add 1 million users every year. Instead, it grew its users exponentially every year. In such cases of rapid growth, the double exponential smoothing method will underestimate the demand for the next period. One way of handling demand data with exponential growth is to not forecast demand y_t, but the logarithm of demand $\log(y_t)$. If demand grows exponentially, the logarithm of demand grows linearly.

- As with the simple exponential smoothing method, we need to pick a value for the smoothing parameter. The only difference, this time, is that we have to pick values for two smoothing parameters. The smoothing parameters need to be numbers between zero and one. Larger values put more weight on recent observations. Again, looking at old data and seeing which values of α and β fit the data best is a good starting point.
- There exist other, more mathematically sophisticated methods of estimating trends, including the previously mentioned regression analysis. However, we find that this increased sophistication often comes at the expense of transparency. The more math we use, the harder it becomes to know what really goes on "under the hood" of a forecasting method. In our view, the double exponential smoothing method is a good compromise between transparency and ease of use on the one side and mathematical sophistication on the other side.
- There exist no big shortcomings of the double exponential smoothing method as long as the data follow a long-term trend with some variation around this trend. In fact, the method also is perfectly applicable in the case of no trend. However, to the extent that there exists some form of seasonality pattern, the method does not work well, especially if low values of β are chosen. In such cases, it is much better to either pick a very high value of β, or, better still, use the method described in the next section.

13.5 Time Series Analysis—Seasonality

Trends are one type of pattern that we can observe in our past demand data. Our logic in the previous section can be summarized as "if it rose in the past, it will rise in the future." Another commonly observed pattern in demand data relates to seasonality. We define *seasonality* as a significant demand change that constitutes a repetitive fluctuation over time. This fluctuation can happen at any frequency, including an hourly, daily, weekly, monthly,

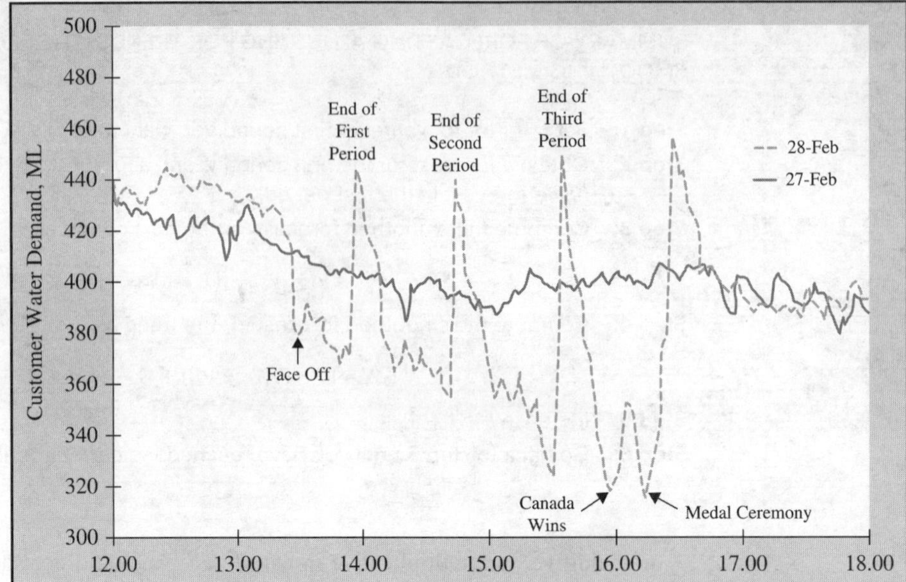

FIGURE 13.7 Water Consumption in Edmonton (Canada) During the Olympic Gold Medal Hockey Game

(Source: http://www.smartplanet.com/blog/smart-takes/infographic-water-consumption-in-edmonton-canada-during-olympic-gold-medal-hockey-game/)

or yearly recurrence of the season. Seasonality stands in contrast to the previously introduced concept of statistical noise. The key difference is that the repetitiveness of the pattern in the old data in the case of seasonality makes us confident to predict that this pattern will continue into the future. In the case of statistical noise, however, we would not be willing to extrapolate the data.

Figure 13.7 shows an illustration of seasonality in water consumption. It is a little odd for an example, but we believe that will make you more likely to remember it. The dotted line shows the water consumption for the city of Edmonton, Canada, on February 28, 2010. February 28, 2010, was a special day for the Canadians because their hockey team was playing for Olympic gold. Half of Canada was glued to their TV screens watching the live broadcast of the game—except, of course, during the breaks between quarters. We can only speculate what Canadians were drinking and what exactly they did during the breaks, but they certainly needed a lot of water (and, we argue, it is unlikely that they took a shower between the quarters).

The pattern in Figure 13.7 is an example of seasonality. The spikes in water consumption are not the outcome of randomness; they reflect significant demand changes causing a repetitive fluctuation of water demand.

Seasonality is by no means limited to bathroom breaks during hockey games. Instead, it is a common pattern in the practice of operations, as the following examples help illustrate:

- *Amazon:* Amazon faces dramatic increases in their demand in the months of November and December. People order gifts for the holidays. These increases oftentimes require a doubling or tripling of capacity. So, predicting them ahead of time is important. And because these demand increases are clearly a result of seasonality (as opposed to resulting from variability), there exists no reason why the company should not be able to plan for it.
- *Flu data:* As you saw in the beginning of the chapter (Figure 13.1), demand for medical services and pharmaceutical products related to the flu is not entirely a result of randomness. True, each flu season might differ in terms of severity and the exact start date, but strong seasonal patterns can be observed.
- *Rush hour traffic:* If you are commuting to school or work during rush hour, you know the effect. Demand for toll booth capacity and road space is much higher from 7–9 a.m.

TABLE 13.12
Number of Patients Showing Up in the Emergency Department

Week	Day of Week	ED Visits
1	Monday	265
	Tuesday	260
	Wednesday	255
	Thursday	261
	Friday	264
	Saturday	220
	Sunday	255
2	Monday	290
	Tuesday	250
	Wednesday	222
	Thursday	230
	Friday	282
	Saturday	211
	Sunday	215
3	Monday	280
	Tuesday	261
	Wednesday	230
	Thursday	240
	Friday	271
	Saturday	223
	Sunday	228

and from 4–6 p.m. The exact seasonal pattern varies by metropolitan area (cities with manufacturing labor tend to work earlier in the day, while bankers show up to work later), but it is certainly predictable.

We now introduce a forecasting method that allows us to handle seasonality. We will again use data from the emergency department, with Table 13.12 showing the last three weeks of arrival data, and Figure 13.8, the distribution of daily arrivals over the seven days in a week (so each day of the week in Figure 13.8 corresponds to three data points in Table 13.12).

The first step of our forecasting method incorporating seasonality is to determine the seasonality pattern. Are we facing a season within a day, within a week, within a year, or

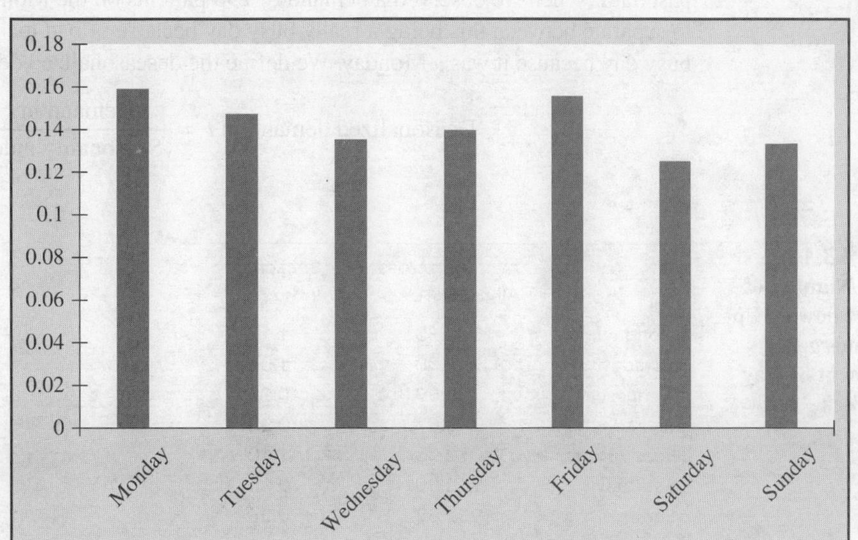

FIGURE 13.8
Day of the Week Seasonality

another recurring fluctuation? For the purpose of this chapter, we find it sufficient to simply "eyeball" past data and apply some basic knowledge about the operations that we face. Patients are most likely to go to the ED on Mondays—the weekends tend to be calmer (see Figure 13.8). More formal statistical tests can be used to confirm such patterns. We thus decide on a seasonality at the level of the day of the week.

In the second step, we try to quantify the effect of seasonality. We will illustrate this with a weekly seasonality, in which the seasonality pattern recurs every seven days (periods). The method easily extends to 24 hours a day, 12 months a year, or any other seasonality you might think of.

We compute the average demand per time period as

$$\text{Average demand} = \text{Average}\,(y_t,\ t = 1\ .\ .\ .\ N)$$

We then compute the average demand for Mondays as

$$\text{Average Monday demand} = \text{Average}\,(y_t,\ t = 1\ .\ .\ .\ N,\ t = \text{Monday})$$

In the same way, we can define the average demand for Tuesdays, Wednesdays, and all other days of the week. Of course, if seasonality is not a weekly pattern, but a monthly pattern, we would do this for each of the 12 months in the year. Or we could do this for the 24 hours in the day or the four quarters in the year. This is entirely a question of what time periods constitute the seasonality. Equipped with the average demand across all periods and average demand for each day in the week, we can then compute the *seasonality index (SI)* for each day of the week:

$$\text{Seasonality index Monday} = \text{SI}_{\text{Monday}} = \frac{\text{Average Monday demand}}{\text{Average total demand}}$$

Table 13.13 shows this for our ED example. We see that the seasonality index for Monday is greater than one, reflecting that more patients go to the ED on Monday. A seasonality index of 1.12 can be interpreted as Monday demand being 12 percent greater than the average demand. Similarly, we interpret the seasonality index for Saturday, which is 0.88, as indicating that Saturday has about 12 percent less demand than the average day of the week.

Equipped with the seasonality indices, we now turn back to our raw data in Table 13.3. For each of the old time periods (in our case, days), we *deseasonalize* the old demand. To deseasonalize (a word that is not in the dictionary) means to remove the seasonal effect from past data. When we observed a demand of 290 patients on the Monday in week 2, we have to separate between this being a really busy day because of bad luck and this being a really busy day because it was a Monday. We define the deseasonalized demand for period t as

$$\text{Deasonalized demand in } t = \frac{\text{Demand in } t}{\text{Seasonality index}}$$

TABLE 13.13
Average Number of Patients Showing Up in the Emergency Department by Day of the Week

	Average across All x-days	Seasonality Index
Monday	278.33	1.12
Tuesday	257.00	1.04
Wednesday	235.67	0.95
Thursday	243.67	0.98
Friday	272.33	1.10
Saturday	218.00	0.88
Sunday	232.67	0.94

TABLE 13.14 Number of Patients Showing Up in the Emergency Department Adjusted for Seasonality Effects

Week	Day of Week	ER Visits	Seasonality Index (SI)	Deasonalized (ER Visits/SI)
1	Monday	265	1.12	236.35
	Tuesday	260	1.04	251.14
	Wednesday	255	0.95	268.60
	Thursday	261	0.98	265.90
	Friday	264	1.10	240.64
	Saturday	220	0.88	250.52
	Sunday	255	0.94	272.07
2	Monday	290	1.12	258.64
	Tuesday	250	1.04	241.48
	Wednesday	222	0.95	233.84
	Thursday	230	0.98	234.32
	Friday	282	1.10	257.05
	Saturday	211	0.88	240.27
	Sunday	215	0.94	229.39
3	Monday	280	1.12	249.72
	Tuesday	261	1.04	252.10
	Wednesday	230	0.95	242.27
	Thursday	240	0.98	244.50
	Friday	271	1.10	247.02
	Saturday	223	0.88	253.93
	Sunday	228	0.94	243.26

In our case, we have

$$\text{Deseasonalized demand in } t = \frac{290}{1.12} = 258.64$$

These calculations are shown in Table 13.14. Note the effect of deasonalizing the data by comparing the Sunday of week 1 (255 patients) with the Monday of week 2 (290 patients). Looking at the demand data alone, one might think of the 290 patients being a much greater demand rate. However, if one adjusts for the effect that Sundays tend to be 6 percent less busy ($SI_{Sunday} = 0.94$) and Mondays tend to be 12 percent more busy ($SI_{Monday} = 1.12$), we actually find that the Sunday of week 1 was the bigger surprise to the ED.

Once we have removed the seasonality from the old demand data by deseasonalizing them, we can proceed as we did before. Each time period still includes a fair bit of noise (see our discussion from the Sunday in week 1 compared to the Monday in week 2). Now that the effect of seasonality is removed, all variation that is left is a result of statistical noise. Some days have more patients and some have less. And we know how to deal with statistical noise—we can rely on either moving averages or exponential smoothing.

Using a smoothing parameter of $\alpha = 0.25$ and an initial forecast for the first Monday of 240, Table 13.15 shows this smoothing process. Each day, we obtain a smoothed forecast, combining the latest data with the old forecast as discussed earlier. As the old data come to an end, we have a last smoothed forecast of 246.45 patients for the next day.

How do we interpret this amount of 246.45 patients? Recall that we are looking at data that have been both deseasonalized and smoothed. Thus, our forecast for an average day in the next week would be 246.45 patients. However, the first day we have to forecast for is a Monday and we know that Monday is not an average day of the week. So, at this last step, in the seasonality-adjusted forecasting method, we have to reseasonalize the data. Again, we are not sure if reseasonalizing is an actual word, but it captures what we mean: We have to bring back the effect of seasonality that we previously took out of the data. This is done

TABLE 13.15 Smoothed Number of Patients Showing Up in the Emergency Department after Adjusting for Seasonality

Week	Day of Week	ER Visits	Seasonality Index (SI)	Deasonalized (ER Visits/SI)	Smoothed Forecast (alpha = 0.25, Week 1 Monday forecast 240)
1	Monday	265	1.12	236.35	239.09
	Tuesday	260	1.04	251.14	242.10
	Wednesday	255	0.95	268.60	248.72
	Thursday	261	0.98	265.90	253.02
	Friday	264	1.10	240.64	249.92
	Saturday	220	0.88	250.52	250.07
	Sunday	255	0.94	272.07	255.57
2	Monday	290	1.12	258.64	256.34
	Tuesday	250	1.04	241.48	252.62
	Wednesday	222	0.95	233.84	247.93
	Thursday	230	0.98	234.32	244.52
	Friday	282	1.10	257.05	247.66
	Saturday	211	0.88	240.27	245.81
	Sunday	215	0.94	229.39	241.70
3	Monday	280	1.12	249.72	243.71
	Tuesday	261	1.04	252.10	245.81
	Wednesday	230	0.95	242.27	244.92
	Thursday	240	0.98	244.50	244.82
	Friday	271	1.10	247.02	245.37
	Saturday	223	0.88	253.93	247.51
	Sunday	228	0.94	243.26	246.45

simply by computing the forecasts as the product of the smoothed forecast for an average day and the appropriate seasonality index:

$$\text{Forecast for next Monday} = \text{Smoothed forecast for an average day} \times SI_{\text{Monday}}$$

Table 13.16 shows these data. We have extrapolated the past demand data by imposing the previously observed seasonality pattern. Simple and elegant!

A couple of further comments on forecasting with seasonality are in order:

- An important building block in the previously introduced method was the estimation of the seasonality indices, SI. We estimated the SI by simply averaging over old data; for example, by computing the SI_{Monday} by averaging across all Mondays. Instead of averaging these values, we could also have applied an exponential smoothing method. In that case, we would have a smoothing parameter for the seasonality index that would get updated in the way we updated the trend forecast in the double exponential smoothing method.

TABLE 13.16 Forecasted Number of Patients Showing Up in the Emergency Department after Reseasonalizing the Data

Week	Day of Week	Base	SI	Forecast (Base × SI)
4	Monday	246.45	1.12	276.33
	Tuesday	246.45	1.04	255.15
	Wednesday	246.45	0.95	233.97
	Thursday	246.45	0.98	241.91
	Friday	246.45	1.10	270.37
	Saturday	246.45	0.88	216.43
	Sunday	246.45	0.94	230.99

Exhibit 13.3

SUMMARY OF FORECASTING WHEN ADJUSTING FOR SEASONALITY

Step 1: Determine the seasonality pattern.

Step 2: Compute the seasonality index for all seasons:

$$SI_{Season} = \frac{\text{Average season demand}}{\text{Average total demand}}$$

Step 3: For all time periods *t*, deseasonalize the data:

$$\text{Deseasonalized demand in } t = \frac{\text{Demand in } t}{SI(t)}$$

Step 4: For all time periods *t*, apply exponential smoothing to deseasonalized demand.

Step 5: Compute the average forecast as the smoothed value for the last period.

Step 6: Reseasonalize the data: Forecast for $s > t$ = Smoothed forecast for last period $\times SI_s$

- We assumed the effect of seasonality to be a multiplicative effect. We deseasonalized by dividing by the appropriate SI and we reseasonalized by multiplying by it. Note that when we handled trends in the previous section, we assumed the trend was additive, as we estimated the new demand and then added the adjustment for the trend. Whether to use an additive or multiplicative model for trends or seasonality really is best answered by trying out the methods on past data.
- There are lots of bells and whistles that could be added to this model. However, we feel that this model is pretty good and gets you as far as you can get without using regression analysis. More sophisticated regression models allow you to combine the effects of trends, seasonality, and other explanatory variables into one single, integrated model. But that really is a story for another day.

Exhibit 13.3 summarizes this forecasting method.

13.6 Expert Panels and Subjective Forecasting

The approaches discussed in the previous sections share two advantages. First, forecasting methods that follow a mathematical algorithm are efficient and thus can be automated. This is especially important in operational settings where we need to make daily or even hourly forecasts across many locations. Second, these methods are based on hard data—there is no wiggle room for feelings, opinions, and other soft stuff.

However, no matter the sophistication of the analytical forecasting methods, all of them have in common that they assume that the future will be like the past. Some patterns will be extrapolated—but there is no room for human intelligence. The forecast is produced by a method, not a human being.

Sometimes, you want to allow for human input into the forecasting method. In such cases, we speak about creating a **subjective forecast.** There are many ways in which you can take the opinion(s) of one or multiple persons as an input and then turn out a forecast as an output. Depending on who gets involved in the process and how the individual opinions are synthesized, we find it helpful to distinguish between three types of subjective forecasting methods.

- *Forecast combination:* Each forecaster will use different mental models to make a forecast. Most likely, each of the forecasters will be wrong at least occasionally, creating some forecast errors. The idea of forecast combination is to average the forecasts of multiple forecasters in the hope that the forecast errors will at least partially average themselves out. John is an optimist, Mary a pessimist, but if we average their forecasts, the hope is that the laws of statistics will kick in and the resulting forecast will be a better one. There exists a fair bit of research supporting this claim. Many ways to combine the forecasts have been presented, but the simplest one is to just take the average across the forecasts done by each forecaster individually.
- *Forecast with consensus building:* Instead of just collecting the forecasts of several experts and then averaging them, we can also ask each expert to explain how she arrived at her forecast. This has the potential to facilitate information sharing: Mary might know that the Chinese market is growing, while John has some insights into the U.S. market. Having Mary and John exchange that knowledge before they forecast is thus a good idea that will make both of their forecasts a better one. A common problem in such meetings is a phenomenon called **groupthink**—where all the experts agree, although the outcome is fundamentally wrong and unlikely. Groupthink can be a result of all experts using the same information (in which case, the idea of forecast errors being averaged out simply does not make sense). Oftentimes, groupthink also reflects fears of disagreement with more senior managers. To counter this problem, we suggest the following: (a) Have participating members first individually and independently create their own forecasts. These data are then a starting point for discussion. During the discussion, special attention should be given to the highest and lowest values of the individual forecasts with the request to the associated forecasters to explain the logic behind their forecasts. (b) Any discussion should start with the most junior experts in the group. A senior executive is more likely to voice her own opinion. A more junior manager is at bigger risk of feeling the pressure to conform. So, by having the senior expert speak last, we get the true beliefs of everybody.
- *Prediction markets:* Imagine you and your classmates go to a horse race but have no knowledge about any of the participating horses. At the race you get asked, "Who is going to win?" You could just ask each of your classmates to make a prediction about the horses' performance and then take some form of an average. This is the idea of the forecast combination. But why not take a look at the betting odds published by the horse track? If, at the betting office, they offer you $25 for a $1 bet for a victory by horse A and only $3 for a victory by horse B, wouldn't you think that horse B is a faster horse? So, instead of relying on yourself and your classmates, unknowledgeable (and potentially even unmotivated) as you are, why not rely on the people who have put their money on this? The idea of prediction markets is that prices can help to aggregate information. For example, if we promise to pay you $1 if our new product sells at least 1 million units, and you are willing to pay us $0.10 for that promise, that means you believe that the likelihood of selling 1 million is low (10 percent to be exact). If somebody feels that he has better information than the current market price, he can trade on that information, thereby moving the future price. If somebody feels that she has better information but would not be willing to trade on this information, we should probably not put too much weight on her opinion either.

Unlike the automated methods of time series extrapolation, subjective forecasts have the potential to be forward looking. They use management intuition and human intelligence to either replace or augment the forecasts done by our models. That is the biggest strength of subjective forecasting. However, as we will discuss in the next section, this is also its biggest weakness.

Sources of Forecasting Biases

We previously defined a biased forecast as a forecast that not only is wrong, but it is wrong on average. In other words, forecasts display a consistent pattern between the outcomes predicted in the forecasts and the actually realized outcomes. Biases exist in all types of human decision making, though they are particularly prevalent in the world of forecasting. The reason for this is that when we forecast, by definition we don't know yet if we are right or wrong. So, "talk is cheap" and the outcome is in a distant future. In forecasting and beyond, the most common biases to be aware of are the following:

- *Overconfidence:* One of the strongest results in the literature on human decision making is that we all overestimate how smart we are. As a result, we are overly confident in succeeding and we are overly confident in being right in terms of our forecast for the future. On the other hand, we underestimate the role of luck (risk) and the effect of others. As a result, we forecast our sales higher and we are more optimistic with respect to the success of our new product launches.
- *Anchoring:* As human decision makers, we oftentimes pick a piece of information and then have this piece dictate how we handle new information. That initial piece of information sets a reference point. Consider a new student venture that is forecasting demand for the future. If the student team uses Facebook's growth as a reference point, it simply will bias the team toward an unrealistic demand trajectory.
- *Incentive alignment:* In the previous two biases, decision makers were caught in their own cognitive decision-making process. They tried their best, but they were subjected to overconfidence and anchoring without realizing it. In forecasting, another bias often results from incentives and personal objectives that the forecasters might have. When asked for their forecast, forecasters know that the forecast is used to make a decision. That decision will most likely impact their work. So, it is only rational for these forecasters to start with the preferred outcome of that decision and then work backward to the forecast that is likely to trigger that decision. For example, a salesperson wants to make sure there is enough inventory in the supply chain so he can fulfill all customer demand. He also knows that the higher the demand he forecasts, the more units the factory will produce and put into the supply chain. For a salesperson who is paid a commission on sales, it is hence only rational to forecast a demand that is much greater than what he truly believes. This behavior of not truthfully sharing one's forecast with the intent of achieving a certain outcome is called *forecast gaming* or **forecast inflation** (because, typically, the resulting forecast is higher than the actual).

The best way to deal with bias is feedback. Those who forecast should always be confronted with the forecasts they made in the past. Forecast errors should be measured and analyzed for the presence of biases. That way, the forecasting process can be improved over time, just as we like to improve any other operational process in our business.

13.7 Conclusion

Forecasting demand has a substantial impact on many operational decisions we take and thus on the future of the overall business. So, forecasting well is critical. In the absence of a crystal ball, good forecasting means to carefully choose the forecasting method. As we saw, each of the quantitative methods had its strengths and weaknesses. No one best method exists.

Beyond the mathematical modeling, the process of forecasting is embedded into an organizational context. Understanding this context is important.

When implementing a forecasting process in practice, we suggest the following five-step approach:

1. Collect data, including old demand forecasts (subjective data) and the actual demand outcomes.
2. Establish the forecasting method: Decide on the balance between subjective and objective data and look for trends and seasonality.
3. Forecast future demand using a forecasting method.
4. Make decisions based on step 3.
5. Measure the forecast error; look for biases and improve the process.

13.8 Practice Problems

The following questions will help in testing your understanding of this chapter. After each question, we show the relevant section in parentheses [Section x].

Q13.1 Jim and John run a barber shop. Every night, both of them predict how many guests will come on the next day. Over the last four days, they have collected some data about their predictions and the actual outcome. Jim predicts the number of guests to be 56 for day 1, 50 for day 2, 45 for day 3, and 59 for day 4. John predicts 47, 49, 51, and 51 for the four respective days. The actual numbers of guests turn out to be 45, 51, 41, and 61. Who has the bigger forecast bias? What are the MSE and the MAE for Jim and John? [13.2]

Q13.2 Tom's Towing LLC operates a fleet of tow trucks that it sends to help drivers in need on the nearby highway. The numbers of calls requesting a tow truck for Monday, Tuesday, Wednesday, and Thursday were 27, 18, 21, and 15, respectively. What would be its forecast for Friday using a naïve forecasting approach? [13.3]

Q13.3 Tom's Towing LLC operates a fleet of tow trucks that it sends to help drivers in need on the nearby highway. The numbers of calls requesting a tow truck for Monday, Tuesday, Wednesday, and Thursday were 27, 18, 21, and 15, respectively. What would be its forecast for Friday using a four-day moving average approach? [13.3]

Q13.4 Tom's Towing LLC operates a fleet of tow trucks that it sends to help drivers in need on the nearby highway. The numbers of calls requesting a tow truck for Monday, Tuesday, Wednesday, and Thursday were 27, 18, 21, and 15, respectively. What would be its forecast for Friday using an exponential smoothing forecasting approach? Use $\alpha = 0.4$ and a forecast for Monday of 18. [13.3]

Q13.5 Online-MBA is an online university that allows students to get credit for various online courses they have taken, as long as they come to campus for a six-week intense boot camp. Demand for this program is quickly increasing. For the last six months, monthly applications were 345, 412, 480, 577, 640, and 711. Using a forecast for the first month of 250, an initial trend forecast of 50, and smoothing parameters of 0.2 for the demand smoothing and 0.5 for the trend smoothing, forecast the demand for the next year using double exponential smoothing. [13.4]

So, the forecast for the next period is 776.8.

Q13.6 GoPro is a training company that helps athletes applying for college improve their sports. Most colleges have their application deadline at the end of December, so the third and fourth quarters tend to be the busiest for the company. Based on the last three years, management has collected a set of old demand data for the various quarters: [13.5]

Year	Quarter	Demand
2012	1	111
	2	120
	3	350
	4	333
2013	1	130
	2	109
	3	299
	4	305
2014	1	143
	2	122
	3	401
	4	307

Using a smoothing parameter of 0.2 and an initial forecast for the deseasonalized demand of 130, forecast demand for the first four quarters in 2015.

Q13.7 Four partners in a big consulting firm try to estimate the number of new recruits needed for the next year. Their forecasts are 32, 44, 21, and 51, respectively. What would be the result of a simple forecast combination? [13.6]

Chapter 14

Betting on Uncertain Demand: The Newsvendor Model[1]

Matching supply and demand is particularly challenging when supply must be chosen before observing demand and demand is stochastic (uncertain). To illustrate this point with a (somewhat anachronistic) example, suppose you are the owner of a simple business: selling newspapers. Each morning you purchase a stack of papers with the intention of selling them at your newsstand at the corner of a busy street. Even though you have some idea regarding how many newspapers you can sell on any given day, you never can predict demand for sure. Some days you sell all of your papers, while other days end with unsold newspapers to be recycled. As the newsvendor, you must decide how many papers to buy at the start of each day. Because you must decide how many newspapers to buy before demand occurs, unless you are very lucky, you will not be able to match supply to demand. A decision tool is needed to make the best out of this difficult situation. The *newsvendor model* is such a tool.

You will be happy to learn that the newsvendor model applies in many more settings than just the newsstand business. The essential issue is that you must take a firm bet (how much inventory to order) before some random event occurs (demand) and then you learn that you either bet too much (demand was less than your order) or you bet too little (demand exceeded your order). This trade-off between "doing too much" and "doing too little" occurs in other settings. Consider a technology product with a long lead time to source components and only a short life before better technology becomes available. Purchase too many components and you risk having to sell off obsolete technology. Purchase too few and you may forgo sizeable profits.

This chapter begins with a description of the production challenge faced by O'Neill Inc., a sports apparel manufacturer. O'Neill's decision also closely resembles the newsvendor's task. We then describe the newsvendor model in detail and apply it to O'Neill's problem. We also show how to use the newsvendor model to forecast a number of performance measures relevant to O'Neill.

[1] Data in this chapter have been disguised to protect confidential information.

14.1 O'Neill Inc.

O'Neill Inc. is a designer and manufacturer of apparel, wetsuits, and accessories for water sports: surf, dive, waterski, wake-board, triathlon, and wind surf. Their product line ranges from entry-level products for recreational users, to wetsuits for competitive surfers, to sophisticated dry suits for professional cold-water divers (e.g., divers that work on oil platforms in the North Sea). O'Neill divides the year into two selling seasons: Spring (February through July) and Fall (August through January). Some products are sold in both seasons, but the majority of their products sell primarily in a single season. For example, waterski is active in the Spring season whereas recreational surf products sell well in the Fall season. Some products are not considered fashionable (i.e., they have little cosmetic variety and they sell from year to year), for example, standard neoprene black booties. With product names like "Animal," "Epic," "Hammer," "Inferno," and "Zen," O'Neill clearly also has products that are subject to the whims of fashion. For example, color patterns on surf suits often change from season to season to adjust to the tastes of the users (e.g., 15–30-year-olds from California).

O'Neill operates its own manufacturing facility in Mexico, but it does not produce all of its products there. Some items are produced by the TEC Group, O'Neill's contract manufacturer in Asia. While TEC provides many benefits to O'Neill (low cost, sourcing expertise, flexible capacity, etc.), they do require a three-month lead time on all orders. For example, if O'Neill orders an item on November 1, then O'Neill can expect to have that item at its distribution center in San Diego, California, ready for shipment to customers, only on January 31.

To better understand O'Neill's production challenge, let's consider a particular wetsuit used by surfers and newly redesigned for the upcoming spring season, the Hammer 3/2. (The "3/2" signifies the thickness of the neoprene on the suit: 3 mm thick on the chest and 2 mm everywhere else.) Figure 14.1 displays the Hammer 3/2 and O'Neill's logo. O'Neill has decided to let TEC manufacture the Hammer 3/2. Due to TEC's three-month lead time, O'Neill needs to submit an order to TEC in November before the start of the spring season. Using past sales data for similar products and the judgment of its designers and sales representatives, O'Neill developed a forecast of 3,200 units for total demand during the spring season for the Hammer 3/2. Unfortunately, there is considerable uncertainty in that forecast despite the care and attention placed on the formation of the forecast. For example, it is O'Neill's experience that 50 percent of the time the actual demand deviates from their initial forecast by more than 25 percent of the forecast. In other words, only 50 percent of the time is the actual demand between 75 percent and 125 percent of their forecast.

Although O'Neill's forecast in November is unreliable, O'Neill will have a much better forecast for total season demand after observing the first month or two of sales. At that time, O'Neill can predict whether the Hammer 3/2 is selling slower than forecast, in which case O'Neill is likely to have excess inventory at the end of the season, or whether the Hammer 3/2 is more popular than predicted, in which case O'Neill is likely to stock out. In the latter case, O'Neill would love to order more Hammers, but the long lead time from Asia prevents O'Neill from receiving those additional Hammers in time to be useful. Therefore, O'Neill essentially must "live or dive" with its single order placed in November.

Fortunately for O'Neill, the economics on the Hammer are pretty good. O'Neill sells the Hammer to retailers for $190 while it pays TEC $110 per suit. If O'Neill has leftover inventory at the end of the season, it is O'Neill's experience that they are able to sell that inventory for $90 per suit. Figure 14.2 summarizes the time line of events and the economics for the Hammer 3/2.

So how many units should O'Neill order from TEC? You might argue that O'Neill should order the forecast for total demand, 3,200, because 3,200 is the most likely outcome.

FIGURE 14.1
O'Neill's Hammer 3/2 Wetsuit and Logo for the Surf Market
Source: O'Neill.

The forecast is also the value that minimizes the expected absolute difference between the actual demand and the production quantity; that is, it is likely to be close to the actual demand. Alternatively, you may be concerned that forecasts are always biased and therefore suggest an order quantity less than 3,200 would be more prudent. Finally, you might argue that because the gross margin on the Hammer is more than 40 percent ((190 − 110)/

FIGURE 14.2
Time Line of Events and Economics for O'Neill's Hammer 3/2 Wetsuit

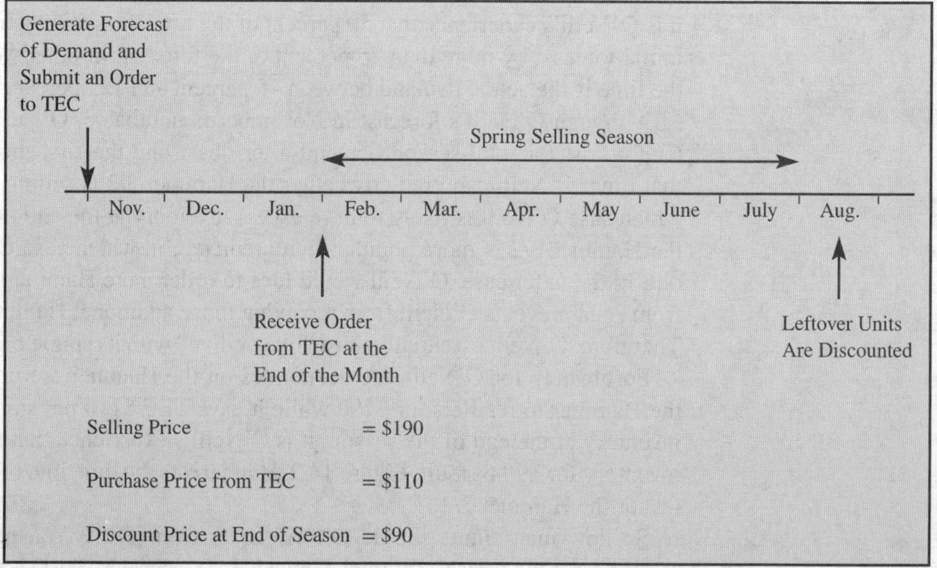

190 = 0.42), O'Neill should order more than 3,200 in case the Hammer is a hit. We next define the newsvendor model and then discuss what the newsvendor model recommends for an order quantity.

14.2 The Newsvendor Model: Structure and Inputs

The newsvendor model considers a setting in which you have only one production or procurement opportunity. Because that opportunity occurs well in advance of a single selling season, you receive your entire order just before the selling season starts. Stochastic demand occurs during the selling season. If demand exceeds your order quantity, then you sell your entire order. But if demand is less than your order quantity, then you have leftover inventory at the end of the season.

There are several critical inputs to the newsvendor model. First, there are some economic parameters. Second, a demand forecast, which we also call a demand model, is needed.

Let's start with the economic parameters. There is a cost to purchase each unit: for the Hammer 3/2, Cost = 110. It is important that Cost includes only costs that depend on the number of units ordered; amortized fixed costs should not be included, because they are unaffected by our order quantity decision. In other words, this cost figure should include all costs that vary with the order quantity and no costs that do not vary with the order quantity. There is a price for each unit you sell; in this case, Price = 190.

If there is leftover inventory at the end of the season, then there is some value associated with that inventory. To be specific, there is a *salvage value* that you earn on each unit of leftover inventory: with the Hammer, the Salvage value = 90. It is possible that leftover inventory has no salvage value whatsoever, that is, Salvage value = 0. It is also possible leftover inventory is costly to dispose of, in which case the salvage value may actually be a salvage cost. For example, if the product is a hazardous chemical, then there is a cost for disposing of leftover inventory; that is, a negative salvage value is possible.

Now consider the demand model. Demand uncertainty is central to the newsvendor model: A single order quantity is chosen but demand is stochastic, meaning that the order quantity could end up being either too high or too low. To manage the demand uncertainty for the Hammer 3/2, we need to be able to answer the following question:

What is the probability demand will be less than or equal to Q units?

for whatever Q value we desire. In short, we need a *distribution function*. Recall from statistics, every random variable is defined by its distribution function, $F(Q)$, which is the probability the outcome of the random variable is Q or lower. In this case the random variable is demand for the Hammer 3/2 and the distribution function is

$$F(Q) = \text{Prob}\{\text{Demand is less than or equal to } Q\}$$

For convenience, we refer to the distribution function, $F(Q)$, as our demand forecast because it gives us a complete picture of the demand uncertainty we face.

Distribution functions come in two forms. *Discrete distribution functions* can be defined in the form of a table: There is a set of possible outcomes and each possible outcome has a probability associated with it. The following is an example of a simple discrete distribution function with three possible outcomes:

Q	$F(Q)$
2,200	0.25
3,200	0.75
4,200	1.00

The Poisson distribution is an example of a discrete distribution function that is used extensively. With *continuous distribution functions* there are an unlimited number of possible outcomes. Both the exponential and the normal are continuous distribution functions. They are defined with one or two parameters. For example, the normal distribution is defined by two parameters: its mean and its standard deviation. We use μ to represent the mean of the distribution and σ to represent the standard deviation. (μ is the Greek letter mu and σ is the Greek letter sigma.) This notation for the mean and the standard deviation is quite common, so we adopt it here.

In some situations, a discrete distribution function provides the best representation of demand, whereas in other situations a continuous distribution function works best.

For the Hammer 3/2, O'Neill has determined that the demand forecast can be represented by the (continuous) normal distribution with a mean of 3,192 units and a standard deviation of 1,181. Section 14.6 provides greater detail on how O'Neill constructed that demand model.

Now that we have the parameters of a normal distribution that express our demand forecast, let's return to the question of how to evaluate $F(Q)$. There are two ways this can be done. The first way is to use spreadsheet software. For example, to determine the value of $F(Q)$, in Excel use the function Normdist(Q, 3192, 1181, 1). The second way, which does not require a computer, is to use the Standard Normal Distribution Function Table in Appendix B.

The *standard normal* is a particular normal distribution: Its mean is 0 and its standard deviation is 1. To introduce another piece of common Greek notation, let $\Phi(z)$ be the distribution function of the standard normal. Even though the standard normal is a continuous distribution, it can be "chopped up" into pieces to make it into a discrete distribution. The Standard Normal Distribution Function Table is exactly that; that is, it is the discrete version of the standard normal distribution. The full table is in Appendix B, but Table 14.1 reproduces a portion of the table.

The format of the Standard Normal Distribution Function Table makes it somewhat tricky to read. For example, suppose you wanted to know the probability that the outcome of a standard normal is 0.51 or lower. We are looking for the value of $\Phi(z)$ with $z = 0.51$. To find that value, pick the row and column in the table such that the first number in the row and the first number in the column add up to the z value you seek. With $z = 0.51$, we are looking for the row that begins with 0.50 and the column that begins with 0.01, because the sum of those two values equals 0.51. The intersection of that row with that column gives $\Phi(z)$; from Table 14.1 we see that $\Phi(0.51) = 0.6950$. Therefore, there is a 69.5 percent probability the outcome of a standard normal is 0.51 or lower.

But it is unlikely that our demand forecast will be a standard normal distribution. So how can we use the standard normal to find $F(Q)$; that is, the probability demand will be Q or lower given that our demand forecast is some other normal distribution? The answer is that we convert the quantity we are interested in, Q, into an equivalent quantity for the standard normal. In other words, we find a z such that $F(Q) = \Phi(z)$; that is, the probability demand

TABLE 14.1
A Portion of the Standard Normal Distribution Function Table, $\Phi(z)$

z	0.00	0.01	0.02	0.03	0.04	0.05	0.06	0.07	0.08	0.09
0.3	0.6179	0.6217	0.6255	0.6293	0.6331	0.6368	0.6406	0.6443	0.6480	0.6517
0.4	0.6554	0.6591	0.6628	0.6664	0.6700	0.6736	0.6772	0.6808	0.6844	0.6879
0.5	0.6915	0.6950	0.6985	0.7019	0.7054	0.7088	0.7123	0.7157	0.7190	0.7224
0.6	0.7257	0.7291	0.7324	0.7357	0.7389	0.7422	0.7454	0.7486	0.7517	0.7549
0.7	0.7580	0.7611	0.7642	0.7673	0.7704	0.7734	0.7764	0.7794	0.7823	0.7852
0.8	0.7881	0.7910	0.7939	0.7967	0.7995	0.8023	0.8051	0.8078	0.8106	0.8133
0.9	0.8159	0.8186	0.8212	0.8238	0.8264	0.8269	0.8315	0.8340	0.8365	0.8389
1.0	0.8413	0.8438	0.8461	0.8485	0.8508	0.8531	0.8554	0.8577	0.8599	0.8621

is less than or equal to Q is the same as the probability the outcome of a standard normal is z or lower. That z is called the *z-statistic*. Once we have the appropriate z-statistics, we then just look up $\Phi(z)$ in the Standard Normal Distribution Function Table to get our answer.

To convert Q into the equivalent z-statistic, use the following equation:

$$z = \frac{Q - \mu}{\sigma}$$

For example, suppose we are interested in the probability that demand for the Hammer 3/2 will be 4,000 units or lower, that is, $Q = 4{,}000$. With a normal distribution that has mean 3,192 and standard deviation 1,181, the quantity $Q = 4{,}000$ has a z-statistic of

$$z = \frac{4{,}000 - 3{,}192}{1{,}181} = 0.68$$

Therefore, the probability demand for the Hammer 3/2 is 4,000 units or lower is $\Phi(0.68)$; that is, it is the same as the probability the outcome of a standard normal is 0.68 or lower. According to the Standard Normal Distribution Function Table (see Table 14.1 for convenience), $\Phi(0.68) = 0.7517$. In other words, there is just over a 75 percent probability that demand for the Hammer 3/2 will be 4,000 or fewer units. Exhibit 14.1 summarizes the process of finding the probability demand will be less than or equal to some Q (or more than Q).

To summarize, the newsvendor model represents a situation in which a decision maker must make a single bet (e.g., the order quantity) before some random event occurs (e.g., demand). There are costs if the bet turns out to be too high (e.g., leftover inventory that is salvaged for a loss on each unit). There are costs if the bet turns out to be too low (the opportunity cost of lost sales). The newsvendor model's objective is to bet an amount that correctly balances those opposing forces. To implement the model, we need to identify our costs and how much demand uncertainty we face. A single "point forecast" (e.g., 3,200 units) is not sufficient. We need to quantify the amount of variability that may occur about our forecast; that is, we need a distribution function.

The next section focuses on the task of choosing an actual order quantity.

14.3 How to Choose an Order Quantity

The next step after assembling all of our inputs (selling price, cost, salvage value, and demand forecast) is to choose an order quantity. The first part in that process is to decide what is our objective. A natural objective is to choose our production/procurement quantity to maximize our expected profit. This section explains how to do this. Section 14.5 considers other possible objectives.

Before revealing the actual procedure for choosing an order quantity to maximize expected profit, it is helpful to explore the intuition behind the solution. Consider again O'Neill's Hammer 3/2 ordering decision. Should we order one unit? If we do, then there is a very good chance we will sell the unit: With a forecast of 3,192 units, it is likely we sell at least one unit. If we sell the unit, then the gain from that unit equals $190 – $110 = $80 (the selling price minus the purchase cost). The *expected* gain from the first unit, which equals the probability of selling the first unit times the gain from the first unit, is then very close to $80. However, there is also a slight chance that we do not sell the first unit, in which case we incur a loss of $110 – $90 = $20. (The loss equals the difference between the purchase cost and the discount price.) But since the probability we do not sell that unit is quite small, the *expected* loss on the first unit is nearly $0. Given that the expected gain from the first unit clearly exceeds the expected loss, the profit from ordering that unit is positive. In this case it is a good bet to order at least one unit.

Exhibit 14.1

A PROCESS FOR EVALUATING THE PROBABILITY DEMAND IS EITHER LESS THAN OR EQUAL TO *Q* (WHICH IS F(*Q*)) OR MORE THAN *Q* (WHICH IS 1 – *F*(*Q*))

If the demand forecast is a normal distribution with mean μ and standard deviation σ, then follow steps A and B:

A. Evaluate the *z*-statistic that corresponds to *Q*:

$$z = \frac{Q - \mu}{\sigma}$$

B. The probability demand is less than or equal to Q is Φ(*z*). With Excel Φ(*z*) can be evaluated with the function Normsdist(*z*); otherwise, look up Φ(*z*) in the Standard Normal Distribution Function Table in Appendix B. If you want the probability demand is greater than Q, then your answer is 1 – Φ(*z*).

If the demand forecast is a discrete distribution function table, then look up *F*(Q), which is the probability demand is less than or equal to Q. If you want the probability demand is greater than Q, then the answer is 1 – *F*(Q).

After deciding whether to order one unit, we can now consider whether we should order two units, and then three units, and so forth. Two things happen as we continue this process. First, the probability that we sell the unit we are considering decreases, thereby reducing the expected gain from that unit. Second, the probability we do not sell that unit increases, thereby increasing the expected loss from that unit. Now imagine we order the 6,400th unit. The probability of selling that unit is quite low, so the expected gain from that unit is nearly zero. In contrast, the probability of *not* selling that unit is quite high, so the expected loss is nearly \$20 on that unit. Clearly it makes no sense to order the 6,400th unit. This pattern is illustrated in Figure 14.3. We see that for some unit just above 4,000 the expected gain on that unit equals its expected loss.

Let's formalize this intuition some more. In the newsvendor model, there is a trade-off between ordering too much (which could lead to costly leftover inventory) and ordering too little (which could lead to the opportunity cost of lost sales). To balance these forces, it is useful to think in terms of a cost for ordering too much and a cost for ordering too little. Maximizing expected profit is equivalent to minimizing those costs. To be specific, let C_o be the

FIGURE 14.3
The Expected Gain and Expected Loss from the *Q*th Hammer 3/2 Ordered by O'Neill

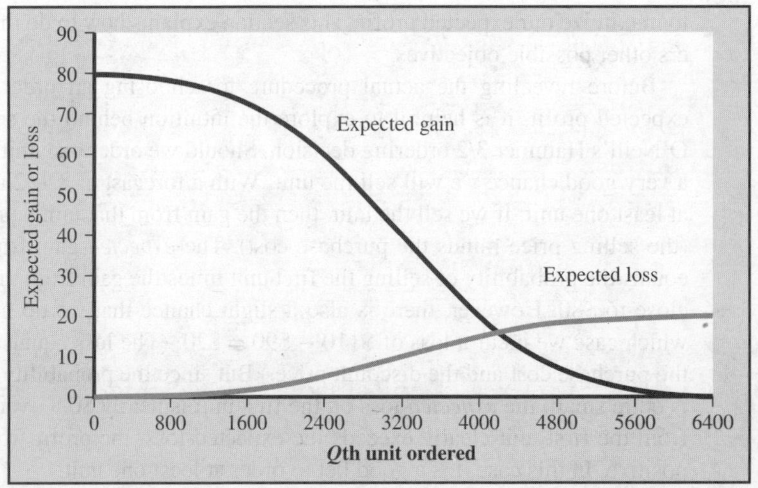

overage cost, the loss incurred when a unit is ordered but not sold. In other words, the overage cost is the per-unit cost of overordering. For the Hammer 3/2, we have $C_o = 20$.

In contrast to C_o, let C_u be the *underage cost*, the opportunity cost of not ordering a unit that could have been sold. The following is an equivalent definition for C_u: C_u is the gain from selling a unit. In other words, the underage cost is the per-unit opportunity cost of underordering. For the Hammer 3/2, $C_u = 80$. Note that the overage and underage costs are defined for a *single unit*. In other words, C_o is not the total cost of all leftover inventory; instead, C_o is the cost *per unit* of leftover inventory. The reason for defining C_o and C_u for a single unit is simple: We don't know how many units will be left over in inventory, or how many units of demand will be lost, but we do know the cost of each unit left in inventory and the opportunity cost of each lost sale.

Now that we have defined the overage and underage costs, we need to choose Q to strike the balance between them that results in the maximum expected profit. Based on our previous reasoning, we should keep ordering additional units until the expected loss equals the expected gain.

The expected loss on a unit is the cost of having the unit in inventory (the overage cost) times the probability it is left in inventory. For the Qth unit, that probability is $F(Q)$: It is left in inventory if demand is less than Q.[2] Therefore, the expected loss is $C_o \times F(Q)$. The expected gain on a unit is the benefit of selling a unit (the underage cost) times the probability the unit is sold, which in this case occurs if demand is greater than Q. The probability demand is greater than Q is $(1 - F(Q))$. Therefore, the expected gain is $C_u \times (1 - F(Q))$.

It remains to find the order quantity Q that sets the expected loss on the Qth unit equal to the expected gain on the Qth unit:

$$C_o \times F(Q) = C_u \times (1 - F(Q))$$

If we rearrange terms in the above equation, we get

$$F(Q) = \frac{C_u}{C_o + C_u} \qquad \textbf{(14.1)}$$

The profit-maximizing order quantity is the order quantity that satisfies the above equation. If you are familiar with calculus and would like to see a more mathematically rigorous derivation of the optimal order quantity, see Appendix D.

So how can we use Equation (14.1) to actually find Q? Let's begin by just reading it. It says that the order quantity that maximizes expected profit is the order quantity Q such that demand is less than or equal to Q with probability $C_u/(C_o + C_u)$. That ratio with the underage and overage costs is called the *critical ratio*. We now have an explanation for why our forecast must be a distribution function. To choose the profit-maximizing order quantity, we need to find the quantity such that demand will be less than that quantity with a particular probability (the critical ratio). The mean alone (i.e., just a sales forecast) is insufficient to do that task.

Let's begin with the easy part. We know for the Hammer 3/2 that $C_u = 80$ and $C_o = 20$, so the critical ratio is

$$\frac{C_u}{C_o + C_u} = \frac{80}{20 + 80} = 0.8$$

[2] That statement might bother you. You might recall that $F(Q)$ is the probability demand is Q or lower. If demand is exactly Q, then the Qth unit will not be left in inventory. Hence, you might argue that it is more precise to say that $F(Q - 1)$ is the probability the Qth unit is left in inventory. However, the normal distribution assumes demand can be any value, including values that are not integers. If you are willing to divide each demand into essentially an infinite number of fractional pieces, as is assumed by the normal, then $F(Q)$ is indeed the probability there is leftover inventory. If you are curious about the details, see Appendix D.

We are making progress, but now comes the tricky part: We need to find the order quantity Q such that there is an 80 percent probability that demand is Q or lower.

There are two ways to find a Q such that there is an 80 percent probability that demand will be Q or smaller. The first is to use the Excel function, Normsinv(), and the second is to use the Standard Normal Distribution Function Table. If you have Excel available, the first method is the easiest, but they both follow essentially the same process, as we will see.

If we have Excel, to find the optimal Q, we begin by finding the z-statistic such that there is an 80 percent probability the outcome of a standard normal is z or lower. Then we convert that z into the Q we seek. To find our desired z, use the following Excel function:

$$z = \text{Normsinv(Critical ratio)}$$

In our case, the critical ratio is 0.80 and Normsinv(0.80) returns 0.84. That means that there is an 80 percent chance the outcome of a standard normal will be 0.84 or lower. That would be our optimal order quantity if demand followed a standard normal distribution. But our demand is not standard normal. It is normal with mean 3,192 and standard deviation 1,181. To convert our z into an order quantity that makes sense for our actual demand forecast, we use the following equation:

$$Q = \mu + z \times \sigma$$

where μ = Mean of the normal distribution

σ = Standard deviation of the normal distribution

Hence, using our Excel method, the expected profit maximizing order quantity for the Hammer 3/2 is $Q = 3{,}192 + 0.84 \times 1{,}181 = 4{,}184$.

The second method to find Q is to use the Standard Normal Distribution Function Table. Again, we want to find the z such that the probability the standard normal is z or less is equal to the critical ratio, which in this case is 0.80. Looking at Table 14.1, we see that $\Phi(0.84) = 0.7995$ and $\Phi(0.85) = 0.8023$, neither of which is exactly the 0.80 probability we are looking for: $z = 0.84$ yields a slightly lower probability (79.95 percent) and $z = 0.85$ yields a slightly higher probability (80.23 percent). What should we do? The rule is simple, which we will call the *round-up rule:*

Round-up rule. Whenever you are looking up a target value in a table and the target value falls between two entries, choose the entry that leads to the larger order quantity.

In this case the larger quantity is $z = 0.85$, so we will go with 0.85. Now, like with our Excel process, we convert that z into $Q = 3{,}192 + 0.85 \times 1{,}181 = 4{,}196$.

Why do our two methods lead to different answers? In short, Excel does not implement the round-up rule. But that raises the next question. Is it OK to use Excel to get our answer? The answer is "yes." To explain, when demand is normally distributed, there will be a small difference between the Excel answer, using the Normsinv() function, and the Standard Normal Distribution Function Table answer. In this case, the difference between the two is only 12 units, which is less than 0.3 percent away from 4,196.

Therefore, the expected profit with either of these order quantities will be essentially the same. Furthermore, Excel provides a convenient means to perform this calculation quickly.

So, if Excel is the quick and easy method, why should we bother with the Standard Normal Distribution Function Table and the round-up rule? Because when our demand forecast is a discrete distribution function, the round-up rule provides the more accurate answer. (Recall, a discrete distribution function assumes that the only possible outcomes are integers.) This is particularly valuable when expected demand is small, say, 10 units,

Exhibit 14.2

A PROCEDURE TO FIND THE ORDER QUANTITY THAT MAXIMIZES EXPECTED PROFIT IN THE NEWSVENDOR MODEL

Step 1 Evaluate the critical ratio: $\frac{C_u}{C_o + C_u}$. In the case of the Hammer 3/2, the underage cost is C_u = Price − Cost and the overage cost is C_o = Cost − Salvage value.

Step 2 If the demand forecast is a normal distribution with mean μ and standard deviation σ, then follow steps A and B:

A. Find the optimal order quantity if demand had a standard normal distribution. One method to achieve this is to find the z value in the Standard Normal Distribution Function Table such that

$$\Phi(z) = \frac{C_u}{C_o + C_u}$$

(If the critical ratio value does not exist in the table, then find the two z values that it falls between. For example, the critical ratio 0.80 falls between $z = 0.84$ and $z = 0.85$. Then choose the larger of those two z values.) A second method is to use the Excel function Normsinv: z = Normsinv(Critical ratio).

B. Convert z into the order quantity that maximizes expected profit, Q: $Q = \mu + z \times \sigma$

or 1 unit, or even 0.25 unit. In those cases, the normal distribution function does not model demand well (in part, because it is a continuous distribution function). Furthermore, it can make a big difference (in terms of expected profit) whether one or two units are ordered. Hence, the value of understanding the round-up rule.

This discussion probably has left you with one final question—Why is the round-up rule the right rule? The critical ratio is actually closer to 0.7995 (which corresponds to $z = 0.84$) than it is to 0.8023 (which corresponds to $z = 0.85$). That is why Excel chooses $z = 0.84$. Shouldn't we choose the z value that leads to the probability that is closest to the critical ratio? In fact, that is not the best approach. The critical ratio equation works with the following logic—keep ordering until you get to the first order quantity such that the critical ratio is less than the probability demand is that order quantity or lower. That logic leads the rule to "step over" the critical ratio and then stop; that is, the round-up rule. Excel, in contrast, uses the "get as close to the critical ratio as possible" rule. If you are hungry for a more in-depth explanation and justification, see Appendix D. Otherwise, stick with the round-up rule, and you will be fine. Exhibit 14.2 summarizes these steps.

14.4 Performance Measures

The previous section showed us how to find the order quantity that maximizes our expected profit. This section shows us how to evaluate a number of relevant performance measures, such as the expected leftover inventory (we don't want too much of that), expected sales (we want more of that), expected lost sales (should be avoided), expected profit (hopefully maximized), and two measures of service, the in-stock probability and the stockout probability, which inform us about how likely it is for customers to be able to find the product they want.

These performance measures can be evaluated for any order quantity, not just the expected profit-maximizing order quantity. To emphasize this point, this section evaluates these performance measures assuming 3,500 Hammer 3/2s are ordered.

Expected Leftover Inventory

If O'Neill orders 3,500 Hammer 3/2s, then at the end of the season there may be some of them left in inventory. How much? Well, if demand is a disappointing 2,000 units, then there will be 3,500 – 2,000 = 1,500 units. But if demand is a robust 4,000 units, then there will be no units leftover at the end of the season. The *expected leftover inventory* is the average (or expected) number of units still not sold at the end of the selling season.

Note that we are interested in the *expected* leftover inventory. Demand can be more than our order quantity, in which case leftover inventory is zero, or demand can be less then our order quantity, in which case there is some positive amount of leftover inventory. Expected leftover inventory is the average of all of those events (the cases with no leftover inventory and all cases with positive leftover inventory) taking into account the likelihood of each possible demand.

How do we find expected leftover inventory for any given order quantity? When demand is normally distributed, use the following equation:

$$\text{Expected leftover inventory} = \sigma \times I(z)$$

where

$$\sigma = \text{Standard deviation of the normal distribution representing demand}$$
$$I(z) = \text{Standard normal inventory function}$$

We already know $\sigma = 1{,}181$ but what is $I(z)$? It is the expected inventory if demand followed a standard normal distribution and we ordered z units.

There are two methods to evaluate $I(z)$, one using Excel and one using a table. With either method, we first find the z-statistic that corresponds to our chosen order quantity, $Q = 3{,}500$:

$$z = \frac{Q - \mu}{\sigma} = \frac{3{,}500 - 3{,}192}{1{,}181} = 0.26$$

The first method then uses the following Excel formula to evaluate the expected inventory if demand were a standard normal distribution, $I(z)$:

$$I(z) = \text{Normdist}(z{,}0{,}1{,}0) + z * \text{Normsdist}(z)$$

(If you are curious about the derivation of the above function, see Appendix D.) In this case, Excel provides the following answer: $I(0.26)$ = Normdist(0.26,0,1,0) + 0.26 * Normsdist(0.26) = 0.5424.

The second method uses the Standard Normal Inventory Function Table in Appendix B to look up the expected inventory. From that table we see that $I(0.26) = 0.5424$. In this case, our two methods yield the same value for $I(z)$, which always is the case when we input into the Excel function a z value rounded to the nearest hundredth (e.g., 0.26 instead of 0.263). Therefore, if the order quantity is 3,500 Hammer 3/2s, then we can expect to have $\sigma \times I(z) = 1{,}181 \times 0.5424 = 641$ units leftover (i.e., remaining) in inventory at the end of the season.

How do we evaluate expected leftover inventory when we do not use a normal distribution to model demand? In that situation we need a table to tell us what expected leftover inventory is for our chosen order quantity. For example, Appendix B provides the inventory function for the Poisson distribution with different means. Appendix C provides a procedure to evaluate the inventory function for any discrete distribution function. We relegate this procedure for creating an inventory function table to the appendix because it is computationally burdensome; that is, it is the kind of calculation you want to do on a spreadsheet rather than by hand.

Exhibit 14.3 summarizes the procedures for evaluating expected leftover inventory.

Exhibit 14.3

EXPECTED LEFTOVER INVENTORY EVALUATION PROCEDURE

If the demand forecast is a normal distribution with mean μ and standard deviation σ, then follow steps A through D:

A. Evaluate the z-statistic for the order quantity Q: $z = \frac{Q - \mu}{\sigma}$.

B. Use the z-statistic to look up in the Standard Normal Inventory Function Table the expected leftover inventory, $I(z)$, with the standard normal distribution.

C. Expected leftover inventory $= \sigma \times I(z)$.

D. With Excel, expected leftover inventory can be evaluated with the following equation:

$$\text{Expected leftover inventory} = \sigma\text{*(Normdist}(z,0,1,0) + z\text{*Normsdist}(z)))$$

If the demand forecast is a discrete distribution function table, then expected leftover inventory equals the inventory function for the chosen order quantity, $I(Q)$. If the table does not include the inventory function, then see Appendix C for how to evaluate it.

Expected Sales

Expected sales is the expected number of units sold given demand and the order quantity. For example, if we order 3,500 Hammer 3/2s and demand is 3,120, then sales is 3,120 units. But if demand is 4,400, then sales is capped at the order quantity of 3,500. Expected sales is evaluated by considering all of the possible demands and the resulting sales.

To understand how to evaluate expected sales, start with the simple fact that each unit purchased either is sold during the season or is unsold (i.e., leftover) at the end of the season. So the sum of sales and leftover inventory must equal the total number of purchased units, Q:

$$\text{Sales} + \text{Leftover inventory} = Q$$

If we take expectation of both sides of the above equation and rearrange the terms we get an equation for expected sales,

$$\text{Expected sales} = Q - \text{Expected leftover inventory}$$

Thus, if O'Neill orders 3,500 Hammer 3/2s, then expected sales = 3,500 – 641 = 2,859. Note, this is only the expected sales. The actual sales will vary depending on demand: Actual sales can be higher or lower than 2,859 units. But if we average across all possible actual sales outcomes, then we get the expected sales of 2,859 units.

See Exhibit 14.4 for a summary of how to evaluate expected sales.

Expected Lost Sales

Expected lost sales is the expected number of units *not* sold because we ran out of inventory. For example, if we order 3,500 Hammer 3/2s and demand is 3,120, then lost sales is 0 units—we had enough inventory to satisfy all demand. But if demand is 4,400, then lost sales is 4,400 – 3,500 = 900 units—we could have sold another 900 units had we ordered at least 4,400 to start the season. Expected lost sales is evaluated by considering all of the possible demands and the resulting lost sales.

Exhibit 14.4

EXPECTED SALES, EXPECTED LOST SALES, AND EXPECTED PROFIT EVALUATION PROCEDURES

Step 1 Evaluate expected leftover inventory (see Exhibit 14.3). All of these performance measures can be evaluated directly in terms of expected leftover inventory and several known parameters: μ = Expected demand; Q = Order quantity; Price; Cost; and Salvage value.

Step 2 Use the following equations to evaluate the performance measure of interest.

Expected sales = Q – Expected leftover inventory
Expected lost sales = μ – Expected sales
= μ – Q + Expected leftover inventory
Expected profit = [(Price – Cost) × Expected sales] – [(Cost – Salvage value) × Expected leftover inventory]

The evaluation of expected lost sales begins with the observation that each unit of demand either generates a sale or becomes a lost sale (because inventory was not available to satisfy that demand). So the sum of sales and lost sales must equal demand:

$$\text{Sales} + \text{Lost sales} = \text{Demand}$$

If we take expectations of both sides of the equation above (and remember that expected demand is μ) and rearrange the terms we get an equation for expected lost sales,

$$\text{Expected lost sales} = \mu - \text{Expected sales}$$

Thus, if O'Neill orders 3,500 Hammer 3/2s, then expected lost sales = 3,192 – 2,859 = 333.

See Exhibit 14.4 for a summary of how to evaluate expected lost sales.

If you happen to find the above method too cumbersome (first evaluate expected leftover inventory, then expected sales), there is a bit of a shortcut to evaluate expected lost sales. And it looks a lot like the process for evaluating expected leftover inventory.

When demand is normally distributed, we can use the following equation for expected lost sales:

$$\text{Expected lost sales} = \sigma \times L(z)$$

where

σ = Standard deviation of the normal distribution representing demand
$L(z)$ = Standard normal loss function

The loss function, $L(z)$, works much like the inventory function, $I(z)$. The first method to evaluate it uses the following Excel formula:

$$L(z) = \text{Normdist}(z,0,1,0) - z*(1 - \text{Normsdist}(z))$$

The second method uses the Standard Normal Loss Function Table in Appendix B to look up the expected lost sales. From that table we see that $L(0.26) = 0.2824$. Therefore, if the order quantity is 3,500 Hammer 3/2s, then we can expect to lose $\sigma \times L(z) = 1{,}181 \times 0.2824 = 334$ units of demand. (We get a slightly different answer with this method because of rounding.)

How do we evaluate expected lost sales when we do not use a normal distribution to model demand? In that situation we need a table to tell us what expected lost sales is for our chosen order quantity. For example, Appendix B provides the loss function for the Poisson distribution with different means. Appendix C provides a procedure to evaluate the loss function for any discrete distribution function.

Expected Profit

We earn Price – Cost on each unit sold and we lose Cost – Salvage value on each unit we do not sell, so our expected profit is

$$\text{Expected profit} = [(\text{Price} - \text{Cost}) \times \text{Expected sales}] - [(\text{Cost} - \text{Salvage value}) \times \text{Expected leftover inventory}]$$

Therefore, we can evaluate expected profit after we have evaluated expected sales and leftover inventory. See Exhibit 14.4 for a summary of this procedure.

With an order quantity of 3,500 units and a normal distribution demand forecast, the expected profit for the Hammer 3/2 is

$$\text{Expected profit} = (\$80 \times 2{,}859) - (\$20 \times 641) = \$215{,}900$$

In-Stock Probability and Stockout Probability

A common measure of customer service is the in-stock probability. The in-stock probability is the probability the firm ends the season having satisfied all demand. (Equivalently, the in-stock probability is the probability the firm has stock available for every customer.) That occurs if demand is less than or equal to the order quantity,

$$\text{In-stock probability} = F(Q)$$

The stockout probability is the probability the firm stocks out for some customer during the selling season (i.e., a lost sale occurs). Because the firm stocks out if demand exceeds the order quantity,

$$\text{Stockout probability} = 1 - F(Q)$$

(The firm either stocks out or it does not, so the stockout probability equals 1 minus the probability demand is Q or lower.) We also can see that the stockout probability and the in-stock probability are closely related:

$$\text{Stockout probability} = 1 - \text{In-stock probability}$$

See Exhibit 14.5 for a summary of the procedure to evaluate these probabilities. With an order quantity of 3,500 Hammer 3/2s, the z-statistic is $z = (3{,}500 - 3{,}192)/1{,}181 = 0.26$. From the Standard Normal Distribution Function Table, we find $\Phi(0.26) = 0.6026$, so the in-stock probability is 60.26 percent. The stockout probability is $1 - 0.6026 = 39.74$ percent.

The in-stock probability is not the only measure of customer service. Another popular measure is the *fill rate*. The fill rate is the probability a customer is able to purchase a unit (i.e., does not experience a stockout). Interestingly, this is not the same as the in-stock probability, which is the probability that all demand is satisfied. For example, say we order $Q = 100$ and demand turns out to be 101. Most customers were able to purchase a unit (the fill rate is high) but the firm did not satisfy all demand (in-stock is not satisfied). See Appendix D for more information regarding how to evaluate the fill rate.

Exhibit 14.5

IN-STOCK PROBABILITY AND STOCKOUT PROBABILITY EVALUATION

If the demand forecast is a normal distribution with mean μ and standard deviation σ, then follow steps A through D:

A. Evaluate the z-statistic for the order quantity: $z = \frac{Q - \mu}{\sigma}$

B. Use the z-statistic to look up in the Standard Normal Distribution Function Table the probability the standard normal demand is z or lower, $\Phi(z)$.

C. In-stock probability = $\Phi(z)$ and Stockout probability = $1 - \Phi(z)$.

D. In Excel, In-stock probability = Normsdist(z) and Stockout probability = 1 – Normsdist(z).

If the demand forecast is a discrete distribution function table, then In-stock probability = $F(Q)$ and Stockout probability = $1 - F(Q)$, where $F(Q)$ is the probability demand is Q or lower.

14.5 How to Achieve a Service Objective

Maximizing expected profit is surely a reasonable objective for choosing an order quantity, but it is not the only objective. As we saw in the previous section, the expected profit-maximizing order quantity may generate an unacceptable in-stock probability from the firm's customer service perspective. This section explains how to determine an order quantity that satisfies a customer service objective, in particular, a minimum in-stock probability.

Suppose O'Neill wants to find the order quantity that generates a 99 percent in-stock probability with the Hammer 3/2. The in-stock probability is $F(Q)$. So we need to find an order quantity such that there is a 99 percent probability that demand is that order quantity or lower. Given that our demand forecast is normally distributed, we first find the z-statistic that achieves our objective with the standard normal distribution. In the Standard Normal Distribution Function Table, we see that $\Phi(2.32) = 0.9898$ and $\Phi(2.33) = 0.9901$. Again, we choose the higher z-statistic, so our desired order quantity is now $Q = \mu = z \times \sigma = 3{,}192 = 2.33 \times 1{,}181 = 5{,}944$. You can use Excel to avoid looking up a probability in the Standard Normal Distribution Function Table to find z:

$$z = \text{Normsinv(In-stock probability)}$$

Notice that a substantially higher order quantity is needed to generate a 99 percent in-stock probability than the one that maximizes expected profit (4,196). Exhibit 14.6 summarizes the process for finding an order quantity to satisfy a target in-stock probability.

14.6 How to Construct a Demand Forecast

So far we have assumed that O'Neill has a demand model, a normal distribution with mean 3,192, and a standard deviation of 1,181. This section discusses one method for deriving a demand model. It is by no means the only possible method—the field of statistics is filled with methods for predicting and modeling uncertain future events, like demand.

As mentioned in Section 14.1, the Hammer 3/2 has been redesigned for the upcoming spring season. As a result, actual sales in the previous season might not be a good guide for expected demand in the upcoming season. In addition to the product redesign, factors that could influence expected demand include the pricing and marketing strategy for the upcoming season, changes in fashion, changes in the economy (e.g., is demand moving toward higher or lower price points), changes in technology, and overall trends for the

Exhibit 14.6

A PROCEDURE TO DETERMINE AN ORDER QUANTITY THAT SATISFIES A TARGET IN-STOCK PROBABILITY

If the demand forecast is a normal distribution with mean μ and standard deviation σ, then follow steps A and B:

A. Find the *z*-statistic in the Standard Normal Distribution Function Table that satisfies the in-stock probability, that is,

$$\Phi(z) = \text{In-stock probability}$$

If the in-stock probability falls between two *z* values in the table, choose the higher *z*. In Excel, *z* can be found with the following formula:

$$z = \text{Normsinv(In-stock probability)}$$

B. Convert the chosen *z*-statistic into the order quantity that satisfies our target in-stock probability,

$$Q = \mu + z \times \sigma$$

If the demand forecast is a discrete distribution function table, then find the order quantity in the table such that $F(Q)$ = In-stock probability. If the in-stock probability falls between two entries in the table, choose the entry with the larger order quantity.

sport. To account for all of these factors, O'Neill surveyed the opinion of a number of individuals in the organization on their personal demand forecast for the Hammer 3/2. The survey's results were averaged to obtain the initial 3,200-unit forecast. This represents the "intuition" portion of our demand forecast. Now we need to analyze O'Neill's available data to further develop the demand forecast.

Table 14.2 presents data from O'Neill's previous spring season with wetsuits in the surf category. Notice that the data include both the original forecasts for each product as well as its actual demand. The original forecast was developed in a process that was comparable to the one that led to the 3,200-unit forecast for the Hammer 3/2 for this season. For example, the forecast for the Hammer 3/2 in the previous season was 1,300 units, but actual demand was 1,696 units.

So how does O'Neill know actual demand for a product that stocks out? For example, how does O'Neill know that actual demand was 1,696 for last year's Hammer 3/2 if they only ordered 1,500 units? Because retailers order via phone or electronically, O'Neill can keep track of each retailer's initial order, that is, the retailer's demand before the retailer knows a product is unavailable. (However, life is not perfect: O'Neill's phone representatives do not always record a customer's initial order into the computer system, so there is even some uncertainty with that figure. We'll assume this is a minor issue and not address it in our analysis.) In other settings, a firm may not be able to know actual demand with that level of precision. For example, a retailer of O'Neill's products probably does not get to observe what demand could be for the Hammer 3/2 once the Hammer is out of stock at the retailer. However, that retailer would know when during the season the Hammer 3/2 stocked out and, hence, could use that information to forecast how many additional units could have been sold during the remainder of the season. Therefore, even if a firm cannot directly observe lost sales, a firm should be able to obtain a reasonable estimate for what demand could have been.

TABLE 14.2 Forecasts and Actual Demand Data for Surf Wetsuits from the Previous Spring Season

Product Description	Forecast	Actual Demand	Error*	A/F Ratio**
JR ZEN FL 3/2	90	140	−50	1.56
EPIC 5/3 W/HD	120	83	37	0.69
JR ZEN 3/2	140	143	−3	1.02
WMS ZEN-ZIP 4/3	170	163	7	0.96
HEATWAVE 3/2	170	212	−42	1.25
JR EPIC 3/2	180	175	5	0.97
WMS ZEN 3/2	180	195	−15	1.08
ZEN-ZIP 5/4/3 W/HOOD	270	317	−47	1.17
WMS EPIC 5/3 W/HD	320	369	−49	1.15
EVO 3/2	380	587	−207	1.54
JR EPIC 4/3	380	571	−191	1.50
WMS EPIC 2MM FULL	390	311	79	0.80
HEATWAVE 4/3	430	274	156	0.64
ZEN 4/3	430	239	191	0.56
EVO 4/3	440	623	−183	1.42
ZEN FL 3/2	450	365	85	0.81
HEAT 4/3	460	450	10	0.98
ZEN-ZIP 2MM FULL	470	116	354	0.25
HEAT 3/2	500	635	−135	1.27
WMS EPIC 3/2	610	830	−220	1.36
WMS ELITE 3/2	650	364	286	0.56
ZEN-ZIP 3/2	660	788	−128	1.19
ZEN 2MM S/S FULL	680	453	227	0.67
EPIC 2MM S/S FULL	740	607	133	0.82
EPIC 4/3	1,020	732	288	0.72
WMS EPIC 4/3	1,060	1,552	−492	1.46
JR HAMMER 3/2	1,220	721	499	0.59
HAMMER 3/2	1,300	1,696	−396	1.30
HAMMER S/S FULL	1,490	1,832	−342	1.23
EPIC 3/2	2,190	3,504	−1,314	1.60
ZEN 3/2	3,190	1,195	1,995	0.37
ZEN-ZIP 4/3	3,810	3,289	521	0.86
WMS HAMMER 3/2 FULL	6,490	3,673	2,817	0.57

*Error = Forecast – Actual demand
**A/F ratio = Actual demand divided by Forecast

As can be seen from the data, the forecasts ranged from a low of 90 units to a high of 6,490 units. There was also considerable forecast error: O'Neill goofed with the Women's Hammer 3/2 Full suit with a forecast nearly 3,000 units above actual demand, while the forecast for the Epic 3/2 suit was about 1,300 units too low. Figure 14.4 gives a scatter plot of forecasts and actual demand. If forecasts were perfect, then all of the observations would lie along the diagonal line.

While the absolute errors for some of the bigger products are dramatic, the forecast errors for some of the smaller products are also significant. For example, the actual demand for the Juniors Zen Flat Lock 3/2 suit was more than 150 percent greater than forecast. This suggests that we should concentrate on the relative forecast errors instead of the absolute forecast errors.

Relative forecast errors can be measured with the *A/F ratio:*

$$\text{A/F ratio} = \frac{\text{Actual demand}}{\text{Forecast}}$$

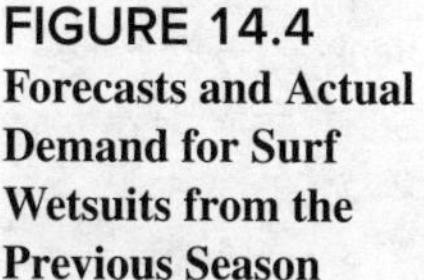
FIGURE 14.4
Forecasts and Actual Demand for Surf Wetsuits from the Previous Season

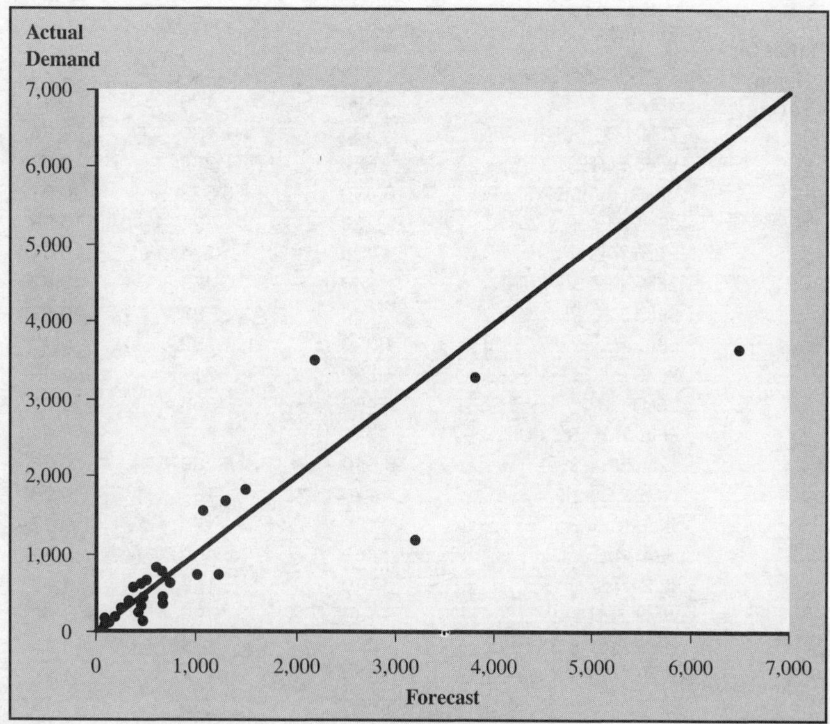

An accurate forecast has an A/F ratio = 1, while an A/F ratio above 1 indicates the forecast was too low and an A/F ratio below 1 indicates the forecast was too high. Table 14.2 displays the A/F ratios for our data in the last column.

Those A/F ratios provide a measure of the forecast accuracy from the previous season. To illustrate this point, Table 14.3 sorts the data in ascending A/F order. Also included in the table is each product's A/F rank in the order and each product's percentile, the fraction of products that have that A/F rank or lower. (For example, the product with the fifth A/F ratio has a percentile of 5/33 = 15.2 percent because it is the fifth product out of 33 products in the data.) We see from the data that actual demand is less than 80 percent of the forecast for one-third of the products (the A/F ratio 0.8 has a percentile of 33.3) and actual demand is greater than 125 percent of the forecast for 27.3 percent of the products (the A/F ratio 1.25 has a percentile of 72.7).

Given that the A/F ratios from the previous season reflect forecast accuracy in the previous season, maybe the current season's forecast accuracy will be comparable. Hence, we want to find a distribution function that will match the accuracy we observe in Table 14.3. We will use the normal distribution function to do this. Before getting there, we need a couple of additional results.

Take the definition of the A/F ratio and rearrange terms to get

$$\text{Actual demand} = \text{A/F ratio} \times \text{Forecast}$$

For the Hammer 3/2, the forecast is 3,200 units. Note that the forecast is not random, but the A/F ratio is random. Hence, the randomness in actual demand is directly related to the randomness in the A/F ratio. Using standard results from statistics and the above equation, we get the following results:

$$\text{Expected actual demand} = \text{Expected A/F ratio} \times \text{Forecast}$$

TABLE 14.3
Sorted A/F Ratios for Surf Wetsuits from the Previous Spring Season

Product Description	Forecast	Actual Demand	A/F Ratio*	Rank	Percentile**
ZEN-ZIP 2MM FULL	470	116	0.25	1	3.0
ZEN 3/2	3,190	1,195	0.37	2	6.1
ZEN 4/3	430	239	0.56	3	9.1
WMS ELITE 3/2	650	364	0.56	4	12.1
WMS HAMMER 3/2 FULL	6,490	3,673	0.57	5	15.2
JR HAMMER 3/2	1,220	721	0.59	6	18.2
HEATWAVE 4/3	430	274	0.64	7	21.2
ZEN 2MM S/S FULL	680	453	0.67	8	24.2
EPIC 5/3 W/HD	120	83	0.69	9	27.3
EPIC 4/3	1,020	732	0.72	10	30.3
WMS EPIC 2MM FULL	390	311	0.80	11	33.3
ZEN FL 3/2	450	365	0.81	12	36.4
EPIC 2MM S/S FULL	740	607	0.82	13	39.4
ZEN-ZIP 4/3	3,810	3,289	0.86	14	42.4
WMS ZEN-ZIP 4/3	170	163	0.96	15	45.5
JR EPIC 3/2	180	175	0.97	16	48.5
HEAT 4/3	460	450	0.98	17	51.5
JR ZEN 3/2	140	143	1.02	18	54.5
WMS ZEN 3/2	180	195	1.08	19	57.6
WMS EPIC 5/3 W/HD	320	369	1.15	20	60.6
ZEN-ZIP 5/4/3 W/HOOD	270	317	1.17	21	63.6
ZEN-ZIP 3/2	660	788	1.19	22	66.7
HAMMER S/S FULL	1,490	1,832	1.23	23	69.7
HEATWAVE 3/2	170	212	1.25	24	72.7
HEAT 3/2	500	635	1.27	25	75.8
HAMMER 3/2	1,300	1,696	1.30	26	78.8
WMS EPIC 3/2	610	830	1.36	27	81.8
EVO 4/3	440	623	1.42	28	84.8
WMS EPIC 4/3	1,060	1,552	1.46	29	87.9
JR EPIC 4/3	380	571	1.50	30	90.9
EVO 3/2	380	587	1.54	31	93.9
JR ZEN FL 3/2	90	140	1.56	32	97.0
EPIC 3/2	2,190	3,504	1.60	33	100.0

*A/F ratio = Actual demand divided by Forecast
**Percentile = Rank divided by total number of wetsuits (33)

and

$$\text{Standard deviation of demand} = \text{Standard deviattion of A/F ratios} \times \text{Forecast}$$

Expected actual demand, or *expected demand* for short, is what we should choose for the mean for our normal distribution, μ. The average A/F ratio in Table 14.3 is 0.9976. Therefore, expected demand for the Hammer 3/2 in the upcoming season is $0.9976 \times 3{,}200 = 3{,}192$ units. In other words, if the initial forecast is 3,200 units and the future A/F ratios are comparable to the past A/F ratios, then the mean of actual demand is 3,192 units. So let's choose 3,192 units as our mean of the normal distribution.

This decision may raise some eyebrows: If our initial forecast is 3,200 units, why do we not instead choose 3,200 as the mean of the normal distribution? Because 3,192 is so close to 3,200, assigning 3,200 as the mean probably would lead to a good order quantity as well. However, suppose the average A/F ratio were 0.90, that is, on average, actual demand is 90 percent of the forecast. It is quite common for people to have overly optimistic forecasts,

Exhibit 14.7

A PROCESS FOR USING HISTORICAL A/F RATIOS TO CHOOSE A MEAN AND STANDARD DEVIATION FOR A NORMAL DISTRIBUTION FORECAST

Step 1 Assemble a data set of products for which the forecasting task is comparable to the product of interest. In other words, the data set should include products that you expect would have similar forecast error to the product of interest. (They may or may not be similar products.) The data should include an initial forecast of demand and the actual demand. We also need a forecast for the item for the upcoming season.

Step 2 Evaluate the A/F ratio for each product in the data set. Evaluate the average of the A/F ratios (that is, the expected A/F ratio) and the standard deviation of the A/F ratios. (In Excel use the average() and stdev() functions.)

Step 3 The mean and standard deviation of the normal distribution that we will use as the forecast can now be evaluated with the following two equations:

$$\text{Expected demand} = \text{A/F ratio Expected A/F ratio} \times \text{Forecast}$$

$$\text{Standard deviation of demand} = \text{Standard deviation of A/F ratios} \times \text{Forecast}$$

where the forecast in the above equations is the forecast for the item for the upcoming season.

so an average A/F ratio of 0.90 is possible. In that case, expected actual demand would only be $0.90 \times 3{,}200 = 2{,}880$. Because we want to choose a normal distribution that represents actual demand, in that situation it would be better to choose a mean of 2,880 even though our initial forecast is 3,200. (Novice golfers sometimes adopt an analogous strategy. If a golfer consistently hooks the ball to the right on her drives, then she should aim to the left of the flag. In an ideal world, there would be no hook to her shot nor a bias in the forecast. But if the data say there is a hook, then it should not be ignored. Of course, the golfer and the forecaster also should work on eliminating the bias.)

Now that we have a mean for our normal distribution, we need a standard deviation. The second equation above tells us that the standard deviation of actual demand equals the standard deviation of the A/F ratios times the forecast. The standard deviation of the A/F ratios in Table 14.3 is 0.369. (Use the "stdev()" function in Excel.) So the standard deviation of actual demand is the standard deviation of the A/F ratios times the initial forecast: $0.369 \times 3{,}200 = 1{,}181$. Hence, to express our demand forecast for the Hammer 3/2, we can use a normal distribution with a mean of 3,192 and a standard deviation of 1,181. See Exhibit 14.7 for a summary of the process of choosing a mean and a standard deviation for a normal distribution forecast.

14.7 Managerial Lessons

Now that we have detailed the process of implementing the newsvendor model, it is worthwhile to step back and consider the managerial lessons it implies.

With respect to the forecasting process, there are three key lessons.

- For each product, it is insufficient to have just a forecast of expected demand. We also need a forecast for how variable demand will be about the forecast. That uncertainty in the forecast is captured by the standard deviation of demand.

- When forecasting, it is important to track actual demand. Two common mistakes are made with respect to this issue. First, do not forget that actual demand may be greater than actual sales due to an inventory shortage. If it is not possible to track actual demand after a stockout occurs, then you should attempt a reasonable estimate of actual demand. Second, actual demand includes potential sales only at the regular price. If you sold 1,000 units in the previous season, but 600 of them were at the discounted price at the end of the season, then actual demand is closer to 400 than 1,000.
- You need to keep track of past forecasts and forecast errors in order to assess the standard deviation of demand. Without past data on forecasts and forecast errors, it is very difficult to choose reasonable standard deviations; it is hard enough to forecast the mean of a distribution, but forecasting the standard deviation of a distribution is nearly impossible with just a "gut feel." Unfortunately, many firms fail to maintain the data they need to implement the newsvendor model correctly. They might not record the data because it is an inherently undesirable task to keep track of past errors: Who wants to have a permanent record of the big forecasting goofs? Alternatively, firms may not realize the importance of such data and therefore do not go through the effort to record and maintain it.

There are also a number of important lessons from the order quantity choice process.

- The profit-maximizing order quantity generally does not equal expected demand. If the underage cost is greater than the overage cost (i.e., it is more expensive to lose a sale than it is to have leftover inventory), then the profit-maximizing order quantity is larger than expected demand. (Because then the critical ratio is greater than 0.50.) On the other hand, some products may have an overage cost that is larger than the underage cost. For such products, it is actually best to order less than the expected demand.
- The order quantity decision should be separated from the forecasting process. The goal of the forecasting process is to develop the best forecast for a product's demand and therefore should proceed without regard to the order quantity decision. This can be frustrating for some firms. Imagine the marketing department dedicates considerable effort to develop a forecast and then the operations department decides to produce a quantity above the forecast. The marketing department may feel that their efforts are being ignored or their expertise is being second-guessed. In addition, they may be concerned that they would be responsible for ensuring that all of the production is sold even though their forecast was more conservative. The separation between the forecasting and the order quantity decision also implies that two products with the same mean forecast may have different expected profit-maximizing order quantities, either because they have different critical ratios or because they have different standard deviations.
- Explicit costs should not be overemphasized relative to opportunity costs. Inventory at the end of the season is the explicit cost of a demand–supply mismatch, while lost sales are the opportunity cost. Overemphasizing the former relative to the latter causes you to order less than the profit-maximizing order quantity.
- It is important to recognize that choosing an order quantity to maximize expected profit is only one possible objective. It is also a very reasonable objective, but there can be situations in which a manager may wish to consider an alternative objective. For example, maximizing expected profit is wise if you are not particularly concerned with the variability of profit. If you are managing many different products so that the realized profit from any one product cannot cause undue hardship on the firm, then maximizing expected profit is a good objective to adopt. But if you are a start-up firm with

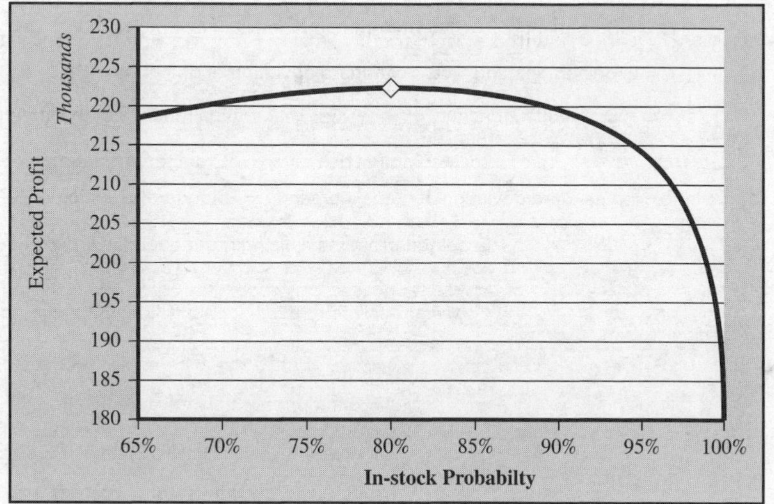

FIGURE 14.5 The Trade-Off between Profit and Service with the Hammer 3/2

The diamond indicates the in-stock probability and the expected profit of the optimal order quantity, 4,196 units.

a single product and limited capital, then you might not be able to absorb a significant profit loss. In situations in which the variability of profit matters, it is prudent to order less than the profit-maximizing order quantity. The expected profit objective also does not consider customer service explicitly in its objective. With the expected profit-maximizing order quantity for the Hammer 3/2, the in-stock probability is about 80 percent. Some managers may feel this is an unacceptable level of customer service, fearing that unsatisfied customers will switch to a competitor. Figure 14.5 displays the trade-off between service and expected profit. As we can see, the expected profit curve is reasonably flat around the maximum, which occurs with an in-stock probability that equals 80 percent. Raising the in-stock probability to 90 percent may be considered worthwhile because it reduces profits by slightly less than 1 percent. However, raising the in-stock dramatically, say, to 99 percent, may cause expected profits to fall too much—in that case by nearly 10 percent.

- Finally, while it is impossible to perfectly match supply and demand when supply must be chosen before random demand, it is possible to make a smart choice that balances the cost of ordering too much with the cost of ordering too little. In other words, uncertainty should not invite ad hoc decision making.

14.8 Summary

The newsvendor model is a tool for making a decision when there is a "too much–too little" challenge: Bet too much and there is a cost (e.g., leftover inventory), but bet too little and there is a different cost (e.g., the opportunity cost of lost sales). (See Table 14.4 for a summary of the key notation and equations.) To make this trade-off effectively, it is necessary to have a complete forecast of demand. It is not enough to just have a single sales forecast; we need to know the potential variation about that sales forecast. With a forecast model of demand (e.g., normal distribution with mean 3,192 and standard deviation 1,181), we can choose a quantity to maximize expected profit or to achieve a desired in-stock probability. For any chosen quantity, we can evaluate several performance measures, such as expected sales and expected profit.

TABLE 14.4 Summary of Key Notation and Equations in Chapter 14

Q = Order quantity C_u = Underage cost C_o = Overage cost   Critical ratio $= \frac{C_u}{C_o + C_u}$

μ = Expected demand σ = Standard deviation of demand

$F(Q)$: Distribution function $\Phi(Q)$: Distribution function of the standard normal

Expected actual demand = Expected A/F ratio × Forecast

Standard deviation of actual demand = Standard deviation of A/F ratios × Forecast

Expected profit-maximizing order quantity: $F(Q) = \frac{C_u}{C_o + C_u}$

z-statistic or normalized order quantity: $z = \frac{Q - \mu}{\sigma}$

$$Q = \mu + z \times \sigma$$

$I(z)$ = Standard normal inventory function

$L(z)$ = Standard normal loss function

Expected Leftover Inventory = $\sigma \times I(z)$

Excel: Expected Leftover Inventory = σ* (Normdist(z,0,1,0) + z × Normsdist(z))

Expected sales = Q – Expected Leftover Inventory

Expected Lost Sales = $\mu - Q$ + Expected Leftover Inventory = $\sigma \times L(z)$

Excel: Expected lost sales = σ* (Normdist(z,0,1,0) – z* (1 – Normsdist(z)))

Expected profit =[(Price – Cost) × Expected sales] – [(Cost – Salvage value) × Expected leftover inventory]

In-stock probability = $F(Q)$ Stockout probability = 1 – In-stock probability

Excel: z = Normsinv(Target in-stock probability)

Excel: In-stock probability = Normsdist(z)

Expected leftover inventory = $\sigma \times I(z)$

Expected sales = Q – Expected leftover inventory

Excel: Expected leftover inventory = σ* (Normdist(z, 0, 1, 0) + z* Normsdist(z))

14.9 Further Reading

The newsvendor model is one of the most extensively studied models in operations management. It has been extended theoretically along numerous dimensions (e.g., multiple periods have been studied, the pricing decision has been included, the salvage values could depend on the quantity salvaged, the decision maker's tolerance for risk can be incorporated into the objective function, etc.)

Several textbooks provide more technical treatments of the newsvendor model than this chapter. See Nahmias (2005), Porteus (2002), or Silver, Pyke, and Peterson (1998).

For a review of the theoretical literature on the newsvendor model, with an emphasis on the pricing decision in a newsvendor setting, see Petruzzi and Dada (1999).

14.10 Practice Problems

The following questions will help in testing your understanding of this chapter. After each question, we show the relevant section in parentheses [Section x].

Solutions to problems marked with an "*" are available in Appendix E. Video solutions to select problems are available in Connect.

Q14.1* **(McClure Books)** Dan McClure owns a thriving independent bookstore in artsy New Hope, Pennsylvania. He must decide how many copies to order of a new book, *Power and Self-Destruction,* an exposé on a famous politician's lurid affairs. Interest in the book will be intense at first and then fizzle quickly as attention turns to other celebrities. The book's retail price is \$20 and the wholesale price is \$12. The publisher will buy back the retailer's leftover copies at a full refund, but McClure Books incurs $4 in shipping and handling costs for each book returned to the publisher. Dan believes his demand forecast can be represented by a normal distribution with mean 200 and standard deviation 80.

a. Dan will consider this book to be a blockbuster for him if it sells more than 400 units. What is the probability *Power and Self-Destruction* will be a blockbuster? [14.2]

b. Dan considers a book a "dog" if it sells less than 50 percent of his mean forecast. What is the probability this exposé is a "dog"? [14.2]

c. What is the probability demand for this book will be within 20 percent of the mean forecast? [14.2]

d. What order quantity maximizes Dan's expected profit? [14.3]

e. Dan prides himself on good customer service. In fact, his motto is "McClure's got what you want to read." How many books should Dan order if he wants to achieve a 95 percent in-stock probability? [14.5]

f. If Dan orders the quantity chosen in part e to achieve a 95 percent in-stock probability, then what is the probability that "Dan won't have what some customer wants to read" (i.e., what is the probability some customer won't be able to purchase a copy of the book)? [14.4]

g. Suppose Dan orders 300 copies of the book. What would Dan's expected profit be in this case? [14.4]

Q14.2* (**EcoTable Tea**) EcoTable is a retailer of specialty organic and ecologically friendly foods. In one of their Cambridge, Massachusetts, stores, they plan to offer a gift basket of Tanzanian teas for the holiday season. They plan on placing one order and any leftover inventory will be discounted at the end of the season. Expected demand for this store is 4.5 units and demand should be Poisson distributed. The gift basket sells for $55, the purchase cost to EcoTable is $32, and leftover baskets will be sold for $20.

a. If they purchase only 3 baskets, what is the probability that some demand will not be satisfied? [14.2]

b. If they purchase 10 baskets, what is the probability that they will have to mark down at least 3 baskets? [14.2]

c. How many baskets should EcoTable purchase to maximize its expected profit? [14.3]

d. Suppose they purchase 4 baskets. How many baskets can they expect to sell? [14.4]

e. Suppose they purchase 6 baskets. How many baskets should they expect to have to mark down at the end of the season? [14.4]

f. Suppose EcoTable wants to minimize its inventory while satisfying all demand with at least a 90 percent probability. How many baskets should they order? [14.5]

g. Suppose EcoTable orders 8 baskets. What is its expected profit? [14.4]

Q14.3* (**Pony Express Creations**) Pony Express Creations Inc. (www.pony-ex.com) is a manufacturer of party hats, primarily for the Halloween season. (80 percent of their yearly sales occur over a six-week period.) One of their popular products is the Elvis wig, complete with sideburns and metallic glasses. The Elvis wig is produced in China, so Pony Express must make a single order well in advance of the upcoming season. Ryan, the owner of Pony Express, expects demand to be 25,000 and the following is his entire demand forecast:

Q	Prob $(D = Q)$	$F(Q)$	$I(Q)$
5,000	0.0181	0.0181	0
10,000	0.0733	0.0914	91
15,000	0.1467	0.2381	548
20,000	0.1954	0.4335	1,738
25,000	0.1954	0.6289	3,906
30,000	0.1563	0.7852	7,050
35,000	0.1042	0.8894	10,976

(*Continued*)

Q	Prob ($D = Q$)	$F(Q)$	$I(Q)$
40,000	0.0595	0.9489	15,423
45,000	0.0298	0.9787	20,168
50,000	0.0132	0.9919	25,061
55,000	0.0053	0.9972	30,021
60,000	0.0019	0.9991	35,007
65,000	0.0006	0.9997	40,002
70,000	0.0002	0.9999	45,001
75,000	0.0001	1.0000	50,000

Prob($D = Q$) = Probability demand D equals Q
$F(Q)$ = Probability demand is Q or lower
$L(Q)$ = Expected lost sales if Q units are ordered

The Elvis wig retails for $25, but Pony Express's wholesale price is $12. Their production cost is $6. Leftover inventory can be sold to discounters for $2.50.

a. Suppose Pony Express orders 40,000 Elvis wigs. What is the chance they have to liquidate 10,000 or more wigs with a discounter? [14.2]

b. What order quantity maximizes Pony Express's expected profit? [14.3]

c. If Pony Express wants to have a 90 percent in-stock probability, then how many Elvis wigs should be ordered? [14.5]

d. If Pony Express orders 50,000 units, then how many wigs can they expect to have to liquidate with discounters? [14.4]

e. If Pony Express insists on a 100 percent in-stock probability for its customers, then what is its expected profit? [14.4]

Q14.4* **(Flextrola)** Flextrola, Inc., an electronics systems integrator, is planning to design a key component for their next-generation product with Solectrics. Flextrola will integrate the component with some software and then sell it to consumers. Given the short life cycles of such products and the long lead times quoted by Solectrics, Flextrola only has one opportunity to place an order with Solectrics prior to the beginning of its selling season. Flextrola's demand during the season is normally distributed with a mean of 1,000 and a standard deviation of 600.

Solectrics' production cost for the component is $52 per unit and it plans to sell the component for $72 per unit to Flextrola. Flextrola incurs essentially no cost associated with the software integration and handling of each unit. Flextrola sells these units to consumers for $121 each. Flextrola can sell unsold inventory at the end of the season in a secondary electronics market for $50 each. The existing contract specifies that once Flextrola places the order, no changes are allowed to it. Also, Solectrics does not accept any returns of unsold inventory, so Flextrola must dispose of excess inventory in the secondary market.

a. What is the probability that Flextrola's demand will be within 25 percent of its forecast? [14.2]

b. What is the probability that Flextrola's demand will be more than 40 percent greater than its forecast? [14.2]

c. Under this contract, how many units should Flextrola order to maximize its expected profit? [14.3]

For parts d through i, assume Flextrola orders 1,200 units.

d. What are Flextrola's expected sales? [14.4]

e. How many units of inventory can Flextrola expect to sell in the secondary electronics market? [14.4]

f. What is Flextrola's expected gross margin percentage, which is (Revenue – Cost)/ Revenue? [14.4]

g. What is Flextrola's expected profit? [14.4]

(* indicates that the solution is in Appendix E)

h. What is Solectrics' expected profit? [14.4]
i. What is the probability that Flextrola has lost sales of 400 units or more? [14.2]
j. A sharp manager at Flextrola noticed the demand forecast and became wary of assuming that demand is normally distributed. She plotted a histogram of demands from previous seasons for similar products and concluded that demand is better represented by the log normal distribution. Figure 14.6 plots the density function for both the log normal and the normal distribution, each with mean of 1,000 and standard deviation of 600. Figure 14.7 plots the distribution function for both the log normal and the normal. Using the more accurate forecast (i.e., the log normal distribution), approximately how many units should Flextrola order to maximize its expected profit? [14.3]

Q14.5* **(Fashionables)** Fashionables is a franchisee of The Limited, the well-known retailer of fashionable clothing. Prior to the winter season, The Limited offers Fashionables the choice of five different colors of a particular sweater design. The sweaters are knit overseas by hand, and because of the lead times involved, Fashionables will need to order its assortment in advance of the selling season. As per the contracting terms offered by The Limited, Fashionables also will not be able to cancel, modify, or reorder sweaters during the selling season. Demand for each color during the season is normally distributed with a mean of 500 and a standard deviation of 200. Further, you may assume that the demands for each sweater are independent of those for a different color.

The Limited offers the sweaters to Fashionables at the wholesale price of \$40 per sweater and Fashionables plans to sell each sweater at the retail price of \$70 per unit. The Limited delivers orders placed by Fashionables in truckloads at a cost of \$2,000 per truckload. The transportation cost of \$2,000 is borne by Fashionables. Assume unless otherwise specified that all the sweaters ordered by Fashionables will fit into one truckload. Also assume that all other associated costs, such as unpacking and handling, are negligible.

FIGURE 14.6 Density Function

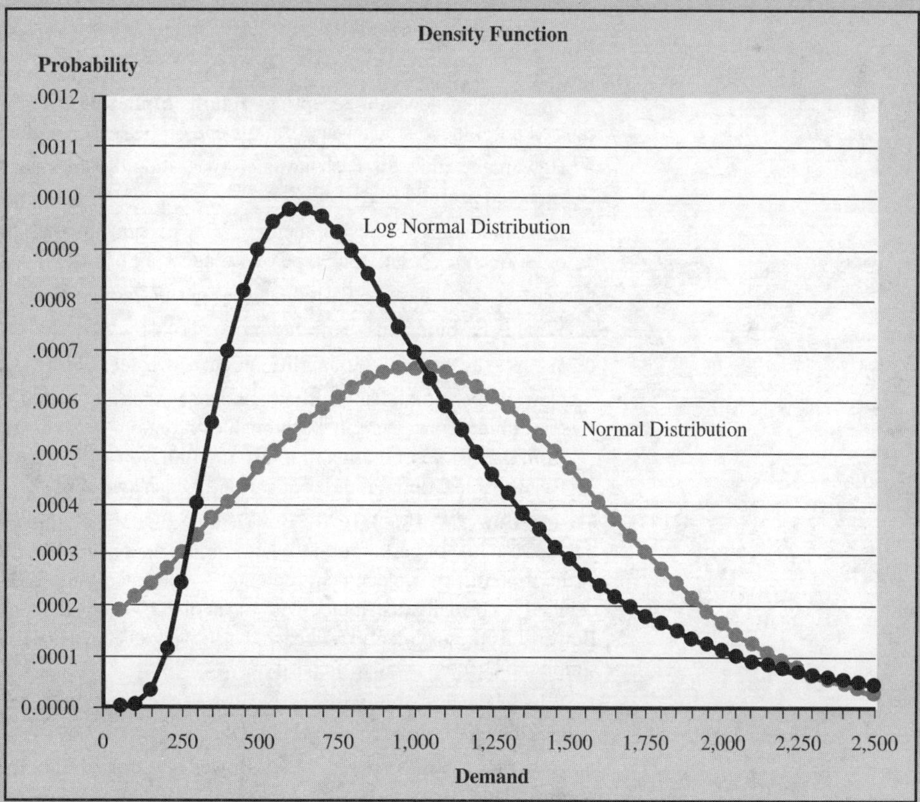

FIGURE 14.7 Distribution Function

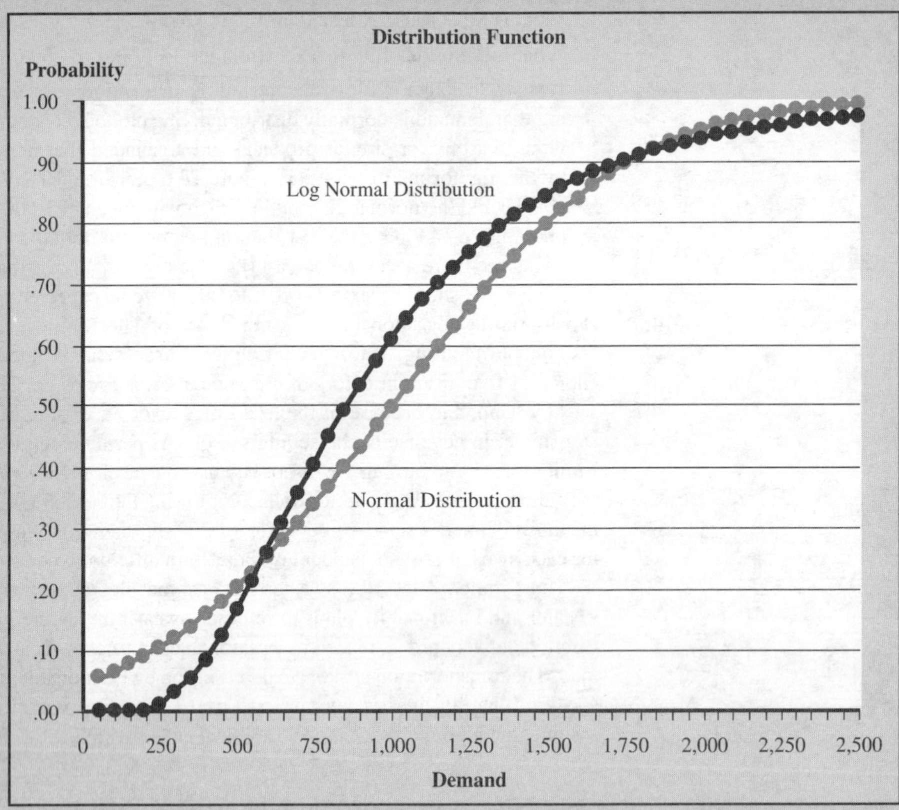

The Limited does not accept any returns of unsold inventory. However, Fashionables can sell all of the unsold sweaters at the end of the season at the fire-sale price of $20 each.

a. How many units of each sweater type should Fashionables order to maximize its expected profit? [14.3]

b. If Fashionables wishes to ensure a 97.5 percent in-stock probability, what should its order quantity be for each type of sweater? [14.5]

For parts c and d, assume Fashionables orders 725 of each sweater.

c. What is Fashionables' expected profit? [14.4]

d. What is the stockout probability for each sweater? [14.4]

e. Now suppose that The Limited announces that the unit of truckload capacity is 2,500 total units of sweaters. If Fashionables orders more than 2,500 units in total (actually, from 2,501 to 5,000 units in total), it will have to pay for two truckloads. What now is Fashionables' optimal order quantity for each sweater? [14.3]

Q14.6 **(Teddy Bower Parkas)** Teddy Bower is an outdoor clothing and accessories chain that purchases a line of parkas at $10 each from its Asian supplier, TeddySports. Unfortunately, at the time of order placement, demand is still uncertain. Teddy Bower forecasts that its demand is normally distributed with mean of 2,100 and standard deviation of 1,200. Teddy Bower sells these parkas at $22 each. Unsold parkas have little salvage value; Teddy Bower simply gives them away to a charity.

a. What is the probability this parka turns out to be a "dog," defined as a product that sells less than half of the forecast? [14.2]

b. How many parkas should Teddy Bower buy from TeddySports to maximize expected profit? [14.3]

c. If Teddy Bower wishes to ensure a 98.5 percent in-stock probability, how many parkas should it order? [14.5]

For parts d and e, assume Teddy Bower orders 3,000 parkas.

d. Evaluate Teddy Bower's expected profit. [14.4]

d. Evaluate Teddy Bower's stockout probability. [14.4]

Q14.7 **(Teddy Bower Boots)** To ensure a full line of outdoor clothing and accessories, the marketing department at Teddy Bower insists that they also sell waterproof hunting boots. Unfortunately, neither Teddy Bower nor TeddySports has expertise in manufacturing those kinds of boots. Therefore, Teddy Bower contacted several Taiwanese suppliers to request quotes. Due to competition, Teddy Bower knows that it cannot sell these boots for more than $54. However, $40 per boot was the best quote from the suppliers. In addition, Teddy Bower anticipates excess inventory will need to be sold off at a 50 percent discount at the end of the season. Given the $54 price, Teddy Bower's demand forecast is for 400 boots, with a standard deviation of 300.

a. If Teddy Bower decides to include these boots in its assortment, how many boots should it order from its supplier? [14.3]

b. Suppose Teddy Bower orders 380 boots. What would its expected profit be? [14.4]

c. John Briggs, a buyer in the procurement department, overheard at lunch a discussion of the "boot problem." He suggested that Teddy Bower ask for a quantity discount from the supplier. After following up on his suggestion, the supplier responded that Teddy Bower could get a 10 percent discount if they were willing to order at least 800 boots. If the objective is to maximize expected profit, how many boots should it order given this new offer? [14.4]

Q14.8 **(Land's End)** Geoff Gullo owns a small firm that manufactures "Gullo Sunglasses." He has the opportunity to sell a particular seasonal model to Land's End. Geoff offers Land's End two purchasing options:

- Option 1. Geoff offers to set his price at $65 and agrees to credit Land's End $53 for each unit Land's End returns to Geoff at the end of the season (because those units did not sell). Since styles change each year, there is essentially no value in the returned merchandise.
- Option 2. Geoff offers a price of $55 for each unit, but returns are no longer accepted. In this case, Land's End throws out unsold units at the end of the season.

This season's demand for this model will be normally distributed with mean of 200 and standard deviation of 125. Land's End will sell those sunglasses for $100 each. Geoff 's production cost is $25.

a. How much would Land's End buy if they chose option 1? [14.3]

b. How much would Land's End buy if they chose option 2? [14.3]

c. Which option will Land's End choose? [14.4]

d. Suppose Land's End chooses option 1 and orders 275 units. What is Geoff Gullo's expected profit? [14.4]

Q14.9 **(CPG Bagels)** CPG Bagels starts the day with a large production run of bagels. Throughout the morning, additional bagels are produced as needed. The last bake is completed at 3 p.m. and the store closes at 8 p.m. It costs approximately $0.20 in materials and labor to make a bagel. The price of a fresh bagel is $0.60. Bagels not sold by the end of the day are sold the next day as "day old" bagels in bags of six, for $0.99 a bag. About two-thirds of the day-old bagels are sold; the remainder are just thrown away. There are many bagel flavors, but for simplicity, concentrate just on the plain bagels. The store manager predicts that demand for plain bagels from 3 p.m. until closing is normally distributed with mean of 54 and standard deviation of 21.

a. How many bagels should the store have at 3 p.m. to maximize the store's expected profit (from sales between 3 p.m. until closing)? (*Hint:* Assume day-old bagels are sold for $0.99/6 = $0.165 each; that is, don't worry about the fact that day-old bagels are sold in bags of six.) [14.3]

b. Suppose that the store manager is concerned that stockouts might cause a loss of future business. To explore this idea, the store manager feels that it is appropriate to assign a stockout cost of $5 per bagel that is demanded but not filled. (Customers frequently purchase more than one bagel at a time. This cost is per bagel demanded that is not satisfied rather than per customer that does not receive a complete order.) Given the additional stockout cost, how many bagels should the store have at 3 p.m. to maximize the store's expected profit? [14.3]

c. Suppose the store manager has 101 bagels at 3 p.m. How many bagels should the store manager expect to have at the end of the day? [14.4]

Q14.10 **(The Kiosk)** Weekday lunch demand for spicy black bean burritos at the Kiosk, a local snack bar, is approximately Poisson with a mean of 22. The Kiosk charges $4.00 for each burrito, which are all made before the lunch crowd arrives. Virtually all burrito customers also buy a soda that is sold for 60¢. The burritos cost the Kiosk $2.00, while sodas cost the Kiosk 5¢. Kiosk management is very sensitive about the quality of food they serve. Thus, they maintain a strict "No Old Burrito" policy, so any burrito left at the end of the day is disposed of. The distribution function of a Poisson with mean 22 is as follows:

Q	*F(Q)*
1	0.0000
2	0.0000
3	0.0000
4	0.0000
5	0.0000
6	0.0001
7	0.0002
8	0.0006
9	0.0015
10	0.0035
11	0.0076
12	0.0151
13	0.0278
14	0.0477
15	0.0769
16	0.1170
17	0.1690
18	0.2325
19	0.3060
20	0.3869
21	0.4716
22	0.5564
23	0.6374
24	0.7117
25	0.7771
26	0.8324
27	0.8775
28	0.9129
29	0.9398
30	0.9595
31	0.9735
32	0.9831
33	0.9895

34	0.9936
35	0.9962
36	0.9978
37	0.9988
38	0.9993
39	0.9996
40	0.9998

a. Suppose burrito customers buy their snack somewhere else if the Kiosk is out of stock. How many burritos should the Kiosk make for the lunch crowd? [14.3]

b. Suppose that any customer unable to purchase a burrito settles for a lunch of Pop-Tarts and a soda. Pop-Tarts sell for 75¢ and cost the Kiosk 25¢. (As Pop-Tarts and soda are easily stored, the Kiosk never runs out of these essentials.) Assuming that the Kiosk management is interested in maximizing profits, how many burritos should they prepare? [14.3]

Chapter 15

Assemble-to-Order, Make-to-Order, and Quick Response with Reactive Capacity[1]

A firm facing the newsvendor problem can manage, but not avoid, the possibility of a demand–supply mismatch: Order too much and inventory is left over at the end of the season, but order too little and incur the opportunity cost of lost sales. The firm finds itself in this situation because it commits to its entire supply before demand occurs. This mode of operation is often called *make-to-stock* because all items enter finished goods inventory (stock) before they are demanded. In other words, with make-to-stock, the identity of an item's eventual owner is not known when production of the item is initiated.

To reduce the demand–supply mismatches associated with make-to-stock, a firm could attempt to delay at least some production until better demand information is learned. For example, a firm could choose to begin producing an item only when it receives a firm order from a customer. This mode of operation is often called *make-to-order* or *assemble-to-order*. Dell Computer is probably the most well-known and most successful company to have implemented the assemble-to-order model.

Make-to-stock and make-to-order are two extremes in the sense that with one all production begins well before demand is received, whereas with the other production begins only after demand is known. Between any two extremes there also must be an intermediate option. Suppose the lead time to receive an order is short relative to the length of the selling season. A firm then orders some inventory before the selling season starts so that some product is on hand at the beginning of the season. After observing early season sales, the firm then submits a second order that is received well before the end of the season (due to the short lead time). In this situation, the firm should make a conservative initial order and use the second order to strategically respond to initial season sales: Slow-selling products are not replenished midseason, thereby reducing leftover inventory, while fast-selling products are replenished, thereby reducing lost sales.

[1] The data in this chapter have been modified to protect confidentiality.

The capability to place multiple orders during a selling season is an integral part of *Quick Response*. Quick Response is a set of practices designed to reduce the cost of mismatches between supply and demand. It began in the apparel industry as a response to just-in-time practices in the automobile industry and has since migrated to the grocery industry under the label *Efficient Consumer Response.*

The aspect of Quick Response discussed in this chapter is the use of *reactive capacity;* that is, capacity that allows a firm to place one additional order during the season, which retailers often refer to as a "second buy." As in Chapter 14, we use O'Neill Inc. for our case analysis. Furthermore, we assume throughout this chapter that the normal distribution with mean 3,192 and standard deviation 1,181 is our demand forecast for the Hammer 3/2.

The first part of this chapter evaluates and minimizes the demand–supply mismatch cost to a make-to-stock firm, that is, a firm that has only a single ordering opportunity, as in the newsvendor model. Furthermore, we identify situations in which the cost of demand–supply mismatches is large. Those are the situations in which there is the greatest potential to benefit from Quick Response with reactive capacity or make-to-order production. The second part of this chapter discusses make-to-order relative to make-to-stock. The third part studies reactive capacity: How should we choose an initial order quantity when some reactive capacity is available? And, as with the newsvendor model, how do we evaluate several performance measures? The chapter concludes with a summary and managerial implications.

15.1 Evaluating and Minimizing the Newsvendor's Demand–Supply Mismatch Cost

In this section, the costs associated in the newsvendor model with demand–supply mismatches are identified, then two approaches are outlined for evaluating the expected demand–supply mismatch cost, and finally we show how to minimize those costs. For ease of exposition, we use the shorthand term *mismatch cost* to refer to the "expected demand–supply mismatch cost."

In the newsvendor model, the mismatch cost is divided into two components: the cost of ordering too much and the cost of ordering too little. Ordering too much means there is leftover inventory at the end of the season. Ordering too little means there are lost sales. The cost for each unit of leftover inventory is the overage cost, which we label C_o. The cost for each lost sale is the underage cost, which we label C_u. (See Chapter 14 for the original discussion of these costs.) Therefore, the mismatch cost in the newsvendor model is the sum of the expected overage cost and the expected underage cost:

$$\begin{aligned}\text{Mismatch cost} = &(C_o \times \text{Expected leftover inventory})\\ &+ (C_u \times \text{Expected lost sales})\end{aligned} \quad \textbf{(15.1)}$$

Notice that the mismatch cost includes both a tangible cost (leftover inventory) and an intangible opportunity cost (lost sales). The former has a direct impact on the profit and loss statement, but the latter does not. Nevertheless, the opportunity cost of lost sales should not be ignored.

Not only does Equation (15.1) provide us with the definition of the mismatch cost, it also provides us with our first method for evaluating the mismatch cost because we already know how to evaluate the expected leftover inventory and the expected lost sales (from Chapter 14). Let's illustrate this method with O'Neill's Hammer 3/2 wetsuit. The Hammer 3/2 has a selling price of \$190 and a purchase cost from the TEC Group of \$110. Therefore, the underage cost is \$190 − \$110 = \$80 per lost sale. Leftover inventory is sold at \$90,

TABLE 15.1 Summary of Performance Measures for O'Neill's Hammer 3/2 Wetsuit When the Expected Profit-Maximizing Quantity Is Ordered and the Demand Forecast Is Normally Distributed with Mean 3,192 and Standard Deviation 1,181

Order quantity, Q	= 4,196 units
Expected demand, μ	= 3,192 units
Standard deviation of demand, σ	= 1,181
z	= 0.85
Expected leftover inventory = σ * $I(z)$	= 1,133.8 units
Expected sales = Q − Expected leftover inventory	= 3,062.2 units
Expected lost sales = μ − Expected sales	= 129.8
Expected profit = (\$190 − \$110) × 3,062.2 − (\$110 − \$90) × 1,133.8	= \$222,300
Expected revenue = Price × Expected sales + Salvage value × Expected leftover inventory = \$190 × 3,062.2 + \$90 × 1,133.8 = \$683,860	

so the overage cost is \$110 − \$90 = \$20 per wetsuit left at the end of the season. The expected profit-maximizing order quantity is 4,196 units. Using the techniques described in Chapter 14, for that order quantity we can evaluate several performance measures, summarized in Table 15.1. Therefore, the mismatch cost for the Hammer 3/2, despite ordering the expected profit-maximizing quantity, is

$$(\$20 \times 1{,}133.8) + (\$80 \times 129.8) = \$33{,}060$$

Now let's consider a second approach for evaluating the mismatch cost. Imagine O'Neill had the opportunity to purchase a magic crystal ball. Even before O'Neill needs to submit its order to TEC, this crystal ball reveals to O'Neill the exact demand for the entire season. O'Neill would obviously order from TEC the demand quantity observed with this crystal ball. As a result, O'Neill would be in the pleasant situation of avoiding all mismatch costs (there would be no excess inventory and no lost sales) while still providing immediate product availability to its customers. In fact, the only function of the crystal ball is to eliminate all mismatch costs: For example, the crystal ball does not change demand, increase the selling price, or decrease the production cost. Thus, the difference in O'Neill's expected profit with the crystal ball and without it must equal the mismatch cost: The crystal ball increases profit by eliminating mismatch costs, so the profit increase must equal the mismatch cost. Therefore, we can evaluate the mismatch cost by first evaluating the newsvendor's expected profit, then evaluating the expected profit with the crystal ball, and finally taking the difference between those two figures.

We already know how to evaluate the newsvendor's expected profit (again, see Chapter 14). So let's illustrate how to evaluate the expected profit with the crystal ball. If O'Neill gets to observe demand before deciding how much to order from TEC, then there will not be any leftover inventory at the end of the season. Even better, O'Neill will not stock out, so every unit of demand turns into an actual sale. Hence, O'Neill's expected sales with the crystal ball equal expected demand, which is μ. We already know that O'Neill's profit per sale is the gross margin, the retail price minus the production cost, Price − Cost. Therefore O'Neill's expected profit with this crystal ball is expected demand times the profit per unit of demand, which is (Price − Cost) × μ. In fact, O'Neill can never earn a higher expected profit than it does with the crystal ball: There is nothing better than having no leftover inventory and earning the full margin on every unit of potential demand. Hence, let's call that profit the *maximum profit:*

$$\text{Maximum profit} = (\text{Price} - \text{Cost}) \times \mu$$

O'Neill's maximum profit with the Hammer 3/2 is \$80 × 3,192 = \$255,360. We already know that the newsvendor expected profit is \$222,300. So the difference between the maximum profit (i.e., crystal ball profit) and the newsvendor expected profit is O'Neill's mismatch costs. That figure is \$255,360 – \$222,300 = \$33,060, which matches our calculation with our first method (as it should). To summarize, our second method for evaluating the mismatch cost uses the following equation:

$$\text{Mismatch cost} = \text{Maximum profit} - \text{Expected profit}$$

Incidentally, you can also think of the mismatch cost as the most O'Neill should be willing to pay to purchase the crystal ball; that is, it is the value of perfect demand information.

The second method for calculating the mismatch cost emphasizes that there exists an easily evaluated maximum profit. We might not be able to evaluate expected profit precisely if there is some reactive capacity available to the firm. Nevertheless, we do know that no matter what type of reactive capacity the firm has, that reactive capacity cannot be as good as the crystal ball we just described. Therefore, the expected profit with any form of reactive capacity must be more than the newsvendor's expected profit but less than the maximum profit.

You now may be wondering about how to minimize the mismatch cost and whether that is any different from maximizing the newsvendor's expected profit. The short answer is that these are effectively the same objective, that is, the quantity that maximizes profit also minimizes mismatch costs. One way to see this is to look at the equation above: If expected profit is maximized and the maximum profit does not depend on the order quantity, then the difference between them, which is the mismatch cost, must be minimized.

Now that we know how to evaluate and minimize the mismatch cost, we need to get a sense of its significance. In other words, is \$33,060 a big problem or a little problem? To answer that question, we need to compare it with something else. The maximum profit is one reference point: The demand–supply mismatch cost as a percentage of the maximum profit is \$33,060/\$255,360 = 13 percent. You may prefer expected sales as a point of comparison: The demand–supply mismatch cost per unit of expected sales is \$33,080/3,062.2 = \$10.8. Alternatively, we can make the comparison with expected revenue, \$683,860, or expected profit, \$222,300: The demand–supply mismatch cost is approximately 4.8 percent of total revenue (\$33,080/\$683,860) and 14.9 percent of expected profit (\$33,080/\$222,300). Companies in the sports apparel industry generally have net profit in the range of 2 to 5 percent of revenue. Therefore, eliminating the mismatch cost from the Hammer 3/2 could potentially double O'Neill's net profit! That is an intriguing possibility.

15.2 When Is the Mismatch Cost High?

No matter which comparison you prefer, the mismatch cost for O'Neill is significant, even if the expected profit-maximizing quantity is ordered. But it is even better to know what causes a large demand–supply mismatch. To answer that question, let's first choose our point of comparison for the mismatch cost. Of the ones discussed at the end of the previous section, only the maximum profit does not depend on the order quantity chosen: unit sales, revenue, and profit all clearly depend on Q. In addition, the maximum profit is representative of the potential for the product: we cannot do better than earn the maximum profit. Therefore, let's evaluate the mismatch cost as a percentage of the maximum profit.

We next need to make an assumption about how much is ordered before the selling season, that is, clearly the mismatch cost depends on the order quantity Q. Let's adopt the natural assumption that the expected profit-maximizing quantity is ordered, which, as we discussed in the previous section, also happens to minimize the newsvendor's mismatch cost.

If we take the equations for expected lost sales and expected leftover inventory from Chapter 14, plug them into our first mismatch cost Equation (15.1), and then do several algebraic manipulations, we arrive at the following observations:

- The expected demand–supply mismatch cost becomes larger as demand variability increases, where demand variability is measured with the coefficient of variation, σ/μ.
- The expected demand–supply mismatch cost becomes larger as the critical ratio, $C_u/(C_o = C_u)$, becomes smaller.

(If you want to see the actual equations and how they are derived, see Appendix D.)

It is intuitive that the mismatch cost should increase as demand variability increases—it is simply harder to get demand to match supply when demand is less predicable. The key insight is how to measure demand variability. The *coefficient of variation* is the correct measure. You may recall in Chapter 9 we discussed the coefficient of variation with respect to the variability of the processing time (CV_p) or the interarrival time to a queue (CV_a). This coefficient of variation, σ/μ, is conceptually identical to those coefficients of variation: It is the ratio of the standard deviation of a random variable (in this case demand) to its mean.

It is worthwhile to illustrate why the coefficient of variation is the appropriate measure of variability in this setting. Suppose you are informed that the standard deviation of demand for an item is 800. Does that tell you enough information to assess the variability of demand? For example, does it allow you to evaluate the probability actual demand will be less than 75 percent of your forecast? In fact, it does not. Consider two cases, in the first the forecast is for 1,000 units and in the second the forecast is for 10,000 units. Demand is less than 75 percent of the 1,000-unit forecast if demand is less than 750 units. What is the probability that occurs? First, normalize the value 750:

$$Z = \frac{Q - \mu}{\sigma} = \frac{750 - 1{,}000}{800} = -0.31$$

Now use the Standard Normal Distribution Function Table to find the probability demand is less than 750: $\Phi\,(-0.31) = 0.3783$. With the forecast of 10,000, the comparable event has demand that is less than 7,500 units. Repeating the same process yields $z = (7{,}500 - 10{,}000)/800 = -3.1$ and $\Phi\,(-3.1) = 0.0009$. Therefore, with a standard deviation of 800, there is about a 38 percent chance demand is less than 75 percent of the first forecast but much less than a 1 percent chance demand is less than 75 percent of the second forecast. In other words, the standard deviation alone does not capture how much variability there is in demand. Notice that the coefficient of variation with the first product is 0.8 (800/1,000), whereas it is much lower with the second product, 0.08 (800/10,000).

For the Hammer 3/2, the coefficient of variation is 1,181/3,192 = 0.37. While there is no generally accepted standard for what is a "low," "medium," or "high" coefficient of variation, we offer the following guideline: Demand variability is rather low if the coefficient of variation is less than 0.25, medium if it is in the range 0.25 to 0.75, and high with anything above 0.75. A coefficient of variation above 1.5 is extremely high, and anything above 3 would imply that the demand forecast is essentially meaningless.

Table 15.2 provides data to allow you to judge for yourself what is a "low," "medium," and "high" coefficient of variation.

TABLE 15.2
Forecast Accuracy Relative to the Coefficient of Variation When Demand Is Normally Distributed

Coefficient of Variation	Probability Demand Is Less Than 75% of the Forecast	Probability Demand Is within 25% of the Forecast
0.10	0.6%	98.8%
0.25	15.9	68.3
0.50	30.9	38.3
0.75	36.9	26.1
1.00	40.1	19.7
1.50	43.4	13.2
2.00	45.0	9.9
3.00	46.7	6.6

Recall from Chapters 9 and 10 that the coefficient of variation with an exponential distribution is always one. Therefore, if two processes have exponential distributions, they always have the same amount of variability. The same is not true with the normal distribution because with the normal distribution the standard deviation is adjustable relative to the mean.

Our second observation above relates mismatch costs to the critical ratio. In particular, products with low critical ratios and high demand variability have high mismatch costs and products with high critical ratios and low demand variability have low mismatch costs. Table 15.3 displays data on the mismatch cost for various coefficients of variation and critical ratios.

As we have already mentioned, it is intuitive that the mismatch cost should increase as demand variability increases. The intuition with respect to the critical ratio takes some more thought. A very high critical ratio means there is a large profit margin relative to the loss on each unit of excess inventory. Greeting cards are good examples of products that might have very large critical ratios: The gross margin on each greeting card is large while the production cost is low. With a very large critical ratio, the optimal order quantity is quite large, so there are very few lost sales. There is also a substantial amount of leftover inventory, but the cost of each unit left over in inventory is not large at all, so the total cost of leftover inventory is relatively small. Therefore, the total mismatch cost is small. Now consider a product with a low critical ratio; that is, the per-unit cost of excess inventory is much higher than the cost of each lost sale. Perishable items often fall into this category as well as items that face obsolescence. Given that excess inventory is expensive, the optimal order quantity is quite low, possibly lower than expected demand. As a result, excess inventory is not a problem, but lost sales are a big problem, resulting in a high mismatch cost.

TABLE 15.3
The Mismatch Cost (as a Percentage of the Maximum Profit) When Demand Is Normally Distributed and the Newsvendor Expected Profit-Maximizing Quantity Is Ordered

	Critical Ratio					
Coefficient of Variation	0.4	0.5	0.6	0.7	0.8	0.9
0.10	10%	8%	6%	5%	3%	2%
0.25	24%	20%	16%	12%	9%	5%
0.40	39%	32%	26%	20%	14%	8%
0.55	53%	44%	35%	27%	19%	11%
0.70	68%	56%	45%	35%	24%	14%
0.85	82%	68%	55%	42%	30%	17%
1.00	97%	80%	64%	50%	35%	19%

15.3 Reducing Mismatch Costs with Make-to-Order

When supply is chosen before demand is observed (make-to-stock), there invariably is either too much or too little supply. A purely hypothetical solution to the problem is to find a crystal ball that reveals demand before it occurs. A more realistic solution is to initiate production of each unit only after demand is observed for that unit, which is often called make-to-order or assemble-to-order. This section discusses the pros and cons of make-to-order with respect to its ability to reduce mismatch costs.

In theory, make-to-order can eliminate the entire mismatch cost associated with make-to-stock (i.e., newsvendor). With make-to-order, there is no leftover inventory because production only begins after a firm order is received from a customer. Thus, make-to-order saves on expensive markdown and disposal expenses. Furthermore, there are no lost sales with make-to-order because each customer order is eventually produced. Therefore, products with a high mismatch cost (low critical ratios, high demand variability) would benefit considerably from a switch to make-to-order from make-to-stock.

But there are several reasons to be wary of make-to-order. For one, even with make-to-order, there generally is a need to carry component inventory. Although components may be less risky than finished goods, there still is a chance of having too many or too few of them. Next, make-to-order is never able to satisfy customer demands immediately; that is, customers must wait to have their order filled. If the wait is short, then demand with make-to-order can be nearly as high as with make-to-stock. But there is also some threshold beyond which customers do not wait. That threshold level depends on the product: Customers are generally less willing to wait for diapers than they are for custom sofas.

It is helpful to think of queuing theory (Chapters 9 and 10) to understand what determines the waiting time with make-to-order. No matter the number of servers, a key characteristic of a queuing system is that customer service begins only after a customer arrives to the system, just as production does not begin with make-to-order until a customer commits to an order. Another important feature of a queuing system is that customers must wait to be processed if all servers are busy, just as a customer must wait with make-to-order if the production process is working on the backlog of orders from previous customers.

To provide a reference point for this discussion, suppose O'Neill establishes a make-to-order assembly line for wetsuits. O'Neill could keep in inventory the necessary raw materials to fabricate wetsuits in a wide array of colors, styles, and quality levels. Wetsuits would then be produced as orders are received from customers. The assembly line has a maximum production rate, which would correspond to the service rate in a queue. Given that demand is random, the interarrival times between customer orders also would be random, just as in a queuing system.

A key insight from queuing is that a customer's expected waiting time depends nonlinearly (a curve, not a straight line) on the system's utilization (the ratio of the flow rate to capacity): As the utilization approaches 100 percent, the waiting time approaches infinity. (See Figure 9.21.) As a result, if O'Neill wishes to have a reasonably short waiting time for customers, then O'Neill must be willing to operate with less than 100 percent utilization, maybe even considerably less than 100 percent. Less than 100 percent utilization implies idle capacity; for example, if the utilization is 90 percent, then 10 percent of the time the assembly line is idle. Therefore, even with make-to-order production, O'Neill experiences demand–supply mismatch costs. Those costs are divided into two types: idle capacity and lost sales from customers who are unwilling to wait to receive their product. When comparing make-to-stock with make-to-order, you could say that make-to-order replaces the cost of leftover inventory with the cost of idle capacity. Whether or not make-to-order is preferable depends on the relative importance of those two costs.

While a customer's expected waiting time may be significant, customers are ultimately concerned with their total waiting time, which includes the processing time. With make-to-order, the processing time has two components: the time in production and the time from production to actual delivery. Hence, successful implementation of make-to-order generally requires fast and easy assembly of the final product. Next, keeping the delivery time to an acceptable level either requires paying for fast shipping (e.g., air shipments) or moving production close to customers (to reduce the distance the product needs to travel). Fast shipping increases the cost of every unit produced, and local production (e.g., North America instead of Asia) may increase labor costs.

In sum, products suitable for make-to-order tend to have the following characteristics: Customers have a strong preference for variety, meaning that a wide assortment must be offered and it is difficult to predict the demand for any one variant of the product; inventory is expensive to hold because of obsolescence and/or falling component prices; final assembly can be completed quickly and relatively efficiently; and there is a reasonable cost to complete the final delivery of the product to the customer in a timely manner.

Dell discovered that all of the above conditions applied to the personal computer in the early days of that industry. Customers (mostly businesses) wanted to customize the computers they purchased to their own specifications. Component prices fell rapidly over time, making holding inventory expensive. Computers were easy to assemble from a set of modular components and final shipping to customers wasn't very expensive relative to the value of the product. Over time, however, the industry has changed and the advantages of make-to-order have diminished. For example, customers are more willing to accept a standard computer configuration (i.e., their preference for variety has diminished) and component prices are not falling as rapidly.

15.4 Quick Response with Reactive Capacity

O'Neill may very well conclude that make-to-order production is not viable either in Asia (due to added shipping expenses) or in North America (due to added labor costs). If pure make-to-order is out of the question, then O'Neill should consider some intermediate solution between make-to-stock (the newsvendor) and make-to-order (a queue). With the newsvendor model, O'Neill commits to its entire supply before *any* demand occurs; whereas with make-to-order, O'Neill commits to supply only after *all* demand occurs. The intermediate solution is to commit to some supply before demand but then maintain the option to produce additional supply after some demand is observed. The capacity associated with that later supply is called *reactive capacity* because it allows O'Neill to react to the demand information it learns before committing to the second order. The ability to make multiple replenishments (even if just one replenishment) is a central goal in Quick Response.

Suppose O'Neill approaches TEC with the request that TEC reduce its lead time. O'Neill's motivation behind this request is to try to create the opportunity for a replenishment during the selling season. Recall that the Spring season spans six months, starting in February and ending in July. (See Figure 14.2.) It has been O'Neill's experience that a hot product in the first two months of the season (i.e., a product selling above forecast) almost always turns out to be a hot product in the rest of the season. As a result, O'Neill could surely benefit from the opportunity to replenish the hot products midseason. For example, suppose TEC offered a one-month lead time for a midseason order. Then O'Neill could submit to TEC a second order at the end of the second month (March) and receive that replenishment before the end of the third month, thereby allowing that inventory to serve demand in the second half of the season. Figure 15.1 provides a time line in this new situation.

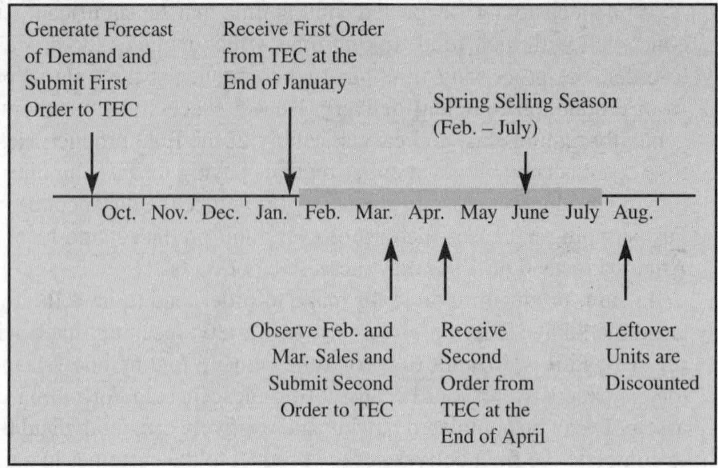

FIGURE 15.1 Time Line of Events for O'Neill's Hammer 3/2 Wetsuit with Unlimited, but Expensive, Reactive Capacity

While it is clear that O'Neill could benefit from the second order, offering a second order with a one-month lead time can be costly to TEC. For example, TEC might need to reserve some capacity to respond to O'Neill's order. If O'Neill's second order is not as large as TEC anticipated, then some of that reserved capacity might be lost. Or O'Neill's order might be larger than anticipated, forcing TEC to scramble for extra capacity, at TEC's expense. In addition, the one-month lead time may force the use of faster shipping, which again could increase costs. The issue is whether the cost increases associated with the second order justify the mismatch cost savings for O'Neill. To address this issue, let's suppose that TEC agrees to satisfy O'Neill's second order but insists on a 20 percent premium for those units to cover TEC's anticipated additional expenses. Given this new opportunity, how should O'Neill adjust its initial order quantity and how much are mismatch costs reduced?

Choosing order quantities with two ordering opportunities is significantly more complex than choosing a single order quantity (i.e., the newsvendor problem). For instance, in addition to our forecast for the entire season's demand, now we need to worry about developing a forecast for demand in the second half of the season given what we observe in the first two months of the season. Furthermore, we do not know what will be our initial sales when we submit our first order, so that order must anticipate all possible outcomes for initial sales and then the appropriate response in the second order for all of those outcomes. In addition, we may stock out within the first half of the season if our first order is not large enough. Finally, even after observing initial sales, some uncertainty remains regarding demand in the second half of the season.

Even though we now face a complex problem, we should not let the complexity overwhelm us. A good strategy when faced with a complex problem is to make it less complex, that is, make some simplifying assumptions that allow for analytical tractability while retaining the key qualitative features of the complex problem. With that strategy in mind, let's assume (1) we do not run out of inventory before the second order arrives and (2) after we observe initial sales we are able to perfectly predict sales in the remaining portion of the season. Assumption 1 is not bad as long as the first order is reasonably large, that is, large enough to cover demand in the first half of the season with a high probability. Assumption 2 is not bad if initial sales are a very good predictor of subsequent sales, which has been empirically observed in many industries.

Our simplifying assumptions are enough to allow us to evaluate the optimal initial order quantity and then to evaluate expected profit. Let's again consider O'Neill's initial order for the Hammer 3/2. It turns out that O'Neill still faces the "too much–too little" problem associated with the newsvendor problem even though O'Neill has the opportunity to make a second order. To explain, note that if the initial order quantity is too large, then there will be leftover inventory at the end of the season. The second order does not help at all with the risk of excess inventory, so the "too much" problem remains.

We also still face the "too little" issue with our initial order, but it takes a different form than in our original newsvendor problem. Recall, with the original newsvendor problem, ordering too little leads to lost sales. But the second order prevents lost sales: After we observe initial sales, we are able to predict total demand for the remainder of the season. If that total demand exceeds our initial order, we merely choose a second order quantity to ensure that all demand is satisfied. This works because of our simplifying assumptions: Lost sales do not occur before the second order arrives, there is no quantity limit on the second order, and initial sales allow us to predict total demand for the season.

Although the second order opportunity eliminates lost sales, it does not mean we should not bother with an initial order. Remember that units ordered during the season are more expensive than units ordered before the season. Therefore, the penalty for ordering too little in the first order is that we may be required to purchase additional units in the second order at a higher cost.

Given that the initial order still faces the "too little–too much" problem, we can actually use the newsvendor model to find the order quantity that maximizes expected profit. The overage cost, C_o, per unit of excess inventory is the same as in the original model; that is, the overage cost is the loss on each unit of excess inventory. Recall that for the Hammer 3/2 Cost = 110 and Salvage value = 90. So $C_o = 20$.

The underage cost, C_u, per unit of demand that exceeds our initial order quantity is the additional premium we must pay to TEC for units in the second order. That premium is 20 percent, which is 20% × 110 = 22. In other words, if demand exceeds our initial order quantity, then the penalty for ordering too little is the extra amount we must pay TEC for each of those units (i.e., we could have avoided that premium by increasing the initial order). Even though we must pay this premium to TEC, we are still better off having the second ordering opportunity: Paying TEC an extra $22 for each unit of demand that exceeds our initial order quantity is better than losing the $80 margin on each of those units if we did not have the second order. So $C_u = 22$.

We are now ready to calculate our optimal initial order quantity. (See Exhibit 14.2 for an outline of this process.) First, evaluate the critical ratio:

$$\frac{C_u}{C_o + C_u} = \frac{22}{20 + 22} = 0.5238$$

Next find the z value in the Standard Normal Distribution Function Table that corresponds to the critical ratio 0.5238: Φ (0.05) = 0.5199 and Φ (0.06) = 0.5239, so let's choose the higher z value, $z = 0.06$. Now convert the z value into an order quantity for the actual demand distribution with $\mu = 3{,}192$ and $\sigma = 1{,}181$:

$$Q = \mu + z \times \sigma = 3{,}192 + 0.06 \times 1{,}181 = 3{,}263$$

Therefore, O'Neill should order 3,263 Hammer 3/2s in the first order to maximize expected profit when a second order is possible. Notice that O'Neill should still order a considerable amount in its initial order so as to avoid paying TEC the 20 percent premium on too many units. However, O'Neill's initial order of 3,263 units is considerably less than its optimal order of 4,196 units when the second order is not possible.

Even though O'Neill must pay a premium with the second order, O'Neill's expected profit should increase by this opportunity. (The second order does not prevent O'Neill from ordering 4,196 units in the initial order, so O'Neill cannot be worse off.) Let's evaluate what that expected profit is for any initial order quantity Q. Our maximum profit has not changed. The best we can do is earn the maximum gross margin on every unit of demand,

$$\text{Maximum profit} = (\text{Price} - \text{Cost}) \times \mu\ (190 - 110) \times 3{,}192 = 255,\ 360$$

The expected profit is the maximum profit minus the mismatch costs:

$$\text{Expected profit} = \text{Maximum profit} - (C_o \times \text{Expected leftover inventory})$$
$$- (C_u \times \text{Expected second order quantity})$$

The first mismatch cost is the cost of leftover inventory and the second is the additional premium that O'Neill must pay TEC for all of the units ordered in the second order. We already know how to evaluate expected leftover inventory for any initial order quantity. (See Exhibit 14.4 for a summary.) We now need to figure out the expected second order quantity.

If we order Q units in the first order, then we make a second order only if demand exceeds Q. In fact, our second order equals the difference between demand and Q, which would have been our lost sales if we did not have a second order. This is also known as the loss function. Therefore,

$$\text{Expected second order quantity} = \text{Newsvendor's expected lost sales}$$

So to evaluate expected profit we need the maximum profit, expected leftover inventory, and expected lost sales.

We evaluated above the maximum profit, \$255,360. To evaluate expected leftover inventory, lookup $I(z)$ in the Standard Normal Inventory Function Table for $z = 0.06$. We find that $I(0.06) = 0.4297$. So expected leftover inventory is $\sigma \times I(z) = 1{,}181 \times 0.4297 = 507$. Expected sales = Q – Expected leftover inventory = 3,263 – 507 = 2,756. Finally, expected lost sales = μ – Expected sales = 3,192 – 2,756 = 436.

We are now ready to evaluate expected profit for the Hammer 3/2 if there is a second order:

$$\begin{aligned}\text{Expected profit} &= \text{Maximum profit} - (C_o \times \text{Expected leftover inventory}) \\ &\quad - (C_u \times \text{Expected second order quantity}) \\ &= \$255{,}360 - (\$20 \times 507) - (\$22 \times 436) \\ &= \$235{,}628\end{aligned}$$

Recall that O'Neill's expected profit with just one ordering opportunity is \$222,300. Therefore, the second order increases profit by (\$235,628 – \$222,300)/\$222,300 = 6.0 percent even though TEC charges a 20 percent premium for units in the second order. We also can think in terms of how much the second order reduces the mismatch cost. Recall that the mismatch cost with only one order is \$33,060. Now the mismatch cost is \$255,360 – \$235,628 = \$19,732, which is a 40 percent reduction in the mismatch cost (1 – \$19,732/\$33,060). In addition, O'Neill's in-stock probability increases from about 80 percent to essentially 100 percent and the number of leftover units at the end of the season that require markdowns to sell is cut in half (from 1,134 to 507). Therefore, even though reactive capacity in the form of a midseason replenishment does not eliminate all mismatch costs, it provides a feasible strategy for significantly reducing mismatch costs.

15.5 Summary

With the newsvendor's make-to-stock system, the firm commits to its entire supply before any updated demand information is learned. As a result, there are demand–supply mismatch costs that manifest themselves in the form of leftover inventory or lost sales. This chapter identifies situations in which the mismatch cost is high and considers several improvements to the newsvendor situation to reduce those mismatch costs.

TABLE 15.4
A Summary of the Key Notation and Equations in Chapter 15

Q = Order quantity
C_u = Underage cost　　C_o = Overage cost
μ = Expected demand　　σ = Standard deviation of demand
Mismatch cost = (C_o × Expected leftover inventory) + (C_u × Expected lost sales)
= Maximum profit − Expected profit
Maximum profit = (Price − Cost) × μ
Coefficient of variation = Standard deviation/Expected demand

Mismatch costs are high (as a percentage of a product's maximum profit) when a product has a low critical ratio and/or a high coefficient of variation. A low critical ratio implies that the cost of leftover inventory is high relative to the cost of a lost sale. Perishable products or products that face obsolescence generally have low critical ratios. The coefficient of variation is the ratio of the standard deviation of demand to expected demand. It is high for products that are hard to forecast. Examples include new products, fashionable products, and specialty products with small markets. The important lesson here is that actions that lower the critical ratio or increase the coefficient of variation also increase demand–supply mismatch costs.

Make-to-order is an extreme solution to the newsvendor situation. With make-to-order, the firm begins producing an item only after the firm has an order from a customer. In other words, production begins only when the ultimate owner of an item becomes known. A key advantage with make-to-order is that leftover inventory is eliminated. However, a make-to-order system is not immune to the problems of demand–supply mismatches because it behaves like a queuing system. As a result, customers must wait to be satisfied and the length of their waiting time is sensitive to the amount of idle capacity.

The intermediate solution between make-to-order and make-to-stock has the firm commit to some production before any demand information is learned, but the firm also has the capability to react to early demand information via a second order, which is called reactive capacity. Reactive capacity can substantially reduce (but not eliminate) the newsvendor's mismatch cost. Still, this approach may be attractive because it does not suffer from all of the challenges faced by make-to-order.

Table 15.4 provides a summary of the key notation and equations presented in this chapter.

15.6 Further Reading

More responsive, more flexible, more reactive operations have been the goal over the last 20 years in most industries, in large part due to the success of Dell Inc. in the personal computer business. For an insightful review of Dell's strategy, see Magretta (1998). See McWilliams and White (1999) for an interview with Michael Dell on his views on how the auto industry should change with respect to its sales and production strategy.

For a comprehensive treatment of Quick Response in the apparel industry, see Abernathy, Dunlop, Hammond, and Weil (1999). Vitzthum (1998) describes how Zara, a Spanish fashion retailer, is able to produce "fashion on demand."

Fisher (1997) discusses the pros and cons of flexible supply chains and Zipkin (2001) does the same for mass customization. Karmarkar (1989) discusses the pros and cons of push versus pull production systems.

See Fisher and Raman (1996) or Fisher, Rajaram, and Raman (2001) for technical algorithms to optimize order quantities when early sales information and reactive capacity are available.

15.7 Practice Problems

The following questions will help in testing your understanding of this chapter. After each question, we show the relevant section in parentheses [Section x].

Solutions to problems marked with an "*" are available in Appendix E. Video solutions to select problems are available in Connect.

Q15.1* **(Teddy Bower)** Teddy Bower sources a parka from an Asian supplier for $10 each and sells them to customers for $22 each. Leftover parkas at the end of the season have no salvage value. The demand forecast is normally distributed with mean 2,100 and standard deviation 1,200. Now suppose Teddy Bower found a reliable vendor in the United States that can produce parkas very quickly but at a higher price than Teddy Bower's Asian supplier. Hence, in addition to parkas from Asia, Teddy Bower can buy an unlimited quantity of additional parkas from this American vendor at $15 each after demand is known.

a. Suppose Teddy Bower orders 1,500 parkas from the Asian supplier. What is the probability that Teddy Bower will order from the American supplier once demand is known? [15.4]

b. Again assume that Teddy Bower orders 1,500 parkas from the Asian supplier. What is the American supplier's expected demand; that is, how many parkas should the American supplier expect that Teddy Bower will order? [15.4]

c. Given the opportunity to order from the American supplier at $15 per parka, what order quantity from its Asian supplier now maximizes Teddy Bower's expected profit? [15.4]

d. Given the order quantity evaluated in part c, what is Teddy Bower's expected profit? [15.4]

e. If Teddy Bower didn't order any parkas from the Asian supplier, then what would Teddy Bower's expected profit be? [15.4]

Q15.2* **(Flextrola)** Flextrola, Inc., an electronics system integrator, is developing a new product. Solectrics can produce a key component for this product. Solectrics sells this component to Flextrola for $72 per unit and Flextrola must submit its order well in advance of the selling season. Flextrola's demand forecast is a normal distribution with mean of 1,000 and standard deviation of 600. Flextrola sells each unit, after integrating some software, for $131. Leftover units at the end of the season are sold for $50.

Xandova Electronics (XE for short) approached Flextrola with the possibility of also supplying Flextrola with this component. XE's main value proposition is that they offer 100 percent in-stock and one-day delivery on all of Flextrola's orders, no matter when the orders are submitted. Flextrola promises its customers a one-week lead time, so the one-day lead time from XE would allow Flextrola to operate with make-to-order production. (The software integration that Flextrola performs can be done within one day.) XE's price is $83.50 per unit.

a. Suppose Flextrola were to procure exclusively from XE. What would be Flextrola's expected profit? [15.2]

b. Suppose Flextrola plans to procure from both Solectrics and XE; that is, Flextrola will order some amount from Solectrics before the season and then use XE during the selling season to fill demands that exceed that order quantity. How many units should Flextrola order from Solectrics to maximize expected profit? [15.4]

c. Concerned about the potential loss of business, Solectrics is willing to renegotiate their offer. Solectrics now offers Flextrola an "options contract": Before the season starts, Flextrola purchases Q options and pays Solectrics $25 per option. During the selling season, Flextrola can exercise up to the Q purchased options with a one-day lead time—that is, Solectrics delivers on each exercised option within one day—and the exercise price is $50 per unit. If Flextrola wishes additional units beyond the options purchased, Solectrics will deliver units at XE's price, $83.50. For example, suppose Flextrola purchases 1,500 options but then needs 1,600 units.

Flextrola exercises the 1,500 options at \$50 each and then orders an additional 100 units at \$83.50 each. How many options should Flextrola purchase from Solectrics? [15.4]

d. Continuing with part c, given the number of options purchased, what is Flextrola's expected profit? [15.4]

Q15.3* **(Wildcat Cellular)** Marisol is new to town and is in the market for cellular phone service. She has settled on Wildcat Cellular, which will give her a free phone if she signs a one-year contract. Wildcat offers several calling plans. One plan that she is considering is called "Pick Your Minutes." Under this plan, she would specify a quantity of minutes, say x, per month that she would buy at 5¢ per minute. Thus, her upfront cost would be $\$0.05x$. If her usage is less than this quantity x in a given month, she loses the minutes. If her usage in a month exceeds this quantity x, she would have to pay 40¢ for each extra minute (that is, each minute used beyond x). For example, if she contracts for $x = 120$ minutes per month and her actual usage is 40 minutes, her total bill is $\$120 \times 0.05 = \$6.00$. However, if actual usage is 130 minutes, her total bill would be $\$120 \times 0.05 = (130 - 120) \times 0.40 = \$10.00$. The same rates apply whether the call is local or long distance. Once she signs the contract, she cannot change the number of minutes specified for a year. Marisol estimates that her monthly needs are best approximated by the normal distribution, with a mean of 250 minutes and a standard deviation of 24 minutes.

a. If Marisol chooses the "Pick Your Minutes" plan described above, how many minutes should she contract for? [15.4]

b. Instead, Marisol chooses to contract for 240 minutes. Under this contract, how much (in dollars) would she expect to pay at 40 cents per minute? [15.4]

c. A friend advises Marisol to contract for 280 minutes to ensure limited surcharge payments (i.e., the 40-cents-per-minute payments). Under this contract, how many minutes would she expect to waste (i.e., unused minutes per month)? [15.4]

d. If Marisol contracts for 260 minutes, what would be her approximate expected monthly cell phone bill? [15.4]

e. Marisol has decided that she indeed does not like surcharge fees (the 40-cents-per-minute fee for her usage in excess of her monthly contracted minutes). How many minutes should she contract for if she wants only a 5 percent chance of incurring any surcharge fee? [15.4]

f. Wildcat Cellular offers another plan called "No Minimum" that also has a \$5.00 fixed fee per month but requires no commitment in terms of the number of minutes per month. Instead, the user is billed 7¢ per minute for her actual usage. Thus, if her actual usage is 40 minutes in a month, her bill would be $\$5.00 = 40 \times 0.07 = \$7.80$. Marisol is trying to decide between the "Pick Your Minutes" plan described above and the "No Minimum" plan. Which should she choose? [15.4]

Q15.4 **(Sarah's Wedding)** Sarah is planning her wedding. She and her fiancé have signed a contract with a caterer that calls for them to tell the caterer the number of guests that will attend the reception a week before the actual event. This "final number" will determine how much they have to pay the caterer; they must pay \$60 per guest that they commit to. If, for example, they tell the caterer that they expect 90 guests, they must pay \$5,400 ($= 90 \times \$60$) even if only, say, 84 guests show up. The contract calls for a higher rate of \$85 per extra guest for the number of guests beyond what the couple commits to. Thus, if Sarah and her fiancé commit to 90 guests but 92 show up, they must pay \$5,570 (the original \$5,400 plus $2 \times \$85$).

The problem Sarah faces is that she still does not know the exact number of guests to expect. Despite asking that friends and family members reply to their invitations a month ago, some uncertainty remains: Her brother may—or may not—bring his new girlfriend; her fiancé's college roommate may—or may not—be able to take a vacation from work; and so forth. Sarah has determined that the expected number of guests (i.e., the mean number) is 100, but the actual number could be anywhere from 84 to 116:

Q	f(Q)	F(Q)	I(Q)	L(Q)	Q	f(Q)	F(Q)	I(Q)	L(Q)
84	0.0303	0.0303	0.00	16.00	101	0.0303	0.5455	4.64	3.64
85	0.0303	0.0606	0.03	15.03	102	0.0303	0.5758	5.18	3.18
86	0.0303	0.0909	0.09	14.09	103	0.0303	0.6061	5.76	2.76
87	0.0303	0.1212	0.18	13.18	104	0.0303	0.6364	6.36	2.36
88	0.0303	0.1515	0.30	12.30	105	0.0303	0.6667	7.00	2.00
89	0.0303	0.1818	0.45	11.45	106	0.0303	0.6970	7.67	1.67
90	0.0303	0.2121	0.64	10.64	107	0.0303	0.7273	8.36	1.36
91	0.0303	0.2424	0.85	9.85	108	0.0303	0.7576	9.09	1.09
92	0.0303	0.2727	1.09	9.09	109	0.0303	0.7879	9.85	0.85
93	0.0303	0.3030	1.36	8.36	110	0.0303	0.8182	10.64	0.64
94	0.0303	0.3333	1.67	7.67	111	0.0303	0.8485	11.45	0.45
95	0.0303	0.3636	2.00	7.00	112	0.0303	0.8788	12.30	0.30
96	0.0303	0.3939	2.36	6.36	113	0.0303	0.9091	13.18	0.18
97	0.0303	0.4242	2.76	5.76	114	0.0303	0.9394	14.09	0.09
98	0.0303	0.4545	3.18	5.18	115	0.0303	0.9697	15.03	0.03
99	0.0303	0.4848	3.64	4.64	116	0.0303	1.0000	16.00	0.00
100	0.0303	0.5152	4.12	4.12					

Q = Number of guests that show up to the wedding
$f(Q)$ = Density function = Prob{Q guests show up}
$F(Q)$ = Distribution function = Prob{Q or fewer guests show up}
$L(Q)$ = Loss function = Expected number of guests above Q

a. How many guests should Sarah commit to with the caterer? [15.2]

b. Suppose Sarah commits to 105 guests. What is Sarah's expected bill? [15.2]

c. Suppose that the caterer is willing to alter the contract so that if fewer than the number of guests they commit to show up, they will get a partial refund. In particular, they only have to pay $45 for each "no-show." For example, if they commit to 90 but only 84 show, they will have to pay 84 × $60 = 6 × $45 = $5,310. Now how many guests should she commit to? [15.4]

d. The caterer offers Sarah another option. She could pay $70 per guest, no matter how many guests show up; that is, she wouldn't have to commit to any number before the wedding. Should Sarah prefer this option or the original option ($60 per committed guest and $85 each guest beyond the commitment)? [15.4]

Q15.5 **(Lucky Smokes)** Lucky Smokes currently operates a warehouse that serves the Virginia market. Some trucks arrive at the warehouse filled with goods to be stored in the warehouse. Other trucks arrive at the warehouse empty to be loaded with goods. Based on the number of trucks that arrive at the warehouse in a week, the firm is able to accurately estimate the total number of labor hours that are required to finish all of the loading and unloading. The following histogram plots these estimates for each week over the past two years. (There are a total of 104 weeks recorded in the graph.) For example, there were three weeks in this period that required 600 total labor hours and only one week that recorded 1,080 hours of required labor.

The mean of the data is 793 and the standard deviation is 111. Labor is the primary variable cost in the operation of a warehouse. The Virginia warehouse employed 20 workers, who were guaranteed at least 40 hours of pay per week. Thus, in weeks with less than 800 hours of required labor, the workers either went home early on some days or were idle.

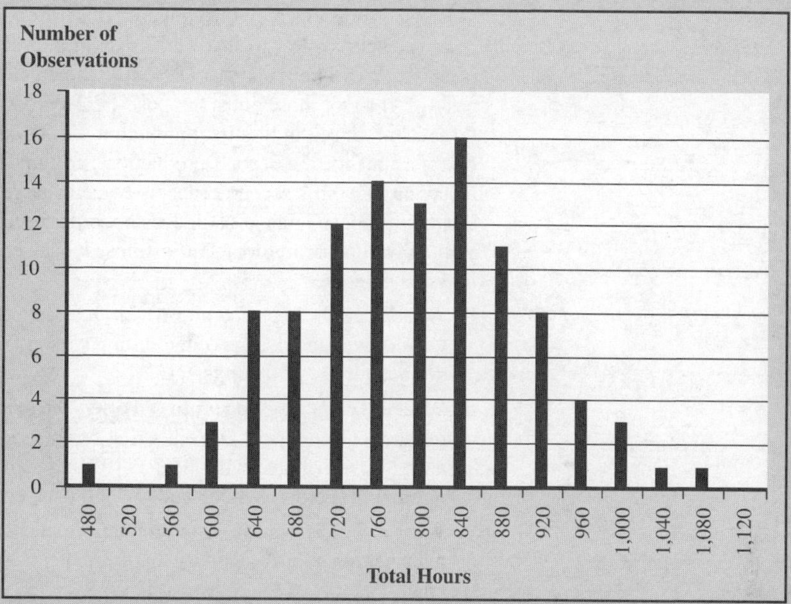

On weeks with more than 800 hours of required labor, the extra hours were obtained with overtime. Workers were paid time and a half for each hour of overtime.

You have been placed in charge of a new warehouse scheduled to serve the North Carolina market. Marketing suggests that the volume for this warehouse should be comparable to the Virginia warehouse. Assume that you must pay each worker for at least 40 hours of work per week and time and a half for each hour of overtime. Assume there is no limit on overtime for a given week. Further, assume you approximate your workload requirement with a normal distribution.

a. If you hire 22 workers, how many weeks a year should you expect to use overtime? [15.2]
b. If you hire 18 workers, how many weeks a year will your workers be underutilized? [15.2]
c. If you are interested in minimizing your labor cost, how many workers should you hire (again, assuming your workload forecast is normally distributed)? [15.4]
d. You are now concerned the normal distribution might not be appropriate. For example, you can't hire 20.5 workers. What is the optimal number of workers to hire if you use the empirical distribution function constructed with the data in the above histogram? [15.4]

Q15.6 **(Shillings)** You are traveling abroad and have only American dollars with you. You are currently in the capital but you will soon be heading out to a small town for an extended stay. In the town, no one takes credit cards and they only accept the domestic currency (shillings). In the capital, you can convert dollars to shillings at a rate of two shillings per dollar. In the town, you learn that one dollar only buys 1.6 shillings. Upon your return to the capital at the end of your trip, you can convert shillings back to dollars at a rate of 2.5 shillings per dollar. You estimate that your expenditures in the town will be normally distributed with mean of 400 shillings and standard deviation of 100 shillings.

a. How many dollars should you convert to shillings before leaving the capital? [15.4]
b. After some thought, you feel that it might be embarrassing if you run out of shillings and need to ask to convert additional dollars, so you really do not want to run out of shillings. How many dollars should you convert to shillings if you want to ensure there is no more than a 1 in 200 chance you will run out of shillings? [15.4]

Q15.7 **(TEC)** Consider the relationship between TEC and O'Neill with unlimited, but expensive, reactive capacity. Recall that TEC is willing to give O'Neill a midseason replenishment (see Figure 15.1) but charges O'Neill a 20 percent premium above the regular wholesale price of $110 for those units. Suppose TEC's gross margin is 25 percent of its selling price for units produced in the first production run. However, TEC estimates that its production cost per unit for the second production run (any units produced during the season after receiving O'Neill's second order) is twice as large as units produced for the initial order. Wetsuits produced that O'Neill does not order need to be salvaged at the end of the season. With O'Neill's permission, TEC estimates it can earn $30 per suit by selling the extra suits in Asian markets.

a. What is TEC's expected profit with the traditional arrangement (i.e., a single order by O'Neill well in advance of the selling season)? Recall that O'Neill's optimal newsvendor quantity is 4,101 units. [15.2]
b. What is TEC's expected profit if it offers the reactive capacity to O'Neill and TEC's first production run equals O'Neill's first production order? Assume the demand forecast is normally distributed with mean 3,192 and standard deviation 1,181. Recall, O'Neill's optimal first order is 3,263 and O'Neill's expected second order is 437 units. [15.4]
c. What is TEC's optimal first production quantity if its CEO authorizes its production manager to choose a quantity that is greater than O'Neill's first order? [15.4]
d. Given the order chosen in part c, what is TEC's expected profit? (*Warning:* This is a hard question.) [15.4]

Q15.8 **(Office Supply Company)** Office Supply Company (OSC) has a spare parts warehouse in Alaska to support its office equipment maintenance needs. Once every six months, a major replenishment shipment is received. If the inventory of any given part runs out before the next replenishment, then emergency air shipments are used to resupply the part as needed. Orders are placed on January 15 and June 15, and orders are received on February 15 and July 15, respectively.

OSC must determine replenishment quantities for its spare parts. As an example, historical data show that total demand for part 1AA-66 over a six-month interval is Poisson with mean 6.5. The cost of inventorying the unneeded part for six months is $5 (which includes both physical and financial holding costs and is charged based on inventory at the end of the six-month period). The variable production cost for 1AA-66 is $37 per part. The cost of a regular, semiannual shipment is $32 per part, and the cost of an emergency shipment is $50 per part.

It is January 15 and there are currently three 1AA-66 parts in inventory. How many parts should arrive on February 15? [15.4]

Q15.9* **(Steve Smith)** Steve Smith is a car sales agent at a Ford dealership. He earns a salary and benefits, but a large portion of his income comes from commissions: $350 per vehicle sold for the first five vehicles in a month and $400 per vehicle after that. Steve's historical sales can be well described with a Poisson distribution with mean 5.5; that is, on average, Steve sells 5.5 vehicles per month. On average, how much does Steve earn in commissions per month? [15.4]

Chapter 16

Service Levels and Lead Times in Supply Chains: The Order-up-to Inventory Model[1]

Many products are sold over a long time horizon with numerous replenishment opportunities. To draw upon a well-known example, consider the Campbell Soup Company's flagship product, chicken noodle soup. It has a long shelf life and future demand is assured. Hence, if in a particular month Campbell Soup has more chicken noodle soup than it needs, it does not have to dispose of its excess inventory. Instead, Campbell needs only wait for its pile of inventory to draw down to a reasonable level. And if Campbell finds itself with less inventory than it desires, its soup factory cooks up another batch. Because obsolescence is not a major concern and Campbell is not limited to a single production run, the newsvendor model (Chapters 14 and 15) is not the right inventory tool for this setting. The right tool for this job is the *order-up-to model.*

Although multiple replenishments are feasible, the order-up-to model still faces the "too little–too much" challenge associated with matching supply and demand. Because soup production takes time (i.e., there is a lead time to complete production), Campbell cannot wait until its inventory draws down to zero to begin production. (You would never let your vehicle's fuel tank go empty before you begin driving to a refueling station!) Hence, production of a batch should begin while there is a sufficient amount of inventory to buffer against uncertain demand while we wait for the batch to finish. Since buffer inventory is not free, the objective with the order-up-to model is to strike a balance between running too lean (which leads to undesirable stockouts, i.e., poor service) and running too fat (which leads to inventory holding costs).

Instead of soup, this chapter applies the order-up-to model to the inventory management of a technologically more sophisticated product: a pacemaker manufactured by Medtronic Inc. We begin with a description of Medtronic's supply chain for pacemakers and then detail the order-up-to model. Next, we consider how to use the model to hit target service levels, discuss what service targets are appropriate, and explore techniques for controlling how frequently we order. We conclude with general managerial insights.

[1] Data in this chapter have been modified to protect confidentiality.

16.1 Medtronic's Supply Chain

Medtronic is a designer and manufacturer of medical technology. They are well known for their line of cardiac rhythm products, and, in particular, pacemakers, but their product line extends into numerous other areas: products for the treatment of cardiovascular diseases and surgery, diabetes, neurological diseases, spinal surgery, and eye/nose/throat diseases.

Inventory in Medtronic's supply chain is held at three levels: manufacturing facilities, distribution centers (DCs), and field locations. The manufacturing facilities are located throughout the world, and they do not hold much finished goods inventory. In the United States there is a single distribution center, located in Mounds View, Minnesota, responsible for the distribution of cardiac rhythm products. That DC ships to approximately 500 sales representatives, each with his or her own defined territory. All of the Medtronic DCs are responsible for providing very high availability of inventory to the sales representatives they serve in the field, where availability is measured with the in-stock probability.

The majority of finished goods inventory is held in the field by the sales representatives. In fact, field inventory is divided into two categories: consignment inventory and trunk inventory. Consignment inventory is inventory owned by Medtronic at a customer's location, usually a closet in a hospital. Trunk inventory is literally inventory in the trunk of a sales representative's vehicle. A sales representative has easy access to both of these kinds of field inventory, so they can essentially be considered a single pool of inventory.

Let's now focus on a particular DC, a particular sales representative, and a particular product. The DC is the one located in Mounds View, Minnesota. The sales representative is Susan Magnotto and her territory includes the major medical facilities in Madison, Wisconsin. Finally, the product is the InSync ICD Model 7272 pacemaker.

A pacemaker is demanded when it is implanted in a patient via surgery. Even though a surgeon can anticipate the need for a pacemaker for a particular patient, a surgeon may not know the appropriate model for a patient until the actual surgery. For this reason, and for the need to maintain a good relationship with each physician, Susan attends each surgery and always carries the various models that might be needed. Susan can replenish her inventory after an implant by calling an order in to Medtronic's Customer Service, which then sends the request to the Mounds View DC. If the model she requests is available in inventory at the DC, then it is sent to her via an overnight carrier. The time between when Susan orders a unit and when she receives the unit is generally one day, and rarely more than two days.

The Mounds View DC requests replenishments from the production facilities on a weekly basis. With the InSync pacemaker, there is currently a three-week lead time to receive each order.

For the InSync pacemaker, Figure 16.1 provides one year's data on monthly shipments and end-of-month inventory at the Mounds View DC. Figure 16.2 provides data on monthly implants (i.e., demand) and inventory for the InSync pacemaker in Susan's territory over the same year. As can be seen from the figures, there is a considerable amount of variation in the number of units demanded at the DC and in particular in Susan's territory. Interestingly, it appears that there is more demand in the summer months in Susan's territory, but the aggregate shipments through the DC do not indicate the same pattern. Therefore, it is reasonable to conclude that the "pattern" observed in Susan's demand data is not real: Just like a splotch of ink might look like something on a piece of paper, random events sometimes appear to form a pattern.

As a sales representative, Susan's primary responsibility is to ensure that Medtronic's products are the choice products of physicians in her territory. To encourage active sales effort, a considerable portion of her yearly income is derived from bonuses to achieve aggressive sales thresholds.

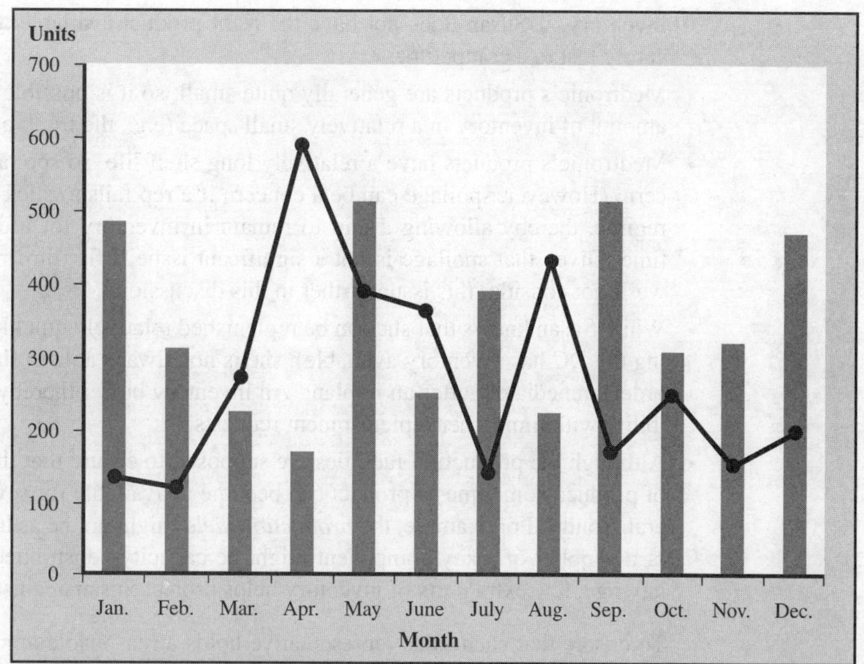

FIGURE 16.1 **Monthly Shipments (Bar) and End-of-Month Inventory (line) for the Insync Pacemaker at the Mounds View Distribution Center**

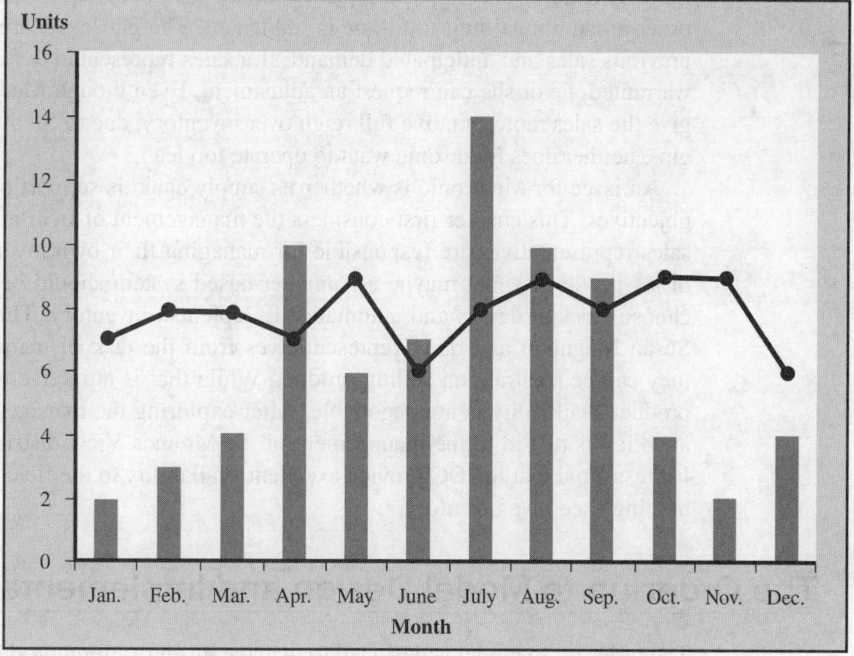

FIGURE 16.2 **Monthly Implants (bar) and End-of-Month Inventory (line) for the InSync Pacemaker in Susan's Territory**

If the decision on inventory investment were left up to Susan, she would err on the side of extra inventory. There are a number of reasons why she would like to hold a considerable amount of inventory:

- Due to the sales incentive system, Susan never wants to miss a sale due to a lack of inventory. Because patients and surgeons do not tolerate waiting for back-ordered inventory, if Susan does not have the right product available, then the sale is almost surely lost to a competitor.

- Medtronic's products are generally quite small, so it is possible to hold a considerable amount of inventory in a relatively small space (e.g., the trunk of a vehicle).
- Medtronic's products have a relatively long shelf life, so spoilage is not a major concern. (However, spoilage can be a concern if a rep fails to stick to a "first-in-first-out" regime, thereby allowing a unit to remain in inventory for a disproportionately long time. Given that spoilage is not a significant issue if first-in-first-out is implemented, we'll not consider this issue further in this discussion.)
- While Susan knows that she can be replenished relatively quickly from the DC (assuming the DC has inventory available), she is not always able to find the time to place an order immediately after an implant. An inventory buffer thereby allows her some flexibility with timing her replenishment requests.
- Although the production facilities are supposed to ensure that the DCs never stock out of product, sometimes a product can become unavailable for several weeks, if not several months. For example, the *production yield* might not be as high as initially planned or a supplier of a key component might be capacity-constrained. Whatever the cause, having a few extra units of inventory helps protect Susan against these shortages.

To ensure that each sales representative holds a reasonable amount of inventory, each sales representative is given a *par level* for each product. The par level specifies the maximum number of units the sales representative can have on-order plus on-hand at any given time. Therefore, once a sales representative's inventory equals her par level, she cannot order an additional unit until one is implanted. The par levels are set quarterly based on previous sales and anticipated demand. If a sales representative feels a higher par level is warranted, he or she can request an adjustment. Even though Medtronic does not wish to give the sales representative full reign over inventory, due to Medtronic's large gross margins, neither does Medtronic want to operate too lean.

An issue for Medtronic is whether its supply chain is supporting its aggressive growth objectives. This chapter first considers the management of field inventory. As of now, the sales representatives are responsible for managing their own inventory (within the limits of set par levels), but maybe a computer-based system should be considered that would choose stocking levels and automatically replenish inventory. This system would relieve Susan Magnotto and other representatives from the task of managing inventory so that they can concentrate on selling product. While that is attractive to Susan, a reduction in product availability is nonnegotiable. After exploring the management of field inventory, attention is turned to the management of the Mounds View distribution center inventory. It is essential that the DC provide excellent availability to the field representatives without holding excessive inventory.

16.2 The Order-up-to Model Design and Implementation

The order-up-to model is designed to manage inventory for a product that has the opportunity for many replenishments over a long time horizon. This section describes the assumptions of the model and how it is implemented in practice. The subsequent sections consider the evaluation of numerous performance measures, how historical data can be used to choose a distribution to represent demand, and how to calibrate the model to achieve one of several possible objectives.

We are working with a single product that is sold over a long period of time. Opportunities to order replenishment inventory occur at regular intervals. The time between two ordering opportunities is called a *period,* and all of the periods are of the same duration. While one day seems like a natural period length for the InSync pacemaker in the field (e.g., in Susan's territory), one week is a more natural period length for the Mounds View DC. In other settings, the appropriate period length could be an hour, a month, or any other interval. See Section 16.8 for additional discussion on the appropriate period length. For the sake of consistency, let's also assume that orders are submitted at the same point in time within the period, say, at the beginning of the period.

Random demand occurs during each period. As with the newsvendor model, among the most critical inputs to the order-up-to model are the parameters of the demand distribution, which is the focus of Section 16.4. However, it is worth mentioning that the model assumes the same demand distribution represents demand in every period. This does not mean that actual demand is the same in every period; it just means that each period's demand is the outcome of a single distribution. The model can be extended to accommodate more complex demand structures, but, as we will see, our simpler structure is adequate for our task.

Receiving a replenishment is the third event within each period. We assume that replenishments are only received at the beginning of a period, before any demand occurs in the period. Hence, if a shipment arrives during a period, then it is available to satisfy demand during that period.

Replenishment orders are received after a fixed amount of time called the *lead time,* which is represented with the variable l. The lead time is measured in periods; if one day is a period, then the lead time to receive an order should be measured in days. Hence, not only should the period length be chosen so that it matches the frequency at which orders can be made and replenishments can be received, it also should be chosen so that the replenishment lead time can be measured in an integer (0, 1, 2, . . .) number of periods.

There is no limit to the quantity that can be ordered within a period, and no matter the order quantity, the order is always received in the lead time number of periods. Therefore, supply in this model is not capacity-constrained, but delivery of an order does take some time.

Inventory left over at the end of a period is carried over to the next period; there is no obsolescence, theft, or spoilage of inventory.

To summarize, at the start of each period, a replenishment order can be submitted and a replenishment can be received, then random demand occurs. There is no limit imposed on the quantity of any order, but an order is received only after l periods. For example, if the period length is one day and $l = 1$, then a Monday morning order is received Tuesday morning. Each period has the same duration and the same sequence of events occurs in each period (order, receive, demand). Figure 16.3 displays the sequence of events over a sample of three periods when the lead time to receive orders is one period, $l = 1$.

Now let's define several terms we use to describe our inventory system and then we show how the order-up-to level is used to choose an order quantity.

FIGURE 16.3
Sample Sequence of Events in the Order-up-to Model with a One-Period Lead Time, l = 1, to Receive Orders

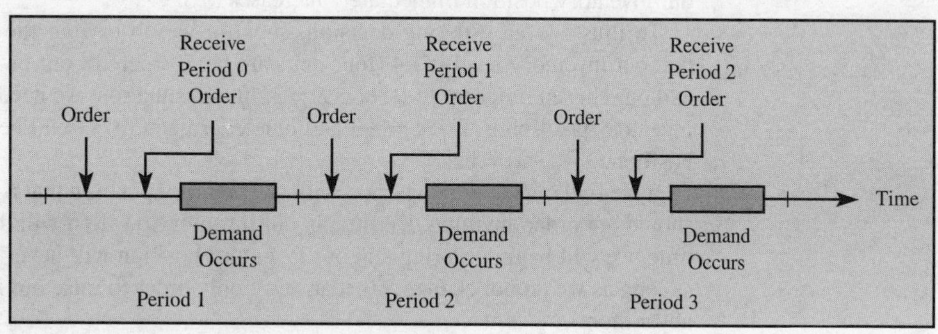

On-order inventory is relatively intuitive: The on-order inventory is the number of units that we ordered in previous periods that we have not yet received. Our on-order inventory should never be negative, but it can be zero.

On-hand inventory is also straightforward: It is the number of units of inventory we have on-hand, immediately available to serve demand.

Back-order is the number of units on back order, that is, the total amount of demand that has occurred but has not been satisfied. To get the mathematics of the order-up-to model to work precisely, it is necessary to assume that *all* demand is eventually filled; that is, if demand occurs and no units are available in current inventory, then that demand is back-ordered and filled as soon as inventory becomes available. In other words, the order-up-to model assumes there are no lost sales. In some settings, this is not a problem: Complete back-ordering is commonplace in the management of inventory between two firms within a supply chain. However, as with the InSync pacemaker in the field, when end consumers generate demand (instead of a firm), the back-order assumption is probably violated (at least to some extent). Nevertheless, if the order-up-to level is chosen so that back orders are rare, then the order-up-to model is a reasonable approximation. Hence, we use it for the InSync pacemaker to manage both the DC inventory as well as Susan's field inventory.

The next measure combines on-hand inventory with the back order:

$$\text{Inventory level} = \text{On-hand inventory} - \text{Back order}$$

Unlike the on-hand inventory and the back order, which are never negative, the inventory level can be negative. It is negative when we have units back-ordered. For example, if the inventory level is −3, then there are three units of demand waiting to be filled.

The following measure combines all of the previous measures:

$$\begin{aligned}\text{Inventory position} &= \text{On-order inventory} + \text{On-hand inventory} - \text{Back order}\\ &= \text{On-order inventory} + \text{Inventory level}\end{aligned}$$

The *order-up-to level* is the maximum inventory position we are willing to have. Let's denote the order-up-to level with the variable S. For example, if $S = 2$, then we are allowed an inventory position up to two units, but no more. Our order-up-to level is essentially equivalent to the par level Medtronic currently uses. It has also been referred to as the *base stock level.* (The order-up-to model is sometimes called the *base stock model.*)

The implementation of our order-up-to policy is relatively straightforward: If we observe at the beginning of any period that our inventory position is less than the order-up-to level S, then we order enough inventory to raise our inventory position to S; that is, in each period, we order the difference between S and the inventory position:

$$\text{Each period's order quantity} = S - \text{Inventory position}$$

Because the inventory position includes our on-order inventory, after we submit the order, our inventory position immediately increases to S.

To illustrate an ordering decision, suppose we observe at the beginning of a period that our inventory level is −4 (four units are back-ordered), our on-order inventory is one, and our chosen order-up-to level is $S = 3$. In this situation, we need to order six units: Our inventory position is $1 - 4 = -3$ and our order quantity should be S minus the inventory position, $3 - (-3) = 6$.

If we find ourselves in a period with an inventory position that is greater than S, then we should not order anything. Eventually our inventory position will drop below S. After that time, we will begin ordering and our inventory position will never again be greater than S as long as we do not change S (because we only order to raise our inventory position to S, never more).

Notice that our inventory position drops below S only when demand occurs. Suppose $S = 3$ and we observe that our inventory position is one at the beginning of the period. If we followed our order-up-to policy in the previous period, then we must have had an inventory position of three after our order in the previous period. The only way that we could then observe an inventory position of one in this period is if two units of demand occurred in the previous period. Thus, we will order two units in this period (to raise our inventory position back to $S = 3$). Hence,

The order quantity in each period exactly equals the demand in the previous period in the order-up-to inventory model.

Due to this observation, an order-up-to policy is sometimes called a *one-for-one ordering policy:* Each unit of demand triggers an order for one replenishment unit.

The order-up-to model is an example of a system that operates on the pull principle of production/inventory control. The key feature of a *pull system* is that production-replenishment of a unit is only initiated when a demand of another unit occurs. Therefore, in a pull system, inventory is pulled through the system only by the occurrence of demand. In contrast, with a *push system,* production-replenishment occurs in anticipation of demand. The newsvendor model is a push system. A kanban system, which is a critical component of any just-in-time system, operates with pull. (See Chapter 8.) Pull systems impose the discipline to prevent the excessive buildup of inventory, but they do not anticipate shifts in future demand. Thus, pull systems are most effective when average demand remains steady, as we have assumed in our order-up-to model.

16.3 The End-of-Period Inventory Level

The inventory level (on-hand inventory minus the back order) is an important metric in the order-up-to model: If the inventory level is high, then we incur holding costs on on-hand inventory, but if the inventory level is low, then we may not be providing adequate availability to our customers. Hence, we need to know how to control the inventory level via our decision variable, the order-up-to level. The following result suggests there actually is a relatively simple relationship between them:

The inventory level measured at the end of a period equals the order-up-to level S *minus demand over $l + 1$ periods.*

If that result is (magically) intuitive to you, or if you are willing to believe it on faith, then you can now skip ahead to the next section. For the rest of us, the remainder of this section explains and derives that result.

We'll derive our result with the help of a seemingly unrelated example. Suppose at a neighborhood picnic you have a large pot with 30 cups of soup in it. Over the course of the picnic, you add 20 additional cups of soup to the pot and a total of 40 cups are served. How many cups of soup are in the pot at the end of the picnic? Not too hard: Start with 30, add 20, and then subtract 40, so you are left with 10 cups of soup in the pot. Does the answer change if you first subtract 40 cups and then add 20 cups? The answer is no as long as people are patient. To explain, if we subtract 40 cups from the original 30 cups, then we will have −10 cups, that is, there will be people waiting in line to receive soup. Once the 20 cups are added, those people in line are served and 10 cups remain. The sequence of adding and subtracting does not matter precisely because everyone is willing to wait in line, that is, there are no lost sales of soup. In other words, the sequence of adding and subtracting does not matter, only the total amount added and the total amount subtracted matter.

Does the answer change in our soup example if the 20 cups are added one cup at a time or in random quantities (e.g., sometimes half a cup, sometime a whole cup, sometimes more than a cup)? Again, the answer is no: The increments by which the soup is added or subtracted do not matter, only the total amount added or subtracted.

Keep the soup example in mind, but let's switch to another example. Suppose a firm uses the order-up-to model, its order-up-to level is $S = 3$, and the lead time is two days, $l = 2$. What is the inventory level at the end of any given day? This seems like a rather hard question to answer, but let's tackle it anyway. To provide a concrete reference, randomly choose a period, say period 10. Let *IL* be the inventory level at the start of period 10. We use a variable for the inventory level because we really do not know the exact inventory level. It turns out, as we will see, that we do not need to know the exact inventory level.

After we submit our order in period 10, we will have a total of 3 – *IL* units on order. When we implement the order-up-to model, we must order so that our inventory level (*IL*) plus our on-order inventory (3 – *IL*) equals our order-up-to level (3 = *IL* + 3 – *IL*). Some of the on-order inventory may have been ordered in period 10, some of it in period 9. No matter when the on-order inventory was ordered, it will *all* be received by the end of period 12 because the lead time is two periods. For example, the period 10 order is received in period 12, so all of the previously ordered inventory should have been received by period 12 as well.

Now recall the soup example. Think of *IL* as the amount of soup you start with. How much is added to the "pot of inventory" over periods 10 to 12? That is the amount that was on order in period 10; that is, 3 – *IL*. So the pot starts with *IL* and then 3 – *IL* is added over periods 10 to 12. How much is subtracted from the pot of inventory over periods 10 to 12? Demand is what causes subtraction from the pot of inventory. So it is demand over periods 10 to 12 that is subtracted from inventory; that is, demand over the $l + 1$ periods (10 to 12 are three periods). So how much is in the pot of inventory at the end of period 12? The answer is simple: Just as in the soup example, it is how much we start with (*IL*), plus the amount we add (3 – *IL*), minus the amount we subtract (demand over periods 10 to 12):

$$\begin{aligned}\text{Inventory level at the end of period 12} &= IL + 3 - IL - \text{Demand in periods 10 to 12}\\ &= 3 - \text{Demand in periods 10 to 12}\end{aligned}$$

In other words, our inventory level at the end of a period is the order-up-to level (in this case 3) minus demand over $l + 1$ periods (in this case, periods 10 to 12). Hence, we have derived our result.

Just as in the soup example, it does not matter the sequence by which inventory is added or subtracted; all that matters is the total amount that is added (3 – *IL*) and the total amount that is subtracted (total demand over periods 10 to 12). (This is why the back-order assumption is needed.) Nor do the increments by which inventory is added or subtracted matter. In other words, we can add and subtract at constant rates, or we could add and subtract at random rates; either way, it is only the totals that matter.

You still may be a bit confused about why it is demand over $l + 1$ periods that is relevant rather than demand over just l periods. Recall that we are interested in the inventory level at the *end* of the period, but we make our ordering decision at the *start* of a period. The time from when an order is placed at the start of a period to the end of the period in which the order arrives is actually $l + 1$ periods' worth of demand.

Now you might wonder why we initiated our analysis at the start of a period, in this case period 10. Why not begin by measuring the inventory position at some other time during a period? The reason is that the inventory position measured at the start of a period is always equal to the order-up-to level, but we cannot be sure about what the inventory position will be at any other point within a period (because of random demand). Hence, we anchor our analysis on something we know for sure, which is that the inventory position equals *S* at the start of every period when an order-up-to policy is implemented.

To summarize, in the order-up-to model, the inventory level at the end of a period equals the order-up-to level S minus demand over $l + 1$ periods. Therefore, while we need to know the distribution of demand for a single period, we also need to know the distribution of demand over $l + 1$ periods.

16.4 Choosing Demand Distributions

Every inventory management system must choose a demand distribution to represent demand. In our case, we need a demand distribution for the Mounds View DC and Susan Magnotto's territory. Furthermore, as discussed in the previous section, we need a demand distribution for one period of demand and a demand distribution for $l + 1$ periods of demand. As we will see, the normal distribution works for DC demand, but the Poisson distribution is better for demand in Susan's territory.

The graph in Figure 16.1 indicates that Mounds View's demand is variable, but it appears to have a stable mean throughout the year. This is a good sign: As we already mentioned, the order-up-to model assumes average demand is the same across periods. Average demand across the sample is 349 and the standard deviation is 122.38. Seven months of the year have demand less than the mean, so the demand realizations appear to be relatively symmetric about the mean. Finally, there do not appear to be any extreme outliers in the data: The maximum is 1.35 standard deviations from the mean and the minimum is 1.46 standard deviations from the mean. Overall, the normal distribution with a mean of 349 and a standard deviation of 122.38 is a reasonable choice to represent the DC's monthly demand.

However, because the DC orders on a weekly basis and measures its lead time in terms of weeks, the period length for our order-up-to model applied to the DC should be one week. Therefore, we need to pick a distribution to represent weekly demand; that is, we have to chop our monthly demand distribution into a weekly demand distribution. If we are willing to make the assumption that one week's demand is independent of another week's demand, and if we assume that there are 4.33 weeks per month (52 weeks per year/12 months), then we can convert the mean and standard deviation for our monthly demand distribution into a mean and standard deviation for weekly demand:

$$\text{Expected weekly demand} = \frac{\text{Expected monthly demand}}{4.33}$$

$$\text{Standard deviation of weekly demand} = \frac{\text{Standard deviation of monthly demand}}{\sqrt{4.33}}$$

Exhibit 16.1 summarizes the process of converting demand distributions from one period length to another.

In the case of the Mounds View DC, expected weekly demand is $349/4.33 = 80.6$ and the standard deviation of weekly demand is $122.38/\sqrt{4.33} = 58.81$. So we will use a normal distribution with mean 80.6 and standard deviation 58.81 to represent weekly demand at the Mounds View DC.

We also need demand for the InSync pacemaker over $l + 1$ periods, which in this case is demand over $3 + 1 = 4$ weeks. Again using Exhibit 16.1, demand over four weeks has mean $4 \times 80.6 = 322.4$ and standard deviation $\sqrt{4} \times 58.81 = 117.6$.

Now consider demand for the InSync pacemaker in Susan's territory. From the data in Figure 16.2, total demand over the year is 75 units, which translates into average demand of 6.25 (75/12) units per month, 1.44 units per week (75/52), and 0.29 (1.44/5) unit per day, assuming a five-day week.

Our estimate of 0.29 unit per day for expected demand implicitly assumes expected demand on any given day of the year is the same as for any other day of the year. In other

Exhibit 16.1

HOW TO CONVERT A DEMAND DISTRIBUTION FROM ONE PERIOD LENGTH TO ANOTHER

If you wish to divide a demand distribution from a long period length (e.g., a month) into n short periods (e.g., a week), then

$$\text{Expected demand in the short period} = \frac{\text{Expected demand in the long period}}{n}$$

$$\text{Standard deviation of demand in the short period} = \frac{\text{Standard deviation of demand in the long period}}{\sqrt{n}}$$

If you wish to combine demand distributions from n short periods (e.g., a week) into one long period (e.g, a three-week period, $n = 3$), then

$$\text{Expected demand in the long period} = n \times \text{Expected demand in the short period}$$

$$\text{Standard deviation of demand in the long period} = \sqrt{n} \times \text{Standard deviation of demand in the short period}$$

The above equations assume the same demand distribution represents demand in each period and demands across periods are independent of each other.

words, there is no seasonality in demand across the year, within a month, or within a week. There probably is not too much promotion-related volatility in demand (buy one pacemaker, get one free), nor is there much volatility due to gift giving (what more could a dad want than a new pacemaker under the Christmas tree?). There probably is not much variation within the week (the same number of implants on average on Friday as on Monday) or within the month. However, those conjectures could be tested with more refined data. Furthermore, from the data in Figure 16.1, it appears demand is stable throughout the year and there are no upward or downward trends in the data. Hence, our assumption of a constant expected daily demand is reasonable.

Using Exhibit 16.1, if average demand over one day is 0.29 unit, then expected demand over $l + 1$ days must be $2 \times 0.29 = 0.58$.

Unlike the normal distribution, which is defined by two parameters (its mean and its standard deviation), the Poisson distribution is defined by only a single parameter, its mean. For the InSync pacemaker, it is natural to choose the mean equal to the observed mean demand rate: 0.29 for demand over one period and 0.58 for demand over two periods. Even though the Poisson distribution does not allow you to choose any standard deviation while holding the mean fixed, the Poisson distribution does have a standard deviation:

$$\text{Standard deviation of a Poisson distribution} = \sqrt{\text{Mean of the distribution}}$$

For example, with a mean of 0.29, the standard deviation is $\sqrt{0.29} = 0.539$. Table 16.1 provides the distribution and density functions for the chosen Poisson distributions.

Because it can be hard to visualize a distribution from a table, Figure 16.4 displays the graphs of the distribution and density functions of the Poisson distribution with mean 0.29. For comparison, the comparable functions for the normal distribution are also included. (The dashed lines with the Poisson distribution are only for visual effect; that is, those functions exist only for integer values.)

The graphs in Figure 16.4 highlight that the Poisson and normal distributions are different in two key respects: (1) The Poisson distribution is discrete (it has integer outcomes),

TABLE 16.1
The Distribution and Density Functions for Two Poisson Distributions

In Excel, $F(S)$ is evaluated with the function POISSON(S, *Expected demand*, 1) and $f(S)$ is evaluated with the function POISSON(S, *Expected demand*, 0).

Mean Demand = 0.29			Mean Demand = 0.58		
S	$F(S)$	$f(S)$	S	$F(S)$	$f(S)$
0	0.74826	0.74826	0	0.55990	0.55990
1	0.96526	0.21700	1	0.88464	0.32474
2	0.99672	0.03146	2	0.97881	0.09417
3	0.99977	0.00304	3	0.99702	0.01821
4	0.99999	0.00022	4	0.99966	0.00264
5	1.00000	0.00001	5	0.99997	0.00031

$F(S)$ = Prob{Demand is less than or equal to S}
$f(S)$ = Prob{Demand is exactly equal to S}

whereas the normal distribution is continuous, and (2) the distribution and density functions for those two distributions have different shapes. The fractional quantity issue is not a major concern if demand is 500 units (or probably even 80 units), but it is a concern when average demand is only 0.29 unit. Ideally, we want a discrete demand distribution like the Poisson.

Yet another argument can be made in support of the Poisson distribution as our model for demand in Susan's territory. Recall that with the queuing models (Chapters 9 and 10) we use the exponential distribution to describe the time between customer arrivals, which is appropriate if customers arrive independently of each other; that is, the arrival time of one customer does not provide information concerning the arrival time of another customer. This is particularly likely if the arrival rate of customers is quite slow, as it is with the InSync pacemaker. So it is likely that the interarrival time of InSync pacemaker demand has an exponential distribution. And here is the connection to the Poisson distribution: If the interarrival times are exponentially distributed, then the number of arrivals in any fixed interval of time has a Poisson distribution. For example, if the interarrival times between InSync pacemaker demand in Susan's territory are exponentially distributed with a mean of 3.45 days, then the average number of arrivals (demand) per day has a Poisson distribution with a mean of $1/3.45 = 0.29$ unit.

If we had daily demand data, we would be able to confirm whether or not our chosen Poisson distribution is a good fit to the data. Nevertheless, absent those data, we have probably made the best educated guess.

FIGURE 16.4
The Distribution (left graph) and Density Functions (right graph) of a Poisson Distribution with a Mean of 0.29 (bullets and dashed lines) and a Normal Distribution with a Mean of 0.29 and a Standard Deviation of 0.539 (solid line)

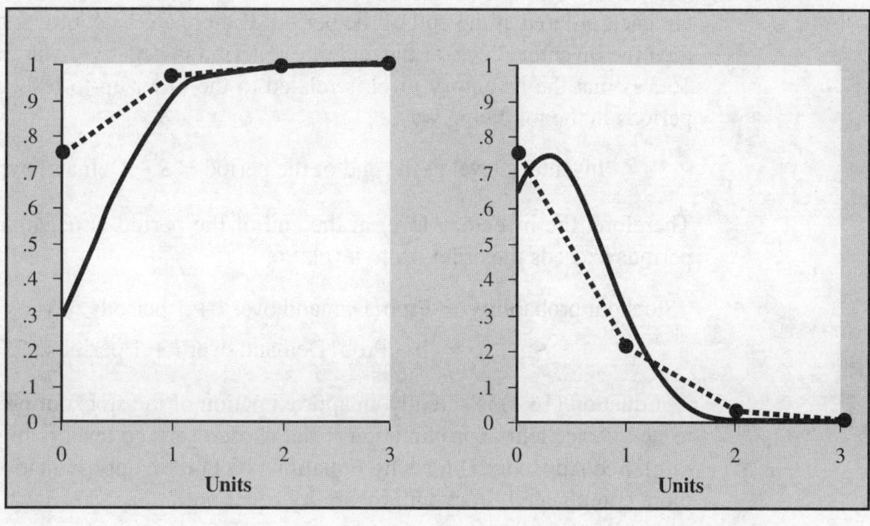

To summarize, we shall use a normal demand distribution with mean 80.6 and standard deviation 58.81 to represent weekly demand for the InSync pacemaker at the Mounds View DC and a normal demand distribution with mean 322.4 and standard deviation 117.6 to represent demand over $l + 1 = 4$ weeks. We will use a Poisson distribution with mean 0.29 to represent daily demand in Susan Magnotto's territory and a Poisson distribution with mean 0.58 to represent demand over $l + 1 = 2$ days.

16.5 Performance Measures

This section considers the evaluation of several performance measures with the order-up-to method. We consider these measures at two locations in the supply chain: Susan Magnotto's territory and the Mounds View distribution center.

Recall we use a Poisson distribution with mean 0.29 to represent daily demand in Susan's territory and a Poisson distribution with mean 0.58 to represent demand over $l + 1 = 2$ days. We shall evaluate the performance measures assuming Susan uses $S = 3$ as her order-up-to level. The Mounds View weekly demand is normally distributed with mean 80.6 and standard deviation 58.81 and over $l + 1 = 4$ weeks it is normally distributed with mean $\mu = 322.4$ and standard deviation $\sigma = 117.6$. We evaluate the performance measures assuming the order-up-to level $S = 625$ is implemented at Mounds View.

In-Stock and Stockout Probability

A *stockout* occurs when demand arrives and there is no inventory available to satisfy that demand immediately. A stockout is not the same as being *out of stock,* which is the condition of having no inventory on hand. With our definition of a stockout, we must be out of stock *and* a demand must occur. Thus, if we are out of stock and no demand occurs, then a stockout never happened. We are *in stock* in a period if all demand was satisfied in that period. With this definition, if we start a period with five units and demand is five units, then we are in stock in that period even though we end the period without inventory.

The *in-stock probability* is the probability we are in stock in a period, and the *stockout probability* is the probability a stockout occurs. We used these same definitions in the newsvendor model, Chapter 14. As in the newsvendor model, an alternative measure is the fill rate, which is the probability a customer will be able to purchase an item. See Appendix D for the procedure to evaluate the fill rate in the order-up-to model.

A stockout causes a back order. Hence, a stockout occurs in a period if one or more units are back-ordered at the end of the period. If there are back orders at the end of the period, then the inventory level at the end of the period is negative. The main result from Section 16.3 is that the inventory level is related to the order-up-to level and demand over $l + 1$ periods in the following way:

$$\text{Inventory level at the end of the period} = S - \text{Demand over } l + 1 \text{ periods}$$

Therefore, the inventory level at the end of the period is negative if demand over $l + 1$ periods exceeds the order-up-to level. So,

$$\begin{aligned} \text{Stockout probability} &= \text{Prob}\{\text{Demand over } l + 1 \text{ periods} > S\} \\ &= 1 - \text{Prob}\{\text{Demand over } l + 1 \text{ periods} \leq S\} \end{aligned} \qquad \textbf{(16.1)}$$

Equation (16.1) is actually an approximation of the stockout probability, but it happens to be an excellent approximation if the chosen service level is high (i.e., if stockouts are rare). See Appendix D for why Equation (16.1) is an approximation and for the exact, but more complicated, stockout probability equation.

Exhibit 16.2

IN-STOCK PROBABILITY AND STOCKOUT PROBABILITY EVALUATION IN THE ORDER-UP-TO MODEL

If the demand over $l + 1$ periods is a normal distribution with mean μ and standard deviation σ, then follow steps A through D (see Exhibit 16.1 for the process of evaluating μ and σ if you have demand over a single period):

A. Evaluate the z-statistic for the order-up-to level: $z = \frac{S - \mu}{\sigma}$.

B. Use the z-statistic to look up in the Standard Normal Distribution Function Table the probability the standard normal demand is z or lower, $\Phi(z)$.

C. In-stock probability = $\Phi(z)$ and Stockout probability = $1 - \Phi(z)$.

D. In Excel, In-stock probability = Normsdist(z) and Stockout probability = 1 − Normsdist(z).

If the demand over $l + 1$ periods is a discrete distribution function, then In-stock probability = $F(S)$ and Stockout probability = $1 - F(S)$, where $F(S)$ is the probability demand over $l + 1$ periods is S or lower.

Because either all demand is satisfied immediately from inventory or not, we know that the

$$\text{In-stock probability} = 1 - \text{Stockout probability}$$

Combining the above equation with Equation (16.1), we get

$$\begin{aligned}\text{In-stock probability} &= 1 - \text{Stockout probability}\\ &= \text{Prob}\{\text{Demand over } l+1 \text{ periods} \le S\}\end{aligned}$$

The above probability equations do not depend on which distribution has been chosen to represent demand, but the process for evaluating those probabilities does depend on the particular demand distribution.

When the demand distribution is given in the form of a table, as with the Poisson distribution, then we can obtain the in-stock probability directly from the table. Looking at Table 16.1, for Susan's territory with an order-up-to level $S = 3$,

$$\begin{aligned}\text{In-stock probability} &= \text{Prob}\{\text{Demand over } l+1 \text{ periods} \le 3\}\\ &= 99.702\%\\ \text{Stockout probability} &= 1 - \text{Prob}\{\text{Demand over } l+1 \text{ periods} \le 3\}\\ &= 1 - 0.99702\\ &= 0.298\%\end{aligned}$$

For the Mounds View distribution center, we need to work with the normal distribution. Recall that with the normal distribution you first do the analysis as if demand is a standard normal distribution and then you convert those outcomes into the answers for the actual normal distribution.

Note that the process for evaluating the in-stock and stockout probabilities in the order-up-to model, which is summarized in Exhibit 16.2, is identical to the one described in Exhibit 14.5 for the newsvendor model except the order quantity Q is replaced with the order-up-to level S. However, it is critical to use the demand forecast for $l + 1$ periods, not the demand forecast for a single period (unless the lead time happens to be 0).

First, we normalize the order-up-to level, which is $S = 625$, using the parameters for demand over $l + 1$ periods:

$$z = \frac{S - \mu}{\sigma} = \frac{625 - 322.4}{117.6} = 2.57$$

Next, we look up $\Phi(z)$ (the probability the outcome of a standard normal is less than or equal to z) in the Standard Normal Distribution Function Table in Appendix B: $\Phi(2.57) = 0.9949$. Therefore, with $S = 625$, the in-stock probability for the DC is 99.49 percent. The stockout probability is $1 - \Phi(z) = 0.0051$, or 0.51 percent.

Expected On-Hand Inventory

Expected on-hand inventory, or just *expected inventory* for short, is the expected number of units of inventory at the end of a period. We choose to measure inventory at the end of the period because that is when inventory is at its lowest point in the period.

Recall that the inventory level at the end of a period is equal to the order-up-to level S minus demand over $l + 1$ periods. Hence, inventory at the end of a period is the difference between S and demand over $l + 1$ periods: If $S = 5$ and demand over $l + 1$ periods is three, then there are two units left in inventory. In other words, expected inventory is the expected amount by which S exceeds demand over $l + 1$ periods. Referring to the insights from the newsvendor model, if we think of S in terms of the order quantity and demand over $l + 1$ periods in terms of "sales," then inventory is analogous to "leftover inventory." Thus, evaluating expected on-hand inventory in the order-up-to model is analogous to evaluating expected leftover inventory in the newsvendor model.

Let's begin with the expected on-hand inventory in Susan's territory. Recall that with a discrete distribution function table, we need to have a column that has the inventory function $I(S)$. Table 16.2 displays the inventory function we need. (Appendix C describes how to use the data in Table 16.1 to evaluate $I(S)$.) Appendix B has the inventory function table for other Poisson distributions. With $S = 3$ and mean demand over $l + 1$ periods equal to 0.58, we see that $I(3) = 2.42335$. Therefore, the expected on-hand inventory in Susan's territory is 2.42335 units if she operates with $S = 3$.

With the Mounds View DC, we follow the process of evaluating expected leftover inventory with a normal distribution. (See Exhibit 14.3.) First, find the z-statistic that corresponds to the order-up-to level:

$$z = \frac{S - \mu}{\sigma} = \frac{625 - 322.4}{117.6} = 2.57$$

Note again that we are using the mean and standard deviation of the normal distribution that represents demand over $l + 1$ periods. Now look up in the Standard Normal Distribution Inventory Function Table the inventory function with the standard normal distribution and a z-statistic of 2.57: $I(2.57) = 2.5716$. Next, convert that expected leftover inventory with the standard normal distribution into the expected on-hand inventory:

$$\text{Expected on-hand inventory} = \sigma \times \text{I}(z) = 117.6 \times 2.5716 = 302.4$$

Exhibit 16.3 summarizes the process.

TABLE 16.2 Distribution and Inventory Function for Two Poisson Distributions

Mean Demand = 0.29			Mean Demand = 0.58		
S	*F(S)*	*I(S)*	*S*	*F(S)*	*I(S)*
0	0.74826	0	0	0.55990	0
1	0.96526	0.74826	1	0.88464	0.55990
2	0.99672	1.71352	2	0.97881	1.44454
3	0.99977	2.71024	3	0.99702	2.42335
4	0.99999	3.71001	4	0.99966	3.42037
5	1.00000	4.71000	5	0.99997	4.42003

$F(S)$ = Prob{Demand is less than or equal to S}
$I(S)$ = Inventory function

Exhibit 16.3

EXPECTED ON-HAND INVENTORY EVALUATION FOR THE ORDER-UP-TO MODEL

If the demand over $l + 1$ periods is a normal distribution with mean μ and standard deviation σ, then follow steps A through D (see Exhibit 16.1 for the process of evaluating μ and σ if you have demand over a single period):

A. Evaluate the z-statistic for the order-up-to level S: $z = \frac{S - \mu}{\sigma}$.

B. Use the z-statistic to look up in the Standard Normal Inventory Function Table the expected inventory with the standard normal distribution, $I(z)$.

C. Expected on-hand inventory $= \sigma \times I(z)$.

D. With Excel, expected on-hand inventory can be evaluated with the following equation:

$$\text{Expected on-hand inventory} = \sigma^*(\text{Normdist}(z, 0, 1, 0) + z^* \text{ Normsdist }(z))$$

If the demand forecast for $l + 1$ periods is a discrete distribution function table, then expected on-hand inventory equals $I(S)$, where $I(S)$ is the inventory function. The inventory function table can be constructed with the procedure described in Appendix C.

Pipeline Inventory/Expected On-Order Inventory

Pipeline inventory, which also will be called *expected on-order inventory,* is the average amount of inventory on order at any given time. It is relevant because Medtronic owns the inventory between the Mounds View distribution center and Susan Magnotto's territory. To evaluate pipeline inventory, we refer to Little's Law, described in Chapter 2,

$$\text{Inventory} = \text{Flow rate } \times \text{Flow time}$$

Now let's translate the terms in the Little's Law equation into the comparable terms in this setting: Inventory is the number of units on order; flow rate is the expected demand in one period (the expected order in a period equals expected demand in one period, so on-order inventory is being created at a rate equal to expected demand in one period); and flow time is the lead time, since every unit spends l periods on order. Therefore,

$$\text{Expected on-order inventory} = \text{Expected demand in one period} \times \text{Lead time}$$

In the case of the InSync pacemaker, Susan's territory has $0.29 \times 1 = 0.29$ unit on order on average and the Mounds View DC has $80.6 \times 3 = 241.8$ units on order. Exhibit 16.4 summarizes the process.

The expected on-order inventory is based on demand over l periods of time, and not $l + 1$ periods of time. Furthermore, the above equation for the expected on-order inventory holds for any demand distribution because Little's Law depends only on average rates, and not on the variability of those rates.

Expected Back Order

The *expected back order* is the expected number of back orders at the end of any period. We need the expected back order to evaluate the expected on-hand inventory, which is of direct interest to any manager.

Recall from Section 16.3 that the inventory level at the end of the period is S minus demand over $l + 1$ periods. Hence, if demand over $l + 1$ periods is greater than S, then there will be back orders. The number of back orders equals the difference between demand over $l + 1$ periods and S. Therefore, in the order-up-to model, the expected back order equals

Exhibit 16.4

EVALUATION OF EXPECTED PIPELINE/EXPECTED ON-ORDER INVENTORY IN THE ORDER-UP-TO MODEL

For the pipeline inventory (which is also known as expected on-order inventory):

Expected on-order inventory = Expected demand in one period × Lead time

the loss function of demand over $l + 1$ periods evaluated at the threshold S. *Note:* This is analogous to the expected lost sales in the newsvendor model. In the order-up-to model, the number of units back-ordered equals the difference between random demand over $l + 1$ periods and S; in the newsvendor model, the expected lost sales are the difference between random demand and Q. So all we need to evaluate the expected back order is the loss function of demand over $l + 1$ periods.

Let's begin with the expected back order in Susan's territory. Recall that with a discrete distribution function table, we need to have a column that has the loss function $L(S)$. Table 16.3 displays the loss function we need. (Appendix C describes how to use the data in Table 16.1 to evaluate $L(S)$.) Appendix B has the loss function table for other Poisson distributions. With $S = 3$ and mean demand over $l + 1$ periods equal to 0.58, we see that $L(3) = 0.00335$. Therefore, the expected back order in Susan's territory is 0.00335 unit if she operates with $S = 3$.

With the Mounds View DC, we follow the process of evaluating expected lost sales with a normal distribution. (See Exhibit 14.3.) First, find the z-statistic that corresponds to the order-up-to level:

$$z = \frac{S - \mu}{\sigma} = \frac{625 - 322.4}{117.6} = 2.57$$

Note again that we are using the mean and standard deviation of the normal distribution that represents demand over $l + 1$ periods. Now look up in the Standard Normal Distribution Loss Function Table the loss function with the standard normal distribution and a z-statistic of 2.57: $L(2.57) = 0.0016$. Next, convert that expected loss with the standard normal distribution into the expected back order:

$$\text{Expected back order} = \sigma \times L(z) = 117.6 \times 0.0016 = 0.19$$

Exhibit 16.5 summarizes the process.

TABLE 16.3
Distribution and Loss Function for Two Poisson Distributions

Mean Demand = 0.29			Mean Demand = 0.58		
S	F(S)	L(S)	S	F(S)	L(S)
0	0.74826	0.29000	0	0.55990	0.58000
1	0.96526	0.03826	1	0.88464	0.13990
2	0.99672	0.00352	2	0.97881	0.02454
3	0.99977	0.00025	3	0.99702	0.00335
4	0.99999	0.00001	4	0.99966	0.00037
5	1.00000	0.00000	5	0.99997	0.00004

$F(S)$ = Prob{Demand is less than or equal to S}
$L(S)$ = Loss function = Expected back order = Expected amount demand exceeds S

Exhibit 16.5

EXPECTED BACK ORDER EVALUATION FOR THE ORDER-UP-TO MODEL

If the demand over $l + 1$ periods is a normal distribution with mean μ and standard deviation σ, then follow steps A through D (see Exhibit 16.1 for the process of evaluating μ and σ if you have demand over a single period):

A. Evaluate the z-statistic for the order-up-to level S: $z = \frac{S - \mu}{\sigma}$.

B. Use the z-statistic to look up in the Standard Normal Loss Function Table the expected loss with the standard normal distribution, $L(z)$.

C. Expected back order $= \sigma \times L(z)$.

D. With Excel, expected back order can be evaluated with the following equation:

Expected back order = σ*(Normdist(z, 0, 1, 0) – z*(1 – Normsdist (z)))

If the demand forecast for $l + 1$ periods is a discrete distribution function table, then expected back order equals $L(S)$, where $L(S)$ is the loss function. If the table does not include the loss function, then see Appendix C for a procedure to evaluate it.

16.6 Choosing an Order-up-to Level to Meet a Service Target

This section discusses the actual choice of InSync order-up-to levels for Susan Magnotto's territory and the Mounds View DC. To refer to a previously mentioned analogy, the order-up-to level is somewhat like the point in the fuel gauge of your car at which you decide to head to a refueling station. The more you are willing to let the dial fall below the "E," the higher the chance you will run out of fuel. However, while increasing that trigger point in the fuel gauge makes you feel safer, it also increases the average amount of fuel you drive around with. With that trade-off in mind, this section considers choosing an order-up-to level to minimize inventory while achieving an in-stock probability no lower than an in-stock target level. This objective is equivalent to minimizing inventory while yielding a stockout probability no greater than one minus the in-stock target level.

Given Medtronic's large gross margin, let's say we want the in-stock probability to be at least 99.9 percent for the InSync pacemaker in Susan's territory as well as at the Mounds View DC. With a 99.9 percent in-stock probability, a stockout should occur no more than 1 in 1,000 days on average. Section 16.7 discusses whether we have chosen a reasonable target.

From Section 16.5 we know that the in-stock probability is the probability demand over $l + 1$ periods is S or lower. Hence, when demand is modeled with a discrete distribution function, we find the appropriate order-up-to level by looking directly into that table. From Table 16.2, we see that in Susan's territory, $S = 0$ clearly does not meet our objective with an in-stock probability of about 56 percent, that is, $F(0) = 0.5599$. Neither is $S = 3$ sufficient because it has an in-stock probability of about 99.7 percent. However, with $S = 4$ our target is met: The in-stock probability is 99.97 percent. In fact, $S = 4$ exceeds our target by a considerable amount: That translates into one stockout every 1/0.00034 = 2,941 days, or one stockout every 11.31 years, if we assume 260 days per year.

With the Mounds View DC, we must work with the normal distribution. We first find the order-up-to level that meets our in-stock probability service requirement with the standard normal distribution and then convert that standard normal order-up-to level to the order-up-to level that corresponds to the actual demand distribution. In the Standard Normal Distribution Function Table, we see that $\Phi(3.08) = 0.9990$, so an order-up-to level of

Exhibit 16.6

HOW TO CHOOSE AN ORDER-UP-TO LEVEL S TO ACHIEVE AN IN-STOCK PROBABILITY TARGET IN THE ORDER-UP-TO MODEL

If the demand over $l + 1$ periods is a normal distribution with mean μ and standard deviation σ, then follow steps A and B (see Exhibit 16.1 for the process of evaluating μ and σ if you have demand over a single period):

A. In the Standard Normal Distribution Function Table, find the probability that corresponds to the target in-stock probability. Then find the *z*-statistic that corresponds to that probability. If the target in-stock probability falls between two entries in the table, choose the entry with the larger *z*-statistic.

In Excel the appropriate *z*-statistic can be found with the following equation:

$$z = \text{Normsinv (Target in-stock probability)}$$

B. Convert the *z*-statistic chosen in part A to an order-up-to level: $S = \mu + z \times \sigma$. Recall that you are using the mean and standard deviation of demand over $l + 1$ periods.

If the demand forecast for $l + 1$ periods is a discrete distribution function table, then find the *S* in the table such that *F*(*S*) equals the target in-stock probability, where *F*(*S*) is the probability demand is less than or equal to *S* over $l + 1$ periods. If the target in-stock probability falls between two entries in the table, choose the larger *S*.

3.08 would generate our desired in-stock probability if demand over $l + 1$ periods followed a standard normal. It remains to convert that *z*-statistic into an order-up-to level: $S = \mu + z \times \sigma$. Remember that the mean and standard deviation should be from the normal distribution of demand over $l + 1$ periods. Therefore,

$$S = 322.4 + 3.08 \times 117.62 = 685$$

See Exhibit 16.6 for a summary of the process to choose an order-up-to level to achieve a target in-stock probability.

16.7 Choosing an Appropriate Service Level

So far in our discussion, we have chosen high service levels because we suspect that a high service level is appropriate. This section puts more rigor behind our hunch. For the sake of brevity, we'll explicitly consider only the management of field inventory. At the end of the section, we briefly discuss the management of distribution center inventory.

The appropriate service level minimizes the cost of holding inventory plus the cost of poor service. The holding cost of inventory is usually expressed as a *holding cost rate,* which is the cost of holding one unit in inventory for one year, expressed as a percentage of the item's cost. For example, if a firm assigns its holding cost rate to be 20 percent, then it believes the cost of holding a unit in inventory for one year equals 20 percent of the item's cost. The holding cost includes the opportunity cost of capital, the cost of spoilage, obsolescence, insurance, storage, and so forth, all variable costs associated with holding inventory. Because Medtronic is a growing company, with a high internal opportunity cost of capital, let's say their holding cost rate is 35 percent for field inventory. We'll use the variable *h* to represent the holding cost. See Chapter 2 for additional discussion on the holding cost rate.

If we assume the InSync pacemaker has a 75 percent gross margin, then the cost of an InSync pacemaker is (1 – 0.75) × Price = 0.25 × Price, where Price is the selling price.[2] Therefore, the annual holding cost is 0.35 × 0.25 × Price = 0.0875 × Price and the daily holding cost, assuming 260 days per year, is 0.875 × Price/260 = 0.000337 × Price.

The cost of poor service requires some thought. We first need to decide how we will measure poor service and then decide on a cost for poor service. In the order-up-to model, a natural measure of poor service is the occurrence of a back order. Therefore, we say that we incur a cost for each unit back-ordered and we'll let the variable b represent that cost. We'll also refer to the variable b as the *back-order penalty cost.* Now we must decide on an appropriate value for b. A natural focal point with field inventory (i.e., inventory for serving final customers) is to assume each back order causes a lost sale and the cost of a lost sale equals the product's gross margin. However, if you believe there are substantial long-run implications of a lost sale (e.g., the customer will switch his or her future business to a competitor), then maybe the cost of a lost sale is even higher than the gross margin. On the other hand, if customers are somewhat patient, that is, a back order does not automatically lead to a lost sale, then maybe the cost of a back order is lower than the gross margin. In the case of Medtronic, the former story is more likely. Let's suppose each back order leads to a lost sale and, to be conservative, the cost of a back order is just the gross margin; that is, $b = 0.75 \times \text{Price}$.

Now let's minimize Medtronic's holding and back-order costs. The holding cost in a period is h times the number of units in inventory (which we measure at the end of the period). The back-order cost in a period is b times the number of units back-ordered.[3] As a result, we face the "too little–too much" challenge: Choose S too high and incur excessive inventory holding costs; but if S is too low, then we incur excessive back-order costs. We can actually use the newsvendor logic to strike the correct balance.

Our overage cost is $C_o = h$: The consequence of setting S too high is inventory and the cost per unit of inventory per period is h. Our underage cost is $C_u = b$: Back orders are the consequence of setting S too low and the cost per back order is b. In the newsvendor model, we chose an order quantity Q such that the critical ratio equals the probability demand is Q or lower, which is the same as the probability that a stockout does not occur. In the order-up-to model, the probability a stockout does not occur in a period is

$$\text{Prob}\{\text{Demand over } l + 1 \text{ periods} \leq S\}$$

Hence, the order-up-to level that minimizes costs in a period satisfies the following newsvendor equation:

$$\text{Prob}\{\text{Demand over } l + 1 \text{ periods} \leq S\} = \frac{C_u}{C_o + C_u} = \frac{b}{h + b} \quad \textbf{(16.2)}$$

For Medtronic, the critical ratio is

$$\frac{b}{h + b} = \frac{(0.75 \times \text{Price})}{(0.00037 \times \text{Price}) + (0.75 \times \text{Price})} = 0.9996$$

[2] Medtronic's gross margin across all products, as reported on their income statement, is approximately 80 percent. Because there are competing products, we assume the actual gross margin of the InSync is slightly lower than this average.

[3] If you have been reading carefully, you might realize that this is not entirely correct. The back-order cost in a period is b times the number of demands *in that period* that are back-ordered; that is, we do not incur the cost b per unit that became back-ordered in a previous period and still is on back order. However, with a high in-stock probability, it should be the case that units are rarely back-ordered, and if they are back-ordered, then they are back-ordered for no more than one period. Hence, with a high in-stock probability, assuming the back-order cost is b times the number of units back-ordered is an excellent approximation.

Notice the following with respect to Equation (16.2):

- We do not need to know the product's actual price, Price, because it cancels out of both the numerator and the denominator of the critical ratio.
- It is important that we use the holding cost per unit per period to evaluate the critical ratio because the order-up-to level determines the expected inventory in a period. In other words, h should be the holding cost for a single unit for a single period.

Now we are ready to justify our service level based on costs. Recall that

$$\text{In-stock probability} = \text{Prob}\{\text{Demand over } l + 1 \text{ periods} \leq S\}$$

If we combine the above equation with Equation (16.2), then the in-stock probability that is consistent with cost minimization is

$$\text{In-stock probability} = \text{Critical ratio} = \frac{b}{h + b} \qquad \textbf{(16.3)}$$

In other words, the appropriate in-stock probability equals the critical ratio. Recall that we chose 99.9 percent as our target in-stock probability. Even though that might seem high, our calculations above suggest that an in-stock probability of up to 99.96 percent is consistent with cost minimization.

Holding inventory is not cheap for Medtronic (35 percent holding cost rate), but due to Medtronic's large gross margins, the underage cost (0.75 × Price) is still about 2,200 times greater than the overage cost (0.000337 × Price)! With such a lopsided allocation of costs, it is no surprise that the appropriate in-stock probability is so high.

Table 16.4 indicates for various gross margins the optimal target in-stock probability. We can see that an obscene gross margin is needed (93 percent) to justify a 99.99 percent in-stock probability, but a modest gross margin (12 percent) is needed to justify a 99 percent in-stock probability.

Now consider the appropriate service level at the distribution center. While the opportunity cost of capital remains the same whether it is tied up in inventory in the field or at the distribution center, all other inventory holding costs are likely to be lower at the distribution center (e.g., physical space, theft, spoilage, insurance, etc.). But even with a lower holding cost, the appropriate service level at the distribution center is unlikely to be as high as it is in the field because the distribution center's back-order cost should be lower. Why? A back order in the field is likely to lead to a lost sale, but a back order at the distribution center does not necessarily lead to a lost sale. Each field representative has a buffer of inventory and that buffer might prevent a lost sale as long as the back order at the distribution center does not persist for too long. This is not to suggest that the appropriate in-stock

TABLE 16.4 The Optimal Target In-Stock Probability for Various Gross Margins

The annual holding cost rate is 35 percent, the back-order penalty cost equals the gross margin, and inventory is reviewed daily.

Gross Margin	Optimal Target In-Stock Probability	Gross Margin	Optimal Target In-Stock Probability
1%	88.24%	35%	99.75%
2	93.81	57	99.90
3	95.83	73	99.95
4	96.87	77	99.96
6	97.93	82	99.97
12	99.02	87	99.98
21	99.50	93	99.99

probability at the distribution center is low. Rather, it suggests that the appropriate in-stock probability might not be 99.9 percent.[4]

The main insight from this section is that the optimal target in-stock probability in the order-up-to model is likely to be quite high (99 percent and above), even with a relatively modest gross margin and high annual holding cost rate. However, that result depends on two key assumptions: Back orders lead to lost sales and inventory does not become obsolete. The latter assumption highlights a connection and a useful contrast between the order-up-to model and the newsvendor model. In the newsvendor model, obsolescence is the primary concern; that is, demand is not expected to continue into the future, so leftover inventory is expensive. As a result, optimal service levels in the newsvendor model are rarely as high as in the order-up-to model. Furthermore, the appropriate model to employ depends on where a *product* is in its *life cycle.* Up to and including the mature stage of a product's life cycle, the order-up-to model is more appropriate. As a product's end of life approaches, the newsvendor model is needed. Some products have very long life cycles—for example, chicken noodle soup—so the newsvendor model is never needed. Others have very short life cycles—for example, O'Neill's Hammer 3/2—so a firm is relegated to the newsvendor model almost immediately. It is the products with an intermediate life cycle (one to two years)—for example, the InSync pacemaker—that can be very tricky to manage. A firm should start thinking in terms of the order-up-to model and then switch to the newsvendor model shortly before the product dies. Many firms botch this "end-of-life" transition: By holding on to high service levels too long, they find themselves with far too much inventory when the product becomes obsolete.

16.8 Controlling Ordering Costs

In our analysis of Medtronic's supply chain, the focus has been on the service level (the in-stock probability) and the expected amount of inventory on hand at the end of each period. Although we have not addressed the issue of *order frequency* (i.e., how many shipments are made each year to the DC or to each sales territory), there are other settings for which it is important to control the order frequency. For example, most online book shoppers realize, due to how online retailers charge for shipping, that five separate orders with one book in each order is generally more expensive than one book order containing the same five books. In other words, when there is a significant cost incurred with each order that is independent of the amount ordered (i.e., a fixed cost), it is necessary to be smart about how often orders are made. The focus of this section is on how we can account for fixed ordering costs in the order-up-to model.

As we have already seen, in the order-up-to model, the order quantity in a period equals the demand in the previous period. Hence, an order is submitted in a period whenever demand in the previous period is not zero. Therefore, the probability we submit an order in a period is 1 – Prob{Demand in one period = 0} and the frequency at which we submit orders is

$$\frac{1 - \text{Prob}\{\text{Demand in one period} = 0\}}{\text{Length of period}}$$

For example, if there is a 90 percent probability we order in a period and a period is two weeks, then our order frequency is 0.9/2 weeks = 0.45 order per week. If demand

[4] Evaluation of the appropriate in-stock probability for the distribution center is beyond the scope of this discussion. However, simulation can be a useful tool to begin to understand the true back-order cost at the distribution center. Via simulation it is possible to estimate the likelihood that a back order at the distribution center causes a lost sale in the field.

TABLE 16.5 Analysis of Ending Inventory for Different Period Lengths

In each case, the delivery time is eight weeks and demand is normally distributed and independent across weeks.

	Period Length (in weeks)			
	1	2	4	8
One period expected demand	100	200	400	800
One period standard deviation	75.0	106.1	150.0	212.1
Lead time (in periods)	8	4	2	1
Target in-stock probability	99.25%	99.25%	99.25%	99.25%
z	2.43	2.43	2.43	2.43
S	1,447	1,576	1,831	2,329
Average back order	0.56	0.59	0.65	0.75
Average ending inventory	548	577	632	730

occurs frequently, so the probability of zero demand is very small no matter the length of the period, then it follows that we can reduce our ordering frequency by increasing the length of our period; that is, we are likely to submit nearly twice as many orders with a one-week period than with a two-week period. But increasing the length of the period is costly from the perspective of inventory holding costs. We illustrate that point via an example.

Suppose all orders are received precisely eight weeks after they are submitted to a supplier, weekly demand is normally distributed with mean 100 and standard deviation 75, the target in-stock probability is 99.25 percent, and demands across weeks are independent. We can choose a period length of one, two, four, or eight weeks. If the period is one week, then the lead time is eight periods, whereas if the period length is four weeks, then the lead time is two periods. Using the methods developed in the previous sections, we can determine the end-of-period average inventory for each period length. Those results are summarized in Table 16.5. The table reveals that our end-of-period inventory is indeed higher as we lengthen the period. But that is not really a fair comparison across our different options.

As we have already stated, the average order quantity equals average demand in the previous period. Thus, our average order quantity with a period length of one week is 100 units, whereas our average order quantity with an eight-week period is 800 units. Figure 16.5 plots the average inventory level over time for our four options; on average, inventory increases at the start of the period by the average order quantity and then decreases at the rate of 100 units per week, that is, average inventory follows a "saw-toothed" pattern. (Due to randomness in demand, the actual inventory pattern varies around those patterns, but those saw-toothed patterns capture the average behavior of inventory.) The average inventory over time is the average end-of-period inventory plus half of the average order quantity, which for our four options is 598, 677, 832, and 1,130, respectively. Hence, longer periods mean less-frequent ordering but more inventory.

Incidentally, you may recall that the graphs in Figure 16.5 resemble Figure 2.11 in Chapter 2. Back in Chapter 2 we used the term *cycle inventory* to refer to the inventory held due to lumpy ordering. In this case, the average cycle inventory would be half of the average order quantity: With four-week periods, the average cycle inventory is 400/2 = 200 units. The average end-of-period inventory is often referred to as *safety inventory* because that is the inventory that is needed to buffer demand variability. The average inventory over time is then safety inventory plus cycle inventory.

To balance the cost of more inventory with the benefit of fewer orders, we need information about holding and ordering costs. Let's say this item costs $50, annual holding costs are 25 percent, and we incur a fixed cost of $275 per shipment (e.g., we could be

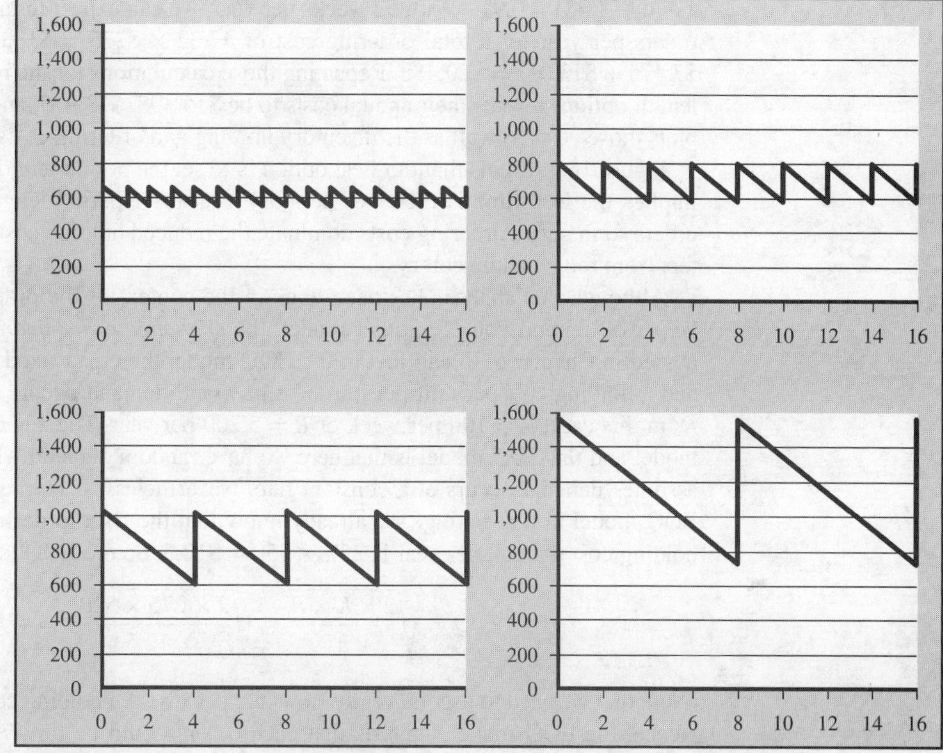

FIGURE 16.5 Average Inventory Pattern over Time for Four Different Period Lengths

Upper left, one week; upper right, two weeks; lower left, four weeks; and lower right, eight weeks.

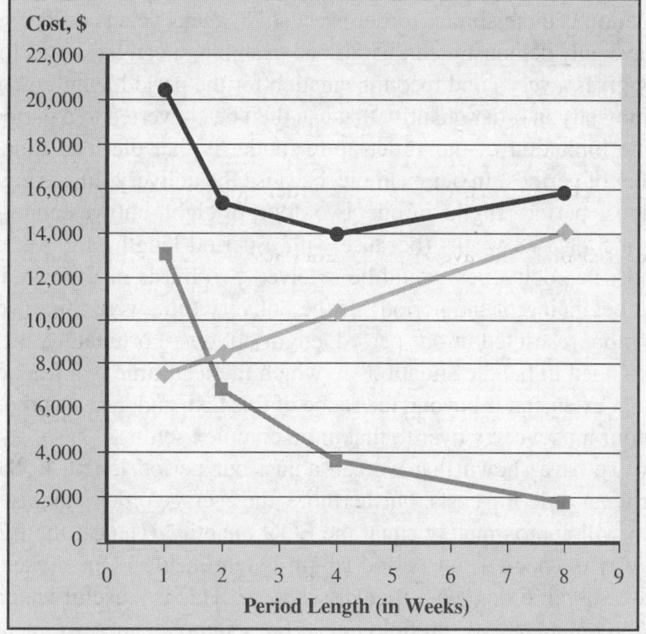

FIGURE 16.6 Annual Ordering Costs (squares), Inventory Costs (diamonds), and Total Costs (circles) for Periods of Length One, Two, Four, and Eight Weeks

talking about a truck delivery). If the period length is one week, then the average inventory is 598 units, which has value 598 × \$50 = \$29,900 and costs us 25% × \$29,900 = \$7,475 per year. With mean demand of 100 and a standard deviation of 75, the *z*-statistic for 0 is (0 − 100)/75 = −1.33. Hence, the probability we order in any given week is

$1 - \Phi(-1.33) = 0.91$.[5] With 52 weeks per year, we can expect to make $0.91 \times 52 = 47.32$ orders per year for a total ordering cost of $47.32 \times \$275 = \$13{,}013$. Total cost is then $\$7{,}475 + \$13{,}013 = \$20{,}488$. Repeating those calculations for the remaining three period-length options reveals their annual costs to be $15,398, $13,975, and $15,913. Figure 16.6 plots those costs as well as the inventory holding and ordering costs of the four options.

Figure 16.6 reveals that our best option is to set the period length to four weeks (which implies the lead time is then two periods). A shorter period length results in too many orders so the extra ordering costs dominate the reduced holding costs. A longer period suffers from too much inventory.

Although this analysis has been done in the context of the order-up-to model, it may very well remind you of another model, the *economic order quantity (EOQ)* model discussed in Chapter 5. Recall that in the EOQ model there is a fixed cost per order/batch K and a holding cost per unit per unit of time h and demand occurs at a constant flow rate R; in this case, $R = 100$ per week or $R = 5{,}200$ per year. The key difference between our model and the EOQ model is that here we have random demand whereas the EOQ model assumes demand occurs at a constant rate. Nevertheless, it is interesting to evaluate the EOQ model in this setting. We already know that the fixed ordering cost is K $275. The holding cost per unit per year is $25\% \times \$50 = \$12.5$. So the EOQ (see Chapter 5) is

$$Q = \sqrt{\frac{2 \times K \times R}{h}} = \sqrt{\frac{2 \times 275 \times 5200}{12.5}} = 478$$

(Note that we need to use the yearly flow rate because the holding cost is per unit per year.) Hence, the EOQ model suggests that each order should be for 478 units, which implies submitting an order every $478/100 = 4.78$ weeks. (This follows from Little's Law.) Hence, even though the order-up-to and the EOQ models are different, the EOQ model's recommendation is quite similar (order every 4.78 weeks versus order every 4 weeks). Although we have only demonstrated this for one example, it can be shown that the EOQ model generally gives a very good recommendation for the period length (note that the EOQ actually recommends an order quantity that can then be converted to a period length).

One limitation of our order-up-to model is that the lead time must equal an integer number of periods. In our example, because the delivery time is eight weeks, this allows us to choose period lengths of one, two, four, or eight, but we cannot choose a period length of 3 or 5 or 4.78 weeks (because with a period length of 3 weeks the lead time is 2.67 periods, i.e., deliveries would be received two-thirds of the way into a period instead of at the beginning of the period). If the delivery time were three weeks, then we would be even more restricted in our period length options. Fortunately, the order-up-to model can be extended to handle situations in which the lead time is a fraction of the period length. But that extension is beyond the scope of this text, and, rest assured, the qualitative insights from our model carry over to that more complex setting.

So we have shown that we can adjust our period length in the order-up-to model to control our ordering costs. Furthermore, the average order quantity with the optimal period length will approximately equal the EOQ quantity. (Hence, the EOQ formula gives us an easy way to check if our period length is reasonable.) One advantage of this approach is that we submit orders on a regular schedule. This is a useful feature if we need to coordinate the orders across multiple items. For example, since we incur a fixed cost per truck shipment, we generally deliver many different products on each truck because no single

[5] We actually just evaluated the probability that demand is *less* than or equal to zero because the normal distribution allows for negative demand. We are implicitly assuming that all negative realizations of demand are really zero demand outcomes.

product's demand is large enough to fill a truck (imagine sending a tractor trailer load of spices to a grocery store). In that situation, it is quite useful to order items at the same time so that the truck can be loaded quickly and we can ensure a reasonably full shipment (given that there is a fixed cost per shipment, it makes sense to utilize the cargo capacity as much as possible). Therefore, we need only ensure that the order times of different products align.

Instead of using fixed order intervals, as in the order-up-to model, we could control ordering costs by imposing a minimum order quantity. For example, we could wait for Q units of demand to occur and then order exactly Q units. With such a policy, we would order on average every Q/R units of time, but due to the randomness in demand, the time between orders would vary. Not surprisingly, the EOQ provides an excellent recommendation for that minimum order quantity, but we omit the analytical details as they are beyond the scope of this text. The important insight from this discussion is that it is possible to control ordering costs by restricting ourselves to a periodic schedule of orders (as in the order-up-to model) or we could restrict ourselves to a minimum order quantity. With the first option, there is little variability in the timing of orders, which facilitates the coordination of orders across multiple items, but the order quantities are variable (which may increase handling costs). With the second option, the order quantities are not variable (we always order Q), but the timing of those orders varies.

16.9 Managerial Insights

This section discusses general managerial insights from the order-up-to model.

One of the key lessons from the queuing and newsvendor chapters is that variability in demand is costly. (Recall that the mismatch cost in the newsvendor model is increasing with the coefficient of variation, which is the ratio of the standard deviation of demand to expected demand.) That result continues to hold in the order-up-to model. Figure 16.7 illustrates the result graphically. The figure presents the trade-off curve between the in-stock probability and expected inventory: As the desired in-stock probability increases,

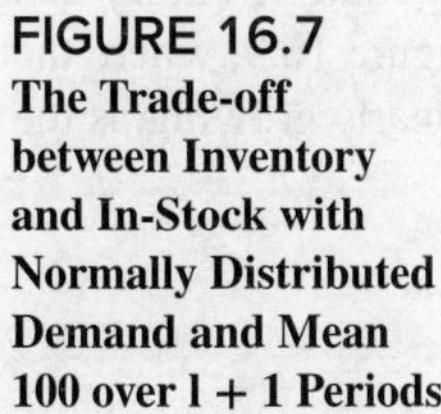

FIGURE 16.7
The Trade-off between Inventory and In-Stock with Normally Distributed Demand and Mean 100 over l + 1 Periods

The curves differ in the standard deviation of demand over $l + 1$ periods: 60, 50, 40, 30, 20, 10 from top to bottom.

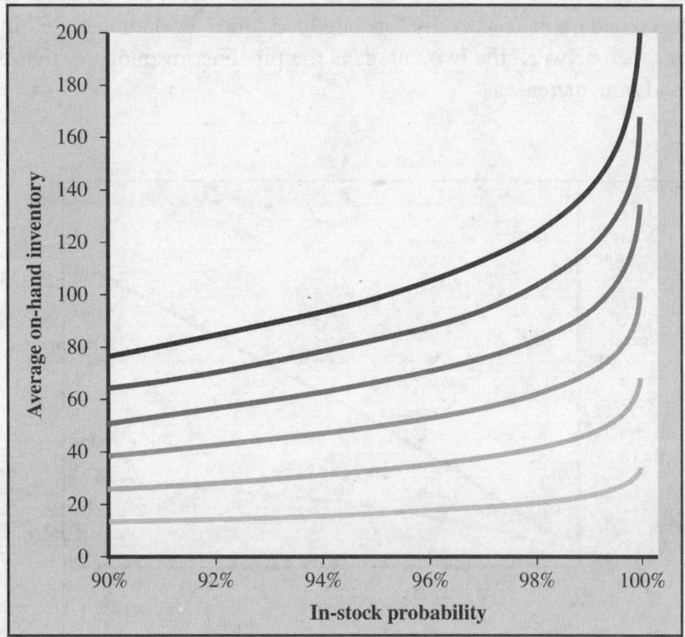

FIGURE 16.8
The Impact of Lead Time on Expected Inventory for Four In-Stock Targets

In-stock targets are 99.9, 99.5, 99.0, and 98 percent, top curve to bottom curve, respectively. Demand in one period is normally distributed with mean 100 and standard deviation 60.

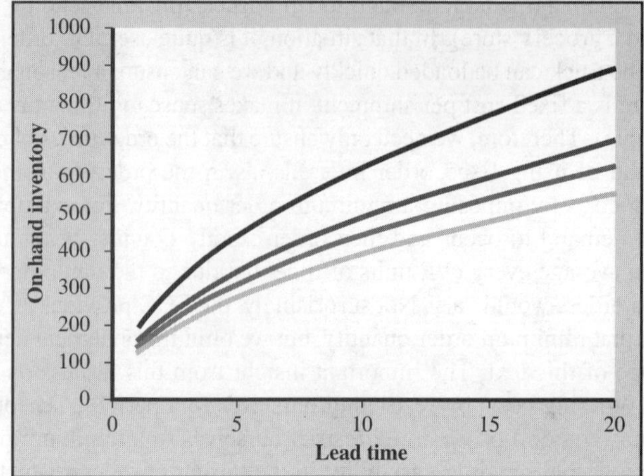

so does the required amount of inventory. Furthermore, we see that for any given in-stock probability, the expected inventory increases in the standard deviation of demand over $l + 1$ periods: Increased variability means more inventory is needed on average to achieve a fixed service level.

In addition to the variability in demand, the expected inventory in the order-up-to model is sensitive to the lead time, as illustrated by Figure 16.8: As the lead time is reduced, so is the required inventory for any service target.

While expected inventory depends on the variability of demand and the lead time, the expected on-order inventory, or pipeline inventory, depends only on the lead time. Therefore, while reducing the uncertainty in demand reduces expected inventory, pipeline inventory can only be reduced with a faster lead time. (Actually, reducing demand also reduces pipeline inventory, but that is rarely an attractive option, and reducing demand does not even reduce pipeline inventory when it is measured relative to the demand rate, e.g., with inventory turns or days of demand.) Furthermore, the amount of pipeline inventory can be considerable, especially for long lead times, as demonstrated in Figure 16.9, where the distance between the two curves is the pipeline inventory, which is clearly growing as the lead time increases.

FIGURE 16.9
Expected Inventory (circles) and Total Inventory (squares), Which Is Expected Inventory Plus Pipeline Inventory, with a 99.9 Percent In-Stock Requirement

Demand in one period is normally distributed with mean 100 and standard deviation 60.

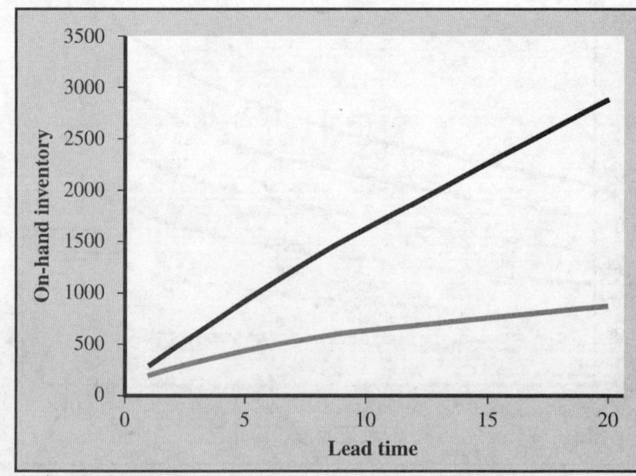

TABLE 16.6
Summary of Key Notation and Equations in Chapter 16

l = Lead time
S = Order-up-to level
Inventory level = On-hand inventory − Back order
Inventory position = On-order inventory + Inventory level
In-stock probability = 1 − Stockout probability
= Prob{Demand over $l + 1$ periods $\leq S$}

Expected on-hand inventory:
If demand over $l + 1$ periods is normally distributed with mean μ and standard deviation σ:
Expected on-hand inventory = $\sigma \times I(z)$, where $z = (S - \mu)/\sigma$

In Excel:
Expected on-hand inventory = σ* (Normdist(z,0,1,0) + z* Normsdist(z))
If demand over $l + 1$ periods is a discrete distribution function table, then
Expected on-hand inventory = $I(S)$
Expected on-order inventory = Expected demand in one period × Lead time

16.10 Summary

This chapter illustrates the application of the order-up-to model to one product, the InSync pacemaker, at two different levels in Medtronic's supply chain: the Mounds View distribution center and Susan Magnotto's Madison, Wisconsin, territory. The order-up-to model periodically reviews (weekly at Mounds View, daily for Susan) the inventory position at a location and submits an order, which is received after a fixed lead time, to raise the inventory position to an order-up-to level. The order-up-to level is chosen, based on the demand distribution, to minimize inventory while maintaining a service standard such as an in-stock probability.

The analysis of the order-up-to model reveals that raising the desired service level increases the required inventory investment and the amount of inventory needed increases nonlinearly as the target service level increases. In other words, as high service levels are desired, proportionally more inventory is needed.

There are two other key factors that determine the amount of inventory that is needed: the variability of demand, measured by the coefficient of variation, and the length of the lead time. Just as we saw in the newsvendor model, an increase in the coefficient of variation leads to an increase in the amount of inventory needed for any fixed service level.

The length of the lead time is critical for two reasons. First, a reduction in the lead time reduces the amount of inventory needed at any location. Second, and maybe even more important, a reduction in the lead time reduces the amount of inventory in transit between locations; that is, the pipeline inventory. In fact, reducing the lead time is the only way to reduce the pipeline inventory: While reducing the variability of demand reduces the expected inventory at a location, it has no effect on pipeline inventory because of Little's Law.

Table 16.6 provides a summary of the key notation and equations presented in this chapter.

16.11 Further Reading

The order-up-to model is just one of many possible inventory policies that could be implemented in practice. For example, there are policies that account for stochastic lead times, lost sales, and/or batch ordering (ordering in integer multiples of a fixed batch quantity). However, no matter what extensions are included, the key insights remain: Inventory increases as demand variability increases or as the lead time increases.

See Zipkin (2000) for an extensive treatment of the theory of inventory management. For less technical, but still sophisticated, treatments, see Nahmias (2005) or Silver, Pyke, and Peterson (1998). Those texts cover the additional polices we discussed in the chapter (for example, a minimum order quantity with a fixed lead time and stochastic demand). In addition, they discuss the issue of the appropriate service level for upstream stages in a supply chain.

See Simchi-Levi, Kaminsky, and Simchi-Levi (2003) and Chopra and Meindl (2004) for managerial discussions of supply chain management.

16.12 Practice Problems

The following questions will help in testing your understanding of this chapter. After each question, we show the relevant section in parentheses [Section x].

Solutions to problems marked with an "*" are available in Appendix E. Video solutions to select problems are available in Connect.

Q16.1* **(Furniture Store)** You are the store manager at a large furniture store. One of your products is a study desk. Weekly demand for the desk is normally distributed with mean 40 and standard deviation 20. The lead time from the assembly plant to your store is two weeks and you order inventory replenishments weekly. You use the order-up-to model to control inventory.

a. Suppose your order-up-to level is $S = 220$. You are about to place an order and note that your inventory level is 100 and you have 85 desks on order. How many desks will you order? [16.2]

b. Suppose your order-up-to level is $S = 220$. You are about to place an order and note that your inventory level is 160 and you have 65 desks on order. How many desks will you order? [16.2]

c. What is the optimal order-up-to level if you want to target a 98 percent in-stock probability? [16.6]

d. Suppose your order-up-to level is $S = 120$. What is your expected on-hand inventory? [16.5]

e. Suppose your order-up-to level is $S = 120$. Your internal cost of capital is 15 percent and each desk costs $200. What is your total cost of capital for the year for inventory in the store? [16.5]

Q16.2* **(Campus Bookstore)** A campus bookstore sells the Palm m505 handheld for $399. The wholesale price is $250 per unit. The store estimates that weekly demand averages 0.5 unit and has a Poisson distribution. The bookstore's annual inventory holding cost is 20 percent of the cost of inventory. Assume orders are made weekly and the lead time to receive an order from the distributor is four weeks.

a. What base stock level minimizes inventory while achieving a 99 percent in-stock probability? [16.6]

b. Suppose the base stock level is $S = 4$. What is the average pipeline inventory? [16.5]

c. Suppose the base stock level is $S = 5$. What is the average inventory held at the end of the week in the store? [16.5]

d. Suppose the base stock level is $S = 6$. What is the probability a stockout occurs during a week (i.e., some customer is back-ordered)? [16.5]

e. Suppose the base stock level is $S = 6$. What is the probability the store is out of stock (i.e., has no inventory) at the end of a week? [16.5]

f. Suppose the base stock level is $S = 6$. What is the probability the store has one or more units of inventory at the end of a week? [16.5]

The bookstore is concerned that it is incurring excessive ordering costs by ordering weekly. For parts g and h, suppose the bookstore now submits orders every two weeks. The demand forecast remains the same and the lead time is still four weeks.

g. What base stock level yields at least a 99 percent in-stock probability while minimizing inventory? [16.6]

h. What is the average pipeline stock? [16.5]

Q16.3* **(Quick Print)** Quick Print Inc. uses plain and three-hole-punched paper for copying needs. Demand for each paper type is highly variable. Weekly demand for the plain paper is estimated to be normally distributed with mean 100 and standard deviation 65 (measured in boxes). Each week, a replenishment order is placed to the paper factory and the order arrives five weeks later. All copying orders that cannot be satisfied immediately due to the lack of paper are back-ordered. The inventory holding cost is about $1 per box per year.

a. Suppose that Quick Print decides to establish an order-up-to level of 700 for plain paper. At the start of this week, there are 523 boxes in inventory and 180 boxes on order. How much will Quick Print order this week? [16.2]

b. What is Quick Print's optimal order-up-to level for plain paper if Quick Print operates with a 99 percent in-stock probability? [16.6]

Q16.4* **(Main Line Auto Distributor)** Main Line Auto Distributor is an auto parts supplier to local garage shops. None of its customers have the space or capital to store all of the possible parts they might need so they order parts from Main Line several times a day. To provide fast service, Main Line uses three pickup trucks to make its own deliveries. Each Friday evening, Main Line orders additional inventory from its supplier. The supplier delivers early Monday morning. Delivery costs are significant, so Main Line only orders on Fridays. Consider part A153QR, or part A for short. Part A costs Main Line $175 and Main Line sells it to garages for $200. If a garage orders part A and Main Line is out of stock, then the garage finds the part from some other distributor. Main Line has its own capital and space constraints and estimates that each unit of part A costs $0.50 to hold in inventory per week. (Assume you incur the $0.50 cost for units left in inventory at the end of the week, not $0.50 for your average inventory during the week or $0.50 for your inventory at the start of the week.) Average weekly demand for this part follows a Poisson distribution with mean 1.5 units. Suppose it is Friday evening and Main Line currently doesn't have any part A's in stock. The distribution and loss functions for a Poisson distribution with mean 1.5 can be found in Appendix B.

a. How many part A's should Main Line order from the supplier? [16.2]

b. Suppose Main Line orders three units. What is the probability Main Line is able to satisfy all demand during the week? [16.5]

c. Suppose Main Line orders four units. What is the probability Main Line is *not* able to satisfy all demand during the week? [16.5]

d. If Main Line seeks to hit a target in-stock probability of 99.5 percent, then how many units should Main Line order? [16.6]

e. Suppose Main Line orders five units. What is Main Line's expected holding cost for the upcoming week? [16.5]

Q16.5* **(Hotspices.com)** You are the owner of Hotspices.com, an online retailer of hip, exotic, and hard-to-find spices. Consider your inventory of saffron, a spice (generally) worth more by weight than gold. You order saffron from an overseas supplier with a shipping lead time of four weeks and you order weekly. Average quarterly demand is normally distributed with a mean of 415 ounces and a standard deviation of 154 ounces. The holding cost per ounce per week is $0.75. You estimate that your back-order penalty cost is $50 per ounce. Assume there are 4.33 weeks per month.

a. If you wish to minimize inventory holding costs while maintaining a 99.25 percent in-stock probability, then what should your order-up-to level be? [16.6]

b. If you wish to minimize holding and back-order penalty costs, then what should your order-up-to level be? [16.6]

c. Now consider your inventory of pepperoncini (Italian hot red peppers). You can order this item daily and your local supplier delivers with a two-day lead time. While not your most popular item, you do have enough demand to sell the five-kilogram bag. Average demand per day has a Poisson distribution with mean 1.0. The holding cost per bag per day is $0.05 and the back-order penalty cost is about $5 per bag. What is your optimal order-up-to level? [16.7]

Q16.6 **(Blood Bank)** Dr. Jack is in charge of the Springfield Hospital's Blood Center. Blood is collected in the regional Blood Center 200 miles away and delivered to Springfield by airplane. Dr. Jack reviews blood reserves and places orders every Monday morning for delivery the following Monday morning. If demand begins to exceed supply, surgeons postpone nonurgent procedures, in which case blood is back-ordered.

Demand for blood on every given week is normal with mean 100 pints and standard deviation 34 pints. Demand is independent across weeks.

a. On Monday morning, Dr. Jack reviews his reserves and observes 200 pints in on-hand inventory, no back orders, and 73 pints in pipeline inventory. Suppose his order-up-to level is 285. How many pints will he order? [16.2]
b. Dr. Jack targets a 99 percent in-stock probability. What order-up-to level should he choose? [16.6]
c. Dr. Jack is planning to implement a computer system that will allow daily ordering (seven days per week) and the lead time to receive orders will be one day. What will be the average order quantity? [16.5]

Q16.7 **(Schmears Shirts)** Schmears Inc. is a catalog retailer of men's shirts. Daily demand for a particular SKU (style and size) is Poisson with mean 1.5. It takes three days for a replenishment order to arrive from Schmears' supplier and orders are placed daily. Schmears uses the order-up-to model to manage its inventory of this shirt.

a. Suppose Schmears uses an order-up-to level of 9. What is the average number of shirts on order? [16.5]
b. Now suppose Schmears uses an order-up-to level of 8. What is the probability during any given day that Schmears does not have sufficient inventory to meet the demand from all customers? [16.5]
c. Schmears is considering a switch from a "service-based" stocking policy to a "cost-minimization" stocking policy. They estimate their holding cost per shirt per day is $0.01. Forty-five percent of customers order more than one item at a time, so they estimate their stockout cost on this shirt is $6 per shirt. What order-up-to level minimizes the sum of their holding and back-order costs? [16.7]

Q16.8 **(ACold)** ACold Inc. is a frozen food distributor with 10 warehouses across the country. Iven Tory, one of the warehouse managers, wants to make sure that the inventory policies used by the warehouse are minimizing inventory while still maintaining quick delivery to ACold's customers. Since the warehouse carries hundreds of different products, Iven decided to study one. He picked Caruso's Frozen Pizza (CFP). Demand for CFPs averages 400 per day with a standard deviation of 200. Weekly demand (five days) averages 2,000 units with a standard deviation of 555. Since ACold orders at least one truck from General Foods each day (General Foods owns Caruso's Pizza), ACold can essentially order any quantity of CFP it wants each day. In fact, ACold's computer system is designed to implement a base stock policy for each product. Iven notes that any order for CFPs arrives four days after the order. Further, it costs ACold $0.01 per day to keep a CFP in inventory, while a back order is estimated to cost ACold $0.45.

a. What base stock level should Iven choose for CFPs if his goal is to minimize holding and back-order costs? [16.7]
b. Suppose the base stock level 2,800 is chosen. What is the average amount of inventory on order? [16.5]
c. Suppose the base stock level 2,800 is chosen. What is the annual holding cost? (Assume 260 days per year.) [16.5]
d. What base stock level minimizes inventory while maintaining a 97 percent in-stock probability? [16.6]

Q16.9 **(Cyber Chemicals)** Cyber Chemicals uses liquid nitrogen on a regular basis. Average daily demand is 178 gallons with a standard deviation of 45. Due to a substantial ordering cost, which is estimated to be $58 per order (no matter the quantity in the order), Cyber currently orders from its supplier on a weekly basis. Cyber also incurs holding costs on its inventory. Cyber recognizes that its inventory is lowest at the end of the week but prefers a more realistic estimate of its average inventory. In particular, Cyber estimates its average inventory to be its average end-of-week inventory plus half of its average order quantity. The holding cost Cyber incurs on that average inventory is $0.08 per gallon per week. Cyber's supplier delivers in less than a day. Assume 52 weeks per year, five days per week.

a. Cyber wishes to maintain a 99.9 percent in-stock probability. If it does so, what is Cyber's annual inventory holding cost? [16.5]
b. What is Cyber's annual ordering cost? [16.8]
c. Should Cyber consider ordering every two weeks? [16.8]

Q16.10 **(Southern Fresh)** Shelf space in the grocery business is a valuable asset. Every good supermarket spends a significant amount of effort attempting to determine the optimal shelf space allocation across products. Many factors are relevant to this decision: the profitability of each product, the size of each product, the demand characteristics of each product, and so forth. Consider Hot Bull corn chips, a local favorite. Average daily demand for this product is 55, with a standard deviation of 30. Bags of Hot Bull can be stacked 20 deep per facing. (A facing is the width on a shelf required to display one item of a product.) Deliveries from Southern Fresh's central warehouse occur two days after a store manager submits an order. (Actually, in most stores, orders are generated by a centralized computer system that is linked to its point-of-sales data. But even these orders are received two days after they are transmitted.)

a. How many facings are needed to achieve a 98.75 percent in-stock probability? [16.6]
b. Suppose Southern Fresh allocates 11 facings to Hot Bull corn chips. On average, how many bags of Hot Bull are on the shelf at the end of the day? [16.5]
c. Although Southern Fresh does not want to incur the cost of holding inventory, it does want to leave customers with the impression that it is well stocked. Hence, Southern Fresh employees continually roam the aisles of the store to adjust the presentation of the product. In particular, they shift product around so that there is an item in each facing whenever possible. Suppose Southern Fresh allocates 11 facings to Hot Bull corn chips. What is the probability that at the end of the day there will be an empty facing, that is, a facing without any product? [16.5]

Chapter 17

Risk-Pooling Strategies to Reduce and Hedge Uncertainty[1]

Uncertainty is the bane of operations. No matter in what form—for example, uncertain demand, uncertain supply, or uncertain quality—operational performance never benefits from the presence of uncertainty. Previous chapters have discussed models for coping with uncertainty (e.g., queuing, newsvendor, and order-up-to) and have emphasized the need to quantify uncertainty. Some strategies for reducing and hedging uncertainty have already been suggested: Combine servers in a queuing system (Chapter 10); reduce uncertainty by collecting data to ensure that the best demand forecast is always implemented (Chapter 14); establish make-to-order production and invest in reactive capacity to better respond to demand (Chapter 15).

This chapter explores several additional strategies based on the concept of risk pooling. The idea behind risk pooling is to redesign the supply chain, the production process, or the product to either reduce the uncertainty the firm faces or hedge uncertainty so that the firm is in a better position to mitigate the consequence of uncertainty. Several types of risk pooling are presented (location pooling, virtual pooling, product pooling, lead time pooling, and capacity pooling), but these are just different names to describe the same basic phenomenon. With each strategy, we work through a practical example to illustrate its effectiveness and to highlight the situations in which the strategy is most appropriate.

17.1 Location Pooling

The newsvendor and the order-up-to inventory models are tools for deciding how much inventory to put at a single location to serve demand. An equally important decision, and one that we have ignored so far, is in how many different locations should the firm store inventory to serve demand. To explain, consider the Medtronic supply chain discussed in Chapter 16. In that supply chain, each sales representative in the field manages a cache of inventory to serve the rep's territory and there is a single distribution center to serve the

[1] Data in this chapter have been disguised to protect confidentiality.

entire U.S. market. Should there be one stockpile of inventory per sales representative or should the demands from multiple territories be served from a single location? Should there be a single distribution center or should the U.S. market demand be divided among multiple distribution centers? We explore those questions in this section.

Pooling Medtronic's Field Inventory

Let's begin with where to locate Medtronic's field inventory. Instead of the current system in which each sales representative manages his or her own inventory, maybe the representatives in adjacent territories could share inventory. For example, Medtronic could rent a small space in a centrally located and easily accessible location (e.g., a back room in a strip mall off the interchange of two major highways) and two to five representatives could pool their inventory at that location. Sharing inventory means that each representative would only carry inventory needed for immediate use; that is, each representative's trunk and consignment inventory would be moved to this shared location. Control of the pooled inventory would be guided by an automatic replenishment system based on the order-up-to model. What impact would this new strategy have on inventory performance?

Recall that average daily demand for Medtronic's InSync pacemaker in Susan Magnotto's Madison, Wisconsin, territory is represented with a Poisson distribution with mean 0.29 unit per day. For the sake of argument, let's suppose there are several other territories adjacent to Susan's, each with a single sales representative and each with average daily demand of 0.29 unit for the InSync pacemaker. Instead of each representative carrying his or her own inventory, now they share a common pool of inventory. We refer to the combined territories in this new system as the *pooled territory* and the inventory there as the *pooled inventory.* In contrast, we refer to the territories in the current system as the *individual territories* and the inventory in one of those territories as the *individual inventory.* We refer to the strategy of combining the inventory from multiple territories/locations into a single location as *location pooling*. We have already evaluated the expected inventory with the current individual territory system, so now we need to evaluate the performance of the system with pooled territories; that is, the impact of location pooling.

The order-up-to model is used to manage the inventory at the pooled territory. The same aggressive target in-stock probability is used for the pooled territory as is used at the individual territories, 99.9 percent. Furthermore, the lead time to replenish the pooled territory is also one day. (There is no reason to believe the lead time to the pooled territory should be different than to the individual territories.)

As discussed in Chapter 16, if the Poisson distribution represents demand at two different territories, then their combined demand has a Poisson distribution with a mean that equals the sum of their means. (See Exhibit 16.1.) For example, suppose Susan shares inventory with two nearby sales representatives and they all have mean demand for the InSync pacemaker of 0.29 unit per day. Then total demand across the three territories is Poisson with mean $3 \times 0.29 = 0.87$ unit per day. We then can apply the order-up-to model to that pooled territory assuming a lead time of one day and a mean demand of 0.87 unit.

Table 17.1 presents data on the impact of pooling the sales representatives' territories. To achieve the 99.9 percent in-stock probability for three sales representatives requires $S = 7$, where S is the order-up-to level. If Susan's inventory is not combined with another representative's, then (as we evaluated in Chapter 16) $S = 4$ is needed to hit the target in-stock probability. The expected inventory at the pooled location is 5.3 units, in contrast to 3.4 units for each individual location. However, the total inventory for three individual locations is $3 \times 3.4 = 10.2$ units. Hence, pooling three locations reduces expected inventory by about 48 percent [(10.2 − 5.3)/10.2], without any degradation in service!

TABLE 17.1 The Impact on InSync Pacemaker Inventory from Pooling Sales Representatives' Territories

Demand at each territory is Poisson with average daily demand of 0.29 unit, the target in-stock probability is 99.9 percent, and the lead time is one day.

Number of Territories Pooled	Pooled Territory's Expected Demand per Day (a)	S	Expected Inventory		Pipeline Inventory	
			Units (b)	Days-of-Demand (b/a)	Units (c)	Days-of-Demand (c/a)
1	0.29	4	3.4	11.7	0.29	1.0
2	0.58	6	4.8	8.3	0.58	1.0
3	0.87	7	5.3	6.1	0.87	1.0
4	1.16	8	5.7	4.9	1.16	1.0
5	1.45	9	6.1	4.2	1.45	1.0
6	1.74	10	6.5	3.7	1.74	1.0
7	2.03	12	7.9	3.9	2.03	1.0
8	2.32	13	8.4	3.6	2.32	1.0

There is another approach to make the comparison between pooled territories and individual territories: Evaluate each inventory quantity relative to the demand it serves; that is, calculate expected inventory measured in days-of-demand rather than units:

$$\text{Expected inventory in days-of-demand} = \frac{\text{Expected inventory in units}}{\text{Expected daily demand}}$$

Table 17.1 also provides that measure of expected inventory. We see that inventory at each individual territory equals 3.4/0.29 = 11.7 days-of-demand whereas inventory at three pooled territories equals only 5.3/0.87 = 6.1 days-of-demand. Using our days-of-demand measure, we see that pooling three territories results in a 48 percent [(11.7 – 6.1)/11.7] reduction in inventory investment. We obtain the same inventory reduction (48 percent) because the two measures of inventory, units and days-of-demand, only differ by a constant factor (the expected daily demand). Hence, we can work with either measure.

While pooling two or three territories has a dramatic impact on inventory, Table 17.1 indicates that there are decreasing marginal returns to pooling territories; that is, each new territory added to the pool brings a smaller reduction in inventory than the previous territory added to the pool. For example, adding two more territories to a pool of six (to make a total of eight combined territories) has very little impact on the inventory investment (3.6 days-of-demand versus 3.7 days-of-demand), whereas adding two more territories to a pool of one (to make a total of three combined territories) has a dramatic impact in inventory (6.1 days-of-demand versus 11.7 days-of-demand). This is good news: The majority of the benefit of pooling territories comes from the first couple of territories combined, so there is little value in trying to combine many territories together.

Although location pooling generally reduces inventory, a careful observer of the data in Table 17.1 would discover that this is not always so: Adding the seventh location to the pool slightly increases inventory (3.9 days-of-demand versus 3.7 days-of-demand). This is due to the restriction that the order-up-to level must be an integer (0, 1, 2, . . .) quantity. As a result, the in-stock probability might be even higher than the target: The in-stock probability with six pooled territories is 99.90 percent, whereas it is 99.97 percent with seven pooled territories. Overall, this issue does not invalidate the general trend that location pooling reduces inventory.

This discussion obviously leads to the question of why does location pooling reduce the required inventory investment? We'll find a good answer by looking at how demand variability changes as locations are added to the pooled location. And, as we have already discussed, the coefficient of variation (the ratio of the standard deviation to the mean) is our choice for measuring demand variability.

Recall that the standard deviation of a Poisson distribution equals the square root of its mean. Therefore,

$$\text{Coefficient of variation of a Poisson distribution} = \frac{\text{Standard deviation}}{\text{Mean}} = \frac{\sqrt{\text{Mean}}}{\text{Mean}} = \frac{1}{\sqrt{\text{Mean}}} \tag{17.1}$$

As the mean of a Poisson distribution increases, its coefficient of variation decreases; that is, the Poisson distribution becomes less variable. Less variable demand leads to less inventory for any given service level. Hence, combining locations with Poisson demand reduces the required inventory investment because a higher demand rate implies less variable demand. However, because the coefficient of variation decreases with the square root of the mean, it decreases at a decreasing rate. In other words, each incremental increase in the mean has a proportionally smaller impact on the coefficient of variation, and, hence, on the expected inventory investment.

Figure 17.1 displays the relationship between inventory and the coefficient of variation for the data in Table 17.1. Notice that the decreasing pattern in inventory closely mimics the decreasing pattern in the coefficient of variation.

In addition to the total expected inventory in the field, we also are interested in the total pipeline inventory (inventory on order between the distribution center and the field). Table 17.1 provides the pipeline inventory in terms of units and in terms of days-of-demand. While location pooling decreases the expected inventory in days-of-demand, it has absolutely no impact on the pipeline inventory in terms of days-of-demand! Why? Little's Law governs pipeline inventory, and Little's Law depends on averages, not variability. Hence,

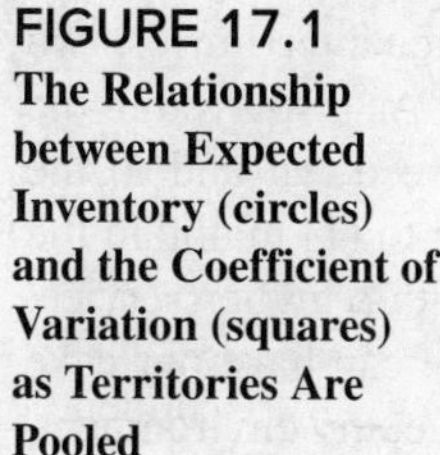

FIGURE 17.1
The Relationship between Expected Inventory (circles) and the Coefficient of Variation (squares) as Territories Are Pooled

Demand in each territory is Poisson with mean 0.29 unit per day, the target in-stock probability is 99.9 percent, and the lead time is one day.

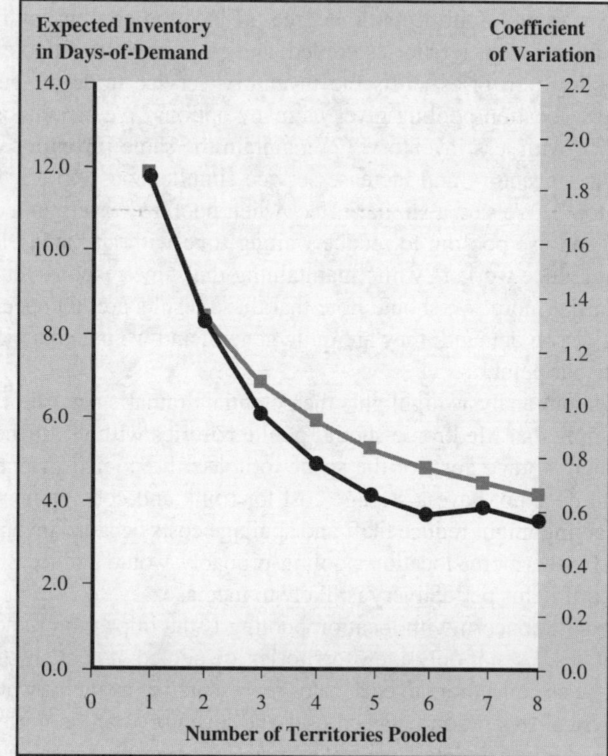

TABLE 17.2
Using Location Pooling to Raise the In-Stock Probability While Maintaining the Same Inventory Investment

Demand at each territory is Poisson with average daily demand of 0.29 unit, and the lead time is one day.

			Expected Inventory		
Number of Territories Pooled	Pooled Territory's Expected Demand per Day	S	Units	Days-of-Demand	In-Stock Probability
1	0.29	4	3.4	11.7	99.96615%
2	0.58	8	6.8	11.7	99.99963
3	0.87	12	10.3	11.8	100.00000

because pooling territories reduces the variability of demand, it reduces expected inventory in the field, but it has no impact on the pipeline inventory. As we mentioned before, the only way to reduce pipeline inventory is to get a faster lead time.

While we can exploit location pooling to reduce inventory while maintaining a service level, we also can use location pooling to increase our service level. For example, we could choose an order-up-to level in the pooled territory that generates the same inventory investment as the individual territories (measured in days-of-demand) and see how much higher our in-stock could be. Table 17.2 presents those data for pooling up to three territories; beyond three territories we can raise the in-stock to essentially 100 percent with the same inventory investment as the individual territories.

Because the in-stock probability target with individual territories is so high (99.9 percent), it probably makes better sense to use location pooling to reduce the inventory investment rather than to increase the service level. However, in other settings it may be more desirable to increase the service level, especially if the target service level is deemed to be too low.

Figure 17.2 provides another perspective on this issue. It displays the inventory–service trade-off curves with four different degrees of location pooling: individual territories, two territories pooled, four territories pooled, and eight territories pooled. As displayed in the figure, pooling territories shifts the inventory–service trade-off curve down and to the right. Hence, location pooling gives us many options: We can choose to (1) maintain the same service with less inventory, (2) maintain the same inventory with a higher service, or (3) reduce inventory and increase service simultaneously (i.e., "we can have our cake and eat it too"). We saw a similar effect when pooling servers in a queuing environment. There you can use pooling to reduce waiting time without having to staff extra workers, or you can reduce workers while maintaining the same responsiveness, or a combination of both. Furthermore, we should note that these results are not specific to the order-up-to model or Poisson demand; they are quite general and we use this model and demand only to illustrate our point.

Although our analysis highlights the potential dramatic benefit of location pooling, this does not imply that Medtronic should pool territories without further thought. There will be an explicit storage cost for the space to house the pooled inventory, whereas the current system does not have a storage cost for trunk and consignment inventory. However, location pooling might reduce theft and spoilage costs because inventory is stored in fewer locations. Furthermore, location pooling probably would reduce shipping costs because the number of items per delivery is likely to increase.

The greatest concern with location pooling is the impact on the efficiency of the sales representatives. Even if only a few territories are pooled, it is likely that the pooled location would not be as convenient to each sales representative as their own individual inventory.

The physical separation between user and inventory can be mitigated via *virtual pooling:* Representatives maintain control of their inventory, but inventory information is shared

FIGURE 17.2
The Inventory–Service Trade-Off Curve for Different Levels of Location Pooling

The curves represent, from highest to lowest, individual territories, two pooled territories, four pooled territories, and eight pooled territories. Demand in each territory is Poisson with mean 0.29 unit per day and the lead time is one day.

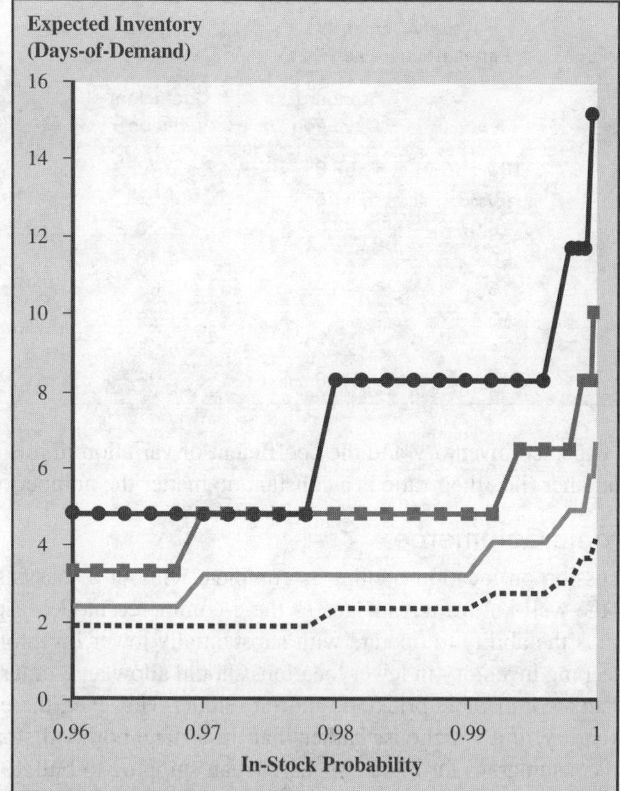

among all representatives so that each rep can obtain inventory from the central distribution center and any other rep that has excess inventory. Although virtual pooling has its own challenges (e.g., the additional cost of maintaining the necessary information systems, the added expense of transshipping inventory among territories, and the sticky design issue of how to decide when inventory can be taken from one rep to be given to another rep), it can still be better than the current system that has isolated pockets of inventory.

Medtronic's Distribution Center(s)

Now let's turn our attention to the distribution center. For the U.S. market, Medtronic currently operates a single distribution center in Mounds View, Minnesota. Suppose Medtronic were to subdivide the United States into two or more regions, with each region assigned a single distribution center. This idea is location pooling in reverse. Hence, the total inventory investment is likely to increase. Let's see by how much.

Recall that weekly demand of the InSync Pacemaker at the Mounds View DC is normally distributed with mean 80.6 and standard deviation 58.81. There is a three-week lead time and the target in-stock probability is 99.9 percent. Table 17.3 provides data on the expected inventory required given the number of DCs Medtronic operates.

Table 17.3 reveals that it is indeed costly to subdivide the U.S. market among multiple distribution centers: Eight DCs require nearly three times more inventory to achieve the same service level as a single DC! (To be precise, it requires 12.8/4.5 = 2.84 times more inventory.)

In this situation, the connection between the coefficient of variation and the expected inventory savings from location pooling (or "dissavings" from location disintegration, as in this case) is even stronger than we saw with field inventory, as displayed in Figure 17.3.

TABLE 17.3 The Increase in Inventory Investment as More Distribution Centers Are Operated

Assume demand is equally divided among the DCs, demands across DCs are independent, total demand is normally distributed with mean 80.6 and standard deviation 58.8, and the lead time is three weeks in all situations.

	Weekly Demand Parameters at Each DC			Expected Inventory at Each DC	
Number of DCs	Mean	Standard Deviation	Coefficient of Variation	Units	Weeks-of-Demand
1	80.6	58.8	0.73	364	4.5
2	40.3	41.6	1.03	257	6.4
3	26.9	34.0	1.26	210	7.8
4	20.2	29.4	1.46	182	9.0
5	16.1	26.3	1.63	163	10.1
6	13.4	24.0	1.79	148	11.0
7	11.5	22.2	1.93	137	11.9
8	10.1	20.8	2.06	127	12.8

In fact, expected inventory and the coefficient of variation in this setting are proportional to one another (i.e., their ratio is a constant no matter the number of distribution centers).

Electronic Commerce

No discussion on location pooling is complete without discussing electronic commerce. One of the well-known advantages to the e-commerce model, especially with respect to e-tailers, is the ability to operate with substantially lower inventory. As our analysis suggests, keeping inventory in fewer locations should allow an e-tailer to turn inventory much faster than a comparable brick-and-mortar retailer. However, there are extra costs to position inventory in a warehouse rather than in a neighborhood store: Shipping individual items to consumers is far more expensive than shipping in bulk to retail stores and, while physical stores need not be constructed, an e-tailer needs to invest in the technology to create an electronic store (i.e., user interface, logistics management, etc.).

We also saw that there are declining returns to location pooling. Not surprisingly, while many e-tailers, such as Amazon.com, started with a single distribution center, they now operate several distribution centers in the United States. This requires that some products are

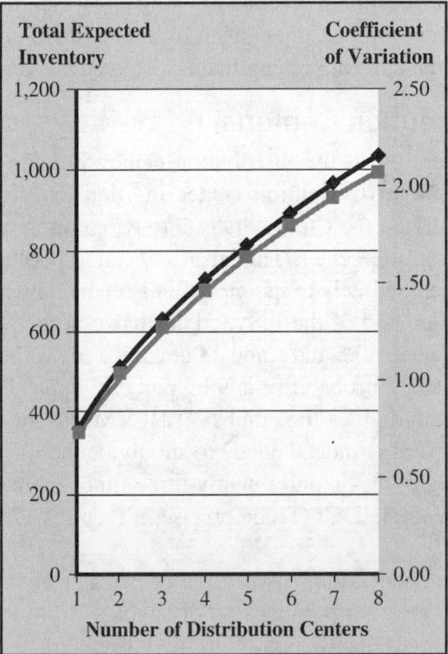

FIGURE 17.3 The Expected Inventory in Units (circles) and the Coefficient of Variation (squares) Depending on the Number of Distribution Centers Medtronic Operates

Demand is assumed to be equally divided and independent across distribution centers. The target in-stock probability is 99.9 percent and the lead time is three weeks in all cases.

stored in multiple locations, but it also means that the average customer is located closer to a distribution center, which accelerates the average delivery time and reduces shipping costs.

The ability to offer customers a huge product selection is another advantage of the e-commerce model, possibly the most important advantage. While we have focused on using location pooling to reduce inventory, location pooling also can enable a broad product assortment. Consider an item that sells but is a rather slow seller. Unfortunately for most businesses, the majority of products fall into that category. To include this item in the product assortment requires at least one unit. Placing one unit in hundreds of locations may not be economical, but it may be economical to place a few units in a single location.

To illustrate this point, consider a slow-moving product that could be sold by a retailer with 200 stores. The product would sell at each store at the average rate of 0.01 unit per week. Consequently, the retailer's total demand across all stores is 0.01 × 200 = 2 per week. You may think this is ridiculously slow, but in fact there are many products that sell at this pace. For example, Brynjolfsson, Hu, and Smith (2003) estimated that 40 percent of Amazon's sales came from items that sold no more than 1.5 units per week. Returning to our example, suppose this retailer must stock at least one unit in each store (the product must be available at the store). Given each store's sales rate, the retailer will stock only one unit and each item will spend nearly two years (1/0.01 = 100 weeks) on the shelf. That sales rate implies a measly 0.5 inventory turn (inventory is turned over once every two years). To finalize this analysis, if inventory costs 20 percent per year to hold (capital cost and, more importantly, the cost of shelf space), then this item will incur 2 × 20% = 40 percent in holding costs. Most retailers do not have anywhere near a 40 percent gross margin, so it is unlikely that this product is profitable—the retailer cannot carry this item profitably because it just doesn't turn fast enough. Now contrast those economics with an e-tailer with one warehouse. If the e-tailer's demand is Poisson with mean two per week, replenishment lead time is two weeks, and the target in-stock is 99 percent, we can use the order-up-to model to determine that the retailer will have on average about six units of inventory. If total yearly demand is about 104 units (52 weeks at 2 per week), then our e-tailer turns inventory 104/6 = 17.3 times per year. The e-tailer stands a chance to make money stocking this item, whereas the brick-and-mortar retailer does not. To summarize, there are many slow-selling products in this world (which can sum up to a lot of sales, as evidenced by Amazon.com), but location pooling may be necessary for a retailer to profitably include them in the assortment.

17.2 Product Pooling

The previous section considered serving demand with fewer inventory locations. A closely related idea is to serve demand with fewer products. To explain, consider O'Neill's Hammer 3/2 wetsuit discussed in Chapters 14 and 15. The Hammer 3/2 we studied is targeted to the market for surfers, but O'Neill sells another Hammer 3/2 that serves the market for recreational divers. The two wetsuits are identical with the exception that the surf Hammer has the "wave" logo (see Figure 14.1) silk screened on the chest, while the dive Hammer has O'Neill's dive logo, displayed in Figure 17.4. O'Neill's current product line has two products to serve demand for a Hammer 3/2 wetsuit, some of it from surfers, the other portion from divers. An alternative is to combine these products into a single product to serve all Hammer 3/2 wetsuit demand, that is, a *universal design*. The strategy of using a universal design is called *product pooling*. This section focuses on the merits of the product-pooling strategy with a universal design.

Recall that demand for the surf Hammer is normally distributed with mean 3,192 and standard deviation 1,181. For the sake of simplicity, let's assume demand for the dive Hammer is also normally distributed with the same mean and standard deviation. Both

FIGURE 17.4
O'Neill's Logo for Dive Wetsuits

wetsuits sell for \$190, are purchased from O'Neill's supplier for \$110, and are liquidated at the end of the season for \$90.

We have already evaluated the optimal order quantity and expected profit for the surf Hammer: Ordering 4,196 units earns an expected profit of \$222,280 (see Table 15.1). Because the dive Hammer is identical to the surf Hammer, it has the same optimal order quantity and expected profit. Therefore, the total profit from both Hammer wetsuits is 2 × \$222,280 = \$444,560.

Now let's consider what O'Neill should do if it sold a single Hammer wetsuit, which we call the universal Hammer. We need a distribution to represent demand for the universal Hammer and then we need an order quantity. Expected demand for the universal Hammer is 3,192 × 2 = 6,384 units. If demand in the dive market is independent of demand in the surf market, then the standard deviation for the universal Hammer is $1,181 \times \sqrt{2} = 1,670$ (see Exhibit 16.1). The underage cost for the universal Hammer is still $C_u = 190 - 110 = 80$ and the overage cost is still $C_o = 110 - 90 = 20$. Hence, the critical ratio has not changed:

$$\frac{C_u}{C_o + C_u} = \frac{80}{20 + 80} = 0.8$$

The corresponding z-statistic is still 0.85, and so the optimal order quantity is

$$Q = \mu + \sigma \times z = 6,384 + 1,670 \times 0.85 = 7,804$$

The expected profit with the universal Hammer is

$$\begin{aligned} \text{Expected profit} &= (C_u \times \text{Expected sales}) - (C_o \times \text{Expected leftover inventory}) \\ &= (80 \times 6,200) - (20 \times 1,604) \\ &= \$463,920 \end{aligned}$$

Therefore, pooling the surf and dive Hammers together can potentially increase profit by 4.4 percent [(463,920 – 444,560)/444,560]. This profit increase is 1.4 percent of the expected revenue when O'Neill sells two wetsuits. Given that net profit in this industry ranges from 2 percent to 5 percent of revenue, this potential improvement is not trivial.

As with the location pooling examples at Medtronic, the potential benefit O'Neill receives from product pooling occurs because of a reduction in the variability of demand. With two Hammer wetsuits, O'Neill faces a coefficient of variation of about 0.37 with each suit. With a universal Hammer, the coefficient of variation is about 1,670/6,384 = 0.26. Recall from Chapter 15 that the mismatch cost in the newsvendor model is directly proportional to the coefficient of variation, hence the connection between a lower coefficient of variation and higher expected profit.

FIGURE 17.5
Random Demand for Two Products

In the graphs, *x*-axis is product 1 and *y*-axis is product 2. In scenario 1 (upper-left graph), the correlation is −0.90; in scenario 2 (upper-right graph), the correlation is 0; and in scenario 3 (the lower graph), the correlation is 0.90. In all scenarios, demand is normally distributed for each product with mean 10 and standard deviation 3.

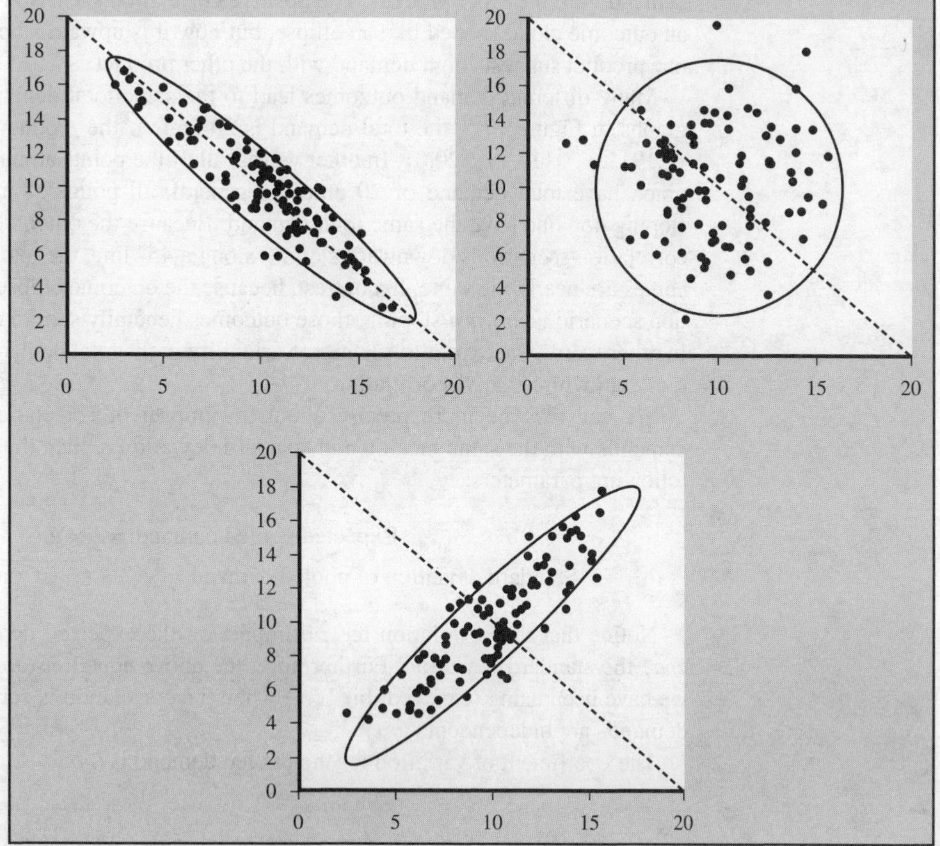

Given this link between the coefficient of variation and the benefit of product pooling, it is important for us to understand how product pooling influences the coefficient of variation. In this example, as well as the Medtronic examples in the previous two sections, we make a key assumption that the demands we are combining are independent. Recall that independence means that the outcome of one demand provides no information about the outcome of the other demand. There are many settings in which demands are indeed independent. But there are also situations in which demands are not independent.

The link between two random events can be measured by their correlation, which ranges from −1 to 1. Independent random events have zero correlation. Positive correlation means two random events tend to move in lockstep; that is, when one is high, the other tends to be high as well, and when one is low, the other tends to be low as well. In contrast, negative correlation means two random events tend to move in opposite directions; that is, when one is high, the other tends to be low, and when one is low, the other tends to be high.

We can illustrate the effect of correlation graphically with two products. Figure 17.5 displays the outcome of 100 random demand realizations for two products in three scenarios. (For example, if the random demands of the two products are five and seven, respectively, then a point is plotted at {5,7}.) In the first scenario, the products' demands are negatively correlated, in the second they are independent, and in the third they are positively correlated. In the independent scenario (scenario two), we see that the outcomes form a "cloud" that roughly fits into a circle; that is, the outcome of one demand says nothing about the outcome of the other demand. In the negative correlation scenario (scenario one), the outcome cloud is a downward-sloping ellipse: High demand with one product suggests low demand with the other product. The positive correlation scenario (scenario three) also has an outcome cloud shaped like an ellipse, but now it is upward sloping: High demand with one product suggests high demand with the other product.

Many different demand outcomes lead to the same total demand. For example, in the graphs in Figure 17.5, the total demand is 20 units if the products' demands are {0,20}, {1,19}, . . . , {19,1}, {20,0}. In other words, all of the points along the dashed line in each graph have total demand of 20 units. In general, all points along the same downward-sloping 45° line have the same total demand. Because the outcome ellipse in the negative correlation scenario is downward sloping along a 45° line, the total demands of those outcomes are nearly the same. In contrast, because the outcome ellipse in the positive correlation scenario is *upward* sloping, those outcomes generally sum to different total demands. In other words, we expect to see more variability in the total demand with positive correlation than with negative correlation.

We can now be more precise about the impact of correlation. If we combine two demands with the same mean μ and standard deviation σ, then the pooled demand has the following parameters:

$$\text{Expected pooled demand} = 2 \times \mu$$

$$\text{Standard deviation of pooled demand} = \sqrt{2 \times (1 + \text{Correlation})} \times \sigma$$

Notice that the correlation has no impact on the expected demand, but it does influence the standard deviation. Furthermore, the above equations are equivalent to the ones we have been using (e.g., Exhibit 16.1) when the correlation is zero; that is, when the two demands are independent.

The coefficient of variation for the pooled demand is then

$$\text{Coefficient of variation of pooled demand} = \sqrt{\frac{1}{2}(1 + \text{Correlation})} \times \left(\frac{\sigma}{\mu}\right)$$

As the correlation increases, the coefficient of variation of pooled demand increases as well, just as the graphs in Figure 17.5 suggest.

Now let's visualize what happens when we choose quantities for both the dive and the surf suits. Figure 17.6 displays the result of our quantity choices for different demand outcomes. For example, if the demand outcome is in the lower-left-hand "square" of the graph, then we have leftover surf and dive suits. The ideal outcome is if demand for each suit happens to equal its order quantity, an outcome labeled with a circle in the graph. The demand–supply mismatch penalty increases as the demand outcome moves further away from that ideal point in any direction.

The comparable graph for the universal Hammer is different, as is shown in Figure 17.7. Now any demand outcome along the downward-sloping 45° line (circles) is an ideal outcome because total demand equals the quantity of universal suits. In other words, the number of ideal demand outcomes with the universal suit has expanded considerably relative to the single ideal demand outcome with two suits. How likely are we to be close to one of those ideal points? Figure 17.7 also superimposes the three "outcome clouds" from Figure 17.5. Clearly, with negative correlation we are more likely to be close to an ideal point (the downward-sloping ellipse) and with positive correlation we are least likely to be near an ideal point.

We can confirm the intuition developed with the graph in Figure 17.7 by actually evaluating O'Neill's optimal order quantity for the universal Hammer 3/2 and its expected profit for the entire range of correlations. We first notice that the optimal order quantity for the Hammer 3/2 is generally *not* the sum of the optimal order quantities of the two suits. For

FIGURE 17.6
The Inventory/Stockout Outcome Given the Order Quantities for Surf and Dive Suits, Q_{surf} and Q_{dive}

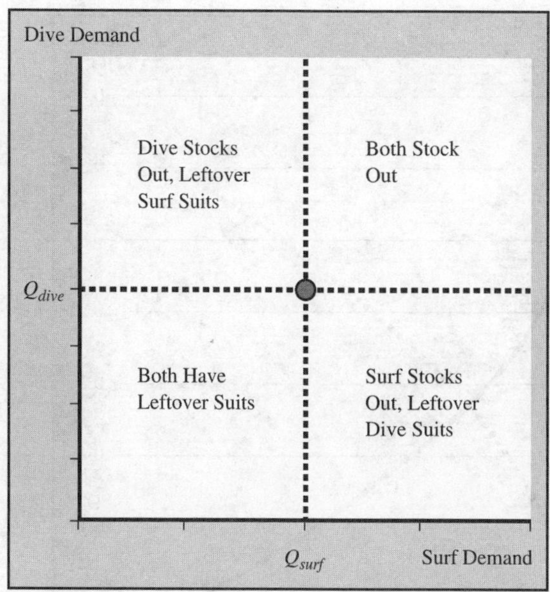

example, O'Neill's total order with two wetsuits is 4,196 × 2 = 8,392 units, but with correlation 0.2 the optimal order for the universal Hammer is 7,929 units and with correlation −0.7 the optimal order is 7,162.

The results with respect to expected profit are displayed in Figure 17.8: We indeed see that the expected profit of the universal Hammer declines as surf and dive demand become more positively correlated.

The extreme ends in Figure 17.8 are interesting. With perfectly positive correlation (i.e., correlation = 1), there is absolutely no benefit from inventory pooling: The expected profit with the universal Hammer is $444,560, and that is also the profit with two Hammer wetsuits! At the other end of the spectrum, correlation = −1, the coefficient of variation of total Hammer demand is 0, and so the maximum profit is achieved, $510,720! In fact, in that

FIGURE 17.7
Outcomes for the Universal Hammer Given Q Units Purchased

Outcomes on the diagonal line with circles are ideal; there is no leftover inventory and no stockouts. Outcomes below and to the left of that line have leftover suits; outcomes to the right and above that line result in stockouts. Ellipses identify likely outcomes under different correlations.

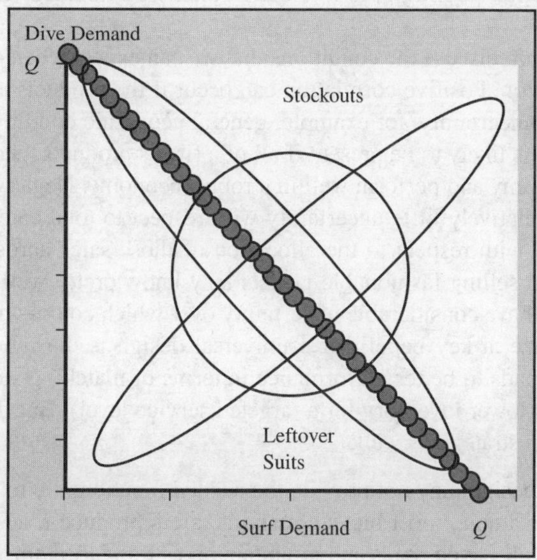

FIGURE 17.8
The Correlation between Surf and Dive Demand for the Hammer 3/2 and the Expected Profit of the Universal Hammer Wetsuit (decreasing curve) and the Coefficient of Variation of Total Demand (increasing curve)

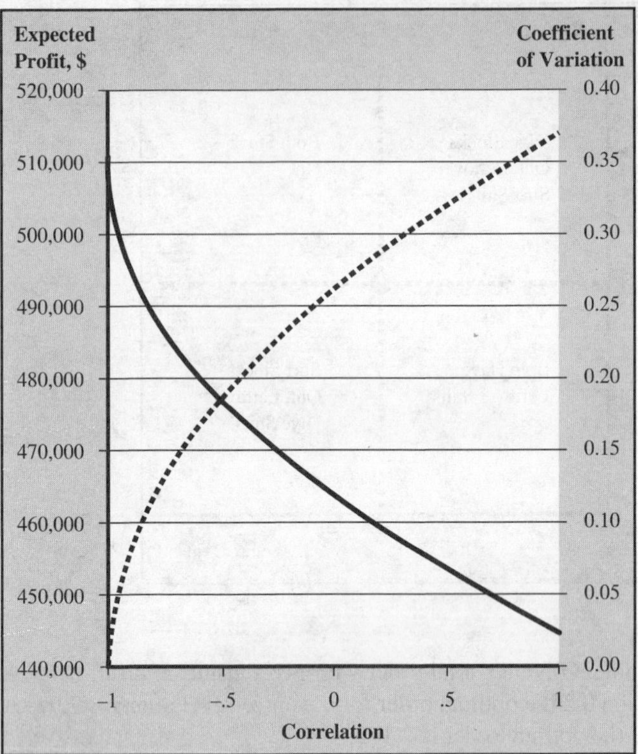

situation, the optimal order quantity for universal suits is just 6,384 units, which also happens to be the expected demand for universal suits. (This makes sense; we only earn the maximum profit if we sell on average the expected demand and we never have leftover inventory.)

While we have been discussing the impact of demand correlation on the efficacy of product pooling, this issue applies even with location pooling. If the demands at two locations are negatively correlated, then location pooling is even more effective than if the demands were merely independent. And if demands are positively correlated across locations, then location pooling is less effective than we evaluated, given our assumption of independence.

We also should discuss the conditions that we can expect when demand has a particular type of correlation. Positive correlation can occur if the products are linked to some common source of uncertainty, for example, general economic conditions. For example, positive correlation is likely to be present if all of a firm's products tend to perform poorly in a depressed economy and perform well in a robust economy. Negative correlation is present when there is relatively little uncertainty with respect to total category sales but substantial uncertainty with respect to the allocation of those sales across the product line. For example, a firm selling fashionable jackets may know pretty well how many jackets will sell in total but have considerable uncertainty over which colors will be hot this season.

To summarize, a key benefit of a universal design is the reduction in demand variability, which leads to better performance in terms of matching supply and demand (e.g., higher profit or lower inventory for a targeted service level). But there are drawbacks to a universal design strategy as well:

- A universal design may not provide the needed functionality to consumers with special needs. For example, most bicycle manufacturers produce road bikes designed for fast touring on well-paved roads and mountain bikes for tearing through rugged trails. They even sell hybrid bikes that have some of the features of a road bike as well as some of the features of a mountain bike. But it is not sufficient to just sell a hybrid bike because it would not satisfy the high-performance portions of the road and mountain bike segments. The lower functionality of a universal design for some segments implies that it might not capture the same total demand as a set of focused designs.

- A universal design may be more expensive or it may be cheaper to produce than focused products. Because a universal design is targeted to many different uses, either it has components that are not necessary to some consumers or it has components that are of better quality than needed by certain consumers. These extra components or the extra quality increases a universal design's cost relative to focused designs. However, it is often cheaper to manufacture or procure a large quantity of a single component than small quantities of a bunch of components; that is, there are economies of scale in production and procurement. In that sense, a universal design may be cheaper.
- A universal design may eliminate some brand/price segmentation opportunities. By definition, a universal design has a single brand/price, but a firm may wish to maintain distinct brands/prices. As with the concern regarding functionality, a single brand/price may not be able to capture the same demand as multiple brands/prices.

With respect to O'Neill's Hammer 3/2 wetsuit, it appears that the first two concerns regarding a universal design are not relevant: Given that the surf and dive Hammers are identical with the exception of the logo, their functionality should be identical as well, and there is no reason to believe their production costs should be much different. However, the universal Hammer wetsuit does eliminate the opportunity to maintain two different O'Neill logos, one geared for the surf market and one geared for the dive market. If it is important to maintain these separate identities (e.g., you might not want serious surfers to think they are purchasing the same product as recreational divers), then maybe two suits are needed. On the other hand, if you wish to portray a single image for O'Neill, then maybe it is even better to have a single logo, in which case two different wetsuits make absolutely no sense.

While we have concentrated on the benefits of serving demand with a universal design, this discussion provides a warning for firms that may be engaging in excessive product proliferation. Every firm wishes to be "customer focused" or "customer oriented," which suggests that a firm should develop products to meet all of the needs of its potential customers. Truly innovative new products that add to a firm's customer base should be incorporated into a firm's product assortment. But if extra product variety merely divides a fixed customer base into smaller pieces, then the demand–supply mismatch cost for each product will increase. Given that some of the demand–supply mismatch costs are indirect (e.g., loss of goodwill due to poor service), a firm might not even realize the additional costs it bears due to product proliferation. Every once in a while a firm realizes that its product assortment has gone amok and *product line rationalization* is sorely needed. The trick to assortment reductions is to "cut the fat, but leave the meat (and surely the bones)"; that is, products should only be dropped if they merely cannibalize demand from other products.

17.3 Lead Time Pooling: Consolidated Distribution and Delayed Differentiation

Location and product pooling, discussed in the previous two sections, have limitations: Location pooling creates distance between inventory and customers and product pooling potentially degrades product functionality. This section studies two strategies that address those limitations: consolidated distribution and delayed differentiation. Both of those strategies use a form of risk pooling that we call lead time pooling.

Consolidated Distribution

The key weakness of location pooling is that inventory is moved away from customers, thereby preventing customers from physically seeing a product before purchase, thus increasing the time a customer must wait to receive a product and generally increasing the delivery cost. However, as we have learned, it also can be costly to position inventory near every customer. A major reason for this cost is the problem of having product in the wrong place. For example, with Medtronic's approximately 500 sales territories, it is highly unlikely that all 500 territories will stock out at the same time. If a stockout occurs in one territory, it is quite likely that there is some other territory that has inventory to spare, even maybe a nearby territory. This imbalance of inventory occurs because a firm faces two different kinds of uncertainty, even with a single product: uncertainty with respect to total demand (e.g., how many InSync pacemakers are demanded in the United States on a particular day) and uncertainty with respect to the allocation of that demand (e.g., how many InSync pacemakers are demanded in each territory in the United States on a particular day). The consolidated-distribution strategy attempts to keep inventory close to customers while hedging against the second form of uncertainty.

We'll demonstrate the consolidated-distribution strategy via a retail example. Imagine demand for a single product occurs in 100 stores and average weekly demand per store follows a Poisson distribution with a mean of 0.5 unit per week. Each store is replenished directly from a supplier with an eight-week lead time. To provide good customer service, the retailer uses the order-up-to model and targets a 99.5 percent in-stock probability. The top panel of Figure 17.9 displays a schematic of this supply chain. Let's evaluate the amount of inventory the retailer needs.

With an eight-week lead time and a mean demand of 0.5 unit per week, the expected demand over $l + 1$ periods is $(8 + 1) \times 0.5 = 4.5$. From the Poisson Distribution Function Table in Appendix B we see that with a mean of 4.5, the order-up-to level $S = 10$ yields an in-stock probability of 99.33 percent and $S = 11$ yields an in-stock probability of 99.76 percent, so we need to choose $S = 11$ for each store. According to the Poisson Inventory Function Table in Appendix B, with mean demand of 4.5 units over $l + 1$ periods and an

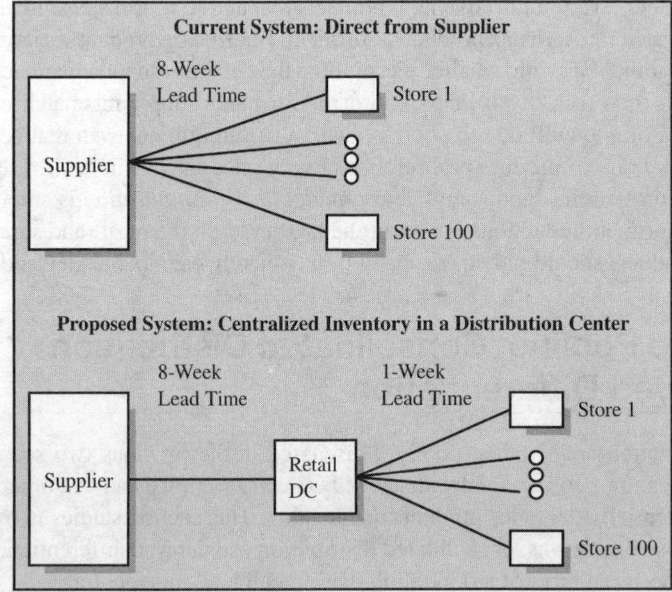

FIGURE 17.9 **Two Retail Supply Chains, One with Direct Shipments from the Supplier, the Other with Consolidated Distribution in a Distribution Center**

Expected weekly demand at each store is 0.5 unit and the target in-stock probability is 99.5 percent.

order-up-to level $S = 11$, the expected inventory is 6.50 units. The total inventory among the 100 stores is then $6.50 \times 100 = 650$ units.

Now suppose the retailer builds a distribution center to provide consolidated distribution. The distribution center receives all shipments from the supplier and then replenishes each of the retail stores; it allows for consolidated distribution. The lead time for the distribution center remains eight weeks from the supplier. The lead time to replenish each of the retail stores is one week. To ensure a reliable delivery to the retail stores, the distribution center operates with a high in-stock probability, 99.5 percent. The bottom panel in Figure 17.9 displays the proposed supply chain with a distribution center.

The distribution center provides the retailer with a centralized location for inventory while still allowing the retailer to position inventory close to the customer. In contrast, the location pooling strategy would just create the centralized-inventory location, eliminating the 100 stores close to customers. Therefore, this centralized-inventory strategy resembles location pooling without the major drawback of location pooling. But what does it do for the total inventory investment?

We can repeat the evaluation of the inventory investment for each store, assuming a 99.5 percent in-stock probability target and now a one-week lead time. From the Poisson Distribution Function Table, given expected demand over $l + 1$ periods is 1.0 unit, the order-up-to level $S = 4$ generates an in-stock probability of 99.63 percent. The resulting expected inventory per store is 3.00 units, nearly a 54 percent reduction in inventory from the direct-supply model (3.00 versus 6.5 units)! Because each store now receives a one-week lead time instead of an eight-week lead time, the inventory at the retail stores is dramatically reduced.

Now we need to evaluate the inventory at the distribution center. The demand at the distribution center equals the orders from the retail stores. On average, the retail stores order 0.5 unit per week; that is, the average inflow (i.e., order) into a store must equal the average outflow (i.e., demand), otherwise inventory either builds up continuously (if the inflow exceeds the outflow) or dwindles down to zero (if the outflow exceeds the inflow). Because the retail stores' total demand is $100 \times 0.5 = 50$ units per week, the average demand at the distribution center also must be 50 units per week.

While we can be very sure of our estimate of the distribution center's expected demand, the distribution center's standard deviation of demand is not immediately apparent. The standard deviation of demand at each retailer is $\sqrt{0.50} = 0.707$. (Recall that with Poisson demand, the standard deviation equals the square root of the mean.) Hence, if demand were independent across all stores, then the standard deviation of total demand would be $0.707 \times \sqrt{100} = 7.07$. However, if there is positive correlation across stores, then the standard deviation would be higher, and with negative correlation the standard deviation would be lower. The only way to resolve this issue is to actually evaluate the standard deviation of total demand from historical sales data (the same data we used to estimate the demand rate of 0.5 unit per week at each store). Suppose we observe that the standard deviation of total weekly demand is 15. Hence, there is evidence of positive correlation in demand across the retail stores.

We now need to choose a distribution to represent demand at the distribution center. In this case, the Poisson is not the best choice. The standard deviation of a Poisson distribution is the square root of its mean, which in this case would be $\sqrt{50} = 7.07$. Because we have observed the standard deviation to be significantly higher, the Poisson distribution would not provide a good fit with the data. Our alternative, and a reasonable choice, is the normal distribution with mean 50 and standard deviation 15. Using the techniques from Chapter 16, we can determine that the distribution center's expected inventory is about 116 units if its target in-stock is 99.5 percent, the lead time is eight weeks, and weekly demand is normally distributed with mean 50 and standard deviation 15.

TABLE 17.4
Retail Inventory with Three Supply Chain Structures

	Direct Delivery Supply Chain	Consolidated-Distribution Supply Chain	Location Pooling
Expected total inventory at the stores	650	300	0
Expected inventory at the DC	0	116	116
Pipeline inventory between the DC and the stores	0	50	0
Total	650	466	116

The only inventory that we have not counted so far is the pipeline inventory. In the direct-delivery model, there is pipeline inventory between the supplier and the retail stores. Using Little's Law, that pipeline inventory equals $0.5 \times 100 \times 8 = 400$ units. The consolidated-distribution model has the same amount of inventory between the supplier and the distribution center. However, with both models let's assume that pipeline inventory is actually owned by the supplier (e.g., the retailer does not start to pay for inventory until it is received). Hence, from the retailer's perspective, that inventory is not a concern. On the other hand, the retailer does own the inventory between the distribution center and the retail stores in the consolidated-distribution model. Again using Little's Law, there are $0.5 \times 100 \times 1 = 50$ units in that pipeline.

Table 17.4 summarizes the retailer's inventory in both supply chain structures. For comparison, the location pooling strategy is also included. With location pooling, all of the stores are eliminated and the retailer ships to customers from a central distribution center. Because that distribution center has an eight-week lead time and faces the same demand distribution as the DC in the consolidated-distribution strategy, its expected inventory is also 116 units.

We see from Table 17.4 that the consolidated-distribution strategy is able to reduce the expected inventory investment 28 percent [(650 – 466)/650] relative to the original direct-delivery structure. In fact, the advantage of the consolidated-distribution strategy is even better than this analysis suggests. The cost of holding one unit of inventory at a retail store is surely substantially higher than the cost of holding one unit in a distribution center: Retail shelf space is more expensive than DC space, shrinkage is a greater concern, and so forth. Because the consolidated-distribution model reduces retail inventory by more than 50 percent, merely adding up the total inventory in the system underestimates the value of the consolidated-distribution model.

Interestingly, the consolidated-distribution model outperforms direct delivery even though the total lead time from the supplier to the retail stores is increased by one week due to the routing of all inventory through the DC. Why is inventory reduced despite the longer total lead time? As mentioned earlier, in this system there are two types of uncertainty: uncertainty with total demand in a given week and uncertainty with the allocation of that demand over the retail stores. When inventory leaves the supplier, the retailer is essentially betting on how much inventory will be needed eight weeks later. However, in the direct-delivery model, the retailer also must predict *where* that inventory is needed; that is, the retailer must gamble on a total quantity and an allocation of that quantity across the retail stores. There is uncertainty with the total inventory needed, but even more uncertainty with where that inventory is needed. The consolidated-distribution model allows the retailer to avoid that second gamble: The retailer only needs to bet on the amount of inventory needed for the central distribution center. In other words, while the retailer must commit to a unit's final destination in the direct-delivery model, in the consolidated-distribution model the retailer delays that commitment until the unit arrives at the distribution center.

FIGURE 17.10
Inventory with the Consolidated-Distribution Supply Chain

Diamonds = total retail store inventory, squares = retail + pipeline inventory, circles = retail + pipeline + DC inventory.

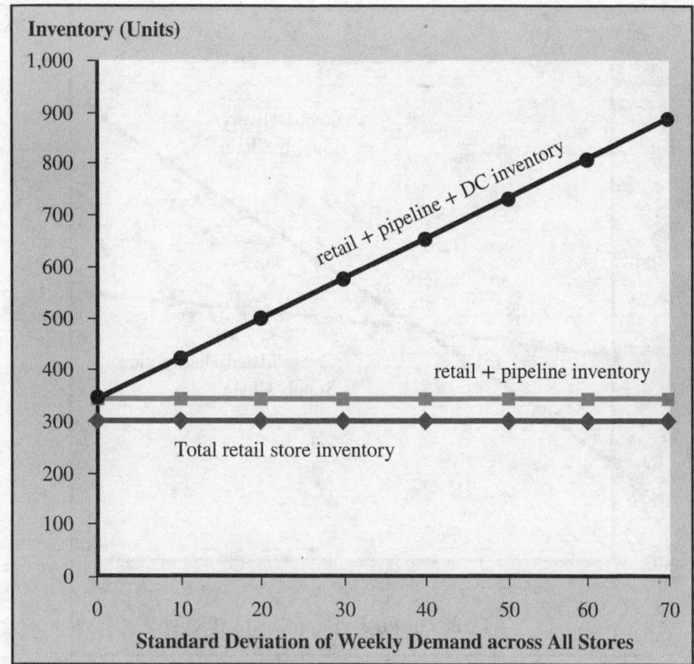

It is precisely because the DC allows the retailer to avoid that second source of uncertainty that the consolidated-distribution model can outperform the direct-delivery model.

The consolidated-distribution model exploits what is often called *lead time pooling*. Lead time pooling can be thought of as combining the lead times for multiple inventory locations. Actually, it is easier to explain graphically: In Figure 17.9 we see that the 100 connections between the supplier and the retail stores in the direct-delivery model (four of which are actually drawn) are pooled into a single connection between the supplier and the DC in the consolidated-distribution model.

We saw that demand correlation influenced the effectiveness of product pooling and location pooling. Not surprisingly, demand correlation has the same effect here. The greater the correlation, the higher the standard deviation of demand at the distribution center. Figure 17.10 displays supply chain inventory with the consolidated-distribution model over a range of demand variability for the distribution center. As retail demand becomes more negatively correlated, the inventory in the consolidated-distribution model declines. However, we have seen that inventory can be reduced even with some positive correlation: The consolidated-distribution model outperforms direct delivery if the DC's standard deviation is about 40 or lower.

Another factor that determines the attractiveness of the consolidated-distribution model relative to the direct-delivery model is the lead time from the supplier. Figure 17.11 displays total supply chain inventory with both models for various supplier lead times. The direct-delivery model performs better than the consolidated-distribution model if the supplier's lead time is three weeks or fewer; otherwise, the consolidated-distribution model does better. This occurs because lead time pooling is most effective as the lead time increases. In particular, the lead time before the distribution center (i.e., from the supplier) should be longer than the lead time after the distribution center (i.e., to the stores).

To summarize, a central inventory location (i.e., a distribution center) within a supply chain can exploit lead time pooling to reduce the supply chain's inventory investment while still keeping inventory close to customers. This strategy is most effective if total

FIGURE 17.11
Inventory with the Consolidated-Distribution Supply Chain (squares) and the Direct-Delivery Supply Chain (circles) with Different Supplier Lead Times

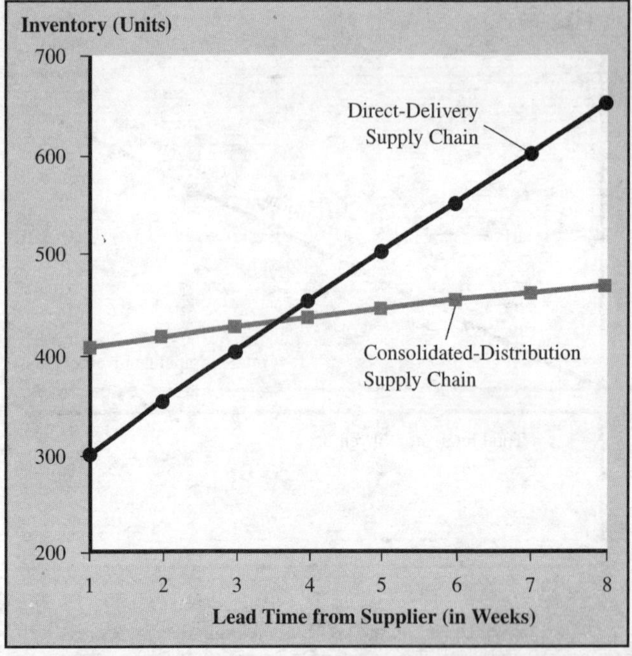

demand is less variable than demand at the individual stores and if the lead time before the distribution center is much longer than the lead time after the distribution center.

While we have concentrated on the inventory impact of the consolidated distribution strategy, that strategy has other effects on the supply chain. We have not included the extra cost of operating the distribution center, even though we did mention that the holding cost for each unit of inventory at the distribution center is likely to be lower than at the retail stores. Furthermore, we have not included the extra transportation cost from the DC to the retailer. A common critique of this kind of supply chain is that it clearly increases the distance a unit must travel from the supplier to the retailer. However, there are some additional benefits of a distribution center that we also have not included.

A DC enables a retailer to take better advantage of temporary price discounts from the supplier; that is, it is easier to store a large buy at the DC than at the retail stores. (See the Trade Promotions and Forward Buying part of Section 19.1 for an analytical model of this issue.) The DC also will facilitate more frequent deliveries to the retail stores. With the direct-delivery model, each store receives a shipment from each supplier. It is generally not economical to make partial truckload shipments, what is referred to as a "less-than-load" or LTL shipment. Therefore, in our example, the retailer receives weekly shipments from the supplier because the retailer would not be able to order a full truckload for each store on a more frequent basis.

But with a DC, more frequent shipments are economical. The DC allows the retailer to put products from multiple suppliers into a truck bound for a store. Because now a truck is filled with products from multiple suppliers, it can be filled more frequently. As a result, with the DC in the supply chain, each store might be able to receive a full truckload per day, whereas without the DC each store can only receive a shipment every week. (This argument also is used to justify the airlines' "hub-and-spoke" systems: It may be difficult to consistently fill a plane from Gainesville to Los Angeles on a daily basis, but Delta Airlines offers service between those two cities via its Atlanta hub because the Atlanta–Los Angeles leg can be filled with passengers flying from other southeast cities.) More frequent deliveries reduce inventory even further than our analysis suggests. (See Section 16.8 for more discussion.) Even the DC may be able to order more frequently from the supplier than weekly because the DC consolidates the orders from all of the retailers. In fact, while the lead time pooling benefit of a DC in this example is significant, it is quite possible that some of these other reasons for operating a DC are even more important.

Delayed Differentiation

Consolidated distribution is a strategy that uses lead time pooling to provide some of the benefits of location pooling without moving inventory far away from customers. Delayed differentiation is the analogous strategy with respect to product pooling; that is, delayed differentiation hedges the uncertainty associated with product variety without taking the variety away from customers. We'll illustrate delayed differentiation with our Hammer 3/2 example from O'Neill.

Recall that the Hammer 3/2 is sold by O'Neill in two versions: a surf wetsuit with the traditional wave logo silk-screened on the chest and a dive wetsuit with O'Neill's dive logo put in the same place. The product-pooling approach to this variety is to eliminate it: sell only one Hammer 3/2 suit with a single logo. However, that is an extreme solution and there may be reasons to maintain two different products.

The problem with two different products is that we might run out of surf Hammers while we have extra dive Hammers. In that situation, it would be great if we could just erase the dive logo and put on the surf logo, since the rest of the wetsuit is identical. Better yet, if we just stocked "logo-less" or generic wetsuits, then we could add the appropriate logo as demand arrives. That strategy is called *delayed differentiation* because we are delaying the differentiation of the wetsuit into its final form until after we observe demand.

Several things are necessary to make this delayed-differentiation strategy work. First, we need to be able to silk-screen the logo onto the generic wetsuit. This is a nontrivial issue. Currently the logo is silk-screened onto the chest piece before it is sewn into the suit. Silk-screening the logo onto a complete suit is substantially harder and may require some redesigning of the silk-screening process. Assuming we can overcome that technical difficulty, we still need to be able to add the silk screen quickly so that there is not much delay between the time a wetsuit is requested and when it is shipped. Hence, we'll need a sufficient amount of idle capacity in that process to ensure fast delivery even though demand may fluctuate throughout the season.

If these challenges are resolved, then we are left with deciding how many of the generic wetsuits to order and evaluating the resulting profit savings. In fact, we have already completed those steps. If we assume that we only silk-screen the logo onto wetsuits when we receive a firm demand for a surf or dive wetsuit, then we never keep finished goods inventory; that is, we only have to worry about our generic wetsuit inventory. The demand for the generic wetsuit is identical to the demand for the universal wetsuit; that is, it is the sum of surf Hammer demand and dive Hammer demand. The economics of the generic suit are the same as well: They sell for the same price, they have the same production cost, and we'll assume they have the same salvage value. (In some cases, the salvage value of the generic suit might be higher or lower than the salvage value of the finished product, but in this case it is plausibly about the same.) Therefore, as with the universal design analysis, we need to decide how many generic wetsuits to order given they are sold for $190 each, they cost $110 each, they will be salvaged for $90 each, and demand is normally distributed with mean 6,384 and standard deviation 1,670.

Using our analysis from the section on product pooling, the optimal order quantity is 7,840 units with the delayed differentiation strategy and expected profit increases to $463,920. Although product pooling and delayed differentiation result in the same numerical analysis, the two strategies are different. Delayed differentiation still offers multiple wetsuits to consumers, so their demands are not pooled together as with a universal design. Instead, delayed differentiation works like lead time pooling with consolidated distribution: A key differentiating feature of the product is delayed until after better demand information is observed; with location pooling that feature is the product's final destination (i.e., store) and with delayed differentiation that feature is the product's logo. Furthermore, product pooling does not require a significant modification to the production process, whereas delayed differentiation does require a change to the silk-screening process. In other applications, delayed differentiation may require a more dramatic change to the process and/or the product design.

In general, delayed differentiation is an ideal strategy when

1. Customers demand many versions, that is, variety is important.
2. There is less uncertainty with respect to total demand than there is for individual versions.
3. Variety is created late in the production process.
4. Variety can be added quickly and cheaply.
5. The components needed to create variety are inexpensive relative to the generic component (i.e., the main body of the product).

Let's explain further each of the five points just mentioned. (1) If variety isn't important, then the firm should offer fewer variants or just a universal design. (2) There should be less uncertainty with total demand so there will be few demand–supply mismatches with the generic component. In general, the more negative correlation across product variants the better, since negative correlation reduces uncertainty in the total demand. (3) Just as we saw that consolidated distribution works best if the supplier lead time to the distribution center is long relative to the lead time from the distribution center to the retail stores, delayed differentiation is most valuable if there is a long lead time to produce the generic component and a short lead time to convert the generic component into a finished product. (4) If adding variety to the generic component is too slow, then the waiting time for customers may be unacceptable, thereby rendering delayed differentiation unacceptable. In addition, if adding variety at the end of the process is costly, then the inventory savings from delayed differentiation may not be worth the extra production cost. (5) Finally, delayed differentiation saves inventory of the generic component (e.g., the generic wetsuit) but does not save inventory of the differentiating components. Hence, delayed differentiation is most useful if the majority of the product's value is in the generic component.

Delayed differentiation is particularly appropriate when variety is associated with the cosmetic features of a product, for example, color, labels, and packaging. For example, suppose a company such as Black and Decker sells power drills to both Home Depot and Walmart. Those are two influential retailers; as a result, they may wish to have slightly different packaging, and, in particular, they might wish to have different product codes on their packages so that consumers cannot make direct price comparisons. The power drill company could store drills in the two different packages, but that creates the possibility of having Home Depot drills available while Walmart drills are stocked out. Because it is relatively easy to complete the final packaging, the delayed-differentiation strategy only completes the packaging of drills after it receives firm orders from the retailers. Furthermore, packaging material is cheap compared to the drill, so while the firm doesn't want to have excessive inventory of drills, it isn't too costly to have plenty of packages available.

Retail paints provide another good example for the application of delayed differentiation. Consumers surely do not want a universal design when it comes to paint color, despite Henry Ford's famous theory of product assortment.[2] But at the same time, a store cannot

[2] Consumers can have any Model T they want, as long as it is black.

afford to keep paint available in every possible shade, hue, tone, sheen, and color. One alternative is for paint to be held in a central warehouse and then shipped to customers as needed; that is, a location pooling strategy. Given the vast variety of colors, it is not clear that even a location pooling strategy can be economical. Furthermore, paint is very costly to ship directly to consumers, so that pretty much kills that idea. Instead, the paint industry has developed equipment so that a retailer can use generic materials to mix any color in their vast catalog. The final production process takes some time, but an acceptable amount of time for consumers (5 to 15 minutes). The in-store production equipment is probably more expensive than mixing paints at a factory, but again, the extra cost here is worth it. Hence, by redesigning the product to add variety at the very end of the production process (i.e., even after delivery to the retail store), paint companies are able to economically provide consumers with extensive variety.

Delayed differentiation can even be used if the "generic component" can be sold to some customers without additional processing. To explain, suppose a company sells two different quality levels of a product, for example, a fast and a slow printer or a fast and a slow microprocessor. These quality differences might allow a firm to price discriminate and thereby increase its overall margins. However, the quality difference might not imply radically different costs or designs. For example, it might be possible to design the fast and the slow printers such that a fast printer could be converted into a slow printer merely by adding a single chip or by flipping a single switch. Hence, the firm might hold only fast printers so they can serve demand for fast printers immediately. When demand for a slow printer occurs, then a fast printer is taken from inventory, the switch is flipped to make it a slow printer, and then it is shipped as a slow printer.

Delayed differentiation is indeed a powerful strategy. In fact, it bears a remarkable resemblance to another powerful strategy, make-to-order production (Chapter 15). With make-to-order production, a firm only begins making a product after it receives a firm order from a customer. Dell Inc. has used the make-to-order strategy with remarkable effectiveness in the personal computer industry. With delayed differentiation, a generic component is differentiated into a final product only after demand is received for that final product. So what is the difference between these two ideas? In fact, they are conceptually quite similar. Their difference is one of degree. Delayed differentiation is thought of as a strategy that stores nearly finished product and completes the remaining few production steps with essentially no delay. Make-to-order is generally thought to apply to a situation in which the remaining production steps from components to a finished unit are more substantial, therefore involving more than a trivial delay. Hence, delayed differentiation and make-to-order occupy two ends of the same spectrum with no clear boundary between them.

17.4 Capacity Pooling with Flexible Manufacturing[3]

Delayed differentiation takes advantage of completely flexible capacity at the end of the manufacturing process; that is, the final production step is capable of taking a generic component and converting it into any final product. Unfortunately, the luxury of complete flexibility is not always available or affordable to a firm, especially if one considers a larger portion of the manufacturing process. This section studies how a firm can use risk pooling with flexible capacity, but not necessarily completely flexible capacity. See also Section 8.7 for additional discussion on capacity flexibility.

To provide a context, consider the manufacturing challenge of an auto manufacturer such as General Motors. GM operates many different assembly plants and produces many

[3] This section is based on the research reported in Jordon and Graves (1995).

different vehicles. Assembly capacity is essentially fixed in this industry over a substantial time horizon due to rigid labor contracts and the extensive capital requirements of an assembly plant. However, demand for individual vehicles can be quite variable: Some products are perennially short on capacity, while others seem to always have too much capacity. To alleviate the resulting demand–supply mismatches, auto manufacturers continually strive for more manufacturing flexibility; that is, the ability to produce more than one vehicle type with the same capacity. GM could use flexible manufacturing to move capacity from slow-selling products to fast-selling products, thereby achieving higher sales and higher capacity utilization. But flexibility is not free: Tooling and assembly equipment capable of making more than one vehicle is more expensive than dedicated equipment and equipment capable of making any vehicle (complete flexibility) is extremely expensive. So how much flexibility does GM need and where should that flexibility be installed?

Let's define a specific problem that is representative of the challenge GM faces. There are 10 manufacturing plants and 10 vehicles (e.g., Chevy Malibu, GMC Yukon XL, etc). For now each plant is assigned to produce just one vehicle; that is, there is no flexibility in the network. Capacity for each vehicle is installed before GM observes the vehicle's demand in the market. Demand is uncertain: A normal distribution represents each vehicle's demand with mean 100 and standard deviation 40. For a slight twist on the distribution, let's assume the minimum demand is 20 and the maximum demand is 180; that is, the normal distribution is truncated so that excessively extreme outcomes are not possible.[4] Even though we impose upper and lower bounds on demand, demand is still quite uncertain, a level of uncertainty that is typical in the auto industry. One last point with respect to demand: We assume the demands for each vehicle are independent; therefore, the correlation between the demands for any two vehicles is zero.

Each plant has a capacity to produce 100 units. If demand exceeds capacity for a vehicle, then the excess is lost. If demand is less than capacity, then demand is satisfied but capacity is idle. Figure 17.12 displays this situation graphically: The left-hand side of the figure represents the 10 production plants; the right-hand side represents the 10 vehicle types; and the lines are "links" that indicate which plant is capable of producing which vehicles. In the "no flexibility" situation, each plant is capable of producing only one vehicle, so there is a total of 10 links. The configuration with the smallest amount of flexibility has 11 links, an example of which is displayed on the right-hand side of Figure 17.12. With 11 links, one plant is capable of producing two different vehicles. As we add more links, we add more flexibility. Total flexibility is achieved when we have 100 links; that is, every plant is able to produce every product. Figure 17.13 displays the full flexibility configuration as well as one of the possible configurations with 20 links.

With each configuration, we are interested in evaluating the expected unit sales and expected capacity utilization. Unfortunately, for most configurations, it is quite challenging to evaluate those performance measures analytically. However, we can obtain accurate estimates of those performance measures via simulation. Each iteration of the simulation draws random demand for each product and then allocates the capacity to maximize unit sales within the constraints of the feasible links. For example, in the configuration with 11 links displayed in Figure 17.12, suppose in one of the iterations that demand for vehicle A is 85 units and vehicle B is 125 units. In that case, plant 2 uses its entire 100 units of capacity to produce vehicle B and plant 1 uses its entire 100 units of capacity to produce 85 units of vehicle A and 15 units of vehicle B, thereby only losing 10 units of potential vehicle B

[4] In other words, any outcome of the normal distribution that is either lower than 20 or higher than 180 is ignored and additional random draws are made until an outcome is received between 20 and 180. There is only a 4.6 percent chance that an outcome of a normal distribution is greater than two standard deviations from the mean (as in this case).

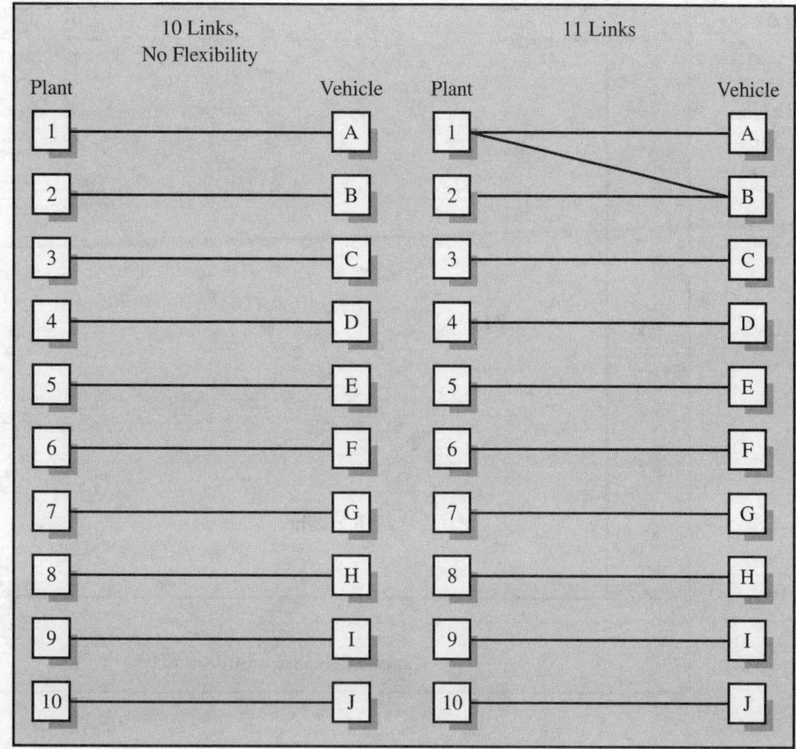

FIGURE 17.12 Two Configurations, One with No Flexibility (10 links) and One with Limited Flexibility (11 links)

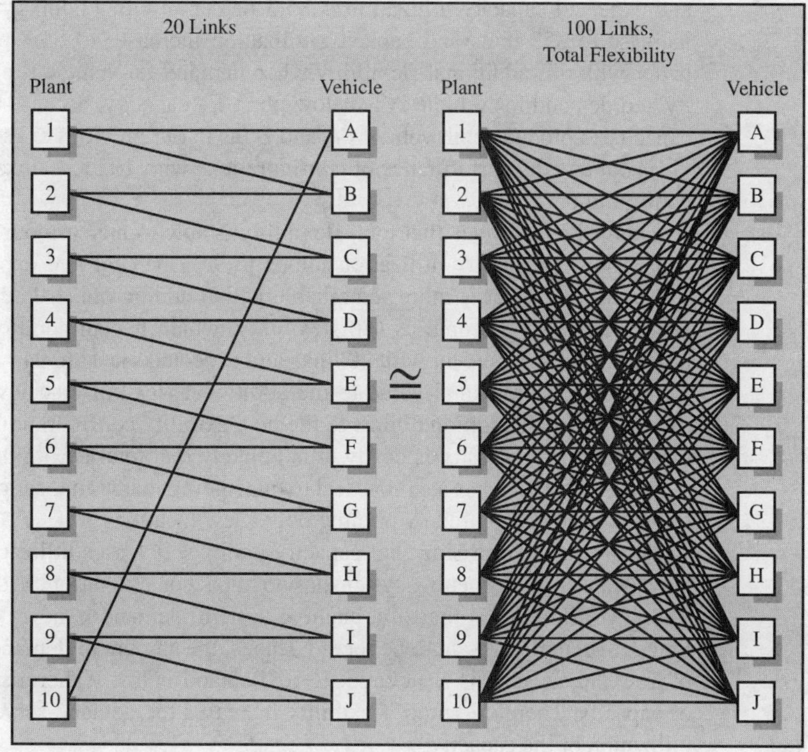

FIGURE 17.13 Flexibility Configurations with Approximately Equal Capability to Respond to Demand Uncertainty

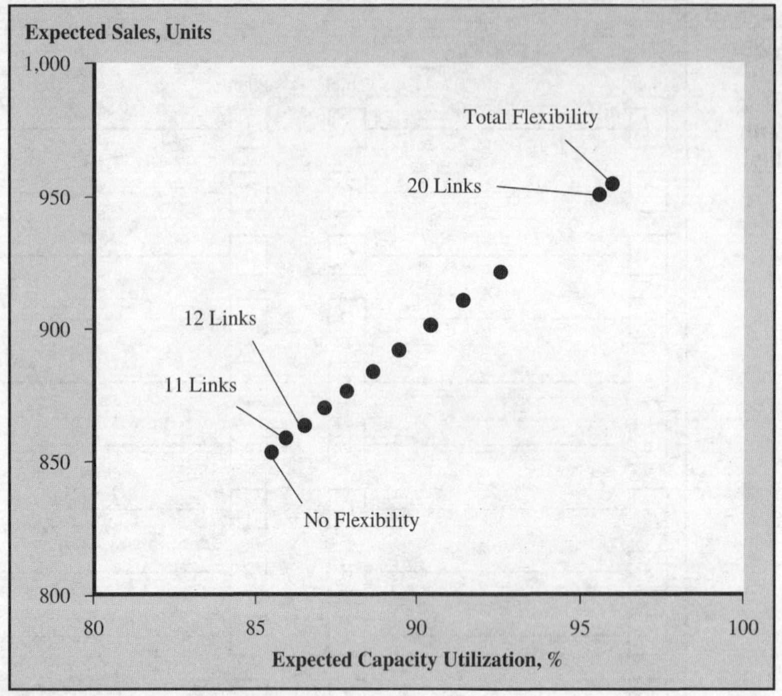

FIGURE 17.14 **Impact of Incrementally Adding Flexibility on Expected Sales and Capacity Utilization**

sales. Our estimate of each performance measure is just its average across the iterations. After many iterations, our estimates will be quite accurate.

Via simulation we find that with no flexibility, expected unit sales are 853 units and expected capacity utilization is 85.3 percent. With 11 links, the expected unit sales increase to 858 units and capacity utilization increases to 85.8 percent. We do slightly better with this additional flexibility when demand for vehicle B exceeds plant 2's capacity and demand for vehicle A is below plant 1's capacity, because then plant 1 can use its capacity to produce both vehicles A and B (as in our previous example). Figure 17.14 provides data on the performance of configurations with 10 to 20 links and the full flexibility configuration.

Figure 17.14 reveals that total flexibility is able to increase our performance measures considerably: Capacity utilization jumps to 95.4 percent and expected sales increase to 954 units. But what is more remarkable is that adding only 10 additional links produces nearly the same outcome as full flexibility, which has an additional 90 links: Capacity utilization is 94.9 percent with 20 links and expected sales are 949 units. Apparently, there is very little incremental value to the additional flexibility achieved by adding the 11th through the 90th additional links to the no-flexibility configuration. In other words, given that installing flexibility is costly, it is unlikely that total flexibility will be economically rational. This result has a similar feel to our finding that with location pooling, the majority of the benefit is captured by pooling only a few locations.

It may seem surprising that capacity pooling increases utilization, given that pooling server capacity in a queuing system has no impact on utilization, as discussed in Chapter 10. The key difference is that in a queuing system, demand is never lost; it just has to wait longer than it might want to be served. Hence, the amount of demand served is independent of how the capacity is structured. Here, demand is lost if there isn't a sufficient amount of capacity. Therefore, more flexibility increases the demand served, which increases the utilization of the capacity.

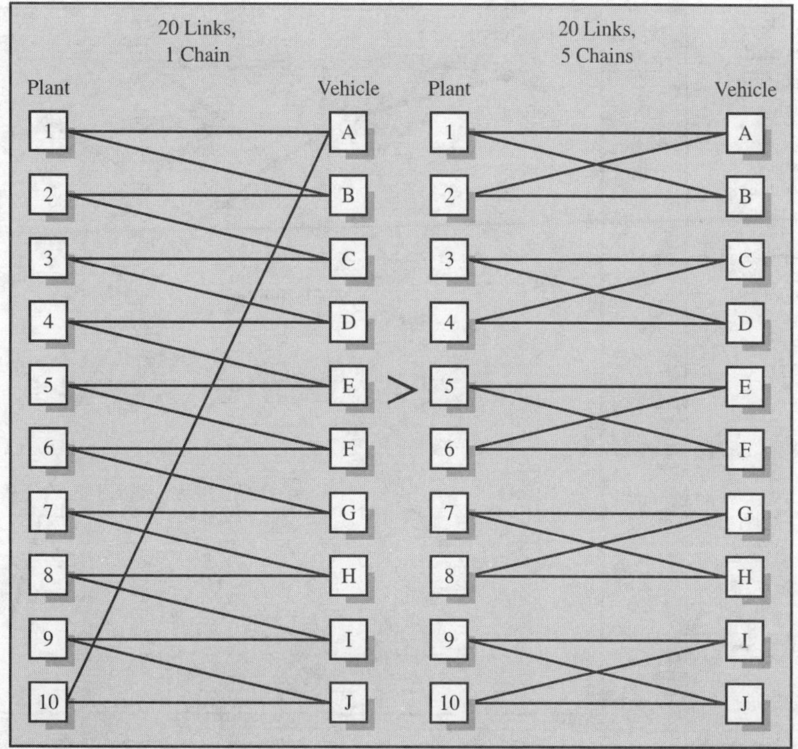

FIGURE 17.15 **Flexibility Configurations with the Same Number of Links but Different Number of Chains**

Although flexibility with 20 links can perform nearly as well as total flexibility with 100 links, not every configuration with 20 links performs that well. Figure 17.13 displays the particular 20-link configuration that nearly equals total flexibility. The effectiveness of that configuration can be explained by the concept of *chaining*. A chain is a group of plants and vehicles that are connected via links. For example, in the 11-link configuration displayed in Figure 17.12, the first two plants and vehicles form a single chain and the remaining plant–vehicle pairs form eight additional chains. With the 20-link configuration displayed in Figure 17.13, there is a single chain, as there is with the total flexibility configuration.

In general, flexibility configurations with the longest and fewest chains for a given number of links perform the best. Figure 17.15 displays two 20-link configurations, one with a single chain (the same one as displayed in Figure 17.13) and the other with five chains. We already know that the single chain configuration has expected sales of 949 units. Again via simulation, we discover that the 20-link configuration with five chains generates expected sales of only 896 units, which compares to the 853 expected unit sales with no-flexibility.

Long chains are beneficial because they facilitate the reallocation of capacity to respond to demand. For example, suppose demand for vehicle A is less than expected, but demand for vehicle G is very strong. If both vehicles are in the same chain, then plant 1's idle capacity can be shifted along the chain to help fill vehicle G's demand: Plant 1 produces some vehicle B's, plant 2 produces some of both vehicles B and C, and so forth so that both plants 6 and 7 can produce some vehicle G. If both of those vehicles are not part of the same chain (as in our five-chain configuration), then this swapping of capacity is not possible.

In addition to how flexibility is configured, there are two additional issues worth mentioning that influence the value of flexibility: correlation and total capacity. So far we have assumed that demands across vehicles are independent. We learned with the other risk-pooling strategies that risk pooling becomes more effective as demand becomes more negatively correlated.

FIGURE 17.16
Expected Sales and Capacity Utilization

Shown are seven different capacities (*C*) and two configurations, one with no flexibility (10 links) and one with 20 links and one chain (displayed in Figure 17.15). In each case, the total capacity is equally divided among the 10 products and expected total demand is 1,000 units.

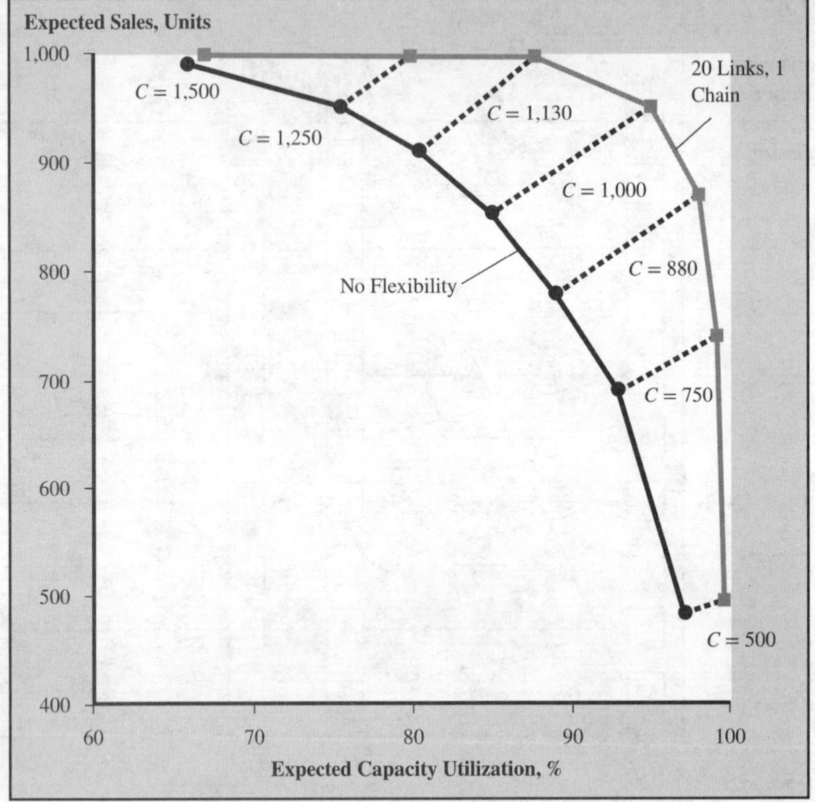

The same holds here: With pooled capacity, the uncertainty in total demand is more important than the uncertainty with individual products; hence, negative correlation is preferred. However, this does not mean that two negatively correlated products must be produced in the same plant. Instead, it is sufficient that two negatively correlated products are produced in the same chain. This is a valuable insight if the negatively correlated products are physically quite different (e.g., a full-size truck and a compact sedan) because producing them in the same chain might be far cheaper than producing them in the same plant.

The total available capacity also influences the effectiveness of flexibility. Suppose capacity for each plant were only 20 units. In that case, each plant would always operate at 100 percent utilization, so flexibility has no value. The end result is the same with the other extreme situation. If each plant could produce 180 units, then flexibility is again not needed because every plant is sure to have idle capacity. In other words, flexibility is more valuable when capacity and demand are approximately equal, as in our numerical examples.

Figure 17.16 further emphasizes that flexibility is most valuable with intermediate amounts of capacity: The biggest gap between the no-flexibility trade-off curve and the 20-link trade-off curve occurs when total capacity equals expected total demand, 1,000 units.

Figure 17.16 illustrates another observation: Flexibility and capacity are substitutes. For example, to achieve expected sales of 950 units, GM can either install total capacity of 1,250 units with no flexibility or 1,000 units of capacity with 20-link flexibility. If capacity is cheap relative to flexibility, then the high-capacity–no-flexibility option may be preferable. But if capacity is expensive relative to flexibility (especially given that we only need 10 additional links of flexibility), then the low-capacity–some-flexibility option may be better.

So far, our discussion has focused on a single firm and its flexibility within its own network of resources. However, if a firm cannot implement flexible capacity on its own,

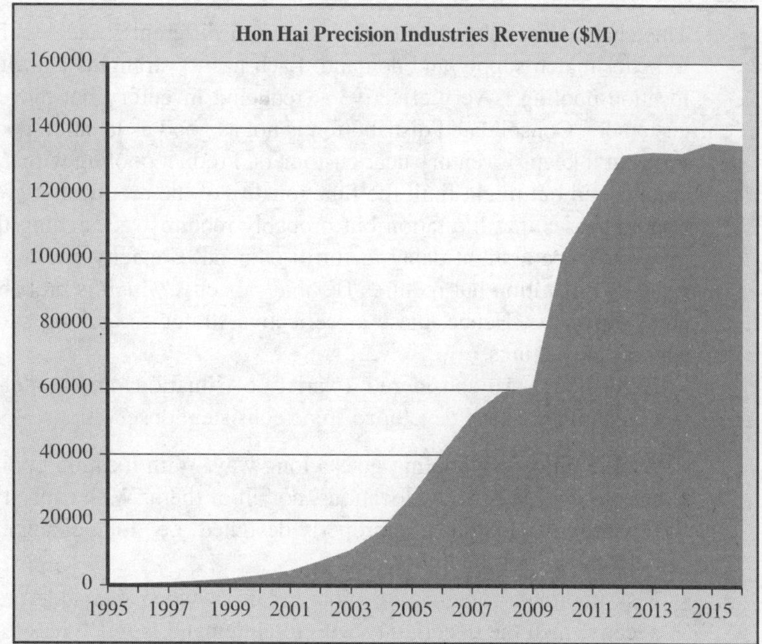

FIGURE 17.17
A Graph of Revenue Growth for Hon Hai

Note: The fiscal years of these firms vary somewhat, so total revenue in a calendar year will be slightly different.

another option is to hire a firm that essentially provides this service for them. In fact, there is an entire industry doing just this—the contract manufacturing industry. These are companies that generally do not have their own products or brands. What they sell is capacity—flexible capacity that is used for all of their clients. For example, Hon Hai Precision Industries could assemble mobile phones for Apple and other brands. The same equipment and often the same components are used by these multiple manufacturers, so, instead of each one investing in its own capacity and component inventory, Hon Hai pools their needs. In other words, while any of these companies could produce its own mobile phones, because of capacity pooling, Hon Hai is able to produce them with higher utilization and therefore lower cost. This added efficiency allows Hon Hai to charge a margin, albeit a rather thin margin (generally in the 5–8 percent range). Furthermore, there is no doubting that Hon Hai (and other contract manufacturers) have been able to grow rapidly—see Figure 17.17.

To summarize, this section considers the pooling of capacity via manufacturing flexibility. The main insights are

- A limited amount of flexibility can accommodate demand uncertainty nearly as well as total flexibility as long as the flexibility is configured to generate long chains.
- Flexibility should be configured so that negatively correlated products are part of the same chain but need not be produced in the same plant.
- Flexibility is most valuable when total capacity roughly equals expected demand.
- It may be possible to purchase flexibility by working with a contract manufacturer.

Therefore, it is generally neither necessary nor economically rational for a firm to sink the huge investment needed to achieve total flexibility. Flexibility is surely valuable, but it should not be installed haphazardly. Finally, while we have used the context of automobile manufacturing to illustrate these insights, they nevertheless apply to workers in service environments. For example, it is not necessary to cross-train workers so that they can handle every task (full flexibility). Instead, it is sufficient to train workers so that long chains of skills are present in the organization.

17.5 Summary

This chapter describes and explores several different strategies that exploit risk pooling to better match supply and demand. Each has its strengths and limitations. For example, location pooling is very effective at reducing inventory but moves inventory away from customers. Consolidated distribution is not as good as location pooling at reducing inventory, but it keeps inventory near customers. Product pooling with a universal design is also quite useful but might limit the functionality of the products offered. Delayed differentiation addresses that limitation but probably requires redesigning the product/process and may introduce a slight delay to fulfill demand. Capacity pooling can increase sales and capacity utilization but requires flexible capacity, which is probably not free and may be quite expensive. Hence, these are effective strategies as long as they are applied in the appropriate settings.

Even though we considered a variety of situations and models (e.g., order-up-to and newsvendor), we have developed some consistent observations:

- A little bit of risk pooling goes a long way. With location pooling, it is usually necessary to pool only a few locations, not all of them. With capacity pooling, a little bit of flexibility, as long as it is properly designed (i.e., long chains), yields nearly the same outcome as full flexibility.
- Risk-pooling strategies are most effective when demands are negatively correlated because then the uncertainty with total demand is much less than the uncertainty with any individual item/location. It follows that these strategies become less effective as demands become more positively correlated.
- Risk-pooling strategies do not help reduce pipeline inventory. That inventory can only be reduced by moving inventory through the system more quickly.
- Risk-pooling strategies can be used to reduce inventory while maintaining the same service (in-stock probability) or they can be used to increase service while holding the same inventory, or a combination of those improvements.

Table 17.5 provides a summary of the key notation and equations presented in this chapter.

TABLE 17.5 Summary of Notation and Key Equations in Chapter 17

The combination of two demands with the same mean and standard deviation yields

$$\text{Expected pooled demand} = 2 \times \mu$$

$$\text{Standard deviation of pooled demand} = \sqrt{2 \times (1 + \text{Correlation})} \times \sigma$$

$$\text{Coefficient of variation of pooled demand} = \sqrt{\frac{1}{2}(1 + \text{Correlation})} \times \left(\frac{\sigma}{\mu}\right)$$

17.6 Further Reading

In recent years, risk-pooling strategies have received considerable attention in the academic community as well as in practice.

Lee (1996) provides a technical treatment of the delayed-differentiation strategy. A more managerial description of delayed differentiation can be found in Feitzinger and Lee (1997). Brown, Lee, and Petrakian (2000) describe the application of delayed differentiation at a semiconductor firm. Simchi-Levi, Kaminsky, and Simchi-Levi (2003) and Chopra and Meindl (2004) cover risk-pooling strategies in the context of supply chain management.

Ulrich and Eppinger (2011) discuss the issues of delayed differentiation and product architecture from the perspective of a product development team.

Upton (1994, 1995) provides broad discussions on the issue of manufacturing flexibility.

17.7 Practice Problems

The following questions will help in testing your understanding of this chapter. After each question, we show the relevant section in parentheses [Section x].

Solutions to problems marked with an "*" are available in Appendix E. Video solutions to select problems are available in Connect.

Q17.1* **(Egghead)** In 1997 Egghead Computers ran a chain of 50 retail stores all over the United States. Consider one type of computer sold by Egghead. Demand for this computer at each store on any given week was independently and normally distributed with a mean demand of 200 units and a standard deviation of 30 units. Inventory at each store is replenished directly from a vendor with a 10-week lead time. At the end of 1997, Egghead decided it was time to close their retail stores, put up an Internet site, and begin filling customer orders from a single warehouse.

a. By consolidating the demand into a single warehouse, what will be the resulting standard deviation of weekly demand for this computer faced by Egghead? Assume Egghead's demand characteristics before and after the consolidation are identical. [17.1]

b. Egghead takes physical possession of inventory when it leaves the supplier and grants possession of inventory to customers when it leaves Egghead's shipping dock. In the consolidated-distribution scenario, what is the pipeline inventory? [17.1]

Q17.2* **(Two Products)** Consider two products, A and B. Demands for both products are normally distributed and have the same mean and standard deviation. The coefficient of variation of demand for each product is 0.6. The estimated correlation in demand between the two products is −0.7. What is the coefficient of variation of the total demand of the two products? [17.2]

Q17.3* **(Fancy Paints)** Fancy Paints is a small paint store. Fancy Paints stocks 200 different SKUs (stock-keeping units) and places replenishment orders weekly. The order arrives one month (let's say four weeks) later. For the sake of simplicity, let's assume weekly demand for each SKU is Poisson distributed with mean 1.25. Fancy Paints maintains a 95 percent in-stock probability.

a. What is the average inventory at the store at the end of the week? [17.3]

b. Now suppose Fancy Paints purchases a color-mixing machine. This machine is expensive, but instead of stocking 200 different SKU colors, it allows Fancy Paints to stock only five basic SKUs and to obtain all the other SKUs by mixing. Weekly demand for each SKU is normally distributed with mean 50 and standard deviation 8. Suppose Fancy Paints maintains a 95 percent in-stock probability for each of the five colors. How much inventory on average is at the store at the end of the week? [17.3]

c. After testing the color-mixing machine for a while, the manager realizes that a 95 percent in-stock probability for each of the basic colors is not sufficient: Since mixing requires the presence of multiple mixing components, a higher in-stock probability for components is needed to maintain a 95 percent in-stock probability for the individual SKUs. The manager decides that a 98 percent in-stock probability for each of the five basic SKUs should be adequate. Suppose that each can costs $14 and 20 percent per year is charged for holding inventory (assume 50 weeks per year). What is the change in the store's holding cost relative to the original situation in which all paints are stocked individually? [17.3]

Q17.4* **(Burger King)** Consider the following excerpts from a *Wall Street Journal* article on Burger King (Beatty, 1996):

> Burger King intends to bring smiles to the faces of millions of parents and children this holiday season with its "Toy Story" promotion. But it has some of them up in arms because local restaurants are running out of the popular toys. . . . Every Kids Meal sold every day of the year comes with a giveaway, a program that has been in place for about six years and has helped Grand Metropolitan PLC's Burger King increase its market share. Nearly all of Burger King's 7,000 U.S. stores are participating in the "Toy Story" promotion. . . . Nevertheless, meeting consumer demand still remains a conundrum for the giants. That is partly because individual

> Burger King restaurant owners make their tricky forecasts six months before such promotions begin. "It's asking you to pull out a crystal ball and predict exactly what consumer demand is going to be," says Richard Taylor, Burger King's director of youth and family marketing. "This is simply a case of consumer demand outstripping supply." The long lead times are necessary because the toys are produced overseas to take advantage of lower costs. . . . Burger King managers in Houston and Atlanta say the freebies are running out there, too. . . . But Burger King, which ordered nearly 50 million of the small plastic dolls, is "nowhere near running out of toys on a national level."

Let's consider a simplified analysis of Burger King's situation. Consider a region with 200 restaurants served by a single distribution center. At the time the order must be placed with the factories in Asia, demand (units of toys) for the promotion at each restaurant is forecasted to be gamma distributed with mean 2,251 and standard deviation 1,600. A discrete version of that gamma distribution is provided in the following table, along with a graph of the density function:

Q	F(Q)	I(Q)	Q	F(Q)	I(Q)
0	0.0000	0	6,500	0.9807	4,280.0
500	0.1312	0	7,000	0.9865	4,770.4
1,000	0.3101	65.6	7,500	0.9906	5,263.6
1,500	0.4728	220.6	8,000	0.9934	5,758.9
2,000	0.6062	457.0	8,500	0.9954	6,255.6
2,500	0.7104	760.1	9,000	0.9968	6,753.3
3,000	0.7893	1,115.3	9,500	0.9978	7,251.7
3,500	0.8480	1,510.0	10,000	0.9985	7,750.6
4,000	0.8911	1,934.0	10,500	0.9989	8,249.8
4,500	0.9224	2,379.5	11,000	0.9993	8,749.3
5,000	0.9449	2,840.7	11,500	0.9995	9,248.9
5,500	0.9611	3,313.2	12,000	1.0000	9,748.7
6,000	0.9726	3,793.7			

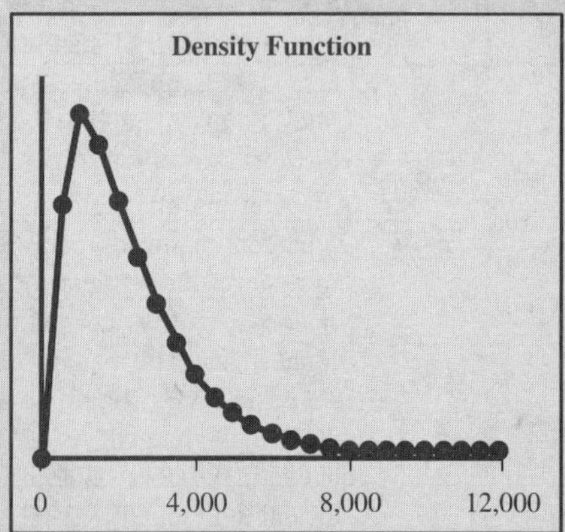

Suppose, six months in advance of the promotion, Burger King must make a single order for each restaurant. Furthermore, Burger King wants to have an in-stock probability of at least 85 percent.

a. Given those requirements, how many toys must each restaurant order? [17.2]

b. How many toys should Burger King expect to have at the end of the promotion? [17.2]

Now suppose Burger King makes a single order for all 200 restaurants. The order will be delivered to the distribution center and each restaurant will receive deliveries from that stockpile as needed. If demands were independent across all restaurants, total demand would be $200 \times 2{,}251 = 450{,}200$ with a standard deviation of $\sqrt{200} \times 1{,}600 = 22{,}627$. But it is unlikely that demands will be independent across restaurants. In other words, it is likely that there is positive correlation. Nevertheless, based on historical data, Burger King estimates the coefficient of variation for the total will be half of what it is for individual stores. As a result, a normal distribution will work for the total demand forecast.

c. How many toys must Burger King order for the distribution center to have an 85 percent in-stock probability? [17.3]

d. If the quantity in part c is ordered, then how many units should Burger King expect to have at the end of the promotion? [17.3]

e. If Burger King ordered the quantity evaluated in part a (i.e., the amount such that each restaurant would have its own inventory and generate an 85 percent in-stock probability) but kept that entire quantity at the distribution center and delivered to each restaurant only as needed, then what would the DC's in-stock probability be? [17.3]

Q17.5* **(Livingston Tools)** Livingston Tools, a manufacturer of battery-operated, hand-held power tools for the consumer market (such as screwdrivers and drills), has a problem. Its two biggest customers are "big box" discounters. Because these customers are fiercely price competitive, each wants exclusive products, thereby preventing consumers from making price comparisons. For example, Livingston will sell the exact same power screwdriver to each retailer, but Livingston will use packing customized to each retailer (including two different product identification numbers). Suppose weekly demand of each product to each retailer is normally distributed with mean 5,200 and standard deviation 3,800. Livingston makes production decisions on a weekly basis and has a three-week replenishment lead time. Because these two retailers are quite important to Livingston, Livingston sets a target in-stock probability of 99.9 percent.

a. Based on the order-up-to model, what is Livingston's average inventory of each of the two versions of this power screwdriver? [17.3]

b. Someone at Livingston suggests that Livingston stock power screwdrivers without putting them into their specialized packaging. As orders are received from the two retailers, Livingston would fulfill those orders from the same stockpile of inventory, since it doesn't take much time to actually package each tool. Interestingly, demands at the two retailers have a slight negative correlation, −0.20. By approximately how much would this new system reduce Livingston's inventory investment? [17.3]

Q17.6 **(Restoration Hardware)** Consider the following excerpts from a *New York Times* article (Kaufman, 2000):

> Despite its early promise . . . Restoration has had trouble becoming a mass-market player. . . . What went wrong? High on its own buzz, the company expanded at breakneck speed, more than doubling the number of stores, to 94, in the year and a half after the stock offering. . . . Company managers agree, for example, that Restoration's original inventory system, which called for all furniture to be kept at stores instead of at a central warehouse, was a disaster.

Let's look at one Restoration Hardware product, a leather chair. Average weekly sales of this chair in each store is Poisson with mean 1.25 units. The replenishment lead time is 12 weeks. (This question requires using Excel to create Poisson distribution and loss function tables that are not included in the appendix. See Appendix C for the procedure to evaluate a loss function table.)

a. If each store holds its own inventory, then what is the company's annual inventory turns if the company policy is to target a 99.25 percent in-stock probability? [17.3]

b. Suppose Restoration Hardware builds a central warehouse to serve the 94 stores. The lead time from the supplier to the central warehouse is 12 weeks. The lead time from the central warehouse to each store is one week. Suppose the warehouse operates with a 99 percent in-stock probability, but the stores maintain a 99.25 percent in-stock probability. If only inventory at the retail stores is considered, what are Restoration's annual inventory turns? [17.3]

Q17.7 **(Study Desk)** You are in charge of designing a supply chain for furniture distribution. One of your products is a study desk. This desk comes in two colors: black and cherry. Weekly demand for each desk type is normal with mean 100 and standard deviation 65 (demands for the two colors are independent). The lead time from the assembly plant to the retail store is two weeks and you order inventory replenishments weekly. There is no finished goods inventory at the plant (desks are assembled to order for delivery to the store).

a. What is the expected on-hand inventory of desks at the store (black and cherry together) if you maintain a 97 percent in-stock probability for each desk color? [17.3]

You notice that only the top part of the desk is black or cherry; the remainder (base) is made of the standard gray metal. Hence, you suggest that the store stock black and cherry tops separately from gray bases and assemble them when demand occurs. The replenishment lead time for components is still two weeks. Furthermore, you still choose an order-up-to level for each top to generate a 97 percent in-stock probability.

b. What is the expected on-hand inventory of black tops? [17.3]

c. How much less inventory of gray bases do you have on average at the store with the new in-store assembly scheme relative to the original system in which desks are delivered fully assembled? (*Hint:* Remember that each assembled desk requires one top and one base.) [17.3]

Q17.8 **(O'Neill)** One of O'Neill's high-end wetsuits is called the Animal. Total demand for this wetsuit is normally distributed with a mean of 200 and a standard deviation of 130. In order to ensure an excellent fit, the Animal comes in 16 sizes. Furthermore, it comes in four colors, so there are actually 64 different Animal SKUs (stock-keeping units). O'Neill sells the Animal for $350 and its production cost is $269. The Animal will be redesigned this season, so at the end of the season leftover inventory will be sold off at a steep markdown. Because this is such a niche product, O'Neill expects to receive only $100 for each leftover wetsuit. Finally, to control manufacturing costs, O'Neill has a policy that at least five wetsuits of any size/color combo must be produced at a time. Total demand for the smallest size (extra small-tall) is forecasted to be Poisson with mean 2.00. Mean demand for the four colors are black = 0.90, blue = 0.50, green = 0.40, and yellow = 0.20.

a. Suppose O'Neill already has no extra small-tall Animals in stock. What is O'Neill's expected profit if it produces one batch (five units) of extra small-tall black Animals? [17.2]

b. Suppose O'Neill announces that it will only sell the Animal in one color, black. If O'Neill suspects this move will reduce total demand by 12.5 percent, then what now is its expected profit from the black Animal? [17.2]

Q17.9* **(Consulting Services)** A small economic consulting firm has four employees, Alice, Bob, Cathy, and Doug. The firm offers services in four distinct areas, Quotas, Regulation, Strategy, and Taxes. At the current time Alice is qualified for Quotas, Bob does Regulation, and so on. But this isn't working too well: The firm often finds it cannot compete for business in one area because it has already committed to work in that area while in another area it is idle. Therefore, the firm would like to train the consultants to be qualified in more than one area. Which of the following assignments is likely to be most beneficial to the firm? [17.4]

a.

	Alice	Bob	Cathy	Doug
Qualified areas:	Quotas	Regulation	Strategy	Taxes
	Regulation	Taxes	Quotas	Strategy

b.

	Alice	Bob	Cathy	Doug
Qualified areas:	Quotas Regulation	Regulation Quotas	Strategy Taxes	Taxes Strategy

c.

	Alice	Bob	Cathy	Doug
Qualified areas:	Quotas Regulation	Regulation Quotas	Strategy Regulation	Taxes Quotas

d.

	Alice	Bob	Cathy	Doug
Qualified areas:	Quotas Strategy	Regulation Taxes	Strategy Quotas	Taxes Regulation

e.

	Alice	Bob	Cathy	Doug
Qualified areas:	Quotas Strategy	Regulation Taxes	Strategy Quotas	Taxes Regulation

Chapter 18

Revenue Management with Capacity Controls

The operations manager constantly struggles with a firm's supply process to better match it to demand. In fact, most of our discussion in this text has concentrated on how the supply process can be better organized, structured, and managed to make it more productive and responsive. But if supply is so inflexible that it cannot be adjusted to meet demand, then another approach is needed. In particular, this chapter takes the opposite approach: Instead of matching supply to demand, we explore how demand can be adjusted to match supply. The various techniques for achieving this objective are collected under the umbrella term *revenue management*, which is also referred to as *yield management*. Broadly speaking, revenue management is the science of maximizing the revenue earned from a fixed supply.

This chapter discusses two specific techniques within revenue management: *protection levels/booking limits* and *overbooking*. (We will see that protection levels and booking limits are really two different concepts that implement the same technique.) Those techniques perform revenue management via capacity controls; that is, they adjust over time the availability of capacity. Prices are taken as fixed, so protection levels and overbooking attempt to maximize revenue without changing prices.

We begin the chapter with a brief introduction to revenue management: its history, its success stories, and some "margin arithmetic" to explain why it can be so powerful. We next illustrate the application of protection levels and overbooking to an example from the hotel industry. The final sections discuss the implementation of these techniques in practice and summarize insights.

18.1 Revenue Management and Margin Arithmetic

Revenue management techniques were first developed in the airline industry in the early 1980s. Because each flown segment is a perishable asset (once a plane leaves the gate, there are no additional opportunities to earn additional revenue on that particular flight), the airlines wanted to maximize the revenue they earned on each flight, which is all the more important given the razor-thin profit margins in the industry. For example, a typical airline operates with about 73 percent of its seats filled but needs to fill about 70 percent of its seats to breakeven: On a 100-seat aircraft, the difference between making and losing money is measured by a handful of passengers.

Firms that implement revenue management techniques generally report revenue increases in the range of 3 to 7 percent with relatively little additional capital investment. The importance of that incremental revenue can be understood with the use of "margin arithmetic." A firm's net profit equation is straightforward:

$$\text{Profit} = R \times M - F = \text{Net profit \%} \times R$$

where

$$\begin{aligned} R &= \text{Revenue} \\ M &= \text{Gross margin as a percentage of revenue} \\ F &= \text{Fixed costs} \\ \text{Net profit \%} &= \text{Net profit as a percentage of revenue} \end{aligned}$$

A firm's net profit as a percentage of its revenue (Net profit %) is generally in the range of 1 to 10 percent.

Now let's suppose we implement revenue management and increase revenue. Let Revenue increase be the percentage increase in revenue we experience, which, as has already been mentioned, is typically in the 3 to 7 percent range. Our percentage change in profit is then

$$\begin{aligned} \text{\% change in profit} &= \frac{[(100\% + \text{Revenue increase}) \times R \times M - F] - [R \times M - F]}{R \times M - F} \\ &= \frac{\text{Revenue increase} \times R \times M}{R \times M - F} \\ &= \frac{\text{Revenue increase} \times M}{\text{Net profit \%}} \end{aligned}$$

(The second line above cancels out terms in the numerator such as the fixed costs. The third line replaces the denominator with Net profit % $\times$ R and then cancels R from both the numerator and denominator.) Table 18.1 presents data evaluated with the above equation for various gross margins, revenue increases, and net profits as a percentage of revenues. The table illustrates that a seemingly small increase in revenue can have a significant impact on profit, especially when the gross margin is large. Thus, a 3 to 7 percent increase in revenue can easily generate a 50 to 100 percent increase in profit, especially in a high-gross-margin setting; revenue management indeed can be an important set of tools. We next illustrate in detail two of the tools in that set with an example from the hotel industry.

TABLE 18.1
Percentage Change in Profit for Different Gross Margins, Revenue Increases, and Net Profits as a Percentage of Revenue

Net Profit % = 2%					Net Profit % = 6%				
	Revenue Increase					Revenue Increase			
Gross Margin	1%	2%	5%	8%	Gross Margin	1%	2%	5%	8%
100%	50%	100%	250%	400%	100%	17%	33%	83%	133%
90	45	90	225	360	90	15	30	75	120
75	38	75	188	300	75	13	25	63	100
50	25	50	125	200	50	8	17	42	67
25	13	25	63	100	25	4	8	21	33
15	8	15	38	60	15	3	5	13	20

18.2 Protection Levels and Booking Limits

The Park Hyatt Philadelphia at the Bellevue, located at Walnut and Broad in downtown Philadelphia, has 118 king/queen rooms that it offers to both leisure and business travelers.[1] Leisure travelers are more price sensitive and tend to reserve rooms well in advance of their stay. Business travelers are generally willing to pay more for a room, in part because they tend to book much closer to the time of their trip and in part because they wish to avoid the additional restrictions associated with the discount fare (e.g., advance purchase requirements and more restrictive cancellation policies). With leisure travelers in mind, the Hyatt offers a \$159 discount fare for a midweek stay, which contrasts with the regular fare of \$225. We'll refer to these as the low and high fares and use the notation $r_l = 159$ and $r_h = 225$ (r stands for revenue and the subscript indicates l for low fare or h for high fare).

Suppose today is April 1, but we are interested in the Hyatt's bookings on May 29th, which is a midweek night. The Hyatt knows that there will be plenty of travelers willing to pay the low fare, so selling all 118 rooms by May 29th is not a problem. However, all else being equal, the Hyatt would like those rooms to be filled with high-fare travelers rather than low-fare travelers. Unfortunately, there is little chance that there will be enough demand at the high fare to fill the hotel and the lost revenue from an empty room is significant: Once May 29th passes, the Hyatt can never again earn revenue from that capacity. So the Hyatt's challenge is to extract as much revenue as possible from these two customer segments for its May 29th rooms; that is, we wish to maximize revenue.

The objective to maximize revenue implicitly assumes that the variable cost of an occupied room is inconsequential. The zero-variable cost assumption is reasonable for an airline. It is probably less appropriate for a hotel, given that an occupied room requires additional utilities and cleaning staff labor. Nevertheless, we stick with the traditional maximize-revenue objective in this chapter. If the variable cost of a customer is significant, then the techniques we present can be easily modified to implement a maximize-profit objective. (For example, see Practice Problems Q18.8 and Q18.10.)

Returning to our example, the Hyatt could just accept bookings in both fare classes as they occur until either it has 118 reservations or May 29th arrives; the first-come-first-served regime is surely equitable. With that process, it is possible the Hyatt has all 118 rooms reserved one week before May 29th. Unfortunately, because business travelers tend to book late, in that situation it is likely some high-fare travelers will be turned away in that last week; the Hyatt is not allowed to cancel a low-fare reservation to make room for a high-fare traveler. Turning away a high-fare reservation is surely a lost revenue opportunity.

There is a better way than just accepting reservations on a first-come-first-served basis. Instead, the Hyatt could reserve a certain number of rooms just for the high-fare travelers; that is, to protect some rooms for last-minute bookings. This is formalized with the concept of protection levels and booking limits.

The *protection level* for a fare is the number of rooms that are reserved for that fare or higher. We let Q represent our protection level for the high fare. If $Q = 35$, then we protect 35 rooms for the high fare. What does it mean to "protect" 35 rooms? It means that at all times there must always be *at least* 35 rooms that could be reserved with

[1] The Park Hyatt in Philadelphia does have 118 king/queen rooms, but the demand and fare data in this case are disguised. Furthermore, the revenue management techniques described in the chapter are meant to be representative of how the Park Hyatt could do revenue management, but should not be taken to represent the Park Hyatt's actual operating procedures.

the high fare. For example, suppose there were 83 rooms reserved at the low fare, 30 rooms reserved at the high fare, and 5 unreserved rooms. Because there are enough unreserved rooms to allow us to possibly have 35 high-fare rooms, we have not violated our protection level.

But now suppose the next traveler requests a low-fare reservation. If we were to allow that reservation, then we would no longer have enough unreserved rooms to allow at least 35 high-fare rooms. Therefore, according to our protection level rule, we would not allow that low-fare reservation. In fact, the limit of 83 has a name; it is called a booking limit: The *booking limit* for a fare is the maximum number of reservations allowed at that fare or lower. There is a relationship between the high-fare protection level and the low-fare booking limit:

$$\text{High-fare protection level} = \text{Capacity} - \text{Low-fare booking limit} \qquad \textbf{(18.1)}$$

In order to have at least 35 rooms available for the high fare (its protection level), the Hyatt cannot allow any more than 83 reservations at the low fare (its booking limit) as long as the total number of allowed reservations (capacity) is 118.

You might now wonder about the protection level for the low fare and the booking limit for the high fare. There is no need to protect any rooms at the low fare because the next best alternative is for the room to go empty. So the protection level for the low fare is 0. Analogously, we are willing to book as many rooms as possible at the high fare because there is no better alternative, so the booking limit on the high fare should be set to at least 118. (As we will see in the next section, we may even wish to allow more than 118 bookings.)

Given that we have defined a booking limit to be the maximum number of reservations allowed for a fare class *or lower,* we have implicitly assumed that our booking limits are *nested.* With *nested booking limits,* it is always true that if a particular fare class is open (i.e., we are willing to accept reservations at that fare class), then we are willing to accept all higher fare classes as well. It is also true that if a particular fare class is closed, then all lower fare classes are closed as well. For reasons beyond the scope of this discussion, nested booking limits may not be optimal. Nevertheless, because nested booking limits make intuitive sense, most revenue management systems operate with nested booking limits. So, throughout our discussion, we shall assume nested booking limits.

So now let's turn to the issue of choosing a booking limit for the low fare or, equivalently, a protection level for the high fare. As in many operational decisions, we again face the "too much–too little" problem. If we protect too many rooms for the high-fare class, then some rooms might remain empty on May 29th. To explain, suppose one week before May 29th we have 83 low-fare bookings but only 10 high-fare bookings. Because we have reached the low-fare booking limit, we "close down" that fare and only accept high-fare bookings in the last week. If only 20 additional high-fare bookings arrive, then on May 29th we have five unreserved rooms, which we might have been able to sell at the low fare. Nevertheless, those five rooms go empty. So protecting too many rooms for a fare class can lead to empty rooms.

But the Hyatt can also protect too few rooms. Suppose one week before May 29th we have 80 low-fare bookings and 35 high-fare bookings. Because only 35 rooms are protected for the high fare, the remaining 3 unreserved rooms could be taken at the low fare. If they are reserved at the low fare, then some high-fare travelers might be turned away; that is, the Hyatt might end up selling a room at the low fare that could have been sold at a high fare. If the protection level were 3 rooms higher, then those 3 unreserved rooms could only go at the high fare. Therefore, because the low-fare bookings tend to come before the high-fare bookings, it is possible to protect too few rooms for the high fare.

TABLE 18.2
The Distribution and Inventory Function for a Poisson with Mean 27.3

Q	F(Q)	I(Q)	Q	F(Q)	I(Q)	Q	F(Q)	I(Q)
10	0.0001	0	20	0.0920	0.15	30	0.7365	3.73
11	0.0004	0	21	0.1314	0.25	31	0.7927	4.47
12	0.0009	0	22	0.1802	0.38	32	0.8406	5.26
13	0.0019	0	23	0.2381	0.56	33	0.8803	6.10
14	0.0039	0	24	0.3040	0.80	34	0.9121	6.98
15	0.0077	0.01	25	0.3760	1.10	35	0.9370	7.89
16	0.0140	0.01	26	0.4516	1.48	36	0.9558	8.83
17	0.0242	0.03	27	0.5280	1.93	37	0.9697	9.79
18	0.0396	0.05	28	0.6025	2.46	38	0.9797	10.76
19	0.0618	0.09	29	0.6726	3.06	39	0.9867	11.74

Our discussion so far suggests the Hyatt could use the newsvendor model logic to choose a protection level. (Peter Belobaba of MIT first developed this approach and labeled it the "Expected Marginal Seat Revenue" analysis. See Belobaba, 1989.) To implement the model, we need a forecast of high-fare demand and an assessment of the underage and overage costs. Let's say the Hyatt believes a Poisson distribution with mean 27.3 represents the number of high-fare travelers on May 29th. (This forecast could be constructed using booking data from similar nights, similar times of the year, and managerial intuition.) Table 18.2 provides a portion of the distribution function for that Poisson distribution.

Now we need an overage cost C_o and an underage cost C_u. The underage cost is the cost per unit of setting the protection level too low (i.e., "under" protecting). If we do not protect enough rooms for the high fare, then we sell a room at the low fare that could have been sold at the high fare. The lost revenue is the difference between the two fares; that is, $C_u = r_h - r_l$.

The overage cost is the cost per unit of setting the protection level too high (i.e., "over" protecting). If we set the protection level too high, it means that we did not need to protect so many rooms for the high-fare customers. In other words, demand at the high fare is less than Q, our protection level. If Q were lower, then we could have sold another room at the low fare. Hence, the overage cost is the incremental revenue of selling a room at the low fare: $C_o = r_l$. According to the newsvendor model, the optimal protection level (i.e., the one that maximizes revenue, which is also the one that minimizes the overage and underage costs) is the Q such that the probability the high-fare demand is less than or equal to Q equals the critical ratio, which is

$$\frac{C_u}{C_o + C_u} = \frac{r_h - r_l}{r_l + (r_h - r_l)} = \frac{r_h - r_l}{r_h} = \frac{225 - 159}{225} = 0.2933$$

In words, we want to find the Q such that there is a 29.33 percent probability high-fare demand is Q or lower. From Table 18.2, we see that $F(23) = 0.2381$ and $F(24) = 0.3040$, so the optimal protection level is $Q = 24$ rooms. (Recall the round-up rule: When the critical ratio falls between two values in the distribution function table, choose the entry that leads to the higher decision variable.) The corresponding booking limit for the low fare is $118 - 24 = 94$ rooms.

In some situations, it is more convenient to express a booking limit as an *authorization level:* The authorization level for a fare class is the percentage of available capacity that can be reserved at that fare or lower. For example, a booking limit of 94 rooms corresponds to an authorization level of 80 percent (94/118) because 80 percent of the Hyatt's rooms can be reserved at the low fare. The process of evaluating protection levels and booking limits is summarized in Exhibit 18.1.

Exhibit 18.1

EVALUATING THE OPTIMAL PROTECTION LEVEL FOR THE HIGH FARE OR THE OPTIMAL BOOKING LIMIT FOR THE LOW FARE WHEN THERE ARE TWO FARES AND REVENUE MAXIMIZATION IS THE OBJECTIVE

Step 1. Evaluate the critical ratio:

$$\text{Critical ratio} = \frac{C_u}{C_o + C_u} = \frac{r_h - r_1}{r_h}$$

Step 2. Find the Q such that $F(Q)$ = Critical ratio, where $F(Q)$ is the distribution function of high-fare demand:

a. If $F(Q)$ is given in table form, then find the Q in the table such that $F(Q)$ equals the critical ratio. If the critical ratio falls between two entries in the table, choose the entry with the higher Q.

b. If high-fare demand is normally distributed with mean μ and standard deviation σ, then find the z-statistic in the Standard Normal Distribution Function Table such that $\Phi(z)$ = Critical ratio. If the critical ratio falls between two entries in the table, choose the entry with the higher z. Finally, convert the chosen z into Q: $Q = \mu + z \times \sigma$.

Step 3. The optimal high-fare protection level is Q evaluated in Step 2. The optimal low-fare booking limit is Capacity – Q, where Capacity is the number of allowed reservations.

If the Hyatt uses a protection level of 24 rooms, then the Hyatt's expected revenue is higher than if no protection level is used. How much higher? To provide some answer to that question, we need to make a few more assumptions. First, let's assume that there is ample low-fare demand. In other words, we could easily book all 118 rooms at the low fare. Second, let's assume the low-fare demand arrives before any high-fare bookings. Hence, if we do not protect any rooms for the high fare, then the low-fare customers will reserve all 118 rooms before any high-fare customer requests a reservation.

Given our assumptions, the Hyatt's revenue without any protection level would be 118 × \$159 = \$18,762: All 118 rooms are filled at the low fare. If we protect 24 rooms, then we surely fill 94 rooms at the low fare, for an expected revenue of 94 × \$159 = \$14,946. What is the expected revenue from the 24 protected rooms? Given that high-fare demand is Poisson with mean 27.3, from Table 18.2 we see that we can expect to have only $I(24) = 0.80$ empty room. That means that 24 – 0.80 = 23.2 rooms will have high-fare customers. If the Hyatt expects to sell 23.2 rooms at the high fare, then the revenue from those rooms is 23.2 × \$225 = \$5,220. Total revenue when protecting 24 rooms is then \$14,946 + \$5,220 = \$20,166. Hence, our expected revenue increases by (20,166 – 18,762) / 18,762 = 7.5 percent. As a point of reference, we can evaluate the *maximum expected revenue,* which is achieved if we sell to every high-fare customer and sell all remaining rooms at the low fare:

$$\text{Maximum expected revenue} = 27.3 \times \$225 + (118 - 27.3) \times \$159 = \$20{,}564$$

Thus, the difference between the maximum expected revenue and the revenue earned by just selling at the low fare is \$20,564 – \$18,762 = \$1,802. The Hyatt's revenue with a protection level falls short of the maximum expected revenue by only \$20,564 – \$20,166 = \$398. Hence, a protection level for the high fare allows the Hyatt to capture about 78 percent (1 – \$398/\$1,802) of its potential revenue improvement.

A revenue increase of 7.5 percent is surely substantial given that it is achieved without the addition of capacity. Nevertheless, we must be reminded of the assumptions that were made. We assumed there is ample demand for the low fare. If low-fare demand is limited, then a protection level for the high fare is less valuable and the incremental revenue gain is smaller. For example, if the sum of low- and high-fare demand is essentially always lower than 118 rooms, then there is no need to protect the high fare. More broadly, revenue management with protection levels is most valuable when operating in a capacity-constrained situation.

The second key assumption is that low-fare demand arrives before high-fare demand. If some high-fare demand "slips in" before the low-fare demand snatches up all 118 rooms, then the revenue estimate without a protection level, \$18,762, is too low. In other words, even if we do not protect any rooms for the high fare, it is possible that we would still obtain some high-fare bookings.

Although we would need to look at actual data to get a more accurate sense of the potential revenue improvement by using protection levels, our estimate is in line with the typical revenue increases reported in practice due to revenue management, 3 to 7 percent.

Now that we have considered a specific example of booking limits at a hotel, it is worth enumerating the characteristics of a business that are conducive to the application of booking limits.

- *The same unit of capacity can be used to sell to different customer segments.* It is easy for an airline to price discriminate between leisure and business travelers when the capacity that is being sold is different, for example, a coach cabin seat and a first-class seat. Those are clearly distinguishable products/services. Booking limits are applied when the capacity sold to different segments is identical; for example, a coach seat on an aircraft or a king/queen room in the Hyatt sold at two different fares.
- *There are distinguishable customer segments and the segments have different price sensitivity.* There is no need for protection levels when the revenue earned from all customers is the same, for example, if there is a single fare. Booking limits are worthwhile if the firm can earn different revenue from different customer segments with the same type of capacity. Because the same unit of capacity is being sold, it is necessary to discriminate between the customer segments. This is achieved with *fences:* additional restrictions that are imposed on the low fare that prevent high-fare customers from purchasing with the low fare. Typical fences include advanced purchase requirements, Saturday night stay requirements, cancellation fees, change fees, and so forth. Of course, one could argue that these fences make the low and high fares different products; for example, a full-fare coach ticket is not the same product as a supersaver coach ticket even if they both offer a seat in the coach cabin. True, these are different products in the broad sense, but they are identical products with respect to the capacity they utilize.
- *Capacity is perishable.* An unused room on May 29th is lost forever, just as an unused seat on a flight cannot be stored until the next flight. In contrast, capacity in a production facility can be used to make inventory, which can be sold later whenever capacity exceeds current demand.
- *Capacity is restrictive.* If the total demand at the leisure and business fares is rarely greater than 118 rooms, then the Hyatt has no need to establish protection levels or booking limits. Because capacity is expensive to install and expensive to change over time, it is impossible for a service provider to always have plenty of capacity. (Utilization would be so low that the firm would surely not be competitive and probably not viable.) But due to seasonality effects, it is possible that the Hyatt has plenty of capacity at some times of the year and not enough capacity at other times. Booking limits are not needed during those lull times but are quite useful during the peak demand periods.

- *Capacity is sold in advance.* If we were allowed to cancel a low-fare reservation whenever someone requested a high-fare reservation (i.e., bump a low-fare passenger off the plane without penalty), then we would not need to protect seats for the high fare: We would accept low-fare bookings as they arrive and then cancel as many as needed to accommodate the high-fare travelers. Similarly, we do not need protection levels if we were to conduct an auction just before the flight departs. For example, imagine a situation in which all potential demand would arrive at the airport an hour or so before the flight departs and then an auction is conducted to determine who would earn a seat on that flight. This is a rather silly way to sell airline seats, but in other contexts there is clearly a movement toward more auctionlike selling mechanisms. Because the auction ensures that capacity is sold to the highest bidders, there is no need for protection levels.
- *A firm wishes to maximize revenue, has the flexibility to charge different prices, and may withhold capacity from certain segments.* A hotel is able to offer multiple fares and withhold fares. In other words, even though the practice of closing a discount fare means the principle of first-come-first-served is violated, this practice is generally not viewed as unethical or unscrupulous. However, there are settings in which the violation of first-come-first-served, or the charging of different prices, or the use of certain fences is not acceptable to consumers; for example, access to health care.
- *A firm faces competition from a "discount competitor."* The low fares charged by People Express, a low-frills airline started after deregulation, were a major motivation for the development of revenue management at American Airlines. In order to compete in the low-fare segment, American was forced to match People Express's fares. But American did not want to have its high-fare customers paying the low fare. Booking limits and low-fare fences were the solution to the problem: American could compete at the low-fare segment without destroying the revenue from its profitable high-fare customers. People Express did not install a revenue management system and quickly went bankrupt after American's response.

18.3 Overbooking

In many service settings, customers are allowed to make reservations and then either are allowed to cancel their reservations with relatively short notice, or just fail to show up to receive their service. For example, on May 28th, the Hyatt might have all of its 118 rooms reserved for May 29th but then only 110 customers might actually show up, leaving eight rooms empty and not generating any revenue. Overbooking, described in this section, is one solution to the no-show problem. If the Hyatt chooses to overbook, then that means the Hyatt accepts more than 118 reservations even though a maximum of 118 guests can be accommodated. Overbooking is also common in the airline industry: In the United States, airlines deny boarding to about one million passengers annually (Stringer, 2002). Furthermore, it has been estimated that prohibiting overbooking would cost the world's airlines \$3 billion annually due to no-shows (Cross, 1995).

Let the variable Y represent the number of additional reservations beyond capacity that the Hyatt is willing to accept, that is, up to $118 + Y$ reservations are accepted. Overbooking can lead to two kinds of outcomes. On a positive note, the number of no-shows can be greater than the number of overbooked reservations, so all the actual customers can be accommodated and more customers are accommodated than would have been without overbooking. For example, suppose the Hyatt accepts 122 reservations and there are six no-shows. As a result, 116 rooms are occupied, leaving only 2 empty rooms, which is almost surely fewer empty rooms than if the Hyatt had only accepted 118 reservations.

TABLE 18.3
Poisson Distribution Function with Mean 8.5

Q	F(Q)	Q	F(Q)
0	0.0002	10	0.7634
1	0.0019	11	0.8487
2	0.0093	12	0.9091
3	0.0301	13	0.9486
4	0.0744	14	0.9726
5	0.1496	15	0.9862
6	0.2562	16	0.9934
7	0.3856	17	0.9970
8	0.5231	18	0.9987
9	0.6530	19	0.9995

On the negative side, the Hyatt can get caught overbooking. For example, if 122 reservations are accepted, but there are only two no-shows, then 120 guests hold reservations for 118 rooms. In that situation, 2 guests need to be accommodated at some other hotel and the Hyatt probably must give some additional compensation (e.g., cash or free future stay) to mitigate the loss of goodwill with those customers.

In deciding the proper amount of overbooking, there is a "too much–too little" trade-off: Overbook too much and the hotel angers some customers, but overbook too little and the hotel has the lost revenue associated with empty rooms. Hence, we can apply the newsvendor model to choose the appropriate *Y*. We first need a forecast of the number of customers that will not show up based on historical data. Let's say the Hyatt believes for the May 29th night that the no-show distribution is Poisson with mean 8.5. Table 18.3 provides the distribution function.[2]

Next, we need underage and overage costs. If the Hyatt chooses *Y* to be too low, then there will be empty rooms on May 29th (i.e., the Hyatt "under" overbooked). If the Hyatt indeed has plenty of low-fare demand, then those empty rooms could have at least been sold for r_l = \$159, so the underage cost is $C_u = r_l = 159$. Surprisingly, the underage cost does not depend on whether customers are allowed to cancel without penalty or not. To explain, suppose we accepted 120 reservations, but there are three no-shows. If reservations are refundable, we collected revenue from 117 customers (because the three no-shows are given a refund) but could have collected revenue from the one empty room. If reservations are not refundable, we collect revenue from 120 customers, but, again, we could have collected revenue from the one empty room. In each case our incremental revenue is \$159 from the one additional room we could have sold had we accepted one more reservation.

If the Hyatt chooses *Y* to be too high, then there will be more guests than rooms. The guests denied a room need to be accommodated at some other hotel and Hyatt offers other compensation. The total cost to Hyatt for each of those guests is estimated to be about \$350, so the overage cost is $C_o = 350$. *Note:* This cost is net of any revenue collected from the customer. For example, if the reservation is not refundable, then the Hyatt incurs \$509 in total costs due to the denial of service, for a net cost of \$350 (\$509—\$159), whereas if the reservation is refundable, then the Hyatt incurs \$350 in total costs due to the denial of service. Either way, the Hyatt is \$350 worse off for each customer denied a room.

[2] A careful reader will notice that our distribution function for no-shows is independent of the number of reservations made. In other words, we have assumed the average number of no-shows is 8.5 whether we make 118 reservations or 150 reservations. Hence, a more sophisticated method for choosing the overbooking quantity would account for the relationship between the number of reservations allowed and the distribution function of no-shows. While that more sophisticated method is conceptually similar to our procedure, it is also computationally cumbersome. Therefore, we shall stick with our heuristic method. Fortunately, our heuristic method performs well when compared against the more sophisticated algorithm.

Exhibit 18.2

THE PROCESS TO EVALUATE THE OPTIMAL QUANTITY TO OVERBOOK

Step 1. Evaluate the critical ratio:

$$\text{Critical ratio} = \frac{C_u}{C_o + C_u} = \frac{r_l}{\text{Cost per bumped customer} + r_l}$$

Step 2. Find the Y such that $F(Y)$ = Critical ratio, where $F(Y)$ is the distribution function of no-shows:

a. If $F(Y)$ is given in table form, then find the Y in the table such that $F(Y)$ equals the critical ratio. If the critical ratio falls between two entries in the table, choose the entry with the higher Y.

b. If no-shows are normally distributed with mean μ and standard deviation σ, then find the z-statistic in the Standard Normal Distribution Function Table such that $\Phi(z)$ = Critical ratio. If the critical ratio falls between two entries in the table, choose the entry with the higher z. Finally, convert the chosen z into Y: $Y = \mu + z \times \sigma$.

Step 3. Y is the optimal amount to overbook; that is, the number of allowed reservations is Y + Capacity, where Capacity is the maximum number of customers that can actually be served.

The critical ratio is

$$\frac{C_u}{C_o + C_u} = \frac{159}{350 + 159} = 0.3124$$

Looking in Table 18.3, we see that $F(6) = 0.2562$ and $F(7) = 0.3856$, so the optimal quantity to overbook is $Y = 7$. In other words, the Hyatt should allow up to $118 + 7 = 125$ reservations for May 29th. Exhibit 18.2 summarizes the process of evaluating the optimal quantity to overbook.

If the Hyatt chooses to overbook by 7 reservations and if the Hyatt indeed receives 125 reservations, then there is about a 26 percent chance ($F(6) = 0.2562$) that the Hyatt will find itself overbooked on May 29th. Because it is not assured that the Hyatt will receive that many reservations, the actual frequency of being overbooked would be lower.

A natural question is how should the Hyatt integrate its protection-level/booking-limit decision with its overbooking decision. The following describes a reasonable heuristic. If the Hyatt is willing to overbook by 7 rooms, that is, $Y = 7$, then its effective capacity is $118 + 7 = 125$ rooms. Based on the forecast of high-fare demand and the underage and overage costs associated with protecting rooms for the high-fare travelers, we determined that the Hyatt should protect 24 rooms for the high fare. Using Equation (18.1), that suggests the booking limit for the low fare should be

$$\begin{aligned}\text{Low-fare booking limit} &= \text{Capacity} - \text{High-fare protection level}\\ &= 125 - 24\\ &= 101\end{aligned}$$

The high-fare booking limit would then be 125; that is, the Hyatt accepts up to 101 low-fare reservations and up to 125 reservations in total.

18.4 Implementation of Revenue Management

Although the applications of revenue management described in this chapter present a reasonably straightforward analysis, in practice there are many additional complications encountered in the implementation of revenue management. A few of the more significant complications are discussed below.

Demand Forecasting

We saw that forecasts are a necessary input to the choice of both protection levels and overbooking quantities. As a result, the choices made are only as good as the inputted forecasts; as the old adage says, "garbage in, garbage out." Fortunately, reservation systems generally provide a wealth of information to formulate these forecasts. Nevertheless, the forecasting task is complicated by the presence of seasonality, special events (e.g., a convention in town), changing fares (both the firm's own fares as well as the competitors' fares), and truncation (once a booking limit is reached, most systems do not capture the lost demand at that fare level), among others. Furthermore, it is possible that the revenue management decisions themselves might influence demand and, hence, the forecasts used to make those decisions. As a result, with any successful revenue management system, a considerable amount of care and effort is put into the demand forecasting task.

Dynamic Decisions

Our analysis provided a decision for a single moment in time. However, fares and forecasts change with time and, as a result, booking limits need to be reviewed frequently (generally daily). In fact, sophisticated systems take future adjustments into consideration when setting current booking limits.

Variability in Available Capacity

A hotel is a good example of a service firm that generally does not have much variation in its capacity: It is surely difficult to add a room to a hotel and the number of rooms that cannot be occupied is generally small. The capacity of an airline's flight is also rigid but maybe less so than a hotel's capacity because the airline can choose to switch the type of aircraft used on a route. However, a car rental company's capacity at any given location is surely variable and not even fully controllable by the firm. Hence, those firms also must forecast the amount of capacity they think will be available at any given time.

Reservations Coming in Groups

If there is a convention in town for May 29th, then the Hyatt may receive a single request for 110 rooms at the low fare. Although this request violates the booking limit, the booking limit was established assuming reservations come one at a time. It is clearly more costly to turn away a single block of 110 reservations than it is to turn away one leisure traveler.

Effective Segmenting of Customers

We assumed there are two types of customers: a low-fare customer and a high-fare customer. In reality, this is too simplistic. There surely exist customers that are willing to pay the high fare, but they are also more than willing to book at the low fare if given the opportunity. Hence, fences are used to separate out customers by their willingness to pay. Well-known fences include advance purchase requirements, cancellation fees, change fees, Saturday night stay requirements, and so on. But these fences are not perfect; that is, they do not perfectly segment out customers. As a result, there is often spillover demand from one fare class to another. It is possible that more effective fences exist, but some fences might generate stiff resistance from customers. For example, a firm could regulate a customer's access to various fare classes based on his or her annual income, or the average price the customer paid in past service encounters, but those schemes will surely not receive a warm reception.

Multiple Fare Classes

In our application of revenue management, we have two fare classes: a low fare and a high fare. In reality there can be many more fare classes. With multiple fare classes, it becomes necessary to forecast demand for each fare class and to establish multiple booking limits.

Software Implementation

While the investment in revenue management software is often reasonable relative to the potential revenue gain, it is nevertheless not zero. Furthermore, revenue management systems often have been constrained by the capabilities of the reservation systems they must work with. In other words, while the revenue management software might be able to make a decision as to whether a fare class should be open or closed (i.e., whether to accept a request for a reservation at a particular fare), it also must be able to communicate that decision to the travel agent or customer via the reservation system. Finally, there can even be glitches in the revenue management software, as was painfully discovered by American Airlines. Their initial software had an error that prematurely closed down the low-fare class on flights with many empty seats (i.e., it set the low-fare class booking limit too low). American Airlines discovered the error only when they realized that the load on those flights was too low (the load is the percent of seats occupied; it is the utilization of the aircraft). By that time it was estimated $50 million in revenue had been lost. Hence, properly chosen booking limits can increase revenue, but poorly chosen booking limits can decrease revenue. As a result, careful observation of a revenue management system is always necessary.

Variation in Capacity Purchase: Not All Customers Purchase One Unit of Capacity

Even if two customers pay the same fare, they might be different from the firm's perspective. For example, suppose one leisure traveler requests one night at the low fare whereas another requests five nights at the low fare. While these customers pay the same amount for a given night, it is intuitive that turning away the second customer is more costly. In fact, it may even be costlier than turning away a single high-fare reservation.

Airlines experience a challenge similar to a hotel's multinight customer. Consider two passengers traveling from Chicago (O'Hare) to New York (JFK) paying the discount fare. For one passenger JFK is the final destination, whereas the other passenger will fly from JFK to London (Heathrow) on another flight with the same airline. The revenue management system should recognize that a multileg passenger is more valuable than a single-leg customer. But booking limits just defined for each fare class on the O'Hare–JFK segment do not differentiate between these two customers. In other words, the simplest version of revenue management does *single-leg* or *single-segment control* because the decision rules are focused on the fares of a particular segment in the airline's network. Our example from the Hyatt could be described as *single-night control* because the focus is on a room for one evening.

One solution to the multileg issue is to create a booking limit for each fare class–itinerary combination, not just a booking limit for each fare class on each segment. This is called *origin-destination control,* or *O-D control* for short. For example, suppose there are three fare classes, Y, M, Q (from highest to lowest), on two itineraries, O'Hare–JFK and O'Hare–Heathrow (via JFK):

Fare Class	O'Hare to JFK	O'Hare to Heathrow
Y	$724	$1,610
M	475	829
Q	275	525

Six booking limits could be constructed to manage the inventory on the O'Hare–JFK leg. For example:

Fare Class	O'Hare to JFK	O'Hare to Heathrow
Y		100
M		68
Y	60	
Q		40
M	35	
Q	20	

Hence, it would be possible to deny a Q fare request to an O'Hare–JFK passenger while accepting a Q fare request to an O'Hare–Heathrow passenger: There could be 20 Q fare reservations on the O'Hare–JFK itinerary but fewer than 40 reservations between the M and Q fares on the O'Hare–JFK itinerary and the Q fare on the O'Hare–Heathrow itinerary. If there were only three booking limits on that leg, then all Q fare requests are either accepted or rejected, but it is not possible to accept some Q fare requests while denying others.

While creating a booking limit for each fare class–itinerary combination sounds like a good idea, unfortunately, it is not a practical idea for most revenue management applications. For example, there could be thousands of possible itineraries that use the O'Hare–JFK leg. It would be a computational nightmare to derive booking limits for such a number of itineraries on each possible flight leg, not to mention an implementation challenge. One solution to this problem is *virtual nesting*. With virtual nesting, a limited number of *buckets* are created, each with its own booking limit, each with its own set of fare class–itinerary combinations. Fare class–itinerary combinations are assigned to buckets in such a way that the fare class–itinerary combinations within the same bucket have similar value to the firm, while fare class–itinerary combinations in different buckets have significantly different values.

For example, four buckets could be created for our example, labeled 0 to 3:

Bucket	Itinerary	Fare class
0	O'Hare to Heathrow	Y
1	O'Hare to Heathrow	M
	O'Hare to JFK	Y
2	O'Hare to Heathrow	Q
	O'Hare to JFK	M
3	O'Hare to JFK	Q

The O'Hare–JFK Y fare is combined into one bucket with the O'Hare–Heathrow M fare because they generate similar revenue ($724 and $829), whereas the O'Hare–Heathrow Y fare is given its own bucket due to its much higher revenue ($1,610). Thus, with virtual nesting, it is possible to differentiate among the customers on the same leg willing to pay the same fare. Furthermore, virtual nesting provides a manageable solution if there are many different fare classes and many different types of customers (e.g., customers flying different itineraries or customers staying a different number of nights in a hotel).

While virtual nesting was the first solution implemented for this issue, it is not the only solution. A more recent, and more sophisticated, solution is called *bid-price control.* Let's explain bid-price controls in the context of our airline example. The many different itineraries that use the O'Hare–JFK segment generate different revenue to the airline, but they all use the same unit of capacity, a coach seat on the O'Hare to JFK flight. With bid-price control, each type of capacity on each flight segment is assigned a *bid price*. Then, a fare class–itinerary combination is accepted as long as its fare exceeds the sum of the bid prices of the flight legs in its itinerary. For example, the bid prices could be

	O'Hare to JFK	JFK to Heathrow
Bid price	$290	$170

Hence, an O'Hare–JFK itinerary is available as long as its fare exceeds $290 and an O'Hare–Heathrow itinerary (via JFK) is available as long as its fare exceeds $290 + $170 = $460. Therefore, on the O'Hare–JFK itinerary, the Y and M fare classes would be open (fares $724 and $475, respectively); while on the O'Hare–Heathrow itinerary, all fares would be available (because the lowest Q fare, $525, exceeds the total bid price of $460).

With bid-price control, there is a single bid price on each flight segment, so it is a relatively intuitive and straightforward technique to implement. The challenge with bid-price control is to find the correct bid prices. That challenge requires the use of sophisticated optimization techniques.

18.5 Summary

Revenue management is the science of using pricing and capacity controls to maximize revenue given a relatively fixed supply/capacity. This chapter focuses on the capacity control tools of revenue management: protection levels/booking limits and overbooking. Protection levels/booking limits take advantage of the price differences between fares and the generally staggered nature of demand arrivals; that is, low-fare reservations made by leisure travelers usually occur before high-fare reservations made by business travelers. By establishing a booking limit for low fares, it is possible to protect enough capacity for the later-arriving high fares. Overbooking is useful when customer reservations are not firm; if a portion of the customers can be expected to not use the capacity they reserved, then it is wise to accept more reservations than available capacity.

The science of revenue management is indeed quite complex and continues to be an extremely active area of research. Despite these challenges, revenue management has been proven to be a robust and profitable tool, as reflected in the following quote by Robert Crandall, former CEO of AMR and American Airlines (Smith, Leimkuhler, and Darrow, 1992):

> I believe that revenue management is the single most important technical development in transportation management since we entered the era of airline deregulation in 1979. . . . The development of revenue management models was a key to American Airlines' survival in the post-deregulation environment. Without revenue management we were often faced with two unsatisfactory responses in a price competitive marketplace. We could match deeply discounted fares and risk diluting our entire inventory, or we could not match and certainly lose market share. Revenue management gave us a third alternative—match deeply discounted fares on a portion of our inventory and close deeply discounted inventory when it is profitable to save space for later-booking higher value customers. By adjusting the number of reservations which are available at these discounts, we can adjust our minimum available fare to account for differences in demand. This creates a pricing structure which responds to demand on a flight-by-flight basis. As a result, we can more effectively match our demand to supply.

Table 18.4 provides a summary of the key notation and equations presented in this chapter.

TABLE 18.4 Summary of Key Notation and Equations in Chapter 18

Choosing protection levels and booking limits:

With two fares, r_h = high fare and r_l = low fare, the high-fare protection level Q has the following critical ratio:

$$\text{Critical ratio} = \frac{C_u}{C_o + C_u} = \frac{r_h - r_l}{r_h}$$

(Find the Q such that the critical ratio is the probability high-fare demand is less than or equal to Q.)

Low-fare booking limit = Capacity − Q

Choosing an overbooking quantity Y:

Let r_l be the low fare. The optimal overbooking quantity Y has the following critical ratio:

$$\text{Critical ratio} = \frac{C_u}{C_o + C_u} = \frac{r_l}{\text{Cost per bumped customer} + r_l}$$

18.6 Further Reading

For a brief history of the development of revenue management, see Cross (1995). For a more extensive history, see Cross (1997). Cross (1997) also provides a detailed overview of revenue management techniques.

See Talluri and van Ryzin (2004) for an extensive treatment of the state of the art in revenue management for both theory and practice. Two already-published reviews on the theory of revenue management are McGill and van Ryzin (1999) and Weatherford and Bodily (1992).

Applications of revenue management to car rentals, golf courses, and restaurants can be found in Geraghty and Johnson (1997); Kimes (2000); and Kimes, Chase, Choi, Lee, and Ngonzi (1998).

18.7 Practice Problems

The following questions will help in testing your understanding of this chapter. After each question, we show the relevant section in parentheses [Section x].

Solutions to problems marked with an "*" are available in Appendix E. Video solutions to select problems are available in Connect.

Q18.1* (**The Inn at Penn**) The Inn at Penn hotel has 150 rooms with standard queen-size beds and two rates: a full price of $200 and a discount price of $120. To receive the discount price, a customer must purchase the room at least two weeks in advance (this helps to distinguish between leisure travelers, who tend to book early, and business travelers, who value the flexibility of booking late). For a particular Tuesday night, the hotel estimates that the demand from leisure travelers could fill the whole hotel while the demand from business travelers is distributed normally with a mean of 70 rooms and a standard deviation of 29.

a. Suppose 50 rooms are protected for full-price rooms. What is the booking limit for the discount rooms? [18.2]

b. Find the optimal protection level for full-price rooms (the number of rooms to be protected from sale at a discount price). [18.2]

c. The Sheraton declared a fare war by slashing business travelers' prices down to $150. The Inn at Penn had to match that fare to keep demand at the same level. Does the optimal protection level increase, decrease, or remain the same? Explain your answer. [18.2]

d. What number of rooms (on average) remain unfilled if we establish a protection level of 61 for the full-priced rooms? [18.2]

e. If The Inn were able to ensure that every full-price customer would receive a room, what would The Inn's expected revenue be? [18.2]

f. If The Inn did not choose to protect any rooms for the full price and leisure travelers book before business travelers, then what would The Inn's expected revenue be? [18.2]

g. Taking the assumptions in part f and assuming now that The Inn protects 50 rooms for the full price, what is The Inn's expected revenue? [18.2]

Q18.2* (**Overbooking The Inn at Penn**) Due to customer no-shows, The Inn at Penn hotel is considering implementing overbooking. Recall from Q18.1 that The Inn at Penn has 150 rooms, the full fare is $200, and the discount fare is $120. The forecast of no-shows is Poisson with a mean of 15.5. The distribution and loss functions of that distribution are as follows:

Y	*F*(*Y*)	*I*(*Y*)	*Y*	*F*(*Y*)	*I*(*Y*)	*Y*	*F*(*Y*)	*I*(*Y*)
8	0.0288	0.02	14	0.4154	0.90	20	0.8944	4.78
9	0.0552	0.05	15	0.5170	1.32	21	0.9304	5.68
10	0.0961	0.11	16	0.6154	1.83	22	0.9558	6.61
11	0.1538	0.20	17	0.7052	2.45	23	0.9730	7.56
12	0.2283	0.36	18	0.7825	3.15	24	0.9840	8.54
13	0.3171	0.58	19	0.8455	3.94	25	0.9909	9.52

The Inn is sensitive about the quality of service it provides alumni, so it estimates the cost of failing to honor a reservation is $325 in lost goodwill and explicit expenses.

a. What is the optimal overbooking limit; that is, the maximum reservations above the available 150 rooms that The Inn should accept? [18.3]

b. If The Inn accepts 160 reservations, what is the probability The Inn will not be able to honor a reservation? [18.3]

c. If The Inn accepts 165 reservations, what is the probability The Inn will be fully occupied? [18.3]

d. If The Inn accepts 170 reservations, what is the expected total cost incurred due to bumped customers? [18.3]

Q18.3* (**WAMB**) WAMB is a television station that has 25 thirty-second advertising slots during each evening. It is early January and the station is selling advertising for Sunday, March 24. They could sell all of the slots right now for $4,000 each, but, because on this particular Sunday the station is televising the Oscar ceremonies, there will be an opportunity to sell slots during the week right before March 24 for a price of $10,000. For now, assume that a slot not sold in advance *and* not sold during the last week is worthless to WAMB. To help make this decision, the salesforce has created the following probability distribution for last-minute sales:

Number of Slots, *x*	Probability Exactly *x* Slots Are Sold
8	0.00
9	0.05
10	0.10
11	0.15
12	0.20
13	0.10
14	0.10
15	0.10
16	0.10
17	0.05
18	0.05
19	0.00

a. How many slots should WAMB sell in advance? [18.2]

b. In practice, there are companies willing to place standby advertising messages: If there is an empty slot available (i.e., this slot was not sold either in advance or during the last week), the standby message is placed into this slot. Since there is no guarantee that such a slot will be available, standby messages can be placed at a much lower cost. Now suppose that if a slot is not sold in advance *and* not sold during the last week, it will be used for a standby promotional message that costs advertisers $2,500. Now how many slots should WAMB sell in advance? [18.2]

c. Suppose WAMB chooses a booking limit of 10 slots on advanced sales. In this case, what is the probability there will be slots left over for standby messages? [18.2]

d. One problem with booking for March 24 in early January is that advertisers often withdraw their commitment to place the ad (typically this is a result of changes in promotional strategies; for example, a product may be found to be inferior or an ad may turn out to be ineffective). Because of such opportunistic behavior by advertisers, media companies often overbook advertising slots. WAMB estimates that in the past the number of withdrawn ads has a Poisson distribution with mean 9. Assume each withdrawn ad slot can still be sold at a standby price of $2,500 although the company misses an opportunity to sell these slots at $4,000 apiece. Any ad that was accepted by WAMB but cannot be accommodated (because there isn't a free slot) costs the company $10,000 in penalties. How many slots (at most) should be sold? [18.3]

e. Over time, WAMB saw a steady increase in the number of withdrawn ads and decided to institute a penalty of $1,000 for withdrawals. (Actually, the company now requires a $1,000 deposit on any slot. It is refunded only if WAMB is unable to provide a slot due to overbooking.) The expected number of withdrawn ads is expected to be cut in half (to only 4.5 slots). Now how many slots (at most) should be sold? [18.3]

Q18.4* **(Designer Dress)** A fashion retailer in Santa Barbara, California, presents a new designer dress at one of the "by invitation only" fashion shows. After the show, the dress will be sold at the company's boutique store for $10,000. Demand at the boutique is limited due to the short time the dress remains fashionable and is estimated to be normal with mean 70 and standard deviation 40. There were only 100 dresses produced to maintain exclusivity and high price. It is the company's policy that all unsold merchandise is destroyed.

a. How many dresses remain unsold on average at the end of the season? [18.2]

b. What is the retailer's expected revenue? [18.2]

c. Fashion companies often sell a portion of new merchandise at exhibitions for a discount while the product is still "fresh" in the minds of the viewers. The company decides to increase revenues by selling a certain number of dresses at a greatly discounted price of $6,000 during the show. Later, remaining dresses will be available at the boutique store for a normal price of $10,000. Typically, all dresses offered at the show get sold, which, of course, decreases demand at the store: It is now normal with mean 40 and standard deviation 25. How many dresses should be sold at the show? [18.2]

d. Given your decision in part c, what is expected revenue? [18.2]

e. Given your decision in part c, how many dresses are expected to remain unsold? [18.2]

Q18.5* **(Overbooking PHL–LAX)** On a given Philadelphia–Los Angeles flight, there are 200 seats. Suppose the ticket price is $475 on average and the number of passengers who reserve a seat but do not show up for departure is normally distributed with mean 30 and standard deviation 15. You decide to overbook the flight and estimate that the average loss from a passenger who will have to be bumped (if the number of passengers exceeds the number of seats) is $800.

a. What is the maximum number of reservations that should be accepted? [18.3]

b. Suppose you allow 220 reservations. How much money do you expect to pay out in compensation to bumped passengers? [18.3]

c. Suppose you allow 220 reservations. What is the probability that you will have to deal with bumped passengers? [18.3]

Q18.6 **(PHL–LAX)** Consider the Philadelphia–Los Angeles flight discussed in Q18.5. Assume the available capacity is 200 seats and there is no overbooking. The high fare is $675 and the low fare is $375. Demand for the low fare is abundant while demand for the high fare is normally distributed with a mean of 80 and standard deviation of 35.

a. What is the probability of selling 200 reservations if you set an optimal protection level for the full fare? [18.2]

b. Suppose a protection level of 85 is established. What is the average number of lost high-fare passengers? [18.2]

c. Continue to assume a protection level of 85 is established. What is the expected number of unoccupied seats? [18.2]

d. Again assume a protection level of 85 is established. What is the expected revenue from the flight? [18.2]

Q18.7 **(Annenberg)** Ron, the director at the Annenberg Center, is planning his pricing strategy for a musical to be held in a 100-seat theater. He sets the full price at $80 and estimates demand at this price to be normally distributed with mean 40 and standard deviation 30. Ron also decides to offer student-only advance sale tickets discounted 50 percent off the full price. Demand for the discounted student-only tickets is usually abundant and occurs well before full-price ticket sales.

a. Suppose Ron sets a 50-seat booking limit for the student-only tickets. What is the number of full-price tickets that Ron expects to sell? [18.2]

b. Based on a review of the show in another city, Ron updates his demand forecast for full-price tickets to be normal with mean 60 and standard deviation 40, but he does not change the prices. What is the optimal protection level for full-price seats? [18.2]

c. Ron realizes that having many empty seats negatively affects the attendees' value from the show. Hence, he decides to change the discount given on student-only tickets from 50 percent off the full price to 55 percent off the full price and he continues to set his protection level optimally. (The demand forecast for full-price tickets remains as in b, normal with mean 60 and standard deviation 40.) How will this change in the student-only discount price affect the expected number of empty seats? (Will they increase, decrease, or remain the same, or is it not possible to determine what will happen?) [18.2]

d. Ron knows that on average eight seats (Poisson distributed) remain empty due to no-shows. Ron also estimates that it is 10 times more costly for him to have one more attendee than seats relative to having one empty seat in the theater. What is the maximum number of seats to sell in excess of capacity? [18.3]

Q18.8 (**Park Hyatt**) Consider the example of the Park Hyatt Philadelphia discussed in the text. Recall that the full fare is $225, the expected full-fare demand is Poisson with mean 27.3, the discount fare is $159, and there are 118 king/queen rooms. Now suppose the cost of an occupied room is $45 per night. That cost includes the labor associated with prepping and cleaning a room, the additional utilities used, and the wear and tear on the furniture and fixtures. Suppose the Park Hyatt wishes to maximize expected profit rather than expected revenue. What is the optimal protection level for the full fare? [18.2]

Q18.9 (**MBA Admissions**) Each year the admissions committee at a top business school receives a large number of applications for admission to the MBA program and they have to decide on the number of offers to make. Since some of the admitted students may decide to pursue other opportunities, the committee typically admits more students than the ideal class size of 720 students. You were asked to help the admissions committee estimate the appropriate number of people who should be offered admission. It is estimated that in the coming year the number of people who will not accept the admission offer is normally distributed with mean 50 and standard deviation 21. Suppose for now that the school does not maintain a waiting list; that is, all students are accepted or rejected.

a. Suppose 750 students are admitted. What is the probability that the class size will be at least 720 students? [18.2]

b. It is hard to associate a monetary value with admitting too many students or admitting too few. However, there is a mutual agreement that it is about two times more expensive to have a student in excess of the ideal 720 than to have fewer students in the class. What is the appropriate number of students to admit? [18.3]

c. A waiting list mitigates the problem of having too few students since at the very last moment there is an opportunity to admit some students from the waiting list. Hence, the admissions committee revises its estimate: It claims that it is five times more expensive to have a student in excess of 720 than to have fewer students accept among the initial group of admitted students. What is your revised suggestion? [18.3]

Q18.10 **(Air Cargo)** An air cargo company must decide how to sell its capacity. It could sell a portion of its capacity with long-term contracts. A long-term contract specifies that the buyer (the air cargo company's customer) will purchase a certain amount of cargo space at a certain price. The long-term contract rate is currently $1,875 per standard unit of space. If long-term contracts are not signed, then the company can sell its space on the spot market. The spot market price is volatile, but the expected future spot price is around $2,100. In addition, spot market demand is volatile: Sometimes the company can find customers; other times it cannot on a short-term basis. Let's consider a specific flight on a specific date. The company's capacity is 58 units. Furthermore, the company expects that spot market demand is normally distributed with mean 65 and standard deviation 45. On average, it costs the company $330 in fuel, handling, and maintenance to fly a unit of cargo.

a. Suppose the company relied exclusively on the spot market; that is, it signed no long-term contracts. What would be the company's expected profit? [18.2]

b. Suppose the company relied exclusively on long-term contracts. What would be the company's expected profit? [18.2]

c. Suppose the company is willing to use both the long-term and the spot markets. How many units of capacity should the company sell with long-term contracts to maximize *revenue*? [18.2]

d. Suppose the company is willing to use both the long-term and the spot markets. How many units of capacity should the company sell with long-term contracts to maximize *profit*? [18.2]

Chapter 19

Supply Chain Coordination

Supply chain performance depends on the actions taken by all of the organizations in the supply chain; one weak link can negatively affect every other location in the chain. While everyone supports in principle the objective of optimizing the supply chain's performance, each firm's primary objective is the optimization of its own performance. And unfortunately, as shown in this chapter, self-serving behavior by each member of the supply chain can lead to less than optimal supply chain performance. In those situations, the firms in the supply chain can benefit from better operational coordination.

In this chapter we explore several challenges to supply chain coordination. The first challenge is the *bullwhip effect:* the tendency for demand variability to increase, often considerably, as you move up the supply chain (from retailer, to distributor, to factory, to raw material suppliers, etc.). Given that variability in any form is problematic for effective operations, it is clear the bullwhip effect is not a desirable phenomenon. We identify the causes of the bullwhip effect and propose several techniques to combat it.

A second challenge to supply chain coordination comes from the *incentive conflicts* among the supply chain's independent firms: An action that maximizes one firm's profit might not maximize another firm's profit. For example, one firm's incentive to stock more inventory, or to install more capacity, or to provide faster customer service, might not be the same as another firm's incentive, thereby creating some conflict between them. We use a stylized example of a supply chain selling sunglasses to illustrate the presence and consequences of incentive conflicts. Furthermore, we offer several remedies to this problem.

19.1 The Bullwhip Effect: Causes and Consequences

Barilla is a leading Italian manufacturer of pasta. Figure 19.1 plots outbound shipments of pasta from its Cortese distribution center over a one-year period along with the orders Cortese placed on Barilla's upstream factories. Think of the outbound shipments as what was demanded of Cortese by its downstream customers and the orders as what Cortese demanded from its upstream suppliers. Clearly, Cortese's demand on its upstream suppliers is more volatile than the demand Cortese faces from its customers.

This pattern, in which a stage in the supply chain amplifies the volatility of its orders relative to its demand, is called the *bullwhip effect*. If there are several stages (or levels) in the supply chain (e.g., retailer, wholesaler, distributor, factory), then this amplification

FIGURE 19.1
Barilla's Cortese Distribution Center Orders and Shipments

Source: Harvard Business School, Barilla Spa case.

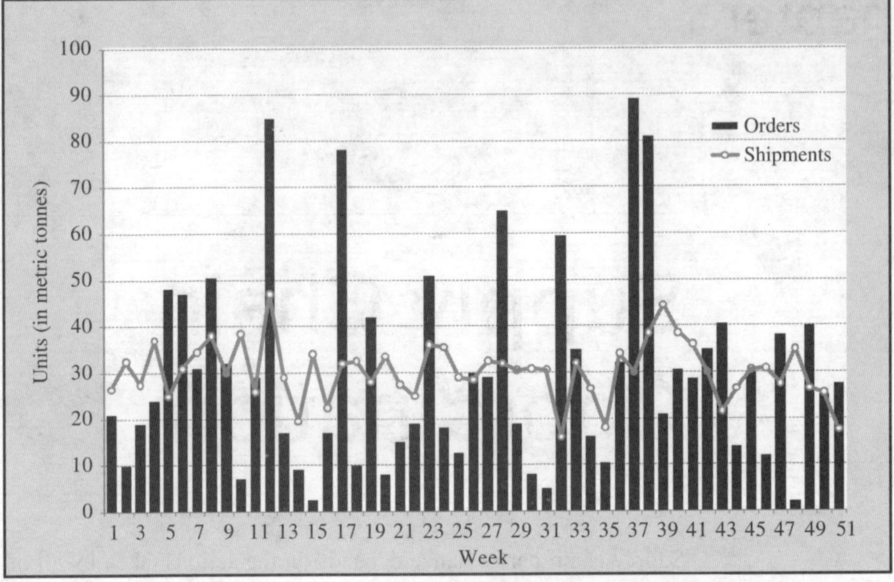

can feed on itself—one level further amplifies the amplified volatility of its downstream customer. This accentuation of volatility resembles the increased amplitude one observes as a whip is cracked—hence the name, the bullwhip effect. In fact, Procter & Gamble coined the term to describe what they observed in their diaper supply chain: They knew that final demand for diapers was reasonably stable (consumption by babies), but the demands requested on their diaper factories were extremely variable. Somehow variability was propagating up their supply chain.

The bullwhip effect does not enhance the performance of a supply chain: Increased volatility at any point in the supply chain can lead to product shortages, excess inventory, low utilization of capacity, and/or poor quality. It impacts upstream stages in the supply chain, which must directly face the impact of variable demand, but it also indirectly affects downstream stages in the supply chain, which must cope with less reliable replenishments from upstream stages. Hence, it is extremely important that its causes be identified so that cures, or at least mitigating strategies, can be developed.

Figure 19.1 provides a real-world example of the bullwhip effect, but to understand the causes of the bullwhip effect, it is helpful to bring it into the laboratory; that is, to study it in a controlled environment. Our controlled environment is a simple supply chain with two levels. The top level has a single supplier and the next level has 20 retailers, each with one store. Let's focus on a single product, a product in which daily demand has a Poisson distribution with mean 1.0 unit at each retailer. Hence, total consumer demand follows a Poisson distribution with mean 20.0 units. (Recall that the sum of Poisson distributions is also a Poisson distribution.) Figure 19.2 displays this supply chain.

Before we can identify the causes of the bullwhip effect, we must agree on how we will measure and identify it. We use the following definition:

The bullwhip effect is present in a supply chain if the variability of demand at one level of the supply chain is greater than the variability of demand at the next downstream level in the supply chain, where variability is measured with the coefficient of variation.

For example, if the coefficient of variation in the supplier's demand (which is the sum of the retailers' orders) is greater than the coefficient of variation of the retailers' total demand, then the bullwhip effect is present in our supply chain.

FIGURE 19.2
A Supply Chain with One Supplier and 20 Retailers

Daily demand at each retailer follows a Poisson distribution with mean 1.0 unit.

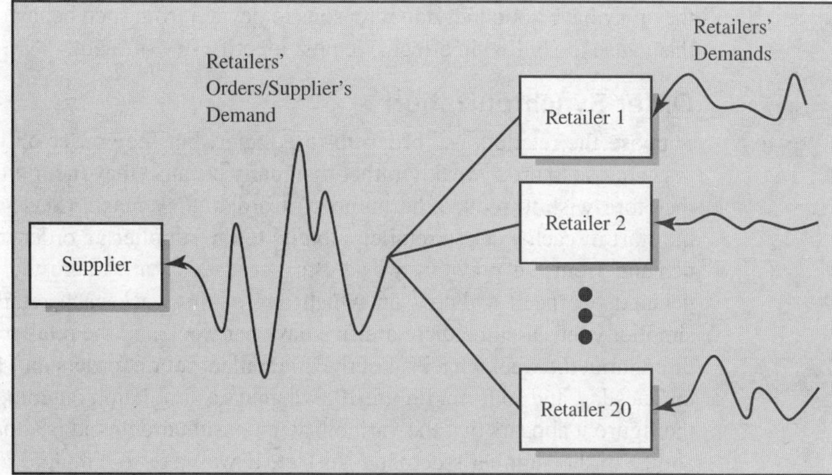

We already know how to evaluate the coefficient of variation in the retailers' total demand: Total demand is Poisson with mean 20, so the standard deviation of demand is $\sqrt{20} = 4.47$ and the coefficient of variation is $4.47/20 = 0.22$. The coefficient of variation of the supplier's demand (i.e., the coefficient of variation of the retailers' orders) depends on how the retailers place orders with the supplier.

Interestingly, while the way in which the retailers submit orders to the supplier can influence the standard deviation of the retailers' orders, it cannot influence the mean of the retailers' orders. To explain, due to the law of the conservation of matter, what goes into a retailer must equal what goes out of the retailer on average; otherwise, the amount inside the retailer will not be stable: If more goes in than goes out, then the inventory at the retailer continues to grow, whereas if less goes in than goes out, then inventory at the retailer continues to fall. Hence, no matter how the retailers choose to order inventory from the supplier, the mean of the supplier's demand (i.e., the retailers' total order) equals the mean of the retailers' total demand. In this case, the supplier's mean demand is 20 units per day, just as the mean of consumer demand is 20 units per day. We can observe this in Figure 19.1 as well: Cortese's average shipment is about 30 tonnes and their average order is also about 30 tonnes.

To evaluate the coefficient of variation in the supplier's demand, we still need to evaluate the standard deviation of the supplier's demand, which does depend on how the retailers submit orders. Let's first suppose that the retailers use an order-up-to policy to order replenishments from the supplier.

A key characteristic of an order-up-to policy is that the amount ordered in any period equals the amount demanded in the previous period (see Chapter 16). As a result, if all of the retailers use order-up-to policies with daily review, then their daily orders will match their daily demands. In other words, there is no bullwhip effect!

If all retailers use an order-up-to policy (with a constant order-up-to level S *), then the standard deviation of the retailers' orders in one period equals the standard deviation of consumer demand in one period; that is, there is no bullwhip effect.*

So we started our experiment with the intention of finding a cause of the bullwhip effect and discovered that the bullwhip effect need not occur in practice. It does not occur when every member at the same level of the supply chain implements a "*demand-pull*" inventory policy each period; that is, their orders each period exactly match their demands. Unfortunately, firms do not always adopt such "distortion-free" inventory management. In fact, they may have good individual reasons to deviate from such behavior. It is those deviations that cause the bullwhip effect. We next identify five of them.

Order Synchronization

Suppose the retailers use order-up-to policies, but they order only once per week. They may choose to order weekly rather than daily because they incur a fixed cost per order and therefore wish to reduce the number of orders they make. (See Section 16.8.) Hence, at the start of each week, a retailer submits to the supplier an order that equals the retailer's demand from the previous week. But because we are interested in the supplier's *daily* demand, we need to know on which day of the week each retailer's week begins. For simplicity let's assume there are five days per week and the retailers are evenly spaced out throughout the week; that is, 4 of the 20 retailers submit orders on Monday, 4 submit orders on Tuesday, and so forth. Figure 19.3 displays a simulation outcome of this scenario. From the figure it appears that the variability in consumer demand is about the same as the variability in the supplier's demand. In fact, if we were to simulate many more periods and evaluate the standard deviations of those two data series, we would, in fact, discover that the standard deviation of consumer demand *exactly* equals the standard deviation of the supplier's demand. In other words, we still have not found the bullwhip effect.

But we made a critical assumption in our simulation. We assumed the retailers' order cycles were evenly spaced throughout the week: The same number of retailers order on Monday as on Wednesday as on Friday. But that is unlikely to be the case in practice: Firms tend to prefer to submit their orders on a particular day of the week or a particular day of the month. To illustrate the consequence of this preference, let's suppose the retailers tend to favor the beginning and the end of the week: Nine retailers order on Monday, five on Tuesday, one on Wednesday, two on Thursday, and three on Friday. Figure 19.4 displays the simulation outcome with that scenario.

We have discovered the bullwhip effect! The supplier's daily demand is clearly much more variable than consumer demand. For this particular sample, the coefficient of variation of the supplier's demand is 0.78 even though the coefficient of variation of consumer demand is only 0.19: The supplier's demand is about four times more variable than consumer demand! And this is not the result of a particularly strange demand pattern; that is,

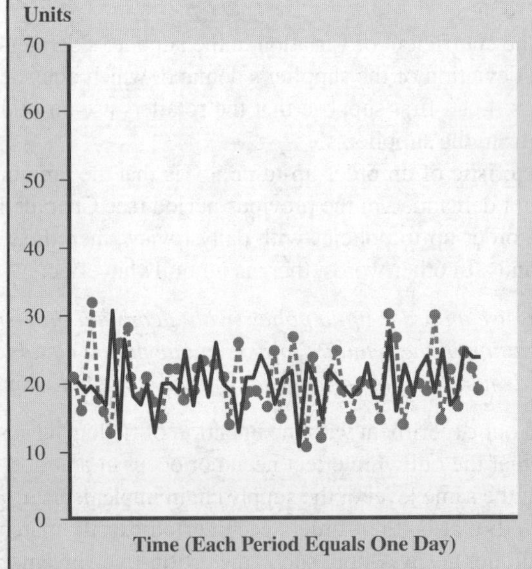

FIGURE 19.3
Simulated Daily Consumer Demand (solid line) and Daily Supplier Demand (circles)

Supplier demand equals the sum of the retailers' orders.

FIGURE 19.4
Simulated Daily Consumer Demand (solid line) and Supplier Demand (circles) When Retailers Order Weekly

Nine retailers order on Monday, five on Tuesday, one on Wednesday, two on Thursday, and three on Friday.

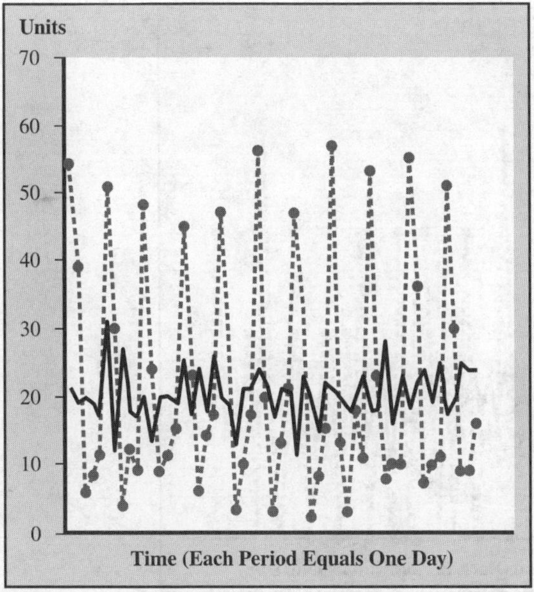

the same qualitative result is obtained if a very long interval of time is simulated. In fact, for comparison, you can note that the consumer demand in Figure 19.4 is identical to consumer demand in Figure 19.3.

Not only do we now observe the bullwhip effect, we have just identified one of its causes, *order synchronization:* If the retailers' order cycles become even a little bit synchronized, that is, they tend to cluster around the same time period, then the bullwhip effect emerges. While the retailers order on average to match average consumer demand, due to their order synchronization there will be periods in which they order considerably more than the average and periods in which they order considerably less than the average, thereby imposing additional demand volatility on the supplier.

Order synchronization also can be observed higher up in the supply chain. For example, suppose the supplier implements a materials requirement planning (MRP) system to manage the replenishment of component inventory. (This is a computer system that determines the quantity and timing of component inventory replenishments based on future demand forecasts and production schedules.) Many firms implement their MRP systems on a monthly basis. Furthermore, many implement their systems to generate replenishment orders in the first week of the month. So a supplier's supplier may receive a flood of orders for its product during the first week of the month and relatively little demand later in the month. This has been called *MRP jitters* or the *hockey stick phenomenon* (the graph of demand over the month looks like a series of hockey sticks, a flat portion and then a spike up).

Order Batching

We argued that the retailers might wish to order weekly rather than daily to avoid incurring excessive ordering costs. This economizing on ordering costs also can be achieved by *order batching:* Each retailer orders so that each order is an integer multiple of some batch size. For example, now let's consider a scenario in which each retailer uses a batch size of 15 units. This batch size could represent a case or a pallet or a full truckload. Let's call it a pallet. By ordering only in increments of 15 units, that is, in pallet quantities, the retailer can facilitate the movement of product around the warehouse and the loading of product onto trucks. How does the retailer decide when to order a pallet? A natural rule is to order a batch whenever the accumulated demand since the last order exceeds the batch size.

FIGURE 19.5
Simulated Daily Consumer Demand (solid line) and Supplier Demand (circles) When Retailers Order in Batches of 15 Units

Every 15th demand, a retailer orders one batch from the supplier that contains 15 units.

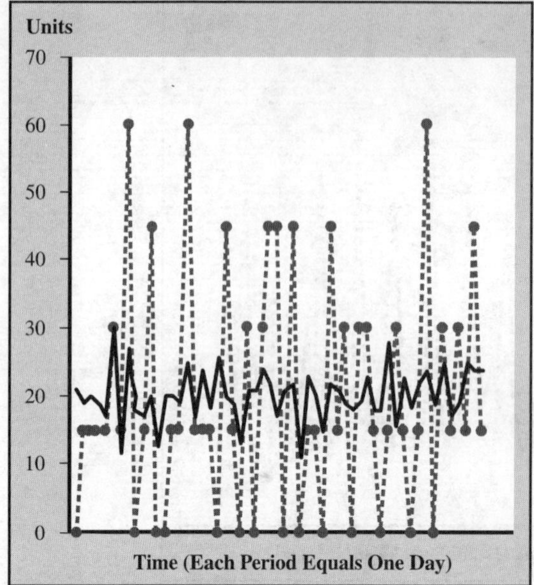

Therefore, in this example, every 15th demand triggers an order for a pallet. Naturally, ordering in batches economizes on the number of orders the retailer must make:

$$\text{Average number of periods between orders} = \frac{\text{Batch size}}{\text{Mean demand per period}}$$

In this situation, the retailer orders on average every 15/1 = 15 periods.

Figure 19.5 displays a simulation outcome with batch ordering. Because the retailers only order in pallet quantities, the supplier's demand equals a multiple of 15: On some days there are no orders, on most days one pallet is ordered by some retailer, on a few days there are up to four pallets ordered.

We again observe the bullwhip effect: The variability of the supplier's demand is considerably greater than the variability of consumer demand. To be specific, the supplier's demand has a coefficient of variation equal to 0.87 in this example, which contrasts with the 0.19 coefficient of variation for consumer demand. Thus, we have identified a second cause of the bullwhip effect, *order batching:* The bullwhip effect emerges when retailers order in batches that contain more than one unit (e.g., pallet quantities or full truckload quantities). Again, the retailers' total order on average equals average consumer demand, but not the variability of their orders. This occurs because, due to the batch quantity requirement, the retailer's order quantity in a period generally does not match the retailer's demand in that period: It tends to be either greater than or less than consumer demand. In other words, the batch quantity requirement forces the retailer to order in a way that is more variable than consumer demand even though, on average, it equals consumer demand.

Trade Promotions and Forward Buying

Suppliers in some industries offer their retailers *trade promotions:* a discount off the wholesale price that is available only for a short period of time. Trade promotions cause retailers to buy on-deal, also referred to as a *forward buy,* which means they purchase much more than they need to meet short-term needs. Trade promotions are a key tool for a supplier when the supplier wants to engage in the practice of *channel stuffing:* providing incentives to induce retailers (the channel) to hold more inventory than needed for

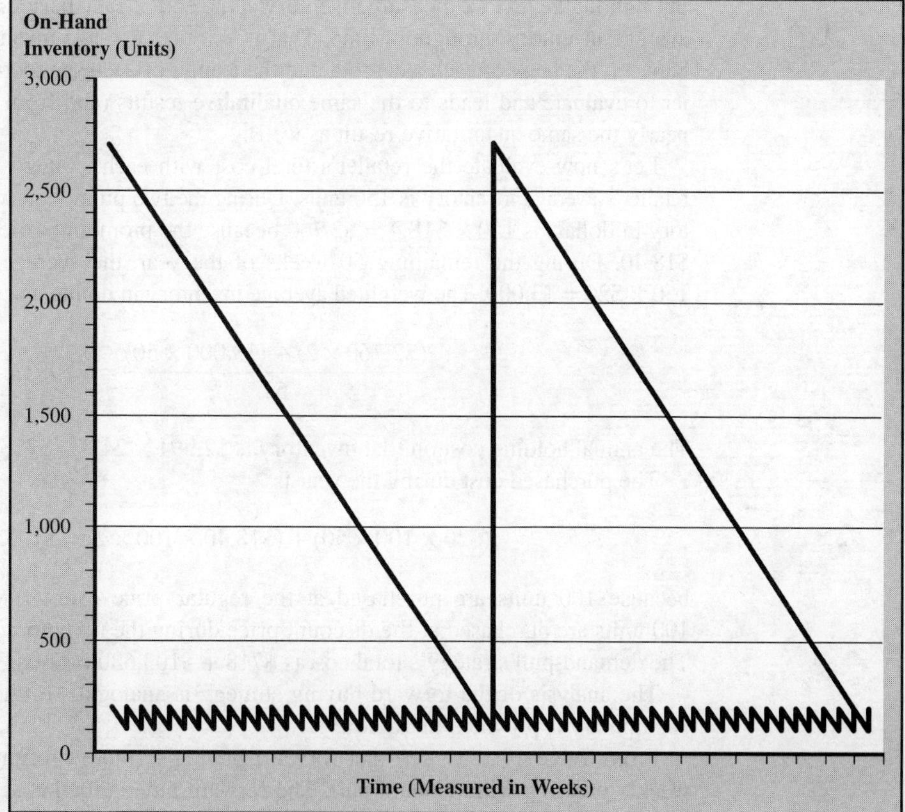

FIGURE 19.6 On-Hand Inventory of Chicken Noodle Soup at a Retailer under Two Procurement Strategies

The first strategy, called demand-pull (lower sawtooth), has the retailer ordering 100 cases each week. The second strategy, called forward buying (upper sawtooth), has the retailer ordering 2,600 cases twice per year.

the short term. Because with trade promotions many retailers purchase at the same time (order synchronization) and because they order in large quantities (order batching), trade promotions are capable of creating an enormous bullwhip. Let's illustrate this with another simple scenario.

Suppose a supplier sells chicken noodle soup; let's consider one of the supplier's retailers. The supplier's regular price of chicken noodle soup is $20 per case, but twice a year the supplier offers an 8 percent discount for cases purchased during a one-week period, for example, the first week in January and the first week in July. The retailer sells on average 100 cases of soup per week and likes to carry a one-week safety stock; that is, the retailer does not let its inventory fall below 100 cases. To avoid unnecessary complications, let's further assume that the retailer's order at the beginning of a week is delivered immediately and demand essentially occurs at a constant rate. The retailer's annual holding cost rate is 24 percent of the dollar value of its inventory.

We now compare the retailer's profit with two different ordering strategies. With the first strategy, the retailer orders every week throughout the year; with the second strategy, the retailer orders only twice per year—during the trade promotion. We call the first strategy *demand-pull* because the retailer matches orders to current demand. The second strategy is called *forward buying* because each order covers a substantial portion of future demand. Figure 19.6 displays the retailer's on-hand inventory over the period of one year with both ordering strategies.

With demand-pull, the retailer's inventory "saw-tooths" between 200 and 100 units, with an average of 150 units. With forward buying, the retailer's inventory also "saw-tooths" but now between 2,700 and 100, with an average of 1,400 units. Note, although throughout the text we measure inventory at the end of each period, here, we are measuring average inventory throughout time. That is, we take average inventory to be the midpoint between the peak of each sawtooth and the trough of each sawtooth. This approach is easier to evaluate and leads to the same qualitative results (and from a practical perspective, nearly the same quantitative result as well).

Let's now evaluate the retailer's total cost with each strategy. With demand-pull, the retailer's average inventory is 150 units. During the two promotion weeks, the average inventory in dollars is $150 \times \$18.4 = \$2,760$ because the promotion price is $\$20 \times (1 - 0.08) = \$18.40$. During the remaining 50 weeks of the year, the average inventory in dollars is $150 \times \$20 = \$3,000$. The weighted average inventory in dollars is

$$\frac{(\$2,760 \times 2) + (\$3,000 \times 50)}{52} = \$2,991$$

The annual holding cost on that inventory is $\$2,991 \times 24\% = \$718$.

The purchased cost during the year is

$$(\$20 \times 100 \times 50) + (\$18.40 \times 100 \times 2) = \$103,680$$

because 100 units are purchased at the regular price over 50 weeks of the year and 100 units are purchased at the discount price during the two promotion weeks of the year. The demand-pull strategy's total cost is $\$718 + \$103,680 = \$104,398$.

The analysis of the forward buying strategy is analogous to the demand-pull strategy. A summary is provided in Table 19.1.

From Table 19.1 we see that forward buying is more profitable to the retailer than weekly ordering with demand-pull: The forward buying total cost is 2.4 percent less than the demand-pull strategy, which is a considerable amount in the grocery industry. We can conclude that a relatively small trade promotion can rationally cause a retailer to purchase a significant volume of product. In fact, the retailer may wish to purchase enough product to cover its demand until the supplier's next promotion. In contrast, it is highly unlikely that an 8 percent discount would induce consumers to purchase a six-month supply of chicken noodle soup; rational retailers are more price sensitive than consumers.

The impact of the trade promotion on the supplier is not good. Imagine the supplier sells to many retailers, all taking advantage of the supplier's trade promotion. Hence, the retailers' orders become synchronized (they order during the same trade promotion weeks of the year) and they order in very large batch quantities (much more than is needed to cover their immediate needs). In other words, trade promotions combine order synchronization and order batching to generate a significant bullwhip effect.

Interestingly, with the forward buying strategy, the retailer does not ever purchase at the regular price. Hence, if the supplier were to offer the retailer the $18.40 price throughout

TABLE 19.1
Analysis of Total Holding and Procurement Costs for Two Ordering Strategies

In demand-pull, the retailer orders every week; in forward buying, the retailer orders twice per year during the supplier's trade promotions.

	Demand-Pull	Forward Buying
Annual purchase (units)	5,200	5,200
Average inventory (units)	150	1,400
Average inventory	$2,991	$25,760
Holding cost (24% of average inventory cost)	$718	$6,182
Units purchased at regular price	5,000	0
Units purchased at discount price	200	5,200
Total purchase cost	$103,680	$95,680
Total holding plus procurement cost	$104,398	$101,862

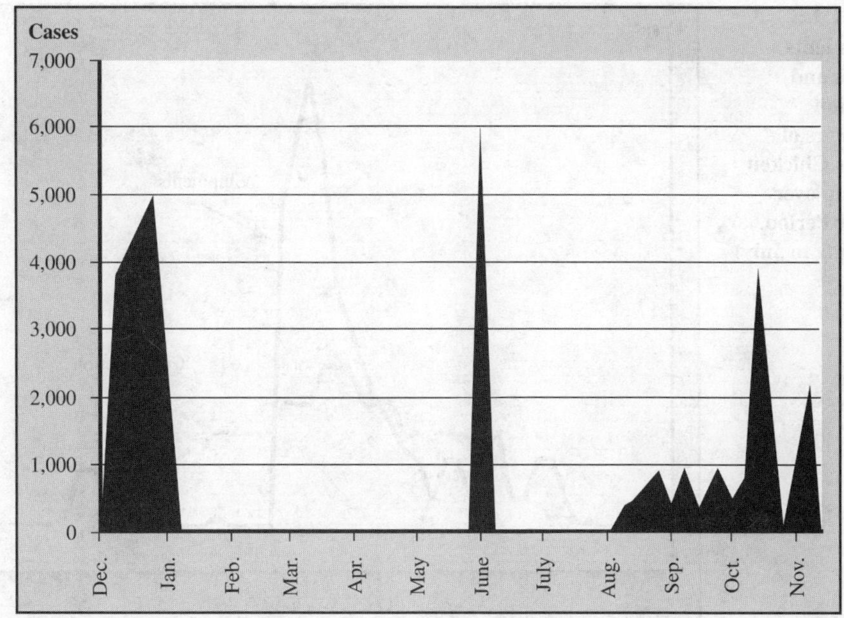

FIGURE 19.7 **One Retailer's Purchases of Campbell's Chicken Noodle Soup over One Year**

the year (instead of just during the two trade promotion weeks), then the supplier's revenue would be the same. However, the retailer could then order on a weekly basis, thereby reducing the retailer's holding cost. It is not too difficult to calculate that the retailer's total cost in this constant-price scenario is $96,342, which is 5.4 percent less than the forward buying cost and 7.7 percent less than the original demand-pull strategy. Thus, due to forward buying, the supply chain's costs are about 5 percent higher than they need be without providing any benefit to the firms in the supply chain (the retailer surely does not benefit from holding extra inventory and the supplier does not benefit from higher revenue).

While our analysis has been with a theoretical supply chain of chicken noodle soup, Campbell Soup would concur that this analysis is consistent with their experience. For example, Figure 19.7 presents data on one retailer's purchases of Campbell's Chicken Noodle Soup over the course of the year. This product is traditionally promoted in January and June even though consumers primarily eat soup during the winter months.[1] As a result, this retailer requires substantial storage space to hold its forward buys. Other retailers may lack the financial and physical capabilities to be so aggressive with forward buying, but they nevertheless will take advantage of trade promotions to some extent. This is confirmed by Figure 19.8, which shows total consumption and shipments of Campbell's Chicken Noodle Soup over a one-year period: Shipments are clearly more volatile than consumption, thereby indicating the presence of the bullwhip effect.

Due to the trade promotion spike in demand in January of every year, Campbell Soup must put its chicken deboning plants on overtime from September through October, its canning plant works overtime November through December, and its shipping facility works overtime throughout January. All of these activities add to production costs, and all because of a spike in demand caused by the company's own pricing.

The negative effects of forward buying also are not limited to the supplier's operational efficiency. Some retailers purchase on-deal with no intention of selling those units to

[1] Campbell's traditionally raises the price of its Chicken Noodle Soup during the summer, so the June buy avoids the imminent price increase. While this is technically not a promotion, the analysis is quite similar and the effect is essentially the same as a trade promotion.

FIGURE 19.8
Total Shipments to Retailers and Consumption by Consumers of Campbell's Chicken Noodle Soup over a One-Year Period (roughly July to July)

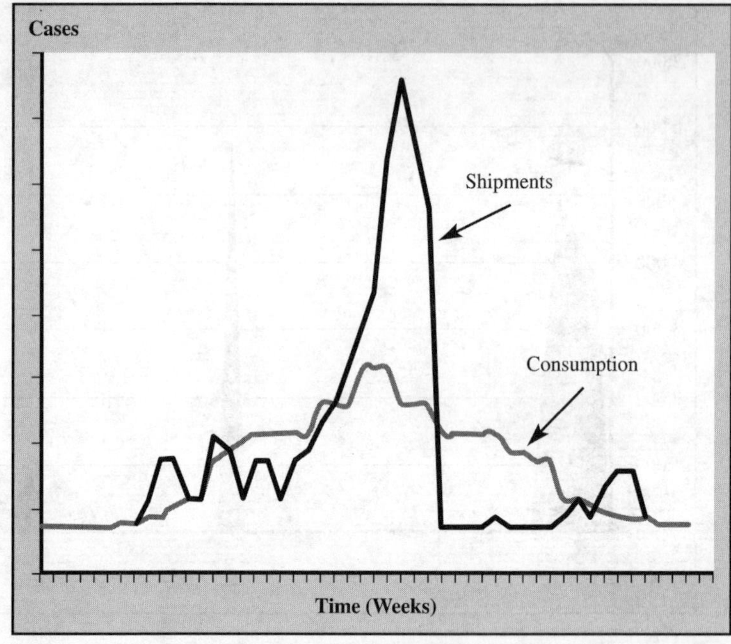

consumers. Instead, they intend on selling to other retailers that cannot take advantage of the deal due to either physical or capital constraints. Those retailers that sell to other retailers are called *diverters* and that practice is called *diversion*. In addition to extra handling (which reduces quality and leads to spoilage), diversion needlessly adds to transportation costs. It also should be mentioned that diversion occurs when a supplier attempts to lower its price in one region of the country while maintaining a higher price in another region, possibly because the supplier faces a regional competitor in the former region. That form of diversion was greatly reduced in the grocery industry when several national grocery chains emerged (Kroger, Safeway, etc.) in the late 1980s and early 1990s. Those national chains insisted that they would receive a single low price from their suppliers, thereby preventing regional price discrimination.

Reactive and Overreactive Ordering

So far in our experimental supply chains, we have assumed the retailer knows what expected demand is in each period even though demand could be stochastic. This is a reasonable assumption for well-established products such as chicken noodle soup. But for many other products, a retailer might not know expected demand with certainty. And this uncertainty creates a complication for the retailer's inventory management.

Suppose the retailer observes higher-than-usual demand in one period. How should the retailer react to this observation? One explanation for this outlier is that it occurred merely due to random fluctuation. In that case, the retailer probably should not change her expectation of future demand and so not change how she manages inventory. But there is another explanation for the outlier: It could signal that demand has shifted, suggesting the product's actual expected demand is higher than previously thought. If that explanation is believed, then the retailer should increase her order quantity to cover the additional future demand; otherwise she will quickly stock out. In other words, it is rational for a retailer to increase her order quantity when faced with an unusually high-demand observation. Analogously, the retailer should decrease her order quantity when faced with an unusually low-demand observation because future demand may be weaker than previously thought. Hence, when a retailer cannot be sure that demand is stable over time, a retailer should rationally react aggressively to possible shifts in demand.

These reactions by the retailer contribute to the bullwhip effect. Suppose the retailer's high-demand observation is really due to random fluctuation. As a result, future demand will not be higher than expected even though the retailer reacted to this information by ordering more inventory. Hence, the retailer will need to reduce future orders so that the excess inventory just purchased can be drawn down. Ordering more than needed now and less than needed later implies the retailer's orders are more volatile than the retailer's demand, which is the bullwhip effect.

While it can be rational to react to extreme demand observations, it is also human nature to *over*react to such information; that is, to act too aggressively. For example, a high-demand signal may rationally warrant a 125 percent increase in a retailer's order quantity, but a retailer may "play it safe" and order 150 percent more just in case. Unfortunately, the retailer might not realize the consequence of this action. Suppose the retailer is replenished by a wholesaler, who is replenished by a distributor, who is replenished by a supplier. The retailer sees a blip in demand and so reacts with a larger order. The retailer's order is the wholesaler's demand, and so the wholesaler sees an even larger blip in demand. The wholesaler reacts and increases his order, which surprises the distributor. So the distributor reacts with an increased order, so large that the supplier only concludes that demand has accelerated substantially. In other words, overreactions can propagate up the supply chain, thereby generating a bullwhip effect.

Shortage Gaming

Under normal circumstances, a retailer will only order as much inventory as needed to cover short-term needs; in particular, the inventory needed to cover demand until the next possible replenishment. But it is not always known when the next possible replenishment will occur. If demand is increasing and capacity is constrained, then a retailer may anticipate a long wait for the next possible replenishment. A rational response is to order plenty of inventory, while inventory is potentially available, in case future replenishment opportunities do not materialize.

Imagine a supply chain with one supplier, a hot-selling product, limited capacity, and multiple retailers. Each retailer knows capacity is tight: While it is possible the supplier will have enough capacity to fill all of the retailers' orders, it is quite likely the supplier will not have enough capacity. The retailers also know that if the supplier runs out of capacity, then the supplier will allocate that scarce capacity to the retailers. The supplier may very well use a proportional allocation scheme: A retailer's share of the capacity is proportional to the retailer's order quantity relative to the total order quantity. For example, if a retailer orders 10 units and the other retailers order a total of 40 units, then the retailer will get a one-fifth share of the capacity (10 / (10 + 40)). When this situation occurs with a product, it is often said that the product is *on allocation;* that is, the supplier must allocate capacity because the total amount demanded by retailers exceeds available capacity.

Knowing that a product may be put on allocation, what should a retailer's ordering strategy be? Returning to our example, the retailer wants 10 units but anticipates only one-fifth of that order will be delivered. Hence, if 10 units are ordered, only 2 units will be received, far less than the retailer wants. An obvious solution is to instead order 50 units: If the retailer receives one-fifth of the order, and 50 units are ordered, then the retailer will receive the desired quantity, 10 units. But the other retailers are probably thinking the same thing. So they too may order much more than needed in anticipation of receiving only a fraction of their order. This behavior of ordering more than needed due to the anticipation of a possible capacity shortage is called *shortage gaming* or *order inflation*.

Shortage gaming can result in quite a mess for the supply chain. Some retailers may receive far less than they could sell (because they did not inflate their order enough) while others might actually receive much more than they can sell (because they inflated their order too much). For instance, the retailer in our example can order 50 units and actually receive 12 units, still only a fraction of the retailer's order, but 2 units more than wanted. Furthermore, order inflation contributes to the bullwhip effect: Once a supplier's customers believe that capacity may be constrained, the supplier's customers may inflate their orders substantially, thereby creating excessive volatility in the supplier's demand. Interestingly, this may occur even if there is enough capacity to satisfy the retailers' desired quantity; all that is needed to create order inflation is the belief among the retailers that they may not get their full order.

A supplier also can exacerbate the bullwhip effect with her own actions via shortage gaming. For example, suppose a supplier allows retailers to return unsold inventory. With little risk associated with having too much inventory, retailers naturally focus on the risk of having too little inventory, leading them to actively participate in shortage gaming.

Another version of allowing retailers to return orders is to allow them to cancel orders they haven't yet received. With the ability to cancel an order without cost, it is obvious that retailers will submit some orders "just in case" they need the inventory or a shortage materializes. In the industry these orders are sometimes called *phantom orders,* because they are orders that are submitted even though they are likely to disappear, like a phantom.

19.2 The Bullwhip Effect: Mitigating Strategies

This section discusses how firms have changed their business practices to combat the bullwhip effect. In the grocery industry, many of these changes came with the *Efficient Consumer Response* initiative.

Not surprisingly, effective change begins with an understanding of root causes. In the case of the bullwhip effect, we identified five causes in the previous section: order synchronization, order batching, trade promotions, overreactive ordering, and shortage gaming.

Sharing Information

Greater information sharing about actual demand between the stages of the supply chain is an intuitive step toward reducing the bullwhip effect. As we saw in the simulations reported in the previous section, the pattern of retail orders may have very little resemblance to the pattern of retail demand. As a result, when retail orders are fluctuating wildly, it can be extremely difficult for a supplier to correctly forecast demand trends and it is not surprising at all if the supplier overreacts to those data. By giving the supplier frequent access to actual consumer demand data, the supplier can better assess trends in demand and plan accordingly.

But sharing current demand data is often not enough to mitigate the bullwhip effect. Demand also can be influenced by retailer actions on pricing, merchandizing, promotion, advertising, and assortment planning. As a result, a supplier cannot accurately forecast sales for a product unless the supplier knows what kind of treatment that product will receive from its retailers. Without that information, the supplier may not build sufficient capacity for a product that the retailers want to support, or the supplier may build too much capacity of a product that generates little interest among the retailers. Both errors may be prevented if the supplier and retailers share with each other their intentions. This sharing process is often labeled *collaborative planning, forecasting, and replenishment (CPFR).*

While it is quite useful for a retailer to share information with its upstream suppliers, it also can be useful for a supplier to share information on availability with its downstream retailers. For example, a supplier may be aware of a component shortage that will lead to a shortage in a product that a retailer intends to promote. By sharing that information, the retailer could better allocate its promotional effort. It also can be useful to share information when the supplier knows that a capacity shortage will not occur, thereby preventing some shortage gaming.

Smoothing the Flow of Product

It is important to recognize that information sharing is quite helpful for reducing the bullwhip effect, but it is unlikely to eliminate it. The bullwhip effect is also a result of physical limitations in the supply chain like order synchronization and order batching.

Order synchronization can be reduced by eliminating reasons why retailers may wish to order at the same time (such as trade promotions). Coordinating with retailers to schedule them on different order cycles also helps.

Reducing order batching means smaller and more frequent replenishments. Unfortunately, this objective conflicts with the desire to control ordering, transportation, and handling costs. The fixed cost associated with each order submitted to the supplier can be reduced with the use of computerized automatic replenishment systems for deciding when and how much to order. In addition, some kind of technology standard, like *electronic data interchange (EDI),* is needed so that orders can be transmitted in an electronic format that can be received by the supplier.

Transportation costs can conflict with small batches because the cost of a truck shipment depends little on the amount that is shipped. Hence, there are strong incentives to ship in full truckloads. There are also economies of scale in handling inventory, which is why it is cheaper to ship in cases than in individual units and cheaper to move pallets rather than individual cases. So the trick is to find a way to have more frequent replenishments while still controlling handling and transportation costs.

One solution is for multiple retailers to consolidate their orders with a supplier through a distributor. By ordering from a distributor rather than directly from a supplier, a retailer can receive the supplier's products on a more frequent basis and still order in full truckloads. The difference is that with direct ordering, the retailer is required to fill a truck with the supplier's products whereas by going through a distributor, the retailer can fill a truck with product from multiple suppliers that sell through that distributor.

Eliminating Pathological Incentives

As we saw in the previous section, trade promotions provide an extremely strong incentive for a retailer to forward buy and forward buying creates a substantial bullwhip effect. A constant wholesale price completely eliminates this incentive. Furthermore, a constant wholesale price might not even cost the supplier too much in revenue, especially if the majority of the retailers never purchased at the regular price.

However, there are perceived negatives associated with eliminating trade promotions. Suppliers began using trade promotions to induce retailers to offer consumer promotions with the objective of using these consumer promotions to increase final consumer demand. And, in fact, trade promotion did succeed somewhat along these lines: Most retailers would cut the retail price during a trade promotion, thereby passing on at least a portion of the deal to consumers. Hence, if trade promotions can no longer be used to induce retailers to conduct consumer promotions, and if consumer promotions are deemed to be necessary, then suppliers must develop some other tool to generate the desired consumer promotions.

Generous returns and order cancellation policies are the other self-inflicted pathological incentives because they lead to shortage gaming and phantom ordering. One solution is to either eliminate these policies or at least make them less generous. For example, the supplier could agree to only partially refund returned units or limit the number of units that can be returned or limit the time in which they can be returned. The supplier also could impose an order cancellation penalty or require a nonrefundable deposit when orders are submitted.

Shortage gaming also can be eliminated by forgoing retailer orders altogether. To explain how this could work, suppose a supplier knows that a product will be on allocation, which means that each retailer will want more than it can receive. So the supplier does not even bother collecting retailer orders. Instead, the supplier could announce an allocation to each retailer proportional to the retailer's past sales. In the auto industry, this scheme is often called *turn-and-earn:* If a dealer turns a vehicle (i.e., sells a vehicle), then the dealer earns the right to another vehicle. Turn-and-earn allocation achieves several objectives: It ensures the supplier's entire capacity is allocated; it allocates more capacity to the higher-selling retailers, which makes intuitive sense; and it motivates retailers to sell more of the supplier's product. For example, in the auto industry, a supplier can use the allocation of a hot-selling vehicle to encourage a dealer to increase its sales effort for all vehicles so that the dealer can defend its allocation. While this extra motivation imposed on dealers is probably beneficial to the auto manufacturers, it is debatable whether it benefits dealers.

Using Vendor-Managed Inventory

Procter & Gamble and Walmart were among the first companies to identify the bullwhip effect and to take multiple significant steps to mitigate it. (Campbell's Soup was another early innovator in North America.) The set of changes they initiated are often collected under the label *vendor-managed inventory (VMI).* While many firms have now implemented their own version of VMI, VMI generally includes the following features:

- The retailer no longer decides when and how much inventory to order. Instead, the supplier decides the timing and quantity of shipments to the retailer. The firms mutually agree on an objective that the supplier will use to guide replenishment decisions (e.g., a target in-stock probability). The supplier's "reach" into the retailer can vary: In some applications, the supplier merely manages product in the retailer's distribution center and the retailer retains responsibility of replenishments from the distribution center to the stores. In other applications, the supplier manages inventory all the way down to the retailer's shelves. The scope of the supplier's reach also can vary by application: Generally, the supplier only controls decisions for its own products, but in some cases the supplier assumes responsibility for an entire category, which generally includes making replenishment decisions for the supplier's competitor's products on behalf of the retailer.
- If the supplier is going to be responsible for replenishment decisions, the supplier also needs information. Hence, with VMI the retailer shares with the supplier demand data (e.g., distribution center withdrawals and/or retail store point-of-sale data, POS data for short). The supplier uses those data as input to an automatic replenishment system; that is, a computer program that decides the timing and quantity of replenishments for each product and at each location managed. In addition to normal demand movements, the supplier must be made aware of potential demand shifts that can be anticipated. For example, if the retailer is about to conduct a consumer promotion that will raise the base level of demand by a factor of 20, then the supplier needs to be aware of when that promotion will occur. These computer-guided replenishment systems are often referred to as *continuous replenishment* or *continuous product replenishment.* However, these are somewhat misnomers since product tends to be replenished more frequently but not continuously.
- The supplier and the retailer eliminate trade promotions. This is surely necessary if the retailer is going to give the supplier control over replenishment decisions because a retailer will not wish to forgo potential forward-buying profits. Hence, the adoption of VMI usually includes some agreement that the supplier will maintain a stable price and that price will be lower than the regular price to compensate the retailer for not purchasing on a deal.

The innovations included in VMI are complementary and are effective at reducing the bullwhip effect. For example, transferring replenishment control from the retailer to the supplier allows the supplier to control the timing of deliveries, thereby reducing, if not eliminating, any order synchronization effects. VMI also allows a supplier to ship in smaller lots than the retailer would order, thereby combating the order-batching cause of the bullwhip. For example, prior to the adoption of VMI, many of Campbell Soup's customers would order three to five pallets of each soup type at a time, where a pallet typically contains about 200 cases. They would order in multiple pallets to avoid the cost of frequent ordering. With VMI Campbell Soup decided to ship fast-moving soups in pallet quantities and slower-moving varieties in mixed pallet quantities (e.g., in one-half- or one-quarter-pallet quantities). Frequent ordering was not an issue for Campbell Soup because they implemented an automatic replenishment system. But Campbell Soup was still concerned about handling and transportation costs. As a result, with VMI Campbell Soup continued to ship in full truckloads, which are about 20 pallets each. However, with VMI each of the 20 pallets could be a different product, whereas before VMI there would be fewer than 20 products loaded onto each truck (because more than one pallet would be ordered for each product). Hence, with VMI it was possible to maintain full truckloads while ordering each product more frequently because each product was ordered in smaller quantities.

In some cases VMI also assists with order batching because it allows the supplier to combine shipments to multiple retailers. Before VMI it would be essentially impossible for two retailers to combine their order to construct a full truckload. But if the supplier has a VMI relationship with both retailers, then the supplier can combine their orders onto a truck as long as the retailers are located close to each other. By replenishing each retailer in smaller than full truckload batches, the supplier reduces the bullwhip effect while still maintaining transportation efficiency.

VMI also can combat the overreaction cause of the bullwhip effect. Because demand information is shared, the supplier is less likely to overreact to changes in the demand. In addition, because VMI is implemented with computer algorithms that codify replenishment strategies, a VMI system is not as emotionally fickle as a human buyer.

While VMI changes many aspects of the supply chain relationship between a supplier and retailer, some aspects of that relationship are generally not disturbed. For example, VMI eliminates trade promotions, but it does not necessarily seek to eliminate consumer promotions. Consumer promotions also can contribute to the bullwhip effect, but there are several reasons why they do not tend to increase volatility as much as trade promotions: Not every retailer runs a consumer promotion at the same time, so order synchronization is not as bad as with a trade promotion, and consumers do not forward buy as much as retailers. In addition, while some companies are willing to forgo trade promotions, only a few are willing to forgo consumer promotions as well: Consumer promotions are viewed as a competitive necessity.

The Countereffect to the Bullwhip Effect: Production Smoothing

Due to the numerous causes of the bullwhip effect, one might expect that the bullwhip effect is a potential problem in nearly any supply chain. But this leads to the following questions: Does the bullwhip effect indeed exist in every supply chain? Is there any natural force that counteracts the bullwhip effect? The short answers are no, the bullwhip effect need not exist everywhere, because there is indeed a force that works to reduce it.

Figure 19.9 shows the monthly inflow and outflow of goods for general merchandisers (such as Walmart, Target, and Kohl's) in the United States over a 10-year period. Outflow of goods is analogous to demand—it is the dollar volume of goods that leaves general

FIGURE 19.9
Inflow and Outflow of Goods to U.S. General Merchandisers

Source: U.S. Census Bureau, Monthly retail trade data.

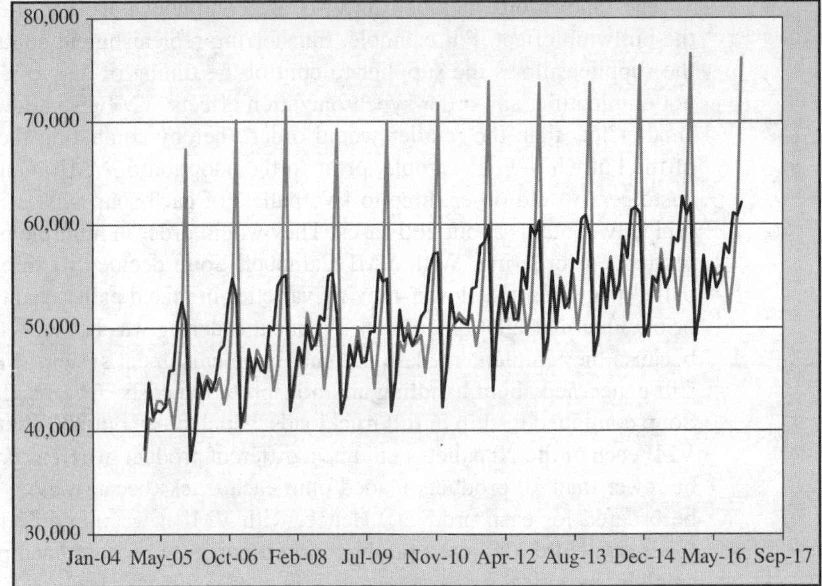

merchandisers, presumably into the hands of final customers. The inflow of goods is the dollar volume of goods purchased by general merchandisers. The figure reveals that the inflow of goods is actually less variable than the outflow of goods. Put another way, the demand seen by the suppliers of the general merchandisers (the inflow series) is less variable than the demand seen by the general merchandisers themselves (the outflow series)—we do not observe the bullwhip effect (at least at the aggregate level of an entire industry and at the monthly time interval). Why?

Looking at these retailers' demand, we see a noticeable fourth-quarter spike each year, which is particularly strong in November and especially in December. Intuitively, this is the annual holiday season sales surge. This annual spike presents retailers with a significant operational challenge—not only do customers need to be helped, shelves need to be replenished. Replenishing on a just-in-time basis requires a substantial amount of labor, but hiring that many seasonal workers for such a short time would be very expensive (just November and December). Instead, retailers start the process of moving product into their warehouses and stores at the start of the quarter, September and October. Each year, as Figure 19.9 reveals, retailers have a net inflow of goods during those months—inflows are greater than outflows (i.e., they build up their inventory). This prepositioning of inventory allows them to smooth out the inflow of product, thereby reducing the amount of work that needs to be done at the very busiest time of the year. In effect, retailers engage in production smoothing–build inventory during slow times and draw down inventory during hectic times so that the burden on their workforce is not too great. Apparently, it is cheaper to preposition inventory than it is to have large fluctuations in the number of employees. Due to this production-smoothing strategy, the suppliers to these retailers actually experience less volatility in their demand than the retailers do.

In general, when a retailer (or any other firm) faces highly seasonal demand (i.e., predictably variable demand), that retailer will have an incentive to engage in production smoothing. This, as we have seen, will act as a force to counteract the bullwhip effect. Whether this force is strong enough to eliminate the bullwhip effect or not depends on how seasonal demand is and how strong the bullwhip forces are. For general merchandisers, the holiday sales spike is sufficiently large and predictable that it overwhelms the bullwhip forces, at least when measured at the industry level and with monthly data. For individual retailers, individual products, and shorter time intervals (weekly or daily), the bullwhip effect may reemerge.

Although seasonality tends to dampen (or eliminate) the bullwhip effect, seasonality is still (almost by definition) a source of variability in the supply chain. But while it creates variability, it does not contribute to amplification—even the suppliers to general merchandisers experience considerable variability and seasonality in their demand, but it is less than the variability faced by their downstream customers.

19.3 Incentive Conflicts in a Sunglasses Supply Chain

The bullwhip effect deteriorates supply chain performance by propagating demand variability up the supply chain. But optimal supply chain performance is also not guaranteed in the absence of the bullwhip effect. This section considers the incentive conflicts that can occur between two firms in a supply chain even without the presence of the bullwhip effect. We illustrate these conflicts with a detailed example based on a supply chain for sunglasses.

Zamatia Ltd. (pronounced zah-MAH-tee-ah, to the cognoscenti) is an Italian upscale maker of eyewear. UV Inc., short for Umbra Visage, is one of their retailers in the United States. To match UV's stylish assortment, UV only operates small boutique stores located in trendy locations. We focus on one of their stores located in Miami Beach, Florida. Zamatia manufactures its sunglasses in Europe and Asia, so the replenishment lead time to the United States is long. Furthermore, the selling season for sunglasses is short and styles change significantly from year to year. As a result, UV receives only one delivery of Zamatia glasses before each season. As with any fashion product, some styles sell out quickly while others are left over at the end of the season.

Consider Zamatia's entry-level sunglasses for the coming season, the Bassano. UV purchases each one of those pairs of sunglasses from Zamatia for \$75 and retails them for \$115. Zamatia's production and shipping costs per pair are \$35. At the end of the season, UV generally needs to offer deep discounts to sell remaining inventory; UV estimates that it will only be able to fetch \$25 per leftover Bassano at the Miami Beach store. UV's Miami Beach store believes this season's demand for the Bassano can be represented by a normal distribution with a mean of 250 and a standard deviation of 125.

UV's procurement quantity decision can be made with the use of the newsvendor model (Chapter 14). Let Q be UV's order quantity. UV's underage cost per unit is $C_u = \$115 - \$75 = \$40$; that is, each lost sale due to underordering costs UV the opportunity cost of \$40. UV's overage cost per unit is $C_o = \$75 - \$25 = \$50$; the consequence of leftover inventory is substantial. UV's critical ratio is

$$\frac{C_u}{C_o + C_u} = \frac{40}{50 + 40} = \frac{4}{9} = 0.4444$$

Hence, to maximize expected profit, UV should choose an order quantity such that 44.4 percent is the probability there is some leftover inventory and 55.6 percent is the probability there is a stockout.

From the Standard Normal Distribution Function Table, we find $\Phi(-0.14) = 0.4443$ and $\Phi(-0.13) = 0.4483$, so the optimal z-statistic is -0.13 and the optimal order quantity is

$$Q = \mu + z \times \sigma = 250 - 0.13 \times 125 = 234$$

Using the equations and procedures described in Chapter 14, we also are able to evaluate several performance measures for UV's store:

$$\text{Expected sales(units)} = 192$$
$$\text{Expected leftover inventory} = 42$$
$$\text{Expected profit} = \$5{,}580$$

Zamatia's profit from selling the Bassano at UV's Miami Beach store is 234 × \$40 = \$9,360, where 234 is the number of Bassano sunglasses that UV purchases and \$40 is Zamatia's gross margin (\$75 – \$35 = \$40).

While Zamatia might be quite pleased with this situation (it does earn \$9,360 relative to UV's \$5,580), it should not be. The total supply chain's profit is \$14,940, but it could be higher. To explain, suppose we choose an order quantity to maximize the supply chain's profit, that is, the combined expected profits of Zamatia and UV. In other words, what order quantity would a firm choose if the firm owned both Zamatia and UV? We call this the *supply chain optimal quantity* because it is the quantity that maximizes the *integrated supply chain*.

We can still use the newsvendor model to evaluate the supply chain's order quantity decision and performance measures. Each lost sale costs the supply chain the difference between the retail price and the production cost, \$115 – \$35 = \$80; that is, the supply chain's underage cost is $C_u = 80$. Each leftover Bassano costs the supply chain the difference between the production cost and the salvage value, \$35 – \$25 = \$10; that is, the supply chain's overage cost is $C_o = 10$. The supply chain's critical ratio is

$$\frac{C_u}{C_o + C_u} = \frac{80}{10 + 80} = 0.8889$$

The appropriate z-statistic for that critical ratio is 1.23 because $\Phi(1.22) = 0.8888$ and $\Phi(1.23) = 0.8907$. The supply chain's expected profit-maximizing order quantity is then

$$Q = \mu + z \times \sigma = 250 + 1.23 \times 125 = 404$$

which is considerably higher than UV's order of 234 units. The supply chain's performance measures can then be evaluated assuming the supply chain optimal order quantity, 404 units:

$$\text{Expected sales(units)} = 243$$
$$\text{Expected leftover inventory} = 161$$
$$\text{Expected profit} = \$17{,}830$$

Thus, while Zamatia and UV currently earn an expected profit of \$14,940, their supply chain could enjoy an expected profit that is about 19 percent higher, \$17,830.

Why does the current supply chain perform significantly worse than it could? The obvious answer is that UV does not order enough Bassanos: UV orders 234 of them, but the supply chain's optimal order quantity is 404 units. But why doesn't UV order enough? Because UV is acting in its own self-interest to maximize its own profit. To explain further, UV must pay Zamatia \$75 per pair of sunglasses and so UV acts as if the cost to produce each Bassano is \$75, not the actual \$35. From UV's perspective, it does not matter if the actual production cost is \$35, \$55, or even \$0; its "production cost" is \$75. UV correctly recognizes that it only makes \$40 on each sale but loses \$50 on each leftover pair. Hence, UV is prudent to order cautiously.

TABLE 19.2
UV's Order Quantity Q and Performance Measures for Several Possible Wholesale Price Contracts

	Wholesale Price			
	$35	$65	$75	$85
C_u	$80	$50	$40	$30
C_o	$10	$40	$50	$60
Critical ratio	0.8889	0.5556	0.4444	0.3333
z	1.23	0.14	−0.13	−0.43
Q	404	268	234	196
Expected sales	243	209	192	169
Expected leftover inventory	161	59	42	27
Umbra's expected profit	$17,830	$8,090	$5,580	$3,450
Zamatia's expected profit	$0	$8,040	$9,360	$9,800
Supply chain's profit	$17,830	$16,130	$14,940	$13,250

UV's trepidation with respect to ordering is due to a phenomenon called *double marginalization*. Because UV's profit margin ($40) is one of two profit margins in the supply chain, and necessarily less than the supply chain's total profit margin ($80), UV orders less than the supply chain optimal quantity. In other words, because UV only earns a portion ($40) of the total benefit of each sale ($80), UV is not willing to purchase as much inventory as would be optimal for the supply chain.

This example illustrates an important finding:

Even if every firm in a supply chain chooses actions to maximize its own expected profit, the total profit earned in the supply chain may be less than the entire supply chain's maximum profit.

In other words, rational and self-optimizing behavior by each member of the supply chain does not necessarily lead to optimal supply chain performance. So what can be done about this? That is the question we explore next.

There is an obvious solution to get UV to order more Bassanos: Zamatia could reduce the wholesale price. A lower wholesale price increases UV's underage cost (gross margin) and decreases the overage cost (loss on leftover inventory), thereby making stockouts costlier and leftover inventory less consequential. More technically, reducing the wholesale price increases UV's critical ratio, which leads UV to order more. Table 19.2 provides some data on supply chain performance with various wholesale prices.

We indeed see that if Zamatia were to reduce its wholesale price from $75 to $65, then UV would increase its Bassano order from 234 to 268 units. UV is quite happy: Its profit increases from $5,580 to $8,090. Furthermore, the supply chain's profit increases from $14,905 to $16,130. In fact, why stop with a $10 wholesale price reduction? If Zamatia were to reduce the wholesale price down to the production cost, $35, then (1) UV orders the supply chain optimal quantity, 404 units, and (2) the supply chain's profit is optimal, $17,830! That strategy is called *marginal cost pricing* because the supplier only charges the retailer the marginal cost of production.

But while marginal cost pricing is terrific for UV and the supply chain, it is disastrous for Zamatia: By definition, Zamatia's profit plunges to zero with marginal cost pricing.

We now see a classic tension within a supply chain: An increase in one firm's profit might come at the expense of a decrease in the other firm's profit. Some might refer to this distributive situation as a *zero-sum game,* but in fact it is even worse! In a zero-sum game, two parties negotiate over how to split a fixed reward (in this case, the total profit), but in this situation the total amount to be allocated between Zamatia and UV is not even fixed: Increasing Zamatia's profit may result in a smaller total profit to be shared.

With respect to the allocation of supply chain profit, firms should care about two things:

1. The size of a firm's piece of the "pie," where the pie refers to the supply chain's total profit.
2. The size of the total "pie," that is, the supply chain's total profit.

Number 1 is obvious: Every firm always wants a larger piece of the pie. Number 2 is less obvious. For a fixed piece of the pie, why should a firm care about the size of the pie; that is, the size of the other firm's piece? "Petty jealousy" is not the answer. The answer is that it is always easier to divide a bigger pie: If a pie gets bigger, then it is possible to give everyone a bigger piece; that is, everyone can be better off if the pie is made bigger. In practice this is often referred to as a *win–win* deal, that is, both parties are better off.

Turning back to our discussion of the wholesale price for Zamatia and UV, we see that arguing over the wholesale price is akin to arguing over each firm's piece of the pie. And in the process of arguing over how to divide the pie, the firms may very well end up destroying part of the pie, thereby serving no one. What these firms need is a tool that first maximizes the size of the pie ($17,830) and then allows them to decide how to divide it between them without damaging any part of it. Such a tool is discussed in the next section.

19.4 Buy-Back Contracts

Without changing the wholesale price, Zamatia would get UV to order more Bassano sunglasses if Zamatia could mitigate UV's downside risk of leftover inventory: UV loses a considerable amount ($50) on each unit it is stuck with at the end of the season. One solution is for Zamatia to buy back from UV all leftover sunglasses for a full refund of $75 per pair; that is, Zamatia could offer UV a *buy-back contract,* also called a *returns policy*.

Unfortunately, buy-back contracts introduce new costs to the supply chain. In particular, UV must ship leftover inventory back to Zamatia, which it estimates costs about $1.50 per pair. And then there is the issue of what Zamatia will do with these leftover Bassano sunglasses when it receives them. One possibility is that Zamatia just throws them out, thereby "earning" a zero salvage value on each leftover Bassano. However, Zamatia may be able to sell a portion of its leftover inventory to a European retailer that may be experiencing higher sales or Zamatia may be able to collect some revenue via an outlet store. It is even possible that Zamatia has higher salvage revenue from each Bassano at the end of the season than UV. But let's suppose Zamatia is able to earn $26.50 per Bassano at the end of the season. Hence, from the perspective of the supply chain, it does not matter whether UV salvages these sunglasses at the end of the season (which earns $25) or if Zamatia salvages these sunglasses at the end of the season (which also earns $25, net of the shipping cost). In contrast, Zamatia and UV might care which firm does the salvaging of leftover inventory. We later expand upon this issue.

Let's begin the analysis of UV's optimal order quantity given the buy-back contract. UV's underage cost with this buy-back contract is still the opportunity cost of a lost sale, which is C_u = $115 − $75 = $40. However, UV's overage cost has changed. Now UV only loses $1.50 per leftover pair due to Zamatia's generous full refund returns policy, C_o = $1.50. UV's critical ratio is

$$\frac{C_u}{C_o + C_u} = \frac{40}{1.5 + 40} = 0.9639$$

With a critical ratio of 0.9639, the optimal z-statistic is 1.8 (i.e., $\Phi(1.79) = 0.9633$ and $\Phi(1.8) = 0.9641$), so UV's optimal order quantity is now

$$Q = \mu + z \times \sigma = 250 + 1.8 \times 125 = 475$$

We can evaluate UV's expected profit and discover that it has increased from $5,580 (with no refund on returns) to $9,580 with the returns policy. Furthermore, with an order quantity of 475 units, UV's expected leftover inventory is 227 units.

Zamatia has surely provided an incentive to UV to increase its order quantity, but is this offer also good for Zamatia? Zamatia's expected profit has several components: It sells 475 units to UV at the beginning of the season, which generates $475 × $75 = $35,625 in revenue; its production cost is 475 × $35 = $16,625; it expects to pay UV 227 × $75 = $17,025 to buy back the expected 227 units of leftover inventory; and it collects 227 × $26.5 = $6,016 in salvage revenue. Combining those components together yields an expected profit of $7,991 for Zamatia, which is *lower* than Zamatia's profit without the returns policy, $9,350.

How did Zamatia go wrong with this buy-back contract? Zamatia did encourage UV to order more Bassano sunglasses by reducing UV's exposure to leftover inventory risk. But Zamatia reduced that risk so much that UV actually ordered more than the supply chain optimal quantity, thereby setting Zamatia up for a large bill when leftover inventory gets shipped back. Is there a compromise between the wholesale price contract with too little inventory and the full refund buy-back contract with too much inventory? (Of course there is.)

Instead of giving a full refund on returned inventory, Zamatia could give a partial refund. For example, suppose Zamatia offers to buy back inventory from UV for $65 per pair. This is still not a bad deal for UV. Its underage cost remains $C_u = 40$, but now its overage cost is $C_o = \$1.50 + \$75 - \$65 = \$11.50$: Each unit left over costs UV the $1.50 to ship back and due to the partial credit, it loses an additional $10 per unit. Table 19.3 provides data on UV's optimal order quantity, expected sales, expected leftover inventory, and expected profit. The table also indicates Zamatia's profit with this partial refund is $9,528, which is slightly better than its profit without a buy-back at all. Furthermore, the supply chain's total profit has jumped to $17,600, which is reasonably close to the maximum profit, $17,830. One way to evaluate the quality of a contract is by its *supply chain efficiency,* which is the fraction of the optimal profit the supply chain achieves. In this case, efficiency is 17,600 / 17,830 = 99 percent; that is, the supply chain earns 99 percent of its potential profit.

Instead of holding the wholesale price fixed and reducing the buy-back price, Zamatia could hold the buy-back price fixed and increase the wholesale price. For example, it could

TABLE 19.3 UV's Order Quantity *Q* and Performance Measures for Several Possible Wholesale Price Contracts

Wholesale price	$75	$75	$75	$85
Buy-back price	$55	$65	$75	$75
C_u	$40	$40	$40	$30
C_o	$21.50	$11.50	$1.50	$11.50
Critical ratio	0.6504	0.7767	0.9639	0.7229
z	0.39	0.77	1.80	0.60
Q	299	346	475	325
Expected sales	221	234	248	229
Expected leftover inventory	78	112	227	96
Expected profits:				
Umbra	$7,163	$8,072	$9,580	$5,766
Zamatia	$9,737	$9,528	$7,990	$11,594
Supply chain	$16,900	$17,600	$17,570	$17,360

increase the wholesale price to $85 and still agree to buy back inventory for $75. That contract indeed works well for Zamatia: it earns a whopping $11,594. It even is not a bad deal for UV: its profit is $5,766, which is still better than the original situation without any refund on returned inventory. But overall supply chain performance has slipped a bit: efficiency is now only 17,360 / 17,830 = 97 percent.

While we seem to be making some progress, we also seem to be fishing around without much guidance. There are many possible combinations of wholesale prices and buy-back prices, so what combinations should we be considering? Recall from the previous section that our objective should be to maximize the size of the pie and then worry about how to divide it. Every firm can be given a bigger piece if the pie is made bigger. So let's first look for wholesale/buy-back price combinations that maximize supply chain profit. In other words, we are looking for a wholesale price and a buy-back price such that UV's expected profit-maximizing order quantity given those terms is the supply chain optimal order quantity, 404 Bassanos. If we find such a contract, then we say that contract "coordinates the supply chain" because the supply chain achieves 100 percent efficiency; that is, it earns the maximum supply chain profit.

We could hunt for our desired wholesale/buy-back price combinations in Excel (for every wholesale price, slowly adjust the buy-back price until we find the one that makes UV order 404 Bassanos), or we could take a more direct route by using the following equation:

$$\text{Buy-back price} = \text{Shipping cost} + \text{Price} - (\text{Price} - \text{Wholesale price}) \times \left(\frac{\text{Price} - \text{Salvage value}}{\text{Price} - \text{Cost}}\right) \qquad \textbf{(19.1)}$$

In other words, if we have chosen a wholesale price, then Equation (19.1) gives us the buy-back price that would cause UV to choose the supply chain optimal order quantity. In that case, the pie would be maximized; that is, we coordinate the supply chain and supply chain efficiency is 100 percent! (If you are curious about how to derive Equation (19.1), see Appendix D.)

Let's evaluate Equation (19.1) with the wholesale price of $75:

$$\text{Buy-back price} = \$1.50 + \$115 - (\$115 - \$75) \times \left(\frac{\$115 - \$25}{\$115 - \$35}\right) = \$71.50$$

Hence, if the wholesale price is $75 and Zamatia agrees to buy back leftover inventory for $71.50 per pair, then UV orders 404 Bassano sunglasses and the supply chain earns the maximum profit, $17,830.

Table 19.4 provides performance data for several different wholesale prices assuming Equation (19.1) is used to choose the buy-back price.

Interestingly, with a wholesale price of $75, the firms split the supply chain's profit, that is, each earns $8,915. In that case, UV does much better than just a wholesale price contract, but Zamatia does worse. However, both firms do significantly better with the wholesale price of $85 and the buy-back price of $82.75 than they do with the original contract we considered (just a $75 wholesale price and no buy-back).

Table 19.4 reveals some remarkable observations:

- There are many different wholesale price/buy-back price pairs that maximize the supply chain's profit. In other words, there are many different contracts that achieve 100 percent supply chain efficiency.

TABLE 19.4 Performance Measures When the Buy-Back Price Is Chosen to Coordinate the Supply Chain—To Ensure 100 Percent Supply Chain Efficiency

Wholesale price	$35	$45	$55	$65	$75	$85	$95	$105
Buy-back price	$26.50	$37.75	$49.00	$60.25	$71.50	$82.75	$94.00	$105.25
C_u	$80	$70	$60	$50	$40	$30	$20	$10
C_o	$10.00	$8.75	$7.50	$6.25	$5.00	$3.75	$2.50	$1.25
Critical ratio	0.8889	0.8889	0.8889	0.8889	0.8889	0.8889	0.8889	0.8889
z	1.23	1.23	1.23	1.23	1.23	1.23	1.23	1.23
Q	404	404	404	404	404	404	404	404
Expected sales	243	243	243	243	243	243	243	243
Expected leftover inventory	161	161	161	161	161	161	161	161
Expected profits:								
Umbra	$17,830	$15,601	$13,373	$11,144	$8,915	$6,686	$4,458	$2,229
Zamatia	$0	$2,229	$4,458	$6,686	$8,915	$11,144	$13,373	$15,601
Supply chain	$17,830	$17,830	$17,830	$17,830	$17,830	$17,830	$17,830	$17,830

- Virtually any allocation of the supply chain's profit between the two firms is feasible; that is, there exist contracts that give the lion's share of the profit to the supplier, contracts that equally divide the profit, and contracts that give the lion's share to the retailer.
- The firms now truly do face a zero-sum game; that is, increasing one firm's profit means the other firm's profit decreases. However, at least now the sum that they can fight over is the maximum possible.

Which contracts will the firms ultimately agree upon? We cannot really say. If Zamatia is the better negotiator or if it is perceived to have more bargaining power than UV, then we would expect Zamatia might get UV to agree to a buy-back contract with a high wholesale price. Even though Zamatia's profit can increase substantially, it is important to note that UV's profit also may increase relative to the status quo because buy-back contracts increase the size of the pie. However, if UV has the stronger negotiating skills, then it is possible UV will secure a contract that it favors (a buy-back contract with a low wholesale price).

19.5 More Supply Chain Contracts

The previous section focused on buy-back contracts, but those are not the only type of contracts that are implemented in supply chains. This section briefly describes several other types of contracts and how they may alleviate supply chain incentive conflicts. This is by no means an exhaustive list of the types of contracts that are observed in practice.

Quantity Discounts

Quantity discounts are quite common, but they come in many different forms. For example, with an all-unit quantity discount, a buyer receives a discount on all units if the quantity ordered exceeds a threshold; whereas with an incremental quantity discount, a buyer receives a discount on all units purchased above a threshold. No matter the form, quantity discounts encourage buyers to order additional inventory because the purchase price of the last unit purchased is decreasing with the amount purchased. (See Section 5.6.) In the context of the newsvendor model, a quantity discount increases the underage cost, thereby increasing the critical ratio. In contrast, recall that the buy-back contract increases the critical ratio by decreasing the overage cost.

Options Contracts

With an options contract, a buyer pays one price to purchase options, say w_o, and another price to exercise the purchased options, w_e. These contracts are often used when a buyer wants a supplier to build capacity well in advance of the selling season. At that time, the buyer has only an uncertain forecast of demand. As the selling season approaches, the buyer anticipates that she will have a much better demand forecast, but by then it is too late to build additional capacity if demand is quite high. Without the options contract, the supplier bears all of the supply chain's risk, so the supplier is likely to build too little capacity. The options contract allows the firms to share the risk of demand–supply mismatches: The supplier earns at least something upfront (the option's price) while the buyer doesn't have to pay for all of the unused capacity (the exercise price is paid only on capacity actually exercised). Hence, just as with buy-back contracts, options contracts are able in some settings to achieve 100 percent supply chain efficiency (i.e., the supplier builds the right amount of capacity) and arbitrarily divide the supply chain's profit between the two firms (i.e., there is more than one options contract that achieves supply chain coordination).

Revenue Sharing

With revenue sharing, a retailer pays a wholesale price per unit purchased to a supplier but then also pays a portion of the revenue earned on that unit to the supplier. As with buy-back contracts, revenue sharing allows the firms in the supply chain to share the risk of demand–supply mismatches: The retailer pays something to the supplier upfront (the wholesale price) but only pays an additional amount if the unit actually generates revenue (the revenue share).

Quantity Flexibility Contracts

Consider an ongoing relationship between a buyer and a supplier. For example, the buyer is Sun Microsystems, the supplier is Sony, and the product is a monitor. Sun's demand fluctuates over time, but Sun nevertheless wants Sony to build enough capacity to satisfy all of Sun's needs, which could be either higher or lower than forecasted. But since Sun probably doesn't incur the cost of idle capacity, Sun is biased toward giving Sony overly rosy forecasts in the hope that Sony will respond to the forecast by building extra capacity. But Sony is no fool; that is, Sony knows that Sun is biased toward optimistic forecasts and so Sony may view Sun's forecasts with a skeptical eye. Unfortunately, Sun may actually have an optimistic forecast, but due to its lack of credibility with Sony, Sony may not respond with additional capacity.

The problem in this relationship is that Sony bears the entire risk of excess capacity; hence, Sun is biased toward rosy forecasts. One solution is to implement *quantity flexibility (QF) contracts:* with a QF contract, Sun provides an initial forecast but then must purchase some quantity within a certain percentage of that forecast. For example, suppose the firms agree to a 25 percent QF contract. Furthermore, it is the first quarter of the year and Sun forecasts its demand for the fourth quarter will be 2,000 units. By the time the fourth quarter rolls around, Sun is committed to purchasing from Sony at least 1,500 units (75 percent of the forecast) and Sony is committed to delivering up to 2,500 units (125 percent of the forecast) should Sun need more than the forecast. If demand turns out to be low, Sony is somewhat protected by the lower collar, whereas if demand turns out to be high, Sun can take advantage of that upside by knowing that Sony has some additional capacity (up to the upper collar). Hence, via quantity flexibility contracts, it can be shown that both firms are better off; that is, the supply chain pie gets bigger and each firm gets a bigger share.

Price Protection

In the tech industry, distributors are concerned with holding too much inventory because that inventory could become obsolete; that is, they must sell that inventory at deeply discounted prices. But there is another concern with holding too much inventory. Suppose a distributor purchases 1,000 units today at $2,000 each, but one week later the supplier cuts the price to $1,800. Unless the distributor sells the entire batch of 1,000 units in the next week, the distributor would be better off to purchase fewer units at $2,000 and to purchase the remainder one week later at $1,800. In other words, the tendency of suppliers to cut their wholesale prices frequently and without notice creates an incentive among distributors to be cautious in the purchase quantities. If distributors then curtail their purchases below the supply chain optimal amount, it can be beneficial to provide them with an incentive to increase their order quantities.

Allowing distributors to return inventory helps to encourage distributors to order more inventory, but it is not the only way. *Price protection* is another way: With price protection, a supplier compensates the distributor for any price reductions on remaining inventory. For example, suppose at the end of the week the distributor sold 700 units purchased at $2,000, but has 300 units remaining. With price protection, the supplier would then send the distributor a check for 300 × ($2,000 – $1,800) = $60,000. In other words, the distributor becomes indifferent between purchasing 1,000 units for $2,000 now and purchasing 700 units for $2,000 now and 300 units for $1,800 in one week.

19.6 Summary

Optimal supply chain performance is not guaranteed even if every firm in the supply chain optimizes its own performance. Self-interest and decentralized decision making do not naturally lead to 100 percent supply chain efficiency. As a result, firms in a supply chain can benefit from better coordination of their actions.

The bullwhip effect (the propagation of demand variability up the supply chain) provides a serious challenge to supply chain operations. There are many causes of the bullwhip effect (order synchronization, order batching, trade promotions, overreactive ordering, and shortage gaming) and more than one of them can be present at the same time. Solutions to the bullwhip effect such as sharing demand information, removing pathological incentives, and vendor-managed inventory are designed to combat those root causes.

The bullwhip effect is not the only challenge posed upon supply chains. Given the terms of trade between supply chain members, it is quite possible that supply chain actions will not be taken because of conflicting incentives. For example, with a simple wholesale price contract, it is generally found that the retailer's incentive to order inventory leads it to order less than the supply chain optimal amount of inventory, a phenomenon called double marginalization. Fortunately, incentive conflicts can be alleviated or even eliminated with the use of carefully designed contractual terms such as buy-back contracts.

19.7 Further Reading

For a description of the causes, consequences, and solutions to the bullwhip effect, see Lee, Padmanabhan, and Whang (1997).

Buzzell, Quelch, and Salmon (1990) provide a history of trade promotions and discuss their pros and cons.

For the original research on buy-back contracts, see Pasternack (1985). For a more managerial description of the application of buy-back contracts, see Padmanabhan and Png (1995). For a review of the theoretical literature on supply chain contracting, see Cachon (2004).

19.8 Practice Problems

The following questions will help in testing your understanding of this chapter. After each question, we show the relevant section in parentheses [Section x].

Solutions to problems marked with an "*" are available in Appendix E. Video solutions to select problems are available in Connect.

Q19.1* **(Buying Tissues)** Procter & Gamble, the maker of Puffs tissues, traditionally sells these tissues for $9.40 per case, where a case contains eight boxes. A retailer's average weekly demand is 25 cases of a particular Puffs SKU (color, scent, etc.). P&G has decided to change its pricing strategy by offering two different plans. With one plan, the retailer can purchase that SKU for the everyday-low wholesale price of $9.25 per case. With the other plan, P&G charges the regular price of $9.40 per case throughout most of the year, but purchases made for a single delivery at the start of each quarter are given a 5 percent discount. The retailer receives weekly shipments with a one-week lead time between ordering and delivery. Suppose with either plan the retailer manages inventory so that at the end of each week there is on average a one-week supply of inventory. Holding costs are incurred at the rate of 0.4 percent of the value of inventory at the end of each week. Assume 52 weeks per year.

a. Suppose the retailer chose the first plan ($9.25 per case throughout the year). What is the retailer's expected annual purchasing and inventory holding cost? [19.1]

b. Suppose the retailer chooses the second plan and only buys at the discount price ($9.40 is the regular price and a 5 percent discount for delivery at the start of each quarter). What is the retailer's expected annual purchasing and inventory holding cost? [19.1]

c. Consider the first plan and propose a new everyday-low wholesale price. Call this the third plan. Design your plan so that both P&G and the retailer prefer it relative to the second plan. [19.1]

Q19.2* **(Returning books)** Dan McClure is trying to decide on how many copies of a book to purchase at the start of the upcoming selling season for his bookstore. The book retails at $28.00. The publisher sells the book to Dan for $20.00. Dan will dispose of all of the unsold copies of the book at 75 percent off the retail price, at the end of the season. Dan estimates that demand for this book during the season is normal with a mean of 100 and a standard deviation of 42.

a. How many books should Dan order to maximize his expected profit? [19.3]

b. Given the order quantity in part a, what is Dan's expected profit? [19.3]

c. The publisher's variable cost per book is $7.50. Given the order quantity in part a, what is the publisher's expected profit? [19.3]

The publisher is thinking of offering the following deal to Dan. At the end of the season, the publisher will buy back unsold copies at a predetermined price of $15.00. However, Dan would have to bear the costs of shipping unsold copies back to the publisher at $1.00 per copy.

d. How many books should Dan order to maximize his expected profits given the buy-back offer? [19.4]

e. Given the order quantity in part d, what is Dan's expected profit? [19.4]

f. Assume the publisher is able on average to earn $6 on each returned book net the publisher's handling costs (some books are destroyed while others are sold at a discount and others are sold at full price). Given the order quantity in part d, what is the publisher's expected profit? [19.4]

g. Suppose the publisher continues to charge $20 per book and Dan still incurs a $1 cost to ship each book back to the publisher. What price should the publisher pay Dan for returned books to maximize the supply chain's profit (the sum of the publisher's profit and Dan's profit)? [19.4]

Q19.3 **(Component options)** Handi Inc., a cell phone manufacturer, procures a standard display from LCD Inc. via an options contract. At the start of quarter 1 (Q1), Handi pays LCD \$4.50 per option. At that time, Handi's forecast of demand in Q2 is normally distributed with mean 24,000 and standard deviation 8,000. At the start of Q2, Handi learns exact demand for Q2 and then exercises options at the fee of \$3.50 per option, (for every exercised option, LCD delivers one display to Handi). Assume Handi starts Q2 with no display inventory and displays owned at the end of Q2 are worthless. Should Handi's demand in Q2 be larger than the number of options held, Handi purchases additional displays on the spot market for \$9 per unit.

For example, suppose Handi purchases 30,000 options at the start of Q1, but at the start of Q2 Handi realizes that demand will be 35,000 units. Then Handi exercises all of its options and purchases 5,000 additional units on the spot market. If, on the other hand, Handi realizes demand is only 27,000 units, then Handi merely exercises 27,000 options.

a. Suppose Handi purchases 30,000 options. What is the expected number of options that Handi will exercise? [19.5]

b. Suppose Handi purchases 30,000 options. What is the expected number of displays Handi will buy on the spot market? [19.5]

c. Suppose Handi purchases 30,000 options. What is Handi's expected total procurement cost? [19.5]

d. How many options should Handi purchase from LCD? [19.5]

e. What is Handi's expected total procurement cost given the number of purchased options from part d? [19.5]

Q19.4 **(Selling Grills)** Smith and Jackson Inc. (SJ) sells an outdoor grill to Cusano's Hardware Store. SJ's wholesale price for the grill is \$185. (The wholesale price includes the cost of shipping the grill to Cusano). Cusano sells the grill for \$250 and SJ's variable cost per grill is \$100. Suppose Cusano's forecast for season sales can be described with a Poisson distribution with mean 8.75. Furthermore, Cusano plans to make only one grill buy for the season. Grills left over at the end of the season are sold at a 75 percent discount.

a. How many grills should Cusano order? [19.3]

b. What is Cusano's expected profit given Cusano's order in part a? [19.3]

c. What is SJ's expected profit given Cusano's order in part a? [19.3]

d. To maximize the supply chain's total profit (SJ's profit plus Cusano's profit), how many grills should be shipped to Cusano's Hardware? [19.3]

Suppose SJ were to accept unsold grills at the end of the season. Cusano would incur a \$15 shipping cost per grill returned to SJ. Among the returned grills, 45 percent of them are damaged and SJ cannot resell them the following season, but the remaining 55 percent can be resold to some retailer for the full wholesale price of \$185.

e. Given the possibility of returning grills to SJ, how many grills should be sent to Cusano's to maximize the supply chain's total profit? [19.4]

Suppose SJ gives Cusano a 90 percent credit for each returned grill; that is, SJ pays Cusano \$166.50 for each returned grill. Cusano still incurs a \$15 cost to ship each grill back to SJ.

f. How many grills should Cusano order to maximize his profit? [19.4]

g. What is Cusano's expected profit given Cusano's order in part f? [19.4]

h. What is SJ's expected profit given Cusano's order in part f? [19.4]

i. To maximize the supply chain's total profit, what should SJ's credit percentage be? (The current credit is 90 percent.) [19.4]

Dave Luna, the director of marketing and sales at SJ, suggests yet another arrangement. He suggests that SJ offer an advanced purchase discount. His plan works as follows: There is a 10 percent discount on any grill purchased before the season starts (the prebook order), but then retailers are able to purchase additional grills as needed during the season at the regular wholesale price (at-once orders). With this plan, retailers are responsible for selling any excess grills at the end of the season; that is, SJ will not accept returns. Assume SJ makes enough grills to satisfy Cusano's demand during the season and any leftover grills can be sold the next season at full price.

j. Given this advanced purchase discount plan, how many grills should Cusano prebook to maximize his profit? [19.5]
k. What is Cusano's expected profit given Cusano's prebook order quantity in part j? [19.5]
l. What is SJ's expected profit from sales to Cusano this season given Cusano's prebook order quantity in part j? [19.5]
m. As a thought experiment, which one of these contractual arrangements would you recommend to SJ? [19.5]

Appendix A

Statistics Tutorial

This appendix provides a brief tutorial to the statistics needed for the material in this book.

Statistics is about understanding and quantifying uncertainty (or, if you prefer, variability). So suppose we are interested in an event that is stochastic, that is, it has an uncertain outcome. For example, it could be the demand for a product, the number of people that call us between 10:00 a.m. and 10:15 a.m., the amount of time until the arrival of the next patient to the emergency room, and so forth. In each case, the outcome of this stochastic event is some number (units of demand, minutes between arrival, etc.). This stochastic event can also be called a *random variable*. Because our random variable could represent a wide variety of situations, for the purpose of this tutorial, let's give our random variable a generic name, X.

All random variables have an *expected value,* which is also called the *mean*. Depending on the context, we use different symbols to represent the mean. For example, we generally use the Greek symbol μ to represent the mean of our stochastic demand whereas we use a to represent the mean of the interarrival time of customers to a queuing system. A random variable is also characterized by its *standard deviation*, which roughly describes the amount of uncertainty in the distribution, or how "spread out" the distribution is. The Greek symbol σ is often used to describe the standard deviation of a random variable. Uncertainty also can be measured with the *variance* of a random variable. The variance of a random variable is closely related to its standard deviation: It is the square of the standard deviation:

$$\text{Variance} = (\text{Standard deviation})^2 = \sigma^2$$

Hence, it is sufficient to just work with the standard deviation because the variance can always be evaluated quickly once you know the standard deviation.

The standard deviation measures the absolute amount of uncertainty in a distribution, but it is often useful to think about the relative amount of uncertainty. For example, suppose we have two random variables, one with mean 20 and the other with mean 200. Suppose further they both have standard deviations equal to 10, that is, they have the same absolute amount of uncertainty. A standard deviation of 10 means there is about a two-thirds chance the outcome of the random variable will be within 10 units of the mean. Being within 10 units of a mean of 20 is much more variable in a relative sense than being within 10 units of a mean of 200: In the first case we have a two-thirds chance of being within 50 percent of the mean, whereas in the second case we have a two-thirds chance of being within 5 percent of the mean. Hence, we need a relative measure of uncertainty.

We'll use the *coefficient of variation*, which is the standard deviation of a distribution divided by its mean, for example, σ/μ. In some cases we will use explicit variables to represent the coefficient of variation. For example, in our work with queuing systems, we will let CV_a be the coefficient of variation of the arrival times to the queue and CV_p be the coefficient of variation of the service times in the queue.

Every random variable is defined by its *distribution function* and its *density function*. (Actually, only one of those functions is sufficient to define the random variable, but that is a picky point.) Let's say $F(Q)$ is the distribution function of X and $f(Q)$ is the density function. The density function returns the probability our stochastic event will be exactly Q, while the distribution function returns the probability our stochastic event will be Q or lower:

$$F(Q) = \text{Prob}\{X \text{ will be less than or equal to } Q\}$$
$$f(q) = \text{Prob}\{X \text{ will be exactly } Q\}$$

There are an infinite number of possible distribution and density functions, but a few of the more useful ones have been given names. The *normal distribution* is probably the most well-known distribution: The density function of the normal distribution is shaped like a bell. The normal distribution is defined with two parameters, its mean and its standard deviation, that is, a μ and a σ. The distribution and density functions of a normal distribution with mean 1,000 and standard deviation 300 are displayed in Figure A.1.

Distribution functions are always increasing from 0 to 1 and often have an S shape. Density functions do not have a typical pattern: Some have the bell shape like the normal; others are downward curving.

While there are an infinite number of normal distributions (essentially any mean and standard deviation combination), there is one normal distribution that is particularly useful, the *standard normal*. The standard normal distribution has mean 0 and standard deviation 1. Because the standard normal is a special distribution, its distribution function is given special notation: The distribution function of the standard normal is $\Phi(z)$; that is, $\Phi(z)$ is

FIGURE A.1 **Distribution (solid line) and Density (circles) Functions of a Normal Distribution with Mean 1,000 and Standard Deviation 300**

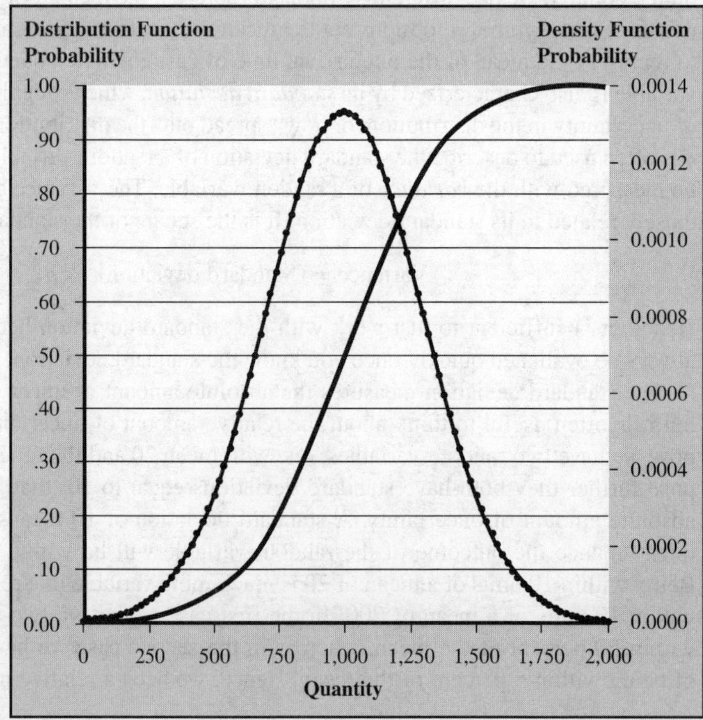

TABLE A.1
The Density Function $f(Q)$ and Distribution Function $F(Q)$ of a Poisson Distribution with Mean 1.25

Q	$f(Q)$	$F(Q)$
0	0.28650	0.28650
1	0.35813	0.64464
2	0.22383	0.86847
3	0.09326	0.96173
4	0.02914	0.99088
5	0.00729	0.99816
6	0.00152	0.99968
7	0.00027	0.99995
8	0.00004	0.99999
9	0.00001	1.00000

the probability the outcome of a standard normal distribution is z or lower. The density function of the standard normal is $\phi(z)$. (Φ and ϕ are the upper- and lowercase, respectively, of the Greek letter phi.)

The normal distribution is a *continuous distribution* because all outcomes are possible, even fractional quantities such as 989.56. The *Poisson distribution* is also common, but it is a *discrete distribution* because the outcome of a Poisson random variable is always an integer value (i.e., 0, 1, 2, . . .). The Poisson distribution is characterized by a single parameter, its mean. The standard deviation of a Poisson distribution equals the square root of its mean:

$$\text{Standard deviation of a Poisson distribution} = \sqrt{\text{Mean of the Poisson distribution}}$$

While the outcome of a Poisson distribution is always an integer, the mean of the Poisson does not need to be an integer. The distribution and density functions of a Poisson distribution with mean 1.25 are displayed in Table A.1. Figure A.2 displays the density function of six different Poisson distributions. Unlike the familiar bell shape of the normal distribution, we can see that there is no standard shape for the Poisson: With a very low mean, the Poisson is a downward-sloping curve, but then as the mean increases, the Poisson begins to adopt a bell-like shape.

FIGURE A.2 **The Density Function of Six Different Poisson Distributions with Means 0.625, 1.25, 2.5, 5,10, and 20**

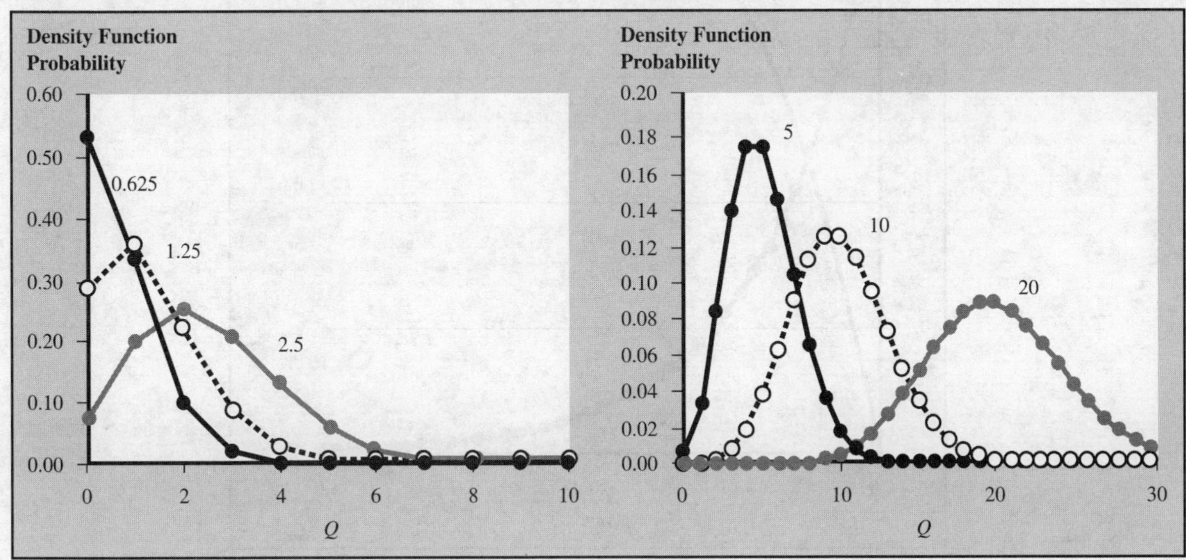

Because the outcome of a Poisson distribution is never negative and always integer, the Poisson generally better fits data with a low mean, say less than 20. For large means (say more than 20), the Poisson generally does not fit data as well as the normal for two reasons: (1) the Poisson adopts a bell-like shape, so it does not provide a shape advantage, and (2) the Poisson's standard deviation *must* equal the square root of the mean, so it does not allow the flexibility to expand or contract the width of the bell like the normal does (i.e., the normal allows for different bell shapes with the same mean but the Poisson only allows one bell shape for a given mean).

We also make extensive use of the exponential distribution in this text because it provides a good representation of the interarrival time of customers (i.e., the time between customer arrivals). The exponential distribution is characterized by a single parameter, its mean. We'll use a as the mean of the interarrival time. So if X is the interarrival time of customers and it is exponentially distributed with mean a, then the distribution function of X is

$$\text{Prob}\{X \text{ is less than or equal to } t\} = F(X) = 1 - e^{-t/a}$$

where e in the above equation is the natural constant that approximately equals 2.718282. In Excel you would write the exponential distribution function with the Exp function: 1 – Exp(–t/a). Notice that the exponential distribution function is a continuous distribution, which makes sense given that we are talking about time. Figure A.3 displays the distribution and density functions of an exponential distribution with mean 0.8.

The exponential distribution and the Poisson distribution are actually closely related. If the interarrival time of customers is exponentially distributed with mean a, then the

FIGURE A.3 **Distribution (solid line) and Density (circles) Functions of an Exponential Distribution with Mean 0.8**

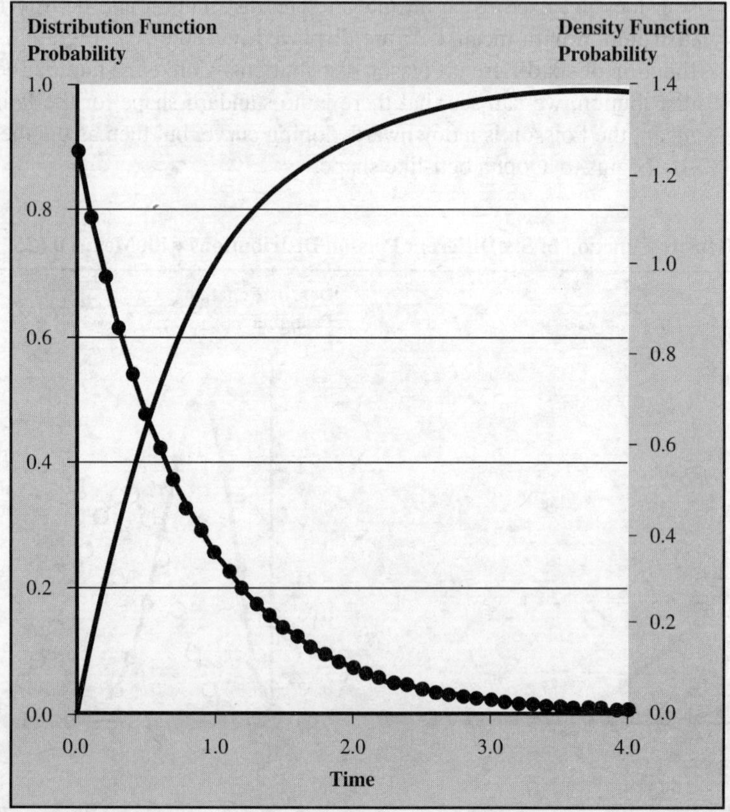

number of customers that arrive over an interval of a unit of time is Poisson distributed with mean $1/a$. For example, if the interarrival time of customers is exponentially distributed with a mean of 0.8 (as in Figure A.3), then the number of customers that arrive in one unit of time has a Poisson distribution with mean $1/0.8 = 1.25$ (as in Table A.1).

Other commonly used distributions include the negative binomial and the gamma, but we will not make much use of them in this text.

Finding the Probability *X* Will Be Less Than Q or Greater Than Q

When working with a random variable, we often need to find the probability the outcome of the random variable will be less than a particular quantity or more than the particular quantity. For example, suppose X has a Poisson distribution with mean 1.25. What is the probability X will be four units or fewer? That can be answered with the distribution function: from Table A.1, $F(4) = 99.088$ percent. What is the probability X will be greater than four units, that is, that it is five or more units? X is either Q or fewer units or it is more than Q units, so

$$\text{Prob}\{X \text{ is } Q \text{ or fewer units}\} + \text{Prob}\{X \text{ is more than } Q \text{ units}\} = 1$$

If we rearrange terms in the above equation, we get

$$\text{Prob}\{X \text{ is more than } Q \text{ units}\} = 1 - \text{Prob}\{X \text{ is } Q \text{ or fewer units}\} = 1 - F(Q)$$

Hence, X will be greater than four units with probability $1 - F(4) = 0.00912$.

A tricky issue in these evaluations is the difference between the "probability X is fewer than Q" and the "probability X is Q or fewer." The first case does not include the outcome that X exactly equals Q, whereas the second case does. For example, when we evaluate the "probability X is more than Q units," we are not including the outcome that X equals Q units. Therefore, be aware of this issue and remember that $F(Q)$ is the probability X is Q or fewer; that is, it includes the probability that X exactly equals Q units.

We also need to find the probability X is more or less than Q when X is normally distributed. Working with the normal distribution is not too hard because all normal distributions, no matter their mean or standard deviation, are related to the standard normal distribution, which is why the standard normal is special and important. Hence, we can find out the probability X will be more or less than Q by working with the standard normal distribution.

Suppose X is normally distributed with mean 1,000 and standard deviation 300 (μ = 1,000, σ = 300) and we want to find the probability X will be less than Q = 1,600 units. First convert Q into the equivalent order quantity if X followed the standard normal distribution. That equivalent order quantity is z, which is called the *z-statistic:*

$$z = \frac{Q - \mu}{\sigma} = \frac{1{,}600 - 1{,}000}{300} = 2.0$$

Hence, the quantity 1,600 relative to a normal distribution with mean 1,000 and standard deviation 300 is equivalent to the quantity 2.0 relative to a standard normal distribution. The probability we are looking for is then $\Phi(2.0)$, which we can find in the Standard Normal Distribution Function Table in Appendix B: Φ (2.0) = 0.9772. In other words, there is a 97.72 percent chance X is less than 1,600 units if X follows a normal distribution with mean 1,000 and standard deviation 300.

What is the probability X will be greater than 1,600 units? That is just $1 - \Phi(2.0) = 0.0228$; that is, the probability X will be greater than 1,600 units is just 1 minus the probability X will be less than 1,600 units.

With the normal distribution, unlike the Poisson distribution, we do not need to worry too much about the distinction between the "probability X is fewer than Q" and the "probability X is Q or fewer." With the Poisson distribution, there can be a significant probability that the outcome is exactly Q units because the Poisson distribution is a discrete distribution and usually has a low mean, which implies that there are relatively few possible outcomes. The normal distribution is continuous, so there essentially is no distinction between "X being exactly Q units" and "X being just a tiny fraction below Q units."

Expected Value

We often need to know the expected value of something happening. For example, suppose we make a decision and there are two possible outcomes, G for good and B for bad; that is, $X = \text{G}$ or $X = \text{B}$. If the outcome is G, then we earn \$100, but if the outcome is B, we lose \$40. Furthermore, we know the following probabilities: $\text{Prob}\{X = \text{G}\} = 0.25$ and $\text{Prob}\{X = \text{B}\} = 0.75$. (Note, these probabilities must sum to 1 because they are the only two possible outcomes.) The expected value of this decision is

$$\begin{aligned} &\$100 \times \text{Prob}\{X = \text{G}\} + (-\$40 \times \text{Prob}\{X = \text{B}\}) \\ &= \$100 \times 0.25 + (-\$40 \times 0.75) \\ &= -\$5 \end{aligned}$$

In words, to evaluate the expected value, we multiply the probability of each outcome with the value of each outcome and then sum up all of those calculations.

Independence, Correlation, and Combining (or Dividing) Random Variables

We often need to combine several random variables or to divide a random variable. For example, if we have five random variables, each one representing demand on a particular day of the week, we might want to combine them into a single random variable that represents weekly demand. Or we might have a random variable that represents monthly demand and we might want to divide it into random variables that represent weekly demand. In addition to combining and dividing random variables across time, we may wish to combine or divide random variables across products or categories.

Suppose you wish to combine n random variables, labeled $X_1, X_2, \ldots, X_n$, into a single random variable X; that is, you want $X + X_1 + X_2 + \ldots = X_n$. Furthermore, we assume each of the n original random variables comes from the same "family," for example, they are all normal or all Poisson. Hence, the combined random variable X is also part of the same family: The sum of two normally random variables is normally distributed; the sum of two Poisson random variables is Poisson; and so forth. So we need a mean to describe X and maybe a standard deviation. The mean of X is easy to evaluate:

$$\mu = \mu_1 + \mu_2 + \cdots + \mu_n$$

In other words, the mean of X is just the sum of the means of the n individual random variables.

If we need a standard deviation for X and the n random variables are independent, then the standard deviation of X is

$$\sigma = \sqrt{\sigma_1^2 + \sigma_2^2 + \cdots + \sigma_n^2}$$

In words, the standard deviation of X is the square root of the sum of the variances of the n random variables. If the n random variables have the same standard deviation (i.e., $\sigma_1 = \sigma_2 = \ldots = \sigma_n$), then the above simplifies to $\sigma = \sqrt{n} \times \sigma_1$.

The key condition in our evaluation of the standard deviation of X is that the n individual random variables are independent. Roughly speaking, two random variables are *independent* if the outcome of one random variable has no influence on the outcome of the other random variable. For example, if one has a rather high demand outcome, then that provides no information as to whether the other random variable will have a high or low outcome.

Two random variables are *correlated* if the outcome of one random variable provides information about the outcome of the other random variable. Two random variables are *positively correlated* if their outcomes tend to move in lock step: If one is high, then the other tends to be high, and if one is low, the other tends to be low. Two random variables are *negatively correlated* if their outcomes tend to move in opposite step: If one is high, then the other tends to be low, and if one is low, the other tends to be high.

The correlation between two random variables can range from −1 to 1. A correlation of −1 means the two are perfectly negatively correlated: As one random variable's outcome increases, the other one's outcome surely decreases. The other extreme is perfectly positively correlated, which means a correlation of 1: As one random variable's outcome increases, the other one's outcome surely increases as well. In the middle is independence: If two random variables are independent, then their correlation is 0.

So how do we evaluate the standard deviation of X when X is the sum of two random variables that may not be independent? Use the following equation:

$$\text{Standard deviation of } X = \sigma = \sqrt{\sigma_1^2 + \sigma_2^2 + 2 \times \sigma_1 \times \sigma_2 \times \text{Correlation}}$$

where *Correlation* in the above equation is the correlation between X_1 and X_2.

Appendix B

Tables

This appendix contains the Erlang Loss Function Table and the distribution, inventory, and loss function tables for the standard normal distribution and several Poisson distributions.

Erlang Loss Function Table

The Erlang Loss Function Table contains the probability that a process step consisting of *m* parallel resources contains *m* flow units, that is, all *m* resources are utilized. Interarrival times of flow units (e.g., customers or data packets, etc.) are exponentially distributed with mean *a* and service times have a mean *p* (service times do not have to follow an exponential distribution).

Because there is no buffer space, if a flow unit arrives and all *m* servers are busy, then that arriving flow unit leaves the system unserved (i.e., the flow unit is lost). The columns in the table correspond to the number of resources *m* and the rows in the table correspond to $r = p/a$; that is, the ratio between the service time and the interarrival time. The following table includes both small values of *r* and larger values of *r*.

Example: Find the probability $P_m(r)$ that a process step consisting of three parallel resources must deny access to newly arriving units. Flow units arrive one every $a = 3$ minutes with exponential interarrival times and take $p = 2$ minutes to serve. First, define $r = p/a = 2/3 = 0.67$ and find the corresponding row heading. Second, find the column heading for $m = 3$. The intersection of that row with that column is $P_m(r) = 0.0255$.

Note that $P_m(r)$ can be computed directly based on the following formula:

$$\text{Probability}\{\text{all } m \text{ servers busy}\} = P_m(r)$$

$$= \frac{\dfrac{r^m}{m!}}{1 + \dfrac{r^1}{1!} + \dfrac{r^2}{2!} + \cdots + \dfrac{r^m}{m!}} \quad \text{(Erlang loss formula)}$$

The exclamation mark (!) in the equation refers to the factorial of an integer number. To compute the factorial of an integer number *x*, write down all numbers from 1 to *x* and then multiply them with each other. For example, $4! = 1 \times 2 \times 3 \times 4 = 24$. This calculation can be done with the Excel function FACT(*x*).

Erlang Loss Table

$r = p / a$	m 1	2	3	4	5	6	7	8	9	10
0.10	0.0909	0.0045	0.0002	0.0000	0.0000	0.0000	0.0000	0.0000	0.0000	0.0000
0.20	0.1667	0.0164	0.0011	0.0001	0.0000	0.0000	0.0000	0.0000	0.0000	0.0000
0.25	0.2000	0.0244	0.0020	0.0001	0.0000	0.0000	0.0000	0.0000	0.0000	0.0000
0.30	0.2308	0.0335	0.0033	0.0003	0.0000	0.0000	0.0000	0.0000	0.0000	0.0000
0.33	0.2500	0.0400	0.0044	0.0004	0.0000	0.0000	0.0000	0.0000	0.0000	0.0000
0.40	0.2857	0.0541	0.0072	0.0007	0.0001	0.0000	0.0000	0.0000	0.0000	0.0000
0.50	0.3333	0.0769	0.0127	0.0016	0.0002	0.0000	0.0000	0.0000	0.0000	0.0000
0.60	0.3750	0.1011	0.0198	0.0030	0.0004	0.0000	0.0000	0.0000	0.0000	0.0000
0.67	0.4000	0.1176	0.0255	0.0042	0.0006	0.0001	0.0000	0.0000	0.0000	0.0000
0.70	0.4118	0.1260	0.0286	0.0050	0.0007	0.0001	0.0000	0.0000	0.0000	0.0000
0.75	0.4286	0.1385	0.0335	0.0062	0.0009	0.0001	0.0000	0.0000	0.0000	0.0000
0.80	0.4444	0.1509	0.0387	0.0077	0.0012	0.0002	0.0000	0.0000	0.0000	0.0000
0.90	0.4737	0.1757	0.0501	0.0111	0.0020	0.0003	0.0000	0.0000	0.0000	0.0000
1.00	0.5000	0.2000	0.0625	0.0154	0.0031	0.0005	0.0001	0.0000	0.0000	0.0000
1.10	0.5238	0.2237	0.0758	0.0204	0.0045	0.0008	0.0001	0.0000	0.0000	0.0000
1.20	0.5455	0.2466	0.0898	0.0262	0.0063	0.0012	0.0002	0.0000	0.0000	0.0000
1.25	0.5556	0.2577	0.0970	0.0294	0.0073	0.0015	0.0003	0.0000	0.0000	0.0000
1.30	0.5652	0.2687	0.1043	0.0328	0.0085	0.0018	0.0003	0.0001	0.0000	0.0000
1.33	0.5714	0.2759	0.1092	0.0351	0.0093	0.0021	0.0004	0.0001	0.0000	0.0000
1.40	0.5833	0.2899	0.1192	0.0400	0.0111	0.0026	0.0005	0.0001	0.0000	0.0000
1.50	0.6000	0.3103	0.1343	0.0480	0.0142	0.0035	0.0008	0.0001	0.0000	0.0000
1.60	0.6154	0.3299	0.1496	0.0565	0.0177	0.0047	0.0011	0.0002	0.0000	0.0000
1.67	0.6250	0.3425	0.1598	0.0624	0.0204	0.0056	0.0013	0.0003	0.0001	0.0000
1.70	0.6296	0.3486	0.1650	0.0655	0.0218	0.0061	0.0015	0.0003	0.0001	0.0000
1.75	0.6364	0.3577	0.1726	0.0702	0.0240	0.0069	0.0017	0.0004	0.0001	0.0000
1.80	0.6429	0.3665	0.1803	0.0750	0.0263	0.0078	0.0020	0.0005	0.0001	0.0000
1.90	0.6552	0.3836	0.1955	0.0850	0.0313	0.0098	0.0027	0.0006	0.0001	0.0000
2.00	0.6667	0.4000	0.2105	0.0952	0.0367	0.0121	0.0034	0.0009	0.0002	0.0000
2.10	0.6774	0.4156	0.2254	0.1058	0.0425	0.0147	0.0044	0.0011	0.0003	0.0001
2.20	0.6875	0.4306	0.2400	0.1166	0.0488	0.0176	0.0055	0.0015	0.0004	0.0001
2.25	0.6923	0.4378	0.2472	0.1221	0.0521	0.0192	0.0061	0.0017	0.0004	0.0001
2.30	0.6970	0.4449	0.2543	0.1276	0.0554	0.0208	0.0068	0.0019	0.0005	0.0001
2.33	0.7000	0.4495	0.2591	0.1313	0.0577	0.0220	0.0073	0.0021	0.0005	0.0001
2.40	0.7059	0.4586	0.2684	0.1387	0.0624	0.0244	0.0083	0.0025	0.0007	0.0002
2.50	0.7143	0.4717	0.2822	0.1499	0.0697	0.0282	0.0100	0.0031	0.0009	0.0002
2.60	0.7222	0.4842	0.2956	0.1612	0.0773	0.0324	0.0119	0.0039	0.0011	0.0003
2.67	0.7273	0.4923	0.3044	0.1687	0.0825	0.0354	0.0133	0.0044	0.0013	0.0003
2.70	0.7297	0.4963	0.3087	0.1725	0.0852	0.0369	0.0140	0.0047	0.0014	0.0004
2.75	0.7333	0.5021	0.3152	0.1781	0.0892	0.0393	0.0152	0.0052	0.0016	0.0004
2.80	0.7368	0.5078	0.3215	0.1837	0.0933	0.0417	0.0164	0.0057	0.0018	0.0005
2.90	0.7436	0.5188	0.3340	0.1949	0.1016	0.0468	0.0190	0.0068	0.0022	0.0006
3.00	0.7500	0.5294	0.3462	0.2061	0.1101	0.0522	0.0219	0.0081	0.0027	0.0008
3.10	0.7561	0.5396	0.3580	0.2172	0.1187	0.0578	0.0249	0.0096	0.0033	0.0010
3.20	0.7619	0.5494	0.3695	0.2281	0.1274	0.0636	0.0283	0.0112	0.0040	0.0013
3.25	0.7647	0.5541	0.3751	0.2336	0.1318	0.0666	0.0300	0.0120	0.0043	0.0014
3.30	0.7674	0.5587	0.3807	0.2390	0.1362	0.0697	0.0318	0.0130	0.0047	0.0016
3.33	0.7692	0.5618	0.3843	0.2426	0.1392	0.0718	0.0331	0.0136	0.0050	0.0017
3.40	0.7727	0.5678	0.3915	0.2497	0.1452	0.0760	0.0356	0.0149	0.0056	0.0019
3.50	0.7778	0.5765	0.4021	0.2603	0.1541	0.0825	0.0396	0.0170	0.0066	0.0023
3.60	0.7826	0.5848	0.4124	0.2707	0.1631	0.0891	0.0438	0.0193	0.0077	0.0028
3.67	0.7857	0.5902	0.4191	0.2775	0.1691	0.0937	0.0468	0.0210	0.0085	0.0031
3.70	0.7872	0.5929	0.4224	0.2809	0.1721	0.0960	0.0483	0.0218	0.0089	0.0033
3.75	0.7895	0.5968	0.4273	0.2860	0.1766	0.0994	0.0506	0.0232	0.0096	0.0036
3.80	0.7917	0.6007	0.4321	0.2910	0.1811	0.1029	0.0529	0.0245	0.0102	0.0039
3.90	0.7959	0.6082	0.4415	0.3009	0.1901	0.1100	0.0577	0.0274	0.0117	0.0046
4.00	0.8000	0.6154	0.4507	0.3107	0.1991	0.1172	0.0627	0.0304	0.0133	0.0053

Erlang Loss Table

$r = p / a$	m									
	1	2	3	4	5	6	7	8	9	10
1.0	0.5000	0.2000	0.0625	0.0154	0.0031	0.0005	0.0001	0.0000	0.0000	0.0000
1.5	0.6000	0.3103	0.1343	0.0480	0.0142	0.0035	0.0008	0.0001	0.0000	0.0000
2.0	0.6667	0.4000	0.2105	0.0952	0.0367	0.0121	0.0034	0.0009	0.0002	0.0000
2.5	0.7143	0.4717	0.2822	0.1499	0.0697	0.0282	0.0100	0.0031	0.0009	0.0002
3.0	0.7500	0.5294	0.3462	0.2061	0.1101	0.0522	0.0219	0.0081	0.0027	0.0008
3.5	0.7778	0.5765	0.4021	0.2603	0.1541	0.0825	0.0396	0.0170	0.0066	0.0023
4.0	0.8000	0.6154	0.4507	0.3107	0.1991	0.1172	0.0627	0.0304	0.0133	0.0053
4.5	0.8182	0.6480	0.4929	0.3567	0.2430	0.1542	0.0902	0.0483	0.0236	0.0105
5.0	0.8333	0.6757	0.5297	0.3983	0.2849	0.1918	0.1205	0.0700	0.0375	0.0184
5.5	0.8462	0.6994	0.5618	0.4358	0.3241	0.2290	0.1525	0.0949	0.0548	0.0293
6.0	0.8571	0.7200	0.5902	0.4696	0.3604	0.2649	0.1851	0.1219	0.0751	0.0431
6.5	0.8667	0.7380	0.6152	0.4999	0.3939	0.2991	0.2174	0.1501	0.0978	0.0598
7.0	0.8750	0.7538	0.6375	0.5273	0.4247	0.3313	0.2489	0.1788	0.1221	0.0787
7.5	0.8824	0.7679	0.6575	0.5521	0.4530	0.3615	0.2792	0.2075	0.1474	0.0995
8.0	0.8889	0.7805	0.6755	0.5746	0.4790	0.3898	0.3082	0.2356	0.1731	0.1217
8.5	0.8947	0.7918	0.6917	0.5951	0.5029	0.4160	0.3356	0.2629	0.1989	0.1446
9.0	0.9000	0.8020	0.7064	0.6138	0.5249	0.4405	0.3616	0.2892	0.2243	0.1680
9.5	0.9048	0.8112	0.7198	0.6309	0.5452	0.4633	0.3860	0.3143	0.2491	0.1914
10.0	0.9091	0.8197	0.7321	0.6467	0.5640	0.4845	0.4090	0.3383	0.2732	0.2146
10.5	0.9130	0.8274	0.7433	0.6612	0.5813	0.5043	0.4307	0.3611	0.2964	0.2374
11.0	0.9167	0.8345	0.7537	0.6745	0.5974	0.5227	0.4510	0.3828	0.3187	0.2596
11.5	0.9200	0.8410	0.7633	0.6869	0.6124	0.5400	0.4701	0.4033	0.3400	0.2811
12.0	0.9231	0.8471	0.7721	0.6985	0.6264	0.5561	0.4880	0.4227	0.3604	0.3019
12.5	0.9259	0.8527	0.7804	0.7092	0.6394	0.5712	0.5049	0.4410	0.3799	0.3220
13.0	0.9286	0.8579	0.7880	0.7192	0.6516	0.5854	0.5209	0.4584	0.3984	0.3412
13.5	0.9310	0.8627	0.7952	0.7285	0.6630	0.5987	0.5359	0.4749	0.4160	0.3596
14.0	0.9333	0.8673	0.8019	0.7373	0.6737	0.6112	0.5500	0.4905	0.4328	0.3773
14.5	0.9355	0.8715	0.8081	0.7455	0.6837	0.6230	0.5634	0.5052	0.4487	0.3942
15.0	0.9375	0.8755	0.8140	0.7532	0.6932	0.6341	0.5761	0.5193	0.4639	0.4103
15.5	0.9394	0.8792	0.8196	0.7605	0.7022	0.6446	0.5880	0.5326	0.4784	0.4258
16.0	0.9412	0.8828	0.8248	0.7674	0.7106	0.6546	0.5994	0.5452	0.4922	0.4406
16.5	0.9429	0.8861	0.8297	0.7739	0.7186	0.6640	0.6102	0.5572	0.5053	0.4547
17.0	0.9444	0.8892	0.8344	0.7800	0.7262	0.6729	0.6204	0.5687	0.5179	0.4682
17.5	0.9459	0.8922	0.8388	0.7859	0.7334	0.6814	0.6301	0.5795	0.5298	0.4811
18.0	0.9474	0.8950	0.8430	0.7914	0.7402	0.6895	0.6394	0.5899	0.5413	0.4935
18.5	0.9487	0.8977	0.8470	0.7966	0.7467	0.6972	0.6482	0.5998	0.5522	0.5053
19.0	0.9500	0.9002	0.8508	0.8016	0.7529	0.7045	0.6566	0.6093	0.5626	0.5167
19.5	0.9512	0.9027	0.8544	0.8064	0.7587	0.7115	0.6647	0.6183	0.5726	0.5275
20.0	0.9524	0.9050	0.8578	0.8109	0.7644	0.7181	0.6723	0.6270	0.5822	0.5380
20.5	0.9535	0.9072	0.8611	0.8153	0.7697	0.7245	0.6797	0.6353	0.5913	0.5480
21.0	0.9545	0.9093	0.8642	0.8194	0.7749	0.7306	0.6867	0.6432	0.6001	0.5576
21.5	0.9556	0.9113	0.8672	0.8234	0.7798	0.7364	0.6934	0.6508	0.6086	0.5668
22.0	0.9565	0.9132	0.8701	0.8272	0.7845	0.7420	0.6999	0.6581	0.6167	0.5757
22.5	0.9574	0.9150	0.8728	0.8308	0.7890	0.7474	0.7061	0.6651	0.6244	0.5842
23.0	0.9583	0.9168	0.8754	0.8343	0.7933	0.7525	0.7120	0.6718	0.6319	0.5924
23.5	0.9592	0.9185	0.8780	0.8376	0.7974	0.7575	0.7177	0.6783	0.6391	0.6003
24.0	0.9600	0.9201	0.8804	0.8408	0.8014	0.7622	0.7232	0.6845	0.6461	0.6079
24.5	0.9608	0.9217	0.8827	0.8439	0.8053	0.7668	0.7285	0.6905	0.6527	0.6153
25.0	0.9615	0.9232	0.8850	0.8469	0.8090	0.7712	0.7336	0.6963	0.6592	0.6224
25.5	0.9623	0.9246	0.8871	0.8497	0.8125	0.7754	0.7385	0.7019	0.6654	0.6292
26.0	0.9630	0.9260	0.8892	0.8525	0.8159	0.7795	0.7433	0.7072	0.6714	0.6358
26.5	0.9636	0.9274	0.8912	0.8552	0.8192	0.7835	0.7479	0.7124	0.6772	0.6422
27.0	0.9643	0.9287	0.8931	0.8577	0.8224	0.7873	0.7523	0.7174	0.6828	0.6483
27.5	0.9649	0.9299	0.8950	0.8602	0.8255	0.7910	0.7565	0.7223	0.6882	0.6543
28.0	0.9655	0.9311	0.8968	0.8626	0.8285	0.7945	0.7607	0.7269	0.6934	0.6600
28.5	0.9661	0.9323	0.8985	0.8649	0.8314	0.7979	0.7646	0.7315	0.6985	0.6656
29.0	0.9667	0.9334	0.9002	0.8671	0.8341	0.8013	0.7685	0.7359	0.7034	0.6710
29.5	0.9672	0.9345	0.9019	0.8693	0.8368	0.8045	0.7722	0.7401	0.7081	0.6763
30.0	0.9677	0.9356	0.9034	0.8714	0.8394	0.8076	0.7758	0.7442	0.7127	0.6813
30.5	0.9683	0.9366	0.9050	0.8734	0.8420	0.8106	0.7793	0.7482	0.7172	0.6863
31.0	0.9688	0.9376	0.9064	0.8754	0.8444	0.8135	0.7827	0.7521	0.7215	0.6910
31.5	0.9692	0.9385	0.9079	0.8773	0.8468	0.8164	0.7860	0.7558	0.7257	0.6957
32.0	0.9697	0.9394	0.9093	0.8791	0.8491	0.8191	0.7892	0.7594	0.7297	0.7002

Distribution, Inventory, and Loss Function Tables

The Standard Normal Distribution Function Table contains the probability that the outcome of a standard normal random variable is z or smaller. The table provides z values up to two significant digits. Find the row and column headings that add up to the z value you are looking for. The intersection of that row and column contains the probability you seek, $\Phi(z)$.

Example (1): Find the probability that a standard normal random variable generates an outcome that is $z = -1.54$ or lower. First, find the row heading -1.5. Second, find the column heading -0.04 because $(-1.5) + (-0.04) = -1.54$. The intersection of that row with that column is $\Phi(-1.54) = 0.0618$.

Example (2): Find the probability that a standard normal random variable generates an outcome that is $z = 0.52$ or lower. First, find the row heading 0.5. Second, find the column heading 0.02 because $(0.5) + (0.02) = 0.52$. The intersection of that row with that column is $\Phi(0.52) = 0.6985$.

The Standard Normal Inventory Table and the Standard Normal Loss Function Table are organized in the same way as the Standard Normal Distribution Function Table.

The Poisson Distribution Function Table provides the probability a Poisson distribution with a given mean (column heading) is S or fewer.

The Poisson Inventory Function Table provides the amount of inventory at the end of a period that has Poisson distributed demand with a given mean (column heading) and an initial inventory of S.

The Poisson Loss Function Table provides the expected amount the outcome of a Poisson distribution with a given mean (column heading) exceeds S.

Example (3): With mean 2.25 and $S = 2$, the Inventory function of a Poisson distribution is 0.44795: Look in the column heading for the mean 2.25 and the row with $S = 2$.

Standard Normal Distribution Function Table, Φ(z)

z	−0.09	−0.08	−0.07	−0.06	−0.05	−0.04	−0.03	−0.02	−0.01	0.00
−4.0	0.0000	0.0000	0.0000	0.0000	0.0000	0.0000	0.0000	0.0000	0.0000	0.0000
−3.9	0.0000	0.0000	0.0000	0.0000	0.0000	0.0000	0.0000	0.0000	0.0000	0.0000
−3.8	0.0001	0.0001	0.0001	0.0001	0.0001	0.0001	0.0001	0.0001	0.0001	0.0001
−3.7	0.0001	0.0001	0.0001	0.0001	0.0001	0.0001	0.0001	0.0001	0.0001	0.0001
−3.6	0.0001	0.0001	0.0001	0.0001	0.0001	0.0001	0.0001	0.0001	0.0002	0.0002
−3.5	0.0002	0.0002	0.0002	0.0002	0.0002	0.0002	0.0002	0.0002	0.0002	0.0002
−3.4	0.0002	0.0003	0.0003	0.0003	0.0003	0.0003	0.0003	0.0003	0.0003	0.0003
−3.3	0.0003	0.0004	0.0004	0.0004	0.0004	0.0004	0.0004	0.0005	0.0005	0.0005
−3.2	0.0005	0.0005	0.0005	0.0006	0.0006	0.0006	0.0006	0.0006	0.0007	0.0007
−3.1	0.0007	0.0007	0.0008	0.0008	0.0008	0.0008	0.0009	0.0009	0.0009	0.0010
−3.0	0.0010	0.0010	0.0011	0.0011	0.0011	0.0012	0.0012	0.0013	0.0013	0.0013
−2.9	0.0014	0.0014	0.0015	0.0015	0.0016	0.0016	0.0017	0.0018	0.0018	0.0019
−2.8	0.0019	0.0020	0.0021	0.0021	0.0022	0.0023	0.0023	0.0024	0.0025	0.0026
−2.7	0.0026	0.0027	0.0028	0.0029	0.0030	0.0031	0.0032	0.0033	0.0034	0.0035
−2.6	0.0036	0.0037	0.0038	0.0039	0.0040	0.0041	0.0043	0.0044	0.0045	0.0047
−2.5	0.0048	0.0049	0.0051	0.0052	0.0054	0.0055	0.0057	0.0059	0.0060	0.0062
−2.4	0.0064	0.0066	0.0068	0.0069	0.0071	0.0073	0.0075	0.0078	0.0080	0.0082
−2.3	0.0084	0.0087	0.0089	0.0091	0.0094	0.0096	0.0099	0.0102	0.0104	0.0107
−2.2	0.0110	0.0113	0.0116	0.0119	0.0122	0.0125	0.0129	0.0132	0.0136	0.0139
−2.1	0.0143	0.0146	0.0150	0.0154	0.0158	0.0162	0.0166	0.0170	0.0174	0.0179
−2.0	0.0183	0.0188	0.0192	0.0197	0.0202	0.0207	0.0212	0.0217	0.0222	0.0228
−1.9	0.0233	0.0239	0.0244	0.0250	0.0256	0.0262	0.0268	0.0274	0.0281	0.0287
−1.8	0.0294	0.0301	0.0307	0.0314	0.0322	0.0329	0.0336	0.0344	0.0351	0.0359
−1.7	0.0367	0.0375	0.0384	0.0392	0.0401	0.0409	0.0418	0.0427	0.0436	0.0446
−1.6	0.0455	0.0465	0.0475	0.0485	0.0495	0.0505	0.0516	0.0526	0.0537	0.0548
−1.5	0.0559	0.0571	0.0582	0.0594	0.0606	0.0618	0.0630	0.0643	0.0655	0.0668
−1.4	0.0681	0.0694	0.0708	0.0721	0.0735	0.0749	0.0764	0.0778	0.0793	0.0808
−1.3	0.0823	0.0838	0.0853	0.0869	0.0885	0.0901	0.0918	0.0934	0.0951	0.0968
−1.2	0.0985	0.1003	0.1020	0.1038	0.1056	0.1075	0.1093	0.1112	0.1131	0.1151
−1.1	0.1170	0.1190	0.1210	0.1230	0.1251	0.1271	0.1292	0.1314	0.1335	0.1357
−1.0	0.1379	0.1401	0.1423	0.1446	0.1469	0.1492	0.1515	0.1539	0.1562	0.1587
−0.9	0.1611	0.1635	0.1660	0.1685	0.1711	0.1736	0.1762	0.1788	0.1814	0.1841
−0.8	0.1867	0.1894	0.1922	0.1949	0.1977	0.2005	0.2033	0.2061	0.2090	0.2119
−0.7	0.2148	0.2177	0.2206	0.2236	0.2266	0.2296	0.2327	0.2358	0.2389	0.2420
−0.6	0.2451	0.2483	0.2514	0.2546	0.2578	0.2611	0.2643	0.2676	0.2709	0.2743
−0.5	0.2776	0.2810	0.2843	0.2877	0.2912	0.2946	0.2981	0.3015	0.3050	0.3085
−0.4	0.3121	0.3156	0.3192	0.3228	0.3264	0.3300	0.3336	0.3372	0.3409	0.3446
−0.3	0.3483	0.3520	0.3557	0.3594	0.3632	0.3669	0.3707	0.3745	0.3783	0.3821
−0.2	0.3859	0.3897	0.3936	0.3974	0.4013	0.4052	0.4090	0.4129	0.4168	0.4207
−0.1	0.4247	0.4286	0.4325	0.4364	0.4404	0.4443	0.4483	0.4522	0.4562	0.4602
0.0	0.4641	0.4681	0.4721	0.4761	0.4801	0.4840	0.4880	0.4920	0.4960	0.5000

(*continued*)

Standard Normal Distribution Function Table, $\Phi(z)$ (Concluded)

z	0.00	0.01	0.02	0.03	0.04	0.05	0.06	0.07	0.08	0.09
0.0	0.5000	0.5040	0.5080	0.5120	0.5160	0.5199	0.5239	0.5279	0.5319	0.5359
0.1	0.5398	0.5438	0.5478	0.5517	0.5557	0.5596	0.5636	0.5675	0.5714	0.5753
0.2	0.5793	0.5832	0.5871	0.5910	0.5948	0.5987	0.6026	0.6064	0.6103	0.6141
0.3	0.6179	0.6217	0.6255	0.6293	0.6331	0.6368	0.6406	0.6443	0.6480	0.6517
0.4	0.6554	0.6591	0.6628	0.6664	0.6700	0.6736	0.6772	0.6808	0.6844	0.6879
0.5	0.6915	0.6950	0.6985	0.7019	0.7054	0.7088	0.7123	0.7157	0.7190	0.7224
0.6	0.7257	0.7291	0.7324	0.7357	0.7389	0.7422	0.7454	0.7486	0.7517	0.7549
0.7	0.7580	0.7611	0.7642	0.7673	0.7704	0.7734	0.7764	0.7794	0.7823	0.7852
0.8	0.7881	0.7910	0.7939	0.7967	0.7995	0.8023	0.8051	0.8078	0.8106	0.8133
0.9	0.8159	0.8186	0.8212	0.8238	0.8264	0.8289	0.8315	0.8340	0.8365	0.8389
1.0	0.8413	0.8438	0.8461	0.8485	0.8508	0.8531	0.8554	0.8577	0.8599	0.8621
1.1	0.8643	0.8665	0.8686	0.8708	0.8729	0.8749	0.8770	0.8790	0.8810	0.8830
1.2	0.8849	0.8869	0.8888	0.8907	0.8925	0.8944	0.8962	0.8980	0.8997	0.9015
1.3	0.9032	0.9049	0.9066	0.9082	0.9099	0.9115	0.9131	0.9147	0.9162	0.9177
1.4	0.9192	0.9207	0.9222	0.9236	0.9251	0.9265	0.9279	0.9292	0.9306	0.9319
1.5	0.9332	0.9345	0.9357	0.9370	0.9382	0.9394	0.9406	0.9418	0.9429	0.9441
1.6	0.9452	0.9463	0.9474	0.9484	0.9495	0.9505	0.9515	0.9525	0.9535	0.9545
1.7	0.9554	0.9564	0.9573	0.9582	0.9591	0.9599	0.9608	0.9616	0.9625	0.9633
1.8	0.9641	0.9649	0.9656	0.9664	0.9671	0.9678	0.9686	0.9693	0.9699	0.9706
1.9	0.9713	0.9719	0.9726	0.9732	0.9738	0.9744	0.9750	0.9756	0.9761	0.9767
2.0	0.9772	0.9778	0.9783	0.9788	0.9793	0.9798	0.9803	0.9808	0.9812	0.9817
2.1	0.9821	0.9826	0.9830	0.9834	0.9838	0.9842	0.9846	0.9850	0.9854	0.9857
2.2	0.9861	0.9864	0.9868	0.9871	0.9875	0.9878	0.9881	0.9884	0.9887	0.9890
2.3	0.9893	0.9896	0.9898	0.9901	0.9904	0.9906	0.9909	0.9911	0.9913	0.9916
2.4	0.9918	0.9920	0.9922	0.9925	0.9927	0.9929	0.9931	0.9932	0.9934	0.9936
2.5	0.9938	0.9940	0.9941	0.9943	0.9945	0.9946	0.9948	0.9949	0.9951	0.9952
2.6	0.9953	0.9955	0.9956	0.9957	0.9959	0.9960	0.9961	0.9962	0.9963	0.9964
2.7	0.9965	0.9966	0.9967	0.9968	0.9969	0.9970	0.9971	0.9972	0.9973	0.9974
2.8	0.9974	0.9975	0.9976	0.9977	0.9977	0.9978	0.9979	0.9979	0.9980	0.9981
2.9	0.9981	0.9982	0.9982	0.9983	0.9984	0.9984	0.9985	0.9985	0.9986	0.9986
3.0	0.9987	0.9987	0.9987	0.9988	0.9988	0.9989	0.9989	0.9989	0.9990	0.9990
3.1	0.9990	0.9991	0.9991	0.9991	0.9992	0.9992	0.9992	0.9992	0.9993	0.9993
3.2	0.9993	0.9993	0.9994	0.9994	0.9994	0.9994	0.9994	0.9995	0.9995	0.9995
3.3	0.9995	0.9995	0.9995	0.9996	0.9996	0.9996	0.9996	0.9996	0.9996	0.9997
3.4	0.9997	0.9997	0.9997	0.9997	0.9997	0.9997	0.9997	0.9997	0.9997	0.9998
3.5	0.9998	0.9998	0.9998	0.9998	0.9998	0.9998	0.9998	0.9998	0.9998	0.9998
3.6	0.9998	0.9998	0.9999	0.9999	0.9999	0.9999	0.9999	0.9999	0.9999	0.9999
3.7	0.9999	0.9999	0.9999	0.9999	0.9999	0.9999	0.9999	0.9999	0.9999	0.9999
3.8	0.9999	0.9999	0.9999	0.9999	0.9999	0.9999	0.9999	0.9999	0.9999	0.9999
3.9	1.0000	1.0000	1.0000	1.0000	1.0000	1.0000	1.0000	1.0000	1.0000	1.0000
4.0	1.0000	1.0000	1.0000	1.0000	1.0000	1.0000	1.0000	1.0000	1.0000	1.0000

Standard Normal Inventory Function Table, $I(z)$

z	−0.09	−0.08	−0.07	−0.06	−0.05	−0.04	−0.03	−0.02	−0.01	0.00
−4.0	0.0000	0.0000	0.0000	0.0000	0.0000	0.0000	0.0000	0.0000	0.0000	0.0000
−3.9	0.0000	0.0000	0.0000	0.0000	0.0000	0.0000	0.0000	0.0000	0.0000	0.0000
−3.8	0.0000	0.0000	0.0000	0.0000	0.0000	0.0000	0.0000	0.0000	0.0000	0.0000
−3.7	0.0000	0.0000	0.0000	0.0000	0.0000	0.0000	0.0000	0.0000	0.0000	0.0000
−3.6	0.0000	0.0000	0.0000	0.0000	0.0000	0.0000	0.0000	0.0000	0.0000	0.0000
−3.5	0.0000	0.0000	0.0000	0.0000	0.0000	0.0000	0.0001	0.0001	0.0001	0.0001
−3.4	0.0001	0.0001	0.0001	0.0001	0.0001	0.0001	0.0001	0.0001	0.0001	0.0001
−3.3	0.0001	0.0001	0.0001	0.0001	0.0001	0.0001	0.0001	0.0001	0.0001	0.0001
−3.2	0.0001	0.0001	0.0001	0.0001	0.0002	0.0002	0.0002	0.0002	0.0002	0.0002
−3.1	0.0002	0.0002	0.0002	0.0002	0.0002	0.0002	0.0002	0.0002	0.0003	0.0003
−3.0	0.0003	0.0003	0.0003	0.0003	0.0003	0.0003	0.0003	0.0004	0.0004	0.0004
−2.9	0.0004	0.0004	0.0004	0.0004	0.0005	0.0005	0.0005	0.0005	0.0005	0.0005
−2.8	0.0006	0.0006	0.0006	0.0006	0.0006	0.0007	0.0007	0.0007	0.0007	0.0008
−2.7	0.0008	0.0008	0.0008	0.0009	0.0009	0.0009	0.0010	0.0010	0.0010	0.0011
−2.6	0.0011	0.0011	0.0012	0.0012	0.0012	0.0013	0.0013	0.0014	0.0014	0.0015
−2.5	0.0015	0.0016	0.0016	0.0017	0.0017	0.0018	0.0018	0.0019	0.0019	0.0020
−2.4	0.0021	0.0021	0.0022	0.0023	0.0023	0.0024	0.0025	0.0026	0.0026	0.0027
−2.3	0.0028	0.0029	0.0030	0.0031	0.0032	0.0033	0.0034	0.0035	0.0036	0.0037
−2.2	0.0038	0.0039	0.0040	0.0041	0.0042	0.0044	0.0045	0.0046	0.0047	0.0049
−2.1	0.0050	0.0052	0.0053	0.0055	0.0056	0.0058	0.0060	0.0061	0.0063	0.0065
−2.0	0.0066	0.0068	0.0070	0.0072	0.0074	0.0076	0.0078	0.0080	0.0083	0.0085
−1.9	0.0087	0.0090	0.0092	0.0094	0.0097	0.0100	0.0102	0.0105	0.0108	0.0111
−1.8	0.0113	0.0116	0.0119	0.0123	0.0126	0.0129	0.0132	0.0136	0.0139	0.0143
−1.7	0.0146	0.0150	0.0154	0.0158	0.0162	0.0166	0.0170	0.0174	0.0178	0.0183
−1.6	0.0187	0.0192	0.0197	0.0201	0.0206	0.0211	0.0216	0.0222	0.0227	0.0232
−1.5	0.0238	0.0244	0.0249	0.0255	0.0261	0.0267	0.0274	0.0280	0.0286	0.0293
−1.4	0.0300	0.0307	0.0314	0.0321	0.0328	0.0336	0.0343	0.0351	0.0359	0.0367
−1.3	0.0375	0.0383	0.0392	0.0400	0.0409	0.0418	0.0427	0.0436	0.0446	0.0455
−1.2	0.0465	0.0475	0.0485	0.0495	0.0506	0.0517	0.0527	0.0538	0.0550	0.0561
−1.1	0.0573	0.0584	0.0596	0.0609	0.0621	0.0634	0.0646	0.0659	0.0673	0.0686
−1.0	0.0700	0.0714	0.0728	0.0742	0.0757	0.0772	0.0787	0.0802	0.0817	0.0833
−0.9	0.0849	0.0865	0.0882	0.0899	0.0916	0.0933	0.0950	0.0968	0.0986	0.1004
−0.8	0.1023	0.1042	0.1061	0.1080	0.1100	0.1120	0.1140	0.1160	0.1181	0.1202
−0.7	0.1223	0.1245	0.1267	0.1289	0.1312	0.1334	0.1358	0.1381	0.1405	0.1429
−0.6	0.1453	0.1478	0.1503	0.1528	0.1554	0.1580	0.1606	0.1633	0.1659	0.1687
−0.5	0.1714	0.1742	0.1771	0.1799	0.1828	0.1857	0.1887	0.1917	0.1947	0.1978
−0.4	0.2009	0.2040	0.2072	0.2104	0.2137	0.2169	0.2203	0.2236	0.2270	0.2304
−0.3	0.2339	0.2374	0.2409	0.2445	0.2481	0.2518	0.2555	0.2592	0.2630	0.2668
−0.2	0.2706	0.2745	0.2784	0.2824	0.2863	0.2904	0.2944	0.2986	0.3027	0.3069
−0.1	0.3111	0.3154	0.3197	0.3240	0.3284	0.3328	0.3373	0.3418	0.3464	0.3509
0.0	0.3556	0.3602	0.3649	0.3697	0.3744	0.3793	0.3841	0.3890	0.3940	0.3989

(*continued*)

Standard Normal Inventory Function Table, $I(z)$ (Concluded)

z	0.00	0.01	0.02	0.03	0.04	0.05	0.06	0.07	0.08	0.09
0.0	0.3989	0.4040	0.4090	0.4141	0.4193	0.4244	0.4297	0.4349	0.4402	0.4456
0.1	0.4509	0.4564	0.4618	0.4673	0.4728	0.4784	0.4840	0.4897	0.4954	0.5011
0.2	0.5069	0.5127	0.5186	0.5244	0.5304	0.5363	0.5424	0.5484	0.5545	0.5606
0.3	0.5668	0.5730	0.5792	0.5855	0.5918	0.5981	0.6045	0.6109	0.6174	0.6239
0.4	0.6304	0.6370	0.6436	0.6503	0.6569	0.6637	0.6704	0.6772	0.6840	0.6909
0.5	0.6978	0.7047	0.7117	0.7187	0.7257	0.7328	0.7399	0.7471	0.7542	0.7614
0.6	0.7687	0.7759	0.7833	0.7906	0.7980	0.8054	0.8128	0.8203	0.8278	0.8353
0.7	0.8429	0.8505	0.8581	0.8658	0.8734	0.8812	0.8889	0.8967	0.9045	0.9123
0.8	0.9202	0.9281	0.9360	0.9440	0.9520	0.9600	0.9680	0.9761	0.9842	0.9923
0.9	1.0004	1.0086	1.0168	1.0250	1.0333	1.0416	1.0499	1.0582	1.0665	1.0749
1.0	1.0833	1.0917	1.1002	1.1087	1.1172	1.1257	1.1342	1.1428	1.1514	1.1600
1.1	1.1686	1.1773	1.1859	1.1946	1.2034	1.2121	1.2209	1.2296	1.2384	1.2473
1.2	1.2561	1.2650	1.2738	1.2827	1.2917	1.3006	1.3095	1.3185	1.3275	1.3365
1.3	1.3455	1.3546	1.3636	1.3727	1.3818	1.3909	1.4000	1.4092	1.4183	1.4275
1.4	1.4367	1.4459	1.4551	1.4643	1.4736	1.4828	1.4921	1.5014	1.5107	1.5200
1.5	1.5293	1.5386	1.5480	1.5574	1.5667	1.5761	1.5855	1.5949	1.6044	1.6138
1.6	1.6232	1.6327	1.6422	1.6516	1.6611	1.6706	1.6801	1.6897	1.6992	1.7087
1.7	1.7183	1.7278	1.7374	1.7470	1.7566	1.7662	1.7758	1.7854	1.7950	1.8046
1.8	1.8143	1.8239	1.8336	1.8432	1.8529	1.8626	1.8723	1.8819	1.8916	1.9013
1.9	1.9111	1.9208	1.9305	1.9402	1.9500	1.9597	1.9694	1.9792	1.9890	1.9987
2.0	2.0085	2.0183	2.0280	2.0378	2.0476	2.0574	2.0672	2.0770	2.0868	2.0966
2.1	2.1065	2.1163	2.1261	2.1360	2.1458	2.1556	2.1655	2.1753	2.1852	2.1950
2.2	2.2049	2.2147	2.2246	2.2345	2.2444	2.2542	2.2641	2.2740	2.2839	2.2938
2.3	2.3037	2.3136	2.3235	2.3334	2.3433	2.3532	2.3631	2.3730	2.3829	2.3928
2.4	2.4027	2.4126	2.4226	2.4325	2.4424	2.4523	2.4623	2.4722	2.4821	2.4921
2.5	2.5020	2.5119	2.5219	2.5318	2.5418	2.5517	2.5617	2.5716	2.5816	2.5915
2.6	2.6015	2.6114	2.6214	2.6313	2.6413	2.6512	2.6612	2.6712	2.6811	2.6911
2.7	2.7011	2.7110	2.7210	2.7310	2.7409	2.7509	2.7609	2.7708	2.7808	2.7908
2.8	2.8008	2.8107	2.8207	2.8307	2.8407	2.8506	2.8606	2.8706	2.8806	2.8906
2.9	2.9005	2.9105	2.9205	2.9305	2.9405	2.9505	2.9604	2.9704	2.9804	2.9904
3.0	3.0004	3.0104	3.0204	3.0303	3.0403	3.0503	3.0603	3.0703	3.0803	3.0903
3.1	3.1003	3.1103	3.1202	3.1302	3.1402	3.1502	3.1602	3.1702	3.1802	3.1902
3.2	3.2002	3.2102	3.2202	3.2302	3.2402	3.2502	3.2601	3.2701	3.2801	3.2901
3.3	3.3001	3.3101	3.3201	3.3301	3.3401	3.3501	3.3601	3.3701	3.3801	3.3901
3.4	3.4001	3.4101	3.4201	3.4301	3.4401	3.4501	3.4601	3.4701	3.4801	3.4901
3.5	3.5001	3.5101	3.5201	3.5301	3.5400	3.5500	3.5600	3.5700	3.5800	3.5900
3.6	3.6000	3.6100	3.6200	3.6300	3.6400	3.6500	3.6600	3.6700	3.6800	3.6900
3.7	3.7000	3.7100	3.7200	3.7300	3.7400	3.7500	3.7600	3.7700	3.7800	3.7900
3.8	3.8000	3.8100	3.8200	3.8300	3.8400	3.8500	3.8600	3.8700	3.8800	3.8900
3.9	3.9000	3.9100	3.9200	3.9300	3.9400	3.9500	3.9600	3.9700	3.9800	3.9900
4.0	4.0000	4.0100	4.0200	4.0300	4.0400	4.0500	4.0600	4.0700	4.0800	4.0900

Standard Normal Loss Function Table, $L(z)$

z	−0.09	−0.08	−0.07	−0.06	−0.05	−0.04	−0.03	−0.02	−0.01	0.00
−4.0	4.0900	4.0800	4.0700	4.0600	4.0500	4.0400	4.0300	4.0200	4.0100	4.0000
−3.9	3.9900	3.9800	3.9700	3.9600	3.9500	3.9400	3.9300	3.9200	3.9100	3.9000
−3.8	3.8900	3.8800	3.8700	3.8600	3.8500	3.8400	3.8300	3.8200	3.8100	3.8000
−3.7	3.7900	3.7800	3.7700	3.7600	3.7500	3.7400	3.7300	3.7200	3.7100	3.7000
−3.6	3.6900	3.6800	3.6700	3.6600	3.6500	3.6400	3.6300	3.6200	3.6100	3.6000
−3.5	3.5900	3.5800	3.5700	3.5600	3.5500	3.5400	3.5301	3.5201	3.5101	3.5001
−3.4	3.4901	3.4801	3.4701	3.4601	3.4501	3.4401	3.4301	3.4201	3.4101	3.4001
−3.3	3.3901	3.3801	3.3701	3.3601	3.3501	3.3401	3.3301	3.3201	3.3101	3.3001
−3.2	3.2901	3.2801	3.2701	3.2601	3.2502	3.2402	3.2302	3.2202	3.2102	3.2002
−3.1	3.1902	3.1802	3.1702	3.1602	3.1502	3.1402	3.1302	3.1202	3.1103	3.1003
−3.0	3.0903	3.0803	3.0703	3.0603	3.0503	3.0403	3.0303	3.0204	3.0104	3.0004
−2.9	2.9904	2.9804	2.9704	2.9604	2.9505	2.9405	2.9305	2.9205	2.9105	2.9005
−2.8	2.8906	2.8806	2.8706	2.8606	2.8506	2.8407	2.8307	2.8207	2.8107	2.8008
−2.7	2.7908	2.7808	2.7708	2.7609	2.7509	2.7409	2.7310	2.7210	2.7110	2.7011
−2.6	2.6911	2.6811	2.6712	2.6612	2.6512	2.6413	2.6313	2.6214	2.6114	2.6015
−2.5	2.5915	2.5816	2.5716	2.5617	2.5517	2.5418	2.5318	2.5219	2.5119	2.5020
−2.4	2.4921	2.4821	2.4722	2.4623	2.4523	2.4424	2.4325	2.4226	2.4126	2.4027
−2.3	2.3928	2.3829	2.3730	2.3631	2.3532	2.3433	2.3334	2.3235	2.3136	2.3037
−2.2	2.2938	2.2839	2.2740	2.2641	2.2542	2.2444	2.2345	2.2246	2.2147	2.2049
−2.1	2.1950	2.1852	2.1753	2.1655	2.1556	2.1458	2.1360	2.1261	2.1163	2.1065
−2.0	2.0966	2.0868	2.0770	2.0672	2.0574	2.0476	2.0378	2.0280	2.0183	2.0085
−1.9	1.9987	1.9890	1.9792	1.9694	1.9597	1.9500	1.9402	1.9305	1.9208	1.9111
−1.8	1.9013	1.8916	1.8819	1.8723	1.8626	1.8529	1.8432	1.8336	1.8239	1.8143
−1.7	1.8046	1.7950	1.7854	1.7758	1.7662	1.7566	1.7470	1.7374	1.7278	1.7183
−1.6	1.7087	1.6992	1.6897	1.6801	1.6706	1.6611	1.6516	1.6422	1.6327	1.6232
−1.5	1.6138	1.6044	1.5949	1.5855	1.5761	1.5667	1.5574	1.5480	1.5386	1.5293
−1.4	1.5200	1.5107	1.5014	1.4921	1.4828	1.4736	1.4643	1.4551	1.4459	1.4367
−1.3	1.4275	1.4183	1.4092	1.4000	1.3909	1.3818	1.3727	1.3636	1.3546	1.3455
−1.2	1.3365	1.3275	1.3185	1.3095	1.3006	1.2917	1.2827	1.2738	1.2650	1.2561
−1.1	1.2473	1.2384	1.2296	1.2209	1.2121	1.2034	1.1946	1.1859	1.1773	1.1686
−1.0	1.1600	1.1514	1.1428	1.1342	1.1257	1.1172	1.1087	1.1002	1.0917	1.0833
−0.9	1.0749	1.0665	1.0582	1.0499	1.0416	1.0333	1.0250	1.0168	1.0086	1.0004
−0.8	0.9923	0.9842	0.9761	0.9680	0.9600	0.9520	0.9440	0.9360	0.9281	0.9202
−0.7	0.9123	0.9045	0.8967	0.8889	0.8812	0.8734	0.8658	0.8581	0.8505	0.8429
−0.6	0.8353	0.8278	0.8203	0.8128	0.8054	0.7980	0.7906	0.7833	0.7759	0.7687
−0.5	0.7614	0.7542	0.7471	0.7399	0.7328	0.7257	0.7187	0.7117	0.7047	0.6978
−0.4	0.6909	0.6840	0.6772	0.6704	0.6637	0.6569	0.6503	0.6436	0.6370	0.6304
−0.3	0.6239	0.6174	0.6109	0.6045	0.5981	0.5918	0.5855	0.5792	0.5730	0.5668
−0.2	0.5606	0.5545	0.5484	0.5424	0.5363	0.5304	0.5244	0.5186	0.5127	0.5069
−0.1	0.5011	0.4954	0.4897	0.4840	0.4784	0.4728	0.4673	0.4618	0.4564	0.4509
0.0	0.4456	0.4402	0.4349	0.4297	0.4244	0.4193	0.4141	0.4090	0.4040	0.3989

(continued)

Standard Normal Loss Function Table, $L(z)$ (Concluded)

z	0.00	0.01	0.02	0.03	0.04	0.05	0.06	0.07	0.08	0.09
0.0	0.3989	0.3940	0.3890	0.3841	0.3793	0.3744	0.3697	0.3649	0.3602	0.3556
0.1	0.3509	0.3464	0.3418	0.3373	0.3328	0.3284	0.3240	0.3197	0.3154	0.3111
0.2	0.3069	0.3027	0.2986	0.2944	0.2904	0.2863	0.2824	0.2784	0.2745	0.2706
0.3	0.2668	0.2630	0.2592	0.2555	0.2518	0.2481	0.2445	0.2409	0.2374	0.2339
0.4	0.2304	0.2270	0.2236	0.2203	0.2169	0.2137	0.2104	0.2072	0.2040	0.2009
0.5	0.1978	0.1947	0.1917	0.1887	0.1857	0.1828	0.1799	0.1771	0.1742	0.1714
0.6	0.1687	0.1659	0.1633	0.1606	0.1580	0.1554	0.1528	0.1503	0.1478	0.1453
0.7	0.1429	0.1405	0.1381	0.1358	0.1334	0.1312	0.1289	0.1267	0.1245	0.1223
0.8	0.1202	0.1181	0.1160	0.1140	0.1120	0.1100	0.1080	0.1061	0.1042	0.1023
0.9	0.1004	0.0986	0.0968	0.0950	0.0933	0.0916	0.0899	0.0882	0.0865	0.0849
1.0	0.0833	0.0817	0.0802	0.0787	0.0772	0.0757	0.0742	0.0728	0.0714	0.0700
1.1	0.0686	0.0673	0.0659	0.0646	0.0634	0.0621	0.0609	0.0596	0.0584	0.0573
1.2	0.0561	0.0550	0.0538	0.0527	0.0517	0.0506	0.0495	0.0485	0.0475	0.0465
1.3	0.0455	0.0446	0.0436	0.0427	0.0418	0.0409	0.0400	0.0392	0.0383	0.0375
1.4	0.0367	0.0359	0.0351	0.0343	0.0336	0.0328	0.0321	0.0314	0.0307	0.0300
1.5	0.0293	0.0286	0.0280	0.0274	0.0267	0.0261	0.0255	0.0249	0.0244	0.0238
1.6	0.0232	0.0227	0.0222	0.0216	0.0211	0.0206	0.0201	0.0197	0.0192	0.0187
1.7	0.0183	0.0178	0.0174	0.0170	0.0166	0.0162	0.0158	0.0154	0.0150	0.0146
1.8	0.0143	0.0139	0.0136	0.0132	0.0129	0.0126	0.0123	0.0119	0.0116	0.0113
1.9	0.0111	0.0108	0.0105	0.0102	0.0100	0.0097	0.0094	0.0092	0.0090	0.0087
2.0	0.0085	0.0083	0.0080	0.0078	0.0076	0.0074	0.0072	0.0070	0.0068	0.0066
2.1	0.0065	0.0063	0.0061	0.0060	0.0058	0.0056	0.0055	0.0053	0.0052	0.0050
2.2	0.0049	0.0047	0.0046	0.0045	0.0044	0.0042	0.0041	0.0040	0.0039	0.0038
2.3	0.0037	0.0036	0.0035	0.0034	0.0033	0.0032	0.0031	0.0030	0.0029	0.0028
2.4	0.0027	0.0026	0.0026	0.0025	0.0024	0.0023	0.0023	0.0022	0.0021	0.0021
2.5	0.0020	0.0019	0.0019	0.0018	0.0018	0.0017	0.0017	0.0016	0.0016	0.0015
2.6	0.0015	0.0014	0.0014	0.0013	0.0013	0.0012	0.0012	0.0012	0.0011	0.0011
2.7	0.0011	0.0010	0.0010	0.0010	0.0009	0.0009	0.0009	0.0008	0.0008	0.0008
2.8	0.0008	0.0007	0.0007	0.0007	0.0007	0.0006	0.0006	0.0006	0.0006	0.0006
2.9	0.0005	0.0005	0.0005	0.0005	0.0005	0.0005	0.0004	0.0004	0.0004	0.0004
3.0	0.0004	0.0004	0.0004	0.0003	0.0003	0.0003	0.0003	0.0003	0.0003	0.0003
3.1	0.0003	0.0003	0.0002	0.0002	0.0002	0.0002	0.0002	0.0002	0.0002	0.0002
3.2	0.0002	0.0002	0.0002	0.0002	0.0002	0.0002	0.0001	0.0001	0.0001	0.0001
3.3	0.0001	0.0001	0.0001	0.0001	0.0001	0.0001	0.0001	0.0001	0.0001	0.0001
3.4	0.0001	0.0001	0.0001	0.0001	0.0001	0.0001	0.0001	0.0001	0.0001	0.0001
3.5	0.0001	0.0001	0.0001	0.0001	0.0000	0.0000	0.0000	0.0000	0.0000	0.0000
3.6	0.0000	0.0000	0.0000	0.0000	0.0000	0.0000	0.0000	0.0000	0.0000	0.0000
3.7	0.0000	0.0000	0.0000	0.0000	0.0000	0.0000	0.0000	0.0000	0.0000	0.0000
3.8	0.0000	0.0000	0.0000	0.0000	0.0000	0.0000	0.0000	0.0000	0.0000	0.0000
3.9	0.0000	0.0000	0.0000	0.0000	0.0000	0.0000	0.0000	0.0000	0.0000	0.0000
4.0	0.0000	0.0000	0.0000	0.0000	0.0000	0.0000	0.0000	0.0000	0.0000	0.0000

Poisson Distribution Function Table

	Mean									
S	0.05	0.10	0.15	0.20	0.25	0.30	0.35	0.40	0.45	0.50
0	0.95123	0.90484	0.86071	0.81873	0.77880	0.74082	0.70469	0.67032	0.63763	0.60653
1	0.99879	0.99532	0.98981	0.98248	0.97350	0.96306	0.95133	0.93845	0.92456	0.90980
2	0.99998	0.99985	0.99950	0.99885	0.99784	0.99640	0.99449	0.99207	0.98912	0.98561
3	1.00000	1.00000	0.99998	0.99994	0.99987	0.99973	0.99953	0.99922	0.99880	0.99825
4	1.00000	1.00000	1.00000	1.00000	0.99999	0.99998	0.99997	0.99994	0.99989	0.99983
5	1.00000	1.00000	1.00000	1.00000	1.00000	1.00000	1.00000	1.00000	0.99999	0.99999
6	1.00000	1.00000	1.00000	1.00000	1.00000	1.00000	1.00000	1.00000	1.00000	1.00000

	Mean									
S	0.55	0.60	0.65	0.70	0.75	0.80	0.85	0.90	0.95	1.00
0	0.57695	0.54881	0.52205	0.49659	0.47237	0.44933	0.42741	0.40657	0.38674	0.36788
1	0.89427	0.87810	0.86138	0.84420	0.82664	0.80879	0.79072	0.77248	0.75414	0.73576
2	0.98154	0.97688	0.97166	0.96586	0.95949	0.95258	0.94512	0.93714	0.92866	0.91970
3	0.99753	0.99664	0.99555	0.99425	0.99271	0.99092	0.98887	0.98654	0.98393	0.98101
4	0.99973	0.99961	0.99944	0.99921	0.99894	0.99859	0.99817	0.99766	0.99705	0.99634
5	0.99998	0.99996	0.99994	0.99991	0.99987	0.99982	0.99975	0.99966	0.99954	0.99941
6	1.00000	1.00000	0.99999	0.99999	0.99999	0.99998	0.99997	0.99996	0.99994	0.99992
7	1.00000	1.00000	1.00000	1.00000	1.00000	1.00000	1.00000	1.00000	0.99999	0.99999
8	1.00000	1.00000	1.00000	1.00000	1.00000	1.00000	1.00000	1.00000	1.00000	1.00000

	Mean									
S	1.25	1.50	1.75	2.00	2.25	2.50	2.75	3.00	3.25	3.50
0	0.28650	0.22313	0.17377	0.13534	0.10540	0.08208	0.06393	0.04979	0.03877	0.03020
1	0.64464	0.55783	0.47788	0.40601	0.34255	0.28730	0.23973	0.19915	0.16479	0.13589
2	0.86847	0.80885	0.74397	0.67668	0.60934	0.54381	0.48146	0.42319	0.36957	0.32085
3	0.96173	0.93436	0.89919	0.85712	0.80943	0.75758	0.70304	0.64723	0.59141	0.53663
4	0.99088	0.98142	0.96710	0.94735	0.92199	0.89118	0.85538	0.81526	0.77165	0.72544
5	0.99816	0.99554	0.99087	0.98344	0.97263	0.95798	0.93916	0.91608	0.88881	0.85761
6	0.99968	0.99907	0.99780	0.99547	0.99163	0.98581	0.97757	0.96649	0.95227	0.93471
7	0.99995	0.99983	0.99953	0.99890	0.99773	0.99575	0.99265	0.98810	0.98174	0.97326
8	0.99999	0.99997	0.99991	0.99976	0.99945	0.99886	0.99784	0.99620	0.99371	0.99013
9	1.00000	1.00000	0.99998	0.99995	0.99988	0.99972	0.99942	0.99890	0.99803	0.99669
10	1.00000	1.00000	1.00000	0.99999	0.99998	0.99994	0.99986	0.99971	0.99944	0.99898
11	1.00000	1.00000	1.00000	1.00000	1.00000	0.99999	0.99997	0.99993	0.99985	0.99971
12	1.00000	1.00000	1.00000	1.00000	1.00000	1.00000	0.99999	0.99998	0.99996	0.99992
13	1.00000	1.00000	1.00000	1.00000	1.00000	1.00000	1.00000	1.00000	0.99999	0.99998
14	1.00000	1.00000	1.00000	1.00000	1.00000	1.00000	1.00000	1.00000	1.00000	1.00000
15	1.00000	1.00000	1.00000	1.00000	1.00000	1.00000	1.00000	1.00000	1.00000	1.00000

(*continued*)

Poisson Distribution Function Table (Concluded)

	Mean											
S	3.75	4.00	4.25	4.50	4.75	5.00	5.25	5.50	5.75	6.00	6.25	6.50
0	0.02352	0.01832	0.01426	0.01111	0.00865	0.00674	0.00525	0.00409	0.00318	0.00248	0.00193	0.00150
1	0.11171	0.09158	0.07489	0.06110	0.04975	0.04043	0.03280	0.02656	0.02148	0.01735	0.01400	0.01128
2	0.27707	0.23810	0.20371	0.17358	0.14735	0.12465	0.10511	0.08838	0.07410	0.06197	0.05170	0.04304
3	0.48377	0.43347	0.38621	0.34230	0.30189	0.26503	0.23167	0.20170	0.17495	0.15120	0.13025	0.11185
4	0.67755	0.62884	0.58012	0.53210	0.48540	0.44049	0.39777	0.35752	0.31991	0.28506	0.25299	0.22367
5	0.82288	0.78513	0.74494	0.70293	0.65973	0.61596	0.57218	0.52892	0.48662	0.44568	0.40640	0.36904
6	0.91372	0.88933	0.86169	0.83105	0.79775	0.76218	0.72479	0.68604	0.64639	0.60630	0.56622	0.52652
7	0.96238	0.94887	0.93257	0.91341	0.89140	0.86663	0.83925	0.80949	0.77762	0.74398	0.70890	0.67276
8	0.98519	0.97864	0.97023	0.95974	0.94701	0.93191	0.91436	0.89436	0.87195	0.84724	0.82038	0.79157
9	0.99469	0.99187	0.98801	0.98291	0.97636	0.96817	0.95817	0.94622	0.93221	0.91608	0.89779	0.87738
10	0.99826	0.99716	0.99557	0.99333	0.99030	0.98630	0.98118	0.97475	0.96686	0.95738	0.94618	0.93316
11	0.99947	0.99908	0.99849	0.99760	0.99632	0.99455	0.99216	0.98901	0.98498	0.97991	0.97367	0.96612
12	0.99985	0.99973	0.99952	0.99919	0.99870	0.99798	0.99696	0.99555	0.99366	0.99117	0.98798	0.98397
13	0.99996	0.99992	0.99986	0.99975	0.99957	0.99930	0.99890	0.99831	0.99749	0.99637	0.99487	0.99290
14	0.99999	0.99998	0.99996	0.99993	0.99987	0.99977	0.99963	0.99940	0.99907	0.99860	0.99794	0.99704
15	1.00000	1.00000	0.99999	0.99998	0.99996	0.99993	0.99988	0.99980	0.99968	0.99949	0.99922	0.99884
16	1.00000	1.00000	1.00000	0.99999	0.99999	0.99998	0.99996	0.99994	0.99989	0.99983	0.99972	0.99957
17	1.00000	1.00000	1.00000	1.00000	1.00000	0.99999	0.99999	0.99998	0.99997	0.99994	0.99991	0.99985
18	1.00000	1.00000	1.00000	1.00000	1.00000	1.00000	1.00000	0.99999	0.99999	0.99998	0.99997	0.99995
19	1.00000	1.00000	1.00000	1.00000	1.00000	1.00000	1.00000	1.00000	1.00000	0.99999	0.99999	0.99998

	Mean											
S	6.75	7.00	7.25	7.50	7.75	8.00	8.25	8.50	8.75	9.00	9.25	9.50
0	0.00117	0.00091	0.00071	0.00055	0.00043	0.00034	0.00026	0.00020	0.00016	0.00012	0.00010	0.00007
1	0.00907	0.00730	0.00586	0.00470	0.00377	0.00302	0.00242	0.00193	0.00154	0.00123	0.00099	0.00079
2	0.03575	0.02964	0.02452	0.02026	0.01670	0.01375	0.01131	0.00928	0.00761	0.00623	0.00510	0.00416
3	0.09577	0.08177	0.06963	0.05915	0.05012	0.04238	0.03576	0.03011	0.02530	0.02123	0.01777	0.01486
4	0.19704	0.17299	0.15138	0.13206	0.11487	0.09963	0.08619	0.07436	0.06401	0.05496	0.04709	0.04026
5	0.33377	0.30071	0.26992	0.24144	0.21522	0.19124	0.16939	0.14960	0.13174	0.11569	0.10133	0.08853
6	0.48759	0.44971	0.41316	0.37815	0.34485	0.31337	0.28380	0.25618	0.23051	0.20678	0.18495	0.16495
7	0.63591	0.59871	0.56152	0.52464	0.48837	0.45296	0.41864	0.38560	0.35398	0.32390	0.29544	0.26866
8	0.76106	0.72909	0.69596	0.66197	0.62740	0.59255	0.55770	0.52311	0.48902	0.45565	0.42320	0.39182
9	0.85492	0.83050	0.80427	0.77641	0.74712	0.71662	0.68516	0.65297	0.62031	0.58741	0.55451	0.52183
10	0.91827	0.90148	0.88279	0.86224	0.83990	0.81589	0.79032	0.76336	0.73519	0.70599	0.67597	0.64533
11	0.95715	0.94665	0.93454	0.92076	0.90527	0.88808	0.86919	0.84866	0.82657	0.80301	0.77810	0.75199
12	0.97902	0.97300	0.96581	0.95733	0.94749	0.93620	0.92341	0.90908	0.89320	0.87577	0.85683	0.83643
13	0.99037	0.98719	0.98324	0.97844	0.97266	0.96582	0.95782	0.94859	0.93805	0.92615	0.91285	0.89814
14	0.99585	0.99428	0.99227	0.98974	0.98659	0.98274	0.97810	0.97257	0.96608	0.95853	0.94986	0.94001
15	0.99831	0.99759	0.99664	0.99539	0.99379	0.99177	0.98925	0.98617	0.98243	0.97796	0.97269	0.96653
16	0.99935	0.99904	0.99862	0.99804	0.99728	0.99628	0.99500	0.99339	0.99137	0.98889	0.98588	0.98227
17	0.99976	0.99964	0.99946	0.99921	0.99887	0.99841	0.99779	0.99700	0.99597	0.99468	0.99306	0.99107
18	0.99992	0.99987	0.99980	0.99970	0.99955	0.99935	0.99907	0.99870	0.99821	0.99757	0.99675	0.99572
19	0.99997	0.99996	0.99993	0.99989	0.99983	0.99975	0.99963	0.99947	0.99924	0.99894	0.99855	0.99804
20	0.99999	0.99999	0.99998	0.99996	0.99994	0.99991	0.99986	0.99979	0.99969	0.99956	0.99938	0.99914
21	1.00000	1.00000	0.99999	0.99999	0.99998	0.99997	0.99995	0.99992	0.99988	0.99983	0.99975	0.99964
22	1.00000	1.00000	1.00000	1.00000	0.99999	0.99999	0.99998	0.99997	0.99996	0.99993	0.99990	0.99985
23	1.00000	1.00000	1.00000	1.00000	1.00000	1.00000	0.99999	0.99999	0.99998	0.99998	0.99996	0.99994
24	1.00000	1.00000	1.00000	1.00000	1.00000	1.00000	1.00000	1.00000	0.99999	0.99999	0.99999	0.99998

Poisson Inventory Function Table

S	Mean 0.05	0.10	0.15	0.20	0.25	0.30	0.35	0.40	0.45	0.50
0	0.00000	0.00000	0.00000	0.00000	0.00000	0.00000	0.00000	0.00000	0.00000	0.00000
1	0.95123	0.90484	0.86071	0.81873	0.77880	0.74082	0.70469	0.67032	0.63763	0.60653
2	1.95002	1.90016	1.85052	1.80121	1.75230	1.70388	1.65602	1.60877	1.56219	1.51633
3	2.95000	2.90000	2.85002	2.80006	2.75014	2.70028	2.65051	2.60084	2.55131	2.50194
4	3.95000	3.90000	3.85000	3.80000	3.75001	3.70002	3.65003	3.60007	3.55011	3.50019
5	4.95000	4.90000	4.85000	4.80000	4.75000	4.70000	4.65000	4.60000	4.55001	4.50002
6	5.95000	5.90000	5.85000	5.80000	5.75000	5.70000	5.65000	5.60000	5.55000	5.50000

S	Mean 0.55	0.60	0.65	0.70	0.75	0.80	0.85	0.90	0.95	1.00
0	0.00000	0.00000	0.00000	0.00000	0.00000	0.00000	0.00000	0.00000	0.00000	0.00000
1	0.57695	0.54881	0.52205	0.49659	0.47237	0.44933	0.42741	0.40657	0.38674	0.36788
2	1.47122	1.42691	1.38342	1.34078	1.29901	1.25812	1.21813	1.17905	1.14089	1.10364
3	2.45276	2.40379	2.35508	2.30664	2.25850	2.21070	2.16325	2.11620	2.06955	2.02334
4	3.45029	3.40044	3.35063	3.30089	3.25121	3.20162	3.15212	3.10274	3.05347	3.00435
5	4.45003	4.40004	4.35007	4.30010	4.25015	4.20021	4.15029	4.10039	4.05052	4.00069
6	5.45000	5.40000	5.35001	5.30001	5.25002	5.20002	5.15003	5.10005	5.05007	5.00009
7	6.45000	6.40000	6.35000	6.30000	6.25000	6.20000	6.15000	6.10001	6.05001	6.00001
8	7.45000	7.40000	7.35000	7.30000	7.25000	7.20000	7.15000	7.10000	7.05000	7.00000

S	Mean 1.25	1.50	1.75	2.00	2.25	2.50	2.75	3.00	3.25	3.50
0	0.00000	0.00000	0.00000	0.00000	0.00000	0.00000	0.00000	0.00000	0.00000	0.00000
1	0.28650	0.22313	0.17377	0.13534	0.10540	0.08208	0.06393	0.04979	0.03877	0.03020
2	0.93114	0.78096	0.65165	0.54134	0.44795	0.36938	0.30366	0.24894	0.20356	0.16609
3	1.79961	1.58980	1.39562	1.21802	1.05729	0.91320	0.78511	0.67213	0.57313	0.48693
4	2.76134	2.52416	2.29481	2.07514	1.86672	1.67077	1.48815	1.31936	1.16454	1.02357
5	3.75221	3.50558	3.26191	3.02249	2.78870	2.56195	2.34353	2.13462	1.93619	1.74901
6	4.75038	4.50113	4.25278	4.00592	3.76134	3.51993	3.28270	3.05070	2.82501	2.60662
7	5.75006	5.50020	5.25058	5.00139	4.75297	4.50574	4.26026	4.01719	3.77728	3.54134
8	6.75001	6.50003	6.25011	6.00029	5.75070	5.50149	5.25292	5.00529	4.75902	4.51460
9	7.75000	7.50000	7.25002	7.00006	6.75015	6.50035	6.25076	6.00149	5.75273	5.50472
10	8.75000	8.50000	8.25000	8.00001	7.75003	7.50008	7.25018	7.00038	6.75076	6.50141
11	9.75000	9.50000	9.25000	9.00000	8.75001	8.50002	8.25004	8.00009	7.75020	7.50039
12	10.75000	10.50000	10.25000	10.00000	9.75000	9.50000	9.25001	9.00002	8.75005	8.50010
13	11.75000	11.50000	11.25000	11.00000	10.75000	10.50000	10.25000	10.00000	9.75001	9.50002
14	12.75000	12.50000	12.25000	12.00000	11.75000	11.50000	11.25000	11.00000	10.75000	10.50001
15	13.75000	13.50000	13.25000	13.00000	12.75000	12.50000	12.25000	12.00000	11.75000	11.50000

(continued)

Poisson Inventory Function Table (Concluded)

S	Mean 3.75	4.00	4.25	4.50	4.75	5.00	5.25	5.50	5.75	6.00	6.25	6.50
0	0.00000	0.00000	0.00000	0.00000	0.00000	0.00000	0.00000	0.00000	0.00000	0.00000	0.00000	0.00000
1	0.02352	0.01832	0.01426	0.01111	0.00865	0.00674	0.00525	0.00409	0.00318	0.00248	0.00193	0.00150
2	0.13523	0.10989	0.08915	0.07221	0.05840	0.04717	0.03804	0.03065	0.02467	0.01983	0.01593	0.01278
3	0.41230	0.34800	0.29286	0.24579	0.20575	0.17182	0.14316	0.11903	0.09877	0.08180	0.06763	0.05582
4	0.89606	0.78147	0.67907	0.58808	0.50763	0.43684	0.37483	0.32073	0.27371	0.23300	0.19788	0.16766
5	1.57361	1.41030	1.25919	1.12019	0.99303	0.87734	0.77260	0.67824	0.59362	0.51806	0.45086	0.39134
6	2.39649	2.19543	2.00413	1.82312	1.65277	1.49330	1.34479	1.20716	1.08024	0.96374	0.85727	0.76038
7	3.31021	3.08476	2.86582	2.65417	2.45052	2.25548	2.06958	1.89320	1.72663	1.57004	1.42348	1.28690
8	4.27259	4.03363	3.79839	3.56758	3.34192	3.12211	2.90882	2.70268	2.50426	2.31402	2.13238	1.95966
9	5.25778	5.01226	4.76861	4.52732	4.28893	4.05402	3.82318	3.59704	3.37620	3.16126	2.95276	2.75123
10	6.25247	6.00413	5.75662	5.51023	5.26529	5.02219	4.78136	4.54326	4.30842	4.07733	3.85056	3.62862
11	7.25073	7.00129	6.75219	6.50356	6.25559	6.00849	5.76253	5.51801	5.27528	5.03471	4.79673	4.56178
12	8.25020	8.00038	7.75067	7.50116	7.25191	7.00304	6.75469	6.50702	6.26026	6.01462	5.77040	5.52790
13	9.25005	9.00010	8.75019	8.50035	8.25061	8.00102	7.75165	7.50257	7.25391	7.00579	6.75838	6.51187
14	10.25001	10.00003	9.75005	9.50010	9.25018	9.00032	8.75054	8.50089	8.25141	8.00217	7.75325	7.50477
15	11.25000	11.00001	10.75001	10.50003	10.25005	10.00010	9.75017	9.50029	9.25048	9.00077	8.75119	8.50181
16	12.25000	12.00000	11.75000	11.50001	11.25001	11.00003	10.75005	10.50009	10.25015	10.00026	9.75042	9.50066
17	13.25000	13.00000	12.75000	12.50000	12.25000	12.00001	11.75001	11.50003	11.25005	11.00008	10.75014	10.50022
18	14.25000	14.00000	13.75000	13.50000	13.25000	13.00000	12.75000	12.50001	12.25001	12.00002	11.75004	11.50007
19	15.25000	15.00000	14.75000	14.50000	14.25000	14.00000	13.75000	13.50000	13.25000	13.00001	12.75001	12.50002

S	Mean 6.75	7.00	7.25	7.50	7.75	8.00	8.25	8.50	8.75	9.00	9.25	9.50
0	0.00000	0.00000	0.00000	0.00000	0.00000	0.00000	0.00000	0.00000	0.00000	0.00000	0.00000	0.00000
1	0.00117	0.00091	0.00071	0.00055	0.00043	0.00034	0.00026	0.00020	0.00016	0.00012	0.00010	0.00007
2	0.01025	0.00821	0.00657	0.00525	0.00420	0.00335	0.00268	0.00214	0.00170	0.00136	0.00108	0.00086
3	0.04599	0.03784	0.03109	0.02551	0.02090	0.01711	0.01399	0.01142	0.00931	0.00759	0.00618	0.00502
4	0.14176	0.11961	0.10072	0.08466	0.07103	0.05949	0.04974	0.04153	0.03462	0.02882	0.02395	0.01988
5	0.33880	0.29260	0.25210	0.21672	0.18589	0.15912	0.13593	0.11589	0.09863	0.08378	0.07105	0.06015
6	0.67257	0.59331	0.52203	0.45815	0.40112	0.35036	0.30532	0.26549	0.23036	0.19947	0.17238	0.14868
7	1.16016	1.04302	0.93519	0.83631	0.74597	0.66373	0.58912	0.52167	0.46087	0.40625	0.35732	0.31362
8	1.79606	1.64173	1.49671	1.36095	1.23434	1.11669	1.00777	0.90726	0.81485	0.73015	0.65277	0.58229
9	2.55712	2.37082	2.19267	2.02292	1.86174	1.70924	1.56546	1.43037	1.30387	1.18580	1.07597	0.97411
10	3.41204	3.20132	2.99694	2.79932	2.60885	2.42586	2.25062	2.08334	1.92418	1.77321	1.63047	1.49594
11	4.33031	4.10280	3.87973	3.66156	3.44876	3.24175	3.04094	2.84671	2.65936	2.47920	2.30644	2.14127
12	5.28746	5.04945	4.81427	4.58232	4.35403	4.12983	3.91013	3.69537	3.48593	3.28221	3.08454	2.89326
13	6.26648	6.02245	5.78007	5.53965	5.30152	5.06603	4.83354	4.60445	4.37913	4.15798	3.94137	3.72968
14	7.25685	7.00964	6.76332	6.51809	6.27418	6.03185	5.79137	5.55304	5.31718	5.08413	4.85422	4.62782
15	8.25270	8.00392	7.75559	7.50783	7.26077	7.01459	6.76947	6.52561	6.28326	6.04266	5.80409	5.56783
16	9.25101	9.00152	8.75223	8.50322	8.25456	8.00636	7.75872	7.51178	7.26569	7.02063	6.77678	6.53436
17	10.25036	10.00056	9.75085	9.50126	9.25184	9.00264	8.75372	8.50517	8.25706	8.00952	7.76266	7.51663
18	11.25012	11.00020	10.75031	10.50047	10.25071	10.00105	9.75152	9.50217	9.25304	9.00420	8.75573	8.50770
19	12.25004	12.00007	11.75011	11.50017	11.25026	11.00040	10.75059	10.50087	10.25125	10.00177	9.75248	9.50342
20	13.25001	13.00002	12.75004	12.50006	12.25009	12.00014	11.75022	11.50033	11.25049	11.00072	10.75103	10.50145
21	14.25000	14.00001	13.75001	13.50002	13.25003	13.00005	12.75008	12.50012	12.25019	12.00028	11.75041	11.50059
22	15.25000	15.00000	14.75000	14.50001	14.25001	14.00002	13.75003	13.50004	13.25007	13.00010	12.75016	12.50023
23	16.25000	16.00000	15.75000	15.50000	15.25000	15.00001	14.75001	14.50001	14.25002	14.00004	13.75006	13.50009
24	17.25000	17.00000	16.75000	16.50000	16.25000	16.00000	15.75000	15.50000	15.25001	15.00001	14.75002	14.50003

Poisson Loss Function Table

S	Mean 0.05	0.10	0.15	0.20	0.25	0.30	0.35	0.40	0.45	0.50
0	0.05000	0.10000	0.15000	0.20000	0.25000	0.30000	0.35000	0.40000	0.45000	0.50000
1	0.00123	0.00484	0.01071	0.01873	0.02880	0.04082	0.05469	0.07032	0.08763	0.10653
2	0.00002	0.00016	0.00052	0.00121	0.00230	0.00388	0.00602	0.00877	0.01219	0.01633
3	0.00000	0.00000	0.00002	0.00006	0.00014	0.00028	0.00051	0.00084	0.00131	0.00194
4	0.00000	0.00000	0.00000	0.00000	0.00001	0.00002	0.00003	0.00007	0.00011	0.00019
5	0.00000	0.00000	0.00000	0.00000	0.00000	0.00000	0.00000	0.00000	0.00001	0.00002
6	0.00000	0.00000	0.00000	0.00000	0.00000	0.00000	0.00000	0.00000	0.00000	0.00000

S	Mean 0.55	0.60	0.65	0.70	0.75	0.80	0.85	0.90	0.95	1.00
0	0.55000	0.60000	0.65000	0.70000	0.75000	0.80000	0.85000	0.90000	0.95000	1.00000
1	0.12695	0.14881	0.17205	0.19659	0.22237	0.24933	0.27741	0.30657	0.33674	0.36788
2	0.02122	0.02691	0.03342	0.04078	0.04901	0.05812	0.06813	0.07905	0.09089	0.10364
3	0.00276	0.00379	0.00508	0.00664	0.00850	0.01070	0.01325	0.01620	0.01955	0.02334
4	0.00029	0.00044	0.00063	0.00089	0.00121	0.00162	0.00212	0.00274	0.00347	0.00435
5	0.00003	0.00004	0.00007	0.00010	0.00015	0.00021	0.00029	0.00039	0.00052	0.00069
6	0.00000	0.00000	0.00001	0.00001	0.00002	0.00002	0.00003	0.00005	0.00007	0.00009
7	0.00000	0.00000	0.00001	0.00001	0.00002	0.00002	0.00003	0.00005	0.00007	0.00009
8	0.00000	0.00000	0.00001	0.00001	0.00001	0.00002	0.00003	0.00004	0.00006	0.00008

S	Mean 1.25	1.50	1.75	2.00	2.25	2.50	2.75	3.00	3.25	3.50
0	1.25000	1.50000	1.75000	2.00000	2.25000	2.50000	2.75000	3.00000	3.25000	3.50000
1	0.53650	0.72313	0.92377	1.13534	1.35540	1.58208	1.81393	2.04979	2.28877	2.53020
2	0.18114	0.28096	0.40165	0.54134	0.69795	0.86938	1.05366	1.24894	1.45356	1.66609
3	0.04961	0.08980	0.14562	0.21802	0.30729	0.41320	0.53511	0.67213	0.82313	0.98693
4	0.01134	0.02416	0.04481	0.07514	0.11672	0.17077	0.23815	0.31936	0.41454	0.52357
5	0.00221	0.00558	0.01191	0.02249	0.03870	0.06195	0.09353	0.13462	0.18619	0.24901
6	0.00038	0.00113	0.00278	0.00592	0.01134	0.01993	0.03270	0.05070	0.07501	0.10662
7	0.00006	0.00020	0.00058	0.00139	0.00297	0.00574	0.01026	0.01719	0.02728	0.04134
8	0.00001	0.00003	0.00011	0.00029	0.00070	0.00149	0.00292	0.00529	0.00902	0.01460
9	0.00000	0.00000	0.00002	0.00006	0.00015	0.00035	0.00076	0.00149	0.00273	0.00472
10	0.00000	0.00000	0.00000	0.00001	0.00003	0.00008	0.00018	0.00038	0.00076	0.00141
11	0.00000	0.00000	0.00000	0.00000	0.00001	0.00002	0.00004	0.00009	0.00020	0.00039
12	0.00000	0.00000	0.00000	0.00000	0.00000	0.00000	0.00001	0.00002	0.00005	0.00010
13	0.00000	0.00000	0.00000	0.00000	0.00000	0.00000	0.00000	0.00000	0.00001	0.00002
14	0.00000	0.00000	0.00000	0.00000	0.00000	0.00000	0.00000	0.00000	0.00000	0.00001
15	0.00000	0.00000	0.00000	0.00000	0.00000	0.00000	0.00000	0.00000	0.00000	0.00000

(continued)

Poisson Loss Function Table (Concluded)

S	Mean 3.75	4.00	4.25	4.50	4.75	5.00	5.25	5.50	5.75	6.00	6.25	6.50
0	3.75000	4.00000	4.25000	4.50000	4.75000	5.00000	5.25000	5.50000	5.75000	6.00000	6.25000	6.50000
1	2.77352	3.01832	3.26426	3.51111	3.75865	4.00674	4.25525	4.50409	4.75318	5.00248	5.25193	5.50150
2	1.88523	2.10989	2.33915	2.57221	2.80840	3.04717	3.28804	3.53065	3.77467	4.01983	4.26593	4.51278
3	1.16230	1.34800	1.54286	1.74579	1.95575	2.17182	2.39316	2.61903	2.84877	3.08180	3.31763	3.55582
4	0.64606	0.78147	0.92907	1.08808	1.25763	1.43684	1.62483	1.82073	2.02371	2.23300	2.44788	2.66766
5	0.32361	0.41030	0.50919	0.62019	0.74303	0.87734	1.02260	1.17824	1.34362	1.51806	1.70086	1.89134
6	0.14649	0.19543	0.25413	0.32312	0.40277	0.49330	0.59479	0.70716	0.83024	0.96374	1.10727	1.26038
7	0.06021	0.08476	0.11582	0.15417	0.20052	0.25548	0.31958	0.39320	0.47663	0.57004	0.67348	0.78690
8	0.02259	0.03363	0.04839	0.06758	0.09192	0.12211	0.15882	0.20268	0.25426	0.31402	0.38238	0.45966
9	0.00778	0.01226	0.01861	0.02732	0.03893	0.05402	0.07318	0.09704	0.12620	0.16126	0.20276	0.25123
10	0.00247	0.00413	0.00662	0.01023	0.01529	0.02219	0.03136	0.04326	0.05842	0.07733	0.10056	0.12862
11	0.00073	0.00129	0.00219	0.00356	0.00559	0.00849	0.01253	0.01801	0.02528	0.03471	0.04673	0.06178
12	0.00020	0.00038	0.00067	0.00116	0.00191	0.00304	0.00469	0.00702	0.01026	0.01462	0.02040	0.02790
13	0.00005	0.00010	0.00019	0.00035	0.00061	0.00102	0.00165	0.00257	0.00391	0.00579	0.00838	0.01187
14	0.00001	0.00003	0.00005	0.00010	0.00018	0.00032	0.00054	0.00089	0.00141	0.00217	0.00325	0.00477
15	0.00000	0.00001	0.00001	0.00003	0.00005	0.00010	0.00017	0.00029	0.00048	0.00077	0.00119	0.00181
16	0.00000	0.00000	0.00000	0.00001	0.00001	0.00003	0.00005	0.00009	0.00015	0.00026	0.00042	0.00066
17	0.00000	0.00000	0.00000	0.00000	0.00000	0.00001	0.00001	0.00003	0.00005	0.00008	0.00014	0.00022
18	0.00000	0.00000	0.00000	0.00000	0.00000	0.00000	0.00000	0.00001	0.00001	0.00002	0.00004	0.00007
19	0.00000	0.00000	0.00000	0.00000	0.00000	0.00000	0.00000	0.00000	0.00000	0.00001	0.00001	0.00002

S	Mean 6.75	7.00	7.25	7.50	7.75	8.00	8.25	8.50	8.75	9.00	9.25	9.50
0	6.75000	7.00000	7.25000	7.50000	7.75000	8.00000	8.25000	8.50000	8.75000	9.00000	9.25000	9.50000
1	5.75117	6.00091	6.25071	6.50055	6.75043	7.00034	7.25026	7.50020	7.75016	8.00012	8.25010	8.50007
2	4.76025	5.00821	5.25657	5.50525	5.75420	6.00335	6.25268	6.50214	6.75170	7.00136	7.25108	7.50086
3	3.79599	4.03784	4.28109	4.52551	4.77090	5.01711	5.26399	5.51142	5.75931	6.00759	6.25618	6.50502
4	2.89176	3.11961	3.35072	3.58466	3.82103	4.05949	4.29974	4.54153	4.78462	5.02882	5.27395	5.51988
5	2.08880	2.29260	2.50210	2.71672	2.93589	3.15912	3.38593	3.61589	3.84863	4.08378	4.32105	4.56015
6	1.42257	1.59331	1.77203	1.95815	2.15112	2.35036	2.55532	2.76549	2.98036	3.19947	3.42238	3.64868
7	0.91016	1.04302	1.18519	1.33631	1.49597	1.66373	1.83912	2.02167	2.21087	2.40625	2.60732	2.81362
8	0.54606	0.64173	0.74671	0.86095	0.98434	1.11669	1.25777	1.40726	1.56485	1.73015	1.90277	2.08229
9	0.30712	0.37082	0.44267	0.52292	0.61174	0.70924	0.81546	0.93037	1.05387	1.18580	1.32597	1.47411
10	0.16204	0.20132	0.24694	0.29932	0.35885	0.42586	0.50062	0.58334	0.67418	0.77321	0.88047	0.99594
11	0.08031	0.10280	0.12973	0.16156	0.19876	0.24175	0.29094	0.34671	0.40936	0.47920	0.55644	0.64127
12	0.03746	0.04945	0.06427	0.08232	0.10403	0.12983	0.16013	0.19537	0.23593	0.28221	0.33454	0.39326
13	0.01648	0.02245	0.03007	0.03965	0.05152	0.06603	0.08354	0.10445	0.12913	0.15798	0.19137	0.22968
14	0.00685	0.00964	0.01332	0.01809	0.02418	0.03185	0.04137	0.05304	0.06718	0.08413	0.10422	0.12782
15	0.00270	0.00392	0.00559	0.00783	0.01077	0.01459	0.01947	0.02561	0.03326	0.04266	0.05409	0.06783
16	0.00101	0.00152	0.00223	0.00322	0.00456	0.00636	0.00872	0.01178	0.01569	0.02063	0.02678	0.03436
17	0.00036	0.00056	0.00085	0.00126	0.00184	0.00264	0.00372	0.00517	0.00706	0.00952	0.01266	0.01663
18	0.00012	0.00020	0.00031	0.00047	0.00071	0.00105	0.00152	0.00217	0.00304	0.00420	0.00573	0.00770
19	0.00004	0.00007	0.00011	0.00017	0.00026	0.00040	0.00059	0.00087	0.00125	0.00177	0.00248	0.00342
20	0.00001	0.00002	0.00004	0.00006	0.00009	0.00014	0.00022	0.00033	0.00049	0.00072	0.00103	0.00145
21	0.00000	0.00001	0.00001	0.00002	0.00003	0.00005	0.00008	0.00012	0.00019	0.00028	0.00041	0.00059
22	0.00000	0.00000	0.00000	0.00001	0.00001	0.00002	0.00003	0.00004	0.00007	0.00010	0.00016	0.00023
23	0.00000	0.00000	0.00000	0.00000	0.00000	0.00001	0.00001	0.00001	0.00002	0.00004	0.00006	0.00009
24	0.00000	0.00000	0.00000	0.00000	0.00000	0.00000	0.00000	0.00000	0.00001	0.00001	0.00002	0.00003

Appendix C

Evaluation of the Expected Inventory and Loss Functions

This appendix describes how the expected inventory and loss functions of a discrete distribution function can be efficiently evaluated.

The expected inventory function is the amount of inventory leftover after demand when Q units are purchased at the beginning of the season. The expected loss function $L(Q)$ is the expected amount a random variable exceeds a fixed value. For example, if the random variable is demand, then $L(Q)$ is the expected amount demand is greater than Q.

It is easiest to describe how to evaluate an expected inventory function with an example. Consider the following distribution function with six possible outcomes and an expected value

Q	F(Q)
0	0.1
1	0.3
2	0.4
3	0.7
4	0.9
5	1.0

$F(Q)$ = Probability demand is less than or equal to the quantity Q

The expected inventory function is evaluated recursively, meaning that we will start with $I(0)$, then evaluate $I(1)$, then evaluate $I(2)$, etcetera. To begin, if $Q = 0$ units are ordered, then clearly there will be 0 units remaining at the end of the season. Hence, $I(0) = 0$. Next, we use the following equation to find the remaining values for the expected inventory function:

$$I(t) = I(t-1) + F(t-1)$$

For example, $I(1) = I(0) + F(0)$, $I(2) = I(1) + F(1)$, $I(3) = I(2) + F(2)$, etcetera. Using that equation we can finish the expected inventory function table:

Q	*F*(*Q*)	*I*(*Q*)
0	0.1	0
1	0.3	$I(0) + F(0) = 0.1$
2	0.4	$I(1) + F(1) = 0.4$
3	0.7	$I(2) + F(2) = 0.8$
4	0.9	$I(3) + F(3) = 1.5$
5	1.0	$I(4) + F(4) = 2.4$

For example, if 5 units are ordered and demand follows the distribution function, $F(Q)$, in the table above, then expected inventory will be 2.4 units.

Once the expected inventory function has been evaluated, the expected loss function can be evaluated with this equation:

$$L(Q) = \mu - Q + I(Q)$$

Applying that equation to the table yields

Q	*F*(*Q*)	*I*(*Q*)	*L*(*Q*)
0	0.1	0	$2.6 - 0 + 0 = 2.6$
1	0.3	0.1	$2.6 - 1 + 0.1 = 1.7$
2	0.4	0.4	$2.6 - 2 + 0.4 = 1$
3	0.7	0.8	$2.6 - 3 + 0.8 = 0.4$
4	0.9	1.5	$2.6 - 4 + 1.5 = 0.1$
5	1.0	2.4	$2.6 - 5 + 2.4 = 0$

Appendix D

Equations and Approximations

This appendix derives in detail some equations and explains several approximations.

Derivation, via Calculus, of the Order Quantity That Maximizes Expected Profit for the Newsvendor (Chapter 14)

Let the selling price be p, the purchase cost per unit be c, and the salvage revenue from leftover inventory be v. The expected profit function is

$$\pi(Q) = -cQ + p\left(\int_0^Q xf(x)dx + (1 - F(Q))Q\right) + v\int_0^Q (Q - x)f(x)dx$$

$$= (p - c)Q + \int_0^Q (p - v)xf(x)dx - (p - v)F(Q)Q$$

where $f(x)$ is the density function and $F(x)$ is the distribution function ($Prob(D = x)$ and $Prob(D \leq x)$, respectively, where D is the random variable representing demand).

Via integration by parts, the profit function can be written as

$$\pi(Q) = (p - c)Q + (p - v)\left(QF(Q) - \int_0^Q F(x)dx\right) - (p - v)F(Q)Q$$

Differentiate the profit function and remember that the derivative of the distribution function equals the density function, that is, $dF(x)/dx = f(x)$:

$$\frac{d\pi(Q)}{dQ} = (p - c) + (p - v)(F(Q) + Qf(Q) - F(Q)) - (p - v)(F(Q) + f(Q)Q)$$

$$= (p - c) - (p - v)F(Q)$$

and

$$\frac{d^2\pi(Q)}{dQ^2} = -(p-v)f(Q)$$

Because the second derivative is negative, the profit function is concave, so the solution to the first-order condition provides the optimal order quantity:

$$\frac{d\pi(Q)}{dQ} = (p-c) - (p-v)F(Q) = 0$$

Rearrange terms in the above equation and you get

$$F(Q) = \frac{p-c}{p-v}$$

Note that $C_o = c - v$ and $C_u = p - c$, so the above can be written as

$$F(Q) = \frac{C_u}{C_u + C_o}$$

The Round-up Rule (Chapter 14)

To understand why the round-up rule is correct, we need to derive the optimal order quantity with a discrete distribution function. Suppose demand will be one of a finite set of outcomes, $D \in \{d_1, d_2, \ldots, d_n\}$. For example, with the empirical distribution function for the Hammer 3/2, the possible demand outcomes included {800, 1,184, . . . , 5,120}. Clearly, the optimal order quantity will equal one of these possible demand outcomes. Suppose we have decided to order d_i units and we are deciding whether to order d_{i+1} units. This is prudent if the expected gain from this larger order quantity is at least as large as the expected cost. The expected gain is

$$C_u(d_{i+1} - d_i)(1 - F(d_i))$$

because we sell an additional $(d_{i+1} - d_i)$ units if demand is greater than d_i, which occurs with probability $1 - F(d_i)$. The expected loss is

$$C_o(d_{i+1} - d_i)F(d_i)$$

because we need to salvage an additional $(d_{i+1} - d_i)$ units if demand is d_i or fewer, which occurs with probability $F(d_i)$. So we should increase our order from d_i to d_{i+1} when

$$C_u(d_{i+1} - d_i)(1 - F(d_i)) \geq C_o(d_{i+1} - d_i)F(d_i)$$

which simplifies to

$$\frac{C_u}{C_o + C_u} \geq F(d_i)$$

Thus, if the critical ratio is greater than $F(d_i)$, then we should increase our order from d_i to d_{i+1}. When the critical ratio is greater than $F(d_i)$ but less than $F(d_{i+1})$, in other words, between the two entries in the table, we should order d_{i+1} units and not increase our order quantity further. Put another way, we choose the larger order quantity when the critical ratio falls between two entries in the table. That is the round-up rule.

The common error is to want to choose the order quantity that yields $F()$ closest to the critical ratio. But that can lead to a suboptimal action. To illustrate, suppose demand was Poisson with mean 1.0, $C_u = 1$, and $C_o = 0.21$. The critical ratio is 0.83, which is about in the middle between $F(1) = 0.74$ and $F(2) = 0.92$. However, expected profit with an order quantity of two units is about 20 percent higher than the profit with an order quantity of one unit. That said, if $F(d_i)$ and $F(d_{i+1})$ are reasonably close together, then choosing the lower order quantity is not going to cause a significant profit loss.

Derivation of the Standard Normal Inventory and Loss Functions (Chapter 14)

We wish to derive the following inventory and loss function equations for the standard normal loss function:

$$I(z) = \phi(z) + z\Phi(z)$$

$$L(z) = \phi(z) - z(1 - \Phi(z))$$

Take the density function of the standard normal distribution,

$$\phi(z) = \frac{1}{\sqrt{2\pi}} e^{-z^2/2}$$

and differentiate

$$\frac{d\phi(z)}{dz} = -z\frac{1}{\sqrt{2\pi}} e^{-z^2/2} = -z\phi(z)$$

The expected inventory function is

$$I(z) = \int_{-\infty}^{z} (z - x)\phi(x)dx$$

$$= \int_{-\infty}^{z} z\phi(x)dx - \int_{-\infty}^{z} x\phi(x)dx$$

The first integral is

$$\int_{-\infty}^{z} z\phi(x)d(x) = z\Phi(z)$$

The second integral is

$$\int_{-\infty}^{z} x\phi(x)dx = -\phi(x)\Big|_{-\infty}^{z} = -\phi(z)$$

because (from above) $d\phi(x)/dx = -x\phi(x)$. Thus, $I(z) = z\Phi(z) + \phi(z)$.

The expected loss function is $L(z) = \mu - S(z)$ where μ is the mean of the standard normal and $S(z)$ is the expected sales function. For the standard normal $\mu = 0$. The expected sales function is related to the expected inventory function: $I(z) = z - S(z)$. Thus, $L(z) = -z + I(z)$, which simplifies to

$$L(z) = \phi(z) - z(1 - \Phi(z))$$

Evaluation of the Fill Rate (Chapter 14)

The fill rate is the probability a customer finds an item available for purchase. This is not the same as the in-stock probability, which is the probability that all demand is satisfied. (To see why, suppose 9 units are available, but 10 customers arrive to make a purchase. The firm is not in-stock, because there will be one person who is unable to purchase a unit. However, each customer has a 9 out of 10 chance to be one of the lucky customers that can purchase an item.)

The fill rate can be evaluated with the following formula:

$$\text{Fill rate} = \frac{\text{Expected sales}}{\text{Expected demand}} = \frac{\text{Expected sales}}{\mu}$$

For example, if O'Neill orders 3,500 Hammer 3/2 wetsuits, then we evaluated in Chapter 14 that their Expected sales = 2,858. Expected demand is 3,192, so the fill rate would be

$$\text{Fill rate} = \frac{2{,}858}{3{,}192} = 89.5\%$$

Mismatch Cost as a Percentage of the Maximum Profit (Chapter 15)

We will use the following notation:

μ = Expected demand

σ = Standard deviation of demand

Q = Expected profit-maximizing order quantity

$z = (Q - \mu)/\sigma$ = Normalized order quantity

$\phi(z)$ = Density function of the standard normal distribution

$\Phi(z)$ = Distribution function of the standard normal

The easiest way to evaluate $\phi(z)$ is to use the Excel function Normdist(z,0,1,0), but it also can be evaluated by hand with the following function:

$$\phi(z) = e^{-(1/2)\times z^2} / \sqrt{2 \times \pi}$$

Begin with the mismatch cost as a percentage of the maximum profit

$$\text{Mismatch cost as a \% of the maximum profit} = (C_o \times \text{Expected leftover inventory}) / (\mu \times C_u) + (C_u \times \text{Expected lost sales}) / (\mu \times C_u) \quad \textbf{(D.1)}$$

We also know the following:

$$\begin{aligned}\text{Expected leftover inventory} &= (Q - \text{Expected sales})\\ &= (Q - \mu + \text{Expected lost sales})\end{aligned} \quad \textbf{(D.2)}$$

and we can rearrange $Q = \mu + z \times \sigma$ into

$$z \times \sigma = (Q - \mu) \tag{D.3}$$

Substitute Equation (D.3) into Equation (D.2), then substitute that equation into Equation (D.1) and simplify:

$$\text{Mismatch cost as a \% of the maximum profit} = ((C_o \times z \times \sigma) + (C_o + C_u) \times \text{Expected lost sales})/(\mu \times C_u) \tag{D.4}$$

Recall that

$$\begin{aligned}\text{Expected lost sales} &= \sigma \times (\phi(z) - z \times (1 - \Phi(z))) \\ &= \sigma \times \left(\phi(z) - z \times \frac{C_o}{C_o + C_u}\right)\end{aligned} \tag{D.5}$$

where the second line in that equation follows from the critical ratio, $\Phi(z) = C_u/(C_o + C_u)$. Substitute Equation (D.5) into Equation (D.4) and simplify to obtain the following:

$$\text{Mismatch cost as a \% of the maximum profit} = \left(\frac{\phi(z)}{\Phi(z)}\right) \times \left(\frac{\sigma}{\mu}\right)$$

The above equation is composed of two terms, $\phi(z)/\Phi(z)$ and σ/μ, so the mismatch cost is high when the product of those two terms is high. The second term is the coefficient of variation, which we discussed in the text. The first term is the ratio of the standard normal density function to the standard normal distribution function evaluated at the normalized order quantity. It depends on z and z depends on the critical ratio (the higher the critical ratio, the higher the optimal z-statistic). In fact, a simple plot reveals that as the critical ratio increases, $\phi(z)/\Phi(z)$ decreases. Thus, the mismatch cost becomes smaller as the critical ratio increases. In other words, all else being equal, between two products, the product with the lower critical ratio has the higher mismatch cost.

Exact Stockout Probability for the Order-up-to Model (Chapter 16)

Recall our main result from Section 16.3 that the inventory level at the end of the period equals S minus demand over $l + 1$ periods. If the inventory level is negative at the end of that interval, then one or more units are back-ordered. A stockout occurs in the last period of that interval if there is at least one unit back-ordered and the most recent back order occurred in that last period. Equation (16.1) in Chapter 16 acknowledges the first part of that statement (at least one unit is back-ordered), but it ignores that second part (the most recent back order must occur in the last period).

For example, suppose $l = 1$ and $S = 2$. If demand over two periods is three units, then there is one unit back-ordered at the end of the second period. As long as one of those three units of demand occurred in the second period, then a stockout occurred in the second period. A stockout does not occur in the second period only if all three units of demand occurred in the first period. Hence, the exact equation for the stockout probability is

$$\begin{aligned}\text{Stockout probability} = \ &\text{Prob}\{\text{Demand over } l + 1 \text{ periods} > S\} \\ &- \text{Prob}\ \{\text{Demand over } l \text{ periods} > S\} \\ &\times \text{Prob}\ \{\text{Demand in one period} = 0\}\end{aligned}$$

Equation (14.1) is an approximation because it ignores the second term in the exact equation above. The second term is the probability that the demand over $l + 1$ periods occurs only in the first l periods; that is, there is no demand in the $(l + 1)$th period. If the service level is high, then the second term should be small. Notice that the approximation overestimates the true stockout probability because it does not subtract the second term. Hence, the approximation is conservative.

If each period's demand is a Poisson distribution with mean 0.29 and there is a two-period lead time, then the approximate and exact stockout probabilities are

	Stockout Probability	
S	Approximation	Exact
0	44.010%	25.174%
1	11.536	8.937
2	2.119	1.873
3	0.298	0.280
4	0.034	0.033
5	0.003	0.003
6	0.000	0.000

Fill Rate for the Order-up-to Model (Chapter 16)

The fill rate is the probability that a customer is able to purchase a unit immediately (i.e., the customer is not backordered). The fill rate can be evaluated with the following equation:

$$\text{Fill rate} = 1 - \frac{\text{Expected back order}}{\text{Expected demand in one period}}$$

The logic behind the above equation is as follows: The number of customers in a period is the expected demand in one period, and the number of customers who are not served in a period is the expected back order, so the ratio of the expected back order to the expected demand is the fraction of customers who are not served. One minus the fraction of customers who are not served is the fraction of customers who are served, which is the fill rate. Note that this logic does not depend on the particular demand distribution (but the evaluation of the expected back order does depend on the demand distribution).

You also might wonder why the denominator of the fraction in the fill rate equation is the expected demand over a single period and not the expected demand over $l + 1$ periods. We are interested in the fraction of customers who are not served immediately from stock (one minus that fraction is the expected fill rate). The lead time influences the fraction of customers in a period who are not served (the expected back order), but it does not influence the number of customers we have. Therefore, the lead time influences the numerator of that ratio (the number of customers who are not served) but not the denominator (the number of customers who arrive).

The above equation for the fill rate is actually an approximation of the fill rate. It happens to be an excellent approximation if the fill rate is reasonably high (say, 90 percent or higher). The advantage of that formula is that it is reasonably easy to work with. However, the remainder of this section derives the exact formula.

The fill rate is one minus the probability of not being served in a period, which is the following:

$$\text{Probability of not being served} = \frac{\text{Expected back orders that occur in a period}}{\text{Expected demand in one period}}$$

We know the denominator of that fraction, the expected demand in one period. We need to determine the numerator. The expected back orders that occur in a period are not quite the same as the expected back order in a period. The difference is that some of the back order might not have occurred in the period. (This is the same issue with the evaluation of the stockout probability.) For example, if the back order in a period is four units and demand in the period was three units, then only three of the four back orders actually occurred in that period; the remaining back-ordered unit was a carryover from a previous period.

Let's define some new notation. Let

$$B(l) = \text{Expected back orders if the lead time is } l$$

Hence, $B(l)$ is what we have been calling the *expected back order.*

The expected back order at the end of the $(l + 1)$th period of an interval of $l + 1$ periods is $B(l)$. If we subtract from those back orders the ones that were back-ordered at the end of the lth period in that interval, then we have the number of back orders that occurred in that last period of the interval. Hence,

$$\text{Probability of not being served} = \frac{B(l) - B(l-1)}{\text{Expected demand in one period}}$$

The numerator of the above fraction, in words, is the expected back order minus what the expected back order would be if the lead time were one period faster. Our exact fill rate equation is thus

$$\text{Expected fill rate} = 1 - \frac{\text{Expected back order} - B(l-1)}{\text{Expected demand in one period}}$$

The first fill rate equation presented in this section is an approximation because it does not subtract $B(l - 1)$ from the expected back order in the numerator. If the service level is very high, then $B(l - 1)$ will be very small, which is why the equation in the chapter is a good approximation.

If demand is Poisson with mean 0.29 per period and the lead time is one period, then

	Expected Fill Rate	
S	Approximation	Exact
0	−100.000%	0.000%
1	51.759	64.954
2	91.539	92.754
3	98.844	98.930
4	99.871	99.876
5	99.988	99.988
6	99.999	99.999

The approximation underestimates the fill rate, especially when the fill rate is low. However, the approximation is accurate for high fill rates.

Coordinating Buy-Back Price (Chapter 19)

If the wholesale price has been chosen, then we want to find the buy-back price that will lead the retailer to order the supply chain profit-maximizing quantity. This can be achieved if the retailer's critical ratio equals the supply chain's critical ratio because it is the critical ratio that determines the optimal order quantity.

Let's define some notation:

p = Retail price

c = Production cost

v = Retailer's salvage value

t = Shipping cost

w = wholesale price

b = buy-back price

The supply chain's critical ratio is $(p - c)/(p - v)$ because $C_u = p - c$ and $C_o = c - v$. The retailer's underage cost with the buy-back contract is $C_u = p - w$ and its overage cost is $C_o = t + w - b$ (i.e., the shipping cost plus the amount not credited by the supplier on returned inventory, $w - b$). Hence, the retailer's critical ratio equals the supply chain's critical ratio when

$$\frac{p-c}{p-v} = \frac{p-w}{(t+w-b)+p-w}$$

If we take the above equation and rearrange terms, we get Equation (19.1).

Appendix 

Solutions to Selected Practice Problems

This appendix provides solutions to marked (*) practice problems.

Chapter 2

Q2.1 (Dell)

The following steps refer directly to Exhibit 2.1.

Step 1. For 2001, we find in Dell's 10-k: Inventory = \$400 (in millions)

Step 2. For 2001, we find in Dell's 10-k: COGS = \$26,442 (in millions)

Step 3. Inventory turns = $\frac{\$26{,}442/\text{Year}}{\$400} = 66.105$ turns per year

Step 4. Per-unit inventory cost = $\frac{40\% \text{ per year}}{66.105 \text{ per year}} = 0.605$ percent per unit

Chapter 3

Q3.1 (Process Analysis with One Flow Unit)

The following steps refer directly to Exhibit 3.1.

Step 1. We first compute the capacity of the three resources:

Resource 1: $\frac{2}{10}$ unit per minute = 0.2 unit per minute

Resource 2: $\frac{1}{6}$ unit per minute = 0.1666 unit per minute

Resource 3: $\frac{3}{16}$ unit per minute = 0.1875 unit per minute

Step 2. Resource 2 has the lowest capacity; process capacity therefore is 0.1666 unit per minute, which is equal to 10 units per hour.

Step 3. Flow rate = Min{Process capacity, Demand}

= Min{8 units per hour, 10 units per hour} = 8 units per hour

This is equal to 0.1333 unit per minute.

Step 4. We find the utilizations of the three resources as

Resource 1: 0.1333 unit per minute/0.2 unit per minute = 66.66 percent
Resource 2: 0.1333 unit per minute/0.1666 unit per minute = 80 percent
Resource 3: 0.1333 unit per minute/0.1875 unit per minute = 71.11 percent

Q3.2 (Process Analysis with Multiple Flow Units)

The following steps refer directly to Exhibit 3.2.

Step 1. Each resource can contribute the following capacity (in minutes of work per day):

Resource	Number of Workers	Minutes per Day
1	2	$2 \times 8 \times 60 = 960$
2	2	$2 \times 8 \times 60 = 960$
3	1	$1 \times 8 \times 60 = 480$
4	1	$1 \times 8 \times 60 = 480$
5	2	$2 \times 8 \times 60 = 960$

Step 2. Process flow diagram:

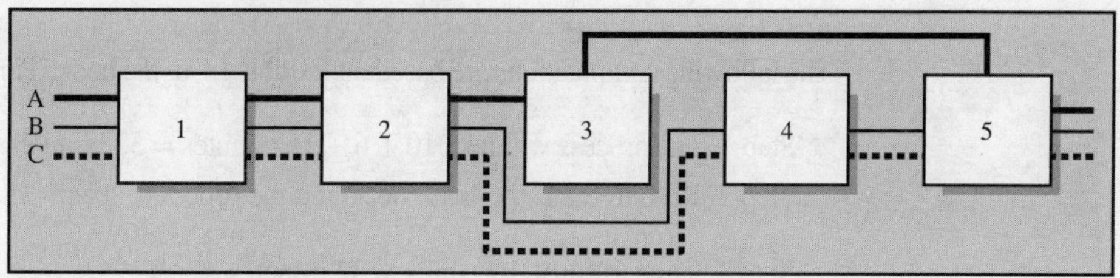

Step 3. We create a table indicating how much capacity will be consumed by the three products at the resources.

Resource	Capacity Requirement from A	Capacity Requirement from B	Capacity Requirement from C
1	$5 \times 40 = 200$	$5 \times 50 = 250$	$5 \times 60 = 300$
2	$3 \times 40 = 120$	$4 \times 50 = 200$	$5 \times 60 = 300$
3	$15 \times 40 = 600$	$0 \times 50 = 0$	$0 \times 60 = 0$
4	$0 \times 40 = 0$	$3 \times 50 = 150$	$3 \times 60 = 180$
5	$6 \times 40 = 240$	$6 \times 50 = 300$	$6 \times 60 = 360$

Step 4. Add up the rows to get the workload for each resource:

Workload for resource 1: 200 + 250 + 300 = 750

Workload for resource 2: 120 + 200 + 300 = 620

Workload for resource 3: 600 + 0 + 0 = 600

Workload for resource 4: 0 + 150 + 180 = 330

Workload for resource 5: 240 + 300 + 360 = 900

Resource	Minutes per Day (see Step 1)	Workload per Day (see Step 4)	Implied Utilization (Step 4/Step 1)
1	960	750	0.78
2	960	620	0.65
3	480	600	1.25
4	480	330	0.69
5	960	900	0.94

Step 5. Compute implied utilization levels. Hence, resource 3 is the bottleneck. Thus, we cannot produce units A at a rate of 40 units per day. Since we are overutilized by 25 percent, we can produce units A at a rate of 32 units per day (four units per hour). Assuming the ratio between A, B, and C is constant (40:50:60), we will produce B at five units per hour and C at six units per hour. If the ratio between A, B, and C is *not* constant, this answer changes. In this case, we would produce 32 units of A and produce products B and C at the rate of demand (50 and 60 units per day, respectively).

Chapter 4

Q4.1 (Empty System, Labor Utilization)

Part a

The following computations are based on Exhibit 4.1 in the book. Time to complete 100 units:

Step 1. The process will take $10 + 6 + 16$ minutes $= 32$ minutes to produce the first unit.

Step 2. Resource 2 is the bottleneck and the process capacity is 0.1666 unit per minute.

Step 3. $\text{Time to finish 100 units} = 32 \text{ minutes} + \dfrac{99 \text{ units}}{0.166 \text{ unit/minute}} = 626 \text{ minutes}$

Parts b, c, and d

We answer these three questions together by using Exhibit 4.2 in the book.

Step 1. Capacities are

$$\text{Resource 1: } \frac{2}{10} \text{unit/minute} = 0.2 \text{ unit/minute}$$

$$\text{Resource 2: } \frac{1}{6} \text{unit/minute} = 0.1666 \text{ unit/minute}$$

$$\text{Resource 3: } \frac{3}{16} \text{unit/minute} = 0.1875 \text{ unit/minute}$$

Resource 2 is the bottleneck and the process capacity is 0.1666 unit/minute.

Step 2. Since there is unlimited demand, the flow rate is determined by the capacity and therefore is 0.1666 unit/minute; this corresponds to a cycle time of 6 minutes/unit.

Step 3. $\text{Cost of direct labor} = \dfrac{6 \times \$10/\text{hour}}{60 \text{ minutes/hour} \times 0.1666 \text{ unit/minute}} = \$6/\text{unit}$

Step 4. Compute the idle time of each worker for each unit:

$$\text{Idle time for workers at resource 1} = 6 \text{ minutes/unit} \times 2 - 10 \text{ minutes/unit} = 2 \text{ minutes/unit}$$

$$\text{Idle time for worker at resource 2} = 6 \text{ minutes/unit} \times 1 - 6 \text{ minutes/unit} = 0 \text{ minutes/unit}$$

$$\text{Idle time for workers at resource 3} = 6 \text{ minutes/unit} \times 3 - 16 \text{ minutes/unit} = 2 \text{ minutes/unit}$$

Step 5. Labor content = 10 + 6 + 16 minutes/unit = 32 minutes/unit

Step 6. Average labor utilization $= \frac{32}{32 + 4} = 0.8888$

Chapter 5

Q5.1 (Window Boxes)

The following computations are based on Exhibit 5.1.

Part a

Step 1. Since there is sufficient demand, the step (other than the stamping machine) that determines flow rate is assembly. Capacity at assembly is $\frac{12}{27}$ unit/minute.

Step 2. The production cycle consists of the following parts:

- Setup for A (120 minutes).
- Produce parts A (360 × 1 minute).
- Setup for B (120 minutes).
- Produce parts B (720 × 0.5 minute).

Step 3. There are two setups in the production cycle, so the setup time is 240 minutes.

Step 4. Every completed window box requires one part A (one minute per unit) and two parts B (2 × 0.5 minute per unit). Thus, the per-unit activity time is two minutes per unit.

Step 5. Use formula

$$\text{Capacity given batch size} = \frac{360 \text{ units}}{240 \text{ minutes} + 360 \text{ units} \times 2 \text{ minutes/unit}} = 0.375 \text{ unit/minute}$$

Step 6. Capacity at stamping for a general batch size is

$$\frac{\text{Batch size}}{240 \text{ minutes} + \text{Batch size} \times 2 \text{ minutes/unit}}$$

We need to solve the equation

$$\frac{\text{Batch size}}{240 \text{ minutes} + \text{Batch size} \times 2 \text{ minutes/unit}} = \frac{12}{27}$$

for the batch size. The batch size solving this equation is Batch size = 960. We can obtain the same number directly by using

$$\text{Recommended batch size} = \frac{\text{Flow rate} \times \text{Setup time}}{1 - \text{Flow rate} \times \text{Time per unit}} = \frac{\frac{12}{27} \times 240}{1 - \frac{12}{27} \times 2} = 960$$

Q5.10 (Cat Food)

$$\frac{7 \times 500}{EOQ} = 1.62$$

Part a

Holding costs are \$0.50 × 15%/50 = 0.0015 per can per week. Note, each can is purchased for \$0.50, so that is the value tied up in inventory and therefore determines the holding cost. The EOQ is then

Part b

The ordering cost is \$7 per order. The number of orders per year is 500/EOQ. Thus, order cost = \$/week = \$81/year.

Part c

The average inventory level is EOQ/2. Inventory costs per week are thus 0.5 × EOQ × 0.0015 = \$1.62. Given 50 weeks per year, the inventory cost per year is \$81

Part d

Inventory Turns = Flow rate/Inventory

Flow Rate = 500 cans per week

Inventory = 0.5 3 EOQ

Thus, Inventory Turns = *R*/(0.5×EOQ) = 0.462 turns per week = 23.14 turns per year

Q5.11 (Beer Distributor)

The holding costs are 25% per year = 0.5% per week = 8*0.005 = \$0.04 per week

(a) $\text{EOQ} = \sqrt{\frac{2 \times 100 \times 10}{0.04}} = 223.6$

(b) Inventory turns = Flow Rate/Inventory = 100 × 50/(0.5 × EOQ) = 5000/EOQ = 44.7 turns per year

(c) $\text{Per unit inventory cost} = \sqrt{\frac{2 \times 0.04 \times 10}{100}} = 0.089\$/unit$

(d) You would never order more than Q = 600.

For Q = 600, we would get the following costs: 0.5 × 600 × 0.04 × 0.95 + 10 × 100/600 = 13.1.

The cost per unit would be 13.1/100 = \$0.131.

The quantity discount would save us 5%, which is \$0.40 per case. However, our operating costs increase by \$0.131 – 0.089 = \$0.042. Hence, the savings outweigh the cost increase and it is better to order 600 units at a time.

Chapter 6

Q6.1 (Crazy Cab)

Part a/b

ROIC Tree:

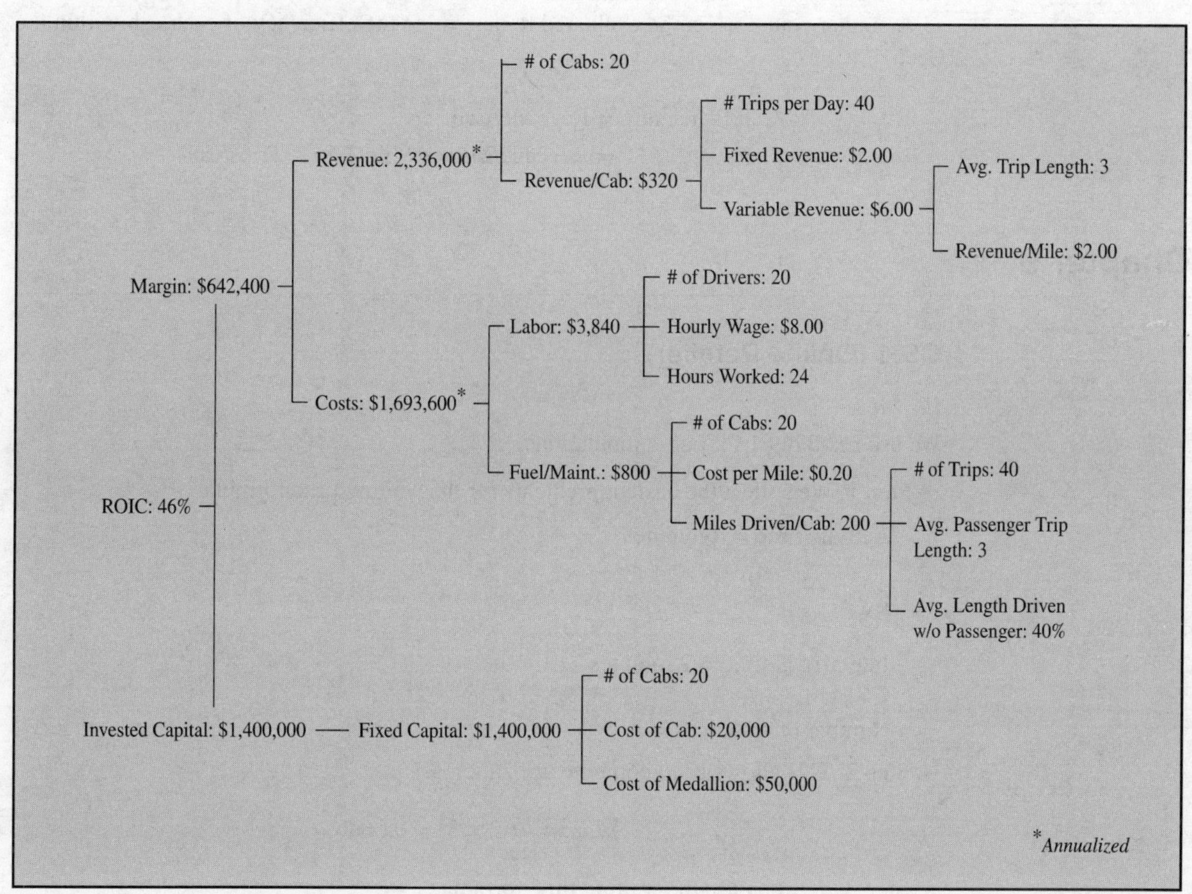

Part c

There are several variables that could be classified as operational value drivers including the number of trips per day, the average trip length, the drivers' hourly wage, and the average distance driven without passengers. Other variables such as the revenue per passenger mile, the fixed fees and the maintenance/fuel cost per mile driven are harder for management to influence because they are either regulated through the cab medallions or are strongly influenced by fuel prices (management could, however, invest in more fuel-efficient cars to reduce this cost).

Given the high capital investments associated with purchasing a cab and medallion, as well as the fixed labor requirements, it is important that each cab maximizes its revenue. An additional trip is almost pure profit, particularly if it replaces idle driving time between passengers.

Part d

Labor Efficiency = Revenue/Labor Costs
= Revenue/Mile × Mile/Trip × Trips/Day × Day/Labor Costs

In this equation, the first ratio measures the company's operational yield, which is largely a reflection of the company's pricing power. The next two ratios are measures of efficiency: the length of each trip and the number of daily trips, respectively. The final ratio is a measure of the cost of a resource, in this instance the company's labor costs.

A similar equation can be evaluated to determine the efficiency of each cab within the fleet:

Cab Efficiency = Revenue/Cab
= Revenue/Mile × Mile/Trip × Trips/Cab

Chapter 9

Q9.1 (Online Retailer)

Part a

We use Exhibit 9.1 for our computations.

Step 1. We collect the basic ingredients for the waiting time formula:

Activity time = 4 minutes

$$CV_p = \frac{2}{4}$$

Interarrival time = 2 minutes
$CV_a = 1$
Number of resources = 3

Step 2. This allows us to compute utilization as

$$p/am = 4/(2 \times 3) = 0.6666$$

Step 3. We then use the waiting time formula

$$T_q \approx \left(\frac{4}{3}\right) \times \left(\frac{0.666^{\sqrt{2(3+1)}-1}}{1-0.6666}\right) \times \left(\frac{1^2+0.5^2}{2}\right) = 1.19 \text{ minutes}$$

Step 4. We find the

Inventory in service: $I_p = m \times u = 3 \times 0.666 = 2$
Inventory in the queue: $I_q = T_q/a = 1.19/2 = 0.596$
Inventory in the system: $I = I_p + I_q = 2.596$

Part b

The number of e-mails that have been received but not yet answered corresponds to the total inventory of e-mails. We find this to be 2.596 e-mails (see Step 4 above).

Chapter 10

Q10.1 (Loss System)

We use Exhibit 10.1 to answer parts a through c.

Step 1. The interarrival time is 60 minutes per hour divided by 55 units arriving per hour, which is an interarrival time of $a = 1.0909$ minutes/unit. The processing time is $p = 6$ minutes/unit; this allows us to compute $r = p/a = 6/1.0909 = 5.5$.

Step 2. With $r = 5.5$ and $m = 7$, we can use the Erlang Loss Formula Table to look up $P_7(5.5)$ as 0.1525. Alternatively, we can use the actual loss formula (see Appendix C) to compute the probability that all seven servers are utilized:

$$\text{Prob}\{\text{all 7 servers are busy}\} = P_7(5.5) = \frac{\frac{5.5^7}{7!}}{1 + \frac{5.5^1}{1!} + \frac{5.5^2}{2!} + \cdots + \frac{5.5^7}{7!}} = 0.1525$$

Step 3. Compute the flow rate: $R = 1/a \times (1 - P_m) = 1/1.0909 \times (1 - 0.153) = 0.77$ unit per minute or 46.585 units per hour.

Step 4. Compute lost customers:

$$\text{Customers lost} = 1/a \times P_m = 1/1.0909 \times 0.153 = 0.14 \text{ unit per minute}$$

which corresponds to 8.415 units per hour.

Thus, from the 55 units that arrive every hour, 46.585 will be served and 8.415 will be lost.

Chapter 12

Q12.1 (Venture Fair)

Part a

Dependency Matrix:

			Information-Providing Activity (Upstream)										
			1	2	3	4	5	6	7	8	9	10	11
Information-Receiving Activity (Downstream)	1	Ideation	■										
	2	Interview Customers	X	■									
	3	Analyze Competing Products	X		■								
	4	User/Customer Observation		X		■							
	5	Send E-Mail Surveys		X			■						
	6	Target Specifications			X	X	X	■					
	7	Product Design						X	■				
	8	Get Price Quotes							X	■			
	9	Build Prototype							X		■		
	10	Test Prototype with Customers									X	■	
	11	Prepare Info for Venture Fair								X		X	■
		Activity	1	2	3	4	5	6	7	8	9	10	11
		Days	3	6	12	10	4	5	10	6	4	5	3

Part b

The critical path is A1→A2→A4→A6→A7→A9→A10→A11, which has a total duration of 3 + 6 + 10 + 5 + 10 + 4 + 5 + 3 = 46. If the project team must have the materials finished by the day before the project fair (April 17th), then they must begin no later than March 3rd (29 days of work in March and 17 days in April).

Chapter 14

Q14.1 (McClure Books)

Part a

We first find the z-statistic for 400 (Dan's blockbuster threshold): $z = (400 - 200)/80 = 2.50$. From the Standard Normal Distribution Function Table, we see that $\Phi(2.50) = 0.9938$. So there is a 99.38 percent chance demand is 400 or fewer. Demand is greater than 400 with probability $1 - \Phi(2.50) = 0.0062$; that is, there is only a 0.62 percent chance this is a blockbuster.

Part b

We first find the z-statistic for 100 units (Dan's dog threshold): $z = (100 - 200)/80 = -1.25$. From the Standard Normal Distribution Function Table, we see that $\Phi(-1.25) = 0.1056$. So there is a 10.56 percent chance demand is 100 or fewer; that is, there is a 10.56 percent chance this book is a dog.

Part c

Demand is within 20 percent of the mean if it is between $1.2 \times 200 = 240$ and $0.8 \times 200 = 160$. Using Exhibit 14.2, we first find the z-statistic for 240 units (the upper limit on that range): $z = (240 - 200)/80 = 0.5$. From the Standard Normal Distribution Function Table, we see that $\Phi(0.5) = 0.6915$. Repeat the process for the lower limit on the range: $z = (160 - 200)/80 = -0.5$ and $\Phi(-0.5) = 0.3085$. The probability demand is between 160 and 240 is $\Phi(0.5) - \Phi(-0.50) = 0.6915 - 0.3085 = 0.3830$; that is, 38.3 percent.

Part d

The underage cost is $C_u = 20 - 12 = 8$. The salvage value is $12 - 4 = 8$ because Dan can return leftover books for a full refund ($12) but incurs a $4 cost of shipping and handling. Thus, the overage cost is cost minus salvage value: $C_o = 12 - 8 = 4$. The critical ratio is $C_u/(C_o + C_u) = 8/12 = 0.6667$. In the Standard Normal Distribution Function Table, we see that $\Phi(0.43) = 0.6664$ and $\Phi(0.44) = 0.6700$, so use the round-up rule and choose $z = 0.44$. Now convert z into the order quantity for the actual demand distribution: $Q = \mu + z \times \sigma = 200 + 0.44 \times 80 = 235.2$.

Part e

We want to find a z such that $\Phi(z) = 0.95$. In the Standard Normal Distribution Function Table, we see that $\Phi(1.64) = 0.9495$ and $\Phi(1.65) = 0.9505$, so use actual $200 + 1.65 \times 80 = 332$.

Part f

If the in-stock probability is 95 percent, then the stockout probability (which is what we are looking for) is 1 minus the in-stock, that is, $1 - 95\% = 5$ percent.

Part g

The z-statistic for 300 units is $z = (300 - 200)/80 = 1.25$. From the Standard Normal Loss Function Table, we see that $L(1.25) = 0.0506$. Expected lost sales are $\sigma \times L(1.25) = 4.05$. Expected sales are 200 – 4.05 = 195.95, expected leftover inventory is 300 – 195.95 = 104.05, and

$$\begin{aligned} \text{Expected profit} &= (\text{Price} - \text{Cost}) \times \text{Expected sales} \\ &\quad - (\text{Cost} - \text{Salvage value}) \times \text{Expected leftover inventory} \\ &= (20 - 12) \times 195.95 - (12 - 8) \times 104.05 \\ &= 1151.4 \end{aligned}$$

Q14.2 (EcoTable Tea)

Part a

We need to evaluate the stockout probability with $Q = 3$. From the Poisson Distribution Function Table, $F(3) = 0.34230$. The stockout probability is $1 - F(3) = 65.8$ percent.

Part b

They will need to mark down three or more baskets if demand is seven or fewer. From the Poisson Distribution Function Table, $F(7) = 0.91341$, so there is a 91.3 percent probability this will occur.

Part c

First evaluate their critical ratio. The underage cost (or cost of a lost sale) is \$55 – \$32 = \$23. The overage cost (or the cost of having a unit left in inventory) is \$32 – \$20 = \$12. The critical ratio is $C_u/(C_o + C_u) = 0.6571$. From the Poisson Distribution Function Table, with a mean of 4.5, we see that $F(4) = 0.53210$ and $F(5) = 0.70293$, so we apply the round-up rule and order five baskets.

Part d

With four baskets, expected lost sales is 1.08808, according to the Poisson Loss Function Table. Expected sales is then 4.5 – 1.08808 = 3.4.

Part e

With six baskets, expected lost sales is 0.32312, according to the Poisson Loss Function Table. Expected sales is then 4.5 – 0.32312 = 4.17688. Expected leftover inventory is then $6 - 4.17688 = 1.72312 \approx 1.8$.

Part f

From the Poisson Distribution Function Table, $F(6) = 0.83105$ and $F(7) = 0.91314$. Hence, order seven baskets to achieve at least a 90 percent in-stock probability (in fact, the in-stock probability will be 91.3 percent).

Part g

If they order eight baskets, then expected lost sales is 0.06758. Expected sales is 4.5 – 0.06758 = 4.43242. Expected leftover inventory is 8 – 4.43242 = 3.56758. Profit is then \$23 × 4.43242 – \$12 × 3.56758 = \$59.13.

Q14.3 (Pony Express Creations)

Part a

If they purchase 40,000 units, then they need to liquidate 10,000 or more units if demand is 30,000 units or lower. From the table provided, $F(30{,}000) = 0.7852$, so there is a 78.52 percent chance they need to liquidate 10,000 or more units.

Part b

The underage cost is $C_u = 12 - 6 = 6$, the overage cost is $C_o = 6 - 2.5 = 3.5$, and the critical ratio is $6/(3.5 + 6) = 0.6316$. Looking in the demand forecast table, we see that $F(25{,}000) = 0.6289$ and $F(30{,}000) = 0.7852$, so use the round-up rule and order 30,000 Elvis wigs.

Part c

We want to find a Q such that $F(Q) = 0.90$. From the demand forecast table, we see that $F(35{,}000) = 0.8894$ and $F(40{,}000) = 0.9489$, so use the round-up rule and order 40,000 Elvis wigs. The actual in-stock probability is then 94.89 percent.

Part d

If $Q = 50{,}000$, then expected lost sales from the table are only 61 units. Expected leftover inventory $= Q - \mu +$ Expected lost sales $= 50{,}000 - 25{,}000 + 61 = 25{,}061$.

Part e

A 100 percent in-stock probability requires an order quantity of 75,000 units. With $Q = 75{,}000$, then expected lost sales from the table are only two units. Use Exhibit 14.5 to evaluate expected sales, expected leftover inventory, and expected profit. Expected sales are expected demand minus expected lost sales $= 25{,}000 - 2 = 24{,}998$. Expected leftover inventory is $75{,}000 - 24{,}998 = 50{,}002$.

$$\begin{aligned}\text{Expected profit} &= (\text{Price} - \text{Cost}) \times \text{Expected sales} \\ &\quad - (\text{Cost} - \text{Salvage value}) \times \text{Expected leftover inventory} \\ &= (12 - 6) \times 24{,}998 - (6 - 2.5) \times 50{,}002 \\ &= -25{,}019\end{aligned}$$

So a 100 percent in-stock probability is a money-losing proposition.

Q14.4 (Flextrola)

Part a

It is within 25 percent of the forecast if it is greater than 750 and less than 1,250. Use Exhibit 14.2. The z-statistic for 750 is $z = (750 - 1{,}000)/600 = -0.42$ and the z-statistic for 1,250 is $z = (1{,}250 - 1{,}000)/600 = 0.42$. From the Standard Normal Distribution Function Table, we see that $\Phi(-0.42) = 0.3372$ and $\Phi(0.42) = 0.6628$. So there is a 33.72 percent chance demand is less than 750 and a 66.28 percent chance it is less than 1,250. The chance it is between 750 and 1,250 is the difference in those probabilities: $0.6628 - 0.3372 = 0.3256$.

Part b

The forecast is for 1,000 units. Demand is greater than 40 percent of the forecast if demand exceeds 1,400 units. Use Exhibit 14.2. Find the z-statistic that corresponds to 1,400 units:

$$z = \frac{Q - \mu}{\sigma} = \frac{1{,}400 - 1{,}000}{600} = 0.67$$

From the Standard Normal Distribution Function Table, $\Phi(0.67) = 0.7486$. Therefore, there is almost a 75 percent probability that demand is less than 1,400 units. The probability that demand is greater than 1,400 units is $1 - \Phi(0.67) = 0.2514$, or about 25 percent.

Part c

To find the expected profit-maximizing order quantity, first identify the underage and overage costs. The underage cost is $C_u = 121 - 72 = 49$ because each lost sale costs Flextrola its gross margin. The overage cost is $C_o = 72 - 50 = 22$ because each unit of leftover inventory can only be sold for $50. Now evaluate the critical ratio:

$$\frac{C_u}{C_o + C_u} = \frac{49}{22 + 49} = 0.6901$$

Look up the critical ratio in the Standard Normal Distribution Function Table: $\Phi(0.49) = 0.6879$ and $\Phi(0.50) = 0.6915$, so choose $z = 0.50$. Now convert the z-statistic into an order quantity: $Q = \mu + z \times \sigma = 1{,}000 + 0.5 \times 600 = 1{,}300$.

Part d

Use Exhibit 14.4 to evaluate expected lost sales and then Exhibit 14.5 to evaluate expected sales. If $Q = 1{,}200$, then the corresponding z-statistic is $z = (Q - \mu)/\sigma = (1{,}200 - 1{,}000)/600 = 0.33$. From the Standard Normal Distribution Loss Table, we see that $L(0.33) = 0.2555$. Expected lost sales are then $\sigma \times L(z) = 600 \times 0.2555 = 153.3$. Finally, recall that expected sales equal expected demand minus expected lost sales: Expected sales = 1,000 – 153.3 = 846.7.

Part e

Flextrola sells its leftover inventory in the secondary market, which equals Q minus expected sales 1,200 – 846.7 = 353.3.

Part f

To evaluate the expected gross margin percentage, we begin with

$$\begin{aligned}\text{Expected revenue} &= (\text{Price} \times \text{Expected sales}) \\ &\quad + (\text{Salvage value} \times \text{Expected leftover inventory}) \\ &= (121 \times 846.7) + (50 \times 353.3) \\ &= 120{,}116\end{aligned}$$

Then we evaluate expected cost $= Q \times c = 1{,}200 \times 72 = 86{,}400$. Finally, expected gross margin percentage = 1 – 86,400/120,116 = 28.1 percent.

Part g

Use Exhibit 14.5 and the results from parts d and e to evaluate expected profit:

$$\begin{aligned}\text{Expected profit} &= (\text{Price} - \text{Cost}) \times \text{Expected sales} \\ &\quad - (\text{Cost} - \text{Salvage value}) \times \text{Expected leftover inventory} \\ &= (121 - 72) \times 846.7 - (72 - 50) \times 353.3 \\ &= 33{,}716\end{aligned}$$

Part h

Solectric's expected profit is $1{,}200 \times (72 - 52) = 24{,}000$ because units are sold to Flextrola for $72 and each unit has a production cost of $52.

Part i

Flextrola incurs 400 or more units of lost sales if demand exceeds the order quantity by 400 or more units; that is, if demand is 1,600 units or greater. The z-statistic that corresponds to 1,600 is $z = (Q - \mu)/\sigma = (1{,}600 - 1{,}000)/600 = 1$. In the Standard Normal Distribution Function Table, $\Phi(1) = 0.8413$. Demand exceeds 1,600 with the probability $1 - \Phi(1) =$ 15.9 percent.

Part j

The critical ratio is 0.6901. From the graph of the distribution function, we see that the probability demand is less than 1,150 with the log normal distribution about 0.70. Hence, the optimal order quantity with the log normal distribution is about 1,150 units.

Q14.5 (Fashionables)

Part a

The underage cost is $C_u = 70 - 40 = 30$ and the overage cost is $C_o = 40 - 20 = 20$. The critical ratio is $C_u/(C_o + C_u) = 30/50 = 0.6$. From the Standard Normal Distribution Function Table, $\Phi(0.25) = 0.5987$ and $\Phi(0.26) = 0.6026$, so we choose $z = 0.26$. Convert that z-statistic into an order quantity $Q = \mu + z \times \sigma = 500 + 0.26 \times 200 = 552$. Note that the cost of a truckload has no impact on the profit-maximizing order quantity.

Part b

We need to find the z in the Standard Normal Distribution Function Table such that $\Phi(z) = 0.9750$ because $\Phi(z)$ is the in-stock probability. We see that $\Phi(1.96) = 0.9750$, so we choose $z = 1.96$. Convert to $Q = \mu + z \times \sigma = 500 + 1.96 \times 200 = 892$.

Part c

If 725 units are ordered, then the corresponding z-statistic is $z = (Q - \mu)/\sigma = (725 - 500)/200 = 1.13$. We need to evaluate lost sales, expected sales, and expected leftover inventory before we can evaluate the expected profit. Expected lost sales with the standard normal is obtained from the Standard Normal Loss Function Table, $L(1.13) = 0.0646$. Expected lost sales are $\sigma \times L(z) = 200 \times 0.0646 = 12.9$. Expected sales are $500 - 12.9 = 487.1$. Expected leftover inventory is $725 - 487.1 = 237.9$. Expected profit is

$$\begin{aligned}\text{Expected profit} &= (70 - 40) \times 487.1 - (40 - 20) \times 237.9 \\ &= 9{,}855\end{aligned}$$

So the expected profit per sweater type is 9,855. The total expected profit is five times that amount, minus 2,000 times the number of truckloads required.

Part d

The stockout probability is the probability demand exceeds the order quantity 725, which is $1 - \Phi(1.13) = 12.9$ percent.

Part e

If we order the expected profit-maximizing order quantity for each sweater, then that equals $5 \times 552 = 2{,}760$ sweaters. With an order quantity of 552 sweaters, expected lost sales are $56.5 = 200 \times L(0.26) = 200 \times 0.2824$, expected sales are $500 - 56.5 = 443.5$, and expected leftover inventory is $552 - 443.5 = 108.5$. Expected profit per sweater type is

$$\begin{aligned}\text{Expected profit} &= (70 - 40) \times 443.5 - (40 - 20) \times 108.5 \\ &= 11{,}135\end{aligned}$$

Because two truckloads are required, the total profit is then 5 × 11,136 – 2 × 2,000 = 51,675. If we order only 500 units per sweater type, then we can evaluate the expected profit per sweater to be 11,010. Total profit is then 5 × 11,010 – 2,000 = 53,050. Therefore, we are better off just ordering one truckload with 500 sweaters of each type.

Chapter 15

Q15.1 (Teddy Bower)

Part a

Teddy will order from the American supplier if demand exceeds 1,500 units. With Q = 1,500, the z-statistic is z = (1,500 – 2,100)/1,200 = –0.5. From the Standard Normal Distribution Function Table, we see that Φ(–0.50) = 0.3085, which is the probability that demand is 1,500 or fewer. The probability that demand exceeds 1,500 is 1 – Φ(–0.50) = 0.6915, or about 69 percent.

Part b

The supplier's expected demand equals Teddy's expected lost sales with an order quantity of 1,500 parkas. From the Standard Normal Loss Function Table, $L(-0.50) = 0.6978$. Expected lost sales are $\sigma \times L(z)$ = 1,200 × 0.6978 = 837.4.

Part c

The overage cost is C_o = 10 – 0 = 10 because leftover parkas must have been purchased in the first order at a cost of $10 and they have no value at the end of the season. The underage cost is C_u = 15 – 10 = 5 because there is a $5 premium on units ordered from the American vendor. The critical ratio is 5/(10 + 5) = 0.3333. From the Standard Normal Distribution Function Table, we see that Φ(–0.44) = 0.3300 and Φ(–0.43) = 0.3336, so choose z = –0.43. Convert to Q: Q = 2,100 – 0.43 × 1,200 = 1,584.

Part d

First evaluate some performance measures. We already know that with Q = 1,584 the corresponding z is –0.43. From the Standard Normal Loss Function Table, $L(-0.43) = 0.6503$. Expected lost sales are then 1,200 × 0.6503 = 780.4; that is the expected order quantity to the American vendor. If the American vendor were not available, then expected sales would be 2,100 – 780.4 = 1,319.6. Expected leftover inventory is then 1,584 – 1,319.6 = 264.4. Now evaluate expected profit with the American vendor option available. Expected revenue is 2,100 × 22 = $46,200. The cost of the first order is 1,584 × 10 = $15,840. Salvage revenue from leftover inventory is 264.4 × 0 = 0. Finally, the cost of the second order is 780.4 × 15 = $11,706. Thus, profit is 46,200 – 15,840 – 11,706 = $18,654.

Part e

If Teddy only sources from the American supplier, then expected profit would be ($22 – $15) × 2,100 = $14,700 because expected sales would be 2,100 units and the gross margin on each unit is $22 – $15 = $7.

Q15.2 (Flextrola)

Part a

Expected sales = 1,000 and the gross margin per sale is 121 – 83.5 = $37.5. Expected profit is then 1,000 × $37.5 = $37,500.

Part b

$C_o = 72 - 50 = 22$; $C_u = 83.5 - 72 = 11.5$; therefore, the premium on orders from XE is \$11.5. The critical ratio is 11.5/(22 + 11.5) = 0.3433. From the Standard Normal Distribution Function Table, $\Phi(-0.41) = 0.3409$ and $\Phi(-0.40) = 0.3446$, so $z = -0.40$. Convert to Q: $Q = 1{,}000 - 0.4 \times 600 = 760$.

Part c

The underage cost on an option is the change in profit if one additional option had been purchased that could be exercised. For example, if 700 options are purchased, but demand is 701, then 1 additional option could have been purchased. The cost of the option plus exercising it is \$25 + \$50 = \$75. The cost of obtaining the unit without the option is \$83.5, so purchasing the option would have saved C_u = \$83.5 – \$75 = \$8.5. The overage cost on an option is the extra profit that could have been earned if the option were not purchased assuming it isn't needed. For example, if demand were 699, then the last option would not be necessary. The cost of that unnecessary option is C_o = \$25. The critical ratio is 8.5/(25 + 8.5) = 0.2537. From the Standard Normal Distribution Function Table, $\Phi(-0.67) = 0.2514$ and $\Phi(-0.66) = 0.2546$, so $z = -0.66$. Convert to Q: $Q = 1{,}000 - 0.66 \times 600 = 604$.

Part d

Evaluate some performance measures. Expected number of units ordered beyond the purchased options (expected lost sales) is $\sigma \times L(-0.66) = 600 \times 0.8128 = 487.7$. Expected number of options exercised (expected sales) is 1,000 – 487.7 = 512.3. Expected revenue is 1,000 × \$121 = \$121,000. So profit is revenue minus the cost of purchasing options (604 × \$25 = \$15,100), minus the cost of exercising options (512.3 × \$50 = \$25,615), minus the cost of units purchased without options (487.7 × \$83.5 = \$40,723): Profit = 121,000 – 15,100 – 25,615 – 40,723 = \$39,562.

Q15.3 (Wildcat Cellular)

Part a

The underage cost is C_u = 0.4 – 0.05 = \$0.35: If her usage exceeds the minutes she purchases then she could have lowered her cost by \$0.35 per minute if she had purchased more minutes. The overage cost is C_o = 0.05 because each minute purchased but not used provides no value. The critical ratio is 0.35/(0.05 + 0.35) = 0.8749. From the Standard Normal Distribution Function Table Func Table $\Phi(1.15) = 0.8749$ and $\Phi(1.16) = 0.8770$, so $z = 1.16$. Convert to Q: $Q = 250 + 1.16 \times 24 = 278$.

Part b

We need to evaluate the number of minutes used beyond the quantity purchased (Expected lost sales). $z = (240 - 250)/24 = -0.42$, $L(-0.42) = 0.6436$, and expected lost sales = 24 × 0.6436 = 15.4 minutes. Each minute costs \$0.4, so the total surcharge is 15.4 × \$0.4 = \$6.16.

Part c

Find the corresponding z-statistic: $z = (280 - 250)/24 = 1.25$. Now evaluate performance measures. $L(1.25) = 0.0506$, and Expected lost sales = 24 × 0.0506 = 1.2 minutes, that is, only 1.2 minutes are needed on average beyond the 280 purchased. The minutes used out of the 280 (Expected sales) is 250 – 1.2 = 248.8. The unused minutes (Expected left over inventory) is 280 – 248.8 = 31.2.

Part d

Find the corresponding z-statistic: $z = (260 - 250)/24 = 0.42$. The number of minutes needed beyond the 260 is Expected lost sales: $L(0.42) = 0.2236$, and Expected lost sales = 24 × 0.2236 = 5.4 minutes. Total bill is 260 × 0.05 + 5.4 × 0.4 = \$15.16.

Part e

From the Standard Normal Distribution Function Table $\Phi(1.64) = 0.9495$ and $\Phi(1.65) = 0.9505$, so with $z = 1.65$ there is a 95.05 percent chance the outcome of a Standard Normal is less than z. Convert to Q: $Q = 250 + 1.65 \times 24 = 290$.

Part f

With "Pick Your Minutes," the optimal number of minutes is 278. The expected bill is then \$14.46: $z = (278 - 250)/24 = 1.17$; $L(1.17) = 0.0596$; Expected surcharge minutes = $24 \times 0.0596 = 1.4$; Expected surcharge = \$0.4 × 1.4 = \$0.56; Purchase cost is 278 × 0.05 = \$13.9; so the total is \$13.9 + 0.56. With "No Minimum," the total bill is \$22.5: Minutes cost \$0.07 × 250 = \$17.5; plus the fixed fee, \$5. So she should stick with the original plan.

Q15.9 (Steve Smith)

For every car Smith sells, he gets \$350 and an additional \$50 for every car sold over five cars. Look in the Poisson Loss Function Table for mean 5.5: The expected amount by which the outcome exceeds zero is $L(0) = 5.5$ (same as the mean) and the expected amount by which the outcome exceeds five is $L(5) = 1.178$. Therefore, the expected commission is $(350 \times 5.5) + (50 \times 1.178) = 1{,}984$.

Chapter 16

Q16.1 (Furniture Store)

Part a

Inventory position = Inventory level + On-order = 100 + 85 = 185. Order enough to raise the inventory position to the order-up-to level, in this case, 220 – 185 = 35 desks.

Part b

As in part a, Inventory position = 160 + 65 = 225. Because the inventory position is above the order-up-to level, 220, you do not order additional inventory.

Part c

Use Exhibit 16.6. From the Standard Normal Distribution Function Table: $\Phi(2.05) = 0.9798$ and $\Phi(2.06) = 0.9803$, so choose $z = 2.06$. The lead time l is 2, so $\mu = (2 + 1) \times 40 = 120$ and $\sigma = \sqrt{2+1} \times 20 = 34.64$

$$S = \mu + z \times \sigma = 120 + 2.06 \times 34.64 = 191.36$$

Part d

Use Exhibit 16.4. The z-statistic that corresponds to $S = 120$ is $S = (120 - 120)/34.64 = 0$. Expected back order is $\sigma \times L(0) = 34.64 \times 0.3989 = 13.82$. Expected on-hand inventory is $S - \mu$ + Expected back order = 120 – 120 + 13.82 = 13.82.

Part e

From part d, on-hand inventory is 13.82 units, which equals 13.82 × \$200 = \$2,764. Cost of capital is 15 percent, so the cost of holding inventory is 0.15 × \$2,764 = \$414.60.

Q16.2 (Campus Bookstore)

Part a

Use Exhibit 16.6. Mean demand over $l + 1$ periods is $0.5 \times (4 + 1) = 2.5$ units. From the Poisson Distribution Function Table, with mean 2.5 we have $F(6) = 0.9858$ and $F(7) = 0.9958$, so choose $S = 7$ to achieve a 99 percent in-stock.

Part b

Use Exhibit 16.4. Pipeline inventory is $l \times$ Expected demand in one period $= 4 \times 0.5 = 2$ units. The order-up-to level has no influence on the pipeline inventory.

Part c

Use Exhibit 16.4. From the Poisson Loss Function Table with mean 2.5, Expected back order $= L(5) = 0.06195$. Expected on-hand inventory $= 5 - 2.5 + 0.06195 = 2.56$ units.

Part d

A stockout occurs if demand is seven or more units over $l + 1$ periods, which is one minus the probability demand is six or fewer in that interval. From the Poisson Distribution Function Table with mean 2.5, we see that $F(6) = 0.9858$ and $1 - F(6) = 0.0142$; that is, there is about a 1.4 percent chance of a stockout occurring.

Part e

The store is out of stock if demand is six or more units over $l + 1$ periods, which is one minus the probability demand is five or fewer in that interval. From the Poisson Distribution Function Table with mean 2.5, we see that $F(5) = 0.9580$ and $1 - F(5) = 0.0420$; that is, there is about a 4.2 percent chance of being out of inventory at the end of any given week.

Part f

The store has one or more units of inventory if demand is five or fewer over $l + 1$ periods. From part e, $F(5) = 0.9580$; that is, there is about a 96 percent chance of having one or more units at the end of any given week.

Part g

Use Exhibit 16.6. Now the lead time is two periods (each period is two weeks and the total lead time is four weeks, or two periods). Demand over one period is 1.0 unit. Demand over $l + 1$ periods is $(2 + 1) \times 1 = 3.0$ units. From the Poisson Distribution Function Table with mean 3.0, we have $F(7) = 0.9881$ and $F(8) = 0.9962$, so choose $S = 8$ to achieve a 99 percent in-stock.

Part h

Use Exhibit 16.4. Pipeline inventory is average demand over l periods $= 2 \times 1 = 2.0$ units.

Q16.3 (Quick Print)

Part a

If $S = 700$ and the inventory position is $523 + 180 = 703$, then 0 units should be ordered because the inventory position exceeds the order-up-to level.

Part b

Use Exhibit 16.6. From the Standard Normal Distribution Function Table, $\Phi(2.32) = 0.9898$ and $\Phi(2.33) = 0.9901$, so choose $z = 2.33$. Convert to $S = \mu + z \times \sigma = 600 + 2.33 \times 159.22 = 971$.

Q16.4 (Main Line Auto Distributor)

Part a

Use Equation (16.2). The critical ratio is $\$25/(\$0.5 + \$25) = 0.98039$. The lead time is $l = 0$, so demand over $(l + 1)$ periods is Poisson with mean 1.5. From the Poisson Distribution

Function Table with mean 1.5, we see $F(3) = 0.9344$ and $F(4) = 0.9814$, so choose $S = 4$. There is currently no unit on order or on hand, so order to raise the inventory position to four: Order four units.

Part b

The in-stock probability is the probability demand is satisfied during the week. With $S = 3$ the in-stock is $F(3) = 0.9344$, that is, a 93 percent probability.

Part c

Demand is not satisfied if demand is five or more units, which is $1 - [F(4) = 0.9814] = 1 - 0.9814 = 0.0186$, or about 1.9 percent.

Part d

Use Exhibit 16.6. From the Poisson Distribution Function Table with mean 1.5, $F(4) = 0.9814$ and $F(5) = 0.9955$, so choose $S = 5$ to achieve a 99.5 percent in-stock probability.

Part e

Use Exhibit 16.4. If $S = 5$, then from the Poisson Loss Function Table with mean 1.5, we see expected back order = $L(5) = 0.0056$. Expected on-hand inventory is S – Demand over $(l + 1)$ periods + Expected back order = $5 - 1.5 + 0.0056 = 3.51$ units. The holding cost is $3.51 \times \$0.5 = \$1.76$.

Q16.5 (Hotspices.com)

Part a

From the Standard Normal Distribution Function Table, $\Phi(2.43) = 0.9925$; so choose $z = 2.43$. Convert to S: $S = \mu + z \times \sigma = 159.62 + 2.43 \times 95.51 = 392$.

Part b

Use Equation (16.3). The holding cost is $h = 0.75$ and the back-order penalty cost is 50. The critical ratio is $50/(0.75 + 50) = 0.9852$. From the Standard Normal Distribution Function Table, $\Phi(2.17) = 0.9850$ and $\Phi(2.18) = 0.9854$, so choose $z = 2.18$. Convert to $S = \mu + z \times \sigma = 159.62 + 2.18 \times 95.51 = 368$.

Part c

Use Equation (16.3). The holding cost is $h = 0.05$ and the back-order penalty cost is 5. The critical ratio is $5/(0.05 + 5) = 0.9901$. Lead time plus one demand is Poisson with mean $1 \times 3 = 3$. From the Poisson Distribution Function Table, with $\mu = 3$, $F(7) = 0.9881$ and $F(8) = 0.9962$, so $S = 8$ is optimal.

Chapter 17

Q17.1 (Egghead)

Part a

New standard deviation is $30 \times \sqrt{50} = 212$.

Part b

Pipeline inventory = Expected demand per week × Lead time = $200 \times 50 \times 10 = 100{,}000$.

Q17.2 (Two Products)

The coefficient of total demand (pooled demand) is the coefficient of the product's demand times the square root of (1 + Correlation)/2. Therefore, $\sqrt{(1-0.7)/2} \times 0.6 = 0.23$.

Q17.3 (Fancy Paints)

Part a

Assume Fancy Paints implements the order-up-to inventory model. Find the appropriate order-up-to level. With a lead time of 4 weeks, the relevant demand is demand over 4 + 1 = 5 weeks, which is 5 × 1.25 = 6.25. From the Poisson Distribution Function Table, $F(10)$ = 0.946 and $F(11)$ = 0.974, a base stock level S = 11 is needed to achieve at least a 95 percent in-stock probability. On-hand inventory at the end of the week is S – 6.25 – Expected back order. From the Poisson Distribution Function Loss Function Table, the Expected back order is $L(11)$ = 0.04673. Thus, on-hand inventory for one SKU is 11 – 6.25 + 0.04673 = 4.8 units. There are 200 SKUs, so total inventory is 200 × 4.8 = 960.

Part b

The standard deviation over (4 + 1) weeks is $\sigma = \sqrt{5} \times 8 = 17.89$ and $\mu = 5 \times 50 = 250$. From the Standard Normal Distribution Function Table, we see that $\Phi(1.64) = 0.9495$ and $\Phi(1.65) = 0.9505$, so we choose $z = 1.65$ to achieve the 95 percent in-stock probability. The base stock level is then $S = \mu + z \times \sigma = 250 + 1.65 \times 17.89 = 279.5$. From the Standard Normal Loss Function Table, $L(1.65) = 0.0206$. So, on-hand inventory for one product is S – 250 + Expected back order = 279.5 – 250 + 17.89 × 0.0206 = 29.9. There are five basic SKUs, so total inventory in the store is 29.9 × 5 = 149.5.

Part c

The original inventory investment is 960 × \$14 = \$13,440, which incurs holding costs of \$13,440 × 0.20 = \$2,688. Repeat part b, but now the target in-stock probability is 98 percent. From the Standard Normal Distribution Function Table, we see that $F(2.05)$ = 0.9798 and $F(2.06)$ = 0.9803, so we choose z = 2.06 to achieve the 98 percent in-stock probability. The base stock level is then $S = \mu + z \times \sigma = 250 + 2.06 \times 17.89 = 286.9$. From the Standard Normal Loss Function Table, $L(2.06) = 0.0072$. So, on-hand inventory for one product is S – 250 + Expected back order = 286.9 – 250 = 17.89 × 0.0072 = 37.0. There are five basic SKUs, so total inventory in the store is 37.0 × 5 = 185. With the mixing machine, the total inventory investment is 185 × \$14 = \$2,590. Holding cost is \$2,590 × 0.2 = \$518, which is only 19 percent (518/2688) of the original inventory holding cost.

Q17.4 (Burger King)

Part a

Use the newsvendor model to determine an order quantity. Use Exhibit 14.6. From the table we see that $F(3{,}500)$ = 0.8480 and $F(4{,}000)$ = 0.8911, so order 4,000 for each store.

Part b

Use Exhibit 14.4 to evaluate expected lost sales and to evaluate the expected leftover inventory. Expected lost sales come from the table, $L(4{,}000)$ = 185.3. Expected sales are μ – 185.3 = 2,251 – 185.3 = 2,065.7. Expected leftover inventory is Q minus expected sales, 4,000 – 2,065.7 = 1,934.3. Across 200 stores there will be 200 × 1,934.3 = 386,860 units left over.

Part c

The mean is 450,200. The coefficient of variation of individual stores is 1,600/2,251 = 0.7108. The coefficient of variation of total demand, we are told, is one-half of that, 0.7108/2 = 0.3554. Hence, the standard deviation of total demand is 450,200 × 0.3554 = 160,001. To find the optimal order quantity to hit an 85 percent in-stock probability, use Exhibit 14.6. From the Standard Normal Distribution Function Table, we see $\Phi(1.03)$ = 0.8485 and $\Phi(1.04)$ = 0.8508, so choose z = 1.04. Convert to Q = 450,200 + 1.04 × 160,001 = 616,601.

Part d

Expected lost sales = 160,001 × $L(z)$ = 160,001 × 0.0772 = 12,352. Expected sales = 450,200 – 12,352 = 437,848. Expected leftover inventory = 616,601 – 437,848 = 178,753, which is only 46 percent of what would be left over if individual stores held their own inventory.

Part e

The total order quantity is 4,000 × 200 = 800,000. With a mean of 450,200 and standard deviation of 160,001 (from part c), the corresponding z is (800,000 – 450,200)/160,001 = 2.19. From the Standard Normal Distribution Function Table, we see $\Phi(2.19)$ = 0.9857, so the in-stock probability would be 98.57 percent instead of 89.11 percent if the inventory were held at each store.

Q17.5 (Livingstion Tools)

Part a

With a lead time of 3 weeks, μ (3 + 1) × 5,200 = 20,800 and $\sigma = \sqrt{3+1} \times 3{,}800$ = 7,600. The target expected back orders is (5,200/7,600) × (1 – 0.999) = 0.0007. From the Standard Normal Distribution Function Table, we see that $\Phi(3.10)$ = 0.9990, so we choose z = 3.10 to achieve the 99.9 percent in-stock probability. Convert to S = 20,800 + 3.10 × 7,600 = 44,360. Expected back order is 7,600 × 0.0003 = 2.28. Expected on-hand inventory for each product is 44,360 – 20,800 + 2.28 = 23,562. The total inventory for the two is 2 × 23,562 = 47,124.

Part b

Weekly demand for the two products is 5,200 × 2 = 10,400. The standard deviation of the two products is $\sqrt{2 \times (1 - \text{Correlation})}$ × Standard deviation of one product = $\sqrt{2 \times (1 - 0.20)} \times 3{,}800 = 4{,}806.66$. Lead time plus one expected demand is 10,400 × 4 = 41,600. Standard deviation over (l + 1) periods is $\sqrt{(3+1)} \times 4{,}806.66 = 9.613$. Now repeat the process in part a with the new demand parameters. Convert to S = 41,600 + 3.10 × 9,613 = 71,401. Expected back order is 9,613 × 0.0003 = 2.88. Expected on-hand inventory is 71,401 – 41,600 + 2.88 = 29,804. The inventory investment is reduced by (47,124 – 29,804)/47,124 = 37 percent.

Q17.9 (Consulting Services)

Option a provides the longest chain, covering all four areas. This gives the maximum flexibility value to the firm, so that should be the chosen configuration. To see that it forms a long chain, Alice can do Regulations, as well as Bob. Bob can do Taxes, as well as Doug. Doug can do Strategy, as well as Cathy. Cathy can do Quota, as well as Alice. Hence, there is a single chain among all four consultants. The other options do not form a single chain.

Chapter 18

Q18.1 (The Inn at Penn)

Part a

The booking limit is capacity minus the protection level, which is 150 – 50 = 100; that is, allow up to 100 bookings at the low fare.

Part b

Use Exhibit 18.1. The underage cost is C_u = 200 – 120 = 80 and the overage cost is C_o = 120. The critical ratio is 80/(120 + 80) = 0.4. From the Standard Normal Distribution Function Table, we see $\Phi(-0.26) = 0.3974$ and $\Phi(-0.25) = 0.4013$, so choose $z = -0.25$. Evaluate Q: $Q = 70 - 0.25 \times 29 = 63$.

Part c

Decreases. The lower price for business travelers leads to a lower critical ratio and hence to a lower protection level; that is, it is less valuable to protect rooms for the full fare.

Part d

The number of unfilled rooms with a protection level of 61 is the same as expected leftover inventory. Evaluate the critical ratio, $z = (61 - 70)/29 = -0.31$. From the Standard Normal Loss Function Table, $L(z) = 0.5730$. Expected lost sales are 29 × 0.5730 = 16.62 and expected leftover inventory is 61 – 70 + 16.62 = 7.62. So we can expect 7.62 rooms to remain empty.

Part e

70 × \$200 + (150 – 70) × \$120 = \$23,600 because, on average, 70 rooms are sold at the high fare and 150 – 70 = 80 are sold at the low fare.

Part f

150 × \$120 = \$18,000.

Part g

If 50 are protected, we need to determine the number of rooms that are sold at the high fare. The z = statistic is (50 – 70)/29 = –0.69. Expected lost sales are 29 × $L(-0.69)$ = 24.22. Expected sales are 70 – 24.22 = 45.78. Revenue is then (150 – 50) × \$120 + 45.78 × \$200 = \$21,155.

Q18.2 (Overbooking The Inn at Penn)

Part a

Use Exhibit 18.2. The underage cost is \$120, the discount fare. The overage cost is \$325. The critical ratio is 120/(325 + 120) = 0.2697. From the table, $F(12) = 0.2283$ and $F(13) = 0.3171$, so the optimal overbook quantity is 13.

Part b

A reservation cannot be honored if there are nine or fewer no-shows. $F(9) = 0.0552$, so there is a 5.5 percent chance the hotel will be overbooked.

Part c

It is fully occupied if there are 15 or fewer no-shows, which has probability $F(15) = 0.5170$.

Part d

Bumped customers equal 20 minus the number of no-shows, so it is equivalent to leftover inventory. Lost sales are $L(20) = 0.28$, expected sales are $15.5 - 0.28 = 15.22$, and expected leftover inventory/bumped customers = $20 - 15.22 = 4.78$. Each one costs \$325, so the total cost is \$325 × 4.78 = \$1,554.

Q18.3 (WAMB)

Part a

First evaluate the distribution function from the density function provided in the table: $F(8) = 0$, $F(9) = F(8) + 0.05 = 0.05$, $F(10) = F(9) + 0.10 = 0.15$, and so on. Let Q denote the number of slots to be protected for sale later and let D be the demand for slots at \$10,000 each. If $D > Q$, we reserved too few slots and the underage penalty is C_u = \$10,000 – \$4,000 = \$6,000. If $D < Q$, we reserved too many slots and the overage penalty is C_o = \$4,000. The critical ratio is 6,000/(4,000 + 6,000) = 0.6. From the table, we find $F(13) = 0.6$, so the optimal protection quantity is 13. Therefore, WAMB should sell 25 – 13 = 12 slots in advance.

Part b

The underage penalty remains the same. The overage penalty is now C_o = \$4,000 – \$2,500 = \$1,500. Setting the protection level too high before meant lost revenue on the slot, but now at least \$2,500 can be gained from the slot, so the loss is only \$1,500. The critical ratio is 6,000/(1,500 + 6,000) = 0.8. From the table, $F(15) = 0.8$, so protect 15 slots and sell 25 – 15 = 10 in advance.

Part c

If the booking limit is 10, there are 15 slots for last-minute sales. There will be standby messages if there are 14 or fewer last-minute sales, which has probability $F(14) = 0.70$.

Part d

Over-overbooking means the company is hit with a \$10,000 penalty, so C_o = 10,000. Under-overbooking means slots that could have sold for \$4,000 are actually sold at the standby price of \$2,500, so C_u = 4,000 – 2,500 = 1,500. The critical ratio is 1,500/(10,000 + 1,500) = 0.1304. From the Poisson Distribution Function Table with mean 9.0, $F(5) = 0.1157$ and $F(6) = 0.2068$, so the optimal overbooking quantity is six, that is, sell up to 31 slots.

Part e

The overage cost remains the same: We incur a penalty of \$10,000 for each bumped customer (and we refund the \$1,000 deposit of that customer, too). The underage cost also remains the same. To explain, suppose they overbooked by two slots but there are three withdrawals. Because they have one empty slot, they sell it for \$2,500. Had they overbooked by one more (three slots), then they would have collected \$4,000 on that last slot instead of the \$2,500, so the difference is C_u = \$4,000 – \$2,500 = \$1,500. Note, the nonrefundable amount of \$1,000 is collected from the three withdrawals in either scenario, so it doesn't figure into the change in profit by overbooking one more unit. The critical ratio is 1,500/(10,000 + 1,500) = 0.1304. From the Poisson Distribution Function Table with mean 4.5, $F(1) = 0.0611$ and $F(2) = 0.17358$, so the optimal overbooking quantity is two, that is, sell up to 27 slots.

Q18.4 (Designer Dress)

Part a

The z-statistic is (100 – 70)/40 = 0.75. Expected lost sales are 40 × $L(z)$ = 40 × 0.1312 = 5.248. Expected sales are 70 – 5.248 = 64.752. Expected leftover inventory is 100 – 64.752 = 35.248.

Part b

Expected revenue is \$10,000 × 64.752 = \$647,520.

Part c

Use Exhibit 18.1. The underage cost is \$10,000 – \$6,000 = \$4,000 because underprotecting boutique sales means a loss of \$4,000 in revenue. Overprotecting means a loss of \$6,000 in revenue. The critical ratio is 4,000/(6,000 + 4,000) = 0.4. From the Standard Normal Distribution Function Table, we see Φ(–0.26) = 0.3974 and Φ(–0.25) = 0.4013, so choose z = –0.25. Evaluate Q: Q = 40 – 0.25 × 25 = 33.75. So protect 34 dresses for sales at the boutique, which means sell 100 – 34 = 66 dresses at the show.

Part d

If 34 dresses are sent to the boutique, then expected lost sales are $\sigma \times L(z)$ = 25 × L(–0.25) = 25 × 0.5363 = 13.41. Expected sales are 40 – 13.41 = 26.59. So revenue is 26.59 × \$10,000 + (100 – 34) × 6,000 = \$661,900.

Part e

From part d, expected sales are 26.59, so expected leftover inventory is 34 – 26.59 = 7.41 dresses.

Q18.5 (Overbooking, PHL–LAX)

Part a

Use Exhibit 18.2. The overage cost is \$800 (over-overbooking means a bumped passenger, which costs \$800). The underage cost is \$475 (an empty seat). The critical ratio is 475/(800 + 475) = 0.3725. From the Standard Normal Distribution Function Table, we see Φ(–0.33) = 0.3707 and Φ(–0.32) = 0.3745, so choose z = –0.32. Evaluate Y: Y = 30 – 0.32 × 15 = 25.2. So the maximum number of reservations to accept is 200 + 25 = 225.

Part b

220 – 200 = 20 seats are overbooked. The number of bumped passengers equals 20 minus the number of no-shows, which is equivalent to leftover inventory with an order quantity of 20. The z-statistic is (20–30)/15 = –0.67. L(–0.67) = 0.8203, so lost sales are 15 × 0.8203 = 12.3. Sales are 30 – 12.3 = 17.7 and expected leftover inventory is 20 – 17.7 = 2.3. If 2.3 customers are bumped, then the payout is \$800 × 2.3 = \$1,840.

Part c

You will have bumped passengers if there are 19 or fewer no-shows. The z-statistic is (19 – 30)/15 = –0.73. Φ(–0.73) = 0.2317, so there is about a 23 percent chance there will be bumped passengers.

Chapter 19

Q19.1 (Buying Tissues)

Part a

If orders are made every week, then the average order quantity equals one week's worth of demand, which is 25 cases. If at the end of the week there is one week's worth of inventory, then the average inventory is $25/2 + 25 = 37.5$. (In this case, inventory "saw-tooths" from a high of two weeks' worth of inventory down to one week, with an average of 1.5 weeks.) On average the inventory value is $37.5 \times 9.25 = \$346.9$. The holding cost per year is $52 \times 0.4\% = 20.8$ percent. Hence, the inventory holding cost with the first plan is $20.8\% \times \$346.9 = \$72$. Purchase cost is $52 \times 25 \times \$9.25 = \$12,025$. Total cost is $12,025 + $72 = $12,097.

Part b

Four orders are made each year; each order on average is for $(52/4) \times 25 = 325$ units. Average inventory is then $325/2 + 25 = 187.5$. The price paid per unit is $\$9.40 \times 0.95 = \$8.93$. The value of that inventory is $187.5 \times \$8.93 = \$1,674$. Annual holding costs are $\$1,674 \times 20.8\% = \$348$. Purchase cost is $52 \times 25 \times \$8.93 = \$11,609$. Total cost is $348 + $11,609 = $11,957.

Part c

P&G prefers our third plan as long as the price is higher than in the second plan, $8.93. But the retailer needs a low enough price so that its total cost with the third plan is not greater than in the second plan, $11,957 (from part b). In part a, we determined that the annual holding cost with a weekly ordering plan is approximately $72. If we lower the price, the annual holding cost will be a bit lower, but $72 is a conservative approximation of the holding cost. So the retailer's purchase cost should not exceed $\$11,957 - \$72 = \$11,885$. Total purchase quantity is $25 \times 52 = 1,300$ units. So if the price is $\$11,885/1,300 = \$9.14$, then the retailer will be slightly better off (relative to the second plan) and P&G is much better off (revenue of $12,012 instead of $11,885).

Q19.2 (Returning Books)

Part a

Use the newsvendor model. The overage cost is C_o = Cost – Salvage value = $20 – $28/4 = $13. The underage cost is C_u = Price – Cost = $28 – $20 = $8. The critical ratio is $8/(13 + 8) = 0.3810$. Look up the critical ratio in the Standard Normal Distribution Function Table to find the appropriate z = statistic = –0.30. The optimal order quantity is $Q = \mu + z \times \sigma = 100 - 0.30 \times 42 = 87$.

Part b

Expected lost sales = $L(z) \times \sigma = 0.5668 \times 42 = 23.81$, where we find $L(z)$ from the Standard Normal Loss Function Table and $z = -0.30$ (from part a). Expected sales = μ – Expected lost sales = 100 – 23.81 = 76.2. Expected leftover inventory = Q – Expected sales = 87 – 76.2 = 10.8. Profit = Price × Expected sales = Salvage value × Expected leftover inventory – Q × Cost = $28 × 76.2 + $7 × 10.8 – 87 × $20 = $469.

Part c

The publisher's profit = Q × (Wholesale price – Cost) = 87 × ($20 – $7.5) = $1,087.5.

Part d

The underage cost remains the same because a lost sale still costs Dan the gross margin, C_u = \$8. However, the overage cost has changed because Dan can now return books to the publisher. He buys each book for \$20 and then returns leftover books for a net salvage value of \$15 – \$1 (due to the shipping cost) = \$14. So his overage cost is now C_o = Cost – Salvage value = \$20 – \$14 = \$6. The critical ratio is 8/(6 + 8) = 0.5714. Look up the critical ratio in the Standard Normal Distribution Function Table to find the appropriate z = statistic = 0.18. The optimal order quantity is $Q = \mu + z \times \sigma = 100 + 0.18 \times 42 = 108$.

Part e

Expected lost sales = $L(z) \times \sigma = 0.3154 \times 42 = 13.2$, where we find $L(z)$ from the Standard Normal Loss Function Table and $z = 0.18$ (from part d). Expected sales = μ – Expected lost sales = 100 – 13.2 = 86.8. Expected leftover inventory = Q – Expected sales = 108 – 86.8 = 21.2. Profit = Price × Expected sales + Salvage value × Expected leftover inventory – Q × Cost = \$28 × 86.8 + \$14 × 21.2 – 108 × \$20 = \$567.

Part f

The publisher's sales revenue is \$20 × 108 = \$2,160. Production cost is \$7.5 × 108 = \$810. The publisher pays Dan \$15 × 21.2 = \$318. The publisher's total salvage revenue on returned books is \$6 × 21.2 = \$127.2. Profit is then \$2,160 – \$810 – \$318 + \$127.2 = \$1,159. Note that both the publisher and Dan are better off with this buy-back arrangement.

Part g

Equation (19.1) in the text gives the buy-back price that coordinates the supply chain (that is, maximizes the supply chain's profit). That buy-back price is \$1 + \$28 – (\$28 – \$20) × (\$28 – \$6)/(\$28 – \$7.5) = \$20.41. Note, the publisher's buy-back price is actually higher than the wholesale price because the publisher needs to subsidize Dan's shipping cost to return books: Dan's net loss on each book returned is \$20 – (20.41 – 1) = \$0.59.

Glossary

A

abandoning Refers to flow units leaving the process because of lengthy waiting times.

abnormal A variation is abnormal if it is not behaving in line with past data; this allows us to conclude that we are dealing with an assignable cause variation and are not just facing randomness in the form of common cause variation.

activity-on-node (AON) representation A way to graphically illustrate the project dependencies in which activities correspond to nodes in a graph.

activity time The duration that a flow unit has to spend at a resource, not including any waiting time; also referred to as service time or processing time.

A/F ratio The ratio of actual demand (A) to forecasted demand (F). Used to measure forecast accuracy.

anchoring bias The fact that human decision makers are selective in their acquisition of new information, looking for what confirms their initially held beliefs.

Andon cord A cord running adjacent to assembly lines that enables workers to stop production if they detect a defect. Just like the jidoka automatic shut-down of machines, this procedure dramatizes manufacturing problems and acts as a pressure for process improvements.

assemble-to-order Also known as make-to-order. A manufacturing system in which final assembly of a product only begins once a firm order has been received. Dell Inc. uses assemble-to-order with personal computers.

assignable cause variation Variation that occurs because of a specific change in input or in environmental variables.

attribute-based control chart A special control chart used for dealing with binary outcomes. It has all the features of the *X*-bar chart, yet does not require a continuous outcome variable. However, attribute-based charts require larger sample sizes, especially if defects occur rarely. Also known as *p*-charts.

authorization level For a fare class, the percentage of capacity that is available to that fare class or lower. An authorization level is equivalent to a booking limit expressed as a percentage of capacity.

automated forecasting Forecasts that are created by computers, typically with no human intervention.

Average labor utilization The average utilization across resources.

B

back-order penalty cost The cost incurred by a firm per back order. This cost can be explicit or implicit (e.g., lost goodwill and future business).

base stock level Also known as the order-up-to level. In the implementation of an order-up-to policy, inventory is ordered so that inventory position equals the base stock level.

batch A collection of units.

biased forecast A forecast that is wrong on average, thus an average forecast error different from zero.

bid price With bid price control, a bid price is assigned to each segment of capacity and a reservation is accepted only if its fare exceeds the bid prices of the segments of capacity that it uses.

bill of materials The list of components that are needed for the assembly of an item.

blocking The situation in which a resource has completed its work on a flow unit, yet cannot move the flow unit to the next step (resource or inventory) downstream as there is not space available.

booking limit The maximum number of reservations that are allowed for a fare class or lower.

bottleneck The resource with the lowest capacity in the process.

buckets A booking limit is defined for a bucket that contains multiple fare class–itinerary combinations.

buffer Another word for inventory, which is used especially if the role of the buffer is to maintain a certain throughput level despite the presence of variability.

bullwhip effect The propagation of demand variability up the supply chain.

buy-back contract A contract in which a supplier agrees to purchase leftover inventory from a retailer at the end of the selling season.

C

capacity Measures the maximum flow rate that can be supported by a resource.

capacity-constrained A process for which demand exceeds the process capacity.

cause–effect diagram A structured way to brainstorm about the potential root causes that have led to a change in an outcome variable. This is done by mapping out all input and environmental variables. Also known as a fishbone diagram or Ishikawa diagram.

channel stuffing The practice of inducing retailers to carry more inventory than needed to cover short-term needs.

coefficient of variation A measure of variability. Coefficient of variation = Standard deviation divided by the mean; that is, the ratio of the standard deviation of a random variable to the mean of the random variable. This is a relative measure of the uncertainty in a random variable.

collaborative planning, forecasting, and replenishment (CPFR) A set of practices designed to improve the exchange of information within a supply chain.

common cause variation Variation that occurs in a process as a result of pure randomness (also known as natural variation).

control charts Graphical tools to statistically distinguish between assignable and common causes of variation. Control charts visualize variation, thereby enabling the user to judge whether the observed variation is due to common causes or assignable causes.

critical path A project management term that refers to all those activities that—if delayed—would delay the overall completion of the project.

critical ratio The ratio of the underage cost to the sum of the overage and underage costs. It is used in the newsvendor model to choose the expected profit-maximizing order quantity.

cycle inventory The inventory that results from receiving (producing) several flow units in one order (batch) that are then used over a time period of no further inflow of flow units.

cycle time The time that passes between two consecutive flow units leaving the process. Cycle time = 1/Flow rate.

D

decision tree A scenario-based approach to map out the discrete outcomes of a particular uncertainty.

decoupling inventory See buffer inventory.

defect probability The statistical probability with which a randomly chosen flow unit does not meet specifications.

defective Not corresponding to the specifications of the process.

demand forecasting The process of creating statements about future realizations of demand.

demand-constrained A process for which the flow rate is limited by demand.

demand-pull An inventory policy in which demand triggers the ordering of replenishments.

density function The function that returns the probability the outcome of a random variable will exactly equal the inputted value.

dependent variable The variable that we try to explain in a regression analysis.

deseasonalize To remove the seasonal effect from past data.

discovery-driven planning A process that emphasizes learning about unknown variables related to a project with the goal of deciding whether or not to invest further resources in the project.

distribution function The function that returns the probability the outcome of a random variable will equal the inputted value or lower.

diversion The practice by retailers of purchasing product from a supplier only to resell the product to another retailer.

diverters Firms that practice diversion.

double exponential smoothing A way of forecasting a demand process with a trend that estimates both the demand and the trend using exponential smoothing. The resulting forecast is the sum of these two estimates. This is a type of momentum-based forecasting.

double marginalization The phenomenon in a supply chain in which one firm takes an action that does not optimize supply chain performance because the firm's margin is less than the supply chain's total margin.

E

earliest completion time (ECT) The earliest time a project activity can be completed, which can be computed as the sum of the earliest start time and the duration of the activity.

earliest due date (EDD) A rule that sequences jobs to be processed on a resource in ascending order of their due dates.

earliest start time (EST) The earliest time a project activity can start, which requires that all information providing activities are completed.

economies of scale Obtaining lower cost per unit based on a higher flow rate. Can happen, among other reasons, because of a spread of fixed cost, learning, statistical reasons (pooling), or the usage of dedicated resources.

Efficient Consumer Response The collective name given to several initiatives in the grocery industry to improve the efficiency of the grocery supply chain.

electronic data interchange (EDI) A technology standard for the communication between firms in the supply chain.

Emergency Severity Index (ESI) A scoring rule used by emergency rooms to rank the severity of a patient's injuries and then to prioritize their care.

environmental variables Variables in a process that are not under the control of management but nevertheless might impact the outcome of the process.

EOQ (economic order quantity) The quantity that minimizes the sum of inventory costs and fixed ordering cost.

Erlang loss formula Computes the proportion of time a resource has to deny access to incoming flow units in a system of multiple parallel servers and no space for inventory.

estimated standard deviation for X-bar The standard deviation of a particular sample mean, *x*-bar.

estimated standard deviation of all parts The standard deviation that is computed across all parts.

expected leftover inventory The expected amount of inventory at the end of the selling season.

expert panel forecasting Forecasts generated using the subjective opinions of management.

exponential distribution Captures a random variable with distribution Prob $\{x < t\} = 1 - \exp(-t/a)$, where a is the mean as well as the standard deviation of the distribution. If interarrival times are exponentially distributed, we speak of a Poisson arrival process. The exponential distribution is known for the memoryless property; that is, if an exponentially distributed service time with mean five minutes has been going on for five minutes, the expected remaining duration is still five minutes.

exponential smoothing forecasting method A forecasting method that predicts that the next value will be a weighted average between the last realized value and the old forecast.

external setups Those elements of setup times that can be conducted while the machine is processing; an important element of setup time reduction/SMED.

extrapolation Estimation of values beyond the range of the original observations by assuming that some patterns in the values present within the range will also prevail outside the range.

F

fences Restrictions imposed on a low-fare class to prevent high-fare customers from purchasing the low fare. Examples include advanced purchase requirements and Saturday night stay over.

fill rate The fraction of demand that is satisfied; that is, that is able to purchase a unit of inventory.

first-come-first-served (FCFS) A rule that sequences jobs to be processed on a resource in the order in which they arrived.

fishbone diagram A structured way to brainstorm about the potential root causes that have led to a change in an outcome variable. This is done by mapping out all input and environmental variables. Also known as a cause–effect diagram or Ishikawa diagram.

Five Whys A brainstorming technique that helps employees to find the root cause of a problem. In order to avoid stopping too early and not having found the real root cause, employees are encouraged to ask "Why did this happen?" at least five times.

flow rate (R) Also referred to as throughput. Flow rate measures the number of flow units that move through the process in a given unit of time. *Example:* The plant produces at a flow rate of 20 scooters per hour. Flow rate = Min{Demand, Capacity}.

flow time (T) Measures the time a flow unit spends in the process, which includes the time it is worked on at various resources as well as any time it spends in inventory. *Example:* A customer spends a flow time of 30 minutes on the phone in a call center.

flow unit The unit of analysis that we consider in process analysis; for example, patients in a hospital, scooters in a kick-scooter plant, and callers in a call center.

forecast combination Combining multiple forecasts that have been generated by different forecasters into one single value.

forecast error The difference between a forecasted value and the realized value.

forecast gaming A purposeful manipulation of a forecast to obtain a certain decision outcome for a decision that is based on the forecast.

forecast with consensus building An iterative discussion among experts about their forecasts and opinions that leads to a single forecast.

forecasting The process of creating statements about outcomes of variables that presently are uncertain and will only be realized in the future.

forward buying If a retailer purchases a large quantity during a trade promotion, then the retailer is said to forward buy.

G

Gantt chart A graphical way to illustrate the durations of activities as well as potential dependencies between the activities.

H

heijunka A principle of the Toyota Production System, proposing that models are mixed in the production process according to their mix in customer demand.

hockey stick phenomenon A description of the demand pattern that a supplier can receive when there is a substantial amount of order synchronization among its customers.

holding cost rate The cost incurred to hold one unit of inventory for one period of time.

horizontal pooling Combining a sequence of resources in a queuing system that the flow unit would otherwise visit sequentially; increases the span of control; also related to the concept of a work cell.

I

idle time The time a resource is not processing a flow unit. Idle time should be reduced as it is a non–value-adding element of labor cost.

ikko-nagashi An element of the Toyota Production System. It advocates the piece-by-piece transfer of flow units (transfer batches of one).

implied utilization The workload imposed by demand of a resource relative to its available capacity. Implied utilization = Demand rate/Capacity.

in-stock probability The probability all demand is satisfied over an interval of time.

incentive alignment bias Forecasting bias resulting from incentives and personal objectives that forecasters might have.

incentive conflicts In a supply chain, firms may have conflicting incentives with respect to which actions should be taken.

independent variables The variables influencing the dependent variable.

information turnaround time (ITAT) The delay between the occurrence of a defect and its detection.

input variables The variables in a process that are under the control of management.

integrated supply chain The supply chain considered as a single integrated unit, that is, as if the individual firms were owned by a single entity.

interarrival time The time that passes between two consecutive arrivals.

internal setups Those elements of setup times that can only be conducted while the machine is not producing. Internal setups should be reduced as much as possible and/or converted to external setups wherever possible (SMED).

inventory (I) The number of flow units that are in the process (or in a particular resource). Inventory can be expressed in (a) flow units (e.g., scooters), (b) days of supply (e.g., three days of inventory), or (c) monetary units ($1 million of inventory).

inventory turns How often a company is able to turn over its inventory. Inventory turns = 1/Flow time, which—based on Little's Law—is COGS/Inventory.

Ishikawa diagram A structured way to brainstorm about the potential root causes that have led to a change in an outcome variable. This is done by mapping out all input and environmental variables. Also known as a fishbone diagram or cause-effect diagram.

J

jidoka In the narrow sense, a specific type of machine that can automatically detect defects and automatically shut down itself. The basic idea is that shutting down the machine forces human intervention in the process, which in turn triggers process improvement.

job A flow unit that requires processing from one or more resources.

K

kaizen The continuous improvement of processes, typically driven by the persons directly involved with the process on a daily basis.

kanban A production and inventory control system in which the production and delivery of parts are triggered by the consumption of parts downstream (pull system).

L

labor content The amount of labor that is spent on a flow unit from the beginning to the end of the process. In a purely manual process, we find labor content as the sum of all the activity times.

lateness The difference between the completion time of a job and its due date. Lateness is negative when the job is completed before the due date (i.e., it is early).

latest completion time (LCT) The latest time a project activity has to be completed by to avoid delaying the overall completion time of the project.

latest start time (LST) The latest time a project activity can start without delaying the overall completion time of the project.

lead time The time between when an order is placed and when it is received. Process lead time is frequently used as an alternative word for flow time.

line balancing The process of evenly distributing work across the resources of a process. Line balancing reduces idle time and can (a) reduce cycle time or (b) reduce the number of workers that are needed to support a given flow rate.

location pooling The combination of inventory from multiple locations into a single location.

long-term forecasts Forecasts used to support strategic decisions with typical time ranges of multiple years.

longest processing time (LPT) A rule that sequences jobs to be processed on a resource in descending order of their processing times.

lower control limit (LCL) A line in a control chart that provides the smallest value that is still acceptable without being labeled an abnormal variation.

lower specification limit (LSL) The smallest outcome value that does not trigger a defective unit.

M

make-to-order A production system, also known as assemble-to-order, in which flow units are produced only once the customer order for that flow unit has been received. Make-to-order production typically requires wait times for the customer, which is why it shares many similarities with service operations. Dell Inc. uses make-to-order with personal computers.

make-to-stock A production system in which flow units are produced in anticipation of demand (forecast) and then held in finished goods inventory.

makespan The total time to process a set of jobs.

marginal cost pricing The practice of setting the wholesale price to the marginal cost of production.

materials requirement planning (MRP) A system that plans the delivery of components required for a manufacturing process so that components are available when needed but not so early as to create excess inventory.

maximum profit In the context of the newsvendor model, the expected profit earned if quantity can be chosen after observing demand. As a result, there are no lost sales and no leftover inventory.

mean The expected value of a random variable.

mean absolute error (MAE) A measure evaluating the quality of a forecast by looking at the average absolute value of the forecast error.

mean squared error (MSE) A measure evaluating the quality of a forecast by looking at the average squared forecast error.

mid-term forecasts Forecasts used to support capacity planning and financial accounting with typical time ranges from weeks to a year.

mismatch cost The sum of the underage cost and the overage cost. In the context of the newsvendor model, the mismatch cost is the sum of the lost profit due to lost sales and the total loss on leftover inventory.

momentum-based forecasts An approach to forecasting that assumes that the trend in the future will be similar to the trend in the past.

moving average forecasting method A forecasting method that predicts that the next value will be the average of the last realized values.

MRP jitters The phenomenon in which multiple firms operate their MRP systems on the same cycle, thereby creating order synchronization.

muda One specific form of waste, namely waste in the form of non–value-adding activities. Muda also refers to unnecessary inventory (which is considered the worst form of muda), as unnecessary inventory costs money without adding value and can cover up defects and other problems in the process.

N

naïve forecasting method A forecasting method that predicts that the next value will be like the last realized value.

natural variation Variation that occurs in a process as a result of pure randomness (also known as common cause variation).

nested booking limits Booking limits for multiple fare classes are nested if each booking limit is defined for a fare class or lower. With nested booking limits, it is always the case that an open fare class implies all higher fare classes are open and a closed fare class implies all lower fare classes are closed.

newsvendor model A model used to choose a single order quantity before a single selling season with stochastic demand.

no-show A customer who does not arrive for his or her appointment or reservation.

normal distribution A continuous distribution function with the well-known bell-shaped density function.

O

one-for-one ordering policy Another name for an order-up-to policy. (With this policy, one unit is ordered for every unit of demand.)

open-access appointment system An appointment system in which appointments are only available one day in advance and are filled on a first-come-first-served basis.

order batching A cause of the bullwhip effect. A firm order batches when it orders only in integer multiples of some batch quantity.

order inflation The practice of ordering more than desired in anticipation of receiving only a fraction of the order due to capacity constraints upstream.

order synchronization A cause of the bullwhip effect. This describes the situation in which two or more firms submit orders at the same moments in time.

order-up-to model A model used to manage inventory with stochastic demand, positive lead times, and multiple replenishments.

origin-destination control A revenue management system in the airline industry that recognizes passengers that request the same fare on a particular segment may not be equally valuable to the firm because they differ in their itinerary and hence total revenue.

outcome variables Measures describing the quality of the output of the process.

overage cost In the newsvendor model, the cost of purchasing one too many units. In other words, it is the increase in profit if the firm had purchased one fewer unit without causing a lost sale (i.e., thereby preventing one additional unit of leftover inventory).

overbooking The practice of accepting more reservations than can be accommodated with available capacity.

overconfidence bias The fact that human decision makers are overly confident in their ability to shape a positive outcome.

P

***p*-chart** A special control chart used for dealing with binary outcomes. It has all the features of the *X*-bar chart, yet does not require a continuous outcome variable. However, *p*-charts require larger sample sizes, especially if defects occur rarely. Also known as attribute-based control charts.

par level Another name for the order-up-to level in the order-up-to model.

Pareto diagram A graphical way to identify the most important causes of process defects. To create a Pareto diagram, we need to collect data on the number of defect occurrences as well as the associated defect types. We can then plot simple bars with heights indicating the relative occurrences of the defect types. It is also common to plot the cumulative contribution of the defect types.

parts per million The expected number of defective parts in a random sample of one million.

percent on time The fraction of jobs that are completed on or before their due date.

phantom orders An order that is canceled before delivery is taken.

pipeline inventory The minimum amount of inventory that is required to operate the process. Since there is a minimum flow time that can be achieved (i.e., sum of the activity times), because of Little's Law, there is also a minimum required inventory in the process. Also known as on-order inventory, it is the number of units of inventory that have been ordered but have not been received.

Poisson distribution A discrete distribution function that often provides an accurate representation of the number of events in an interval of time when the occurrences of the events are independent of each other. In other words, it is a good distribution to model demand for slow-moving items.

Poisson process An arrival process with exponentially distributed interarrival times.

poka-yoke A Toyota technique of "fool-proofing" many assembly operations, that is, by making mistakes in assembly operations physically impossible.

pooling The concept of combining several resources (including their buffers and their arrival processes) into one joint resource. In the context of waiting time problems, pooling reduces the expected wait time.

prediction markets A betting game in which forecasters can place financial bets on their forecasts.

price protection The industry practice of compensating distributors due to reductions in a supplier's wholesale price. As a result of price protection, the price a distributor pays to purchase inventory is effectively always the current price; that is, the supplier rebates the distributor whenever a price reduction occurs for each unit the distributor is holding in inventory.

process capability index The ratio between the width of the specification interval of the outcome variable and the variation in the outcome variable (measured by six times its estimated standard deviation). It tells us how many standard deviations we can move away from the statistical mean before causing a defect.

process capacity Capacity of an entire process, which is the maximum flow rate that can be achieved in the process. It is based on the capacity of the bottleneck.

process flow diagram Maps resources and inventory and shows graphically how the flow unit travels through the process in its transformation from input to output.

processing time The duration that a flow unit has to spend at a resource, not including any waiting time; also referred to as activity time or service time.

product pooling The practice of using a single product to serve two demand segments that were previously served by their own product version.

production cycle The processing and setups of all flow units before the resource starts to repeat itself.

protection level The number of reservations that must always be available for a fare class or higher. For example, if a flight has 120 seats and the protection level is 40 for the high-fare class, then it must always be possible to have 40 high-fare reservations.

pull system A manufacturing system in which production is initiated by the occurrence of demand.

push system A manufacturing system in which production is initiated in anticipation of demand.

Q

quantity discount Reduced procurement costs as a result of large order quantities. Quantity discounts have to be traded off against the increased inventory costs.

quantity flexibility (QF) contracts With this contract, a buyer provides an initial forecast to a supplier. Later on the buyer is required to purchase at least a certain percentage of the initial forecast (e.g., 75 percent), but the buyer also is allowed to purchase a certain percentage above the forecast (e.g., 125 percent of the forecast). The supplier must build enough capacity to be able to cover the upper bound.

Quick Response A series of practices in the apparel industry used to improve the efficiency of the apparel supply chain.

R

random variable A variable that represents a random event. For example, the random variable *X* could represent the number of times the value 7 is thrown on two dice over 100 tosses.

reactive capacity Capacity that can be used after useful information regarding demand is learned; that is, the capacity can be used to react to the learned demand information.

regression analysis A statistical process of estimating the relationship of one variable with multiple variables that influence this one variable.

reseasonalize To reintroduce the seasonal effect to the forecasted data.

resource The entity of a process that the flow unit has to visit as part of its transformation from input to output.

returns policy See buy-back contract.

revenue management Also known as yield management. The set of tools used to maximize revenue given a fixed supply.

rework An approach of handling defective flow units that attempts to invest further resource time into the flow unit in the attempt to transform it into a conforming (nondefective) flow unit.

rework loops An iteration/repetition of project or process activities done typically because of quality problems.

robust The ability of a process to tolerate changes in input and environmental variables without causing the outcomes to be defective.

root cause A root cause for a defect is a change in an input or an environmental variable that initiated a defect.

round-up rule When looking for a value inside a table, it often occurs that the desired value falls between two entries in the table. The round-up rule chooses the entry that leads to the larger quantity.

S

safety inventory The inventory that a firm holds to protect itself from random fluctuations in demand.

salvage value The value of leftover inventory at the end of the selling season in the newsvendor model.

scheduling The process of deciding what work to assign to which resources and when to assign the work.

seasonality A significant demand change that constitutes a repetitive fluctuation over time.

seasonality index (SI) The estimated multiplicative adjustment factor that allows us to move from the average overall demand to the average demand for a particular season.

service level The probability with which a unit of incoming demand will receive service as planned. In the context of waiting time problems, this means having a waiting time less than a specified target wait time; in other contexts, this also can refer to the availability of a product.

service time The duration that a flow unit has to spend at a resource, not including any waiting time; also referred to as activity time or processing time.

set of specifications A set of rules that determine if the outcome variable of a unit is defective or not.

short-term forecasts Forecasts used to support tactical decision making with typical time ranges from hours to weeks.

shortage gaming A cause of the bullwhip effect. In situations with a capacity constraint, retailers may inflate their orders in anticipation of receiving only a portion of their order.

shortest processing time (SPT) A rule that sequences jobs to be processed on a resource in ascending order of their processing times.

six-sigma process A process that has 6 standard deviations on either side of the mean and the specification limit.

slack time The difference between the earliest completion time and the latest completion time; measures by how much an activity can be delayed without delaying the overall project.

smoothing parameter The parameter that determines the weight new realized data have in creating the next forecast with exponential smoothing.

span of control The scope of activities a worker or a resource performs. If the resource is labor, having a high span of control requires extensive training. Span of control is largest in a work cell.

standard deviation A measure of the absolute variability around a mean. The square of the standard deviation equals the variance.

standard normal A normal distribution with mean 0 and standard deviation 1.

starving The situation in which a resource has to be idle as there is no flow unit completed in the step (inventory, resource) upstream from it.

stationary arrivals When the arrival process does not vary systemically over time; opposite of seasonal arrivals.

statistical noise Variables influencing the outcomes of a process in unpredictable ways.

statistical process control (SPC) A framework in operations management built around the empirical measurement and the statistical analysis of input, environmental, and outcome variables.

stockout Occurs if a customer demands a unit but a unit of inventory is not available. This is different from "being out of stock," which merely requires that there is no inventory available.

stockout probability The probability a stockout occurs over a predefined interval of time.

supply chain efficiency The ratio of the supply chain's actual profit to the supply chain's optimal profit.

supply-constrained A process for which the flow rate is limited by either capacity or the availability of input.

T

takotei-mochi A Toyota technique to reduce worker idle time. The basic idea is that a worker can load one machine and while this machine operates, the worker—instead of being idle—operates another machine along the process flow.

tandem queue A set of queues aligned in a series so that the output of one server flows to only one other server.

tardiness If a job is completed after its due date, then tardiness is the difference between the completion time of a job and its due date. If the job is completed before its due date, then tardiness is 0. Tardiness is always positive.

target variation The largest amount of variation in a process that does not exceed a given defect probability.

target wait time (TWT) The wait time that is used to define a service level concerning the responsiveness of a process.

tasks The atomic pieces of work that together constitute activities. Tasks can be moved from one activity/resource to another in the attempt to improve line balance.

theory of constraints An operation guideline that recommends managerial attention be focused on the bottleneck of a process.

time series analysis Analysis of old demand data.

time series–based forecast An approach to forecasting that uses nothing but old demand data.

trade promotion A temporary price discount off the wholesale price that a supplier offers to its retailer customers.

trend A continuing increase or decrease in a variable that is consistent over a long period of time.

tsukurikomi The Toyota idea of integrating quality inspection throughout the process. This is therefore an important enabler of the quality-at-the-source idea.

turn-and-earn An allocation scheme in which scarce capacity is allocated to downstream customers proportional to their past sales.

U

unbiased forecast A forecast that is correct on average, thus an average forecast error equal to zero.

underage cost In the newsvendor model, the profit loss associated with ordering one unit too few. In other words, it is the increase in profit if one additional unit had been ordered and that unit is sold.

universal design/product A product that is designed to serve multiple functions and/or multiple customer segments.

unknown unknowns (unk-unks) Project management parlance to refer to uncertainties in a project that are not known at the outset of the project.

upper control limit (UCL) A line in a control chart that provides the largest value that is still acceptable without being labeled an abnormal variation.

upper specification limit (USL) The largest outcome value that does not trigger a defective unit.

utilization The extent to which a resource uses its capacity when supporting a given flow rate. Utilization = Flow rate/Capacity.

V

variance A measure of the absolute variability around a mean. The square root of the variance equals the standard deviation.

vendor-managed inventory (VMI) The practice of switching control of inventory management from a retailer to a supplier.

virtual nesting A revenue management system in the airline industry in which passengers on different itineraries and paying different fare classes may nevertheless be included in the same bucket for the purchase of capacity controls.

virtual pooling The practice of holding inventory in multiple physical locations that share inventory information data so that inventory can be moved from one location to another when needed.

W

weighted shortest processing time (WSPT) A rule that sequences jobs to be processed on a resource in descending order of the ratio of their weight to their processing time. Jobs with high weights and low processing times tend to be sequenced early.

work in process (WIP) The inventory that is currently in the process (as opposed to inventory that is finished goods or raw material).

worker-paced line A process layout in which a worker moves the flow unit to the next resource or buffer when he or she has completed processing it; in contrast to a machine-paced line, where the flow unit moves based on a conveyor belt.

workload The request for capacity created by demand. Workload drives the implied utilization.

X

X-bar The average of a sample.

X-bar charts A special control chart in which we track the mean of a sample (also known as **X**-bar).

X-double-bar The average of a set of sample averages.

yield management Also known as revenue management. The set of tools used to maximize revenue given a fixed supply.

Z

z-statistic Given quantity and any normal distribution, that quantity has a unique *z*-statistic such that the probability the outcome of the normal distribution is less than or equal to the quantity equals the probability the outcome of a standard normal distribution equals the *z*-statistic.

zero-sum game A game in which the total payoff to all players equals a constant no matter what outcome occurs.

References

Abernathy, F. H., J.T. Dunlop, J. Hammond, and D. Weil. *A Stitch in Time: Lean Retailing and the Transformation of Manufacturing—Lessons from the Apparel and Textile Industries.* New York: Oxford University Press, 1999.

Anupindi, R., S. Chopra, S. D. Deshmukh, J. A. Van Mieghem, and E. Zemel. *Managing Business Process Flows.* Upper Saddle River, NJ: Prentice Hall, 1999.

Bartholdi, J. J., and D. D. Eisenstein. "A Production Line That Balances Itself." *Operations Research* 44, no. 1 (1996), pp. 21–34.

Beatty, S. "Advertising: Infinity and Beyond? No Supply of Toys at Some Burger Kings." *The Wall Street Journal,* November 25, 1996, p. B-10.

Belobaba, P. "Application of a Probabilistic Decision Model to Airline Seat Inventory Control." *Operations Research* 37, no. 2 (1989), pp. 183–97.

Bohn, R. E., and R. Jaikumar. "A Dynamic Approach to Operations Management: An Alternative to Static Optimization." *International Journal of Production Economics* 27, no. 3 (1992), pp. 265–82.

Bohn, R. E., and C. Terwiesch. "The Economics of Yield-Driven Processes." *Journal of Operations Management* 18 (December 1999), pp. 41–59.

Breyfogle, F. W. *Implementing Six Sigma.* New York: John Wiley & Sons, 1999.

Brown, A., H. Lee, and R. Petrakian. "Xilinx Improves Its Semiconductor Supply Chain Using Product and Process Postponement." *Interfaces* 30, no. 4 (2000), p. 65.

Brynjolfsson, E., Y. Hu, and M. D. Smith. "Consumer Surplus in the Digital Economy: Estimating the Value of Increased Product Variety." *Management Science* 49, no. 11 (2003), pp. 1580–96.

Buzzell, R., J. Quelch, and W. Salmon. "The Costly Bargain of Trade Promotion." *Harvard Business Review* 68, no. 2 (1990), pp. 141–49.

Cachon, G. "Supply Chain Coordination with Contracts." In *Handbooks in Operations Research and Management Science: Vol. 11. Supply Chain Management, I: Design, Coordination, and Operation,* ed. T. Kok and S. Graves. Amsterdam: North-Holland, 2004.

Cannon, J., T. Randall, and C. Terwiesch. "Improving Earnings Prediction Based on Operational Variables: A Study of the U.S. Airline Industry." Working paper, The Wharton School and The Eccles School of Business, 2007.

W. Chan Kim and Renée Mauborgne. *Blue Ocean Strategy.* Harvard Business School Press. 2005.

Chase, R. B., and N. J. Aquilano. *Production and Operations Management: Manufacturing and Services.* 7th ed. New York: Irwin, 1995.

Chopra, S., and P. Meindl. *Supply Chain Management: Strategy, Planning and Operation.* 2nd ed. Upper Saddle River, NJ: Pearson Prentice Hall, 2004.

Cross, R. "An Introduction to Revenue Management." In *Handbook of Airline Economics,* ed. D. Jenkins, pp. 453–58. New York: McGraw-Hill, 1995.

Cross, R. *Revenue Management: Hard-Core Tactics for Market Domination.* New York: Broadway Books, 1997.

De Groote, X. Inventory Theory: A Road Map. Unpublished teaching note. INSEAD. March 1994.

Diwas Singh KC, Christian Terwiesch, (2012) An Econometric Analysis of Patient Flows in the Cardiac Intensive Care Unit. Manufacturing & Service Operations Management 14(1):50-65. https://doi.org/10.1287/msom.1110.0341

Drew, J., B. McCallum, and S. Roggenhofer. *Journey to Lean: Making Operational Change Stick.* New York: Palgrave Macmillan, 2004.

Feitzinger, E., and H. Lee. "Mass Customization at Hewlett-Packard: The Power of Postponement." *Harvard Business Review* 75 (January–February 1997), pp. 116–21.

Fisher, M. "What Is the Right Supply Chain for Your Product?" *Harvard Business Review* 75 (March–April) 1997, pp. 105–16.

Fisher, M., K. Rajaram, and A. Raman. "Optimizing Inventory Replenishment of Retail Fashion Products." *Manufacturing and Service Operations Management* 3, no. 3 (2001), pp. 230–41.

Fisher, M., and A. Raman. "Reducing the Cost of Demand Uncertainty through Accurate Response to Early Sales." *Operations Research* 44 (1996), pp. 87–99.

Fujimoto, T. *The Evolution of a Manufacturing System at Toyota.* New York: Oxford University Press, 1999.

Gans, N., G. Koole, and A. Mandelbaum. "Telephone Call Centers: Tutorial, Review, and Research Prospects." *Manufacturing & Service Operations Management* 5 (2003), pp. 79–141.

Gaur, V., M. Fisher, and A. Raman. "An Econometric Analysis of Inventory Turnover Performance in Retail Services." *Management Science* 51 (2005), pp. 181–94.

Geraghty, M., and E. Johnson. "Revenue Management Saves National Rental Car." *Interfaces* 27, no. 1 (1997), pp. 107–27.

Hall, R. W. *Queuing Methods for Services and Manufacturing.* Upper Saddle River, NJ: Prentice Hall, 1997.

Hansell, S. "Is This the Factory of the Future?" *New York Times,* July 26, 1998.

Harrison, M. J., and C. H. Loch. "Operations Management and Reengineering." Working paper, Stanford University, 1995.

Hayes, R. H., and S. C. Wheelwright. "Link Manufacturing Process and Product Life Cycles." *Harvard Business Review,* January–February 1979, pp. 133–40.

Hayes, R. H., S. C. Wheelwright, and K. B. Clark. *Dynamic Manufacturing: Creating the Learning Organization.* New York: Free Press, 1988.

Hillier, F. S., and G. J. Lieberman. *Introduction to Operations Research.* 7th ed. New York: McGraw-Hill, 2002.

Holweg, M., and F. K. Pil. *The Second Century: Reconnecting Customer and Value Chain through Build-to-Order, Moving beyond Mass and Lean Production in the Auto Industry.* New ed. Cambridge, MA: MIT Press, 2005.

Hopp, W. J., and M. L. Spearman. *Factory Physics I: Foundations of Manufacturing Management.* New York: Irwin/McGraw-Hill, 1996.

Jordon, W., and S. Graves. "Principles on the Benefits of Manufacturing Process Flexibility." *Management Science* 41 (1995), pp. 577–94.

Juran, J. *The Quality Control Handbook.* 4th ed. New York: McGraw-Hill, 1951.

Juran, J. *Juran on Planning for Quality.* New York: Free Press, 1989.

Karmarkar, U. "Getting Control of Just-in-Time." *Harvard Business Review* 67 (September–October 1989), pp. 122–31.

Kaufman, L. "Restoration Hardware in Search of a Revival." *New York Times,* March 21, 2000.

Kavadias, S., C. H. Loch, and A. DeMeyer, "DragonFly: Developing a Proposal for an Uninhabited Aerial Vehicle (UAV)." Insead case 600-003-1.

Kimes, S. "Revenue Management on the Links I: Applying Yield Management to the Golf-Course Industry." *Cornell Hotel and Restaurant Administration Quarterly* 41, no. 1 (February 2000), pp. 120–27.

Kimes, S., R. Chase, S. Choi, P. Lee, and E. Ngonzi. "Restaurant Revenue Management: Applying Yield Management to the Restaurant Industry." *Cornell Hotel and Restaurant Administration Quarterly* 39, no. 3 (1998), pp. 32–39.

Koller, T., M. Goedhart, and D. Wessels. *Valuation.* 4th ed. New York: John Wiley & Sons, 2005.

Lee, H. "Effective Inventory and Service Management through Product and Process Redesign." *Operations Research* 44, no. 1 (1996), pp. 151–59.

Lee, H., V. Padmanabhan, and S. Whang. "The Bullwhip Effect in Supply Chains." *MIT Sloan Management Review* 38, no. 3 (1997), pp. 93–102.

Loch C. H., A. DeMeyer, and M. T. Pich, *Managing the Unknown: A New Approach to Managing High Uncertainty and Risk in Projects.* John Wiley & Sons, 2006.

Magretta, J. 1998. "The Power of Virtual Integration: An Interview with Dell Computer's Michael Dell." *Harvard Business Review* 76 (March–April 1998), pp. 72–84.

McGill, J., and G. van Ryzin. "Revenue Management: Research Overview and Prospects." *Transportation Science* 33, no. 2 (1999), pp. 233–56.

McWilliams, G., and J. White. "Others Want to Figure Out How to Adopt Dell Model." *The Wall Street Journal,* December 1, 1999.

Antonio Moreno, Christian Terwiesch (2015) Pricing and Production Flexibility: An Empirical Analysis of the U.S. Automotive Industry. Manufacturing & Service Operations Management 17(4):428-444. https://doi.org/10.1287/msom.2015.0534

Motorola. "What Is Six Sigma?" Summary of Bill Weisz's videotape message, 1987.

Nahmias, S. *Production and Operations Analysis.* 5th ed. New York: McGraw-Hill, 2005.

Ohno, T. *Toyota Production System: Beyond Large-Scale Production.* Productivity Press, March 1, 1998.

Olivares, Marcelo, Christian Terwiesch, and Lydia Cassorla, "Structural Estimation of the Newsvendor Model: An Application to Reserving Operating Room Time," *Management Science,* Vol. 54, No. 1, 2008 (pp. 45–55).

Padmanabhan,V., and I. P. L. Png. "Returns Policies: Make Money by Making Good." *Sloan Management Review,* Fall 1995, pp. 65–72.

Papadakis, Y. "Operations Risk and Supply Chain Design." Working paper. The Wharton Risk Center, 2002.

Pasternack, B. "Optimal Pricing and Returns Policies for Perishable Commodities." *Marketing Science* 4, no. 2 (1985), pp. 166–76.

Petruzzi, N., and M. Dada. "Pricing and the Newsvendor Problem: A Review with Extensions." *Operations Research* 47 (1999), pp. 183–94.

Porter, M., M. Kramer. "Creating Shared Value: How to Reinvent Capitalism and Unleash a Wave of Innovation and Growth." *Harvard Business Review.* Jan–Feb, 2011.

Porteus, E. *Stochastic Inventory Theory.* Palo Alto, CA: Stanford University Press, 2002.

Ramstad, E. "Koss CEO Gambles on Inventory Buildup: Just-in-Time Production Doesn't Always Work." *The Wall Street Journal,* March 15, 1999.

Sakasegawa, H. "An Approximation Formula $L_q = \alpha\beta^{\rho}(1 - \rho)$." *Annals of the Institute of Statistical Mathematics* 29, no. 1 (1977), pp. 67–75.

Sechler, B. "Special Report: E-commerce, behind the Curtain." *The Wall Street Journal,* July 15, 2002.

Silver, E., D. Pyke, and R. Peterson. *Inventory Management and Production Planning and Scheduling.* New York: John Wiley & Sons, 1998.

Simchi-Levi, D., P. Kaminsky, and E. Simchi-Levi. *Designing and Managing the Supply Chain: Concepts, Strategies, and Case Studies.* 2nd ed. New York: McGraw-Hill, 2003.

Simison, R. "Toyota Unveils System to Custom-Build Cars in Five Days." *The Wall Street Journal,* August 6, 1999.

Smith, B., J. Leimkuhler, and R. Darrow. "Yield Management at American Airlines." *Interfaces* 22, no. 1 (1992), pp. 8–31.

Stevenson, W. *Operations Management.* 8th ed. McGraw-Hill/ Irwin, 2006.

Stringer, K. "As Planes Become More Crowded, Travelers Perfect Getting 'Bumped.'" *The Wall Street Journal,* March 21, 2002.

Talluri, K., and G. van Ryzin. *The Theory and Practice of Revenue Management.* Boston: Kluwer Academic Publishers, 2004.

Terwiesch, Christian, and Karl T. Ulrich, *Innovation Tournaments: Creating and Selecting Exceptional Opportunities,* Harvard Business School Press, 2009.

Terwiesch, C. "Paul Downs Cabinet Maker." Teaching case at The Wharton School, 2004.

Terwiesch, C., and C. H. Loch. "Pumping Iron at Cliffs and Associates I: The Cicored Iron Ore Reduction Plant in Trinidad." Wharton-INSEAD Alliance case, 2002.

Tucker, A. L. "The Impact of Operational Failures on Hospital Nurses and Their Patients." *Journal of Operations Management* 22, no. 2 (April 2004), pp. 151–69.

Ulrich, K. T., and S. Eppinger. *Product Design and Development.* 5th ed. McGraw Hill Irwin, 2011.

Upton, D. "The Management of Manufacturing Flexibility." *California Management Review* 36 (Winter 1994), pp. 72–89.

Upton, D. "What Really Makes Factories Flexible." *Harvard Business Review* 73 (July–August 1995), pp. 74–84.

Vitzthum, C. "Spain's Zara Cuts a Dash with 'Fashion on Demand.'" *The Wall Street Journal,* May 29, 1998.

Wadsworth, H. M., K. S. Stephens, and A. B. Godfrey. *Modern Methods for Quality Control and Improvement.* New York: John Wiley & Sons, 1986.

Weatherford, L. R., and S. E. Bodily. "A Taxonomy and Research Overview of Perishable-Asset Revenue Management: Yield Management, Overbooking and Pricing." *Operations Research* 40, no. 5 (1992), pp. 831–43.

Whitney, D. *Mechanical Assemblies: Their Design, Manufacture, and Role in Product Development.* New York: Oxford University Press, 2004.

Whitt, W. "The Queuing Network Analyzer." *Bell System Technology Journal* 62, no. 9 (1983).

Womack, J. P., D. T. Jones, and D. Roos. *The Machine That Changed the World: The Story of Lean Production.* Reprint edition. New York: Harper Perennial, 1991.

Zipkin, P. *Foundations of Inventory Management.* New York: McGraw-Hill, 2000.

Zipkin, P. "The Limits of Mass Customization." *Sloan Management Review,* Spring 2001, pp. 81–87.

Index of Key "How to" Exhibits

Summary of Key Notation and Equations

Chapter 2: The Process View of the Organization

$$\text{Little's Law: Average inventory} = \text{Average flow rate} \times \text{Average time}$$

Chapter 3: Understanding the Supply Process: Evaluating Process Capacity

$$\text{Implied utilization} = \frac{\text{Capacity requested by demand}}{\text{Available capacity}}$$

Chapter 4: Estimating and Reducing Labor Costs

$$\text{Flow rate} = \text{Min}\{\text{Available input, Demand, Process capacity}\}$$

$$\text{Cycle time} = \frac{1}{\text{Flow rate}}$$

$$\text{Cost of direct labor} = \frac{\text{Total wages}}{\text{Flow rate}}$$

$$\text{Idle time across all workers at resource } i = \text{Cycle time} \times (\text{Number of workers at resource } i) - \text{Processing time at resource } i$$

$$\text{Average labor utilization} = \frac{\text{Labor content}}{\text{Labor content} + \text{Total idle time}}$$

Chapter 5: Batching and Other Flow Interruptions: Setup Times and the Economic Order Quantity Model

$$\text{Capacity given batch size} = \frac{\text{Batch size}}{\text{Setup time} + \text{Batch size} \times \text{Time per unit}}$$

$$\text{Recommended batch size} = \frac{\text{Flow rate} \times \text{Setup time}}{1 - \text{Flow rate} \times \text{Time per unit}}$$

$$\text{Economic order quantity} = \sqrt{\frac{2 \times \text{Setup cost} \times \text{Flow rate}}{\text{Holding cost}}}$$

Chapter 9: Variability and Its Impact on Process Performance: Waiting Time Problems

m = number of servers
p = processing time
a = interarrival time

CV_a = coefficient of variation for interarrivals
CV_p = coefficient of variation of processing time

$$\text{Utilization } u = \frac{p}{a \times m}$$

$$T_q = \left(\frac{\text{Processing time}}{m}\right) \times \left(\frac{\text{Utilization}^{\sqrt{2(m+1)}-1}}{1 - \text{Utilization}}\right) \times \left(\frac{CV_a^2 + CV_p^2}{2}\right)$$

$$\text{Flow time } T = T_q + p$$

$$\text{Inventory in service } I_p = m \times u$$

$$\text{Inventory in the queue } I_q = T_q / a$$

$$\text{Inventory in the system } I = I_p + I_q$$

Chapter 10: Quality

$$\text{Yield of resource} = \frac{\text{Flow rate of units processed correctly at the resource}}{\text{Flow rate}}$$

Chapter 14: Betting on Uncertain Demand: The Newsvendor Model

Q = order quantity
C_u = Underage cost
C_o = Overage cost
μ = Expected demand
σ = Standard deviation of demand

$F(Q)$ = Distribution function
$\Phi(Q)$ = Distribution function of the standard normal
$L(Q)$ = Loss function
$L(z)$ = Loss function of the standard normal distribution

$$\text{Critical ratio} = \frac{C_u}{C_o + C_u}$$

$$\text{A/F ratio} = \frac{\text{Actual demand}}{\text{Forecast}}$$

$$\text{Expected profit-maximizing order quantity: } F(Q) = \frac{C_u}{C_o + C_u}$$

$$z\text{-statistic or normalized order quantity: } z = \frac{Q - \mu}{\sigma}$$

$$Q = \mu + z \times \sigma$$

$$\text{Expected lost sales with a standard normal distribution} = L(z)$$

$$\text{Expected lost sales with a normal distribution} = \sigma \times L(z)$$

In Excel: $L(z) = \sigma$*Normdist(z, 0 , 1, 0) – z*(1 – Normsdist(z))

Expected lost sales for nonnormal distributions = $L(Q)$ (from loss function table)

Expected sales = μ – Expected lost sales

Expected leftover inventory = Q – Expected sales

Expected profit = [(Price – Cost) × Expected sales]
– [(Cost – Salvage value) × Expected leftover inventory]

In-stock probability = $F(Q)$

Stockout probability = 1 – In-stock probability

In Excel: In-stock probability = Normsdist(z)

In Excel: z = Normsinv(Target in-stock probability)

Chapter 15: Assemble-to-Order, Make-to-Order, and Quick Response with Reactive Capacity

Mismatch cost = (C_o × Expected leftover inventory) + (C_u × Expected lost sales)
= Maximum profit – Expected profit

Maximum profit = (Price – Cost) × μ

Coefficient of variation = Standard deviation/Expected demand

Chapter 16: Service Levels and Lead Times in Supply Chains: The Order-up-to Inventory Model

l = Lead time
S = Order-up-to level

Inventory level = On-hand inventory – Back order
Inventory position = On-order inventory + Inventory level
In-stock probability = 1 – Stockout probability
= Prob{Demand over (l + 1) periods ≤ S}

$$z\text{-statistic for normalized order quantity: } z = \frac{S - \mu}{\sigma}$$

$$\text{Expected back order with a normal distribution} = \sigma \times L(z)$$

$$\text{In Excel: Expected back order} = \sigma^*(\text{Normdist}(z, 0, 1, 0) - z^*(1 - \text{Normsdist}(z)))$$

$$\text{Expected back order for nonnormal distributions} = L(S) \text{ (from loss function table)}$$

$$\text{Expected inventory} = S - \text{Expected demand over } l + 1 \text{ periods} + \text{Expected back order}$$

$$\text{Expected on-order inventory} = \text{Expected demand in one period} \times \text{Lead time}$$

Chapter 17: Risk-Pooling Strategies to Reduce and Hedge Uncertainty

$$\text{Expected pooled demand} = 2 \times \mu$$

$$\text{Standard deviation of pooled demand} = \sqrt{2 \times (1 + \text{Correlation})} \times \sigma$$

$$\text{Coefficient of variation of pooled demand} = \sqrt{\frac{1}{2}(1 + \text{Correlation})} \times \left(\frac{\sigma}{\mu}\right)$$

Chapter 18: Revenue Management with Capacity Controls

$$\text{Protection level: Critical ratio} = \frac{C_u}{C_o + C_u} = \frac{r_h - r_l}{r_h}$$

$$\text{Low-fare booking limit} = \text{Capacity} - Q$$

$$\text{Overbooking: Critical ratio} = \frac{C_u}{C_o + C_u} = \frac{r_l}{\text{Cost per bumped customer} + r_l}$$

Index